Alan Westmuckett.

Oracle Built-in Packages

Oracle Built-in Packages

Steven Feuerstein, Charles Dye,
and John Beresniewicz

O'REILLY™

Cambridge · Köln · Paris · Sebastopol · Tokyo

Oracle Built-in Packages

by Steven Feuerstein, Charles Dye, and John Beresniewicz

Published by O'Reilly & Associates, Inc., 101 Morris Street, Sebastopol, CA 95472.

Editor: Deborah Russell

Production Editor: John Files

Printing History:

April 1998:   First Edition.

ISBN: 1-56592-375-8

To Veva Silva, the woman who brought me to life.

—Steven Feuerstein

To Natalie.

—Charles Dye

To Arlene.

—John Beresniewicz

Table of Contents

Preface

After publishing more than 1,600 pages on Oracle PL/SQL in two previous books, I marvel at the existence now of this third book covering yet other aspects of the PL/SQL language. I can still remember quite distinctly a moment in September, 1994, when I embarked on writing the first draft of *Oracle PL/SQL Programming* and wondered: are there really 400 pages worth of material on that much-used and often-maligned procedural language from a nonprocedural (SQL) company? If the answer to that question was a resounding "yes" in 1994, then the answer is a deafening roar today!

Maybe PL/SQL isn't the answer to every object-oriented programmer's deepest desires. Maybe developers are badly in need of—and unreservedly deserve—better tools with which to write, debug, and reuse PL/SQL programs. Maybe PL/SQL isn't perfect, but the reality is that hundreds of thousands of people around the world work (and struggle) with PL/SQL on a daily basis. We all need as much information as possible about how we can make the best possible use of Oracle PL/SQL.

And that is the objective of *Oracle Built-in Packages*. If you are going to build complex applications using PL/SQL, you will not succeed unless you learn about and figure out how to utilize many of the packages described in this book. Packages are the method of choice for Oracle and third parties like RevealNet, Inc., to *extend* the base PL/SQL language, to improve ease of use, and to provide brand-new functionality in the language. Writing PL/SQL code without knowing about or using built-in packages is akin to building an automobile and ignoring the last 20 years of technological advances. The resulting machine will run more slowly, use more gas, and be harder to repair.

Oracle Built-in Packages grew out of Chapter 15 of the first edition of *Oracle PL/ SQL Programming*. When Oracle released Oracle8, it was time to update that book to include the wide-ranging new PL/SQL8 functionality. It was clear from the start that this second edition, if organized like the first, would have been well over 1,500 pages in length—a totally impractical size for a developer's handbook.

What to do? Based on feedback from developers about *Oracle PL/SQL Programming*, there was an enormous amount of interest in, and often confusion surrounding, the built-in packages. These Oracle-provided "add-ons" to PL/SQL clearly needed more detailed coverage, more examples, more tips, more of just about everything. My single chapter of 100 pages was woefully inadequate. We made the decision to move that single chapter out of *Oracle PL/SQL Programming* and expand it into a book all its own. You are holding the result.

I recognized early in the process that I couldn't personally cover all of the Oracle built-in packages discussed in this book. I didn't have the necessary expertise, nor the time to learn, nor the time to write it all. So I sought and received the help of two excellent Oracle technologists: John Beresniewicz and Charles Dye.

Over the past six months, John, Charles, and I have researched the packages provided by Oracle in the database, verified the documentation, uncovered aberrant behavior, and discovered neat tricks. We also made it a priority to construct package-based utilities that you will be able to put to immediate use.

While *Oracle Built-in Packages* is a collaborative effort, it is also a combination of very individual efforts. As such, you will find differences in coding styles and philosophies. Rather than try to enforce a single standard throughout, I welcomed the variations (as long as all contributed in their own way to a deeper, clearer understanding of the PL/SQL technology). There is rarely a single right way to do anything, and there is an enormous amount we can learn from the different journeys each of us takes to a solution.

For purposes of directing feedback and questions, you may find it useful to know who wrote each of the chapters. In the next section, "Structure of this Book," you will find the names of the authors listed with their chapters. You will also see that there are two other names: Chuck Sisk and Chip Dawes. While many people helped in many ways to produce *Oracle Built-in Packages* (see the "Acknowledgements" for details), Chuck and Chip actually contributed entire chapters.

Structure of This Book

This book is divided into four parts:

Part I, *Overview*

Chapter 1, *Introduction*, introduces you to PL/SQL packages generally and built-in packages specifically. It shows you how to call packaged code from your own programs and includes tips for handling the exceptions raised when you call a packaged program. (Steven)

Part II, *Application Development Packages*

Chapter 2, *Executing Dynamic SQL and PL/SQL*, shows you how to use the DBMS_SQL package to construct and execute SQL statements and PL/SQL blocks at runtime. (Steven)

Chapter 3, *Intersession Communication*, shows you how to use DBMS_PIPE and DBMS_ALERT to communicate information between different Oracle sessions. You can also use DBMS_PIPE to communicate with processes external to Oracle. (John)

Chapter 4, *User Lock and Transaction Management*, introduces DBMS_LOCK, a handy but rarely used package that provides an interface to the Oracle lock manager, and DBMS_TRANSACTION, which offers several programs that affect transaction behavior in your PL/SQL program. (DBMS_LOCK—John; DBMS_TRANSACTION—Steven)

Chapter 5, *Oracle Advanced Queuing*, contains an extensive treatment of Oracle Advanced Queuing, a powerful queuing mechanism available with Oracle8. You'll use this mechanism through the DBMS_AQ and DBMS_AQADM packages. (Steven)

Chapter 6, *Generating Output from PL/SQL Programs*, shows you how to send information from your program either to the screen, using DBMS_OUTPUT, or to a server-side file, using UTL_FILE. (Steven)

Chapter 7, *Defining an Application Profile*, familiarizes you with a handy package, DBMS_APPLICATION_INFO. You'll use it to "register" the current execution status of your application with the Oracle database. (John)

Chapter 8, *Managing Large Objects*, shows you how Oracle8 provides robust support for large objects (sometimes known as "BLOBs" or "LOBs"), and how the DBMS_LOB built-in package allows you to access and manipulate these LOBs from within a PL/SQL program. (Chuck)

Chapter 9, *Datatype Packages*, collects together several packages that specialize in manipulating different types of data. DBMS_ROWID makes it easy to work with the two different ROWID formats available in Oracle8. UTL_RAW allows you to work with raw data. UTL_REF, new in Oracle8 Release 8.1, provides a PL/SQL interface to select and modify objects (instances of an object type) in an object table without having to specify or know about the underlying database table. (DBMS_ROWID—Steven; UTL_RAW—Chip; UTL_REF—Steven)

Chapter 10, *Miscellaneous Packages*, contains coverage of a number of packages: DBMS_UTILITY (the actual "miscellaneous" package), DBMS_DDL (contains programs to recompile stored code, analyze objects in your schema, and modify how object identifiers may be referenced in Oracle8), DBMS_RANDOM (a random number generator), and DBMS_DESCRIBE (use it to get information about the parameters of a stored program). (Steven)

Part III, *Server Management Packages*

Chapter 11, *Managing Session Information*, introduces you to DBMS_SESSION and DBMS_SYSTEM, two packages that help you analyze and manage information about your current session. (John)

Chapter 12, *Managing Server Resources*, presents DBMS_SPACE and DBMS_ SHARED_POOL, which contain handy tools for database administrators to help them manage database-related resources on the server. (John)

Chapter 13, *Job Scheduling in the Database*, shows you how to use DBMS_JOB to schedule the execution of stored procedures without the use of operating sytem-specific schedulers, such as UNIX's *cron*. (John)

Part IV, *Distributed Database Packages*

Chapter 14, *Snapshots*, explores the packages, DBMS_SNAPSHOT, DBMS_ REFRESH, and DBMS_OFFLINE_SNAPSHOT, and some programs in DBMS_REP-CAT, showing how to maintain snapshots, snapshot groups, and snapshot logs. (Charles)

Chapter 15, *Advanced Replication*, explains how to use DBMS_REPCAT, DBMS_ REPUTIL, DBMS_OFFLINE_OG, DBMS_REPCAT_ADMIN, DBMS_REPCAT_AUTH, and DBMS_RECTIFIER_DIFF to create and administer your replicated databases. (Charles)

Chapter 16, *Conflict Resolution*, shows you how to configure Oracle to automatically detect, correct, and report many forseeable conflicts by using procedures in DBMS_REPCAT to create and maintain custom resolution methods. (Charles)

Chapter 17, *Deferred Transactions and Remote Procedure Calls*, introduces the DBMS_DEFER package and shows you how to queue deferred remote procedure calls (RPCs) and use DBMS_DEFER_QUERY and DBMS_DEFER_SYS to perform administrative and diagnostic activities. (Charles)

Appendix A, *What's on the Companion Disk?*, explains how to install and use the software on the companion diskette. (A group effort)

Conventions Used in This Book

The following conventions are used in this book:

Italic
  Used for file and directory names and URLs.

`Constant width`
  Used for code examples.

`Constant width bold`
  In some code examples, highlights the statements being discussed.

`Constant width italic`
  In some code examples, indicates an element (e.g., a filename) that you supply.

UPPERCASE
  In code examples, indicates PL/SQL keywords.

lowercase
  In code examples, indicates user-defined items such as variables, parameters, etc.

Punctuation
  In code examples, enter exactly as shown.

Indentation
  In code examples, helps to show structure (but is not required).

`--` In code examples, a double hyphen begins a single-line comment, which extends to the end of a line.

/* and */
  In code examples, these characters delimit a multiline comment, which can extend from one line to another.

. In code examples and related discussions, a dot qualifies a reference by separating an object name from a component name. For example, dot notation is used to select fields in a record and to specify declarations within a package.

< > In syntax descriptions, angle brackets enclose the name of a syntactic element.

[ ] In syntax descriptions, square brackets enclose optional items.

{ } In syntax descriptions, curly brackets enclose a set of items; you must choose only one of them.

| In syntax descriptions, a vertical bar separates the items enclosed in curly brackets, as in {VARCHAR2 | DATE | NUMBER}.

Indicates that the code example described in the text appears on the companion disk.

Versions of Oracle

The built-in packages of Oracle PL/SQL discussed in this book are installed in the Oracle database. Each version of the Oracle database comes with its corresponding version of PL/SQL and its set of built-in packages. Most of the built-in packages became available with Oracle Release 7.1. A number of new packages were provided with Oracle8. The text describes which packages are available only with specific versions of Oracle.

About the Disk

You'll find a high-density Windows disk included with this book. This disk contains the Companion Utilities Guide for *Oracle Built-in Packages*, an online tool developed by RevealNet, Inc., that gives you point-and-click access to more than 175 files of source code and documentation that we developed. Many of the code examples are also printed in the book. We've included these to give you a jump-start on writing your own PL/SQL code and to keep you from having to type many pages of PL/SQL statements from printed text.

Throughout the book, disk icons (see the earlier "Conventions Used in This Book" section) will indicate where a code example shown or mentioned in the text is included on the disk. Appendix A, *What's on the Companion Disk?*, describes how to install the Windows-based interface. You can run the software in any Microsoft Windows environment (3.1, 95, NT 3.5, NT 4.0). If you are working in a non-Windows environment, you can obtain a compressed file containing the utilities on the desk from the RevealNet PL/SQL Pipeline Archives at *http://www.revealnet.com/plsql-pipeline*.

About PL/Vision

You will find a number of references to PL/Vision in this book. PL/Vision is a library of PL/SQL packages from RevealNet. PL/Vision was designed and implemented by Steven Feuerstein; it is described in great detail in his second book,

Advanced Oracle PL/SQL Programming with Packages (O'Reilly & Associates, 1996*)*. Several points to keep in mind about PL/Vision:

- You do not need to install PL/Vision in order to use the built-in packages described in this book. Hovever, a number of PL/Vision packages make it easier for you to take advantage of built-in package functionality (including PLVdyn, PLVfile and the p package).

- You do not have to purchase PL/Vision in order to take advantage of at least *some* of its functionality (certainly anything mentioned in this book). You can download PL/Vision Lite, the companion software for *Advanced Oracle PL/ SQL Programming with Packages,* from *www.revealnet.com.*

- You can also get information about PL/Vision Professional (and download a trial version) from the *www.revealnet.com* web site. PL/Vision Professional is the full-use version of PL/Vision, consisting of more than 50 packages (as of January 1998).

About Q

John Beresniewicz is one of the principal designers and implementers of the Q family of products from Savant Corporation. Q is a major application based primarily on PL/SQL code that uses the Oracle built-in packages; John's knowledge and experience with the built-ins is largely derived from his work on Q.

Q is designed to help DBAs and developers address performance tuning, problem diagnosis, and space management issues in networked database environments. Q includes facilities for database tuning and diagnostics, SQL tuning, event and alarm generation, network diagnostics, PC troubleshooting, and broadcast messaging. The Q Diagnostic Center for Oracle is a powerful diagnostic tool for analyzing Oracle performance problems. The product architecture combines a unique graphical interface utilizing principles of visual intelligence, which communicates with a data access layer implemented entirely as PL/SQL packages. Q also includes a PL/SQL server-side agent executing under the Oracle job queue.

If you are interested in Savant Corporation and the Q product family, please visit *www.savant-corp.com.* A fully functional trial copy of the Q Diagnostic Center for Oracle and PC can be downloaded from the site.

Comments and Questions

Please address comments and questions concerning this book to the publisher:

O'Reilly & Associates
101 Morris Street
Sebastopol, CA 95472
800-998-9938 (in the U.S. or Canada)
707-829-0515 (international or local)
707-829-0104 (fax)

You can also send us messages electronically. See the ads in the book for information about O'Reilly & Associates' online services.

For corrections and amplifications for the book, check out *www.oreilly.com/catalog/oraclebip/*.

If you have any questions about the disk supplied with this book, contact Reveal-Net, Inc. at *www.revealnet.com*.

Acknowledgments

We have many people to thank. Here are acknowledgments from all three of us.

Steven

Help! I started writing big, fat books about PL/SQL and I just can't stop myself!

It almost feels that way sometimes. As I was finishing up my first book, *Oracle PL/SQL Programming*, I sighed as I thought about the summer of 1996: the workload would let up and I could actually enjoy the sun and the season. As my son, Eli, would say: "Yeah, right." By the summer of 1996, I was busy writing *Advanced Oracle PL/SQL Programming with Packages*, turning PL/Vision into an actual product people would buy, and, due largely to the enthusiastic reception for *Oracle PL/SQL Programming*, doing more and more training.

Now it is the winter of 1998 and I am at it again. So, yes, it is true that I just cannot stop myself (Debby Russell, my editor, is already talking about a Quick Reference), but it is also very true that I received loads of help in writing this book. A saving grace of my busy life right now is that I am getting help from sharp, enthusiastic PL/SQL developers from all around the world—and it is time to name names.

First and foremost, I thank my coauthors: John Beresniewicz ("John B") and Charles Dye ("Daddy," being the father of a newborn—I cannot even imagine writing a book in the midst of becoming a new dad, and he is already working on another book!). While there are challenges aplenty in a writing coauthorship, the rewards are also numerous. Charles explored and made available to all of us in great detail a chunk of Oracle technology about which I am ignorant. John B was my "dream come true:" an experienced developer with an orientation towards constructing generic, reusable components that will be enriching the lives of PL/SQL developers for years to come. And while they will without a doubt be heaping praise on their spouses, I would also like to thank Arlene Haskins and Kathy Dye for their toleration of my imposition on their husbands' time and attention.

Next! Even with Charles and John lined up to write significant chunks of this book, I was still more than happy to "share the opportunity" with others. Chuck Sisk (*csisk@saraswati.com*) and Chip Dawes *(chipd@mcs.net)*, both consultants with SSC in Chicago, volunteered to take on the DBMS_LOB and UTL_RAW packages, respectively. Their involvement has enriched the book, and I deeply appreciate their willingness to help. I also thank Bert Scalzo for his very early efforts as a contributor. He was not able to continue, due to an illness in his family, but his enthusiasm and effort did have its impact on the book.

Several people got involved in the critical task of technical review. Any errors you discover in this book are the responsibility of its authors, but there are many fewer errors due to the hard work of Dan Clamage, Ken Denny, Ken Geis, Eric Givler, Shobana Gurumurthy, Dwayne King, Phil Pitha, Bill Pribyl, Kevin Taufner, Rick Wessman, Jay Weiland, and Solomon Yakobson. And when it comes to technical review, it is hard to beat the keen eye of members of the Oracle PL/SQL team (and elsewhere within Oracle). Many thanks to Shirish Puranik for coordinating the effort, as well as the detailed feedback provided by Sashikanth Chandrasekaran, Brajesh Goyal, Radhakrishna Hari, Susan Kotsovolos, Amit Jasuja, and Alex Tsukerman.

I promised Debby that my acknowledgments would be shorter in length than the chapter on Oracle Advanced Queueing, so let me simply add that I am grateful to:

- Steve Hilker of RevealNet, Inc. for putting together an excellent Companion Disk resource, and to the rest of the crew at RevealNet for supporting my writing in the midst of aggressive, exciting productive development cycles.

- Bill Hinman, Barrie Hinman, and Sandra Wilbert for providing a solid foundation from which I do all of my work here in Chicago.

- Tony Ziemba for his continued support (and publication through *Oracle Developer* from Pinnacle) of my writing and PL/SQL evangelism.

Many thanks to the staff of O'Reilly & Associates for another wonderful effort: John Files, the production editor for the book; Nancy Wolfe Kotary, who copyedited this enormous book in record time; Claire LeBlanc, who coordinated the production work in Cambridge (and did a good deal of it herself); Mike Sierra, who converted the files to Frame and performed all kinds of system wizardry; Sebastian Banker, Kimo Carter, Mary Costulas, Will Plummer, and Susan Reinbold, who entered edits into the files; Rob Romano, who created the figures; Edie Freedman, who designed the cover; Nancy Priest, who designed the interior format; and Joel Berson, who prepared the index (and improved the text while he was at it); and finally Debby Russell, my editor and friend, whose enthusiasm for this book never wavered, even as the page count increased.

And what about my family? Don't I want to thank them, too? Sure! Thanks, Veva, for putting up with me being around the house so much this past year—except when I was on the road, and then thanks for never forgetting what I look like. Thanks, Eli, for becoming an adolescent at the same time that I got really busy and travelled too much. You had and have more important things in your life going on than seeking out Dad for entertainment. Though we did, come to think of it, play lots of darts and pool and ping pong.

From Charles

At last the fun part has arrived: acknowledging those who have helped me to nurture my contribution to this book from an enticing proposition to a finished product. While I may have shouldered the responsibility for actually researching and writing about the distributed database packages, there are several individuals without whose assistance I would not be a position to pen this acknowledgment.

My wife Kathy has been unwavering in her support and enthusiasm for my work with O'Reilly & Associates. It's one thing to come home from the salt mines each day to work on a project like this, and another to come home to somebody who encourages you when you just don't feel like it, and who understands when her mate overlooks domestic responsibilities such as washing the dishes. Also, at about the same time that this book project was hatched, Kathy assumed the role of mother, and brought little Natalie into this world on December 19, 1997. Happily, that date corresponds favorably with the completion of this book!

Of course, without Steven Feuerstein, I would not have had the opportunity to contribute to this book in the first place. Even before this project, I had a great deal of respect for Steven's work: all of his other O'Reilly titles adorn my shelves, well thumbed. Needless to say, it was a tremendous honor when he selected me to assist him with this book. And, after working with him for the past several months, I have found that he is a friendly, helpful, and reliable guy, in addition to being an outstanding technical resource. I hope we have the opportunity to collaborate on future projects.

Debby Russell, our editor from O'Reilly & Associates is the person who put Steven and me in touch with each other. Now, I seriously doubt that Debby spends much time administering replicated Oracle databases or cutting PL/SQL code, and I think that's precisely the reason why she has been able to craft this book into something you would want to purchase. She has been both a referee and a cheerleader as Steven, John, and I have agreed and disagreed on format and organization. Debby is also supporting my writing of another O'Reilly book: *Distributed Oracle Systems.*

The person most responsible for sparking my interest in Oracle's replication technology is Jenny Tsai of Oracle Education. She was my instructor for the Symmetric Replication class, which I took back in 1995. Besides successfully teaching a complex and perhaps esoteric topic to students of varying aptitudes, Jenny has also provided clarification and confirmation of various Oracle replication functionality as I have deployed the technology in the real world. Additionally, Jenny has reviewed my material for this book with the utmost diligence and has found answers to the most obscure conundra. Many thanks as well to Sue Jang, Gordon Smith, and Norman Woo from Oracle, who helped me a great deal in reviewing this book. I am also very grateful to two technical reviewers from outside Oracle Corporation: Lu Cheng and Peter Grendler.

Finally, I thank John Sullivan. I do actually have a *real* job. When I was writing this book, I was the DBA for The Dialog Corporation (formally Knight-Ridder Information, Inc.), and John Sullivan was my boss. Unlike Dilbert's pointy-haired dolt boss, John understood that a happy employee is a productive employee. He granted immeasurable latitude in how I met my workday responsibilities, and indulged my requests for the equipment and time required to research the topics covered in this and my upcoming book.

From John

There are so many to thank and acknowledge: my parents first of all for their guidance, love, and support; my friend, and first Oracle mentor, John Cullen; my employer (and friend) Bill Wynn, founder of Savant Corporation, whose confidence in me often exceeds my own. Thanks also to Steven, Charles, and Debby Russell for making this book happen; it's been hard work, but well worth it. Very special thanks and so much more to Arlene, whose personal sacrifices for this book and my career exceed all others. Her love and support have been heroic. Finally, I offer the greatest praise and recognition to my Guru, Avatar Adi Da Samraj. It is my sincere hope that the great event of His appearance in this time will soon be widely recognized worldwide.

I

Overview

This part of the book contains a single chapter that introduces the built-in packages and provides some quick-reference tools to help you use the remainder of the book. Chapter 1, *Introduction*, introduces you to PL/SQL packages generally and to built-in packages specifically. It shows you how to call packaged code from your own programs and includes tips for handling the exceptions raised when you call a packaged program.

1

Introduction

Ah, for the good old days of Version 1.0 of PL/SQL! Life was so simple then. No stored procedures or functions—and certainly no packages. You had your set of built-in functions, like SUBSTR and TO_DATE. You had the IF statement and various kinds of loops. With these tools at hand, you built your batch-processing scripts for execution in SQL*Plus, and you coded your triggers in SQL*Forms 3.0, and you went home at night content with a good day's work done.

Of course, there was an awful lot you *couldn't* do with PL/SQL 1.0—such as build complex, robust, large-scale applications, or read and write operating system files, or manipulate data in array structures, or debug your code effectively, or store your business formulas in reusable program units.

Sure, life was simpler back when you were stuck with PL/SQL 1.0. You just too frequently told your manager or your users that what they wanted done was, well, impossible. Fortunately, Oracle recognized that it would be so much nicer for both its users and its bottom line if its bedrock technology (most importantly, the Oracle RDBMS and PL/SQL) could actually meet user needs. So it came out with PL/SQL Version 2 (which works with Version 7 of the Oracle Server) and then, most recently, PL/SQL Version 8.0 (to accompany Oracle8). In each major version and its sub-releases (2.1, 2.2, 2.3, and, sometime in 1998, 8.1), Oracle has added major new functionality. As a result, hundreds of thousands of software programmers now use PL/SQL to implement sophisticated applications.

Easily the most important new feature of PL/SQL2 was the introduction of packages. Packages (explored in more detail in the next section) allow you to collect together related program elements and control access to those elements. Anyone who develops PL/SQL applications should employ packages at the very core of their layers of reusable code—and Oracle Corporation itself is no exception. Starting with PL/SQL 2.0 and continuing through every subsequent release, Oracle has made available to PL/SQL developers a series of *built-in packages*, which extend the functionality of PL/SQL in many fascinating and important directions.

It is no longer sufficient to be aware of and expert in only the core elements of PL/SQL. Getting a handle on IF statements, loops, and the built-in functions like INSTR and TO_CHAR is now only the first phase in your journey towards PL/SQL expertise. To take full advantage of the PL/SQL language, developers must now also learn how to use the programs contained in the built-in packages. And, believe me, once you make a few discoveries in these built-in packages, you will be amazed—and you will be addicted. You will eagerly troll this book for features you can apply in new and creative ways to solve your problems.

This first chapter introduces you to basic concepts of package usage in PL/SQL, shows you how to use built-in packaged functionality in your programs, and explains how to find and learn from the source code for these packages.

The Power of Built-in Packages

Most of the built-in packages extend the PL/SQL language to support features that would otherwise be unavailable to you. This is possible because when Oracle Corporation builds a package, they have the luxury of writing elements of the package in C, giving them full access to the underlying operating system and other areas of technology that are off-limits to the rest of us poor PL/SQL programmers. The result is that Oracle is making something available to us which we could not get ourselves, no matter how proficient a PL/SQL programmer we become.*

However, I don't want to sound as if I'm complaining. I'm very glad Oracle took advantage of packages and C and whatever else they could (and not just because it gave me the excuse to write another book!). The result is a much more powerful and useful PL/SQL. Let's look at an example to give you a feeling for the way Oracle used the package structure to revolutionize the code you write.

Consider Oracle7 Server Version 7.1: the "Parallel Everything" database, as Oracle Corporation called it in its marketing materials. Oracle 7.1 offered parallel query, parallel index update, and many other features that take advantage of the symmetric multiprocessors widely available today. This parallelization of the RDBMS offered significant improvements in database performance, and we should all be glad for that. But there is, fortunately, so much more for which to be thankful.

---

* With Oracle8 and its support for external programs in PL/SQL, this is no longer quite true. With PL/SQL8, you will be able to build your own packages that, in turn, call C programs. See Chapter 21 of *Oracle PL/SQL Programming*, Second Edition, for more information about this feature.

A Kinder, More Sharing Oracle

Oracle Corporation didn't simply utilize this parallelization technology inside its own code. It also made this same technology available to us in a "safe" way: through the specification of the DBMS_PIPE package. While DBMS_PIPE is probably not used by the Oracle Server itself, that built-in package certainly accesses the same parallelization technology used by the RDBMS. The advantages for a PL/SQL developer are far-reaching.

Even if DBMS_PIPE originally grew out of a need by Oracle Corporation to enhance its own performance, the advantages of DBMS_PIPE are not confined to the Oracle RDBMS. Any developer can use DBMS_PIPE in all sorts of new and creative ways. You can parallelize your own programs. You can communicate between a client program in Oracle Forms and a server-based process, without having to commit any data. You can build a debugger for your server-side PL/SQL programs.

And, given the fact that the technology accessed by DBMS_PIPE is also used by the Oracle Server, you are all but guaranteed that DBMS_PIPE will be very efficient and (relatively) bug-free.

The DBMS_PIPE package is just one of many such mind- and functionality-expanding new resources made available through the built-in packages. Do you need to issue your own locks? Do you need to detect whether another process in your current session has committed data? Use the DBMS_LOCK package. Do you want to issue messages from within your PL/SQL programs to help trace and debug your program? Check out the DBMS_OUTPUT package. Would you like to schedule jobs within the RDBMS itself? Explore the DBMS_JOB package. The list goes on and on, and is constantly growing. With the Oracle-supplied packages, you have at your disposal many of the same tools available to the internal Oracle product developers. With these tools, you can do things never before possible!

Built-in Packages Covered in This Book

Oracle Corporation provides many built-in packages, in a variety of its products. You may find it hard to believe, but even this large book cannot document *all* of those packages. Oracle Developer/2000 contains a set of built-in packages, including DDE and TEXT_IO. Oracle WebServer offers its own built-in packages, from HTP to OWA_UTIL, for use in web-based development. This book does *not* discuss those packages. Instead, its focus is on the core database built-in packages, generally those with a DBMS_ or UTL_ prefix.

Within that context, this book discusses all of the built-in packages that you are likely to use. Although (as noted above) it does not offer descriptions for every single package ever created by Oracle Corporation and stored in the database, I would be very surprised if you ever needed to use one of the few packages not found in these pages. The rest of this section introduces you to the packages covered in this book; I have organized these packages into three general areas:

Application development packages

> Used primarily by developers as they build applications.

Server management packages

> Used mostly by database administrators to manage their database servers.

Distributed database packages

> Used by database administrators and developers to manage data across a distributed enterprise.

It is, of course, quite possible and not uncommon for a DBA to use a package we have designated in this book as an "application developer package." In addition, a single package may contain both administrative and development programs. These categories are not meant to restrict your use of the built-in packages; instead, we hope to give some structure to a long, complex list of functional areas so that you will be able to access the technology with more ease and minimal confusion.

The following sections briefly describe each of the packages found in the chapters of this book. Table 1-1 provides a quick summary. Some of these packages, or the programs within them, are available only under certain Oracle versions, as explained in the following chapters.

Table 1-1. Oracle Built-in Packages

Package	Description	Chapter
DBMS_AQ	Creates messages in, and consumes messages from, specific queues provided by the Oracle Advanced Queuing facility.	5
DBMS_AQADM	Performs Oracle Advanced Queueing administrative tasks such as creating and dropping queue tables and altering queues.	5
DBMS_APPLICATION_ INFO	Monitors the execution of an application.	7
DBMS_ALERT	Broadcasts notification to multiple users that specific database events have occurred.	3
DBMS_DDL	Recompiles stored code, analyzes objects in a schema, and modifies referenceability of object identifiers in Oracle8.	10
DBMS_DEFER	Queues deferred remote procedure calls (RPCs).	17

Table 1-1. Oracle Built-in Packages (continued)

Package	Description	Chapter
DBMS_DEFER_QUERY	Provides access to parameters passed to deferred calls, primarily for diagnostic purposes.	17
DBMS_DEFER_SYS	Performs administrative tasks such as scheduling, executing, and deleting queued transactions.	17
DBMS_DESCRIBE	Gets information about the parameters of a stored program.	10
DBMS_JOB	Provides an interface to Oracle's job scheduler (for noninteractive execution of PL/SQL programs).	13
DBMS_LOB	Acesses and manipulates large objects (LOBs) from within PL/SQL programs.	8
DBMS_LOCK	Helps you manage contention for resources used by complex multiuser applications.	4
DBMS_OFFLINE_OG	Instantiates sites (i.e., exports data from an existing master site and imports it into the new master site).	15
DBMS_OFFLINE_ SNAPSHOT	Instantiates a new snapshot using an export of a master table.	14
DBMS_OUTPUT	Displays information to your screen.	6
DBMS_PIPE	Lets applications communicate with routines external to the database.	3
DBMS_RANDOM	Provides a random number generator.	10
DBMS_RECTIFIER_DIFF	Compares replicated tables at two master sites and synchronizes them if necessary.	15
DBMS_REFRESH	Administers snapshot groups at a snapshot site.	14
DBMS_REPCAT	Performs many advanced replication operations, including maintenance, snapshots, and conflict resolution.	14. 15. 16
DBMS_REPCAT_ADMIN	Creates administrator accounts for replication.	15
DBMS_REPCAT_AUTH	Grants and revokes "surrogate SYS" privileges for administrator accounts, and grants and revokes propagator accounts for Oracle8.	15
DBMS_REPUTIL	Enables and disables replication at the session level.	15
DBMS_ROWID	Works with ROWID formats, both extended (Oracle8 only) and restricted (traditional Oracle7).	9
DBMS_SESSION	Modifies and inspects session roles and settings, and manipulates session memory and package states.	11

Table 1-1. Oracle Built-in Packages (continued)

Package	Description	Chapter
DBMS_SHARED_POOL	Allows PL/SQL objects and SQL cursors to be pinned (kept) in the Oracle shared pool; used mainly for memory management.	12
DBMS_SNAPSHOT	Maintains snapshots and snapshot logs.	14
DBMS_SPACE	Analyzes space in tables, indexes, and clusters, and provides information about segment free list sizes.	12
DBMS_SQL	Executes dynamically constructed SQL statements and PL/SQL blocks of code.	2
DBMS_SYSTEM	Lets administrators set trace events in other users' sessions (for debugging).	11
DBMS_TRANSACTION	Provides a programmatic interface to a number of transaction-oriented SQL statements.	4
DBMS_UTILITY	Performs miscellaneous operations such as freeing unused memory, calculating elapsed program time, etc.	10
UTL_FILE	Reads and writes information in server-side files.	6
UTL_RAW	Works with raw data, performing such operations as concatenation, byte translation, etc.	9
UTL_REF	Provides a PL/SQL interface to select and modify objects in an object table (Oracle8 only).	9

Part II, Application Development Packages

This part of the book collects together packages that are used predominantly by application developers. However, this designation should most definitely *not* keep DBAs away from these packages. The DBMS_SQL package, for example, can be and has been used by DBAs to construct powerful, efficient scripts for maintaining database objects and extracting information about a database.

Chapter 2, Executing Dynamic SQL and Pl/SQL

The DBMS_SQL package offers the ability to execute dynamically (at runtime) constructed SQL statements, including DDL, and PL/SQL blocks of code. DBMS_SQL is simultaneously one of the most complex, useful, and rewarding of the built-in packages. It may take some time for you to get comfortable with the way to apply this technology. Once you are up and running, however, you will be amazed at the feats you will be able to perform!

Chapter 3, Intersession Communication

It seems that everything these days has something to do with communication. Messaging technologies are consequently receiving lots of attention, but they are nothing new for Oracle. Oracle has already provided, through the DBMS_

PIPE and DBMS_ALERT packages, mechanisms for communication between database sessions. For instance, using database pipes with DBMS_PIPE, an application can communicate with a service routine external to the database. Or, debuggers that capture PL/SQL errors can utilize the fact that DBMS_PIPE is asynchronous with database transactions, getting the errors logged whether the transaction issued a COMMIT or a ROLLBACK. DBMS_ALERT is a little different in that it allows synchronous notification to multiple users that specific database events have occurred.

Chapter 4, User Lock and Transaction Management

Complex, multiuser applications managing new types of resources (objects, BLOBs, etc.) will require the ability to manage contention for those resources. The Oracle database manages concurrent, multiuser contention for data using sophisticated locking mechanisms. Well, Oracle has now provided developers with the "keys" to those locking mechanisms through the DBMS_LOCK package. Watch out, though. This deceptively powerful package might also put your applications to "sleep"! DBMS_TRANSACTION provides a programmatic interface to a number of transaction-oriented SQL statements.

Chapter 5, Oracle Advanced Queuing

Oracle8 offers a new capability called Oracle Advanced Queuing, which will make it much easier for developers to build applications requiring deferred execution of activity. Oracle is positioning Oracle AQ as an alternative to the queuing mechanisms of teleprocessing monitors and messaging interfaces. Oracle AQ will serve as a foundation technology for workflow management applications, both those delivered by Oracle Corporation itself and those implemented by third parties. Two packages, DBMS_AQ and DBMS_AQADM, make Advanced Queuing available from within PL/SQL programs.

Chapter 6, Generating Output from PL/SQL Programs

The built-in packages offer a number of ways to generate output from within your PL/SQL program. While updating a database table is, of course, a form of "output" from PL/SQL, this chapter shows you how to use DBMS_OUTPUT to display information to your screen and UTL_FILE to read and write information in server-side files.

Chapter 7, Defining an Application Profile

It can be difficult to tell what is going on while an application is running. Wouldn't it be nice to know that the big performance problem was because users were spending 90% of their time in a module that someone else wrote? Seriously, though, one key to providing accurate, quantitative information about utilization and resource consumption is to instrument applications such that they can be tracked externally. The DBMS_APPLICATION_INFO package lets an application register itself in a way that can be monitored at runtime through the V$SESSION and V$SQLAREA virtual tables.

Chapter 8, Managing Large Objects

With Oracle8, Oracle finally offers native, robust support for large objects. Oracle LOBs can be stored in a column in a table or as an attribute of an object type. The database supports objects of up to four gigabytes of data, including character text, graphic images, video, or "raw" data. The DBMS_ LOB package provides procedures and functions to access and manipulate LOBs within PL/SQL programs.

Chapter 9, Datatype Packages

This chapter introduces you to several packages that specialize in working with specific types of Oracle data. The DBMS_ROWID package allows you to work with the two different ROWID formats available in Oracle8: extended (new to Oracle8) and restricted (traditional Oracle7 ROWIDs). The UTL_RAW package offers a set of functions allowing you to perform concatenation, substring, bit-wise logical analysis, byte translation, and length operations on RAW data. The UTL_REF package, new in Oracle8 Release 8.1, provides a PL/ SQL interface to select and modify objects (instances of an object type) in an object table without having to specify or know about the underlying database table.

Chapter 10, Miscellaneous Packages

You can't find a neat category for eveything, can you? This chapter collects together a variety of useful packages you are sure to dip into on a regular basis. DBMS_UTILITY is the actual "miscellaneous" package. It offers programs to free unused user memory, parse comma-delimited lists, calculate the elapsed time of PL/SQL programs, and much more. You never know what you'll find popping up next in DBMS_UTILITY! DBMS_DESCRIBE contains a single procedure, DESCRIBE_PROCEDURE, which you can use to get information about the parameters of a stored program. DBMS_DDL contains programs to recompile stored code, analyze objects in your schema, and modify the referenceability of object identifiers in Oracle8. DBMS_RANDOM supplies PL/SQL developers with a random number generator.

Part III, Server Management Packages

This part of the book groups together packages used to monitor, modify, or manage server-side resources in various ways. These packages will be of definite interest to DBAs; however, developers will also benefit from becoming familiar with them. The packages include facilities for managing session and shared pool memory, monitoring internal space utilization in segments, and executing PL/SQL procedures automatically in background processes.

Chapter 11, Managing Session Information

Oracle technologies allow for a great deal of user customization and security. Language preferences can be specified at the session level using the NLS options of the ALTER SESSION command. Roles can be used to distinguish groups of users from each other and to modify application behavior accordingly. The DBMS_SESSION package contains programs that can modify and inspect session roles and settings from within PL/SQL. This package also contains programs for manipulating session memory and package states; these programs are very instructive to understand, even if not often used. This chapter also describes the DBMS_SYSTEM package, which lets administrators set various trace events in other users' sessions. This can be invaluable when tracking down difficult application performance or database issues.

Chapter 12, Managing Server Resources

With the built-in packages, Oracle is exposing information about database internals—information that is not directly visible in the catalog. The DBMS_SPACE package gives DBAs an analysis of the amount of space both used and free within a table, index, or cluster segment. It also provides information about segment free list sizes, of special interest to Oracle parallel server administrators. On the memory side, the DBMS_SHARED_POOL package gives DBAs some measure of control over the Oracle System Global Area's (SGA's) shared pool. By pinning large packages into the shared pool, expensive runtime memory management (and even errors) can be avoided.

Chapter 13, Job Scheduling in the Database

The job queue is a powerful facility introduced with Version 7.2 of Oracle that gives DBAs and developers the ability to schedule noninteractive execution of PL/SQL programs. It's ideal for handling regular administrative tasks like analyzing tables and for automatically kicking off long-running batch jobs without requiring operator attention. The DBMS_JOB package is your interface to this facility, and it's a little tricky to use. This chapter explains how the job queue works and how to get it to work for you.

Part IV, Distributed Database Packages

This part of the book describes the packages used for simple and advanced replication. It provides details about each package's procedures and functions, and explains how to use them together to create a replicated environment.

Chapter 14, Snapshots

The packages DBMS_SNAPSHOT, DBMS_REFRESH, and DBMS_OFFLINE_SNAPSHOT, and some of the programs in DBMS_REPCAT, embody the functionality to maintain snapshots, snapshot groups, and snapshot logs. This includes refreshing snapshots, changing refresh intervals, adding and removing snapshots from snapshot groups, and purging uneccessary data from snapshot logs. You can use DBMS_OFFLINE_SNAPSHOT to instantiate a new snapshot using an export of a master table instead of using the CREATE SNAPSHOT command. In some cases, this type of instantiation is quicker because of network constraints.

Chapter 15, Advanced Replication

This chapter explains how to use the DBMS_REPCAT, DBMS_REPUTIL, DBMS_OFFLINE_OG, DBMS_REPCAT_ADMIN, DBMS_REPCAT_AUTH, and DBMS_RECTIFIER_DIFF packages to create and administer your replicated databases. DBMS_REPCAT and DBMS_REPUTIL contain the bulk of the procedures required to use the advanced replication option (formerly referred to as "symmetric replication"). Use these procedures to define and modify replication groups, replicated objects, master sites, and snapshot sites.

Chapter 16, Conflict Resolution

Inevitably, conflicts will arise in a replicated environment. You can configure Oracle to automatically detect, correct, and report many of the forseeable conflicts by using procedures in DBMS_REPCAT to create and maintain resolution methods.

Chapter 17, Deferred Transactions and Remote Procedure Calls

The advanced replication option relies heavily on DBMS_DEFER to propagate data changes among master sites, but you can also use it yourself to queue deferred remote procedure calls (RPCs). DBMS_DEFER_QUERY is primarily a diagnostic tool that reports on queued RPCs. Use this package to determine the values of passed parameters and more. DBMS_DEFER_SYS contains the procedures you will need to add and remove default destinations for your RPCs, schedule propagation, and manage transactions.

Using Built-in Packages

There are several steps involved in using a built-in package:

1. Install the built-in package into the database. In most cases, this will be done for you automatically. However, some packages, such as UTL_RAW, are not automatically installed or made publicly accessible, at least in the most recent version of Oracle as this book went to press. The individual chapters in this book will tell you about any special steps you need to take to ensure that the package is installed.

2. Learn about what is available in the package. You can do this by reading the appropriate section of this book and also by looking at the source code (explained later in this chapter).

3. Place references to elements of the package in your own code. To do this, you need to know the correct syntax for referencing package elements (read on to find out how to do this).

What Is a Package?

This section offers a brief introduction to packages. You can find more detailed treatments in both *Oracle PL/SQL Programming* (O'Reilly & Associates, 1995 and 1997), and *Advanced Oracle PL/SQL Programming with Packages* (O'Reilly & Associates, 1996), my two previous books on PL/SQL.

A package is a *collection* of PL/SQL elements that are "packaged" or grouped together within a special BEGIN-END syntax, a kind of "meta-block" of code. Here is a partial list of the kinds of elements you can place in a package:

- Cursors

- Variables (scalars, records, tables, etc.) and constants

- Exception names and PRAGMAs for associating an error number with an exception

- PL/SQL table and record TYPE statements

- Procedures and functions

Packages are among the least understood and most underutilized features of PL/SQL. That's a shame, because the package structure is also one of the most useful constructs for building well-designed PL/SQL-based applications. Packages provide a structure in which you can organize your modules and other PL/SQL elements. They encourage proper structured programming techniques in an environment that often befuddles the implementation of structured programming. When you place a program unit into a package, you automatically create a "context" for that program. By collecting related PL/SQL elements in a package, you express that relationship *in the very structure of the code itself.* Packages are often called "the poor man's objects" because they support some, but not all, object-oriented rules.

The PL/SQL package is a deceptively simple yet powerful construct. It consists of up to two distinct parts: the specification and the body. The *package specification* defines the public interface or API (Application Programming Interface) of the package: those elements that can be referenced outside of the package. The *package body* contains the implementation of the package. In just a few hours you can learn the basic elements of package syntax and rules; there's not all that much to it. You can spend weeks and months, however, uncovering all the nuances and implications of the package structure.

Of course, if you are working with built-in packages, you can leave those details to Oracle. You just have to figure out how to make the best use of the packages provided.

Controlling Access with Packages

Probably the most important implication of package structure is how the builder of the package has complete control over what you can see or do. The users of a package can do either of the following:

- Execute programs listed in the package specification

- Reference elements (variables, constants, exceptions, etc.) listed in the package specification

What *can't* a user of a package do? You can't look inside the package and see how the code was implemented. You can't bypass the programs in the package specification in order to modify (corrupt) data structures managed *inside* the package body.

These restrictions are closely tied to the power and usefulness of the package structure. To illustrate this point, consider the following simple timer package. First, the specification:

```
PACKAGE tmr
IS
   PROCEDURE capture;
   PROCEDURE show_elapsed;
END tmr;
```

The tmr.capture procedure captures the current time. The tmr.show_elapsed procedure shows the elapsed time. The following script, for example, displays the amount of time it takes to run the calc_totals procedure:

```
BEGIN
   tmr.capture;
   calc_totals;
   tmr.show_elapsed;
END;
/
```

Now let's take a look at the package body (where all the code for those two procedures resides):

```
PACKAGE BODY tmr
IS
   last_timing NUMBER := NULL;

   PROCEDURE capture IS
   BEGIN
      last_timing := DBMS_UTILITY.GET_TIME;
```

```
     END;

     PROCEDURE show_elapsed IS
     BEGIN
         DBMS_OUTPUT.PUT_LINE (DBMS_UTILITY.GET_TIME - last_timing);
     END;
  END tmr;
```

The DBMS_UTILITY.GET_TIME program is a function from the built-in package, DBMS_UTILITY, which returns the number of hundredths of seconds that have elapsed since an arbitrary point in time. DBMS_OUTPUT is another built-in package; its PUT_LINE procedure displays output from a PL/SQL program to your screen.

Notice that there is another code element defined inside the package body besides the capture and show_elapsed procedures: the last_timing variable. This variable holds the timing value from the last call to tmr.capture. Since last_timing does not appear in the package specification, an external program (i.e., one that is not defined in this package) cannot directly reference that variable. This restriction is illustrated in the Booch diagram[*] in Figure 1-1.

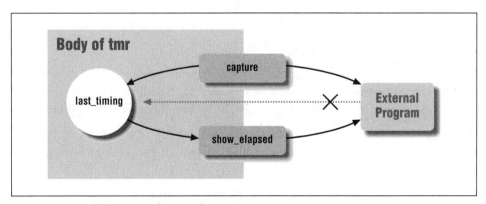

Figure 1-1. Booch diagram of tmr package

So if I try to access the last_timing variable from outside the tmr package, I get an error. This is shown as follows:

```
SQL> exec tmr.last_timing := 100;
begin tmr.last_timing := 100; end;
*
ERROR at line 1:
ORA-06550: line 1, column 14:
PLS-00302: component 'LAST_TIMING' must be declared
```

---

[*] This diagram is named after Grady Booch, who pioneered many of the ideas of the package, particularly in the context of object-oriented design.

Why should you or anyone else care about where you define the last_timing variable? Because it illustrates a critical aspect of a package's value: integrity. If I had placed the variable in the specification, then a user of the package could write over the value of last_timing—and completely invalidate the integrity of the package. Suppose my package specification looked like this:

```
PACKAGE tmr
IS
    last_timing NUMBER;
    PROCEDURE capture;
    PROCEDURE show_elapsed;
END tmr;
```

The package compiles and seems to work as before. But consider the following rewrite of my script to time the calc_totals procedure:

```
BEGIN
    tmr.capture;
    calc_totals;

    tmr.last_timing := DBMS_UTILITY.GET_TIME;

    tmr.show_elapsed;
END;
/
```

Since tmr.last_timing is now in the package specification, this code will compile, and completely subvert the usefulness of the tmr package. For no matter how much time calc_totals actually takes to execute, the tmr.show_elapsed procedure will always display 0—or *very* close to 0—hundredths of seconds for elapsed time.

If, on the other hand, I keep last_timing inside the body of the package, only the tmr.capture procedure can modify its value. A user of tmr is, therefore, guaranteed to get dependable results.

This absolute control is the reason that the package structure has been so useful to Oracle Corporation—and one of the reasons the company has constructed dozens of built-in packages. Since you can perform only the operations and access the data structures listed in the package specification, Oracle can make technology available in a highly controlled fashion. As long as *its* developers write their code properly, there will never be any danger that we can disrupt Oracle Server internals by calling built-in packaged functionality.

Referencing Built-in Package Elements

As noted earlier, a package can have up to two parts: the specification and the body. When it comes to built-in packages, you really don't need to concern yourself with the package body. That is the *implementation* of the package, and something that is the responsibility of Oracle Corporation. With very few exceptions, those package bodies are "wrapped," which means that they are distributed in an encrypted format that you cannot read. This is just as well, because what you really need to do is study the specification to learn about the capabilities offered in that package.

There are two ways to use a built-in package in your own code:

1. Run a function or procedure defined in the package specification.
2. Reference a nonprogram element defined in the package specification.

Notice that you never actually execute a package itself. The package is simply a "container" for the various code elements defined in the package. Let's take a look at an example to make all this very clear. The DBMS_SQL package (examined at great length in Chapter 2) allows you to execute dynamic SQL (SQL statements constructed at runtime), a feature previously unavailable in the PL/SQL language. Here is a portion of the specification of that package:

```
CREATE OR REPLACE PACKAGE DBMS_SQL
IS
   --   CONSTANTS
   --
   v6 constant integer := 0;
   native constant integer := 1;
   v7 constant integer := 2;
   --
   --   PROCEDURES AND FUNCTIONS
   --
   FUNCTION open_cursor RETURN INTEGER;

   PROCEDURE parse
      (c IN INTEGER,
       statement IN VARCHAR2,
       language_flag IN INTEGER);
```

What this tells you is that there are three different constants, one procedure, and one function defined in the package. (There is actually much, much more, of course, but this is all we need to get the point across.) To reference any of the elements, you will use the same "dot notation" used to specify columns in tables.

So if I want to open a dynamic cursor, I use this:

```
DECLARE
   dyncur PLS_INTEGER;
BEGIN
   dyncur := DBMS_SQL.OPEN_CURSOR;
```

And if I want to parse a string using the "native" database method, I would write the following code:

```
PROCEDURE showemps (where_in IN VARCHAR2)
IS
```

```
    dyncur PLS_INTEGER := DBMS_SQL.OPEN_CURSOR;
BEGIN
    DBMS_SQL.PARSE (dyncur,
        'SELECT ename FROM emp WHERE ' || NVL (where_in, '1=1'),
        DBMS_SQL.NATIVE);
    ...
END;
```

In this case, I have qualified my references to the OPEN_CURSOR, PARSE, and NATIVE elements of the DBMS_SQL package. The first two instances are programs (a function and a procedure). The third instance is a constant, passed as the third argument in my call to DBMS_SQL.PARSE.

Exception Handling and Built-in Packages

Programs in built-in packages can raise exceptions. You will often want to write code to check for and handle these exceptions. You should know about the different ways that exceptions can be defined and raised by programs in the built-in packages. This will affect the way you write your exception handlers.

At the beginning of each package's coverage, you will find a description of the exceptions defined within that package. Within the documentation of many of the programs within a package, you will also find an explanation of the specific exceptions that may be raised by those individual programs. When references are made to named exceptions in these explanations, they will appear in one of two forms:

```
PACKAGE.exception_name
```

or:

```
exception_name
```

If the exception name is unqualified (i.e., no package name appears before the exception name), then this exception is defined either:

- In the package currently under discussion, or

- In the STANDARD package; examples are VALUE_ERROR and NO_DATA_ FOUND.

In this section, I will review the four types of exceptions you may encounter when working with built-in packages. I will then show you the kind of code you will need to write to handle exceptions properly when they propagate out from built-in packages. The following sections demonstrate how to write code to work with these different types of exceptions.

Table 1-2 summarizes these types.

Table 1-2. Types of Exceptions

Type	How Exception Is Defined	How Exception Is Raised	SQLCODE Behavior	SQLERRM Behavior	How to Handle Exception
Package-named system exception	The package gives a name to a specific Oracle error number using the PRAGMA EXCEPTION_INIT statement.	The packaged program issues a RAISE statement.	Returns the Oracle error number.	Returns the standard Oracle error message text.	You can handle it by number within a WHEN OTHERS clause, or by name with its own exception handler; the latter improves the readability of your code.
Package-defined exception	The package declares one or more exceptions; these exceptions have names, but no message text and no unique number.	The packaged program RAISEs that exception by name.	Returns 1.	Returns "Unhandled user-defined exception" message.	You can only handle it by name or with a WHEN OTHERS clause, in which case it is impossible to tell which exception was raised.
Standard system exception	It is previously given a name in the STANDARD package or it is simply an error number.	The packaged program issues a RAISE statement.	Returns the Oracle error number.	Returns the standard Oracle error message text.	You can handle it by name in its own exception handler, if a name has been associated with that error number. Otherwise, you handle the exception by number in a WHEN OTHERS clause.
Package-specific exception	In this case, Oracle has rudely appropriated for itself one or more of the application-specific error numbers between −20,999 and −20,000 set aside for customers.	The packaged program calls RAISE_APPLICATION_ERROR.	Returns the number in the −20NNN range.	Returns the message text provided in the call to RAISE_APPLICATION_ERROR.	You can handle these exceptions by number within a WHEN OTHERS clause.

Package-named system exception

In this scenario, the package gives a name to a specific Oracle error number using the PRAGMA EXCEPTION_INIT statement. You can then handle the exception by name with its own exception handler or by number within a WHEN OTHERS clause. Let's look at an example.

The DBMS_DEFER package associates names with a number of Oracle errors. Here is an example of one such association:

```
updateconflict EXCEPTION;
PRAGMA EXCEPTION_INIT (updateconflict, -23303);
```

If a program in DBMS_DEFER raises this exception, you can handle it in either of the following ways:

```
EXCEPTION
    WHEN DBMS_DEFER.UPDATECONFLICT
    THEN
        /* SQLCODE returns -23303 and SQLERRM returns the standard
           Oracle error message */
```

or:

```
EXCEPTION
    WHEN OTHERS
    THEN
        IF SQLCODE = -23303
        THEN
            /* SQLERRM returns the standard Oracle error message */
```

NOTE   You will not be able to write a statement like WHEN DBMS_
              DEFER.UPDATECONFLICT in the Oracle Developer/2000 Release 1
              environment. See "Calling Built-in Packaged Code from Oracle
              Developer/2000 Release 1" for more information on this restriction.

Package-defined exception

In this scenario, the package declares one or more exceptions by name only; these exceptions do not have message text or a unique number associated with them. When this exception has been raised, SQLCODE will always return 1 and SQLERRM will always return the "Unhandled user-defined exception" message. As a consequence, you have two basic options for handling these exceptions:

- You handle by name; write an exception handler that references the packaged exception by name.

- You rely on the WHEN OTHERS clause, in which case there is no way for you to know precisely which exception was raised.

Let's look at the UTL_FILE package for an example. The following exceptions are defined in the package specification:

```
PACKAGE UTL_FILE
IS
    invalid_path EXCEPTION;
    invalid_mode EXCEPTION;
    invalid_filehandle EXCEPTION;
    invalid_operation EXCEPTION;
    read_error EXCEPTION;
    write_error EXCEPTION;
    internal_error EXCEPTION;
END;
```

The UTL_FILE.FOPEN function can raise the INVALID_MODE, INVALID_OPERATION, or INVALID_PATH exceptions. I can write an exception section for a program using UTL_FILE.FOPEN in one of two ways:

```
PROCEDURE my_program
IS
    fid UTL_FILE.FILE_TYPE;
BEGIN
    fid := UTL_FILE.FOPEN ('/tmp', 'myfile.txt', 'R');
    ...
EXCEPTION
    WHEN UTL_FILE.INVALID_OPERATION
    THEN
        ...
    WHEN UTL_FILE.INVALID_MODE
    THEN
        ...
    WHEN UTL_FILE.INVALID_PATH
    THEN
        ...
END;
```

or:

```
PROCEDURE my_program
IS
    fid UTL_FILE.FILE_TYPE;
BEGIN
    fid := UTL_FILE.FOPEN ('/tmp', 'myfile.txt', 'R');
    ...
EXCEPTION
    WHEN OTHERS /* Not recommended! Information is lost... */
    THEN
        ...
END;
```

When working with this kind of exception, always use the first approach. With the WHEN OTHERS clause, there is no way for you to know *which* of the three UTL_FILE exceptions was raised. SQLCODE returns the same value of 1 regardless of the specific exception raised.

NOTE   You will not be able to write a statement like WHEN UTL_
                FILE.INVALID_MODE in the Oracle Developer/2000 Release 1 envi-
                ronment. See "Calling Built-in Packaged Code from Oracle Devel-
                oper/2000 Release 1" for more information on this restriction.

Standard system exception

In this scenario, the package does not contain any statements that define new
exceptions, nor does it give names to existing Oracle error numbers. Instead, a
program in the package simply raises one of the errors defined in the Oracle documentation. You can then handle this exception by its name (if there is one) or
by its number within a WHEN OTHERS clause. Let's look at an example.

The UTL_FILE.GET LINE procedure raises the NO_DATA_FOUND exception
(ORA-01403, but SQLCODE actually returns a value of 100) if you try to read past
the end of a file. You can handle this error in either of the following ways:

```
EXCEPTION
   WHEN NO_DATA_FOUND
   THEN
      ...
```

or:

```
EXCEPTION
   WHEN OTHERS
   THEN
      IF SQLCODE = 100
      THEN
         /* SQLERRM returns the standard Oracle error message */
         ...
END;
```

Of course, if you need to handle an exception that does not have a name associated with it, you can only rely on the WHEN OTHERS clause and an IF statement
with SQLCODE to handle that error specifically.

Package-specific exception

In some packages, Oracle developers decided to appropriate for their own use
error numbers in the range set aside by Oracle Corporation for customer use
(–20999 through –20000). This is very poor practice, as it can cause conflicts with
your own use of these values. Unfortunately, it does happen and you need to
know what to do about it.

For example, the DBMS_OUTPUT package uses the –20000 error number to communicate back to the calling program either one of these errors:

```
ORU-10027: buffer overflow, limit of <buf_limit> bytes.
ORU-10028: line length overflow, limit of 255 bytes per line.
```

Here is a attempt to call DBMS_OUTPUT.PUT_LINE that raises an unhandled exception in a SQL*Plus session:

```
SQL> exec dbms_output.put_line (rpad ('abc', 300, 'def'))
*
ERROR at line 1:
ORA-20000: ORU-10028: line length overflow, limit of 255 bytes per line
ORA-06512: at "SYS.DBMS_OUTPUT", line 99
ORA-06512: at "SYS.DBMS_OUTPUT", line 65
ORA-06512: at line 1
```

I can handle this error if I call the built-in procedure from within a PL/SQL block as follows:

```
/* Filename on companion disk: myput.sp */
CREATE OR REPLACE PROCEDURE myput (str IN VARCHAR2)
IS
BEGIN
   DBMS_OUTPUT.PUT_LINE (str);
EXCEPTION
   WHEN OTHERS
   THEN
      IF SQLCODE = -20000
      THEN
         IF SQLERRM LIKE '%ORU-10027%'
         THEN
            DBMS_OUTPUT.ENABLE (1000000);
            myput (str);

         ELSIF SQLERRM LIKE '%ORU-10028%'
         THEN
            myput (SUBSTR (str, 1, 255));
            myput (SUBSTR (str, 256));
         END IF;
      END IF;
END;
/
```

The myput procedure implements the following logic: try to display the string. If an exception is raised, check to see if it is a −20000 error. If so, see if the error message indicates that it is a "buffer too small" error. If so, expand the buffer to the maximum size and try again to display the string. If the error message indicates a "string too long" error, display the first 255 bytes and then call myput again recursively to display the rest of the string.

Same exception, different causes

One interesting situation you may run into when working with some of the built-in packages is that the same exception can be raised from different circumstances.

Specifically, the NO_DATA_FOUND exception is raised by the PL/SQL runtime engine under any of these conditions:

- You execute a SELECT INTO query (an implicit cursor) that does not identify any rows.

- You attempt to access a row in a PL/SQL or index-by table that is not yet defined.

- You try to read past the end of a file using UTL_FILE.GET_LINE.

- You read past the end of a large object with DBMS_LOB.READ.

If you are writing code that could raise NO_DATA_FOUND for different reasons, you may not be able to get by with a single exception handler like this:

```
EXCEPTION
   WHEN NO_DATA_FOUND
   THEN
      /* ?? What caused the problem? */
      ...
END;
```

You will want to know in the exception handler whether the problem was that the query returned no rows, or you read past the end of the file, or you tried to access an undefined row in an index-by table, or something else. If you face this problem, you may want to use a technique I call *exception aliasing*. Consider the very short program below:

```
CREATE OR REPLACE PROCEDURE just_a_demo
   (file IN UTL_FILE.FILE_TYPE, empno_in IN emp.empno%TYPE)
IS
   line VARCHAR2(1000);
   end_of_file EXCEPTION;
   v_ename emp.ename%TYPE;
BEGIN
   SELECT ename
     INTO v_ename
     FROM emp
    WHERE empno = empno_in;

   BEGIN
      UTL_FILE.GET_LINE (file, line);
   EXCEPTION
      WHEN NO_DATA_FOUND
      THEN
         RAISE end_of_file;
   END;
EXCEPTION
   WHEN end_of_file
   THEN
      DBMS_OUTPUT.PUT_LINE ('Read past end of file!');

   WHEN NO_DATA_FOUND
   THEN
```

```
        DBMS_OUTPUT.PUT_LINE
            ('No employee found for ' || TO_CHAR (empno_in));
    END:
    /
```

I have embedded the call to UTL_FILE.GET_LINE inside its own block. If that program reads past the end of a file and raises NO_DATA_FOUND, that block's exception section "translates" NO_DATA_FOUND into another, distinct exception: end_of_file (declared in the procedure itself). The exception section of the procedure as a whole can then distinguish between the two different NO_DATA_ FOUND scenarios.

Encapsulating Access to the Built-in Packages

You will discover (both through reading this book and through your own experience) that there are many reasons to avoid directly accessing built-in packaged functionality. In a number of cases, you will want to build your own package *on top of* the built-in package. This process is usually referred to as *encapsulation.*

Why would you bother with an encapsulation package? Any of the following reasons will do:

- The built-in packages offer lots of interesting technology, but they are not always very easy to use. You can hide the complexity, or in some cases, the poor design, and make it much easier for yourself and others to reap the benefits.

- Some of the packages contain programs that you would not want to make generally or widely available. Conversely, other programs in that same package might be very useful for the "general public." An encapsulation package can offer only those programs that *should* be available, while hiding the others. (In this case, you will want to revoke any EXECUTE privileges on the underlying package.)

- Write less code. Have you ever noticed the really impressive lengths of the names of Oracle built-in packages and their programs? Studies conducted by the Institute for Study Conduction estimate that by the year 2000, developers using PL/SQL will have experienced a $150 trillion loss in productivity due to having to type names like DBMS_DESCRIBE.DESCRIBE_PROCEDURE. Your encapsulations can use shorter names and thereby erase the federal deficit.

- Take full advantage of built-in packages from Oracle Developer/2000 Release 1. As you will read in the next section, there are many restrictions on accessing stored code from products like Oracle Forms. Encapsulation can help you work around these restrictions.

Roughly speaking, there are two types of encapsulation to consider when working with the built-in packages:

Extension encapsulation

This is the most common type of encapsulation for built-in packages. In this case, you provide one or more programs that *extend* the functionality or usability of the underlying package.

Covering encapsulation

When you create a cover for a built-in package, you create a package with a specification that matches that of the built-in package (same program names, same parameter lists). You can even give your package the same name as the built-in package, but you install it in a schema other than SYS.

When you revoke EXECUTE authority on the built-in package and grant EXECUTE authority on your package, users of the built-in package will automatically be directed to your replacement. Oracle recommends this technique, for example, with the DBMS_APPLICATION_INFO package.

Examples of encapsulation packages

This book (and the accompanying disk) contains many packages that encapsulate or cover an underlying built-in package (or, in some cases, a subset of the package). Table 1-3 shows the encapsulation packages in the book.

Table 1-3. Encapsulation Packages for Built-ins

Built-in Package/ Program	Encapsulation Package Name	File	Description
DBMS_AQ DBMS_AQADM	aq	*aq.spp*	Hides details of creating, starting, stopping, and dropping queues and queue tables. The package allows you to write less code and also handles common errors.
DBMS_APPLICATION_ INFO	register_app	*register.sql*	Allows developers to easily register applications and track resource usage statistics.
DBMS_APPLICATION_ INFO.SET_SESSION_ LONGOPS	longops	*longops.sql*	Simplifies use of this difficult procedure.
DBMS_UTILITY. GET_PARAMETER_ VALUE	dbparm	*dbparm.spp*	Makes it easier to obtain specific initialization values from the database instance.

Table 1-3. Encapsulation Packages for Built-ins (continued)

Built-in Package/ Program	Encapsulation Package Name	File	Description
DBMS_UTILITY. DB_VERSION	db	*dbver.spp*	Converts through encapsulation the DB_VERSION procedure into two separate functions, so you can ask for the version or the compatibility value, as desired.
DBMS_SQL. DESCRIBE_ COLUMNS	desccols	*desccols.spp*	Provides a general, flexible interface to DBMS_ SQL.DESCRIBE_COLUMNS so you don't need to declare PL/SQL tables and call that wordy built-in procedure to obtain the column information.
DBMS_SQL.PARSE	dynconst	*dynconst.spp*	Hides the need to provide a DBMS_SQL database mode when you parse a SQL statement. This technique is especially useful when you are writing code in Oracle Developer/2000 Release 1. (See the next section for details.)
DBMS_DESCRIBE	psdesc	*psdesc.spp*	Hides the need to declare a dozen different PL/SQL tables just so you can use DBMS_DESCRIBE. DESCRIBE_PROCEDURE.
DBMS_IJOB.REMOVE	remove_all_ jobs (procedure)	*job3.sql*	Allows the DBA to remove all jobs regardless of owner.
DBMS_LOCK	dblock	*dblock.sql*	Simplifies the use of user-named locks, as well as maximizing their efficiency.
DBMS_IJOB.BROKEN	break_all_jobs (procedure)	*job3.sql*	Allows the DBA to set the broken flag in all jobs regardless of owner.
DBMS_PIPE	dbpipe	*dbpipe.sql*	Provides some useful and interesting pipe utilities, including generic message pack/unpack and message forwarding.
DBMS_SESSION	my_session	*mysess.sql*	Simplifies use of some of the programs and adds some additional conveniences.

Table 1-3. Encapsulation Packages for Built-ins (continued)

Built-in Package/ Program	Encapsulation Package Name	File	Description
DBMS_SHARED_POOL. KEEP	object_keeper (procedure)	*keeper.sql*	Allows configurable auto-keeping of packages in database startup scripts.
DBMS_SPACE	segspace	*segspace.sql*	Transforms the unwieldy procedure calls into simple, SQL-callable functions.
DBMS_SYSTEM. SET_SQL_TRACE_ IN_SESSION	trace	*trace.sql*	Allows the DBA to set SQL tracing on or off in other sessions by username or session id.

Calling Built-in Packaged Code from Oracle Developer/2000 Release 1

If you use Oracle Developer/2000 Release 1 to build your client-side application, you can use the built-in packages, but you should be aware of the following restrictions:[*]

- You can reference only packaged procedures and functions. You cannot, for example, make reference in your client-side code to DBMS_SQL.NATIVE (a constant) or UTL_FILE.INVALID_OPERATION (an exception).

- You must supply a value for each argument in a packaged procedure or function. You cannot rely on default values in the headers of those programs. This is true even if those default values do not reference elements in the built-in packages (in other words, are literal values).

- You must be connected to the Oracle database before you can compile program units that reference built-in packages. While it is possible to work on your client-side module without connecting to Oracle, the PL/SQL compiler cannot resolve references to server-side objects like built-in packages unless you are connected.

The following sections explore these restrictions in more detail and suggest work-arounds for making full use of the built-in packages from within products like Oracle Forms and Oracle Reports.

Referencing packaged constants and variables

Consider the DBMS_SQL.PARSE procedure. Here is the header for this program:

---

[*] These restrictions are not likely to affect you when you work with Oracle Developer/2000 Release 2 or above.

```
PROCEDURE DBMS_SQL.PARSE
   (c IN INTEGER,
    statement IN VARCHAR2,
    language_flag IN INTEGER);
```

The third argument, language_flag, can be any of the following values, as defined by constants in the DBMS_SQL specification:

```
DBMS_SQL.V6
DBMS_SQL.V7
DBMS_SQL.NATIVE
```

Now, if you try to execute this program in an Oracle Forms program unit, as in the following,

```
BEGIN
   DBMS_SQL.PARSE (cur, 'SELECT ...', DBMS_SQL.NATIVE);
   ...
```

you will receive this error:

```
Error 302: component NATIVE must be declared
```

Oracle Forms simply does not know how to interpret anything but procedures and functions in stored packages. So what's a developer to do? You have several options:

- Find out the literal value *behind* the named constant and use that, or

- Create a stored function that encapsulates the constant and call that, or

- Create a stored procedure that calls DBMS_SQL.PARSE and hides the use of the constant.

The first option would result in code like this:

```
BEGIN
   DBMS_SQL.PARSE (cur, 'SELECT ...', 1);
   ...
```

I suggest that you do not take this approach. You are always better off not proliferating the use of literals like this one in your code. They are hard to understand and leave you vulnerable to errors caused by changes in the way that DBMS_SQL behaves.

The second option (encapsulating the constant inside a function) is better. I could, for example, create a tiny package as follows:

```
/* Filename on companion disk: dynconst.spp */
CREATE OR REPLACE PACKAGE dynsql_value
IS
     FUNCTION v6 RETURN INTEGER;
     FUNCTION v7 RETURN INTEGER;
     FUNCTION native RETURN INTEGER;
END;
```

```
/
CREATE OR REPLACE PACKAGE BODY dynsql_value
IS
    FUNCTION v6 RETURN INTEGER
        IS BEGIN RETURN DBMS_SQL.V6; END;

    FUNCTION v7 RETURN INTEGER;
        IS BEGIN RETURN DBMS_SQL.V7; END;

    FUNCTION native RETURN INTEGER;
        IS BEGIN RETURN DBMS_SQL.NATIVE; END;
END;
/
```

With this code in place on the server, I can then call DBMS_SQL.PARSE as follows:

```
BEGIN
    DBMS_SQL.PARSE (cur, 'SELECT ...', dynsql_value.native);
    ...
```

This code is almost identical to my first example, but I am calling a function rather than referencing a literal, and that makes all the difference.

The third option, encapsulating the call to DBMS_SQL.PARSE, is perhaps the optimal solution. Why should you even have to bother passing the database mode? You might as well just always make it "native." Here is some code that hides this argument entirely:

```
*Filename on companion disk: dynconst.spp */
CREATE OR REPLACE PACKAGE dynsql_value
IS
    PROCEDURE parse (cur IN INTEGER, sql_str IN VARCHAR2);
END;
/
CREATE OR REPLACE PACKAGE BODY dynsql_value
IS
    PROCEDURE parse (cur IN INTEGER, sql_str IN VARCHAR2)
    IS
    BEGIN
        DBMS_SQL.PARSE (cur, sql_str, DBMS_SQL.NATIVE)
    END;
END;
/
```

Now I can parse a SQL statement from within Oracle Forms as follows:

```
BEGIN
    dynsql_value.parse (cur, 'SELECT ...');
    ...
```

I recommend this last technique, because you will inevitably find other workaround needs having to do with DBMS_SQL or another built-in package. Why not collect them all together in a single encapsulator package? This point is driven home in the next section.

Handling exceptions in Oracle Developer/2000 Release 1

An earlier section in this chapter ("Exception Handling and Built-in Packages") explored the different types of exceptions that can be raised from within built-in packages. One type in particular, the package-specific exception, presents a challenge to Oracle Developer/2000 programmers.

Consider once again the UTL_FILE package. It declares a number of exceptions and, as noted previously, the only way to handle those exceptions (and know which exception was raised) is to create an explicit exception handler, as in:

```
EXCEPTION
   WHEN UTL_FILE.INVALID_MODE
   THEN
      ...
END;
```

Unfortunately, you cannot write this kind of code from Oracle Forms. It cannot resolve the reference to UTL_FILE.INVALID_MODE. What can you do? If you are going to make extensive use of UTL_FILE from Oracle Forms (or Oracle Reports), and you want to build in some robust error handling, you should probably consider building a wrapper package around UTL_FILE.

Instead of calling UTL_FILE.FOPEN directly, for example, and risk raising an exception you cannot interpret accurately, you might want to consider something like this:

```
/* Filename on companion disk: myfile.spp */
CREATE OR REPLACE PACKAGE myfile
IS
   /* Document in the package specification that:
      - INVALID_MODE is returned as -20100.
      - INVALID_PATH is returned as -20101.
      - INVALID_OPERATION is returned as -20102.
   */
   PROCEDURE fopen
      (loc IN VARCHAR2, file IN VARCHAR2, fmode IN VARCHAR2);
END;
/
CREATE OR REPLACE PACKAGE BODY myfile
IS
   g_file UTL_FILE.FILE_TYPE;

   PROCEDURE fopen
      (loc IN VARCHAR2, file IN VARCHAR2, fmode IN VARCHAR2)
   IS
   BEGIN
      g_file := UTL_FILE.FOPEN (loc, file, fmode);
   EXCEPTION
      WHEN UTL_FILE.INVALID_MODE
      THEN
```

```
              RAISE_APPLICATION_ERROR (-20100, 'Invalid mode ' || fmode);

          WHEN UTL_FILE.INVALID_PATH
          THEN
              RAISE_APPLICATION_ERROR (-20101, 'Invalid path ' || loc);

          WHEN UTL_FILE.INVALID_MODE
          THEN
              RAISE_APPLICATION_ERROR (-20102, 'Invalid operation');

      END;
   END;
   /
```

I accomplish two things with this prototype package:

1. I translate the package-specific exceptions to –20NNN exceptions. Therefore, my UTL_FILE exception now has a number. I can check for that number within my client-side application and take appropriate action.

2. I hide the UTL_FILE.FILE_TYPE record. From Oracle Forms, I cannot even declare a record of this type (it is not a program, so UTL_FILE.FILE_TYPE cannot be referenced from within Oracle Developer/2000 Release 1).

With this wrapper approach, you can build a package that allows you to read and write a particular server-side file from Oracle Forms. You would still need to build read, write, and close procedures, but the technique should be clear.

Accessing Built-in Packaged Technology from Within SQL

Throughout this book, you will find documentation indicating whether a particular packaged function can be called from within an SQL statement, or whether a packaged procedure can be called by a function that, in turn, is called from within SQL. This section explains the significance of that capability.

If you are running a version of Oracle Server 7.1 and beyond, you can call PL/SQL functions from within SQL statements. (If you are not running at least Oracle Server 7.1, you can skip this section—but you should also certainly upgrade your database software as soon as possible!) Let's take a look at an example to give you a feel for this capability.

Suppose that my formula for calculating total compensation for an employee is "salary plus commission." Here is that formula implemented in PL/SQL:

```
CREATE OR REPLACE FUNCTION totcomp
   (sal_in IN NUMBER, comm_in IN NUMBER)
RETURN NUMBER
IS
BEGIN
```

```
      RETURN sal_in + NVL (comm_in, 0);
END;
/
```

Once this program is stored in the database, I can call it from within a query as follows:

```
SQL> SELECT ename, totcomp (sal, comm) total_compensation FROM emp;

ENAME       TOTAL_COMPENSATION
----------  ------------------
SMITH                      800
...
MILLER                    1300
```

You can also call a packaged function from within a SQL statement. In this case, however, you must also provide a special statement, the RESTRICT_REFERENCES pragma, to enable that function for use inside SQL. Here, for example, is the code you would have to write to place totcomp inside a package and still call it from a query:

```
CREATE OR REPLACE PACKAGE empcomp
IS
   FUNCTION totcomp
      (sal_in IN NUMBER, comm_in IN NUMBER)
   RETURN NUMBER;

   PRAGMA RESTRICT_REFERENCES (total, WNDS, RNDS, WNPS, RNPS);
END;
/
CREATE OR REPLACE PACKAGE BODY empcomp
IS
   FUNCTION totcomp
      (sal_in IN NUMBER, comm_in IN NUMBER)
   RETURN NUMBER
   IS
   BEGIN
      RETURN (sal_in + NVL (comm_in, 0));
   END;
END;
/
```

The line in bold is the statement asserting that the empcomp.total function does not violate any of the restrictions on functions in SQL. Here is how you would call this packaged function inside SQL:

```
SQL> SELECT ename, empcomp.total (sal, comm) total_comp from emp;

ENAME       TOTAL_COMP
----------  ----------
SMITH              800
...
MILLER            1300
```

The same rules apply for built-in packaged programs callable from SQL. Oracle Corporation itself must provide a RESTRICT_REFERENCES pragma in its own package specifications for any procedure or function that is to be used from within SQL. And since Oracle did not pragmatize built-in packages prior to Oracle 7.3.3, you will not be able to call built-in packaged programs from SQL (directly or indirectly) until you install Oracle 7.3.4 or later.

If you try to call a packaged function in SQL that does not have such a pragma, you will receive this error:

```
SQL> SELECT utl_file.fopen ('/tmp', ename || '.dat', 'R')
  2     FROM employee;
select utl_file.fopen ('a', 'b', 'r') from employee
       *
ERROR at line 1:
ORA-06571: Function FOPEN does not guarantee not to update database
```

Don't you hate those double negatives?

You will also encounter this same error if you try to execute a function in SQL that, in turn, calls a packaged procedure that does not have a pragma. For example, the DBMS_JOB.SUBMIT procedure is not "pragma-tized" for use in SQL. Consequently, the following function (exactly the same as that shown earlier, except for the addition of the procedure call) will not be executable within SQL:

```
CREATE OR REPLACE FUNCTION totcomp
   (sal_in IN NUMBER, comm_in IN NUMBER)
RETURN NUMBER
IS
   myjob INTEGER;
BEGIN
   DBMS_JOB.SUBMIT (myjob, 'calc_totals;');
   RETURN (sal_in + NVL (comm_in, 0));
END;
/
```

Here is the error I get when I try to execute my new and "improved" function:

```
SQL> SELECT totcomp (salary, NULL) FROM employee;
SELECT totcomp (salary, NULL) FROM employee
       *
ERROR at line 1:
ORA-06571: Function TOTCOMP does not guarantee not to update database
```

Calling a packaged function in SQL

If you want to use a packaged function in a SQL statement, it must have a RESTRICT_REFERENCES pragma. If that is the case, you are all set! Just call the function as you would call a built-in function such as SUBSTR or TO_CHAR.

Suppose that I am working on the large objects stored in files. The DBMS_LOB package includes several RESTRICT_REFERENCES pragmas. Here is the program for the GETLENGTH function:

```
PRAGMA RESTRICT_REFERENCES (getlength, WNDS, RNDS, WNPS, RNPS);
```

Here are the meanings for each of those *purity levels*:

WNDS

Writes No Database State. In other words, does not make any changes to database structures by calling an INSERT, UPDATE, or DELETE.

WNPS

Writes No Package State. In other words, does not change the values of any package data structures.

RNDS

Read No Database State. In other words, does not SELECT from any database tables or other database objects.

RNPS

Reads No Package State. In other words, does not reference any package data structures.

The absolute minimum purity level required to allow a program to be used (directly or indirectly) inside SQL is WNDS. You can *never* update the database. In some situations, such as when you want to call a function from within a WHERE clause, the program will also need to have asserted the WNPS purity level.

Since DBMS_LOB.GETLENGTH asserts all four purity levels, I can use it in SQL, both in the SELECT list of a query and even in the WHERE clause. Here is an example; in it, I display the length of each photograph stored in the archives for my family:

```
SELECT DBMS_LOB.GETLENGTH (portrait_lob_loc)
   FROM photo_archive
  WHERE family = 'FEUERSTEIN AND DBMS_LOB.GETLENGTH (portrait_lob_loc) < 1000;
```

Table 1-4 provides a complete list of all packaged programs that can be called (directly or indirectly) from within a SQL statement, the purity levels for each, and the Oracle versions in which these purity levels become available (thus enabling you to call the programs from within SQL). The rest of this section explains how to use packaged functions and procedures, and the meaning of the various purity levels.

Table 1-4. Purity Levels for Oracle Built-in Package Programs

Package	Program	WNDS	WNPS	RNDS	RNPS
DBMS_LOB	COMPARE[a]	X	X	X	X
	FILEEXISTS[a]	X	X	X	X
	FILEISOPEN	X	X	X	X
	GETLENGTH	X	X	X	X
	INSTR	X	X	X	X
	SUBSTR	X	X	X	X
DBMS_OUTPUT	DISABLE[b]	X		X	
	ENABLE[b]	X		X	
	GET_LINE[b]	X		X	
	GET_LINES[b]	X		X	
	NEW_LINE[b]	X		X	
	PUT[b]	X		X	
	PUT_LINE[b]	X		X	
DBMS_PIPE	CREATE_PIPE[b]	X		X	
	NEXT_ITEM_TYPE[b]	X		X	
	PACK_MESSAGE[b]	X		X	
	PACK_MESSAGE_RAW[b]	X		X	
	PACK_MESSAGE_ROWID[b]	X		X	
	PURGE[b]	X		X	
	RECEIVE_MESSAGE[b]	X		X	
	REMOVE_PIPE[b]	X		X	
	RESET_BUFFER[b]	X		X	
	SEND_MESSAGE[b]	X		X	
	UNIQUE_SESSION_NAME[b]	X	X	X	
	UNPACK_MESSAGE[b]	X		X	
	UNPACK_MESSAGE_RAW[b]	X		X	
	UNPACK_MESSAGE_ROW-ID[b]	X		X	
DBMS_ROWID	ROWID_BLOCK_NUMBER[a]	X	X	X	X
	ROWID_CREATE[a]	X	X	X	X
	ROWID_INFO[a]	X	X	X	X
	ROWID_OBJECT[a]	X	X	X	
	ROWID_RELATIVE_FNO[a]	X	X		X
	ROWID_ROW_NUMBER[a]	X	X	X	X
	ROWID_TO_ABSOLUTE[a]	X	X	X	X
	ROWID_TO_EXTENDED[a]	X	X		X
	ROWID_TO_RESTRICTED[a]	X	X	X	X

Table 1-4. Purity Levels for Oracle Built-in Package Programs (continued)

Package	Program	WNDS	WNPS	RNDS	RNPS
	ROWID_TYPE[a]	X	X	X	X
	ROWID_VERIFY[a]	X	X		X
DBMS_SESSION	UNIQUE_SESSION_ID[b]	X	X	X	
DBMS_STANDARD	DELETING[b]	X	X		X
	INSERTING[b]	X	X		X
	RAISE_APPLICATION_ ERROR[b]	X	X	X	X
	UPDATING[b]	X	X		X
DBMS_UTILITY	DATA_BLOCK_ADDRESS_ BLOCK[b]	X	X	X	X
	DATA_BLOCK_ADDRESS_ FILE[b]	X	X	X	X
	GET_HASH_VALUE[b]	X	X	X	X
	MAKE_DATA_BLOCK_ ADDRESS[b]	X	X	X	X
	PORT_STRING[b]	X	X	X	X
UTL_RAW	BIT_AND[b]	x	x	x	x
	BIT_COMPLEMENT[b]	X	X	X	X
	BIT_OR[b]	X	X	X	X
	BIT_XOR[b]	X	X	X	X
	CAST_TO_RAW[b]	X	X	X	X
	COMPARE[b]	X	X	X	X
	CONCAT[b]	X	X	X	X
	CONVERT[b]	X	X	X	X
	COPIES[b]	X	X	X	X
	LENGTH[b]	X	X	X	X
	OVERLAY[b]	X	X	X	X
	REVERSE[b]	X	X	X	X
	SUBSTR[b]	X	X	X	X
	TRANSLATE[b]	X	X	X	X
	TRANSLITERATE[b]	X	X	X	X
	XRANGE[b]	X	X	X	X

[a] Indicates availability in Oracle8 and above only.
[b] Indicates availability in Oracle7.3 and above only.

Using a packaged procedure from within SQL

You cannot call a PL/SQL procedure directly inside an SQL statement. Instead, you would call that procedure from within a function that is called in SQL (or within another program that is, in turn, called by that function, and so on). That function will not work within SQL unless the procedure it calls has a RESTRICT_ REFERENCES pragma.

You will most likely run into this situation when you want to add some trace capabilities to your SQL statement. Suppose that I want to write a general trace function that I can add to any SELECT statement to obtain information about the rows' queries. Here is one possible implementation:

```
CREATE OR REPLACE FUNCTION sql_trace (str IN VARCHAR2) RETURN NUMBER
IS
BEGIN
   DBMS_OUTPUT.PUT_LINE ('Display from SQL: ' || str);
   RETURN 0;
EXCEPTION
   WHEN OTHERS THEN RETURN SQLCODE;
END;
/
```

Now I will use this function inside SQL:

```
SQL> SELECT last_name, sql_trace (first_name) trc
  2    FROM employee
  3    WHERE department_id = 20;
```

And here are the results:

```
LAST_NAME              TRC
--------------- ----------
SMITH                    0
JONES                    0
SCOTT                    0
ADAMS                    0
FORD                     0
```

Wait a minute! Where's the trace output from the function? It turns out that you must call DBMS_OUTPUT.ENABLE to flush out the current contents of the buffer (a "standalone" call to DBMS_OUTPUT.PUT_LINE will also do the trick). Here we go:

```
SQL> exec dbms_output.enable
Display from SQL: JOHN
Display from SQL: TERRY
Display from SQL: DONALD
Display from SQL: DIANE
Display from SQL: JENNIFER
```

Examining Built-in Package Source Code

When you install the Oracle database, the source code files for all of the built-in packages are placed on your hard disk (either on your own personal computer or on some "remote" server). I recommend strongly that you take some time to examine these files for several reasons:

1. The files contain documentation that may complement the contents of this book and improve your understanding of how to use the packages.

2. The files are the source code. They contain the definitive listing of what is available in the package. This book makes a valiant effort to offer up-to-date information on almost every one of the most commonly used packages, but it never hurts to check the original. For example, I suggest that every time you install a new version of the database, you should check (at a minimum) the *dbmsutil.sql* file, to see if Oracle Corporation has added anything to its miscellaneous package, DBMS_UTILITY.

3. It can be an awful lot of fun to see how Oracle's own developers construct and document their own PL/SQL packages. This is particularly true of the file containing the STANDARD package, *standard.sql*.

4. Dependencies. The built-in package file can provide you with other valuable information, including which built-in packages and/or other objects must already be in the database before you can proceed with the installation.

Where do you find all of this interesting code? If you are working in a UNIX environment, the files that define the built-in packages may be found in,

```
$ORACLE_HOME/rdbmsNN/admin
```

where NN is the version number. So if you are running Oracle 7.3, you will find the source code files in /this directory/:

```
$ORACLE_HOME/rdbms73/admin
```

If you are working in Windows NT, these files are located in,

```
C:\OraNT\RdbmsNN\admin
```

where C is the drive on which Oracle was installed. You can probably deduce the pattern at this point for other operating systems.

If you are working in a UNIX environment that conforms to the OFA (Optimal Flexible Architecture) configuration standards, the catalog scripts will be found under,

```
$ORACLE_HOME/rdbms/admin
```

with the $ORACLE_HOME environment variable containing the Oracle version information.

If you are working with VAX/VMS, the software directory tree structure often looks like this:

```
[ORACLE733.RDBMS.ADMIN]
[ORACLE803.RDBMS.ADMIN]
```

Note that you do not necessarily have read access on these directories, so I cannot guarantee that you will be able to view the contents of these files. If you can, however, I suggest that you first stop at *standard.sql* (present up through Oracle 7.3, but seems to disappear with some installations of Oracle 8.0). This file contains the definition of the STANDARD package, which is explained in the next section.

The STANDARD Package

One of the most surprising things I ever learned about the PL/SQL language is that the most basic elements of that language are defined in a PL/SQL package called STANDARD. According to the modification history in the *standard.sql* file, this package was created on November 21, 1992. Contained inside it are many lessons about the very nature of the PL/SQL language.

Consider the TO_DATE and SUBSTR functions. Although they seem like basic, low-level language elements, both of these are functions defined (and overloaded) in the STANDARD package. Even more astonishing, the most basic operators in the PL/SQL language, such as +, IN, and LIKE, are actually defined as functions in that same package.

Here, for example, are the definitions of the LIKE and = operators,

```
function 'LIKE' (str VARCHAR2, pat VARCHAR2) return BOOLEAN;
function '='  (LEFT NUMBER, RIGHT NUMBER) return BOOLEAN;
```

and here is the implementation of LIKE:

```
function 'LIKE' (str varchar2, pat varchar2) return boolean is
begin
  return peslik(str, pat);
end;
```

What is this peslik function? Ah, that is where, when, and how Oracle "cheats" (or, at least, makes the rest of us PL/SQL developers jealous):

```
function peslik(str varchar2, pat varchar2) return boolean;
    pragma interface (c,peslik);
```

The peslik function is a stub program for a callout to C.

You will also discover that all PL/SQL datatypes are defined in the STANDARD package specification as types and subtypes:

```
subtype INTEGER is NUMBER(38,0);
subtype BINARY_INTEGER is INTEGER range '-2147483647'..2147483647;
subtype NATURAL is BINARY_INTEGER range 0..2147483647;
subtype NATURALN is NATURAL not null;
subtype SIGNTYPE is BINARY_INTEGER range '-1'..1;  -- for SIGN functions
```

Interestingly, the subtype SIGNTYPE is not listed in PL/SQL manual. Once discovered here, though, you can put it to use in your code.* If, for example, you need a variable that can only have values −1, 0, 1, and NULL, you can write something like this:

```
/* Filename on companion disk: creind.sp */
DECLARE my_variable SIGNTYPE;
```

Trying to assign my_variable outside of SIGNTYPE range results in an error:

```
SQL> DECLARE my_variable SIGNTYPE;
  2  BEGIN
  3    my_variable := 2;
  4  END;
  5  /
DECLARE my_variable SIGNTYPE;

*

ERROR at line 1:
ORA-06502: PL/SQL: numeric or value error
ORA-06512: at line 3
```

All predefined exceptions are also defined in the STANDARD package specification:

```
LOGIN_DENIED exception;
   pragma EXCEPTION_INIT(LOGIN_DENIED, '-1017');
```

If you are still running Oracle7, take a look at *standard.sql*. You might even want to copy it to some other location, so that when you upgrade to Oracle8, you won't lose access to this file and all of its fascinating contents.

The DBMS_STANDARD Package

The other default package, DBMS_STANDARD, deserves some mention. It can be found in the *dbmsstdx.sql* file, and it contains, according to the file's own documentation, "kernel extensions to package STANDARD... mostly utility routines for triggers." You will find in DBMS_STANDARD the following programs:

```
PROCEDURE raise_application_error
   (num BINARY_INTEGER,
    msg VARCHAR2,
    keeperrorstack BOOLEAN DEFAULT FALSE);

FUNCTION inserting RETURN BOOLEAN;
FUNCTION deleting  RETURN BOOLEAN;
FUNCTION updating  RETURN BOOLEAN;
FUNCTION updating (colnam varchar2) RETURN BOOLEAN;
```

---

* This insight was provided by Solomon Yakobson.

So whenever you write code like this,

```
IF hiredate < ADD_MONTHS (SYSDATE, -216)
THEN
   RAISE_APPLICATION_ERROR
      (-20000, ' Employee must be at least 18 years old.');
END IF;
```

you are actually calling a program in the DBMS_STANDARD package. Again, this package is defaulted, so you do not need to qualify references to these procedures and functions.

II

Application Development Packages

This part of the book describes the built-in application development packages:

- Chapter 2, *Executing Dynamic SQL and PL/SQL*, shows you how to use the DBMS_SQL package to construct and execute SQL statements and PL/SQL blocks at runtime.

- Chapter 3, *Intersession Communication*, shows you how to use DBMS_PIPE and DBMS_ALERT to communicate information between different Oracle sessions. You can also use DBMS_PIPE to communicate with processes external to Oracle.

- Chapter 4, *User Lock and Transaction Management*, introduces DBMS_LOCK, a handy but rarely used package that interfaces to the Oracle lock manager, and DBMS_TRANSACTION, which offers several programs that affect transaction behavior in your PL/SQL program.

- Chapter 5, *Oracle Advanced Queuing*, contains an extensive treatment of Oracle Advanced Queuing, a powerful queuing mechanism available with Oracle8, and the DBMS_AQ and DBMS_AQADM packages.

- Chapter 6, *Generating Output from PL/SQL Programs*, shows you how to send information from your program either to the screen, using DBMS_OUTPUT, or to a server-side file, using UTL_FILE.

- Chapter 7, *Defining an Application Profile*, familiarizes you with a handy package, DBMS_APPLICATION_INFO. You'll use it to "register" the current execution status of your application with the Oracle database.

- Chapter 8, *Managing Large Objects*, shows you how Oracle8 provides robust support for large objects (sometimes known as BLOBs or LOBs), and how the DBMS_LOB built-in package allows you to access and manipulate these LOBs from within a PL/SQL program.

- Chapter 9, *Datatype Packages*, collects together several packages that manipulate different types of data. DBMS_ROWID makes it easy to work with the two different ROWID formats available in Oracle8. UTL_RAW allows you to work with raw data. UTL_REF, new in Oracle8 Release 8.1, provides a PL/SQL interface to select and modify objects (instances of an object type) in an object table without having to specify or know about the underlying database table.

- Chapter 10, *Miscellaneous Packages*, contains coverage of a number of packages: DBMS_UTILITY (the actual "miscellaneous" package), DBMS_DESCRIBE (gets information about the parameters of a stored program), DBMS_DDL (contains programs to recompile stored code, analyze objects in your schema, and modify the referenceability of object identifiers in Oracle8), and DBMS_RANDOM (a random number generator).

2

Executing Dynamic SQL and PL/SQL

The DBMS_SQL package offers access to dynamic SQL and dynamic PL/SQL from within PL/SQL programs. "Dynamic" means that the SQL statements you execute with this package are not prewritten into your programs. They are, instead, constructed at runtime as character strings and then passed to the SQL engine for execution.

The DBMS_SQL package allows you to perform actions that are otherwise impossible from within PL/SQL programs, including:

Execute DDL statements

DDL (Data Definition Language) statements, such as DROP TABLE or CREATE INDEX, are not legal in native PL/SQL. On the other hand, you can use DBMS_SQL to issue any DDL statement and create generic programs to perform such actions as dropping the specified table. Of course, your session will still need the appropriate database privileges to perform the requested actions.

Build an ad-hoc query interface

With DBMS_SQL, you no longer have to hard-code a SELECT statement for a query or a cursor. Instead, you can let a user specify different sort orders, conditions, and any other portion of a SELECT statement.

Execute dynamically constructed PL/SQL programs

In a database table you can store the names of procedures that perform certain calculations. Then build a front-end to that table, which allows a user to select the computation of interest, provide the inputs to that program, and then execute it. When other computations need to be offered to the user, you add a row in a table, instead of modifying one or more screens.

DBMS_SQL is simultaneously one of the most complex, most useful, and most rewarding of the built-in packages. It may take some time for you to get comfortable with how to apply the technology. Once you are up and running, however, you will be amazed at the feats you will be able to perform!

Examples of Dynamic SQL

Before explaining the details of DBMS_SQL, let's look at a few concrete examples.

When you issue a SQL statement via DBMS_SQL, you will have to write much more code than you would by simply executing a native SQL statement, such as an implicit cursor created with a SELECT statement. To get a feel for the differences between these two approaches, consider the following code. This first procedure uses native SQL to give every employee in the specified department a raise:

```
PROCEDURE giveraise (dept_in IN INTEGER, raise_in IN NUMBER) IS
BEGIN
    UPDATE employee
        SET salary = salary + raise_in
      WHERE department_id = dept_in;
END;
```

The following procedure does the same thing, but with DBMS_SQL. Given the volume of code (and the subsequent overhead), you should only use DBMS_SQL when your SQL statement is truly dynamic or involves DDL.

```
PROCEDURE giveraise (dept_in IN INTEGER, raise_in IN NUMBER)
IS
    cursor_handle INTEGER;
    emps_updated INTEGER;
BEGIN
    /* Create a cursor to use for the dynamic SQL */
    cursor_handle := DBMS_SQL.OPEN_CURSOR;
    /*
    || Construct the SQL statement and parse it in Version 7 mode.
    || Notice that the statement includes two bind variables; these
    || are "placeholders" in the SQL statement.
    */
    DBMS_SQL.PARSE
       (cursor_handle,
         'UPDATE employee SET salary = salary + :raise_amount ' ||
            'WHERE department_id = :dept',
         DBMS_SQL.V7);

    /* Now I must supply values for the bind variables */
    DBMS_SQL.BIND_VARIABLE (cursor_handle, 'raise_amount', raise_in);
    DBMS_SQL.BIND_VARIABLE (cursor_handle, 'dept', dept_in);

    /* Execute the SQL statement */
```

```
    emps_updated := DBMS_SQL.EXECUTE (cursor_handle);

    /* Close the cursor */
    DBMS_SQL.CLOSE_CURSOR (cursor_handle);
EXCEPTION
    WHEN OTHERS
    THEN
        /* Clean up on failure too. */
        DBMS_SQL.CLOSE_CURSOR (cursor_handle);
END;
```

Truly dynamic SQL occurs when you literally construct the SQL statement from runtime variable values. This is shown in the next example. The create_index procedure creates an index where the name of the index, the name of the table, and the column on which the index is to be created are passed as parameters to the procedure. This action would be impossible without DBMS_SQL for two reasons: this is a DDL call and the SQL statement isn't known until the procedure is called.

```
/* Filename on companion disk: creind.sp */
CREATE OR REPLACE PROCEDURE create_index
    (index_in IN VARCHAR2, table_in IN VARCHAR2, column_in in VARCHAR2)
IS
    cursor_handle INTEGER;
    feedback INTEGER;
BEGIN
    /* Create a cursor to use for the dynamic SQL */
    cursor_handle := DBMS_SQL.OPEN_CURSOR;

    /* Construct the SQL statement and parse it in native mode. */
    DBMS_SQL.PARSE
        (cursor_handle,
         'CREATE INDEX ' || index_in || ' ON ' || table_in ||
            '( ' || column_in || ')',
         DBMS_SQL.NATIVE);

    /* You should always execute your DDL! */
    feedback := DBMS_SQL.EXECUTE (cursor_handle);

    DBMS_SQL.CLOSE_CURSOR (cursor_handle);
END create_index;
/
```

Getting Started with DBMS_SQL

Before you start using DBMS_SQL, you need to make sure that it is installed and that the appropriate users have access to this package. In addition, you should be aware of how privileges are applied to programs that execute dynamic SQL.

Creating the DBMS_SQL Package

The DBMS_SQL package is created when the Oracle database is installed. The *dbmssql.sql* script (found in the built-in packages source code directory, as described in Chapter 1, *Introduction*) contains the source code for this package's specification. This script is called by *catproc.sql*, which is normally run immediately after database creation. The script creates the public synonym DBMS_SQL for the package and grants EXECUTE privilege on the package to public. All Oracle users can reference and make use of this package.

Given the power, flexibility, and potential impact of dynamic SQL, you may actually want to revoke public access to DBMS_SQL and instead grant EXECUTE privilege to only those users who need to perform dynamic SQL.

To "hide" DBMS_SQL, issue this command from the SYS account:

```
REVOKE EXECUTE ON DBMS_SQL FROM PUBLIC;
```

To grant EXECUTE privilege to a specific user, issue this command from SYS:

```
GRANT EXECUTE ON DBMS_SQL TO whatever_user;
```

Security and Privilege Issues

Generally, when you run stored code (and all DBMS_* built-in packages are certainly stored in the database!), that code executes under the authority and using the privileges associated with the owner of the code. If this rule were applied to DBMS_SQL, then anyone who had EXECUTE privilege on DBMS_SQL would be able to act as SYS. This is clearly not a viable approach.

When you execute a DBMS_SQL program from within an anonymous block, that program is executed using the privileges of the current schema. If you embed DBMS_SQL programs within a stored program, those dynamic SQL programs will execute using the privileges of the owner of the stored program. DBMS_SQL is, in other words, a "run as user" package, rather than a "run as owner" package. This can lead to a number of complications, discussed in more detail in the "Tips on Using Dynamic SQL" section later in this chapter.

DBMS_SQL Programs

DBMS_SQL is one of the most complex built-in packages, with a large number of programs and data structures defined in the package specification. Table 2-1 summarizes the programs defined in the DBMS_SQL package.

Table 2-1. DBMS_SQL Programs

Name	Description	Use in SQL?
BIND_ARRAY	Binds a specific value to a host array (PL/SQL8 only).	No
BIND_VARIABLE	Binds a specific value to a host variable.	No
CLOSE_CURSOR	Closes the cursor.	No
COLUMN_VALUE	Retrieves a value from the cursor into a local variable.	No
COLUMN_VALUE_LONG	Retrieves a selected part of a LONG value from a cursor's column defined with DEFINE_COLUMN_LONG.	No
DEFINE_ARRAY	Defines an array to be selected from the specified cursor (PL/SQL8 only).	No
DEFINE_COLUMN	Defines a column to be selected from the specified cursor.	No
DEFINE_COLUMN_LONG	Defines a LONG column to be selected from the specified cursor.	No
DESCRIBE_COLUMNS	Describes the columns for a dynamic cursor (PL/SQL8 only).	No
EXECUTE	Executes the cursor.	No
EXECUTE_AND_FETCH	Executes the cursor and fetches its row(s).	No
FETCH_ROWS	Fetches the row(s) from the cursor.	No
IS_OPEN	Returns TRUE if the cursor is open.	No
LAST_ERROR_POSITION	Returns the byte offset in the SQL statement where the error occurred.	No
LAST_ROW_COUNT	Returns the total number of rows fetched from the cursor.	No
LAST_ROW_ID	Returns the ROWID of the last row fetched from the cursor.	No
LAST_SQL_FUNCTION_CODE	Returns the SQL function code for the SQL statement.	No
OPEN_CURSOR	Opens the cursor.	No
PARSE	Parses the specified SQL statement. If the statement is a DDL statement, then the parse also executes the statement.	No
VARIABLE_VALUE	Gets a value of a variable in a cursor.	No

Types of Dynamic SQL

There are four distinct types, or methods, of dynamic SQL that you can execute with the programs of DBMS_SQL; these are listed in Table 2-2. Familiarity with these methods and the kinds of code you need to write for each will help you use DBMS_SQL most effectively.

Table 2-2. Types of Dynamic SQL

Type	Description	DBMS_SQL Programs Used
Method 1	No queries; just DDL statements and UPDATEs, INSERTs, or DELETEs, which have no bind variables.	OPEN_CURSOR PARSE EXECUTE
Method 2	No queries; just UPDATEs, INSERTs, or DELETEs, with a fixed number of bind variables.	OPEN_CURSOR PARSE BIND_VARIABLE EXECUTE
Method 3	Queries (SELECT statements) with a fixed numbers of columns and bind variables.	OPEN_CURSOR PARSE DEFINE_COLUMN BIND_VARIABLE EXECUTE FETCH_ROWS COLUMN_VALUE VARIABLE_VALUE
Method 4	Queries (SELECT statements) with a variable numbers of columns and bind variables. In other words, you don't know until runtime how many bind variables there may be.	Same as for Method 3, but the code you must write is much more complex.

The following DDL statement is an example of Method 1 dynamic SQL:

```
CREATE INDEX emp_ind_1 on emp (sal, hiredate)
```

And this update statement is also Method 1 dynamic SQL:

```
UPDATE emp SET sal = 10000 WHERE empno = 1506
```

Of course, that UPDATE statement also is not very dynamic. If I now add a place-holder to this DML statement (indicated by the colon) so that I do not "hard-code" the employee number, I then have Method 2 dynamic SQL:

```
UPDATE emp SET sal = 10000 WHERE empno = :employee_id
```

A call to BIND_VARIABLE will be required for the previous statement to be executed successfully with DBMS_SQL.

A Method 3 dynamic SQL statement is a query with a fixed number of bind variables (or none). This will be the most common type of dynamic SQL you will execute. Here is an example:

```
SELECT ename, :second_column FROM emp WHERE deptno = :dept_id
```

In this case, I am leaving until runtime the decision about which column I will retrieve with my query. Now, this statement looks like Method 3 dynamic SQL, but this dynamic stuff can get very tricky. What if I substituted the string "hire-date, sal" for the placeholder "second_column"? I could then have a variable number of columns in the select list, and this would be Method 4 dynamic SQL.

How can you tell the difference? Well, you really *can't* just by looking at the string. The code, however, will tell. If you do not *plan* for Method 4 (variable number of columns in the select list, in this case), then your PL/SQL program will fail. It will not issue the right number of calls to DEFINE_COLUMN.

Usually, when you are dealing with Method 4 dynamic SQL, you will have strings that look more like this:

```
SELECT :select_list FROM emp WHERE :where_clause
```

Now there can be no doubt: there is no way to know how many columns you are retrieving. So how do you write your PL/SQL program to handle this complexity? Slowly and carefully, with lots of debugging. You will need to write logic to parse strings, locate placeholders, and then call the appropriate DBMS_SQL program.

Very few developers will have to deal with Method 4 dynamic SQL. You can find an example of the kind of code you will have to write in the later section, "Displaying Table Contents with Method 4 Dynamic SQL."

DBMS_SQL Exceptions

The DBMS_SQL defines a single exception in its specification as follows:

```
DBMS_SQL.INCONSISTENT_TYPE EXCEPTION;
PRAGMA EXCEPTION_INIT(DBMS_SQL.INCONSISTENT_TYPE, -6562);
```

This exception can be raised by either the COLUMN_VALUE or the VARIABLE_VALUE procedure if the type of the specified OUT argument is different from the type of the value which is being returned. You can trap this exception and handle it with the following syntax in your exception section:

```
EXCEPTION
   WHEN DBMS_SQL.INCONSISTENT_TYPE
   THEN
        . . .
```

You may encounter other exceptions when working with dynamic SQL (in fact, there will be times when you believe that all you can do with DBMS_SQL is raise exceptions). The table on the following page displays some of the most common errors.

Error Number	Description
ORA-00942	Table or view does not exist. You have referenced an object that does not exist in your schema. Remember that when you execute SQL from within a programmatic interface, that SQL is executed under the schema of the owner of the program, not that of the account running the PL/SQL program.
ORA-01001	Invalid cursor. You have tried to use a value which has not been initialized as a DBMS_SQL cursor through a call to OPEN_CURSOR.
ORA-01002	Fetch out of sequence. If you execute FETCH_CURSOR more than once after the cursor's result set is exhausted, you will raise this exception.
ORA-01008	Not all variables bound. You have included a placeholder in your SQL statement string in the form :BINDVAR, but you did not call BIND_VARIABLE to bind a value to that placeholder.
ORA-01027	Bind variables not allowed for data definition operations. You cannot include a bind variable (an identifier with a colon in front of it) in a DDL statement executed dynamically.
ORA-01031	Insufficient privileges. You have tried to execute a SQL statement for which you do not have the appropriate privileges. Remember that when you execute a SQL statement inside a PL/SQL program, all roles are disabled. You will need to have *directly granted* privileges on your objects to affect them from within PL/SQL and the DBMS_SQL package.
ORA-29255	This occurs with array processing in PL/SQL8. The cursor may not contain both bind and define arrays. For more information, see the section "Array Processing with DBMS_SQL."

DBMS_SQL Nonprogram Elements

DBMS_SQL defines three constants that you use in calls to the PARSE procedure to specify how Oracle handles the SQL statement:

```
DBMS_SQL.NATIVE CONSTANT INTEGER := 1;
DBMS_SQL.V6 CONSTANT INTEGER := 0;
DBMS_SQL.V7 CONSTANT INTEGER := 2;
```

The PL/SQL8 version of the DBMS_SQL package also predefines a number of data structures for use in array processing and column describes.

When you want to parse very long SQL statements (in excess of 32Kbytes), you'll need to declare a table based on the DBMS_SQL.VARCHAR2S index-by table TYPE defined as follows:

```
SUBTYPE VARCHAR2S IS SYS.DBMS_SYS_SQL.VARCHAR2S;
```

A little investigation reveals that this table is, in turn, defined as:

```
TYPE VARCHAR2S IS TABLE OF VARCHAR2(256)
   INDEX BY BINARY_INTEGER;
```

When you use the DESCRIBE_COLUMNS procedure, you'll need to declare records based on the DBMS_SQL.DESC_REC record TYPE and index-by tables based on the DBMS_SQL.DESC_TAB table TYPE. These are defined as:

```
TYPE DESC_REC IS RECORD (
    col_type BINARY_INTEGER := 0, /* type of column */
    col_max_len BINARY_INTEGER := 0, /* maximum length of column */
    col_name VARCHAR2(32) := 0, /* name of column */
    col_name_len BINARY_INTEGER := 0, /* length of column name */
    col_schema_name BINARY_INTEGER := 0,
        /* name of column type schema if an object type */
    col_schema_name_len VARCHAR2(32) := 0, /* length of schema name */
    col_precision BINARY_INTEGER := 0, /* precision if number */
    col_scale BINARY_INTEGER := 0, /* scale if number */
    col_charsetid BINARY_INTEGER := 0, /* character set identifier */
    col_charsetform BINARY_INTEGER := 0, /* character set form */
    col_null_ok BOOLEAN := TRUE /* TRUE if column can be NULL */
    );

TYPE DESC_TAB IS TABLE OF DESC_REC INDEX BY BINARY_INTEGER;
```

When you perform array processing with the BIND_ARRAY and DEFINE_ARRAY procedures, you will rely on the following predefined index-by tables to set up and manipulate those arrays:

```
TYPE NUMBER_TABLE IS TABLE OF NUMBER INDEX BY BINARY_INTEGER;
TYPE VARCHAR2_TABLE IS TABLE OF VARCHAR2(2000) INDEX BY BINARY_INTEGER;
TYPE DATE_TABLE IS TABLE OF DATE INDEX BY BINARY_INTEGER;
TYPE BLOB_TABLE IS TABLE OF BLOB INDEX BY BINARY_INTEGER;
TYPE CLOB_TABLE IS TABLE OF CLOB INDEX BY BINARY_INTEGER;
TYPE BFILE_TABLE IS TABLE OF BFILE INDEX BY BINARY_INTEGER;
```

Remember that these index-by tables are also available for your use even when you are not using, for example, the DEFINE_ARRAY procedure. You can still declare your own CLOB index-by tables based on DBMS_SQL.CLOB_TABLE any time you want and under whichever circumstances. This will save you the trouble of defining the table TYPE.

NOTE   BLOB, CLOB, NCLOB, and BFILE are various large object (LOB) datatypes available with PL/SQL8. See the discussion of the DBMS_LOB package in Chapter 8, *Datatype Packages*, for more information on manipulating LOBs from within PL/SQL.

The DBMS_SQL Interface

DBMS_SQL is an extremely powerful package, but it is also one of the most complicated built-in packages to use. Sure, you can construct and execute any SQL statement you desire. The trade-off for that flexibility is that you have to do lots more work to get your SQL-related job done. You must specify all aspects of the SQL statement, usually with a wide variety of procedure calls, from the SQL statement itself down to the values of bind variables and the datatypes of columns in SELECT statements. Before I explore each of the programs that implement these steps, let's review the general flow of events that must occur in order to use DBMS_SQL successfully.

Processing Flow of Dynamic SQL

In order to execute dynamic SQL with DBMS_SQL you must follow these steps; see Figure 2-1 for a graphical summary:

1. *Open a cursor.* When you open a cursor, you ask the RDBMS to set aside and maintain a valid cursor structure for your use with future DBMS_SQL calls. The RDBMS returns an INTEGER handle to this cursor. You will use this handle in all future calls to DBMS_SQL programs for this dynamic SQL statement. Note that this cursor is completely distinct from normal, native PL/SQL cursors.

2. *Parse the SQL statement.* Before you can specify bind variable values and column structures for the SQL statement, it must be parsed by the RDBMS. This parse phase verifies that the SQL statement is properly constructed. It then associates the SQL statement with your cursor handle. Note that when you parse a DDL statement, it is also executed immediately. Upon successful completion of the DDL parse, the RDBMS also issues an implicit commit. This behavior is consistent with that of SQL*Plus.

3. *Bind all host variables.* If the SQL statement contains references to host PL/SQL variables, you will include placeholders to those variables in the SQL statement by prefacing their names with a colon, as in :salary. You must then bind the actual value for that variable into the SQL statement.

4. *Define the columns in SELECT statements.* Each column in the list of the SELECT must be defined. This define phase sets up a correspondence between the expressions in the list of the SQL statement and the local PL/SQL variables receiving the values when a row is fetched (see COLUMN_VALUE). This step is only necessary for SELECT statements and is roughly equivalent to the INTO clause of an implicit SELECT statement in PL/SQL.

5. *Execute the SQL statement.* Execute the specified cursor—that is, its associated SQL statement. If the SQL statement is an INSERT, UPDATE, or DELETE, the EXECUTE command returns the numbers of rows processed. Otherwise, you should ignore that return value.

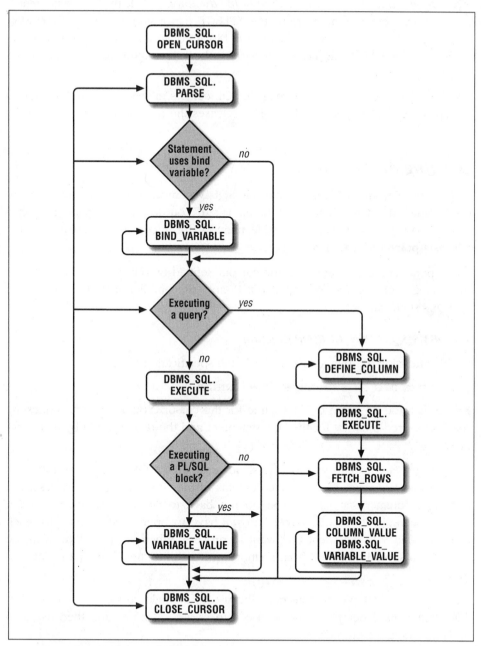

Figure 2-1. DBMS_SQL execution flow

6. *Fetch rows from the dynamic SQL query.* If you execute a SQL statement, you
   must then fetch the rows from the cursor, as you would with a normal
   PL/SQL cursor. When you fetch, however, you do not fetch directly into local
   PL/SQL variables.

7. *Retrieve values from the execution of the dynamic SQL.* If the SQL statement is a query, retrieve values from the SELECT expression list using COLUMN_VALUE. If you have passed a PL/SQL block containing calls to stored procedures, use VARIABLE_VALUE to retrieve the values returned by those procedures.

8. *Close the cursor.* As with normal PL/SQL cursors, always clean up by closing the cursor when you are done. This releases the memory associated with the cursor.

Opening the Cursor

Before you perform any kind of dynamic SQL, you must obtain a pointer to memory in which the dynamic SQL will be managed. You do this by "opening the cursor," at which point Oracle sets aside memory for a cursor data area and then returns a pointer to that area.

These pointers are different from the cursors defined by other elements of Oracle, such as the Oracle Call Interface (OCI) and precompiler interfaces and even PL/SQL's static cursors.

The DBMS_SQL.OPEN_CURSOR function

Use this function to open a cursor. Here's the specification:

```
FUNCTION DBMS_SQL.OPEN_CURSOR RETURN INTEGER;
```

Notice that you do not provide a name for the cursor. You are simply requesting space in shared memory for the SQL statement and the data affected by that statement.

You can use a cursor to execute the same or different SQL statements more than once. When you reuse a cursor, the contents of the cursor data area are reset if a new SQL statement is parsed. You do not have to close and reopen a cursor before you reuse it. You absolutely do *not* have to open a new cursor for each new dynamic SQL statement you want to process. When you are done with the cursor, you should remove it from memory with a call to the CLOSE_CURSOR procedure.

The following example demonstrates the use of a single cursor for two different SQL statements. I declare a cursor, use it to create an index, and then use it to update rows in the emp table.

```
CREATE OR REPLACE PROCEDURE do_two_unrelated_actions
    (tab_in IN VARCHAR2, col_in IN VARCHAR2, val_in IN NUMBER)
IS
    cur BINARY_INTEGER := DBMS_SQL.OPEN_CURSOR;
    fdbk BINARY_INTEGER;
```

```
  BEGIN
     /* Piece together a CREATE INDEX statement. */
     DBMS_SQL.PARSE (cur,
        'CREATE INDEX ind_' || tab_in || '$' || col_in || ' ON ' ||
        tab_in || '(' || col_in || ')',
        DBMS_SQL.NATIVE);
     fdbk := DBMS_SQL.EXECUTE (cur);

     /* Use the same cursor to do the update. */
     DBMS_SQL.PARSE (cur,
        'UPDATE ' || tab_in || ' SET ' || col_in || ' = :newval',
        DBMS_SQL.NATIVE);
     DBMS_SQL.BIND_VARIABLE (cur, 'newval', val_in);
     fdbk := DBMS_SQL.EXECUTE (cur);

     /* Free up the memory from the cursor. */
     DBMS_SQL.CLOSE_CURSOR (cur);
  END;
  /
```

The DBMS_SQL.IS_OPEN function

The IS_OPEN function returns TRUE if the specified cursor is already open, and FALSE if the cursor has been closed or if the value does not point to a dynamic cursor,

```
FUNCTION DBMS_SQL.IS_OPEN (c IN INTEGER) RETURN BOOLEAN;
```

where c is the pointer to the cursor. This function corresponds to the %ISOPEN attribute for regular PL/SQL cursors.

Parsing the SQL Statement

Once you have allocated a pointer to a cursor, you can then associate that pointer with a SQL statement. You do this by *parsing* the SQL statement with a call to the PARSE procedure. The parse phase checks the statement's syntax, so if there is a syntax error, the call to PARSE will fail and an exception will be raised.

The DBMS_SQL.PARSE procedure

The PARSE procedure immediately parses the statement specified. It comes in two formats. The first, as follows, will be used in almost every case. For very large SQL statments, use the PL/SQL table-based version described in the next section.

```
PROCEDURE DBMS_SQL.PARSE
   (c IN INTEGER,
    statement IN VARCHAR2,
    language_flag IN INTEGER);
```

The parameters for this procedure are summarized in the following table.

Parameter	Description
c	The pointer to the cursor or memory area for this SQL statement.
statement	The SQL statement to be parsed and associated with the cursor. This statement should not be terminated with a semicolon unless it is a PL/SQL block.
language_flag	A flag determing how Oracle will handle the statement. Valid options are DBMS_SQL.V6, DBMS_SQL.V7, and DBMS_SQL.NATIVE. Use DBMS_SQL.NATIVE unless otherwise instructed by your DBA.

Note that you cannot defer the parsing of this statement, as is possible with OCI. Statements in DBMS_SQL are parsed immediately. Oracle documentation does mention that this "may change in future versions; you should not rely on this behavior." This means that at some point in the future, Oracle Corporation may allow parsing to be deferred to the execute phase, thereby reducing network traffic. If this change occurs, let's hope that a flag is offered to preserve earlier functionality.

NOTE   The common understanding among long-time Oracle programmers is that when you parse DDL, it always executes, so a call to the EXECUTE procedure is not necessary when calling DBMS_SQL.PARSE for a DDL statement. *You should not take this shortcut!* Oracle will not guarantee that this behavior will continue in future releases. If you want to make sure that your DDL has executed, call the DBMS_SQL.EXECUTE procedure.

Parsing very long SQL statements

PL/SQL8 offers a second, overloaded version of PARSE, which comes in handy when you have very large SQL statements. If your SQL statement exceeds the largest possible contiguous allocation on your system (and it is machine-dependent) or 32Kbytes (the maximum size for VARCHAR2), then use this version of the PARSE procedure:

```
PROCEDURE DBMS_SQL.PARSE
    (c IN INTEGER,
     statement IN DBMS_SQL.VARCHAR2S,
     lb IN INTEGER,
     ub IN INTEGER,
     lfflg IN BOOLEAN,
     language_flag IN INTEGER);
```

The parameters for this procedure are summarized in the following table.

Parameter	Description
c	The pointer to the cursor or memory area for this SQL statement.
statement	The SQL statement to be parsed and associated with the cursor. In this case, you will be passing a PL/SQL table of the DBMS_SQL.VARCHAR2S type.
lb	The lower bound or first row in the statement table to be parsed.
ub	The upper bound or last row in the statement table to be parsed.
lfflg	If TRUE, then a line-feed should be concatenated after each row in the table.
language_flag	A flag determining how Oracle will handle the statement. Valid options are DBMS_SQL.V6, DBMS_SQL.V7, and DBMS_SQL.NATIVE. Use DBMS_SQL.NATIVE unless otherwise instructed by your DBA.

My own parse_long_one procedure offers an example of using the array-based version of the PARSE procedure:

```
/* Filename on companion disk: parslong.sp */
CREATE OR REPLACE PROCEDURE parse_long_one
    (select_list IN VARCHAR2,
     from_list IN VARCHAR2,
     where_clause IN VARCHAR2,
     maxlen IN BINARY_INTEGER := 256, /* Can change the max. */
     dbg IN BOOLEAN := FALSE /* Built-in debugging toggle */
    )
IS
    /* Open the cursor as I declare the variable */
    cur BINARY_INTEGER := DBMS_SQL.OPEN_CURSOR;

    /* Declare the index-by table based on the DBMS_SQL TYPE. */
    sql_table DBMS_SQL.VARCHAR2S;

    /* Local module to extract up to the next maxlen chars. */
    FUNCTION next_row
        (string_in IN VARCHAR2,
         start_inout IN OUT BINARY_INTEGER,
         len_in IN BINARY_INTEGER)
    RETURN VARCHAR2
    IS
        v_start BINARY_INTEGER := start_inout;
    BEGIN
        start_inout := LEAST (len_in + 1, start_inout + maxlen);
        RETURN SUBSTR (string_in, v_start, maxlen);
    END;

    /* Local module to transfer string to index-by table. */
    PROCEDURE fill_sql_table (string_in IN VARCHAR2)
    IS
        v_length BINARY_INTEGER;
```

```
         v_start BINARY_INTEGER := 1;
     BEGIN
         IF string_in IS NOT NULL
         THEN
             v_length := LENGTH (string_in);
             LOOP
                sql_table (NVL (sql_table.LAST, 0)+1) :=
                    next_row (string_in, v_start, v_length);
                EXIT WHEN v_start > v_length;
             END LOOP;
         END IF;
     END;

  BEGIN
     /* Move each portion of the SELECT string to the table. */
     fill_sql_table (select_list);
     fill_sql_table (from_list);
     fill_sql_table (where_clause);

     /* Parse everything from first to last row of table. */
     DBMS_SQL.PARSE (cur,
         sql_table, sql_table.FIRST, sql_table.LAST,
         FALSE, DBMS_SQL.NATIVE);

     /* Execute and fetch rows if doing something for real... */
     /* If debugging, then display contents of the table. */
     IF dbg
     THEN
         DBMS_OUTPUT.PUT_LINE
             ('Parsed into lines of length ' || TO_CHAR (maxlen));
         FOR rowind IN sql_table.FIRST .. sql_table.LAST
         LOOP
             DBMS_OUTPUT.PUT_LINE (sql_table(rowind));
         END LOOP;
     END IF;

     /* Close the cursor when done. */
     DBMS_SQL.CLOSE_CURSOR (cur);
  END;
  /
```

Here is a little test script (and the results of execution) for this procedure:

```
SQL> BEGIN
parse_long_one ('select empno, ename, sal, hiredate, mgr, comm ',
    'from emp ', 'where empno = empno and sal = sal', 10, TRUE);
END;
/

Parsed into lines of length 10
select emp
no, ename,
sal, hire
date, mgr,
comm
```

```
from emp
where empn
o = empno
and sal =
sal
/
```

Notice that the SELECT statement is broken without any concern for keeping identifiers intact. The lfflg value passed in to the PARSE procedure is set to FALSE so linefeeds are not concatenated. As a result, the broken identifiers are concatenated back together and the SQL statement parses without any difficulty.

Binding Values into Dynamic SQL

The SQL (or PL/SQL) statement you execute is constructed as a string at runtime. In most scenarios, you are using dynamic SQL because all the information about the SQL statement is not known at compile time. You therefore have values that you want to pass *into* the SQL statement at runtime. You have two ways of doing this: concatenation and binding. With concatenation, you convert all elements of the SQL statement into strings and concatenate them together. With binding, you insert *placeholders* in your string (identifiers prefaced with a colon) and then explicitly bind or associate a value with that placeholder before executing the SQL statement.

If you concatenate the value into the string, then you are not really binding values and you do not have to make calls to the BIND_VARIABLE or BIND_ARRAY procedures. Here is an example of the parsing of a dynamically constructed string relying on concatenation:

```
DBMS_SQL.PARSE
   (cur, 'SELECT * FROM emp WHERE ename LIKE ' || v_ename);
```

At runtime the string is cobbled together and passed to the SQL engine for parsing. With binding, you would write code like this:

```
DBMS_SQL.PARSE
   (cur, 'SELECT * FROM emp WHERE ename LIKE :varname');
DBMS_SQL.BIND_VARIABLE (cur, 'varname', 'a', 100);
```

Binding involves writing more code, but offers much more flexibility and power. The following comparison between concatenation and binding techniques will help you decide which to use:

- When you concatenate, you convert to a string format. This can become awkward and error-prone. With binding, you do not perform any conversions. Instead, the native datatypes are employed.

- When you execute DDL statements dynamically, you *cannot* use bind variables. Your only choice is to concatenate together the strings and then pass that to the engine. This makes sense, since, at least in the current version of DBMS_SQL, there is no such thing as deferred parsing. When you parse, you also execute DDL.

• You can execute the same dynamic cursor more than once, and each time you bind in different values to the SQL statement. This is not possible if you concatenate the values into the string at the time of parsing.

• With bind variables, you can take advantage of the new array-processing features of PL/SQL8's DBMS_SQL package. You can bind an entire array of scalar values into the SQL string and then apply each of those values in a single SQL execution.

So if you decide that you really do want to bind variables into your dynamic SQL, use one of the programs described in the following sections.

The DBMS_SQL.BIND_VARIABLE procedure

The BIND_VARIABLE procedure binds a scalar value to a placeholder in your SQL statement. A placeholder is an identifier prefaced by a colon, as in :myval. Call BIND_VARIABLE after DBMS_SQL.PARSE, but before calls to EXECUTE and EXECUTE_AND_FETCH. This procedure is overloaded to allow you to bind a number of different types of data. This is the header:

```
PROCEDURE DBMS_SQL.BIND_VARIABLE
    (c IN INTEGER,
     name IN VARCHAR2,
     value IN <datatype>);
```

The parameters for this procedure are summarized in the following table.

Parameter	Description
c	The handle or pointer to the cursor originally returned by a call to OPEN_CURSOR.
name	The name of the placeholder included in the SQL statement passed to PARSE.
value	The value to be bound to the placeholder variable.

<datatype> may be any of the following:

```
BFILE
BLOB
CLOB CHARACTER SET ANY_CS
DATE
MLSLABEL /*Trusted Oracle only*/
NUMBER
VARCHAR2 CHARACTER SET ANY_CS_ARRAY
```

Here is an example of binding the current date/time into a placeholder called "now:"

```
DBMS_SQL.BIND_VARIABLE (cur, 'now', SYSDATE);
```

Here is an example of binding the literal value "Liberation Theology" into a place-holder called "progress:"

```
DBMS_SQL.BIND_VARIABLE (cur, ':progress', 'Liberation Theology');
```

Notice that you can include or leave out the colon when you specify the place-holder name.

The DBMS_SQL package also offers more specific variants of BIND_VARIABLE for less-common datatypes,

```
PROCEDURE DBMS_SQL.BIND_VARIABLE
    (c IN INTEGER,
     name IN VARCHAR2,
     value IN VARCHAR2 CHARACTER SET ANY_CS,
     [,out_value_size IN INTEGER]);

PROCEDURE DBMS_SQL.BIND_VARIABLE_CHAR
    (c IN INTEGER,
     name IN VARCHAR2,
     value IN CHAR CHARACTER SET ANY_CS,
     [,out_value_size IN INTEGER]);

PROCEDURE DBMS_SQL.BIND_VARIABLE_RAW
    (c IN INTEGER,
     name IN VARCHAR2,
     value IN RAW
     [,out_value_size IN INTEGER]);

PROCEDURE DBMS_SQL.BIND_VARIABLE_ROWID
    (c IN INTEGER,
     name IN VARCHAR2,
     value IN ROWID);
```

where out_value_size is the maximum size expected for the value that might be passed to this variable. Square brackets indicate optional parameters. If you do not provide a value for out_value_size, the size is the length of the current value provided.

Examples. For every placeholder you put in your SQL string, you must make a call to BIND_VARIABLE (or BIND_ARRAY). For example, the SELECT statement in the call to PARSE below contains two bind variables, :call_date and :call_type:

```
DBMS_SQL.PARSE
    (the_cursor,
     'SELECT COUNT(*) freq FROM call WHERE call_date = :call_date ' ||
       'AND call_type_cd = :call_type',
     DBMS_SQL.V7);
```

I will therefore need to issue the following two calls to BIND_VARIABLE before I can execute the query,

```
DBMS_SQL.BIND_VARIABLE (the_cursor, 'call_date', :call.last_date_called);
DBMS_SQL.BIND_VARIABLE (the_cursor, 'call_type', :call.call_status);
```

where the two bind values are items in an Oracle Forms screen. Since BIND_VARIABLE is overloaded, I can call it with either a date value or a string, and PL/SQL will execute the appropriate code. Notice that the name of the bind variable does *not* have to match any particular column name in the SELECT statement, and it does not have to match the name of the PL/SQL variable that may hold the value. The name is really just a placeholder into which a value is substituted.

You can also include the colon in the placeholder name when you bind the value to the variable:

```
DBMS_SQL.BIND_VARIABLE (the_cursor, ':call_date', :call.last_date_called);
```

If you want to avoid having to make these separate calls to BIND_VARIABLE, you can substitute these values into the SQL statement yourself at the time the statement is parsed. The code shows the same SELECT statement, but without any bind variables.

```
DBMS_SQL.PARSE
    (the_cursor,
     'SELECT COUNT(*) freq FROM call WHERE call_date = ''' ||
     TO_CHAR (:call.last_date_called) ||
     ''' AND call_type_cd = ''' || :call.call_status || '''',
     DBMS_SQL.V7);
```

Kind of ugly, isn't it? All of those single quotes glommed together (three consecutive single quotes at the end of a string result in one single quote around the literal values stuffed into the SQL statement), the concatenation, datatype conversions, etc. This is the tradeoff for not using the programmatic interface provided by DBMS_SQL.

You will also call BIND_VARIABLE for every placeholder in a dynamic PL/SQL block, even if the placeholder is an OUT argument or is otherwise simply receiving a value. Consider the following PL/SQL procedure, which performs an assignment dynamically when it could simply do it explicitly:

```
CREATE OR REPLACE PROCEDURE assign_value (newval_in IN NUMBER)
IS
    cur PLS_INTEGER := DBMS_SQL.OPEN_CURSOR;
    fdbk PLS_INTEGER;
    local_var NUMBER; /* Receives the new value */
BEGIN
    DBMS_SQL.PARSE
        (cur, 'BEGIN :container := :newval; END;', DBMS_SQL.NATIVE);
    DBMS_SQL.BIND_VARIABLE (cur, 'newval', newval_in);
    DBMS_SQL.BIND_VARIABLE (cur, 'container', 1);
```

```
      fdbk := DBMS_SQL.EXECUTE (cur);
      DBMS_SQL.VARIABLE_VALUE (cur, 'container', local_var);
   END;
   /
```

Notice that even though the container placeholder's value *before execution* is irrelevant, I still needed to bind that placeholder to a value for the PL/SQL block to execute successfully.

The DBMS_SQL.BIND_ARRAY procedure

With PL/SQL8, you can use the new BIND_ARRAY procedure to perform bulk selects, inserts, updates, and deletes to improve the performance of your application. This same procedure will allow you to use and manipulate index-by tables (previously known as PL/SQL tables) within dynamically constructed PL/SQL blocks of code. To perform bulk or array processing, you will associate one or more index-by tables with columns or placeholders in your cursor.

The BIND_ARRAY procedure establishes this association for you. Call this procedure after PARSE, but before calls to EXECUTE and EXECUTE_AND_FETCH:

```
PROCEDURE DBMS_SQL.BIND_ARRAY
   (c IN INTEGER,
   name IN VARCHAR2,
   <table_variable> IN <datatype>,
   [,index1 IN INTEGER,
   ,index2 IN INTEGER)]);
```

The parameters for this procedure are summarized in the following table.

Parameter	Description
c	The handle or pointer to the cursor originally returned by a call to OPEN_CURSOR.
name	The name of the host variable included in the SQL statement passed to PARSE.
index1	The lower bound or row in the index-by table <table_variable> for the first table element.
table_variable	See the following description.
index2	The upper bound or row in the index-by table <table_variable> for the last table element.

The <table_variable> IN <datatype> clause may be any of the following:

```
n_tab IN DBMS_SQL.NUMBER_TABLE
c_tab IN DBMS_SQL.VARCHAR2_TABLE
d_tab IN DBMS_SQL.DATE_TABLE
bl_tab IN DBMS_SQL.BLOB_TABLE
cl_tab IN DBMS_SQL.CLOB_TABLE
bl_tab IN DBMS_SQL.BFILE_TABLE
```

The following example shows how I can use BIND_ARRAY to update multiple numeric rows of any table that has a numeric primary key:

```
/* Filename on companion disk: updarray.sp */
CREATE OR REPLACE PROCEDURE updarray
     (tab IN VARCHAR2,
      keycol IN VARCHAR2,
      valcol IN VARCHAR2,
      keylist IN DBMS_SQL.NUMBER_TABLE,
      vallist IN DBMS_SQL.NUMBER_TABLE)
   IS
     cur INTEGER := DBMS_SQL.OPEN_CURSOR;
     fdbk INTEGER;
     mytab DBMS_SQL.NUMBER_TABLE;
   BEGIN
     DBMS_SQL.PARSE
       (cur,
        'UPDATE ' || tab ||
          ' SET ' || valcol || ' = :vals ' ||
        ' WHERE ' || keycol || ' = :keys',
        DBMS_SQL.NATIVE);

     DBMS_SQL.BIND_ARRAY (cur, 'keys', keylist);
     DBMS_SQL.BIND_ARRAY (cur, 'vals', vallist);

     fdbk := DBMS_SQL.EXECUTE (cur);

     DBMS_SQL.CLOSE_CURSOR (cur);
   END;
   /
```

Now I can execute this "update by array" procedure for the sal column of the emp table.

```
DECLARE
   emps DBMS_SQL.NUMBER_TABLE;
   sals DBMS_SQL.NUMBER_TABLE;
BEGIN
   emps (1) := 7499;
   sals (1) := 2000;
   emps (2) := 7521;
   sals (2) := 3000;

   updarray ('emp', 'empno', 'sal', emps, sals);
END;
/
```

The section on the DEFINE_ARRAY procedure and the section called "Array Processing with DBMS_SQL" provide additional examples of using BIND_ARRAY.

Rules for array binding. There are a number of factors to keep in mind when you are binding with index-by tables.

- At the time of binding, the contents of the nested table are copied from your private global area to the DBMS_SQL buffers. Consequently, if you make changes to the nested table after your call to DBMS_SQL.BIND_ARRAY, those changes will not affect the cursor when executed.

- If you specify values for index1 and/or index2, then those rows must be defined in the nested table. The value of index1 must be less than or equal to index2. All elements between and included in those rows will be used in the bind, but the table does not have to be densely filled.

- If you do not specify values for index1 and index2, the first and last rows defined in the nested table will be used to set the boundaries for the bind.

- Suppose that you have more than one bind array in your statement and the bind ranges (or the defined rows, if you did not specify) for the arrays are different. DBMS_SQL will then use the smallest common range—that is, the greatest of the lower bounds and the least of the upper bounds.

- You can mix array and scalar binds in your dynamic SQL execution. If you have a scalar bind, the same value will be used for each element of the arrays.

- When fetching data using dynamic SQL, you cannot use arrays in both the bind and define phases. You may not, in other words, specify multiple bind values and at the same time fetch multiple rows into an array.

Defining Cursor Columns

The OPEN_CURSOR procedure allocates memory for a cursor and its result set and returns a pointer to that area in memory. It does not, however, give any structure to that cursor. And even after you parse a SQL statement for that pointer, the cursor itself still does not have any internal structure. If you are going to execute a SELECT statement dynamically and extract values of columns in retrieved rows, you will need to take the additional step of defining the datatype of the individual columns in the cursor.

Each cursor column is, essentially, a *container* which will hold fetched data. You can use the DEFINE_COLUMN procedure to define a "scalar" column—one that will hold a single value. You can also (with PL/SQL8) call DEFINE_ARRAY to create a column that will hold multiple values, allowing you to fetch rows in bulk from the database.

The DBMS_SQL.DEFINE_COLUMN procedure

When you call the PARSE procedure to process a SELECT statement, you need to pass values from the database into local variables. To do this, you must tell DBMS_SQL the datatypes of the different columns or expressions in the SELECT list by making a call to the DEFINE_COLUMN procedure:

```
PROCEDURE DBMS_SQL.DEFINE_COLUMN
    (c IN INTEGER,
     position IN INTEGER,
     column IN <datatype>);
```

The parameters for this procedure are summarized in the following table.

Parameter	Description
c	Pointer to the cursor.
position	The relative position of the column in the SELECT list.
column	A PL/SQL variable or expression whose datatype determines the datatype of the column being defined. The particular value being passed in is irrelevant.

<datatype> may be one of the following data types:

```
NUMBER
DATE
MLSLABEL
BLOB
CLOB CHARACTER SET ANY_CS
BFILE
```

The DBMS_SQL package also offers more specific variants of DEFINE_COLUMN for less-common datatypes.

```
PROCEDURE DBMS_SQL.DEFINE_COLUMN
    (c IN INTEGER
    ,position IN INTEGER
    ,column IN VARCHAR2 CHARACTER SET ANY_CS
    ,column_size IN INTEGER);

PROCEDURE DBMS_SQL.DEFINE_COLUMN_CHAR
    (c IN INTEGER
    ,position IN INTEGER
    ,column IN CHAR CHARACTER SET ANY_CS
    ,column_size IN INTEGER);

PROCEDURE DBMS_SQL.DEFINE_COLUMN_RAW
    (c IN INTEGER
    ,position IN INTEGER
    ,column IN RAW
    ,column_size IN INTEGER);

PROCEDURE DBMS_SQL.DEFINE_COLUMN_ROWID
    (c IN INTEGER
    ,position IN INTEGER
    ,column IN ROWID);
```

You call DEFINE_COLUMN after the call to the PARSE procedure, but before the call to EXECUTE or EXECUTE_AND_FETCH. Once you have executed the SELECT statement, you will then use the COLUMN_VALUE procedure to grab a column value from the select list and pass it into the appropriate local variable.

The following code shows the different steps required to set up a SELECT statement for execution with DBMS_SQL:

```
DECLARE
    /* Declare cursor handle and assign it a pointer */
    c INTEGER := DBMS_SQL.OPEN_CURSOR;

    /* Use a record to declare local structures. */
    rec employee%ROWTYPE;

    /* return value from EXECUTE; ignore in case of query */
    execute_feedback INTEGER;
BEGIN
    /* Parse the query with two columns in SELECT list */
    DBMS_SQL.PARSE
       (c,
        'SELECT employee_id, last_name FROM employee',
        DBMS_SQL.V7);

    /* Define the columns in the cursor for this query */
    DBMS_SQL.DEFINE_COLUMN (c, 1, rec.empno);
    DBMS_SQL.DEFINE_COLUMN (c, 2, rec.ename, 30);

    /* Now I can execute the query */
    execute_feedback := DBMS_SQL.EXECUTE (c);
    ...
    DBMS_SQL.CLOSE_CURSOR (c)
END;
```

Notice that with the DEFINE_COLUMN procedure, you define columns (their datatypes) using a sequential position. With BIND_VARIABLE, on the other hand, you associate values to placeholders by name.

The DBMS_SQL.DEFINE_ARRAY procedure

If you are working with PL/SQL8, you have the option of defining a column in the cursor which is capable of holding the values of multiple fetched rows. You accomplish this with a call to the DEFINE_ARRAY procedure:

```
PROCEDURE DBMS_SQL.DEFINE_ARRAY
     (c IN INTEGER
     ,position IN INTEGER
     ,<table_parameter> IN <table_type>
     ,cnt IN INTEGER
     ,lower_bound IN INTEGER);
```

The DEFINE_ARRAY parameters are summarized in the following table.

Parameter	Description
c	Pointer to cursor.
position	The relative position of the column in the select list.

Parameter	Description
<table_parameter>	The nested table which is used to tell DBMS_SQL the datatype of the column.
cnt	The maximum number of rows to be fetched in the call to the FETCH_ROWS or EXECUTE_AND_FETCH functions.
lower_bound	The starting row (lower bound) in which column values will be placed in the nested table you provide in the corresponding call to the COLUMN_VALUE or VARIABLE_VALUE procedures.

<table_parameter> IN <table_type> is one of the following:

```
n_tab IN DBMS_SQL.NUMBER_TABLE
c_tab IN DBMS_SQL.VARCHAR2_TABLE
d_tab IN DBMS_SQL.DATE_TABLE
bl_tab IN DBMS_SQL.BLOB_TABLE
cl_tab IN DBMS_SQL._TABLE
bf_tab IN DBMS_SQL.BFILE_TABLE
```

When you call the COLUMN_VALUE or VARIABLE_VALUE procedures against an array-defined column, the Nth fetched column value will be placed in the lower_bound+N–1th row in the nested table. In other words, if you have fetched three rows and your call to DEFINE_ARRAY looked like this,

```
DECLARE
    datetab DBMS_SQL.DATE_TABLE;
BEGIN
    DBMS_SQL.DEFINE_ARRAY (cur, 2, datetab, 10, 15);

    ... execute and fetch rows ...

    DBMS_SQL.COLUMN_VALUE (cur, 2, datetab);
END;
```

then the data will be placed in datetab(15), datetab(16), and datetab(17).

Executing the Cursor

So you've opened and parsed the cursor. You've bound your variables and defined your columns. Now it's time to get some *work* done.

The DBMS_SQL.EXECUTE function

The EXECUTE function executes the SQL statement associated with the specified cursor,

```
FUNCTION DBMS_SQL.EXECUTE (c IN INTEGER) RETURN INTEGER;
```

where c is the pointer to the cursor. This function returns the number of rows processed by the SQL statement if that statement is an UPDATE, INSERT, or DELETE.

For all other SQL (queries and DDL) and PL/SQL statements, the value returned by EXECUTE is undefined and should be ignored.

If the SQL statement is a query, you can now call the FETCH_ROWS function to fetch rows that are retrieved by that query. If you are executing a query, you can also use EXECUTE_AND_FETCH to execute the cursor and fetch one or more rows with a single program call.

Fetching Rows

You can fetch one or more rows of data from a dynamically constructed query with either the FETCH_ROWS or EXECUTE_AND_FETCH functions.

NOTE   Prior to PL/SQL8, both of these functions would return either 0 (no rows fetched) or 1 (one row fetched). With PL/SQL8 and array processing, these functions will return 0 (no rows fetched) or the actual number of rows fetched.

The DBMS_SQL.FETCH_ROWS function

The FETCH_ROWS function corresponds to the FETCH statement for regular PL/SQL cursors. It fetches the next N rows from the cursor (a maximum of one if not using array processing in PL/SQL8). Here's the specification for the function,

```
FUNCTION DBMS_SQL.FETCH_ROWS
    (c IN INTEGER) RETURN INTEGER;
```

where c is the pointer to the cursor. The function returns 0 when there are no more rows to fetch. You can therefore use FETCH_ROWS much as you would FETCH and the %FOUND (or %NOTFOUND) attributes. The following two sets of statements are equivalent:

- Use a normal, static cursor:

```
FETCH emp_cur INTO emp_rec;
IF emp_cur%FOUND
THEN
    ... process data ...
END IF;
```

- Use DBMS_SQL to fetch rows:

```
IF DBMS_SQL.FETCH_ROWS (c) > 0
THEN
    ... process data ...
END IF;
```

So hat happens when you fetch past the end of the cursor's result set? With static cursors, you can fetch all you want and never raise an error. In the following block, for example, I fetch 1000 times from a table with 14 rows. (C'mon, you knew that, right? The emp table has 14 rows.)

```
DECLARE
    CURSOR empcur IS SELECT * FROM emp;
    emprec empcur%ROWTYPE;
BEGIN
    OPEN empcur;
    FOR rowind IN 1 .. 1000
    LOOP
        FETCH empcur INTO emprec;
    END LOOP;
END;
/
```

No problem—and no exceptions! After the fourteenth fetch, the FETCH statement simply does nothing (and the record continues to hold the fourteenth row's information).

However, the "fetch past last record" behavior with dynamic SQL is different. The FETCH_ROWS function will raise the ORA-01002 exception: fetch out of sequence, if you fetch again *after* a call to FETCH_ROWS has returned 0. The following anonymous block raises the ORA-01002 error, because there are only three employees in department 10:

```
DECLARE
    cur PLS_INTEGER := DBMS_SQL.OPEN_CURSOR;
    fdbk PLS_INTEGER;
BEGIN
    DBMS_SQL.PARSE
        (cur, 'SELECT * FROM emp WHERE deptno = 10', DBMS_SQL.NATIVE);

    fdbk := DBMS_SQL.EXECUTE_CURSOR (cur);
    FOR Nfetch IN 1 .. 5
    LOOP
        /* On fetch #5 this will raise ORA-01002 */
        fdbk := DBMS_SQL.FETCH_ROWS (cur);
    END LOOP;
    DBMS_SQL.CLOSE_CURSOR (cur);
END;
/
```

The following procedure shows how you can employ the FETCH_ROWS logic inside of a loop to fetch each of the rows from a cursor and place column values in an Oracle Forms block:

```
/* Filename on companion disk: fillblck.fp */
PROCEDURE fill_block (where_clause_in IN VARCHAR2)
    /*
    || Query data from table using a dynamic where clause and then
    || pass those values to an Oracle Forms block.
    */
    IS
```

```
    /*
    || Declare cursor handle and parse the query, all in a single
    || statement using open_and_parse (see PARSE description).
    */
    c INTEGER := DBMS_SQL.OPEN_CURSOR;

    emprec employee%ROWTYPE;

    /* return value from EXECUTE; ignore in case of query */
    fdbk INTEGER;
BEGIN
    /* Parse the query  with a dynamic WHERE clause */
    DBMS_SQL.PARSE (c,
        'SELECT employee_id, last_name ' ||
        ' FROM employee WHERE ' || where_clause_in,
        DBMS_SQL.NATIVE);

    /* Define the columns in the cursor for this query */
    DBMS_SQL.DEFINE_COLUMN (c, 1, emprec.empno);
    DBMS_SQL.DEFINE_COLUMN (c, 2, emprec.ename, 30);

    /* Now I can execute the query */
    fdbk:= DBMS_SQL.EXECUTE (c);
    LOOP
        /* Try to fetch next row. If done, then exit the loop. */
        EXIT WHEN DBMS_SQL.FETCH_ROWS (c) = 0;
        /*
        || Retrieve data via calls to COLUMN_VALUE and place those
        || values in a new record in the block.
        */
        DBMS_SQL.COLUMN_VALUE (c, 1, emprec.empno);
        DBMS_SQL.COLUMN_VALUE (c, 2, emprec.ename);
        CREATE_RECORD;
        :employee.employee_id := emprec.empno;
        :employee.employee_nm := emprec.ename;
    END LOOP;

    /* Clean up the cursor */
    DBMS_SQL.CLOSE_CURSOR (c);
END;
```

In this example, you can fetch only one row at a time, because you defined each of your columns in the cursor to hold a single value. If, on the other hand, you defined a column as an array, then the fetch could receive multiple rows in a single call. This approach is explored in more detail in the section "Array Processing with DBMS_SQL."

The DBMS_SQL.EXECUTE_AND_FETCH function

The EXECUTE_AND_FETCH function executes the SELECT statement associated with the specified cursor and immediately fetches the rows associated with the query. Here's the specification for the function.

```
FUNCTION DBMS_SQL.EXECUTE_AND_FETCH
    (c IN INTEGER
    ,exact IN BOOLEAN DEFAULT FALSE)
RETURN INTEGER;
```

Parameters are summarized in the following table.

Parameter	Description
c	The handle or pointer to the cursor originally returned by a call to OPEN_CURSOR.
exact	Set to TRUE if you want the function to raise an exception when it fetches more than one row.

Even if EXECUTE_AND_FETCH does raise an exception (TOO_MANY_ROWS), the rows will still be fetched and available. The value returned by the function will, however, be NULL.

This function is designed to make it easy to execute and fetch a single row from a query. It is very similar to the implicit SELECT cursor in native PL/SQL, which either returns a single row, multiple rows (for PL/SQL8 array access only), or raises the TOO_MANY_ROWS exception (ORA-01422).

See the sidebar entitled "Oracle: The Show Me Technology," for a script you can use to examine the behavior of this built-in function.

Retrieving Values

If you construct a dynamic SELECT or PL/SQL block, you can retrieve values from the cursor after execution. Use the COLUMN_VALUE procedure to obtain the values of individual columns in the fetched row of a SELECT. Use the COLUMN_VALUE_LONG procedure to obtain the values of a LONG column in the fetched row of a SELECT. Use the VARIABLE_VALUE procedure to extract the values of variables in a dynamic PL/SQL block.

The DBMS_SQL.COLUMN_VALUE procedure

The COLUMN_VALUE procedure retrieves a value from the cursor into a local variable. Use this procedure when the SQL statement is a query and you are fetching rows with EXECUTE_AND_FETCH or FETCH_ROWS. You can retrieve the value for a single column in a single row or, with PL/SQL8, you can retrieve the values for a single column across multiple rows fetched. The header for the single-row version of the procedure is as follows:

Oracle: The Show Me Technology

If there is one thing I have learned over the years, it is that if I am not absolutely sure about the way a particular feature works, I have to try it out and see what happens. I have two primary references for writing about PL/SQL technology: the Oracle documentation and the Oracle software. The former is helpful for guiding my "first draft." The latter is helpful for making sure that my "final draft" is accurate and honest. See, unfortunately, just because the documentation says that something works a certain way, that doesn't necessarily mean it really does operate as advertised.

I built the following script (designed for use in SQL*Plus) to make it easier for Oracle to "show me" exactly the kind of variations in behavior of DBMS_SQL.EXECUTE_AND_FETCH I might encounter. You use the first argument to indicate whether or not you want rows to be found. The second argument dictates the error-handling behavior. I thought I would share it with you to give you a sense of how these kinds of scripts can make it very easy to test functionality and behavior.

```
/* Filename on companion disk: execftch.sql */
DECLARE
    cur INTEGER := DBMS_SQL.OPEN_CURSOR;
    fdbk INTEGER;
BEGIN
    DBMS_SQL.PARSE
       (cur, 'SELECT empno FROM emp where 1=&1', DBMS_SQL.NATIVE);

    DBMS_SQL.DEFINE_COLUMN (cur, 1, 1);

    fdbk := DBMS_SQL.EXECUTE_AND_FETCH (cur, &2);
    DBMS_OUTPUT.PUT_LINE (fdbk);
    DBMS_SQL.CLOSE_CURSOR (cur);
EXCEPTION
    WHEN OTHERS
    THEN
        DBMS_OUTPUT.PUT_LINE ('error code ' || SQLCODE);
        DBMS_OUTPUT.PUT_LINE
          ('returned by e_and_f ' || NVL (TO_CHAR (fdbk), '[NULL]'));
END;
/
```

Here are the results of executing this script in SQL*Plus:

```
SQL> @execftch 1 false
1
SQL> @execftch 2 false
0
SQL> @execftch 1 true
error code -1422
returned by e_and_f [NULL]
SQL> @execftch 2 true
error code 100
returned by e_and_f [NULL]ORA-01403: no data found
```

```
PROCEDURE DBMS_SQL.COLUMN_VALUE
(c IN INTEGER,
    position IN INTEGER,
   value OUT <datatype>,
   [, column_error OUT NUMBER]
   [, actual_length OUT INTEGER ]);
```

The COLUMN_VALUE parameters are summarized in the following table.

Parameter	Description
c	Pointer to the cursor.
position	Relative position of the column in the select list.
value	The PL/SQL structure that receives the column value. If the <datatype> of this argument does not match that of the cursor's column, DBMS_SQL will raise the DBMS_SQL.INCONSISTENT_ DATATYPE exception.
<table_parameter>	The PL/SQL table (of type <table_type>) holding one or more colum values, depending on how many rows were previously fetched.
column_error	Returns an error code for the specified value (the value might be too large for the variable, for instance).
actual_length	Returns the actual length of the returned value before any truncation takes place (due to a difference in size between the retrieved value in the cursor and the variable).

<datatype> can be one of the following types:

```
NUMBER
DATE
MLSLABEL
VARCHAR2 CHARACTER SET ANY_CS
BLOB
CLOB CHARACTER SET ANY_CS
BFILE
```

The header for the multiple-row version of COLUMN_VALUE is as follows:

```
PROCEDURE DBMS_SQL.COLUMN_VALUE
    (c IN INTEGER,
    position IN INTEGER,
    <table_parameter> OUT <table_type>);
```

<table_parameter> OUT <table_type> can be one of the following:

```
n_tab OUT DBMS_SQL.NUMBER_TABLE
c_tab OUT DBMS_SQL.VARCHAR2_TABLE
d_tab OUT DBMS_SQL.DATE_TABLE
bl_tab OUT DBMS_SQL.BLOB_TABLE
cl_tab OUT DBMS_SQL.CLOB_TABLE
bf_tab OUT DBMS_SQL.BFILE_TABLE
```

The DBMS_SQL package also offers more specific variants of COLUMN_VALUE for less common datatype:

```
PROCEDURE DBMS_SQL.COLUMN_VALUE_CHAR
    (c IN INTEGER,
```

```
        position IN INTEGER,
        value OUT CHAR,
        [, column_error OUT NUMBER]
        [, actual_length OUT INTEGER ]);

    PROCEDURE DBMS_SQL.COLUMN_VALUE_RAW
        (c IN INTEGER,
        position IN INTEGER,
        value OUT RAW,
        [, column_error OUT NUMBER]
        [, actual_length OUT INTEGER ]);

    PROCEDURE DBMS_SQL.COLUMN_VALUE_ROWID
        (c IN INTEGER,
        position IN INTEGER,
        value OUT ROWID,
        [, column_error OUT NUMBER]
        [, actual_length OUT INTEGER ]);
```

You call COLUMN_VALUE after a row has been fetched to transfer the value from the SELECT list of the cursor into a local variable. For each call to the single-row COLUMN_VALUE, you should have made a call to DEFINE_COLUMN in order to define that column in the cursor. If you want to use the multiple-row version of COLUMN_VALUE, use the DEFINE_ARRAY procedure to define that column as capable of holding an array of values.

The following procedure displays employees by defining a cursor with two columns and, after fetching a row, calls COLUMN_VALUE to retrieve both column values:

```
/* Filename on companion disk: showemps.sp */
CREATE OR REPLACE PROCEDURE showemps (where_in IN VARCHAR2 := NULL)
IS
    cur INTEGER := DBMS_SQL.OPEN_CURSOR;
    rec emp%ROWTYPE;
    fdbk INTEGER;
BEGIN
    DBMS_SQL.PARSE
        (cur, 'SELECT empno, ename FROM emp ' ||
            ' WHERE ' || NVL (where_in, '1=1'),
        DBMS_SQL.NATIVE);

    DBMS_SQL.DEFINE_COLUMN (cur, 1, rec.empno);
    DBMS_SQL.DEFINE_COLUMN (cur, 2, rec.ename, 30);

    fdbk := DBMS_SQL.EXECUTE (cur);
    LOOP
        /* Fetch next row. Exit when done. */
        EXIT WHEN DBMS_SQL.FETCH_ROWS (cur) = 0;
        DBMS_SQL.COLUMN_VALUE (cur, 1, rec.empno);
        DBMS_SQL.COLUMN_VALUE (cur, 2, rec.ename);
        DBMS_OUTPUT.PUT_LINE (TO_CHAR (rec.empno) || '=' || rec.ename);
```

```
      END LOOP;

      DBMS_SQL.CLOSE_CURSOR (cur);
   END;
   /
```

This next PL/SQL8 block fetches the hiredate and employee ID for all rows in the emp table and deposits values into two separate PL/SQL tables. Notice that since I know there are just 14 rows in the emp table, I need only one call to the EXECUTE_AND_FETCH function to fetch all rows.

```
/* Filename on companion disk: arrayemp.sp */
CREATE OR REPLACE PROCEDURE showall
   IS
      cur INTEGER := DBMS_SQL.OPEN_CURSOR;
      fdbk INTEGER;

      empno_tab DBMS_SQL.NUMBER_TABLE;
      hiredate_tab DBMS_SQL.DATE_TABLE;
   BEGIN
      DBMS_SQL.PARSE
         (cur, 'SELECT empno, hiredate FROM emp', DBMS_SQL.NATIVE);

      /* Allow fetching of up to 100 rows. */
      DBMS_SQL.DEFINE_ARRAY (cur, 1, empno_tab, 100, 1);
      DBMS_SQL.DEFINE_ARRAY (cur, 2, hiredate_tab, 100, 1);

      fdbk := DBMS_SQL.EXECUTE_AND_FETCH (cur);

      /* This will show total numbers of rows fetched. */
      DBMS_OUTPUT.PUT_LINE (fdbk);

      /* Get values for all rows in one call. */
      DBMS_SQL.COLUMN_VALUE (cur, 1, empno_tab);
      DBMS_SQL.COLUMN_VALUE (cur, 2, hiredate_tab);

      FOR rowind IN empno_tab.FIRST .. empno_tab.LAST
      LOOP
         DBMS_OUTPUT.PUT_LINE (empno_tab(rowind));
         DBMS_OUTPUT.PUT_LINE (hiredate_tab(rowind));
      END LOOP;

      DBMS_SQL.CLOSE_CURSOR (cur);
   END;
   /
```

The "DBMS_SQL Examples" section provides other examples of array processing in DBMS_SQL.

The DBMS_SQL.COLUMN_VALUE_LONG procedure

DBMS_SQL provides a separate procedure, COLUMN_VALUE_LONG, to allow you to retrieve LONG values from a dynamic query. The header for this program is as follows:

```
PROCEDURE DBMS_SQL.COLUMN_VALUE_LONG
    (c IN INTEGER
    ,position IN INTEGER
    ,length IN INTEGER
    ,offset IN INTEGER
    ,value OUT VARCHAR2
    ,value_length OUT INTEGER);
```

The COLUMN_VALUE_LONG parameters are summarized in the following table.

Parameter	Description
c	Pointer to the cursor.
position	Relative position of the column in the select list.
length	The length in bytes of the portion of the LONG value to be retrieved.
offset	The byte position in the LONG column at which the retrieval is to start.
value	The variable that will receive part or all of the LONG column value.
value_length	The actual length of the retrieved value.

The COLUMN_VALUE_LONG procedure offers just about the only way to obtain a LONG value from the database and move it into PL/SQL data structures in your program. You cannot rely on a static SELECT to do this. Instead, use DBMS_SQL and both the DEFINE_COLUMN_LONG and COLUMN_VALUE_LONG procedures.

The following example demonstrates the technique, and, in the process, offers a generic procedure called dump_long that you can use to dump the contents of a long column in your table into a local PL/SQL table. The dump_long procedure accepts a table name, column name, and optional WHERE clause. It returns a PL/SQL table with the LONG value broken up into 256-byte chunks.

```
/* Filename on companion disk: dumplong.sp */
CREATE OR REPLACE PROCEDURE dump_long (
    tab IN VARCHAR2,
    col IN VARCHAR2,
    whr IN VARCHAR2 := NULL,
    pieces IN OUT DBMS_SQL.VARCHAR2S)
/* Requires Oracle 7.3 or above */
IS
    cur PLS_INTEGER := DBMS_SQL.OPEN_CURSOR;
    fdbk PLS_INTEGER;

    TYPE long_rectype IS RECORD (
        piece_len PLS_INTEGER,
        pos_in_long PLS_INTEGER,
        one_piece VARCHAR2(256),
        one_piece_len PLS_INTEGER
        );
    rec long_rectype;

    BEGIN
```

```
/* Construct the query, sticking in a non-restricting filter
      if whr is NULL */
DBMS_SQL.PARSE (
    cur,
    'SELECT ' || col ||
    '  FROM ' || tab ||
    ' WHERE ' || NVL (whr, '1 = 1'),
    DBMS_SQL.NATIVE);

/* Define the long column and then execute and fetch... */
DBMS_SQL.DEFINE_COLUMN_LONG (cur, 1);
fdbk := DBMS_SQL.EXECUTE (cur);
fdbk := DBMS_SQL.FETCH_ROWS (cur);

/* If a row was fetched, loop through the long value until
|| all pieces are retrieved.
*/
IF fdbk > 0
THEN
    rec.piece_len := 256;
    rec.pos_in_long := 0;
    LOOP
       DBMS_SQL.COLUMN_VALUE_LONG (
          cur,
          1,
          rec.piece_len,
          rec.pos_in_long,
          rec.one_piece,
          rec.one_piece_len);
       EXIT WHEN rec.one_piece_len = 0;

       /* Always put the new piece in the next available row */
       pieces (NVL (pieces.LAST, 0) + 1) := rec.one_piece;
       rec.pos_in_long := rec.pos_in_long + rec.one_piece_len;
    END LOOP;
END IF;
DBMS_SQL.CLOSE_CURSOR (cur);
END;
/
```

To test this procedure, I created a table with a LONG column as follows (the table creation, INSERT, and test script may all be found in dumplong.tst):

```
DROP TABLE nextbook;
CREATE TABLE nextbook
    (title VARCHAR2(100), text LONG);
INSERT INTO nextbook VALUES
    ('Oracle PL/SQL Quick Reference',
    RPAD ('INSTR ', 256, 'blah1 ') ||
    RPAD ('SUBSTR ', 256, 'blah2 ') ||
    RPAD ('TO_DATE ', 256, 'blah3 ') ||
    RPAD ('TO_CHAR ', 256, 'blah4 ') ||
    RPAD ('LOOP ', 256, 'blah5 ') ||
    RPAD ('IF ', 256, 'blah6 ') ||
```

```
        RPAD ('CURSOR ', 256, 'blah7 ')
        );
```

I then put together this short test script. It extracts the single value from the table. (I pass a NULL WHERE clause, so it simply returns the first—and only—row fetched.) It then uses a numeric FOR loop to scan through the returned table to display the results.

```
    DECLARE
       mytab DBMS_SQL.VARCHAR2S;
    BEGIN
       dump_long ('nextbook', 'text', NULL, mytab);
       FOR longind IN 1 .. mytab.COUNT
       LOOP
          DBMS_OUTPUT.PUT_LINE  (SUBSTR (mytab(longind), 1, 60));
       END LOOP;
    END;
    /
```

Here is the output displayed in my SQL*Plus window:

```
    INSTR blah1 blah1 blah1 blah1 blah1 blah1 blah1 blah1 blah1
    SUBSTR blah2 blah2 blah2 blah2 blah2 blah2 blah2 blah2 blah2
    TO_DATE blah3 blah3 blah3 blah3 blah3 blah3 blah3 blah3 blah
    TO_CHAR blah4 blah4 blah4 blah4 blah4 blah4 blah4 blah4 blah
    LOOP blah5 blah5 blah5 blah5 blah5 blah5 blah5 blah5 blah5 b
    IF blah6 blah6 blah6 blah6 blah6 blah6 blah6 blah6 blah6 bla
    CURSOR blah7 blah7 blah7 blah7 blah7 blah7 blah7 blah7 blah7
```

The DBMS_SQL.VARIABLE_VALUE procedure

The VARIABLE_VALUE procedure retrieves the value of a named variable from the specified PL/SQL block. You can retrieve the value for a single variable, or, with PL/SQL8, you can retrieve the values for an array or PL/SQL table of values. This is the header for the single-row version of the procedure:

```
    PROCEDURE DBMS_SQL.VARIABLE_VALUE
        (c IN INTEGER
        ,name IN VARCHAR2
        ,value OUT <datatype>);
```

The VARIABLE_VALUE parameters are summarized in the following table.

Parameter	Description
c	The handle or pointer to the cursor originally returned by a call to OPEN_CURSOR.
name	The name of the host variable included in the PL/SQL statement passed to PARSE.
value	The PL/SQL data structure (either a scalar variable, <datatype>, or a PL/SQL table, <table_type>) that receives the value from the cursor.

<datatype> can be one of the following:

```
NUMBER
DATE
MLSLABEL
VARCHAR2 CHARACTER SET ANY_CS
BLOB
CLOB CHARACTER SET ANY_CS
BFILE
```

The header for the multiple-row version of VARIABLE_VALUE is the following:

```
PROCEDURE DBMS_SQL.VARIABLE_VALUE
    (c IN INTEGER
    ,name IN VARCHAR2
    ,value IN <table_type>);
```

<table_type> can be one of the following:

```
DBMS_SQL.NUMBER_TABLE
DBMS_SQL.VARCHAR2_TABLE
DBMS_SQL.DATE_TABLE
DBMS_SQL.BLOB_TABLE
DBMS_SQL.CLOB_TABLE
DBMS_SQL.BFILE_TABLE
```

The DBMS_SQL package also offers more specific variants of VARIABLE_VALUE for less common datatypes:

```
PROCEDURE DBMS_SQL.VARIABLE_VALUE_CHAR
    (c IN INTEGER
    ,name IN VARCHAR2
    ,value OUT CHAR CHARACTER SET ANY_CS);

PROCEDURE DBMS_SQL.VARIABLE_VALUE_RAW
    (c IN INTEGER
    ,name IN VARCHAR2
    ,value OUT RAW);

PROCEDURE DBMS_SQL.VARIABLE_VALUE_ROWID
    (c IN INTEGER
    ,name IN VARCHAR2
    ,value OUT ROWID);
```

If you use the multiple-row version of VARIABLE_VALUE, you must have used the BIND_ARRAY procedure to define the bind variable in the PL/SQL block as an array of values.

The following program allows you to provide the name of a stored procedure, a list of IN parameters, and a single OUT variable. It then uses dynamic PL/SQL to construct and execute that stored procedure, and finally retrieves the OUT value and returns it to the calling block.

```
/* Filename on companion disk: runprog.sp */
CREATE OR REPLACE PROCEDURE runproc
```

```
        (proc IN VARCHAR2, arglist IN VARCHAR2, outval OUT NUMBER)
   IS
        cur INTEGER := DBMS_SQL.OPEN_CURSOR;
        fdbk INTEGER;
   BEGIN
        DBMS_SQL.PARSE
          (cur, 'BEGIN ' || proc || '(' || arglist || ', :outparam); END;',
           DBMS_SQL.NATIVE);

        DBMS_SQL.BIND_VARIABLE (cur, 'outparam', 1);

        fdbk := DBMS_SQL.EXECUTE (cur);

        DBMS_SQL.VARIABLE_VALUE (cur, 'outparam', outval);

        DBMS_SQL.CLOSE_CURSOR (cur);
   END;
   /
```

Now if I have the following procedure defined:

```
CREATE OR REPLACE PROCEDURE testdyn
    (in1 IN NUMBER, in2 IN DATE, out1 OUT NUMBER)
IS
BEGIN
    out1 := in1 + TO_NUMBER (TO_CHAR (in2, 'YYYY'));
END;
/
```

Then I can execute testdyn dynamically as follows:

```
DECLARE
    n NUMBER;
BEGIN
    runproc ('testdyn', '1, sysdate', n);
    DBMS_OUTPUT.PUT_LINE (n);
END;
/
```

As you have likely discerned, this is not a very good general-purpose program. It will work only with procedures that have parameter lists in which the last argument is a numeric OUT parameter and that argument must be the only OUT or IN OUT parameter in the list.

There can be many complications when attempting to execute dynamic PL/SQL. For suggestions on how best to perform these tasks, see the "Tips on Using Dynamic SQL" section.

Closing the Cursor

When you are done working with a cursor, you should close it and release associated memory.

The DBMS_SQL.CLOSE_CURSOR procedure

The CLOSE_CURSOR procedure closes the specified cursor and sets the cursor handle to NULL. It releases all memory associated with the cursor. The specification for the procedure is,

```
PROCEDURE DBMS_SQL.CLOSE_CURSOR
    (c IN OUT INTEGER);
```

where c is the handle or pointer to the cursor that was originally returned by a call to OPEN_CURSOR. The parameter is IN OUT because once the cursor is closed, the pointer is set to NULL.

If you try to close a cursor that is not open or that is not a valid cursor ID, this program will raise the INVALID_CURSOR exception. You might consider building a "wrapper" for CLOSE_CURSOR to avoid this exception.

```
CREATE OR REPLACE PROCEDURE closeif (c IN OUT INTEGER)
IS
BEGIN
   IF DBMS_SQL.IS_OPEN (c)
   THEN
       DBMS_SQL.CLOSE_CURSOR (c);
   END IF;
END;
/
```

Checking Cursor Status

Several functions allow you to check the status of a cursor.

The DBMS_SQL.LAST_ERROR_POSITION function

The LAST_ERROR_POSITION function returns the byte offset in the SQL statement where the error occurred. The first character in the statement is at position 0. This function offers the same kind of feedback SQL*Plus offers you when it displays a syntax or value error while executing a SQL statement: it displays the problematic text with an asterisk (*) under the character that caused the problem. Here's the specification for this function:

```
FUNCTION DBMS_SQL.LAST_ERROR RETURN INTEGER;
```

You must call this function immediately after a call to EXECUTE or EXECUTE_AND_FETCH in order to obtain meaningful results. The following script demonstrates when and how this function's return value can come in handy:

```
/* Filename on companion disk: file errpos.sql */
DECLARE
    cur BINARY_INTEGER := DBMS_SQL.OPEN_CURSOR;
    errpos BINARY_INTEGER;
    fdbk BINARY_INTEGER;
```

```
BEGIN
   DBMS_SQL.PARSE (cur, 'SELECT empno, ^a FROM emp', DBMS_SQL.NATIVE);
   DBMS_SQL.DEFINE_COLUMN (cur, 1, 1);
   fdbk := DBMS_SQL.EXECUTE_AND_FETCH (cur, false);
   DBMS_SQL.CLOSE_CURSOR (cur);
EXCEPTION
   WHEN OTHERS
   THEN
      errpos := DBMS_SQL.LAST_ERROR_POSITION;
      DBMS_OUTPUT.PUT_LINE (SQLERRM || ' at pos ' || errpos);
      DBMS_SQL.CLOSE_CURSOR (cur);
END;
/
```

When I run this script in SQL*Plus, I get the following output:

```
SQL> @errpos
ORA-00936: missing expression at pos 14
```

One of the greatest frustrations with dynamic SQL is getting your string strung together improperly. It is very easy to introduce syntax errors. The DBMS_SQL.LAST_ERROR_POSITION function can be a big help in uncovering the source of your problem.

NOTE   Some readers may be wondering why I declared a local variable called errpos and assigned the value to it before calling DBMS_OUTPUT.PUT_LINE to examine the error. The reason (discovered by Eric Givler, ace technical reviewer for this book) is that if I do not grab the value from this function before calling SQLERRM, the function will return 0 instead of the 14 for which I am looking.

If my exception section looks, for example, as follows,

```
WHEN OTHERS
THEN
   DBMS_OUTPUT.PUT_LINE
      (SQLERRM || ' at pos ' || DBMS_SQL.LAST_ERROR_POSITION);
   DBMS_SQL.CLOSE_CURSOR (cur);
```

then the output from running the program will become:

```
SQL> @errpos
ORA-00936: missing expression at pos 0
```

Why does this happen? The SQLERRM function must be executing an implicit SQL statement (probably a query!). This action resets the values returned by this DBMS_SQL function, since it is tied to the underlying, generic implicit cursor attribute.

The DBMS_SQL.LAST_ROW_COUNT function

The LAST_ROW_COUNT function returns the total number of rows fetched at that point. This function corresponds to the %ROWCOUNT attribute of a normal, static cursor in PL/SQL. Here's the specification for this function:

```
FUNCTION DBMS_SQL.LAST_ROW_COUNT RETURN INTEGER;
```

You must call this function immediately after a call to EXECUTE_AND_FETCH or FETCH_ROWS in order to obtain meaningful results. You will most likely use this function when fetching from within a loop:

```
CREATE OR REPLACE PROCEDURE show_n_emps (lim IN INTEGER)
IS
    cur PLS_INTEGER := DBMS_SQL.OPEN_CURSOR;
    fdbk PLS_INTEGER;
    v_ename emp.ename%TYPE;
BEGIN
    DBMS_SQL.PARSE (cur, 'SELECT ename FROM emp', DBMS_SQL.NATIVE);
    DBMS_SQL.DEFINE_COLUMN (cur, 1, v_ename, 100);
    fdbk := DBMS_SQL.EXECUTE (cur);
    LOOP
        EXIT WHEN DBMS_SQL.FETCH_ROWS (cur) = 0;
        IF DBMS_SQL.LAST_ROW_COUNT <= lim
        THEN
            DBMS_SQL.COLUMN_VALUE (cur, 1, v_ename);
            DBMS_OUTPUT.PUT_LINE (v_ename);
        ELSE
            /* Hit maximum. Display message and exit. */
            DBMS_OUTPUT.PUT_LINE
                ('Displayed ' || TO_CHAR (lim) || ' employees.');
            EXIT;
        END IF;
    END LOOP;
    DBMS_SQL.CLOSE_CURSOR (cur);
END;
/
```

The DBMS_SQL.LAST_ROW_ID function

The LAST_ROW_ID function returns the ROWID of the row fetched most recently. The specification for this function is as follows:

```
FUNCTION DBMS_SQL.LAST_ROW_ID RETURN ROWID;
```

You must call this function immediately after a call to EXECUTE_AND_FETCH or FETCH_ROWS in order to obtain meaningful results. This function is useful mostly for debugging purposes and perhaps to log which records have been affected.

The DBMS_SQL.LAST_SQL_FUNCTION_CODE function

The LAST_SQL_FUNCTION_CODE function returns the SQL function code for the SQL statement. The specification for this function is as follows:

```
FUNCTION DBMS_SQL.LAST_SQL_FUNCTION_CODE RETURN INTEGER;
```

You must call this function immediately after a call to EXECUTE_AND_FETCH or EXECUTE in order to obtain meaningful results. It will tell you which type of SQL statement was executed.

The SQL function codes are listed in Table 2-3.

Table 2-3. SQL Function Codes

Code	SQL Function	Code	SQL Function	Code	SQL Function
01	CREATE TABLE	35	LOCK	69	(NOT USED)
02	SET ROLE	36	NOOP	70	ALTER RESOURCE COST
03	INSERT	37	RENAME	71	CREATE SNAP-SHOT LOG
04	SELECT	38	COMMENT	72	ALTER SNAP-SHOT LOG
05	UPDATE	39	AUDIT	73	DROP SNAPSHOT LOG
06	DROP ROLE	40	NO AUDIT	74	CREATE SNAP-SHOT
07	DROP VIEW	41	ALTER INDEX	75	ALTER SNAPSHOT
08	DROP TABLE	42	CREATE EXTER-NAL DATABASE	76	DROP SNAPSHOT
09	DELETE	43	DROP EXTERNAL DATABASE	77	CREATE TYPE
10	CREATE VIEW	44	CREATE DATA-BASE	78	DROP TYPE
11	DROP USER	45	ALTER DATABASE	79	ALTER ROLE
12	CREATE ROLE	46	CREATE ROLL-BACK SEGMENT	80	ALTER TYPE
13	CREATE SEQUENCE	47	ALTER ROLL-BACK SEGMENT	81	CREATE TYPE BODY
14	ALTER SEQUENCE	48	DROP ROLLBACK SEGMENT	82	ALTER TYPE BODY
15	(NOT USED)	49	CREATE TABLESPACE	83	DROP TYPE BODY
16	DROP SEQUENCE	50	ALTER TABLESPACE	84	DROP LIBRARY
17	CREATE SCHEMA	51	DROP TABLESPACE	85	TRUNCATE TABLE
18	CREATE CLUSTER	52	ALTER SESSION	86	TRUNCATE CLUS-TER
19	CREATE USER	53	ALTER USER	87	CREATE BITMAP-FILE

Table 2-3. SQL Function Codes (continued)

Code	SQL Function	Code	SQL Function	Code	SQL Function
20	CREATE INDEX	54	COMMIT (WORK)	88	ALTER VIEW
21	DROP INDEX	55	ROLLBACK	89	DROP BITMAP-FILE
22	DROP CLUSTER	56	SAVEPOINT	90	SET CON-STRAINTS
23	VALIDATE INDEX	57	CREATE CON-TROL FILE	91	CREATE FUNC-TION
24	CREATE PROCE-DURE	58	ALTER TRACING	92	ALTER FUNCTION
25	ALTER PROCE-DURE	59	CREATE TRIGGER	93	DROP FUNCTION
26	ALTER TABLE	60	ALTER TRIGGER	94	CREATE PACK-AGE
27	EXPLAIN	61	DROP TRIGGER	95	ALTER PACKAGE
28	GRANT	62	ANALYZE TABLE	96	DROP PACKAGE
29	REVOKE	63	ANALYZE INDEX	97	CREATE PACK-AGE BODY
30	CREATE SYN-ONYM	64	ANALYZE CLUS-TER	98	ALTER PACKAGE BODY
31	DROP SYNONYM	65	CREATE PROFILE	99	DROP PACKAGE BODY
32	ALTER SYSTEM SWITCH LOG	66	DROP PROFILE	157	CREATE DIREC-TORY
33	SET TRANSAC-TION	67	ALTER PROFILE	158	DROP DIREC-TORY
34	PL/SQL EXECUTE	68	DROP PROCE-DURE	159	CREATE LIBRARY

Describing Cursor Columns

With PL/SQL8, you can now obtain information about the structure of the columns of your dynamic cursor.

The DBMS_SQL.DESCRIBE_COLUMNS procedure

The DESCRIBE_COLUMNS prodecure obtains information about your dynamic cursor. Here is the header:

```
PROCEDURE DBMS_SQL.DESCRIBE_COLUMNS
      (c IN INTEGER
      ,col_cnt OUT INTEGER
      ,desc_t OUT DBMS_SQL.DESC_TAB);
```

The parameters for the DESCRIBE_COLUMNS procedure are summarized in the following table.

Parameter	Description
c	The pointer to the cursor.
col_cnt	The number of columns in the cursor, which equals the number of rows defined in the PL/SQL table.
desc_t	The PL/SQL table, which contains all of the column information. This is a table of records of type DBMS_SQL.DESC_REC (<table_type), which is described later.

The following table lists the DBMS_SQL.DESC_REC record type fields.

<table_type>	Datatype	Description
col_type	BINARY_INTEGER	Type of column described
col_max_len	BINARY_INTEGER	Maximum length of column value
col_name	VARCHAR2(32)	Name of the column
col_name_len	BINARY_INTEGER	Length of the column name
col_schema_name	VARCHAR2(32)	Name of column type schema if an object type
col_schema_name_len	BINARY_INTEGER	Length of schema name
col_precision	BINARY_INTEGER	Precision of column if a number
col_scale	BINARY_INTEGER	Scale of column if a number
col_charsetid	BINARY_INTEGER	ID of character set
col_charsetform	BINARY_INTEGER	Character set form
col_null_ok	BOOLEAN	TRUE if column can be NULL

The values for column types are as follows:

Datatype	Number
VARCHAR2	1
NVARCHAR2	1
NUMBER	2
INTEGER	2
LONG	8
ROWID	11
DATE	12
RAW	23
LONG RAW	24
CHAR	96
NCHAR	96

Datatype	Number
MLSLABEL	106
CLOB (Oracle8)	112
NCLOB (Oracle8)	112
BLOB (Oracle8)	113
BFILE (Oracle8)	114
Object type (Oracle8)	121
Nested table Type (Oracle8)	122
Variable array (Oracle8)	123

When you call this program, you need to have declared a PL/SQL table based on the DBMS_SQL.DESC_T. You can then use PL/SQL table methods to traverse the table and extract the needed information about the cursor. The following anonymous block shows the basic steps you will perform when working with this built-in:

```
DECLARE
    cur PLS_INTEGER := DBMS_SQL.OPEN_CURSOR;
    cols DBMS_SQL.DESC_T;
    ncols PLS_INTEGER;
BEGIN
    DBMS_SQL.PARSE
        (cur, 'SELECT hiredate, sal FROM emp', DBMS_SQL.NATIVE);
    DBMS_SQL.DEFINE_COLUMN (cur, 1, SYSDATE);
    DBMS_SQL.DEFINE_COLUMN (cur, 2, 1);
    DBMS_SQL.DESCRIBE_COLUMNS (cur, ncols, cols);
    FOR colind IN 1 .. ncols
    LOOP
        DBMS_OUTPUT.PUT_LINE (cols.col_name);
    END LOOP;
    DBMS_SQL.CLOSE_CURSOR (cur);
END;
/
```

If you are going to use this procedure to extract information about a dynamic cursor, you will likely want to build a "wrapper" around it to make it easier for you to get at this data. The "DBMS_SQL Examples" section at the end of this chapter offers an example of this wrapper.

How'd He Get Those Numbers?

The Oracle documentation for DBMS_SQL tells us only that the col_type field
of the DBMS_REC record contains the "type of the column being described"
and that the type is an INTEGER. Well, what exactly are those integer values?
I could have sent email to someone at Oracle Corporation and waited for a
response. But even then, how would I be sure that those values are correct?
And why depend on another person, when I can depend on the software itself?

To figure out the different column type values, I first constructed a table as
follows:

```
CREATE TABLE coltypes
   (vc VARCHAR2(10),
    nvc NVARCHAR2(10),
    ch CHAR(10),
    nch NCHAR(10),
    d DATE,
    n NUMBER,
    i INTEGER,
    l LONG,
    r RAW(100),
    rid ROWID,
    cl CLOB,
    ncl NCLOB,
    bl BLOB,
    bf BFILE,
    msl MLSLABEL
    )
/
```

These columns pretty much cover all of the datatypes through Oracle8. I then
built a script which relies on the desccols package to call the DESCRIBE_
COLUMNS procedure (see the "DBMS_SQL Examples" section) and display the
column information, including the column types.

```
/* Filename on companion disk: desccols.xmn */
DECLARE
    cur integer := dbms_sql.open_cursor;
    cl CLOB;
    bl BLOB;
    ncl NCLOB;
    bf BFILE;
    msl MLSLABEL;
    r RAW(100);
    rid ROWID;
BEGIN
    dbms_sql.PARSE (cur, 'SELECT vc, nvc, ch, nch, d, n, i, l, r
        , rid, cl, ncl, bl, bf, msl FROM coltypes', DBMS_SQL.NATIVE);
```

```
   DBMS_SQL.DEFINE_COLUMN (cur, 1, 'a', 10);
   DBMS_SQL.DEFINE_COLUMN (cur, 2, 'a', 10);
   DBMS_SQL.DEFINE_COLUMN_CHAR (cur, 3, 'a', 10);
   DBMS_SQL.DEFINE_COLUMN_CHAR (cur, 4, 'a', 10);
   DBMS_SQL.DEFINE_COLUMN (cur, 5, SYSDATE);
   DBMS_SQL.DEFINE_COLUMN (cur, 6, 1);
   DBMS_SQL.DEFINE_COLUMN (cur, 7, 1);
   DBMS_SQL.DEFINE_COLUMN_LONG (cur, 8);
   DBMS_SQL.DEFINE_COLUMN_RAW (cur, 9, r, 10);
   DBMS_SQL.DEFINE_COLUMN_ROWID (cur, 10, rid);
   DBMS_SQL.DEFINE_COLUMN (cur, 11, cl);
   DBMS_SQL.DEFINE_COLUMN (cur, 12, ncl);
   DBMS_SQL.DEFINE_COLUMN (cur, 13, bl);
   DBMS_SQL.DEFINE_COLUMN (cur, 14, bf);
   DBMS_SQL.DEFINE_COLUMN (cur, 15, msl);
   dyncur.desccols (cur);
   dyncur.show;
   DBMS_SQL.CLOSE_CURSOR (cur);
END;
/
```

and I got this output:

```
Column 1
VC
1
Column 2
NVC
1
Column 3
CH
96
Column 4
NCH
96
Column 5
D
12
Column 6
N
2
Column 7
I
2
Column 8
L
8
Column 9
R
23
Column 10
RID
11
```

```
Column 11
CL
112
Column 12
NCL
112
Column 13
BL
113
Column 14
BF
114
Column 15
MSL
106
```

I could then document those values with confidence in this book. I wanted to show you this so that you understand that even when a person knows an *awful* lot about PL/SQL, he doesn't necessarily know everything. In fact, knowing everything is completely impossible and anyone claiming to "know it all" should not be trusted. Recognize your areas of ignorance and then search out the answers, perferably by going to the source—the source code, that is.

Tips on Using Dynamic SQL

This section offers advice about how best to take advantage of dynamic SQL and the DBMS_SQL package. Following this section is a series of detailed examples of putting DBMS_SQL to use.

Some Restrictions

You can do a lot of awfully interesting stuff with DBMS_SQL, but some things are off-limits:

- You cannot manipulate cursor variables from within dynamic SQL. Cursor variables are a relatively new, advanced, and little-used feature of PL/SQL (see Chapter 6 of *Oracle PL/SQL Programming* for more information). But if you want to use them, you'll have to do it in static PL/SQL code.

- Unless otherwise noted, DBMS_SQL does not support many of the new data structures in Oracle8. For example, you cannot bind an object or a nested table or a variable array.

Privileges and Execution Authority with DBMS_SQL

There are two basic rules to remember when working with DBMS_SQL:

- Stored programs execute under the privileges of the owner of that program. So if you parse and execute dynamic SQL from within a program, references to database objects in that SQL statement are resolved according to the schema of the program, not the schema of the person running the program.

- Roles are disabled when compiling and executing PL/SQL code. Privileges must be granted directly in order to be used with PL/SQL code. So when you execute dynamic SQL from within a PL/SQL program, you must have directly granted privileges to any database objects referenced in the dynamically constructed string.

The following anecdotes demonstrate the kinds of problems you can face with dynamic SQL.

The tale of Jan

Jan is a sharp DBA. She keeps up on the latest in Oracle technology, both within her discipline and in the wider array of Oracle software. When Oracle Server Release 7.1 hit the street, she checked for new features and came across the built-in DBMS_SQL package. DBMS_SQL, she discovered, allows you to execute dynamic SQL and PL/SQL from within PL/SQL programs.

Jan immediately saw the possibilities and built herself a suite of procedures to perform DBA tasks, all inside that most wonderful of PL/SQL constructs, the package. Among other great features, the Janfast/jandyn package she developed contains a procedure called create_index to create an index for any table and column(s) on the table. The code for this procedure is shown at the beginning of this chapter.

Jan installed the Janfast/jandyn package in the JANDBA account (what can I say? She likes her name!) and granted EXECUTE privilege on that package to all users, including her account named (yep, you guessed it) JAN. To make things even more exciting, she built an Oracle Forms front-end to her package (Janfast/jandyn). She could then take advantage of the stored code through a fill-in-the-form interface, rather than the command-line approach of SQL*Plus.

One day Jan receives a call: it seems that the company has added many employees over the years, and the emp table now has six million rows. All of the user accounts (working against a shared data source in the PERSONNEL Oracle account) are experiencing serious performance problems. A new index (at least one) is needed on the emp table to improve query performance.

So Jan connects to the production PERSONNEL account and starts up Janfast/jan-dyn. Just a few keystrokes and mouse clicks later, she has constructed the following statement,

```
jandyn.create_index ('empname_idx', 'emp', 'ename, sal');
```

which is to say: create an index named empname_idx on the emp table on the ename and sal columns (in that order). She clicks on the Execute button and Jan-fast does its thing. Notified through a chime of the successful completion of her task, Jan is impressed at how rapidly the index was built. She notifies the application development team that all is better now. Fifteen minutes of quiet contemplation pass before she gets an angry call from a developer: "The performance hasn't changed one bit!" he says angrily. "The screens still work just as slowly as before when I try to search for an employee by name."

Jan the DBA is bewildered and quickly runs the following script to examine the indexes on the emp table:

```
SQL> SELECT i.index_name, i.tablespace_name,
            uniqueness u, column_name col, column_position pos
       FROM all_indexes i, all_ind_columns c
      WHERE i.index_name = c.index_name
        AND i.table_name = 'EMP';

INDEX_NAME        TABLESPACE_NAME       U          COL       POS
----------------  --------------------  ---------  --------- ---
EMP_PRIMARY_KEY   USER_DATA             UNIQUE     EMPNO     1
```

There is no empname_idx index! What has gone wrong? Where did the index go? How and why did Janfast/jandyn fail our industrious and creative database administrator?

Remember: when you execute stored code, you run it under the privileges of the *owner* of that code, not the privileges of the account that called the program. When Jan executed the index creation statement from within a call to jandyn.cre-ind, the DDL statement was processed as though it were being executed *by* JAN-DBA, not by PERSONNEL. If the DBA had wanted to create an index in her own schema, she should have entered the following command:

```
jandyn.creind
    ('personnel.empname_idx', 'personnel.emp', 'ename, sal');
```

If this command had been executed, Jan would have had a much better chance at solving her performance problems.

The tale of Scott

Here's another common gotcha: my SCOTT account has been granted the standard CONNECT and RESOURCE roles. As a result, I can create a table as follows:

```
SQL> CREATE TABLE upbeat (tempo NUMBER);

Table created
```

Now suppose that I have created a little program to make it easier for me to execute DDL from within PL/SQL:

```
/* Filename on companion disk: runddl.sp */
CREATE OR REPLACE PROCEDURE runddl (ddl_in in VARCHAR2)
IS
    cur INTEGER:= DBMS_SQL.OPEN_CURSOR;
    fdbk INTEGER;
BEGIN
    DBMS_SQL.PARSE (cur, ddl_in, DBMS_SQL.V7);

    fdbk := DBMS_SQL.EXECUTE (cur);

    DBMS_SQL.CLOSE_CURSOR (cur);
END;
/
```

I then issue the same CREATE TABLE statement as before, this time within PL/SQL, but now I get an error:

```
SQL> exec runddl ('CREATE TABLE upbeat (tempo NUMBER)');
*
ERROR at line 1:
ORA-01031: insufficient privileges
ORA-06512: at "SYS.DBMS_SYS_SQL", line 239
```

Don't beat your head against the wall when this happens! Just remember that role-based privileges do not help you when executing SQL from within PL/SQL. The RESOURCE role is ignored when the CREATE TABLE statement is executed. SCOTT doesn't have any CREATE TABLE *privileges*, so the dynamic SQL fails.

Combining Operations

Every PARSE must be preceded by a call to OPEN_CURSOR. Every call to PARSE must include a DBMS mode argument, even though 99.99% of the time, it is going to be DBMS_SQL.NATIVE.

When I find myself repeating the same steps over and over again in using a package or particular feature, I look for ways to bundle these steps into a single procedure or function call to save myself time. The next function shows such a function, open_and_parse, which opens a cursor and parses the specified SQL statement. Using open_and_parse, I can replace the following statements,

```
cursor_handle := DBMS_SQL.OPEN_CURSOR;
DBMS_SQL.PARSE (cursor_handle, 'UPDATE emp ... ', DBMS_SQL.NATIVE);
```

with just this:

```
   cursor_handle := open_and_parse ('UPDATE emp ... ');
```

Here, then, is the open_and_parse bundled procedure:

```
/* Filename  on companion disk: openprse.sf */
CREATE OR REPLACE FUNCTION open_and_parse
   (sql_statement_in IN VARCHAR2,
    dbms_mode_in IN INTEGER := DBMS_SQL.NATIVE)
RETURN INTEGER
IS
   /* Declare cursor handle and assign it a pointer */
   return_value INTEGER := DBMS_SQL.OPEN_CURSOR;
BEGIN
   /* Parse the SQL statement */
   DBMS_SQL.PARSE (return_value, sql_statement_in, dbms_mode_in);

   /* Pass back the pointer to this parsed statement */
   RETURN return_value;
END;
```

Now, one problem with this otherwise handy little procedure is that it *always* declares a new cursor. What if you already have a cursor? Then you should go straight to the parse step. You can combine the functionality of open_and_parse with the initcur procedure shown in the next section to produce your own enhanced program.

Minimizing Memory for Cursors

As noted earlier, you will not want to allocate a cursor via the OPEN_CURSOR procedure if you can instead use an already defined cursor that is not currently in use. The best way to minimize memory usage with dynamic SQL cursors is to encapsulate the open action inside a procedure. The initcur procedure shown below demonstrates this technique.

With initcur, you pass a variable into the procedure. If that variable points to a valid, open DBMS_SQL cursor, then it is returned unchanged. If, on the other hand, that cursor is closed (the IS_OPEN function returns FALSE) *or* IS_OPEN for any reason raises the INVALID_CURSOR exception, then OPEN_CURSOR is called and the new cursor pointer is returned.

```
CREATE OR REPLACE PROCEDURE initcur (cur_inout IN OUT INTEGER) IS
BEGIN
   IF NOT DBMS_SQL.IS_OPEN (cur_inout)
   THEN
      cur_inout := DBMS_SQL.OPEN_CURSOR;
   END IF;
EXCEPTION
   WHEN invalid_cursor
   THEN
      cur_inout := DBMS_SQL.OPEN_CURSOR;
END;
/
```

You could also implement this functionality as a function, or could overload both inside a package, as follows:

```
CREATE OR REPLACE PACKAGE dyncur
IS
    PROCEDURE initcur (cur_inout IN OUT INTEGER);
    FUNCTION initcur (cur_in IN INTEGER) RETURN INTEGER;
END dyncur;
/
```

In addition to allocating cursor areas only when necessary, you should make sure that you close your cursors when you are done with them. Unlike static cursors, which close automatically when their scope terminates, a dynamic SQL cursor will remain open even if the block in which it was defined finishes execution. And remember that you should perform the close operation at the end of the executable code, but also in any exception sections in the block. This technique is shown here:

```
CREATE OR REPLACE PROCEDURE do_dynamic_stuff
IS
    cur1 INTEGER := DBMS_SQL.OPEN_CURSOR;
    cur2 INTEGER := DBMS_SQL.OPEN_CURSOR;

    PROCEDURE closeall IS
    BEGIN
        /* Only close if open. Defined in Closing the Cursor section. */
        closeif (cur1);
        closeif (cur2);
    END;
BEGIN
    /* Do the dynamic stuff, then close the cursors.*/
    ...
    closeall;
EXCEPTION
    WHEN DUP_VAL_ON_INDEX
    THEN
        /* Special handling, then cleanup */
        ...
        closeall;

    WHEN OTHERS
    THEN
        /* Catch-all cleanup, then reraise to propagate out the error.*/
        closeall;
        RAISE;
END;
/
```

The *openprse.ssp* file contains a package that implements both the initcur
and an enhanced version of open_and_parse (see the section called "Combining Operations"). This package allows you to keep to an absolute minimum
the number of cursors allocated to perform dynamic SQL operations.

Improving the Performance of Dynamic SQL

You can improve the performance of your dynamic SQL operations by taking
advantage of two aspects of DBMS_SQL:

- Reuse DBMS_SQL cursors whenever possible (this technique was demonstrated in the last section).

- Avoid reparsing your dynamic SQL when the only thing that changes is a
  bind variable.

The following script (written with the help of John Beresniewicz) demonstrates
the gains you can see by paying attention to both of these considerations. The
script illustrates three different ways to do the same thing in dynamic SQL using
DBMS_SQL, namely fetch rows from a table.

- Approach 1 parses and executes each query without using any bind variables.
  It is the most inefficient, performing 1000 parses, executing 1000 statements,
  and requiring room in the shared pool for up to 1000 different SQL statements.

- Approach 2 parses and executes for each query, but uses bind variables, so it
  works a bit more efficiently. With this approach, you still perform 1000 parses
  and execute 1000 times, but at least you need room for only one SQL statement in the shared pool.

- Approach 3 parses just once and executes each query using host variables. It
  is by far the most efficient technique: requiring just one parse, 1000 executions, and a single preparsed SQL statement in the shared pool.

I have used a very large and cumbersome SELECT in this test to make sure that
there was enough overhead in parsing to both simulate a "real-world" query and
also to demonstrate a clear difference in performance between the second and
third approaches (for very simple SQL statements, you will not see too much of a
difference). For the sake of brevity, I will not show the entire query in the code.

```
/* Filename on companion disk: effdsql.tst */
DECLARE
   /*
   || Approach 1: the worst
   */
```

```
    v_start INTEGER;
    cursor_id INTEGER;
    exec_stat INTEGER;
BEGIN
    v_start := DBMS_UTILITY.GET_TIME;
    cursor_id := DBMS_SQL.OPEN_CURSOR;
    FOR i IN 1..&1
    LOOP
        /*
        || parse and excecute each loop iteration
        || without using host vars, this is worst case
        */
        DBMS_SQL.PARSE (cursor_id, 'SELECT ...', DBMS_SQL.native);
        exec_stat := DBMS_SQL.EXECUTE(cursor_id);
    END LOOP;
    DBMS_SQL.CLOSE_CURSOR(cursor_id);
    DBMS_OUTPUT.PUT_LINE
        ('Approach 1: ' || TO_CHAR (DBMS_UTILITY.GET_TIME - v_start));
END;
/
DECLARE
/*
|| Approach 2: a little better
*/
    v_start INTEGER;
    cursor_id INTEGER;
    exec_stat INTEGER;
BEGIN
    v_start := DBMS_UTILITY.GET_TIME;
    cursor_id := DBMS_SQL.OPEN_CURSOR;
    FOR i IN 1..&1
    LOOP
        /*
        || parse and excecute each loop iteration using host vars
        */
        DBMS_SQL.PARSE (cursor_id, 'SELECT ...', DBMS_SQL.native);
        DBMS_SQL.BIND_VARIABLE(cursor_id,'i',i);
        exec_stat := DBMS_SQL.EXECUTE(cursor_id);
    END LOOP;
    DBMS_SQL.CLOSE_CURSOR(cursor_id);
    DBMS_OUTPUT.PUT_LINE
        ('Approach 2: ' || TO_CHAR (DBMS_UTILITY.GET_TIME - v_start));
END;
/
DECLARE
/*
|| Approach 3: the best
*/
    v_start INTEGER;
    cursor_id INTEGER;
    exec_stat INTEGER;
BEGIN
    v_start := DBMS_UTILITY.GET_TIME;
    cursor_id := DBMS_SQL.OPEN_CURSOR;
```

```
    /*
    || Parse first, outside of loop
    */
    DBMS_SQL.PARSE (cursor_id, 'SELECT ...', DBMS_SQL.native);
    FOR i IN 1..&1
    LOOP
        /*
        || bind and excecute each loop iteration using host vars
        */
        DBMS_SQL.BIND_VARIABLE(cursor_id,'i',i);
        exec_stat := DBMS_SQL.EXECUTE(cursor_id);
    END LOOP;
    DBMS_SQL.CLOSE_CURSOR(cursor_id);
    DBMS_OUTPUT.PUT_LINE
        ('Approach 3: ' || TO_CHAR (DBMS_UTILITY.GET_TIME - v_start));
END;
/
```

And here are the results from running this script twice:

```
SQL>  @effdsql.tst 10000
Approach 1: 860
Approach 2: 981
Approach 3: 479
```

Problem-Solving Dynamic SQL Errors

Sometimes the hardest aspect to building and executing dynamic SQL programs is getting the string of dynamic SQL right. You might be combining a list of columns in a query with a list of tables and then a WHERE clause that changes with each execution. You have to concatenate that stuff together, getting the commas right, and the ANDs and ORs right, and so on. What happens if you get it wrong? Well, let's take the nightmare scenario and work it through.

I am building the most complicated PL/SQL application ever. It uses dynamic SQL left and right, but that's OK. I am a pro at dynamic SQL. I can, in a flash, type OPEN_CURSOR, PARSE, DEFINE_COLUMN, and other commands. I know the right sequence, I know how to detect when there are no more rows to fetch, and I *blast* through the development phase. I also rely on some standard exception-handling programs I have built that display an error message when encountered.

Then the time comes to test my application. I build a test script that runs through a lot of my code; I place it in a file named *testall.sql*. With trembling fingers I start my test:

```
SQL> @testall
```

And, to my severe disappointment, here is what shows up on my screen:

```
ORA-00942: table or view does not exist
ORA-00904: invalid column name
```

```
ORA-00921: unexpected end of SQL command
ORA-00936: missing expression
ORA-00911: invalid character
```

Ugh. A whole bunch of error messages, clearly showing that various SQL statements have been constructed improperly and are causing parse errors—but *which*
SQL statements are the troublemakers? That is a very difficult question to answer.
One way to get at the answer is to place all calls to the PARSE procedure inside
an exception section and then display the string causing the error.

```
CREATE OR REPLACE PROCEDURE whatever
IS
    v_sql VARCHAR2 (32767);
BEGIN
    construct_sql (v_sql);

    DBMS_SQL.PARSE (cur, v_sql, DBMS_SQL.NATIVE);
EXCEPTION
    WHEN OTHERS
    THEN
        DBMS_OUTPUT.PUT_LINE ('Error in ' || v_sql);
END;
/
```

This certainly would have helped explain those earlier error messages. The problem with this approach is that I would need to build this exception section every
time I call PARSE. I also might be raising exceptions from lines of code other than
those containing the call to PARSE. How could I distinguish between the errors
and the information I should display? Furthermore, I might discover after writing
the previous code ten or twenty times that I need *more* information, such as the
error code. I would then have to go back to all those occurrences and enhance
them. This is a very tedious, high-maintenance, and generally nonproductive way
of doing things.

A different and better approach is to provide your own substitute for PARSE that
encapsulates, or hides away, all of these details. You don't have to add exception
sections in each call to this substitute, because it would come with its own exception section. And if you decide you want to do things differently, you just change
this one program. Doesn't that sound so much better?

Let's go through the steps involved in creating a layer over PARSE that enhance its
error-detection capabilities. First, we will build the interface to the underlying
DBMS_SQL call. That is easy enough:

```
/* Filename on companion disk: dynsql.spp */
/* Final version of package */
CREATE OR REPLACE PACKAGE dynsql
IS
    PROCEDURE parse
        (cur IN INTEGER,
```

```
        sqlstr IN VARCHAR2,
        dbmsmode IN INTEGER := NULL);
  END;
  /
```

Why did I bother to put this single procedure inside a package? I always start with packages, because sooner or later I want to add more related functionality, or I need to take advantage of package features, like persistent data. In this case, I could foresee providing an overloaded parse function, which opens and returns a cursor. I also expect to be defining some package data pertaining to error information, which would require a package.

Notice that the parse procedure looks just like the DBMS_SQL version, except that the database mode has a default value of NULL (which will translate into DBMS_SQL.NATIVE). This way (a) you do not have to bother with providing a mode, and (b) the default value is not a packaged constant, which could cause problems for calling this program from within Oracle Developer Release 1.

It would be a good idea to compare using DBMS_SQL with dynsql before we even try to implement this package; that will be a validation of the design of the interface. So instead of this,

```
  DECLARE
      cur PLS_INTEGER := DBMS_SQL.OPEN_CURSOR;
      fdbk PLS_INTEGER;
  BEGIN
      DBMS_SQL.PARSE (cur, 'CREATE INDEX ... ', DBMS_SQL.NATIVE);
```

I could use dynsql.parse as follows:

```
  DECLARE
      cur PLS_INTEGER := DBMS_SQL.OPEN_CURSOR;
  BEGIN
      dynsql.parse (cur, 'CREATE INDEX ... ');
```

I get to write a little bit less code, but that isn't really the main objective. I just want to make sure that I can do whatever I can do with DBMS_SQL (with parse, anyway) through dynsql. Now let's build the package body and add some value:

```
  CREATE OR REPLACE PACKAGE BODY dynsql
  IS
      PROCEDURE parse
        (cur IN INTEGER, sqlstr IN VARCHAR2, dbmsmode IN INTEGER := NULL)
      IS
      BEGIN
        DBMS_SQL.PARSE (cur, sqlstr, NVL (dbmsmode, DBMS_SQL.NATIVE));
      EXCEPTION
        WHEN OTHERS
        THEN
           DBMS_OUTPUT.PUT_LINE ('Error in ' || sqlstr);
      END;
  END;
  /
```

With this program installed, I can replace all calls to PARSE with dynsql.parse and then see precisely which dynamic SQL statements are causing me problems. As I mentioned earlier, though, I really want to get more information. Suppose, for example, that I needed to see the error number (as surely I would), as well as the position in the SQL statement in which the error was detected. No problem! I just go to the package body and add a couple lines of code:

```
CREATE OR REPLACE PACKAGE BODY dynsql
IS
    PROCEDURE parse
        (cur IN INTEGER, sqlstr IN VARCHAR2, dbmsmode IN INTEGER := NULL)
    IS
    BEGIN
        DBMS_SQL.PARSE (cur, sqlstr, NVL (dbmsmode, DBMS_SQL.NATIVE));
    EXCEPTION
        WHEN OTHERS
        THEN
            DBMS_OUTPUT.PUT_LINE ('Parse error: ' || TO_CHAR (SQLCODE) ||
                ' at position ' || TO_CHAR (DBMS_SQL.LAST_ERROR_POSITION));
            DBMS_OUTPUT.PUT_LINE ('SQL string: ' || sqlstr);
    END;
END;
/
```

This should put me in good stead, except for one problem: what if my SQL string is more than 243 bytes in length? The PUT_LINE procedure will raise a VALUE_ERROR if the string passed to it exceeds 255 bytes in length. What an annoyance! But since I have had the foresight to hide all my calls to PARSE away in this single program, I can even address this difficulty. PL/Vision Lite* offers a display_wrap procedure in the PLVprs package. So I can avoid any VALUE_ERROR exceptions as follows:

```
CREATE OR REPLACE PACKAGE BODY dynsql
IS
    PROCEDURE parse
        (cur IN INTEGER, sqlstr IN VARCHAR2, dbmsmode IN INTEGER := NULL)
    IS
    BEGIN
        DBMS_SQL.PARSE (cur, sqlstr, NVL (dbmsmode, DBMS_SQL.NATIVE));
    EXCEPTION
        WHEN OTHERS
        THEN
            DBMS_OUTPUT.PUT_LINE ('Parse error: ' || TO_CHAR (SQLCODE) ||
                ' at position ' || TO_CHAR (DBMS_SQL.LAST_ERROR_POSITION));
            PLVprs.display_wrap ('SQL string: ' || sqlstr);
    END;
END;
/
```

---

* This software comes with my book *Advanced Oracle PL/SQL Programming with Packages* (O'Reilly & Associates, 1996). You can also download it from *www.revealnet.com*.

See how easy it is to upgrade your programs and fix shortcomings once you have encapsulated your repetitive actions behind a programmatic interface?

Executing DDL in PL/SQL

DBMS_SQL allows you to execute almost any DDL statements from within PL/SQL. Here are some considerations to keep in mind:

- You should explicitly execute and then close your DDL cursors. Currently, Oracle will automatically execute DDL statements when they are parsed with a call to PARSE. Oracle Corporation warns users of DBMS_SQL that this behavior might not be supported in the future.

- You cannot establish a new connection to Oracle through PL/SQL. You cannot, in other words, issue a CONNECT command from within PL/SQL; you will get an "ORA-00900: invalid SQL statement" error. From this, one can deduce that CONNECT is not a SQL statement. It is, rather, a SQL*Plus command.

- You must have the necessary privileges to execute that DDL statement granted explicitly to the account owning the program in which the DDL is being run. Remember that roles are disabled during PL/SQL compilation and execution. If you want to create a table using dynamic SQL, you must have CREATE TABLE or CREATE ANY TABLE privileges granted directly to your schema.

- Your dynamic DDL execution can result in your program hanging. When I call a procedure in a package, that package is locked until execution of that program ends. If another program attempts to obtain a conflicting lock (this might occur if you try to drop that package using dynamic DDL), that program will lock waiting for the other program to complete execution.

Executing Dynamic PL/SQL

Dynamic PL/SQL is an awful lot of fun. Just think: you can construct your PL/SQL block "on the fly" and then execute it from within another PL/SQL program. Here are some factors to keep in mind as you delve into this relatively esoteric aspect of PL/SQL development:

- The string you execute dynamically must start with a DECLARE or BEGIN statement and terminate with "END." It must, in other words, be a valid anonymous block.

- The string must end with a semicolon, unlike DDL and DML statements, which cannot end with a semicolon.

- The dynamic PL/SQL block executes *outside* the scope of the block in which the EXECUTE function is called, but that calling block's exception section will trap exceptions raised by the dynamic PL/SQL execution.

- As a direct consequence of the previous rule, you can only reference globally available data structures and program elements from within the dynamic PL/SQL block.

Let's explore those last two restrictions so as to avoid any confusion. First of all, I will build a little utility to execute dynamic PL/SQL.

```
/* Filename on companion disk: dynplsql.sp */
CREATE OR REPLACE PROCEDURE dyn_plsql (blk IN VARCHAR2)
IS
    cur PLS_INTEGER := DBMS_SQL.OPEN_CURSOR;
    fdbk PLS_INTEGER;
BEGIN
    DBMS_SQL.PARSE (cur,
        'BEGIN ' || RTRIM (blk, ';') || '; END;',
        DBMS_SQL.NATIVE);

    fdbk := DBMS_SQL.EXECUTE (cur);
    DBMS_SQL.CLOSE_CURSOR (cur);
END;
/
```

This one program encapsulates many of the rules mentioned previously for PL/SQL execution. It guarantees that whatever I pass in is executed as a valid PL/SQL block by enclosing the string within a BEGIN-END pairing. For instance, I can execute the calc_totals procedure dynamically as simply as this:

```
SQL> exec dyn_plsql ('calc_totals');
```

Now let's use this program to examine what kind of data structures you can reference within a dynamic PL/SQL block. In the following anonymous block, I want to use DBMS_SQL to assign a value of 5 to the local variable num:

```
<<dynamic>>
DECLARE
    num NUMBER;
BEGIN
    dyn_plsql ('num := 5');
END;
/
```

This string is executed within its own BEGIN-END block, which would *appear* to be a nested block within the anonymous block named "dynamic" with the label. Yet when I execute this script I receive the following error:

```
PLS-00302: component 'NUM' must be declared
ORA-06512: at "SYS.DBMS_SYS_SQL", line 239
```

The PL/SQL engine is unable to resolve the reference to the variable named num. I get the same error even if I qualify the variable name with its block name.

```
<<dynamic>>
DECLARE
   num NUMBER;
BEGIN
   /* Also causes a PLS-00302 error! */
   dyn_plsql ('dynamic.num := 5');
END;
/
```

Now suppose that I define the num variable inside a package called dynamic:

```
CREATE OR REPLACE PACKAGE dynamic
IS
   num NUMBER;
END;
/
```

I am then able to execute the dynamic assignment to this newly defined variable successfully.

```
BEGIN
   dyn_plsql ('dynamic.num := 5');
END;
/
```

What's the difference between these two pieces of data? In the first attempt, the variable num is defined locally in the anonymous PL/SQL block. In my second attempt, num is a public "global" defined in the dynamic package. This distinction makes all the difference with dynamic PL/SQL.

It turns out that a dynamically constructed and executed PL/SQL block is not treated as a *nested* block. Instead, it is handled like a procedure or function called from within the current block. So any variables local to the current or enclosing blocks are not recognized in the dynamic PL/SQL block. You can only make references to globally defined programs and data structures. These PL/SQL elements include stand alone functions and procedures and any elements defined in the specification of a package.

Fortunately, the dynamic block *is* executed within the context of the calling block. If you have an exception section within the calling block, it will trap exceptions raised in the dynamic block. So if I execute this anonymous block in SQL*Plus,

```
BEGIN
   dyn_plsql ('undefined.packagevar := ''abc''');
EXCEPTION
   WHEN OTHERS THEN DBMS_OUTPUT.PUT_LINE (sqlcode);
END;
/
```

I will not get an unhandled exception.

The *dynpl/sql.tst* file compares the performance of static PL/SQL execution (assigning a value to a global variable) with dynamic PL/SQL.

DBMS_SQL Examples

This section contains extended examples of using the DBMS_SQL package.

A Generic Drop_Object Procedure

The dynamic SQL of DBMS_SQL allows you to create completely generic modules to manipulate objects in the Oracle7 Server. You can, for instance, write a procedure that drops the specified table, but you can also create a module that will drop whatever kind of object you specify, as shown in this first version of drop_object:

```
CREATE OR REPLACE PROCEDURE drop_object
    (type_in IN VARCHAR2, name_in IN VARCHAR2)
IS
    /* Declare and create a cursor to use for the dynamic SQL */
    cur PLS_INTEGER := DBMS_SQL.OPEN_CURSOR;
    fdbk PLS_INTEGER;
BEGIN
    /* Construct the SQL statement, parse it and execute it. */
    DBMS_SQL.PARSE
        (cur, 'DROP ' || type_in || ' ' || name_in, DBMS_SQL.NATIVE);

    fdbk := DBMS_SQL.EXECUTE (cur);
    DBMS_SQL.CLOSE_CURSOR (cur);
END;
/
```

Well, that was straightforward enough. But how useful is it? Sure, it lets me execute DDL in PL/SQL, which wasn't possible before. But assuming that I have written this procedure as part of a broader interface to manage database objects from a screen, it is fairly limited. It is, in fact, simply equivalent to a DROP OBJECT statement. Boooring. Why not utilize the flexibility of the PL/SQL language to provide additional productivity, above and beyond the "straight" DDL? Wouldn't it be nice to, for example, drop all packages with names like "STR%" or drop all objects of any type in a schema with a single command?

To implement these kinds of requests, I need to let the user pass in wildcarded object names and types. I can then use these values to identify N number of matching objects. Where are these objects defined? In the USER_OBJECTS or ALL_OBJECTS data dictionary view. Interestingly, then, in my final version of drop_object, I combine the use of both static and dynamic SQL to add value to the standard DROP OBJECT command:

```
/* Filename on companion disk: dropobj.sp */
CREATE OR REPLACE PROCEDURE drop_object
    (type_in IN VARCHAR2, name_in IN VARCHAR2)
IS
    /* The static cursor retrieving all matching objects */
    CURSOR obj_cur IS
        SELECT object_name, object_type
          FROM user_objects
         WHERE object_name LIKE UPPER (name_in)
           AND object_type LIKE UPPER (type_in)
         ORDER BY object_name;

    cur PLS_INTEGER := DBMS_SQL.OPEN_CURSOR;
    fdbk PLS_INTEGER;
BEGIN
    /* For each matching object ... */
    FOR obj_rec IN obj_cur
    LOOP
        /* Reusing same cursor, parse and execute the drop statement. */
        DBMS_SQL.PARSE
           (cur,
            'DROP ' || obj_rec.object_type || ' ' || obj_rec.object_name,
            DBMS_SQL.NATIVE);

        fdbk := DBMS_SQL.EXECUTE (cur);
    END LOOP;
    DBMS_SQL.CLOSE_CURSOR (cur);
END;
/
```

Using this enhanced utility, I can now remove all objects in my schema that are used in the Order Entry system with this single command:

```
SQL> exec drop_object ('%', 'oe%');
```

Or I could be more selective and simply drop all tables containing the substring "emp."

```
SQL> exec drop_object ('table', '%emp%');
```

The drop_object procedure demonstrates the flexiblity and power that PL/SQL can bring to administrative tasks. It also clearly points out the inherent dangers of this power. With drop_object in place, you can remove everything in your schema with one program! Use this procedure—and any other similar utilities you build—with the utmost of care.

A Generic Foreign Key Lookup Function

I am always looking for ways to cut down on the code I need to write to maintain foreign keys in Oracle-based applications. For all its great features, Oracle Forms—just like its predecessor, SQL*Forms V3—does not offer comprehensive support for handling foreign keys. Sure, there is the LOV object and its associated record group, which can be used to look up and validate entries on the screen. This object cannot, however, be used to perform Post-Query lookups of a foreign key's description—a ubiquitous operation in an application built on a normalized database.

This same lookup process could also take place in a report, in a graph, in an embedded C program, and so on. Before the advent of DBMS_SQL, the only solution was to build a function for each separate entity that serves as a foreign key in a table. This function would take the foreign key and return the name or description. The specifications for such functions would look like these,

```
FUNCTION caller_name (caller_id IN caller.caller_id%TYPE)
   RETURN VARCHAR2;

FUNCTION company_name (company_id IN company.company_id%TYPE)
   RETURN VARCHAR2;

FUNCTION company_type (company_type_cd IN company.company_type_cd%TYPE)
   RETURN VARCHAR2;
```

and so on, for as many foreign keys as you've got. And every time a new foreign key is added to the mix, you must write a new function.

Wouldn't it be just fabulous if you could construct a single generic function using dynamic SQL that would work for all foreign keys? Let's give it a shot.

First, what information would I need to pass to this function in order to construct the SQL statement to retrieve the name or description? Here are some possibilities:

Foreign key value
    The ID or code of the record we wish to locate.

Table name
    The table containing the record identified by the foreign key value.

Primary key column name
    The name of the column in the previous table that contains the foreign key value (in this, the "source table" for the foreign key, it is actually the table's primary key).

Primary key name or description column name
    The name of the column in the previous table that contains the name or description of the primary key.

These parameters would allow me to construct SQL statements that look like the following:

```
SELECT caller_nm FROM caller WHERE caller_id = 154
SELECT call_type_nm FROM call_type WHERE call_type_id = 2
```

The steps I need to perform are straightforward:

1. Construct the SQL statement along the lines of the examples.

2. Fetch the matching record.

3. Retrieve the value from the cursor and return it to the calling program.

My first version of this function, fk_name, shows a generic function that returns the name and description of a foreign key.

```
/* Filename on companion disk: fkname.sf */
CREATE OR REPLACE FUNCTION fk_name
    (fk_id_in IN INTEGER,
     fk_table_in IN VARCHAR2,
     fk_id_col_in IN VARCHAR2,
     fk_nm_col_in IN VARCHAR2)
RETURN VARCHAR2
IS
    /* Declare and obtain a pointer to a cursor */
    cur INTEGER := DBMS_SQL.OPEN_CURSOR;

    /* Variable to receive feedback from package functions */
    fdbk INTEGER;
    /*
    || The return value of the function. Notice that I have
    || to hardcode a size in my declaration.
    */
    return_value VARCHAR2(100) := NULL;
BEGIN
    /*
    || Parse the query. I construct most of the SQL statement from
    || the parameters with concatenation. I also include a single
    || bind variable for the actual foreign key value.
    */
    DBMS_SQL.PARSE
       (cur,
        'SELECT ' || fk_nm_col_in ||
        '  FROM ' || fk_table_in ||
        ' WHERE ' || fk_id_col_in || ' = :fk_value',
        DBMS_SQL.NATIVE);

    /* Bind the variable with a specific value -- the parameter */
    DBMS_SQL.BIND_VARIABLE (cur, 'fk_value', fk_id_in);

    /* Define the column in the cursor for the FK name */
    DBMS_SQL.DEFINE_COLUMN (cur, 1, fk_nm_col_in, 100);
    /* Execute the cursor, ignoring the feedback */
    fdbk := DBMS_SQL.EXECUTE (cur);

    /* Fetch the row. If feedback is 0, no match found */
    fdbk := DBMS_SQL.FETCH_ROWS (cur);
    IF fdbk > 0
    THEN
        /* Found a match. Extract the value/name for the key */
```

```
          DBMS_SQL.COLUMN_VALUE (cur, 1, return_value);
      END IF;
      /*
      || Close the cursor and return the description, which
      || could be NULL if no records were fetched.
      */
      DBMS_SQL.CLOSE_CURSOR (cur);
      RETURN return_value;
   END;
   /
```

I can now use this function in a Post-Query trigger in Oracle Forms, as follows:

```
:call.name :=
   fk_name (:call.caller_id, 'caller', 'caller_id', 'caller_nm');

:call.call_type_ds :=
   fk_name (:call.call_type_id,
            'call_type', 'call_type_id', 'call_type_nm');
```

Well, that was fun. I now have a generic look-up for foreign keys. Instead of stopping at this point, however, let's explore some ways to improve the functionality and ease of use of this function. Several things caught my eye on the first pass:

- The programmer has to type in a lot of information in the parameter list in order to look up the foreign key. One might argue that it is almost as easy to type a SQL statement. While that's not true, I have found that programmers are resistant to using new toys unless their advantage is overwhelming.

- The size of the value returned by COLUMN_VALUE is hardcoded at 100 bytes. Any sort of hardcoding is always something to be avoided.

- There is a clear pattern to the names of the tables and columns in the previous examples. The foreign key column is always the table name with an "_ID" suffix. The description column is always the table name with an "_NM" suffix. It seems to me that the function should be able to take advantage of these kinds of naming conventions.

- The function assumes that the datatype of the foreign key is INTEGER; I have encountered many tables with VARCHAR2 foreign keys. True, the reasons are usually suspect, but it happens just the same.

Can I change fk_name to handle some of these concerns? I can certainly add a parameter with a maximum name length to use in the call to COLUMN_VALUE. I can support VARCHAR2 datatypes for foreign keys by placing the function inside a package and overloading the definition of the function. What about all those parameters and the naming conventions? Ideally, I would like to allow a developer to call fk_name with no more information than in the following examples:

```
:call.name := fk_name (:call.caller_id, 'caller');

:call.call_type_ds := fk_name (:call.call_type_id, 'call_type');
```

In this scenario, the function would use the name of the table to generate the names of the key and name columns and stuff them into the SQL statement. Sounds reasonable to me. The second version of fk_name supports default names for these two columns.

In this version, the last three parameters have default values. If the user does not specify an ID column name, the default is the table name with the default suffix. The same goes for the fk_name column. If the user includes a value for either of these arguments, then if the value starts with an underscore (_), it will be used as a suffix to the table name. Otherwise, the value will be used as a complete column name. The following table shows how parameter values will be converted inside the program.

Column	Argument Supplied to fk_name	Converted Value
ID column	NULL	caller_id
Name column	NULL	caller_nm
ID column	caller_number	caller_number
ID column	caller_name	caller_name
ID column	_#	caller_#
Name column	_fullname	caller_fullname

Here, then, in Version 2, we have an even more generic function to return foreign key names.

```
/* Filename on companion disk: fkname2.sf */
CREATE OR REPLACE FUNCTION fk_name
    (fk_id_in IN INTEGER,
     fk_table_in IN VARCHAR2,
     fk_id_col_in IN VARCHAR2 := '_ID',
     fk_nm_col_in IN VARCHAR2 := '_NM',
     max_length_in IN INTEGER := 100)
RETURN VARCHAR2
/* I will not repeat any comments from first version of fk_name. */
IS
    /*
    || Local variables to hold column names, since I must construct
    || those names based on the values provided. If the column names
    || are NULL, then fall back on the defaults.
    */
    fk_id_column VARCHAR2(60) := NVL (fk_id_col_in, '_ID');
    fk_nm_column VARCHAR2(60) := NVL (fk_nm_col_in, '_NM');

    cur INTEGER := DBMS_SQL.OPEN_CURSOR;
    fdbk INTEGER;
    /*
    || The return value of the function. Notice that even though one
    || of the parameters now specifies a maximum size for the return
    || value, I still do have to hardcode a size in my declaration.
```

```
        */
        return_value VARCHAR2(100) := NULL;

        /*---------------------- Local Module -------------------------*/

        PROCEDURE convert_column (col_name_inout IN OUT VARCHAR2)
        /*
        || Construct the column name. If the argument begins with a "_",
        || use as suffix to table name. Otherwise, substitute completely.
        */
        IS
        BEGIN
            IF SUBSTR (col_name_inout, 1, 1) = '_'
            THEN
                col_name_inout := fk_table_in || col_name_inout;
            ELSE
                /* Default value on variable declaration already handles it */
                NULL;
            END IF;
        END;

    BEGIN
        /* Convert the column names as necessary based on arguments */
        convert_column (fk_id_column);
        convert_column (fk_nm_column);

        /* Parse statement using converted column names */
        DBMS_SQL.PARSE
            (cur,
             'SELECT ' || fk_nm_column ||
             '  FROM ' || fk_table_in ||
             ' WHERE ' || fk_id_column || ' = :fk_value',
             DBMS_SQL.NATIVE);

        DBMS_SQL.BIND_VARIABLE (cur, 'fk_value', fk_id_in);
        DBMS_SQL.DEFINE_COLUMN (cur, 1, fk_nm_column, max_length_in);
        fdbk := DBMS_SQL.EXECUTE (cur);
        fdbk := DBMS_SQL.FETCH_ROWS (cur);
        IF fdbk > 0
        THEN
            DBMS_SQL.COLUMN_VALUE (cur, 1, return_value);
        END IF;
        DBMS_SQL.CLOSE_CURSOR (cur);
        RETURN return_value;
    END;
```

With this new version of fk_name, I can certainly retrieve the caller's name and the call type description without specifying all the columns, assuming that their columns match my conventions.

- Assume that table caller has caller_id and caller_nm columns:

  ```
  :call.name := fk_name (:call.caller_id, 'caller');
  ```

- Assume that call_type table has call_type_id and call_type_nm columns:

  ```
  :call.call_type_ds := fk_name (:call.call_type_id, 'call_type');
  ```

Of course, conventions do not hold so consistently in the real world. In fact, I have found that database administrators and data analysts will often treat an entity like caller, with its caller ID number and caller name, differently from the way they would treat a caller type, with its type code and description. The columns for the caller type table are more likely to be caller_typ_cd and caller_typ_ds. Fortunately, fk_name will still handle this situation as follows:

- A full set of defaults works just fine:

    ```
    :call.name := fk_name (:call.caller_id, 'caller');
    ```

- Use alternative suffixes for a code table:

    ```
    :call.call_type_ds :=
    fk_name (:call.call_type_id, 'call_type', '_cd', '_ds');
    ```

You might scoff and say, "Why bother providing just the suffixes? Might as well go ahead and provide the full column names." But there is a value to this approach: if the data analysts have adopted standards for their naming conventions of tables and key columns, the fk_name interface supports and reinforces these standards, and avoids supplying redundant information.

Is that it, then? Have we gone as far as we can go with fk_name? Surely some of you have looked at those rather simple SELECT statements and thought, "Gee, very few of my lookups actually resemble such queries." I agree. Sometimes you will need to check an additional column on the table, such as a "row active?" flag. You might even have several records, all for the same primary key, but active for different periods. So you should also pass a date against which to check.

How can you handle these application-specific situations? When in doubt, just add another parameter!

Sure. Why not add a parameter containing either a substitute WHERE clause for the SQL statement, or a clause to be appended to the rest of the default WHERE clause? The specification for fk_name would then change to the following:

```
/* Filename on companion disk: fkname3.sf */
FUNCTION fk_name
    (fk_id_in IN INTEGER,
     fk_table_in IN VARCHAR2,
     fk_id_col_in IN VARCHAR2 := '_ID',
     fk_nm_col_in IN VARCHAR2 := '_NM',
     max_length_in IN INTEGER := 100,
     where_clause_in IN VARCHAR2 := NULL)
    RETURN VARCHAR2;
```

The rule for this WHERE clause would be as follows: if the string starts with the keywords AND or OR, then the text is appended to the default WHERE clause. Otherwise, the argument substitutes completely for the default WHERE clause.

Rather than repeat the entire body of fk_name, I offer only the modifications necessary to PARSE, and thus effect this change in the following code:

```
IF UPPER (where_clause_in) LIKE 'AND%' OR
   UPPER (where_clause_in) LIKE 'OR%'
THEN
   /* Append the additional Boolean expressions to default */
   where_clause :=
      ' WHERE ' || fk_id_column || ' = :fk_value ' || where_clause_in;

ELSIF where_clause_in IS NOT NULL
THEN
   /* Substitute completely the WHERE clause */
   where_clause := ' WHERE ' || where_clause_in;

ELSE
   /* Just stick with default */
   where_clause := ' WHERE ' || fk_id_column || ' = :fk_value';
END IF;

/* Now the call to PARSE uses the pre-processed WHERE clause */
DBMS_SQL.PARSE
   (cur,
    'SELECT ' || fk_nm_column || '  FROM ' ||
    fk_table_in || where_clause, DBMS_SQL.NATIVE);
```

Using this final version of fk_name, I can perform lookups as follows:

- Retrieve only the description of the call type if that record is still flagged as
  active. Notice that I must stick several single quotes together to get the right
  number of quotes in the evaluated argument passed to fk_name.

```
:call.call_type_ds :=
   fk_name (:call.call_type_id, 'call_type', '_cd', '_ds', 25,
            'AND row_active_flag = ''Y''');
```

- Retrieve the name of the store kept in the record for the current year. Notice
  that the ID and name arguments in the call to fk_name are NULL. I have to
  include values here since I want to provide the WHERE clause, but I will pass
  NULL and thereby use the default values (without having to know what those
  defaults are!).

```
/* Only the record for this year should be used */
year_number := TO_CHAR (SYSDATE, 'YYYY');
/*
|| Pass check for year to WHERE clause. */
:store.description :=
   fk_name (:store.store_id, 'store_history', NULL, NULL, 60,
            'AND TO_CHAR (eff_date, ''YYYY'') = ''' ||
            year_number || '''');
```

The fragment of the WHERE clause passed to fk_name can be arbitrarily complex,
including subselects, correlated subqueries, and a whole chain of conditions
joined by ANDs and ORs.

A Wrapper for DBMS_SQL .DESCRIBE_COLUMNS

The DESCRIBE_COLUMNS procedure provides a critical feature for those of us writing generic, flexible code based on dynamic SQL. With earlier versions of DBMS_SQL, there was no way to query runtime memory to find out the internal structure of a cursor. Now you can do this with DESCRIBE_COLUMNS, but it is very cumbersome. As shown in the section "Describing Cursor Columns," you must declare a PL/SQL table, read the cursor structure into that table, and then traverse the table to get the information you need.

A much better approach is to write the code to perform these steps *once* and then encapsulate all that knowledge into a package. Then you can simply call the programs in the package and not have to worry about all the internal data structures and operations that have to be performed.

You will find an example of this "wrapper" around DESCRIBE_COLUMNS on your companion disk. Here is the specification of that package:

```
/* Filename on companion disk: desccols.spp */
CREATE OR REPLACE PACKAGE desccols
IS
    varchar2_type CONSTANT PLS_INTEGER := 1;
    number_type CONSTANT PLS_INTEGER := 2;
    date_type CONSTANT PLS_INTEGER := 12;
    char_type CONSTANT PLS_INTEGER := 96;
    long_type CONSTANT PLS_INTEGER := 8;
    rowid_type CONSTANT PLS_INTEGER := 11;
    raw_type CONSTANT PLS_INTEGER := 23;
    mlslabel_type CONSTANT PLS_INTEGER := 106;
    clob_type CONSTANT PLS_INTEGER := 112;
    blob_type CONSTANT PLS_INTEGER := 113;
    bfile_type CONSTANT PLS_INTEGER := 114;

    PROCEDURE forcur (cur IN INTEGER);

    PROCEDURE show (fst IN INTEGER := 1, lst IN INTEGER := NULL);
    FUNCTION numcols RETURN INTEGER;
    FUNCTION nthcol (num IN INTEGER) RETURN DBMS_SQL.DESC_REC;
END desccols;
/
```

Before we look at the implementation of this package, let's explore how you might use it. I declare a set of constants that give names to the various column types. This way, you don't have to remember or place in your code the literal values. Now notice that there are no other data structures defined in the specification. Most importantly, there is no declaration of a PL/SQL table based on DBMS_SQL.DESC_T to hold the description information. That table is instead hidden away inside the package body. You call the desccols.forcur procedure to "describe the columns for a cursor," passing it your cursor ID or handle, to load

·up that table by calling DESCRIBE_COLUMNS. You then can take any of the following actions against that PL/SQL table of column data:

* Show the column information by calling desccols.show (the prototype on disk shows only the column name and column type).

* Retrieve the total number of columns in the table with a call to desccols.numcols.

* Retrieve all the information for a specific column by calling the desccols.nthcol function.

The following script defines a cursor, extracts the cursor information with a call to desccols.forcur, and then shows the cursor information:

```
/* Filename on companion disk: desccols.tst */
DECLARE
    cur INTEGER := DBMS_SQL.OPEN_CURSOR;
BEGIN
    DBMS_SQL.PARSE
       (cur, 'SELECT ename, sal, hiredate FROM emp', DBMS_SQL.NATIVE);
    DBMS_SQL.DEFINE_COLUMN (cur, 1, 'a', 60);
    DBMS_SQL.DEFINE_COLUMN (cur, 1, 1);
    DBMS_SQL.DEFINE_COLUMN (cur, 1, SYSDATE);
    desccols.forcur (cur);
    desccols.show;
    DBMS_SQL.CLOSE_CURSOR (cur);
END;
/
```

Here is the output in SQL*Plus:

```
Column 1
ENAME
1
Column 2
SAL
2
Column 3
HIREDATE
12
```

In this next example, I load up the column information, use the nthcol function to get the information about just one column, deposit it in a locally declared record, and then check the column type.

```
DECLARE
    cur integer := dbms_sql.open_cursor;
    rec DBMS_SQL.DESC_REC;
BEGIN
    dbms_sql.PARSE
       (cur, 'SELECT ename, sal, hiredate FROM emp', DBMS_SQL.NATIVE);
    DBMS_SQL.DEFINE_COLUMN (cur, 1, 'a', 60);
    DBMS_SQL.DEFINE_COLUMN (cur, 1, 1);
```

```
        DBMS_SQL.DEFINE_COLUMN (cur, 1, SYSDATE);
        desccols.forcur (cur);
        rec := desccols.nthcol (1);
        IF rec.col_type = desccols.varchar2_type
        THEN
            DBMS_OUTPUT.PUT_LINE ('Process as string!');
        END IF;
        DBMS_SQL.CLOSE_CURSOR (cur);
    END;
    /
```

And I get this output when executed:

```
    Process as string!
```

Notice how I have shifted from dealing with the low-level details of the
DESCRIBE_COLUMNS built-in to manipulating all that data through a clear, easy-
to-use API. It is not as though the code you need to write (and you will find in
the body of the next package) is all that complicated. But why bother with this
code again and again when you can write it once and then just pass in the
pointer to the cursor and let the package do all the work?

The implementation of the desccols package is straightforward.

```
/* Filename on companion disk: desccols.spp */
CREATE OR REPLACE PACKAGE BODY desccols
IS
    /* Here is the PL/SQL table holding the column information. */
    desctab DBMS_SQL.DESC_TAB;
    desccnt PLS_INTEGER;
    firstrow PLS_INTEGER;
    lastrow PLS_INTEGER;

    PROCEDURE forcur (cur IN INTEGER)
    IS
    BEGIN
        /* Clear out the PL/SQL table */
        desctab.DELETE;

        /* Fill up the PL/SQL table */
        DBMS_SQL.DESCRIBE_COLUMNS (cur, desccnt, desctab);

        /* Get the first and last row numbers to avoid future lookups */
        firstrow := desctab.FIRST;
        lastrow := desctab.LAST;
    END;

    PROCEDURE show (fst IN INTEGER := 1, lst IN INTEGER := NULL)
    IS
    BEGIN
        IF desccnt > 0
        THEN
            /* Show the specified rows. */
            FOR colind IN
```

```
                    GREATEST (fst, firstrow) ..
                    LEAST (NVL (lst, lastrow), lastrow)
              LOOP
                    /* Add additional lines of output as you desire */
                    DBMS_OUTPUT.PUT_LINE ('Column ' || TO_CHAR (colind));
                    DBMS_OUTPUT.PUT_LINE (desctab(colind).col_name);
                    DBMS_OUTPUT.PUT_LINE (desctab(colind).col_type);
              END LOOP;
          END IF;
      END;


      FUNCTION numcols RETURN INTEGER
      IS
      BEGIN
          RETURN desccnt;
      END;


      FUNCTION nthcol (num IN INTEGER) RETURN DBMS_SQL.DESC_REC
      IS
          retval DBMS_SQL.DESC_REC;
      BEGIN
          /* If a valid row number, retrieve that entire record. */
          IF num BETWEEN firstrow AND lastrow
          THEN
              retval := desctab(num);
          END IF;
          RETURN retval;
      END;
END;
/
```

Displaying Table Contents with Method 4
Dynamic SQL

This section examines the kind of code you need to write to perform dynamic
SQL Method 4. Method 4, introduced early in this chapter, supports queries that
have a variable (defined only at runtime) number of items in the SELECT list
and/or a variable number of host variables. Here is an example of Method 4
dynamic SQL:

```
'SELECT ' || variable_select_list ||
'   FROM ' || table_name ||
' WHERE sal > :minsal
'    AND ' || second_clause ||
order_by_clause
```

Notice that with this SQL statement, I do not know how many columns or expressions are returned by the query. The names of individual columns are "hidden" in
the variable select list. I also do not know the full contents of the WHERE clause;
the minsal bind variable is obvious, but what other bind variable references might
I find in the second_clause string? As a result of this uncertainty, Method 4

dynamic SQL is the most complicated kind of dynamic query to handle with DBMS_SQL.

What's so hard about that? Well, if I am going to use the DBMS_SQL package to execute and fetch from such a query, I need to write and compile a PL/SQL program. Specifically, to parse the SQL statement, I need to define the columns in the cursor with calls to DEFINE_COLUMN—yet I do not know the list of columns at the time I am writing my code. To execute the query, I must associate values to all of my bind variables (identifiers with a ":" in front of them) by calling BIND_VARIABLE—yet I do not know the names of those bind variables at the time I write my code. Finally, to retrieve data from the result set of the query I also need to call COLUMN_VALUE for each column. But, again, I do not know the names or datatypes of those columns up front.

Sounds challenging, doesn't it? In fact, working with these incredibly dynamic SQL strings requires some interesting string parsing and some even more creative thinking.

When would you run into Method 4? It arises when you build a frontend to support ad-hoc query generation by users, or when you want to build a generic report program, which constructs the report format and contents dynamically at runtime. I also encountered it recently when I decided to build a PL/SQL procedure to display the contents of a table—any table, as specified by the user at runtime. This section explores what it took for me to implement this "in table" procedure.

The "in table" procedural interface

Before I dive into the PL/SQL required to create my procedure, I should explore my options. After all, it is certainly very easy for me to build a script in SQL*Plus to display the contents of any table.

```
SELECT * FROM &1
```

I could even spice it up with a variable select list and WHERE clause as follows:

```
SELECT &1
  FROM &2
 WHERE &3
 ORDER BY &4
```

In fact, SQL*Plus is a very flexible, powerful front-end tool for SQL scripts. Yet no matter how fancy I get with substitution parameters in SQL*Plus, this is not code I can run from within PL/SQL. Furthermore, PL/SQL gives me more procedural control over how to specify the data I want to see and how to display the data. Finally, if I use PL/SQL, then I get to play with DBMS_SQL! On the downside, however, from within PL/SQL I must rely on DBMS_OUTPUT (described in

Chapter 7, *Defining an Application Profile*) to display my table contents, so I must reckon with the buffer limitations of that built-in package (a maximum of 1,000,000 bytes of data—you will clearly not use my procedure to display very large quantities of data).

So I will use PL/SQL and DBMS_SQL. But before building any code, I need to come up with a specification. How will the procedure be called? What information do I need from my user (a developer, in this case)? What should a user have to type to retrieve the desired output? I want my procedure (which I call "intab" for "in table") to accept the inputs in the following table.

Parameter	Description
Name of the table	Required. Obviously, a key input to this program.
Maximum length of string displayed	Optional. Sets an upper limit on the size of string columns. I do not even attempt to do the kind of string wrapping performed in SQL*Plus. Instead, SUBSTR simply truncates the values.
WHERE clause	Optional. Allows you to restrict the rows retrieved by the query. If not specified, all rows are retrieved. You can also use this parameter to pass in ORDER BY and HAVING clauses, since they follow immediately after the where clause.
Format for date columns	Optional. Allows you to set the standard format for date displays. The default includes date and time information. When using SQL*Plus, I find it very irritating to constantly have to use TO_CHAR to see the time portion of my date fields.

Given these inputs, the specification for my procedure becomes the following:

```
PROCEDURE intab
   (table_in IN VARCHAR2,
    string_length_in IN INTEGER := 20,
    where_in IN VARCHAR2 := NULL,
    date_format_in IN VARCHAR2
       := 'MM/DD/YY HHMISS')
```

Here are some examples of calls to intab:

```
execute intab ('emp');

execute intab
   ('emp', 20,  'deptno = ' || v_deptno || ' order by sal');
```

These two calls to intab produce the following output:

```
execute intab ('emp');
----------------------------------------------------------------------------
                         Contents of emp
----------------------------------------------------------------------------
EMPNO ENAMEJOBMGR  HIREDATESALCOMMDEPTNO
```

```
-------------------------------------------------------------------------
   7839   KINGPRESIDENT11/17/81 120000500010
   7698   BLAKE MANAGER7839 05/01/81 120000285030
   7782   CLARKMANAGER7839 06/09/81 120000245010
   7566   JONESMANAGER7839 04/02/81 120000297520
   7654   MARTINSALESMAN7698 09/28/81 1200001250    140030
   7499   ALLENSALESMAN7698 02/20/81 1200001600   3000
   7844   TURNERSALESMAN7698 09/08/81 1200001500      0    30
   7900   JAMESCLERK7698 12/03/81 12000095030
   7521   WARDSALESMAN7698 02/22/81 1200001250    500  30
   7902   FORDANALYST7566 12/03/81 120000300020
   7369   SMITHCLERK7902 12/17/80 12000080020
   7788   SCOTTANALYST7566 12/09/82 120000300020
   7876   ADAMSCLERK7788 01/12/83 120000110020
   7934   MILLERCLERK7782 01/23/82 120000130010

execute intab ('emp', 20, 'deptno = 10 order by sal');
-------------------------------------------------------------------------
                         Contents of emp
-------------------------------------------------------------------------
EMPNO ENAMEJOB       MGR   HIREDATESALCOMMDEPTNO
-------------------------------------------------------------------------
   7934   MILLERCLERK7782 01/23/82 120000130010
   7782   CLARKMANAGER7839 06/09/81 120000245010
   7839   KINGPRESIDENT11/17/81 120000500010
```

Notice that the user does not have to provide any information about the structure of the table. My program will get that information itself—precisely the aspect of intab that makes it a Method 4 dynamic SQL example.

While this version of intab will certainly be useful, I am the first to recognize that there are many other possible enhancements to intab, including:

- Supplying a list of only those columns you wish to display. This will bypass the full list of columns for the table (which, as you will see, is extracted from the data dictionary).

- Supplying a list of those columns you wish to *exclude* from display. If your table has 50 columns, and you don't want to display three of those columns, it's a lot easier to list the three you don't want than the 47 you *do* want.

- Supplying an ORDER BY clause for the output. You *could* do this through the WHERE clause, but it is certainly more structured to provide a separate input.

- Providing a format for numeric data in addition to the date format.

So, yes, there is always more one can do, but this one (yours truly) would like to leave some interesting work for his readers. To encourage you to take my intab and "run with it," I will, in this section, step you through the usage of DBMS_SQL required to implement the intab procedure. (The full program is contained on the companion disk.)

Steps for intab construction

In order to display the contents of a table, follow these steps:

1. Construct and parse the SELECT statement (using OPEN_CURSOR and PARSE).

2. Bind all local variables with their placeholders in the query (using BIND_
   VARIABLE).

3. Define each column in the cursor for this query (using DEFINE_COLUMN).

4. Execute and fetch rows from the database (using EXECUTE and FETCH_
   ROWS).

5. Retrieve values from the fetched row and place them into a string for display
   purposes (using COLUMN_VALUE). Then display that string with a call to the
   PUT_LINE procedure of the DBMS_OUTPUT package.

NOTE   My intab implementation does not currently support bind variables.
                I assume, in other words, that the where_clause_in argument does
                not contain any bind variables. As a result, I will not be exploring in
                detail the code required for step 2.

Constructing the SELECT

In order to extract the data from the table, I have to construct the SELECT
statement. The structure of the query is determined by the various inputs to the
procedure (table name, WHERE clause, etc.) and the contents of the data
dictionary. Remember that the user does not have to provide a list of columns.
Instead, I must identify and extract the list of columns for that table from a data
dictionary view. I have decided to use all_tab_columns in intab so the user can
view the contents not only of tables he, or she, owns (which are accessible in
user_tab_columns), but also any table for which he, or she, has SELECT access.

Here is the cursor I use to fetch information about the table's columns:

```
CURSOR col_cur
   (owner_in IN VARCHAR2,
    table_in IN VARCHAR2)
IS
   SELECT column_name, data_type,
          data_length,
          data_precision, data_scale
     FROM all_tab_columns
    WHERE owner = owner_in
      AND table_name = table_in;
```

With this column cursor, I extract the name, datatype, and length information for
each column in the table. How should I store all of this information in my PL/SQL

Using Dot Notation

Notice that my cursor takes two parameters, owner_in and table_in, but that my program itself only accepts a single table name parameter. Rather than have the user pass this information in as two separate parameters, she can use standard dot notation, as in SCOTT.EMP, and the intab procedure will parse them as follows:

```
dot_loc := INSTR (table_nm, '.');
IF dot_loc > 0
THEN
    owner_nm := SUBSTR (table_nm, 1, dot_loc-1);
    table_nm := SUBSTR (table_nm, dot_loc+1);
END IF;
```

You should always try to make the interface as seamless and intelligent as possible for your users. You should also always try to make use of existing programs to implement your own. In this case (as pointed out to me by Dan Clamage, a technical reviewer), you can also use DBMS_UTILITY.NAME_TOKENIZE to parse this object name.

program? To answer this question, I need to think about how that data will be used. It turns out that I will use it in many ways, for example:

- I will use the column names to build the select list for the query.

- To display the output of a table in a readable fashion, I need to provide a column header that shows the names of the columns over their data. These column names must be spaced out across the line of data in, well, columnar format. So I need the column name and the length of the data for that column.

- To fetch data into a dynamic cursor, I need to establish the columns of the cursor with calls to DEFINE_COLUMN. For this, I need the column datatype and length.

- To extract the data from the fetched row with COLUMN_VALUE, I need to know the datatypes of each column, as well as the number of columns.

- To display the data, I must construct a string containing all the data (using TO_CHAR to convert numbers and dates). Again, I must pad out the data to fit under the column names, just as I did with the header line.

Therefore, I need to work with the column information several times throughout my program, yet I do not want to read repeatedly from the data dictionary. As a result, when I query them out of the all_tab_columns view, I will store the column data in three PL/SQL tables.

Table	Description
colname	The name of each column.
coltype	The datatype of each column, a string describing the datatype.
collen	The number of characters required to display the column data.

So if the third column of the emp table is SAL, then colname(3) = 'SAL', coltype(3) = 'NUMBER', and collen(3) = 7, and so forth.

The name and datatype information is stored directly from the data dictionary. When I work with the DBMS_SQL built-ins, however, they do not use the strings describing the datatypes (such as "CHAR" and "DATE"). Instead, DEFINE_COLUMN and COLUMN_VALUE rely on PL/SQL variables to *infer* the correct datatypes. So I use three local functions, is_string, is_date, and is_number, to help me translate a datatype into the correct variable usage. The is_string function, for example, validates that both CHAR and VARCHAR2 are string datatypes:

```
FUNCTION is_string (row_in IN INTEGER) RETURN BOOLEAN
IS
BEGIN
   RETURN (coltype(row_in) IN ('CHAR', 'VARCHAR2'));
END;
```

Figuring out the appropriate number of characters required to fit the column's data (the contents of the collen PL/SQL table) is a bit more complicated.

Computing column length

I need to take several different aspects of the column into account:

1. The length of the column name (you don't want the column length to be smaller than the header).

2. The maximum length of the data. If it's a string column, that information is contained in the data_length column of all_tab_columns.

3. If it's a number column, that information is contained in the data_precision column of the view (unless the datatype is unconstrained, in which case that information is found in the data_length column).

4. If it's a date column, the number of characters will be determined by the length of the date format mask.

As you can see, the type of data partially determines the type of calculation I perform for the length. Here's the formula for computing a string column's length:

```
GREATEST
  (LEAST (col_rec.data_length, string_length_in),
   LENGTH (col_rec.column_name))
```

The formula for a numeric column length is as follows:

```
GREATEST
  (NVL (col_rec.data_precision, col_rec.data_length),
   LENGTH (col_rec.column_name))
```

Finally, here's the formula for a date column length:

```
GREATEST (LENGTH (date_format_in), LENGTH (col_rec.column_name))
```

I use these formulas inside a cursor FOR loop that sweeps through all the columns for a table (as defined in all_tab_columns). This loop (shown following) fills my PL/SQL tables:

```
FOR col_rec IN
    col_cur (owner_nm, table_nm)
LOOP
   /* Construct select list for query. */
   col_list := col_list || ', ' || col_rec.column_name;

   /* Save datatype and length for calls to DEFINE_COLUMN. */
   col_count := col_count + 1;
   colname (col_count) := col_rec.column_name;
   coltype (col_count) := col_rec.data_type;

   /* Compute the column length with the
      above formulas in a local module. */
   collen (col_count) := column_lengths;

   /* Store length and keep running total. */
   line_length := line_length + v_length + 1;

   /* Construct column header line. */
   col_header := col_header || ' ' || RPAD (col_rec.column_name, v_length);
END LOOP;
```

When this loop completes, I have constructed the select list, populated my PL/SQL tables with the column information I need for calls to DEFINE_COLUMN and COLUMN_VALUE, and also created the column header line. Now that was a busy loop!

Next step? Construct the WHERE clause. In the following code, I check to see if the "WHERE clause" might actually just be a GROUP BY or ORDER BY clause. In those cases, I'll skip the WHERE part and attach this other information.

```
IF where_clause IS NOT NULL
THEN
   IF (where_clause NOT LIKE 'GROUP BY%' AND
       where_clause NOT LIKE 'ORDER BY%')
```

```
        THEN
            where_clause := 'WHERE ' || LTRIM (where_clause, 'WHERE');
        END IF;
    END IF;
```

I have now finished construction of the SELECT statement. Time to parse it, and then construct the various columns in the dynamic cursor object.

Defining the cursor structure

The parse phase is straightforward enough. I simply cobble together the SQL statement from its processed and refined components.

```
DBMS_SQL.PARSE
    (cur,
     'SELECT ' || col_list ||
     ' FROM ' || table_in || ' ' || where_clause,
     DBMS_SQL.NATIVE);
```

Of course, I want to go far beyond parsing. I want to execute this cursor. Before I do that, however, I must give some structure to the cursor. Remember: when you open a cursor, you have merely retrieved a handle to a chunk of memory. When you parse the SQL statement, you have associated a SQL statement with that memory. But as a next step, you must define the columns in the cursor so that it can actually store fetched data.

With Method 4 dynamic SQL, this association process is complicated. I cannot "hard-code" the number or type of calls to DEFINE_COLUMN in my program; I do not have all the information until runtime. Fortunately, in the case of intab, I *have* kept track of each column to be retrieved. Now all I need to do is issue a call to DEFINE_COLUMN for each row defined in my PL/SQL table colname. Before we go through the actual code, here are some reminders about DEFINE_COLUMN.

The header for this built-in procedure is as follows:

```
PROCEDURE DBMS_SQL.DEFINE_COLUMN
    (cursor_handle IN INTEGER,
     position IN INTEGER,
     datatype_in IN DATE|NUMBER|VARCHAR2)
```

There are three things to keep in mind with this built-in:

1. The second argument is a number; DEFINE_COLUMN does not work with column *names*—only with the sequential position of the column in the list.

2. The third argument establishes the datatype of the cursor's column. It does this by accepting an expression of the appropriate type. You do not, in other words, pass a string like "VARCHAR2" to DEFINE_COLUMN. Instead, you would pass a variable defined as VARCHAR2.

3. When you are defining a character-type column, you must also specify the maximum length of values retrieved into the cursor.

In the context of intab, the row in the PL/SQL table is the Nth position in the column list. The datatype is stored in the coltype PL/SQL table, but must be converted into a call to DEFINE_COLUMN using the appropriate local variable. These complexities are handled in the following FOR loop:

```
FOR col_ind IN 1 .. col_count
LOOP
  IF is_string (col_ind)
  THEN
    DBMS_SQL.DEFINE_COLUMN
      (cur, col_ind, string_value, collen (col_ind));

  ELSIF is_number (col_ind)
  THEN
    DBMS_SQL.DEFINE_COLUMN (cur, col_ind, number_value);

  ELSIF is_date (col_ind)
  THEN
    DBMS_SQL.DEFINE_COLUMN (cur, col_ind, date_value);
  END IF;
END LOOP;
```

When this loop is completed, I will have called DEFINE_COLUMN for each column defined in the PL/SQL tables. (In my version this is all columns for a table. In your enhanced version, it might be just a subset of all these columns.) I can then execute the cursor and start fetching rows. The execution phase is no different for Method 4 than it is for any of the other simpler methods,

```
fdbk := DBMS_SQL.EXECUTE (cur);
```

where fdbk is the feedback returned by the call to EXECUTE. Now for the finale: retrieval of data and formatting for display.

Retrieving and displaying data

I use a cursor FOR loop to retrieve each row of data identified by my dynamic cursor. If I am on the first row, I will display a header (this way, I avoid displaying the header for a query which retrieves no data). For each row retrieved, I build the line and then display it:

```
LOOP
    fdbk := DBMS_SQL.FETCH_ROWS (cur);
    EXIT WHEN fdbk = 0;

    IF DBMS_SQL.LAST_ROW_COUNT = 1
    THEN
```

```
        /* We will display the header information here */
        ...
    END IF;

    /* Construct the line of text from column information here */
    ...

    DBMS_OUTPUT.PUT_LINE (col_line);
END LOOP;
```

The line-building program is actually a numeric FOR loop in which I issue my calls to COLUMN_VALUE. I call this built-in for each column in the table (information that is stored in—you guessed it—my PL/SQL tables). As you can see below, I use my is_* functions to determine the datatype of the column and therefore the appropriate variable to receive the value.

Once I have converted my value to a string (necessary for dates and numbers), I pad it on the right with the appropriate number of blanks (stored in the collen PL/SQL table) so that it lines up with the column headers.

```
col_line := NULL;
FOR col_ind IN 1 .. col_count
LOOP
    IF is_string (col_ind)
    THEN
        DBMS_SQL.COLUMN_VALUE (cur, col_ind, string_value);

    ELSIF is_number (col_ind)
    THEN
        DBMS_SQL.COLUMN_VALUE (cur, col_ind, number_value);
        string_value := TO_CHAR (number_value);

    ELSIF is_date (col_ind)
    THEN
        DBMS_SQL.COLUMN_VALUE (cur, col_ind, date_value);
        string_value := TO_CHAR (date_value, date_format_in);
    END IF;

    /* Space out the value on the line
       under the column headers. */
    col_line := col_line || ' ' || RPAD (NVL (string_value, ' '),
        collen (col_ind));
END LOOP;
```

There you have it. A very generic procedure for displaying the contents of a database table from within a PL/SQL program. It all fell pretty smoothly into place once I got the idea of storing my column structures in a set of PL/SQL tables. Drawn on repeatedly, those in-memory tables made it easy to implement Method 4 dynamic SQL—another example of how taking full advantage of everything PL/SQL has to offer strengthens your ability to implement quickly and cleanly.

Build those utilities!

I suppose you could read this section and shrug, thinking: "Well, I don't feel like I have the time to write these kinds of generic utilities." I urge you to reject this line of reasoning. You *always* have time to create a more generic, generally useful implementation. Any time you spend up-front to craft high-quality, well-designed modules will pay off—for you personally, and for all others who benefit from your labors.

PL/SQL offers endless possibilities for building reusable code, which will save you many hours of development, debugging, and maintenance. The DBMS_SQL package in particular is a veritable gold mine. Dive in and try your hand at dynamic SQL!

Full text of intab procedure

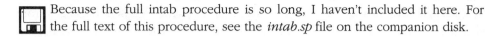 Because the full intab procedure is so long, I haven't included it here. For the full text of this procedure, see the *intab.sp* file on the companion disk.

Indirect Referencing in PL/SQL

I cut my teeth, so to speak, with Oracle software on a product called SQL*Forms. Back around 1987–1989, it was a really hot product for application development, and I was a guru. I wrote recursive triggers. I wrote a debugger for this product so thoroughly lacking in a debugger. I could produce robust forms in little or no time. It was very sad, then, for many of us, when Windows and other GUIs came along, and Oracle Corporation did not keep up. Of course, Oracle Forms has come a long way and is competing well with PowerBuilder and SQL*Windows and Visual Basic. That makes me happy because it has some really neat features, one of which is indirect referencing.

Oracle Forms offers two built-ins, the NAME_IN function and the COPY procedure, which allow you to retrieve and set by name the values of variables inside your form. For example, I can set the value of the global variable GLOBAL.right_now to SYSDATE with the following call,

```
COPY (TO_CHAR (SYSDATE), 'global.right_now');
```

and I can retrieve the value of that same global with a call to NAME_IN:

```
v_date := TO_DATE (NAME_IN ('global.right_now'));
```

Some of you might, and should, be saying to yourself, "Well, heck, why not just use the assignment operator," as in,

```
v_date := TO_DATE (:GLOBAL.right_now);
```

and you would of course be right—in this situation. The power of NAME_IN and COPY, however, become clear when instead of using them with "hard-coded" variable names, you construct the name of the variable at runtime. Here is an example:

```
COPY (TO_CHAR (SYSDATE), 'global.date_in_year' || TO_CHAR (v_yearnum));
```

In this case, the name of the variable to which SYSDATE is assigned is not determined until this line of code is executed and the v_yearnum variable is evaluated. This "indirect reference" to the GLOBAL variable in question offers developers a tremendous amount of flexibility. Indirect referencing will come in most handy when you are building generic utilities in which the very structure of your PL/SQL in-memory data is not defined until runtime.

I encountered the need for indirect referencing when building a PL/SQL code generator (now a product called PL/Generator from RevealNet). I wanted to provide a utility that would read a template file and then generate PL/SQL packages from that file. I found that by using indirect referencing, I could make these templates user-extensible. While this is neither the time nor place to really explore the generator technology, the following text shows a fragment of the template file. The square brackets ([and]) are used to "tag" template commands. The [IF] command implements "meta-conditional" logic, and that is where my indirect referencing comes into play:

```
[IF]myvars.checkstatus
   IF SQL%ROWCOUNT = 0
   THEN
      DBMS_OUTPUT.PUT_LINE ('No records updated!');
   END IF;
[ENDIF]
```

That is the code to be processed by PL/Generator. So before I do the generation, I will set the myvars.checkstatus packaged global variable to "T" with a statement like this:

```
SQL> exec myvars.checkstatus := 'T';
```

When I run my utility, I employ indirect referencing to "look up" the value of the variable with the name "myvars.checkstatus." That lookup will return TRUE and the check against ROWCOUNT thus will be included in the package that is generated. To accomplish this feat, follow these steps:

1. Grab the variable name from within the template file.

2. Use dynamic PL/SQL to evaluate the packaged variable. (Remember: with dynamic SQL, you can only read/modify "global" or package-based data.)

In this section, I will show you how to build a package called dynvar to perform this kind of dynamic or indirect referencing for string values. You can easily over-

load the programs in dynvar to support other datatypes. Here is the specification
of the package:

```
/* Filename on companion disk: dynvar.spp */
CREATE OR REPLACE PACKAGE dynvar
IS
    PROCEDURE assign (expr_in IN VARCHAR2, var_inout IN OUT VARCHAR2);
    FUNCTION val (var_in IN VARCHAR2) RETURN VARCHAR2;
    PROCEDURE copyto (val_in IN VARCHAR2, nm_in IN VARCHAR2)

END dynvar;
/
```

These three programs function as follows:

dynvar.assign

Assigns a value returned by the expression to the specified variable. This procedure is most helpful when you want to use dynamic PL/SQL to assign a
value to a *locally declared* variable.

dynvar.val

This is similar to the Oracle Forms NAME_IN function. It retrieves the value
currently held by the specified variable. In this case, var_in is a string containing the name of the variable you want to evaluate, not the variable itself.

dynvar.copyto

This is similar to the Oracle Forms COPY procedure. It "copies" the specified
value, which can be an expression, to the variable. In this case, you provide
the name of the variable, not a direct reference to the variable.

Here is a demonstration script using all three of these programs:

```
/* Filename on companion disk: dynvar.tst */
CREATE OR REPLACE PACKAGE TSTVAR
IS
    str1 varchar2(2000);
    str2 varchar2(2000);
END;
/
DECLARE
    v_pkg CHAR(7) := 'tstvar.';
    localstr VARCHAR2(100);
BEGIN
    dynvar.assign ('abc' || 'def' , localstr); /* Note 1 below */
    DBMS_OUTPUT.PUT_LINE ('local string set to ' || localstr);

    dynvar.copyto ('abcdefghi', v_pkg || 'str1'); /* Note 2 below */
    DBMS_OUTPUT.PUT_LINE ('global string set to ' || tstvar.str1);

    DBMS_OUTPUT.PUT_LINE ('value retrieved dynamically ' ||
        dynvar.val (v_pkg || 'str1')); /* Note 3 below */

    tstvar.str2 := 'tstvar.str1';
```

```
    DBMS_OUTPUT.PUT_LINE ('double indirection gets us ' ||
        dynvar.val (dynvar.val (v_pkg || 'str2'))); /* Note 4 below */

    DBMS_OUTPUT.PUT_LINE ('expression retrieved dynamically ' ||
        dynvar.val (v_pkg || 'str1' || '|| '' wow!''')); /* Note 5 below */
END;
/
```

This is the output from the program:

```
SQL> @dynvar.tst

Package created.

local string set to abcdef
global string set to abcdefghi
value retrieved dynamically abcdefghi
double indirection gets us abcdefghi
expression retrieved dynamically abcdefghi wow!
```

Here are some notes on program behavior:

1. The call to dynvar.assign assigned the concatenated string to the local variable, which is not possible with "normal" dynamic PL/SQL, since the data structures referenced in your dynamic PL/SQL block must be global.

2. The call to dynvar.copyto copied the string "abcdefghi" to the PL/SQL variable tstvar.str1 *indirectly*, since the name of the variable was constructed at runtime.

3. In the first call to dynvar.val, I construct the name of the variable and pass that to dynvar for processing. It returns "abcdefghi."

4. I then use two levels of indirection to get the value of the tstvar.str1 variable. In this case, I assign to tstvar.str2 the name of its sister variable in the package, tstvar.str1. I then call dynvar.val twice, first to evaluate tstvar.str2 and retrieve the value "tstvar.str1." Then I call dynvar.val to evaluate tstvar.str1 and return the first nine letters of the alphabet.

5. In this last call to dynvar.val, I do not pass a variable name. Instead, I pass an expression, a concatenation of the variable with the string "wow." This function doesn't mind in the least. As long as the string you pass is a valid string expression, it will be evaluated and returned.

The following sections show the implementations of the dynvar programs (all found in the *dynvar.spp* file), along with an explanation. A few comments for clarification: in each of these I make use of two variables, cur and fdbk. These are defined at the package level. In addition, to improve performance, I open the cursor when the package is initialized and therefore do not need to open and close it in each program.

Assigning a value

The dynvar.assign procedure performs a dynamic assignment of a string expression to a string variable. That variable can be either locally or globally (in a package) defined.

```
PROCEDURE assign (expr_in IN VARCHAR2, var_inout IN OUT VARCHAR2) IS
BEGIN
   DBMS_SQL.PARSE (cur,
      'BEGIN :var := ''' || expr_in || '''; END;', DBMS_SQL.NATIVE);
   DBMS_SQL.BIND_VARIABLE (cur, 'var', 'a', 2000);
   fdbk := DBMS_SQL.EXECUTE (cur);
   DBMS_SQL.VARIABLE_VALUE (cur, 'var', var_inout);
END;
```

Here are the basic steps performed in this procedure:

- Parse the assignment statement constructed with a bind variable and the expression. (Remember that the cursor was previously opened and remains open for the duration of your session.)

- Bind the variable (even though it is an OUT value) that will receive the value of the expression. The value I bind into it is irrelevant, but dynamic PL/SQL requires that you call the BIND_VARIABLE procedure for each placeholder in your string.

- Execute the PL/SQL block.

- Extract the value assigned to the placeholder variable and pass it to the variable you provided in the call to the procedure.

There are several interesting aspects to dynvar.assign:

- In the parse, I construct my assignment string, making sure to enclose the expression within single quotes. I do this because expr_in will be evaluated to a string when it is passed into the procedure. If I do not enclose it in quotes, the PL/SQL compiler will try to interpret the string as *code* rather than as a literal.

- The second argument to dynvar.assign must be declared as IN OUT because, when I perform the call to the VARIABLE_VALUE procedure, I deposit a new value directly into the variable provided in the call to the procedure.

- When you call dynvar.assign, you pass the actual variable in the second argument, not a string (whether literal or a variable) containing the *name* of the variable. If you want to assign a value to a variable, but reference the variable by its name, use the dynvar.copyto procedure.

Retrieving a value

The dynvar.val function extracts the value contained in the variable you have named in the argument to this program.

```
FUNCTION val (var_in IN VARCHAR2) RETURN VARCHAR2 IS
    retval VARCHAR2(2000);
BEGIN
    DBMS_SQL.PARSE
        (cur, 'BEGIN :val := ' || var_in || '; END;', DBMS_SQL.NATIVE);
    DBMS_SQL.BIND_VARIABLE (cur, 'val', 'a', 2000);
    fdbk := DBMS_SQL.EXECUTE (cur);
    DBMS_SQL.VARIABLE_VALUE (cur, 'val', retval);
    RETURN retval;
END;
```

Here are the steps performed by dynvar.val:

- Parse the assignment string. Notice that in this case I do not surround the var_ in value with single quotes. It's not a string expression in this case, but is instead the *name* of the variable. If you try to use dynvar.val to extract the value of a local, nonpackaged variable, you will receive a compile error.

- Bind the placeholder variable. As with assign, the value I bind is irrelevant, since it actually is an OUT placeholder, about to receive the value from the variable name that is passed in.

- Execute the dynamic PL/SQL block, extract the value into a *local* variable (whereas in dynvar.assign, it was extracted directly into the variable you provide), and then return the value.

Copying a value to a packaged variable

The dynvar.copyto procedure copies the value to the variable named in the second argument. This corresponds to Oracle Forms' COPY and allows you to indirectly reference the variable you want to modify.

```
PROCEDURE copyto (val_in IN VARCHAR2, nm_in IN VARCHAR2) IS
BEGIN
    DBMS_SQL.PARSE
        (cur,
         'BEGIN ' || nm_in || ' := ''' || val_in || '''; END;',
         DBMS_SQL.NATIVE);
    fdbk := DBMS_SQL.EXECUTE (cur);
END;
```

This procedure constructs and parses the string and then executes; there's not much to it. There is no need to call VARIABLE_VALUE because I do not need to extract any values. I am modifying the named variable right in the execution of the PL/SQL block.

I also do not call BIND_VARIABLE, because I have not used any placeholders. Instead, I concatentate directly (into the PL/SQL block) the value I want to assign to the named variable. Why do I do this? Let's examine the consequences of using a placeholder.

Suppose my dynamic PL/SQL block were constructed as follows:

```
'BEGIN ' || nm_in || ' := :val; END;',
```

When I bind in my value with a call to DBMS_SQL.BIND_VARIABLE, it is not treated as a literal. For example, if I call dynvar.copyto with the following arguments,

```
dynvar.copyto ('steven''s hairline', 'rapid.retreat');
```

then the PL/SQL block I would execute is,

```
BEGIN rapid.retreat := steven's hairline; END;
```

which would definitely run into compile problems. When I first encountered this problem, I figured that I would embed the :val placeholder inside single quotes to make sure that the value I pass in was treated as literal. My parse statement then looked like this:

```
DBMS_SQL.PARSE
    (cur, 'BEGIN ' || nm_in || ' := ''':val''; END;', DBMS_SQL.NATIVE);
```

But this would not work; DBMS_SQL did not recognize :val as a placeholder, any longer since it was inside single quotes. Sigh. The only solution was to remove :val, and, instead of using placeholders, simply concatenate the value directly into the string inside single quotes.

The dynvar package should get you comfortable with executing dynamic PL/SQL code and also with the concept of indirect referencing. I suggest that you try extending dynvar to support other datatypes (numbers and dates, in particular). See what challenges you encounter. You will definitely need to make some changes to incorporate these different datatypes into your dynamically constructed blocks.

Array Processing with DBMS_SQL

One of the most significant advances for DBMS_SQL in Oracle8 is the support for "array processing" through use of the BIND_ARRAY and DEFINE_ARRAY procedures. Using these procedures, you can greatly speed up dynamic SQL processing that involves multiple rows of data. This section offers some general suggestions and then provides detailed examples of using array processing in DBMS_SQL to perform fetches, queries, and dynamic PL/SQL.

In order to take advantage of array processing, you will need to be comfortable with the use of index-by tables (called *PL/SQL tables* in Oracle7). These structures are like single-dimension arrays and are described in detail in Chapter 10 of *Oracle PL/SQL Programming*. With this feature under your belt, you are ready to implement array processing with DBMS_SQL. As you do so, keep in mind the following tips:

- When you declare index-by tables to be used in DBMS_SQL processing, you must declare them based on one of the DBMS_SQL table TYPES:

```
DBMS_SQL.NUMBER_TABLE
DBMS_SQL.VARCHAR2_TABLE
DBMS_SQL.DATE_TABLE
DBMS_SQL.BLOB_TABLE
DBMS_SQL.CLOB_TABLE
DBMS_SQL.BFILE_TABLE
```

  Here is an example of declaring a table used to receive multiple pointers to BFILEs from a dynamically constructed query:

```
DECLARE
    bfiles_list DBMS_SQL.BFILE_TABLE;
```

  One very significant downside to the approach taken by Oracle to support array processing with DBMS_SQL is that you cannot use index-by tables of records. Instead, you will need to declare individual tables for each of the columns you wish to query or placeholders you wish to put in your SQL statements.

- If you are going to fetch more than one row with a single call to FETCH_ROWS, you must define the columns in that cursor as "array columns." To do this, you must provide an index-by table in the call to DEFINE_ARRAY. The following example shows the steps required to fetch a whole bunch of salaries (up to 100 at a time) from the emp table:

```
DECLARE
    cur PLS_INTEGER := DBMS_SQL.OPEN_CURSOR;
    sal_table DBMS_SQL.NUMBER_TABLE;
BEGIN
    DBMS_SQL.PARSE (cur, 'SELECT sal FROM emp', DBMS_SQL.NATIVE);
    DBMS_SQL.DEFINE_COLUMN (cur, 1, sal_table, 100, 10);
```

- When you call DEFINE_ARRAY, you also can specify the starting row in which data is to be placed when you call DBMS_SQL.COLUMN_VALUE (in the previous example, I specified that the starting row to be 10). This is a little bit odd and worth emphasizing. That fifth argument does not have anything to do with the index-by table you pass as the third argument to DEFINE_ARRAY. It applies to the index-by table that is passed to the call to COLUMN_VALUE (which might or might not actually *be* the same index-by table). If you don't provide a value for this starting row, values are assigned to the receiving index-by table from row 1. In all cases, the rows are filled sequentially. Why would you *not* use the default value of 1 for starting row? You might want to preserve the values already stored in the index-by table, and simply add the new rows of data to the table.

- If you want to bind multiple values into a SQL statement, you must call BIND_ARRAY instead of the scalar BIND_VARIABLE procedure. You will do this when you want to modify more than one row in the table with a single DML statement.

- If you are using more than one array or index-by table in a single SQL statement, remember that DBMS_SQL applies a "lowest common denominator" rule. It determines the highest starting row number and the lowest ending row number across all arrays and then uses only those rows between those endpoints in *all* of the arrays.

The following section shows in more detail how to use array processing in DBMS_SQL to fetch multiple rows with a single call to DBMS_SQL.FETCH_ROWS, update multiple rows of data with multiple bind variables, and manipulate index-by table contents with dynamic PL/SQL.

Using array processing to insert

There are three different ways to change the contents of a table: INSERT, DELETE, and UPDATE. This section shows examples of the first of these DML statements, INSERT, utilizing the array features of DBMS_SQL. The next two sections show examples of DELETE and UPDATE.

The following procedure inserts the contents of a index-by table into a database table using single-row INSERTs (the Version 7 behavior). Notice that I parse once, but bind and execute for each individual row in the index-by table. I do not need to reparse, since I am not changing the SQL statement, only the value I am binding *into* that SQL statement.

Notice also that I first create a package to define two index-by table types. Why do I do this? I am passing in index-by tables as arguments to my insert procedure. The parameter list of the procedure must therefore reference existing index-by table types in order to compile. I could also have put the table type declarations and the procedure into a single package.

```
/* Filename on companion disk: dynins.sp */
CREATE OR REPLACE PACKAGE mytables
IS
    TYPE number_table IS TABLE OF NUMBER INDEX BY BINARY_INTEGER;
    TYPE varchar2_table IS TABLE OF VARCHAR2(2000) INDEX BY BINARY_INTEGER;
END;
```

```
/
CREATE OR REPLACE PROCEDURE instab7
   (empnotab IN mytables.number_table,
    enametab IN mytables.varchar2_table)
IS
   cur PLS_INTEGER := DBMS_SQL.OPEN_CURSOR;
   fdbk PLS_INTEGER;
   totfdbk PLS_INTEGER := 0;
BEGIN
   DBMS_SQL.PARSE (cur,
      'INSERT INTO emp2 (empno, ename) VALUES (:empno, :ename)',
      DBMS_SQL.NATIVE);

   FOR emprow IN empnotab.FIRST .. empnotab.LAST
   LOOP
      DBMS_SQL.BIND_VARIABLE (cur, 'empno', empnotab(emprow));
      DBMS_SQL.BIND_VARIABLE (cur, 'ename', enametab(emprow));
      fdbk := DBMS_SQL.EXECUTE (cur);
      totfdbk := totfdbk + fdbk;
   END LOOP;

   DBMS_OUTPUT.PUT_LINE ('Rows inserted: ' || TO_CHAR (totfdbk));

   DBMS_SQL.CLOSE_CURSOR (cur);
END;
/
```

How would this implementation change with Oracle8? You no longer have to perform separate INSERTs for each of the rows in the index-by table. Instead, you can bind an index-by table directly into the SQL statement. The following version of the instab procedure relies on this new feature. Notice that the FOR LOOP is gone. Instead, I call BIND_ARRAY once for each column in the INSERT statement, passing in the appropriate index-by table. Notice that I must now use the DBMS_ SQL table types, whereas in the previous example I created my own index-by table types and used those in the parameter list.

```
/* Filename on companion disk: dynins.sp */
CREATE OR REPLACE PROCEDURE instab8
   (empnotab IN DBMS_SQL.NUMBER_TABLE,
    enametab IN DBMS_SQL.VARCHAR2_TABLE)
IS
   cur PLS_INTEGER := DBMS_SQL.OPEN_CURSOR;
   fdbk PLS_INTEGER;
BEGIN
   DBMS_SQL.PARSE (cur,
      'INSERT INTO emp2 (empno, ename) VALUES (:empno, :ename)',
      DBMS_SQL.NATIVE);

   DBMS_SQL.BIND_ARRAY (cur, 'empno', empnotab);
   DBMS_SQL.BIND_ARRAY (cur, 'ename', enametab);

   fdbk := DBMS_SQL.EXECUTE (cur);
```

```
              DBMS_OUTPUT.PUT_LINE ('Rows inserted: ' || TO_CHAR (fdbk));

              DBMS_SQL.CLOSE_CURSOR (cur);
          END;
```

So in this case I end up with less code to write. In other situations, you may have to copy your data from your own index-by tables, perhaps a table or record that is not supported by DBMS_SQL, into the appropriate DBMS_SQL-declared index-by tables before you can call BIND_ARRAY. But putting aside code volume, what about the impact on performance? To compare these two approaches, I wrote the following SQL*Plus script:

```
/* Filename on companion disk: dynins.tst */
DECLARE
    timing PLS_INTEGER;

    empnos7 mytables.number_table;
    enames7 mytables.varchar2_table;

    empnos8 DBMS_SQL.NUMBER_TABLE;
    enames8 DBMS_SQL.VARCHAR2_TABLE;
BEGIN
    /* Load up the index-by tables. */
    FOR i IN 1 .. &1
    LOOP
        empnos&2(i) := 10000 + i;
        enames&2(i) := 'Eli ' || TO_CHAR (i);
    END LOOP;

    timing := DBMS_UTILITY.GET_TIME;
    instab&2 (empnos&2, enames&2);
    DBMS_OUTPUT.PUT_LINE
        ('V&2 style = ' || TO_CHAR (DBMS_UTILITY.GET_TIME - timing));
END;
/
```

Though SQL*Plus is a fairly crude tool, those substitution parameters let you write some clever, concise utilities. In this case, I populate my index-by tables with &1 number of rows—but the index-by table I fill up depends on the &2 or second argument: the Oracle7 or Oracle8 versions. Once the tables have their data, I pass them to the appropriate version of "instab," and, using DBMS_UTILITY.GET_ TIME, display the number of hundredths of seconds that elapsed.

I ran this script a number of times to even out the bumps of initial load and parse and so on. The following numbers are representative:

```
SQL> @dynins.tst 1000 7
Rows inserted: 1000
V7 style = 90
SQL> @dynins.tst 1000 8
```

```
Rows inserted: 1000
V8 style = 2
```

As you can see, dynamic SQL using arrays or index-by tables will perform significantly better than the single-row processing available in Oracle7.

So that's how you do INSERTs: for each column for which you are inserting a value, you must bind in an array or index-by table. You can also mix together scalars and arrays. If, for example, I wanted to insert a set of new employees and make the hiredate the value returned by SYSDATE, the bind steps in my instab8 procedure would be modified as follows:

```
DBMS_SQL.BIND_ARRAY (cur, 'empno', empnotab);
DBMS_SQL.BIND_ARRAY (cur, 'ename', enametab);
DBMS_SQL.BIND_VARIABLE (cur, 'hiredate', SYSDATE);
```

In other words: two array binds and one scalar bind. The same value returned by SYSDATE is then applied to *all* rows inserted.

Using array processing to delete

The process for deleting multiple rows with a single call to the EXECUTE function is similar to that for INSERTSs: one call to BIND_ARRAY for each placeholder in the SQL statement. With DELETEs, however, the placeholders are in the WHERE clause, and each row in the index-by table is used to identify one or more rows in the database table.

The following procedure removes all rows as specified in the array of names. Notice the use of LIKE and UPPER operators to increase the flexibility of the table entries (if that is what you want!).

```
/* Filename on companion disk: dyndel.sp */
CREATE OR REPLACE PROCEDURE delemps
    (enametab IN DBMS_SQL.VARCHAR2_TABLE)
IS
    cur PLS_INTEGER := DBMS_SQL.OPEN_CURSOR;
    fdbk PLS_INTEGER;
BEGIN
    DBMS_SQL.PARSE (cur,
        'DELETE FROM emp WHERE ename LIKE UPPER (:ename)',
        DBMS_SQL.NATIVE);

    DBMS_SQL.BIND_ARRAY (cur, 'ename', enametab);

    fdbk := DBMS_SQL.EXECUTE (cur);

    DBMS_OUTPUT.PUT_LINE ('Rows deleted: ' || TO_CHAR (fdbk));

    DBMS_SQL.CLOSE_CURSOR (cur);
END;
/
```

The standard emp table contains the following 14 names:

ADAMS	JAMES	SCOTT
ALLEN	JONES	SMITH
BLAKE	KING	TURNER
CLARK	MARTIN	WARD
FORD	MILLER	

Now let's run the following script:

```
/* Filename on companion disk: dyndel.tst */
DECLARE
    empnos8 DBMS_SQL.NUMBER_TABLE;
    enames8 DBMS_SQL.VARCHAR2_TABLE;
BEGIN
    /* Load up the index-by table. */
    enames8(1) := '%S%';
    enames8(2) := '%I%';

    delemps (enames8);
END;
/

SQL> @dyndel.tst
Rows deleted: 8
```

And we are then left with the following employees:

ALLEN	FORD
BLAKE	TURNER
CLARK	WARD

In many situations, you will have the primary key sitting in the row of the index-by table, and the array-based DELETE will simply delete one row of the database table for each row in the array. As you can see from the previous example, however, that is not the only way to use arrays to delete multiple rows.

NOTE   As you try out these various examples, don't forget to perform ROLL-BACKs to restore the data to the original state before continuing or exiting!

Using array processing to update

Finally, we have UPDATE statements, where you can have placeholders both in the SET clause and in the WHERE clause. Be careful about how you utilize arrays in updates; the behavior will not always be as you might expect. Here are some different scenarios or combinations and the behaviors I have encountered:

Conditions:

Array placeholder in SET, no placeholders in the WHERE clause.

Behavior:

The value in the *last* row of the array will be applied to all rows identified by the WHERE clause (or lack of one). All other rows in the array are ignored.

Conditions:

Array placeholder in WHERE clause, no placeholders in SET.

Behavior:

As expected, all rows identified in the WHERE clause have their column values set as determined in the SET statement (all scalar binds or no binds at all).

Conditions:

There are N rows in a SET clause array and M rows in a WHERE clause array, and N is different from M.

Behavior:

The rule of thumb is that smallest number of rows across all arrays are used. So if the SET array has ten rows and the WHERE array has six rows, then only the *first* six rows of the SET array are used (assuming that both arrays are filled sequentially from same row number).

Conditions:

You use an array in the SET clause. In addition, the WHERE clause uses one or more arrays and is also structured so that each row in the array could identify more than one row of data in the database table (as would be the case with use of a LIKE statement and wildcarded values).

Behavior:

In this situation, for all database records identified by row N in the WHERE array, the values will be set from row N in the SET array.

Generally, you should think of the arrays in the SET clause as being "correlated" to the arrays in the WHERE clause. This correlation is demonstrated in the following procedure. I use dynamic SQL to update the salaries of employees whose names match the strings provided in the enames table.

```
/* Filename on companion disk: dynupd.sp */
CREATE OR REPLACE PROCEDURE updemps
    (enametab IN DBMS_SQL.VARCHAR2_TABLE,
```

```
          saltab IN DBMS_SQL.NUMBER_TABLE)
   IS
      cur PLS_INTEGER := DBMS_SQL.OPEN_CURSOR;
      fdbk PLS_INTEGER;
   BEGIN
      DBMS_SQL.PARSE (cur,
         'UPDATE emp SET sal = :sal WHERE ename LIKE UPPER (:ename)',
         DBMS_SQL.NATIVE);

      DBMS_SQL.BIND_ARRAY (cur, 'sal', saltab);
      DBMS_SQL.BIND_ARRAY (cur, 'ename', enametab);

      fdbk := DBMS_SQL.EXECUTE (cur);

      DBMS_OUTPUT.PUT_LINE ('Rows updated: ' || TO_CHAR (fdbk));

      DBMS_SQL.CLOSE_CURSOR (cur);
   END;
   /
```

I then use the following script to test the procedure. Notice that there are four salaries and only two employee names, each of which is actually a wildcarded pattern.

```
/* Filename on companion disk: dynupd.tst */
DECLARE
   timing PLS_INTEGER;
   sals DBMS_SQL.NUMBER_TABLE;
   enames DBMS_SQL.VARCHAR2_TABLE;
BEGIN
   /* Load up the index-by tables. */
   sals(1) := 1111;
   sals(2) := 2222;
   sals(3) := 3333;
   sals(4) := 4444;

   enames(1) := '%I%'; /* any name containing an I */
   enames(2) := '%S';  /* any name containing an S */

   updemps (enames, sals);
END;
/
```

When I run this script, I update nine rows as shown in the following output:

```
SQL> @dynupd.tst
Rows updated: 9

ENAME SAL
---------- ----------
SMITH2222
ALLEN1600
WARD1250
JONES2222
MARTIN1111
```

```
BLAKE2850
CLARK2450
SCOTT2222
KING1111
TURNER1500
ADAMS2222
JAMES2222
FORD3000
MILLER1111
```

What has happened here? All the employees with an I in their name have a salary of 1111, and all the employees with S in their name have a salary of 2222. If you have both an I and S, as with SMITH, notice that you get the S salary of 2222 and not the I salary of 1111. The salaries of 3333 and 4444 are completely ignored by the procedure, since there are only two rows in the enames table.

For a final example of array processing for updates, the following program reads data from a file and performs a batch update of employee salaries, correlating the key value (first column in the file's line) with the new column value (second column in the file's line).

```
/* Filename on companion disk: fileupd.sp */
CREATE OR REPLACE PROCEDURE upd_from_file
    (loc IN VARCHAR2, file IN VARCHAR2)
IS
    /* DBMS_SQL related elements */
    cur PLS_INTEGER := DBMS_SQL.OPEN_CURSOR;
    fdbk PLS_INTEGER;
    empnos DBMS_SQL.NUMBER_TABLE;
    sals DBMS_SQL.NUMBER_TABLE;

    /UTL_FILE related elements */
    fid UTL_FILE.FILE_TYPE;
    v_line VARCHAR2(2000);
    v_space PLS_INTEGER;

BEGIN
    /* Load the index-by tables from the file. */

    fid := UTL_FILE.FOPEN (loc, file, 'R');

    BEGIN
        LOOP
            UTL_FILE.GET_LINE (fid, v_line);
            v_space := INSTR (v_line, ' ', 1, 1);
            empnos (NVL (empnos.LAST, 0) + 1) :=
                TO_NUMBER (SUBSTR (v_line, 1, v_space-1));
            sals (NVL (empnos.LAST, 0) + 1) :=
                TO_NUMBER (SUBSTR (v_line, v_space+1));
        END LOOP;
    EXCEPTION
        WHEN NO_DATA_FOUND
        THEN
```

```
            UTL_FILE.FCLOSE (fid);
      END;

      /* Perform the multiple row updates. */

      DBMS_SQL.PARSE (cur,
         'UPDATE emp SET sal = :sal WHERE empno = :empno',
         DBMS_SQL.NATIVE);

      DBMS_SQL.BIND_ARRAY (cur, 'empno', empnos);
      DBMS_SQL.BIND_ARRAY (cur, 'sal', sals);

      fdbk := DBMS_SQL.EXECUTE (cur);

      DBMS_SQL.CLOSE_CURSOR (cur);
   END;
   /
```

You can run this procedure against the *fileupd.dat* data file by executing the *fileupd.tst* script to confirm the results. In this case, each row in the empnos index-by table identifies a specific record in the database; the corresponding row in the sals index-by table is then used in the update of the sal column value. Notice that I need to put the loop that reads the file inside its own block, because the only way to know that I have read the whole file is to call UTL_FILE.GET_ LINE until it raises a NO_DATA_FOUND exception (which means "EOF" or end of file).

As a final treat, check out the package in the *arrayupd.spp* file (and the corresponding *arrayupd.tst* test script). It offers a completely dynamic interface allowing array-based updates of any number, date, or string column in any table based on a single integer primary key. For example, using the arrayupd.col procedure, all of the dynamic SQL code in the upd_from_file procedure could be replaced with the following:

```
BEGIN
   ... Load arrays from file as before ...

   /* Then call arrayupd to perform the array-based update. */
   arrayupd.cols ('emp', 'empno', 'sal', empnos, sals);
END;
```

And the really wonderful thing about this overloaded procedure is that while it certainly is not as fast as static UPDATE statements, it competes very nicely and is efficient enough for many applications.

Using array processing to fetch

For all the value of array processing to update a database table, you are most likely to use BIND_ARRAY and DEFINE_ARRAY to fetch rows from the database and then process them in a front-end application. If the claims of Oracle Corporation about improved performance of dynamic SQL are true (see Chapter 10 of

Oracle PL/SQL Programming), then this array-processing feature of DBMS_SQL could offer a crucial solution to the problem of passing multiple rows of data between the server and the client application through a PL/SQL application.

Let's examine how to perform fetches with arrays in DBMS_SQL—and analyze the performance impact—by building a package called empfetch to retrieve employee numbers and names. In the process, I will construct a "wrapper" around this fantastic new technology so that it can be made available in client environments where index-by tables and other Oracle8 features are not available directly.

First, the basics of querying into arrays: you must use the DEFINE_ARRAY procedure to define a specific column in the cursor as an array column. When you do this, you also specify the number of rows which are to be fetched in a single call to FETCH_ROWS (or EXECUTE_AND_FETCH). Here, for example, is the code required to set up a cursor to retrieve 100 rows from the orders table:

```
DECLARE
    ordernos DBMS_SQL.NUMBER_TABLE;
    orderdates DBMS_SQL.DATE_TABLE;
     cur PLS_INTEGER := DBMS_SQL.OPEN_CURSOR
BEGIN
    DBMS_SQL.PARSE
        (cur, 'SELECT orderno, order_date FROM orders', DBMS_SQL.NATIVE);

    DBMS_SQL.DEFINE_ARRAY (cur, 1, ordernos, 100, 1);
    DBMS_SQL.DEFINE_ARRAY (cur, 1, orderdates, 100, 1);
```

You then use COLUMN_VALUE to retrieve column values, just as you would with scalar, non-array processing. You simply provide an array to accept the multiple values, and in they come.

Moving on to our example, here is the specification for the package to query employee data using dynamic SQL and array processing:

```
/* Filename on companion disk: empfetch.spp */
CREATE OR REPLACE PACKAGE empfetch
  IS
    PROCEDURE rows (numrows_in IN INTEGER,
        where_clause_in IN VARCHAR2 := NULL,
        append_rows_in IN BOOLEAN := FALSE);

    FUNCTION ename_val (row_in IN INTEGER) RETURN emp.ename%TYPE;

    FUNCTION empno_val (row_in IN INTEGER) RETURN emp.empno%TYPE;

    FUNCTION numfetched RETURN INTEGER;
END empfetch;
/
```

The empfetch.rows procedure fetches the specified maximum number of rows from the database, using an optional WHERE clause. You can also request "append rows," which means that the newly fetched rows are appended to employee numbers and names already in the index-by tables. The default behavior is to delete all existing rows in the arrays.

Once the rows are loaded with a call to empfetch.rows, you can retrieve the Nth employee name and employee number, as well as find out how many rows were fetched. This is a nice enhancement over normal cursor-based processing: this way, I have random, bidirectional access to my data.

Finally, notice that there is no indication in this package specification that I am using dynamic SQL or array processing or index-by tables. These programs are callable from any environment supporting the most basic versions of PL/SQL, from 1.1 in Oracle Developer/2000 Release 1 to any variant of PL/SQL Release 2.X. This is especially important for third-party tools like PowerBuilder, which do not always keep up with the latest enhancements of PL/SQL.

Before exploring the implementation of the empfetch package, let's see an example of its use, combined with an analysis of its performance. Once the package compiled, I built a script to compare using static and dynamic SQL to fetch rows from the database table. The *empfetch.tst* script first uses an explicit cursor to fetch all the rows from the emp table and copy the ename and empno column values to local variables. Can't get much leaner than that. I then use the empfetch package to perform the same steps.

```
/*  Filename on companion disk: empfetch.tst */
DECLARE
   timing PLS_INTEGER;
   v_ename emp.ename%TYPE;
   v_empno emp.empno%TYPE;
BEGIN
   /* The static approach */
   timing := DBMS_UTILITY.GET_TIME;
   FOR i IN 1 .. &1
   LOOP
      DECLARE
         CURSOR cur IS SELECT empno, ename FROM emp;
      BEGIN
         FOR rec IN cur
         LOOP
            v_ename := rec.ename;
            v_empno := rec.empno;
         END LOOP;
      END;
   END LOOP;
   DBMS_OUTPUT.PUT_LINE
      ('static = ' || TO_CHAR (DBMS_UTILITY.GET_TIME - timing));

   timing := DBMS_UTILITY.GET_TIME;
   FOR i IN 1 .. &1
   LOOP
```

```
    /* Fetch all the rows from the table, putting them in arrays
       maintained inside the package body. */
    empfetch.rows (20);

    /* For each row fetched, copy the values from the arrays to the
       local variables by calling the appropriate functions.
       Notice that there is no exposure here of the fact that
       arrays are being used. */
    FOR i IN 1 .. empfetch.numfetched
    LOOP
        v_ename := empfetch.ename_val (i);
        v_empno := empfetch.empno_val (i);
    END LOOP;
    END LOOP;
    DBMS_OUTPUT.PUT_LINE
        ('dynamic = ' || TO_CHAR (DBMS_UTILITY.GET_TIME - timing));
END;
/
```

And here are the astounding results from execution of this test script:

```
SQL>  @empfetch.tst 10
static = 114
dynamic = 119
SQL>  @empfetch.tst 100
static = 1141
dynamic = 1167
```

In other words, there was virtually no difference in performance between these two approaches. This closeness exceeded my expectations, and is more than one might expect simply from the array processing. My hat is off to the PL/SQL development team! They really *have* reduced the overhead of executing dynamic SQL and anonymous blocks.

You will find the full implementation of the empfetch body in the *empfetch.spp* file; later I will show the different elements of the package and offer some observations. First, the following data structures are declared at the package level:

1. A cursor for the dynamic SQL. I open the cursor when the package is initialized and keep that cursor allocated for the duration of the session, minimizing memory requirements and maximizing performance.

   ```
   c PLS_INTEGER := DBMS_SQL.OPEN_CURSOR;
   ```

2. Two arrays to hold the employee IDs and the names. Notice that I must use the special table types provided by DBMS_SQL.

   ```
   empno_array DBMS_SQL.NUMBER_TABLE;
   ename_array DBMS_SQL.VARCHAR2_TABLE;
   ```

3. A global variable keeping track of the number of rows fetched. I could retrieve this value with the empno.COUNT operator, but this would be mis-

leading if you were appending rows, and it would also entail more overhead than simply storing the value in this variable.

```
g_num_fetched PLS_INTEGER := 0;
```

Now we will look at the programs that make use of these data structures. First, the rows procedure, which populates the arrays:

```
PROCEDURE rows (numrows_in IN INTEGER,
    where_clause_in IN VARCHAR2 := NULL,
    append_rows_in IN BOOLEAN := FALSE)
IS
    v_start PLS_INTEGER := 1;
BEGIN
    IF append_rows_in
    THEN
        v_start :=
            NVL (GREATEST (empno_array.LAST, ename_array.LAST), 0) + 1;
    ELSE
        /* Clean out the tables from the last usage. */
        empno_array.DELETE;
        ename_array.DELETE;
    END IF;

    /* Parse the query  with a dynamic WHERE clause */
    DBMS_SQL.PARSE (c,
        'SELECT empno, ename FROM emp WHERE ' || NVL (where_clause_in, '1=1'),
        DBMS_SQL.NATIVE);

    /* Define the columns in the cursor for this query */
    DBMS_SQL.DEFINE_ARRAY (c, 1, empno_array, numrows_in, v_start);
    DBMS_SQL.DEFINE_ARRAY (c, 2, ename_array, numrows_in, v_start);

    /* Execute the query and fetch the rows. */
    g_num_fetched:= DBMS_SQL.EXECUTE_AND_FETCH (c);

    /* Move the column values into the arrays */
    DBMS_SQL.COLUMN_VALUE (c, 1, empno_array);
    DBMS_SQL.COLUMN_VALUE (c, 2, ename_array);
END;
```

Areas of interest in this program include:

- I set the starting row for the call to DEFINE_ARRAY according to the append_ rows argument. If not appending, I clean out the arrays and start at row 1. If appending, I determine the highest-defined row in both of the arrays and start from the next row.

- If the user does not provide a WHERE clause, I append a trivial "1=1" condition after the WHERE keyword. This is admittedly kludgy and little more than a reflection of this programmer's laziness. The alternative is to do more complex string analysis and concatenation.

- Both calls to DBMS_SQL.DEFINE_ARRAY use the same number of rows and the starting row, ensuring that their contents are correlated properly.

- I execute and fetch with a single line of code. When performing array processing, there is no reason to separate these two steps, unless you will be fetching N number of rows more than once to make sure you have gotten them all.

That takes care of most of the work and complexity of the empfetch package. Let's finish up by looking at the functions that retrieve individual values from the arrays. These are very simple pieces of code; I will show ename_val, but empno_val is almost exactly the same:

```
FUNCTION ename_val (row_in IN INTEGER) RETURN emp.ename%TYPE
IS
BEGIN
    IF ename_array.EXISTS (row_in)
    THEN
        RETURN ename_array (row_in);
    ELSE
        RETURN NULL;
    END IF;
END;
```

Notice that I avoid raising the NO_DATA_FOUND exception by checking whether the row exists before I try to return it.

As you can see from empfetch, it doesn't necessarily take lots of code to build a solid encapsulation around internal data structures. From the performance of this package, you can also see that array processing with dynamic SQL offers some new opportunities for building an efficient programmatic interface to your data.

Using array processing in dynamic PL/SQL

The first release of Oracle8 (8.0.3) contained a number of bugs relating to the use of array processing in dynamic PL/SQL. The 8.0.4 and 8.0.5 releases, however, fix many (if not all) of these problems. I offer in this section one example to demonstrate the techniques involved in order to copy the contents of one index table to another index table. You can find another example of array processing with index tables in the next section.

The following testarray procedure moves the rows of one index table to another.

```
    on companion disk: plsqlarray.sp */
CREATE OR REPLACE PROCEDURE testarray
  IS
     cur INTEGER := DBMS_SQL.OPEN_CURSOR;
     fdbk INTEGER;
     mytab1 DBMS_SQL.NUMBER_TABLE;
     mytab2 DBMS_SQL.NUMBER_TABLE;
  BEGIN
     mytab1 (25) := 100;
```

```
    mytab1 (100) := 1000;
    mytab2 (25) := -100;
    mytab2 (100) := -1000;
    DBMS_SQL.PARSE (cur, 'BEGIN :newtab := :oldtab; END;', DBMS_SQL.NATIVE);

    DBMS_SQL.BIND_ARRAY (cur, 'newtab', mytab2, 25, 100);
    DBMS_SQL.BIND_ARRAY (cur, 'oldtab', mytab1, 25, 100);

    fdbk := DBMS_SQL.EXECUTE (cur);
    DBMS_SQL.VARIABLE_VALUE (cur, 'newtab', mytab2);

    DBMS_OUTPUT.PUT_LINE('mytab2(1) := ' || mytab2(1));
    DBMS_OUTPUT.PUT_LINE('mytab2(2) := ' || mytab2(2));
    DBMS_OUTPUT.PUT_LINE('mytab2(25) := ' || mytab2(25));
    DBMS_OUTPUT.PUT_LINE('mytab2(100) := ' || mytab2(100));

    DBMS_SQL.CLOSE_CURSOR (cur);
END;
/
```

Notice that I must call DBMS_SQL.BIND_VARIABLE twice, once for the "IN" index table (the "old table," mytab1) and once for the "OUT" index table (the "new table," mytab2). Finally, I call DBMS_SQL.VARIABLE_VALUE to transfer the result of the assignment into my local index table.

Here are the results from execution of this procedure:

```
SQL> exec testarray
mytab2(1) := -1000
mytab2(2) := 100
mytab2(25) := -100
mytab2(100) := -1000
```

Ah! Not quite what we might have expected. This procedure *did* transfer the contents of mytab1 to mytab2, but it filled rows sequentially in mytab2 starting from row 1—definitely something to keep in mind when you take advantage of this technology. You might want to DELETE from the index table before the copy.

Using the RETURNING Clause in Dynamic SQL

One of the many enhancements in Oracle8 is the addition of the RETURNING clause to INSERTs, UPDATEs, and DELETEs. You can use the RETURNING clause to retrieve data (or expressions derived from the data) from the rows affected by the DML statement.

Here is an example of an INSERT statement that returns the just-generated primary key:

```
DECLARE
    mykey emp.empno%TYPE;
    total_comp NUMBER;
BEGIN
```

```
      INSERT INTO emp (empno, ename, deptno)
         VALUES (emp_seq.NEXTVAL, 'Feuerstein', 10)
         RETURNING empno, sal + NVL (comm, 0) INTO mykey, total_comp;
   END;
   /
```

You return data into scalar values when the DML has modified only one row. If the DML modifies more than one row, you can return data into index tables using DBMS_SQL. If you modify more than one row and try to return values into a scalar variable, then you will raise an exception, as follows:

```
SQL> DECLARE
        mykey emp.empno%TYPE;
     BEGIN
        /* Updating all rows in the table... */
        UPDATE emp SET sal = 1000 RETURNING empno INTO mykey;
     END;
     /

     ERROR at line 1:
     ORA-01422: exact fetch returns more than requested number of rows
```

If you are changing more than one row of data and employing the RETURNING clause, you *must* use DBMS_SQL to pass back those values into an index table. You cannot simply specify an index table in the RETURNING clause with static SQL. If you try this, you will receive the following error:

```
     PLS-00385: type mismatch found at '<index table>' in SELECT...INTO statement
```

The rest of this section demonstrates the use of the RETURNING clause for both single- and multiple-row operations from within DBMS_SQL.

RETURNING from a single-row insert

Suppose that you want to insert a row into a table with the primary key generated from a sequence, and then return that sequence value to the calling program. In this example, I will create a table to hold notes (along with a sequence and an index, the latter to show the behavior when an INSERT fails):

```
/*Filename on companion disk: insret.sp */
CREATE TABLE note (note_id NUMBER, text VARCHAR2(500));
CREATE UNIQUE INDEX note_text_ind ON note (text);
CREATE SEQUENCE note_seq;
```

I then build a procedure around the INSERT statement for this table:

```
/* Filename on companion disk: insret.sp */
CREATE OR REPLACE PROCEDURE ins_note
   (text_in IN note.text%TYPE, note_id_out OUT note.note_id%TYPE)
IS
   cur INTEGER := DBMS_SQL.OPEN_CURSOR;
   fdbk INTEGER;
   v_note_id note.note_id%TYPE;
```

```
BEGIN
    DBMS_SQL.PARSE (cur,
        'INSERT INTO note (note_id, text) ' ||
        '   VALUES (note_seq.NEXTVAL, :newtext) ' ||
        '   RETURNING note_id INTO :newid',
        DBMS_SQL.NATIVE);

    DBMS_SQL.BIND_VARIABLE (cur, 'newtext', text_in);
    DBMS_SQL.BIND_VARIABLE (cur, 'newid', v_note_id);

    fdbk := DBMS_SQL.EXECUTE (cur);
    DBMS_SQL.VARIABLE_VALUE (cur, 'newid', v_note_id);
    note_id_out := v_note_id;

    DBMS_SQL.CLOSE_CURSOR (cur);
EXCEPTION
    WHEN OTHERS
    THEN
        DBMS_OUTPUT.PUT_LINE ('Note insert failure:');
        DBMS_OUTPUT.PUT_LINE (SQLERRM);
END;
/
```

These operations should be familiar to you by this time. Here are the steps to perform:

1. Open a cursor and then parse the INSERT statement. Notice that I reference the next value of the sequence right in the VALUES list. The RETURNING clause passes the primary key, note_id, into a placeholder.

2. Bind both the incoming text value and the outgoing primary key. (I am not really binding a value in the second call to DBMS_SQL.BIND_VARIABLE, but I have to perform the bind step anyway.)

3. Execute the cursor and retrieve the primary key from the bind variable in the RETURNING clause. Notice that I pass back the value into a local variable, which is then copied to the OUT argument. Otherwise, I would need to define the note_id_out parameter as an IN OUT parameter.

4. I include an exception section to display any errors that might arise.

The following anonymous block tests this procedure by inserting a row and then trying to insert it again:

```
/* Filename on companion disk: insret.sp */
DECLARE
    myid note.note_id%TYPE;
BEGIN
    ins_note ('Note1', myid);
    DBMS_OUTPUT.PUT_LINE ('New primary key = ' || myid);
    myid := NULL;
    ins_note ('Note1', myid);
EXCEPTION
```

```
        WHEN OTHERS
        THEN
            NULL;
    END;
    /
```

Here is the result:

```
SQL> @insret.sp
New primary key = 41

Note insert failure:
ORA-00001: unique constraint (SCOTT.NOTE_TEXT_IND) violated
```

The same technique and steps can be used for using the RETURNING clause in UPDATEs and DELETEs when affecting single rows. Let's now take a look at the slightly more complex scenario: changing multiple rows of data and returning values from those rows.

RETURNING from a multiple-row delete

I want to use dynamic SQL to provide a generic delete mechanism for tables with single integer primary keys. You provide the name of the table, the name of the primary key, and the WHERE clause. I do the delete. But such a general utility will never be used unless it can be trusted, unless its actions can be confirmed. That is where the RETURNING clause comes into play.

```
/* Filename on companion disk: delret.sp */
CREATE OR REPLACE PROCEDURE delret
    (tab_in IN VARCHAR2,
     pkey_in IN VARCHAR2,
     where_in IN VARCHAR2,
     pkeys_out OUT DBMS_SQL.NUMBER_TABLE)
IS
    cur INTEGER := DBMS_SQL.OPEN_CURSOR;
    delstr VARCHAR2(2000) :=
        'DELETE FROM ' || tab_in || ' WHERE ' || where_in ||
        ' RETURNING ' || pkey_in || ' INTO :idarray';
    fdbk INTEGER;
    v_pkeys DBMS_SQL.NUMBER_TABLE;
BEGIN
    DBMS_OUTPUT.PUT_LINE ('Dynamic Delete Processing: ');
    DBMS_OUTPUT.PUT_LINE (delstr);

    DBMS_SQL.PARSE (cur, delstr, DBMS_SQL.NATIVE);
    DBMS_SQL.BIND_ARRAY (cur, 'idarray', v_pkeys);

    fdbk := DBMS_SQL.EXECUTE (cur);
    DBMS_SQL.VARIABLE_VALUE (cur, 'idarray', v_pkeys);
    pkeys_out := v_pkeys;

    DBMS_SQL.CLOSE_CURSOR (cur);
```

```
EXCEPTION
   WHEN OTHERS
   THEN
      DBMS_OUTPUT.PUT_LINE ('Dynamic Delete Failure:');
      DBMS_OUTPUT.PUT_LINE (SQLERRM);
END;
/
```

In this program, I construct the DELETE statement and save it to a local variable. I do this so that I can display the string for confirmation purposes and then parse it without duplicating the code. I will go to great lengths (and do so on a regular basis) to avoid even the slightest repetition of code.

When I bind, I call DBMS_SQL.BIND_ARRAY instead of DBMS_SQL.BIND_VARI-ABLE so that I can retrieve an entire list of values. My call to DBMS_SQL.VARIABLE_VARIABLE performs the retrieval, and I close the cursor. The following anonymous block exercises my generic "delete and return" procedure. Notice that since I am returning an index table, I must always declare such a table to hold the values.

```
/* Filename on companion disk: delret.sp */
DECLARE
   v_pkeys DBMS_SQL.NUMBER_TABLE;
BEGIN
   delret ('emp', 'empno', 'deptno = 10', v_pkeys);
   IF v_pkeys.COUNT > 0
   THEN
      FOR ind IN v_pkeys.FIRST .. v_pkeys.LAST
      LOOP
         DBMS_OUTPUT.PUT_LINE ('Deleted ' || v_pkeys(ind));
      END LOOP;
   END IF;
   ROLLBACK;
END;
/
```

Here are the results from execution of the previous script:

```
Dynamic Delete Processing:
DELETE FROM emp WHERE deptno = 10 RETURNING empno INTO :idarray
Deleted 7782
Deleted 7839
Deleted 7934
```

3

Intersession Communication

It seems that everything these days has something to do with communication. Messaging technologies are consequently receiving lots of attention, but they are nothing new for Oracle. Through the packages described in this chapter, Oracle has already provided mechanisms for communication between database sessions:

DBMS_PIPE

Using database pipes with DBMS_PIPE, an application can communicate with a service routine external to the database. Or, debuggers that capture PL/SQL errors can utilize the fact that DBMS_PIPE is asynchronous with database transactions, getting the errors logged whether the transaction issued a COMMIT or a ROLLBACK.

DBMS_ALERT

This package is a little different, in that it allows synchronous notification to multiple users that specific database events have occurred.

DBMS_PIPE: Communicating Between Sessions

The DBMS_PIPE package provides services that allow Oracle sessions connected to the same instance to communicate messages with each other without the need for a COMMIT. Sessions use DBMS_PIPE programs to pack data into a message buffer and then send the message to a memory area in the Oracle shared pool (the *pipe*), where another session can receive it and unpack the message data into local variables. The database pipes implemented by DBMS_PIPE are roughly modeled after UNIX pipes. Pipes may be *private* to the user or *public*, and can be written to, or read from, independent of database transactions.

The basic functionality that DBMS_PIPE introduces is the ability for Oracle sessions to communicate with each other. Before the existence of database pipes, users connected to an Oracle database could communicate or interact with each other only through the database. If users needed to somehow exchange information with each other, this had to be done by reading, writing, and committing data to tables (i.e., the database was itself the communications medium). This communications model suffers from the following problems:

- It is transactional; it relies on COMMIT for users to see messages.

- Communications are slow; they involve physical writing to disk.

- There is limited capacity due to locking issues in message tables.

- There are space management issues.

The database pipes introduced through the DBMS_PIPE package establish a fast, lightweight, memory-based, nontransactional mechanism of intersession communications.

The DBMS_PIPE package is most often used to provide an interface between sessions connected to an Oracle instance and service routines external to Oracle in the host operating environment. In this kind of application, the service routine connects to Oracle and listens for service requests on a specific database pipe. Sessions in the database request services by placing messages on the request pipe, and they receive data from the service routine on session-specific response pipes.

Other applications you might consider developing with DBMS_PIPE include:

- Debuggers that place error messages into pipes

- Auditing of security violations independent of transaction success

- Transaction concentrators to multiplex many user transactions through a single session

- Complex calculation servers to offload long or memory-intensive computations

- Alerters that notify sessions of important events

An example of the last application has actually been built by Oracle as the DBMS_ALERT package (described later in this chapter), which makes extensive use of DBMS_PIPE programs to implement database alerts.

Getting Started with DBMS_PIPE

The DBMS_PIPE package is created when the Oracle database is installed. The *dbmspipe.sql* script (found in the built-in packages source code directory, as described in Chapter 1, *Introduction*) contain the source code for this package's specification. This script is called by *catproc.sql*, which is normally run immediately after database creation. The script creates the public synonym DBMS_PIPE

for the package. Under Oracle7, no privileges are automatically granted on DBMS_
PIPE. Under Oracle8, the EXECUTE_CATALOG_ROLE role is granted EXECUTE
privilege on DBMS_PIPE. Thus, the DBMS_PIPE programs are not generally available to users.

DBMS_PIPE programs

Table 3-1 lists the programs included in the DBMS_PIPE package.

Table 3-1. DBMS_PIPE Programs

Name	Description	Use in SQL?
CREATE_PIPE	Creates a public or private pipe	Yes
NEXT_ITEM_TYPE	Returns datatype of next item in message buffer	Yes
PACK_MESSAGE	Packs item into message buffer	No
PACK_MESSAGE_RAW	Packs RAW item into message buffer	No
PACK_MESSAGE_ROWID	Packs ROWID item into message buffer	No
PURGE	Empties named pipe of all messages	No
RECEIVE_MESSAGE	Receives message from pipe into local buffer	Yes
REMOVE_PIPE	Removes the named pipe	Yes
RESET_BUFFER	Resets buffer message pointers	No
SEND_MESSAGE	Sends local message buffer out on pipe	Yes
UNIQUE_SESSION_NAME	Returns string unique to the session	Yes
UNPACK_MESSAGE	Unpacks item from message buffer	No
UNPACK_MESSAGE_RAW	Unpacks RAW item from message buffer	No
UNPACK_MESSAGE_ROWID	Unpacks ROWID item from message buffer	No

DBMS_PIPE does not declare any package exceptions of its own. Many of the
individual programs raise Oracle exceptions under certain circumstances, as
described in the following sections.

DBMS_PIPE nonprogram elements

The DBMS_PIPE package contains one nonprogram element, maxwait. It is
defined as follows:

```
maxwait CONSTANT INTEGER := 86400000;
```

The maxwait constant is used as the default maximum time to wait for calls to the
SEND_MESSAGE or RECEIVE_MESSAGE functions to complete. The units are in
seconds, so the value of 86400000 equates to 1000 days.

How Database Pipes Work

It is important to understand how DBMS_PIPE implements the concept of a communications pipe between Oracle sessions—and this implementation is not necessarily obvious.

Memory structures

The pipes themselves are named memory areas in the Oracle SGA's shared pool where communications messages can be written or read. DBMS_PIPE works through the interaction of these memory areas with a private memory buffer in each user's session. There is only one private memory buffer per user that is used to send and receive messages on database pipes. Private buffers can be thought of as "mailboxes"—one for each user—and the database pipes are like the "post office." The difference is that users are responsible for delivering and retrieving messages to and from the post office.*

Nontransactional communications

One very important property of the DBMS_PIPE programs is that they are nontransactional. This means that they are not bound to the current database transaction, and they will succeed or fail independently of any COMMIT or ROLLBACK processing. Transaction independence is one reason why DBMS_PIPE is often used to implement debugging software, since problems in uncommitted transactions can still be logged into database pipes.

Pipe communications logic

The basic sequence of events for DBMS_PIPE-based communications, follows:

- The sending user loads his private buffer with a "message," which can be composed of multiple items of various datatypes. This is done via successive calls to the PACK_MESSAGE procedure.

- The sending user moves the message from the private buffer into the pipe with the SEND_MESSAGE function.

- The receiving user pulls the message off the pipe into his private buffer using the RECEIVE_MESSAGE function.

- The receiving user "unpacks" the message items into local variables using the UNPACK_MESSAGE procedure.

---

* Dan Clamage (technical reviewer extraordinaire) points out that the single-session message buffer is actually implemented as a private global variable in the DBMS_PIPE package body. He laments, and I join him, that Oracle did not implement the ability to declare several message buffers of your own.

Figure 3-1 illustrates the architecture and basic logic of pipe-based communications.

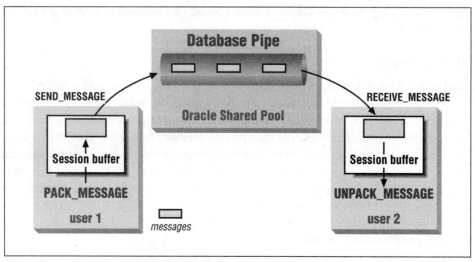

Figure 3-1. Sending messages between sessions through a database pipe

The post office analogy helps me keep in mind how DBMS_PIPE works. Think of the message as something physical (such as a postcard or letter) that moves from one user buffer (mailbox) into the pipe (post office), and then out of the pipe and into another session buffer (mailbox). The pipe itself acts like a first-in-first-out (FIFO) queue—that is, messages are extracted in the order in which they are put in the queue. This understanding helps clear up the following common points of confusion:

Q: Is the message still in my buffer after calling SEND_MESSAGE?

A: No, it physically left your session and went into the pipe.

Q: Can two users pull the same message from a pipe using RECEIVE_MESSAGE?

A: No, the first user to make the call has physically removed the message from the pipe.

Q: Can a user pull a specific message from a pipe using RECEIVE_MESSAGE?

A: No, the pipe will always return the next message in the queue.

NOTE   Note that Oracle8's Advanced Queuing features, covered in Chapter 5, *Oracle Advanced Queuing*, offer more sophisticated and robust messaging capabilities, which may be used instead of database pipes for more complex applications.

Managing Pipes and the Message Buffer

Use DBMS_PIPE's CREATE_PIPE, REMOVE_PIPE, RESET_PIPE, RESET_BUFFER, PURGE, and UNIQUE_SESSION_NAME programs to create and remove pipes and to perform some additional pipe management operations.

The DBMS_PIPE.CREATE_PIPE function

The CREATE_PIPE function is used to create a new public or private named database pipe. Note that database pipes can also be created implicitly by the SEND_MESSAGE function. Here's the header for this function:

```
FUNCTION DBMS_PIPE.CREATE_PIPE
    (pipename IN VARCHAR2
    ,maxpipesize IN INTEGER DEFAULT 8192
    ,private IN BOOLEAN DEFAULT TRUE)
RETURN INTEGER;
```

Parameters are summarized in the following table.

Name	Description
pipename	Name of the database pipe
maxpipesize	Maximum size in bytes of the pipe
private	TRUE means pipe is private to user

Return values. The CREATE_PIPE procedure has a single return value of 0, indicating success. This value is returned even if the pipe already existed and can be used by the user.

Exceptions. The program does not raise any package exceptions. The following Oracle exceptions are raised if the user attempts to create a pipe that already exists and is private to another user or uses a NULL pipename:

Number	Description
ORA-23322	Insufficient privileges to access pipe
ORA-23321	Pipename may not be NULL

Restrictions. Note the following restrictions on calling CREATE_PIPE:

- Pipenames are limited to 128 byes in length, are case-insensitive, and cannot contain NLS characters.

- Pipenames must not begin with "ORA$", as these names are reserved for use by Oracle Corporation.

Example. This example is a function that encapsulates CREATE_PIPE and returns either the Boolean value TRUE, indicating that the pipe can be used by the caller, or FALSE otherwise. The function traps the ORA-23322 exception using PRAGMA EXCEPTION_INIT and returns FALSE if this exception is raised.

The makepipe function can be found in the dbpipe package discussed in the "DBMS_PIPE Examples" section. It is created by the *dbpipe.sql* script.

```
/* Filename on companion disk:  dbpipe.sql */
PACKAGE BODY dbpipe
IS
    cannot_use_pipe    EXCEPTION;
    PRAGMA EXCEPTION_INIT(cannot_use_pipe,-23322);
    null_pipename    EXCEPTION;
    PRAGMA EXCEPTION_INIT(null_pipename,-23321);

    /*
    || encapsulates DBMS_PIPE.CREATE_PIPE and returns
    || FALSE if ORA-23322 is raised indicating
    || the pipename is already used and not accessible
    || to the caller
    */
    FUNCTION makepipe
        (pipename_IN IN VARCHAR2
        ,maxsize_bytes_IN IN INTEGER DEFAULT 8192
        ,private_IN IN BOOLEAN DEFAULT TRUE)
    RETURN BOOLEAN
    IS
        call_status  INTEGER;

    BEGIN
        call_status := DBMS_PIPE.CREATE_PIPE
                        (pipename_IN
                        ,maxsize_bytes_IN
                        ,private_IN);
        RETURN call_status = 0;
    EXCEPTION
        WHEN cannot_use_pipe OR null_pipename
        THEN
            RETURN FALSE;
    END makepipe;

END dbpipe;
```

The CREATE_PIPE function creates a private pipe by default. Private pipes may be used only by sessions connected to the same username (schema) as the pipe's creator or executing stored PL/SQL programs owned by that schema. Public pipes may be accessed by all sessions with execute privileges on DBMS_PIPE. Note that CREATE_PIPE is the only way to create a private database pipe. Pipes created implicitly by the SEND_MESSAGE function are always public.

Pipes created using CREATE_PIPE should be explicitly removed using the REMOVE_PIPE function.

Database pipes are empty upon creation. However, if the named database pipe already exists and is available to the user calling CREATE_PIPE, the function will return 0, but the pipe is not emptied. Avoid writing code that assumes that a successful call to CREATE_PIPE results in an empty pipe.

The maxpipesize parameter of CREATE_PIPE determines the maximum size in memory of the database pipe. This places a limit both on the amount of Oracle shared pool memory and on the maximum size of all messages the pipe can hold at any time. When designing applications that use database pipes, it is important to estimate the number and the size of the messages that the pipe will need to contain, so that maxpipesize can be determined. Basically, the objective is to size the pipe as small as possible while making sure that there is plenty of room to handle anticipated message traffic. Note that after creation, a pipe's maximum size can be increased using the SEND_MESSAGE function or by destroying and recreating the pipe.

The DBMS_PIPE.REMOVE_PIPE function

The REMOVE_PIPE function is used to destroy a database pipe and free the memory used by the pipe back to the Oracle shared pool. The header for this program is,

```
FUNCTION DBMS_PIPE.REMOVE_PIPE
    (pipename IN VARCHAR2)
RETURN INTEGER;
```

where the pipename is the name of the database pipe to be removed.

Return values. The REMOVE_PIPE procedure has a single return value of 0, indicating success. This value is returned even if the pipe did not exist.

Exceptions. The program does not raise any package exceptions. The following Oracle exceptions are raised if the user attempts to remove a pipe belonging to another user or passes a NULL pipename:

Number	Description
ORA-23322	Insufficient privileges to access pipe
ORA-23321	Pipename may not be NULL

Restrictions. Pipenames must not begin with "ORA$" as these names are reserved for use by Oracle Corporation.

Example. This example is a function that encapsulates REMOVE_PIPE and returns the Boolean value TRUE indicating that the pipe was successfully removed (or did not exist) or FALSE indicating that the pipe exists but cannot be removed by the caller. The function traps the ORA-23322 error using PRAGMA EXCEPTION_INIT and returns FALSE if this exception is raised.

The closepipe function can be found in the dbpipe package discussed in the "DBMS_PIPE Examples" section and defined in the *dbpipe.sql* script.

```
/* Filename on companion disk: dbpipe.sql */
PACKAGE BODY dbpipe
IS
    cannot_use_pipe    EXCEPTION;
    PRAGMA EXCEPTION_INIT(cannot_use_pipe,-23322);
    null_pipename    EXCEPTION;
    PRAGMA EXCEPTION_INIT(null_pipename,-23321);
    /*
    || encapsulates DBMS_PIPE.REMOVE_PIPE and returns
    || FALSE if ORA-23322 is raised indicating
    || the pipename exists and is not removable
    || by the caller
    */
    FUNCTION closepipe
        (pipename_IN IN VARCHAR2)
    RETURN BOOLEAN
    IS
        call_status  INTEGER;

    BEGIN
        call_status := DBMS_PIPE.REMOVE_PIPE(pipename_IN);
        RETURN (call_status = 0);

    EXCEPTION
        WHEN cannot_use_pipe OR null_pipename
        THEN
            RETURN FALSE;
    END closepipe;

END dbpipe;
```

TIP   It is good practice to remove pipes explicitly when they are no longer needed. This can sometimes be difficult, since database pipes are typically shared by multiple sessions, so it is hard to know when they can be removed. Empty pipes that have not been removed will eventually be aged out of the shared pool by Oracle.

The DBMS_PIPE.RESET_BUFFER procedure

The DBMS_PIPE.RESET_BUFFER procedure resets the session message buffer's internal pack and unpack indicators, effectively discarding the contents of the buffer. The header for this procedure follows:

```
PROCEDURE DBMS_PIPE.RESET_BUFFER;
```

The program does not raise any package exceptions.

Example. This example shows the use of RESET_BUFFER at the beginning of a program that packs a PL/SQL record into a message.

The pack_send_request procedure can be found in the pipesvr package discussed in the "DBMS_PIPE Examples" section. The following code has been excerpted from that example package:

```
/* Filename on companion disk: pipesvr.sql */
PROCEDURE pack_send_request
    (request_rec_IN IN request_rectype
    ,return_code_OUT OUT NUMBER)
IS
BEGIN
    /* discard any previous unsent message items */
    DBMS_PIPE.RESET_BUFFER;

    /* pack message in standard order */
    DBMS_PIPE.PACK_MESSAGE(request_protocol);
    DBMS_PIPE.PACK_MESSAGE(request_rec_IN.response_pipe);
    DBMS_PIPE.PACK_MESSAGE(request_rec_IN.service);

    /*
    || send message to request pipe nowait
    */
    return_code_OUT := DBMS_PIPE.SEND_MESSAGE
                          (pipename => request_pipe
                          ,timeout  => 0);
END pack_send_request;
```

Oracle advises that the RESET_BUFFER procedure should not generally be needed. I make sure, however, to use it in the following places:

- Exception handlers of programs using UNPACK_MESSAGE procedures

- At the beginning of programs designed to pack specific messages into the buffer using PACK_MESSAGE procedures

In handling unpack exceptions, it is safe practice to initialize the message buffer after an unexpected item type is encountered. When packing messages, it is important to be sure that only the intended message items are packed into the buffer. By resetting the message buffer, programs can protect themselves from sending any previously packed but unsent message items.

The DBMS_PIPE.PURGE procedure

The PURGE procedure empties the named pipe of all messages. The header for this procedure is,

```
PROCEDURE DBMS_PIPE.PURGE
    (pipename IN VARCHAR2);
```

where the pipename parameter is the name of the database pipe to be emptied.

Exceptions. The program does not raise any package exceptions. The following Oracle exceptions are raised if the user attempts to purge a pipe belonging to another user or passes a NULL pipename:

Number	Description
ORA-23322	Insufficient privileges to access pipe
ORA-23321	Pipename may not be NULL

Restrictions. Note the following restrictions on calling PURGE:

- Pipenames are limited to 128 bytes in length, are case-insensitive, and cannot contain NLS characters.

- Pipenames must not begin with "ORA$", as these names are reserved for use by Oracle Corporation.

Example. This example shows a procedure that will purge all pipes to which the calling user has access. The purge_all_pipes procedure can be found in the dbpipe package discussed in "DBMS_PIPE Examples." You will need SELECT privilege on SYS.V_$DB_PIPES to create the package.

```
/* Filename on companion disk: dbpipe.sql */
PACKAGE BODY dbpipe
IS
    cannot_use_pipe    EXCEPTION;
    PRAGMA EXCEPTION_INIT(cannot_use_pipe,-23322);

    PROCEDURE purge_all_pipes
    IS
        /* gets names of all pipes */
        CURSOR all_pipes_cur
        IS
        SELECT name
          FROM sys.v_$db_pipes;

    BEGIN
        FOR all_pipes_rec IN all_pipes_cur
        LOOP
            BEGIN
```

```
                    DBMS_PIPE.PURGE(all_pipes_rec.name);

             /* ignore cannot_use_pipe exception */
             EXCEPTION
                WHEN cannot_use_pipe
                THEN
                   null;
                WHEN OTHERS
                THEN
                      RAISE;
             END;
          END LOOP;
       END purge_all_pipes;

   END dbpipe;
```

Emptying a pipe using PURGE releases the SGA memory associated with the pipe. Oracle can then reclaim this memory for other uses based on normal least-recently-used (LRU) aging of the shared pool.

WARNING   Pipes that are not in use, but still have unpurged messages in them, waste SGA memory because they cannot be aged out of the shared pool. Very large pipes in this condition can lead to serious database performance problems.

Note also that calling PURGE may cause the user session's message buffer to be overwritten by messages discarded from the pipe. Be sure to send any message packed in the session buffer prior to calling PURGE. Expert technical reviewer Dan Clamage points out that this is because the implementation of PURGE is "to simply do RECEIVE_MESSAGE with timeout = 0 until the pipe is empty."

The PURGE procedure will implicitly create a public pipe of the given name if one does not already exist. This is somewhat nonintuitive, in that emptying a non-existent pipe causes a new empty pipe to exist.

The DBMS_PIPE.UNIQUE_SESSION_NAME function

The UNIQUE_SESSION_NAME function returns a string value that is constant for a given session and unique among all sessions currently connected to the database. Here's the header for this program:

```
FUNCTION DBMS_PIPE.UNIQUE_SESSION_NAME
RETURN VARCHAR2;
```

The program does not raise any package exceptions.

Example. This example creates a pipe with a name unique to the session for receiving messages intended specifically for this session.

```
DECLARE
   /*
   || declare and initialize my_pipename variable with
   || string unique to session
   */
   my_pipename VARCHAR2(128) := DBMS_PIPE.UNIQUE_SESSION_NAME;

   call_status INTEGER;

BEGIN
   /*
   || create pipe as public so anyone can send message to it
   */
   call_status := DBMS_PIPE.CREATE_PIPE
                     (pipename => my_pipename
                     ,private => FALSE);
END;
```

Applications in which user sessions receive messages on database pipes usually create a unique pipe for each session to use. This helps ensure that sessions get only messages intended for them. As illustrated in the previous example, UNIQUE_SESSION_NAME is often used to generate pipe names that are unique to the session.

Packing and Unpacking Messages

The PACK_MESSAGE, PACK_MESSAGE_RAW, PACK_MESSAGE_ROWID, UNPACK_MESSAGE, UNPACK_MESSAGE_RAW, UNPACK_MESSAGE_ROWID, and NEXT_ITEM_TYPE programs are used to pack messages into your session's local message buffer and unpack them from this buffer.

The DBMS_PIPE.PACK_MESSAGE procedure

The PACK_MESSAGE procedure is used to pack items of datatypes VARCHAR2, NUMBER, or DATE into the user's session's local message buffer. The header for this program follows:

```
PROCEDURE DBMS_PIPE.PACK_MESSAGE
       (item IN VARCHAR2 | NUMBER | DATE);
```

Note that you must specify VARCHAR2 *or* NUMBER *or* DATE.

In Oracle8, the VARCHAR2 version of PACK_MESSAGE is somewhat different, as follows:

```
PROCEDURE DBMS_PIPE.PACK_MESSAGE
       (item IN VARCHAR2 CHARACTER SET ANY_CS);
```

The item parameter is the message of the particular type that is packed into the message buffer.

Exceptions. The program does not raise any package exceptions. The Oracle.06558 Oracle exception is raised if the message buffer becomes full and no more items can be packed.

Restrictions. Note that the user session message buffer is limited to 4096 bytes.

Example. The following example creates a procedure to pack and send a PL/SQL record to a database pipe. Notice the overloading of PACK_MESSAGE, which packs items of different datatypes into the local message buffer using the same procedure call.

```
/* Filename on companion disk: pipex1.sql */
DECLARE
    /*
    || PL/SQL block illustrating use of
    || DBMS_PIPE.PACK_MESSAGE to pack and send
    || a PL/SQL record to a pipe
    */
    TYPE friend_rectype IS RECORD
        (name       VARCHAR2(60)
        ,birthdate  DATE
        ,weight_lbs NUMBER
        );

    friend_rec  friend_rectype;

    PROCEDURE pack_send_friend
        (friend_rec_IN IN friend_rectype
        ,pipename_IN IN VARCHAR2)
    IS
        call_status    INTEGER;
    BEGIN
        /*
        ||notice the PACK_MESSAGE overloading
        */
        DBMS_PIPE.PACK_MESSAGE(friend_rec_IN.name);
        DBMS_PIPE.PACK_MESSAGE(friend_rec_IN.birthdate);
        DBMS_PIPE.PACK_MESSAGE(friend_rec_IN.weight_lbs);

        call_status := DBMS_PIPE.SEND_MESSAGE
                        (pipename=>pipename_IN,timeout=>0);

        IF call_status != 0
        THEN
            DBMS_OUTPUT.PUT_LINE('Send message failed');
        END IF;

    END pack_send_friend;

BEGIN

    /*
```

```
   || OK, now use the procedure to send a friend_rec
   */
   friend_rec.name := 'John Smith';
   friend_rec.birthdate := TO_DATE('01/14/55','MM/DD/YY');
   friend_rec.weight_lbs := 175;

   pack_send_friend(friend_rec,'OPBIP_TEST_PIPE');
END;
```

As in the example, it is good practice to encapsulate the packing and sending of
an entire message as part of a logical program unit. Otherwise, additional calls to
PACK_MESSAGE could add unexpected items to a message before sending, perhaps causing confusion on the receiving end.

The DBMS_PIPE.PACK_MESSAGE_RAW procedure

The PACK_MESSAGE_RAW procedure packs an item of datatype RAW into the
user session's local message buffer. Here's the header for this program:

```
PROCEDURE DBMS_PIPE.PACK_MESSAGE_RAW
     (item IN RAW);
```

The parameter is the item to be packed into the message buffer.

Exceptions. The program does not raise any package exceptions. The ORA-06558
Oracle exception is raised if the message buffer becomes full and no more items
can be packed.

Restrictions. Note that the user session's local message buffer is limited to 4096
bytes.

Example. In this example, a hex string is converted to RAW, packed into the session buffer using the PACK_MESSAGE_RAW procedure, and sent to a pipe.

```
/* Filename on companion disk: pipex1.sql */
DECLARE
    hex_data    VARCHAR2(12):='FFEEDDCCBBAA';
    raw_data    RAW(6);
    call_status INTEGER;
BEGIN
    /* create some raw data */
    raw_data := HEXTORAW(hex_data);

    /*
    || pack and send raw data on pipe
    */
    DBMS_PIPE.PACK_MESSAGE_RAW(raw_data);
    call_status := DBMS_PIPE.SEND_MESSAGE('OPBIP_TEST_PIPE');

    IF call_status != 0
    THEN
```

```
            DBMS_OUTPUT.PUT_LINE('Send message failed');
        END IF;
    END;
```

Applications that need to send large or sensitive data items through database pipes may benefit from using compression and/or encryption on the data and packing the results using PACK_MESSAGE_RAW.

The DBMS_PIPE.PACK_MESSAGE_ROWID procedure

The PACK_MESSAGE_ROWID procedure packs an item of datatype ROWID into the user session's local message buffer. The header for this program follows:

```
PROCEDURE DBMS_PIPE.PACK_MESSAGE_ROWID
    (item IN ROWID);
```

The item parameter is the ROWID to pack into the message buffer.

Exceptions. The program does not raise any package exceptions. The ORA-06558 Oracle exception is raised if the message buffer becomes full and no more items can be packed.

Restrictions. Note that the user session's local message buffer is limited to 4096 bytes.

Example. This (somewhat contrived) example shows a trigger that places the ROWIDs of new or modified rows of the emp table into a database pipe.

```
/* Filename on companion disk: pipex1.sql */
CREATE OR REPLACE TRIGGER emp_AIU
    AFTER INSERT OR UPDATE ON emp
    FOR EACH ROW
DECLARE
    rowid_pipename  VARCHAR2(20) := 'ROWID_PIPE';
    call_status     INTEGER;
BEGIN
    /*
    || pack and send the rowid to a pipe
    */
    DBMS_PIPE.PACK_MESSAGE_ROWID(:NEW.rowid);
    call_status := DBMS_PIPE.SEND_MESSAGE(rowid_pipename);

    IF call_status != 0
    THEN
        RAISE_APPLICATION_ERROR(-20001, 'Trigger emp_AIU failed');
    END IF;
END;
```

The DBMS_PIPE.UNPACK_MESSAGE procedure

The UNPACK_MESSAGE procedure unpacks the next item from the local message buffer when the item is of datatype VARCHAR2, NUMBER, or DATE. The header for this procedure follows:

```
PROCEDURE DBMS_PIPE.UNPACK_MESSAGE
    (item OUT VARCHAR2 | NUMBER | DATE);
```

In Oracle8, the VARCHAR2 version of UNPACK_MESSAGE is somewhat different, as follows:

```
PROCEDURE DBMS_PIPE.UNPACK_MESSAGE
    (item OUT VARCHAR2 CHARACTER SET ANY_CS);
```

The item parameter is the variable into which the next buffer item is unpacked.

Exceptions. The program does not raise any package exceptions. The following Oracle exceptions are raised if the message buffer contains no more items, or if the item parameter does not match the datatype of the next item in the buffer:

Number	Description
ORA-06556	The pipe is empty; cannot fulfill the UNPACK_MESSAGE request
ORA-06559	Wrong datatype requested, 2; actual datatype is 1

Example. This example shows a procedure using UNPACK_MESSAGE to receive and unpack the PL/SQL record type used in the example for PACK_MESSAGE. Note that even though UNPACK_MESSAGE is overloaded on datatype, the correct version needs to be called for the next item in the buffer, or an ORA-06559 error will be raised. This example is a companion to the PACK_MESSAGE example. Together these two examples illustrate a complete pack, send, receive, and unpack DBMS_PIPE communications cycle.

```
/* Filename on companion disk: pipex1.sql */
set serveroutput on size 100000

DECLARE
    /*
    || PL/SQL block illustrating use of
    || DBMS_PIPE.UNPACK_MESSAGE to receive and
    || unpack a PL/SQL record from a pipe
    */
    TYPE friend_rectype IS RECORD
        (name         VARCHAR2(60)
        ,birthdate    DATE
        ,weight_lbs   NUMBER
        );

    friend_rec   friend_rectype;
```

```
PROCEDURE receive_unpack_friend
   (friend_rec_OUT OUT friend_rectype
   ,pipename_IN IN VARCHAR2)
IS
   call_status    INTEGER;
BEGIN

   call_status := DBMS_PIPE.RECEIVE_MESSAGE
                     (pipename=>pipename_IN,timeout=>0);
   /*
   ||NOTE: UNPACK_MESSAGE overloaded but we must
   ||      call the correct version
   */
   DBMS_PIPE.UNPACK_MESSAGE(friend_rec_OUT.name);
   DBMS_PIPE.UNPACK_MESSAGE(friend_rec_OUT.birthdate);
   DBMS_PIPE.UNPACK_MESSAGE(friend_rec_OUT.weight_lbs);

END receive_unpack_friend;

BEGIN
   /*
   || OK test the procedure, get rec from other example
   */
   receive_unpack_friend(friend_rec,'OPBIP_TEST_PIPE');

   /* display results */
   DBMS_OUTPUT.PUT_LINE('Friend name: '||friend_rec.name);
   DBMS_OUTPUT.PUT_LINE('Friend birthdate: '||
                   TO_CHAR(friend_rec.birthdate));
   DBMS_OUTPUT.PUT_LINE('Friend weight: '||
                   TO_CHAR(friend_rec.weight_lbs));
END;
```

Here is output from running the previous script after running the PACK_MESSAGE example script:

```
Friend name: John Smith
Friend birthdate: 14-JAN-55
Friend weight: 175

PL/SQL procedure successfully completed.
```

As illustrated in the example, it is good practice to encapsulate the receipt and unpacking of messages into a single logical program unit. Message items must be unpacked in the same order in which they were packed.

NOTE   The numeric datatype identifiers in the ORA-06559 message do not match the item type values returned by the NEXT_ITEM_TYPE function.

The DBMS_PIPE.UNPACK_MESSAGE_RAW procedure

The UNPACK_MESSAGE_RAW procedure unpacks the next item from the local message buffer when the item is of datatype RAW. The header for this program follows:

```
PROCEDURE DBMS_PIPE.UNPACK_MESSAGE_RAW
    (item OUT RAW);
```

The item parameter is the RAW variable into which the next buffer item is unpacked.

Exceptions. The program does not raise any package exceptions. The following Oracle exceptions are raised if the message buffer contains no more items or the item parameter does not match the datatype of the next item in the buffer:

Number	Description
ORA-06556	The pipe is empty; cannot fulfill the UNPACK_MESSAGE request
ORA-06559	Wrong datatype requested, 2; actual datatype is 1

Example. In this example, a message with a raw data item is received, unpacked using the UNPACK_MESSAGE_RAW procedure, and displayed.

```
/* Filename on companion disk: pipex1.sql */
set serveroutput on size 100000

DECLARE
    hex_data    VARCHAR2(12);
    raw_data    RAW(6);
    call_status INTEGER;
BEGIN
    /*
    || receive and unpack the raw message
    */
    call_status := DBMS_PIPE.RECEIVE_MESSAGE('OPBIP_TEST_PIPE');
    DBMS_PIPE.UNPACK_MESSAGE_RAW(raw_data);

    /* display results */
    hex_data := RAWTOHEX(raw_data);
    DBMS_OUTPUT.PUT_LINE('hex of raw: '||hex_data);
END;
```

Output from running this script immediately after the PACK_MESSAGE_RAW example script:

```
hex of raw: FFEEDDCCBBAA

PL/SQL procedure successfully completed.
```

Note that the numeric datatype identifiers in the ORA-06559 message do not match the item type values returned by the NEXT_ITEM_TYPE function.

The DBMS_PIPE.UNPACK_MESSAGE_ROWID procedure

The UNPACK_MESSAGE_ROWID procedure unpacks the next item from the local message buffer when the item is of datatype ROWID. Here's the header for this program:

```
PROCEDURE DBMS_PIPE.UNPACK_MESSAGE_ROWID
    (item OUT ROWID);
```

The item parameter is the ROWID variable into which the next message buffer item is unpacked.

Exceptions. The program does not raise any declared exceptions. The following Oracle errors are raised if the message buffer contains no more items or the item parameter does not match the datatype of the next item in the buffer:

Number	Description
ORA-06556	The pipe is empty; cannot fulfill the UNPACK_MESSAGE request
ORA-06559	Wrong datatype requested, 2; actual datatype is 1

Example. In this example, the database pipe that is filled by the EMP_AIU trigger from the example for PACK_MESSAGE_ROWID is emptied using UNPACK_MESSAGE_ROWID.

```
/* Filename on companion disk: pipex1.sql */
set serveroutput on size 100000

DECLARE
    rowid_pipename  VARCHAR2(20) := 'ROWID_PIPE';
    temp_rowid      ROWID;
    call_status     INTEGER:=0;
BEGIN
    /*
    || receive and unpack all rowids from pipe
    */
    WHILE call_status = 0
    LOOP
        call_status := DBMS_PIPE.RECEIVE_MESSAGE
            (pipename=>rowid_pipename, timeout=>0);

        IF call_status = 0
        THEN
            DBMS_PIPE.UNPACK_MESSAGE_ROWID(temp_rowid);

            /* display rowid results */
            DBMS_OUTPUT.PUT_LINE(ROWIDTOCHAR(temp_rowid));
        END IF;
    END LOOP;
END;
/
```

The script output looks like this:

```
SQL>
14 rows updated.

Commit complete.

AAAA6OAAGAAAAOFAAA
AAAA6OAAGAAAAOFAAB
AAAA6OAAGAAAAOFAAC
AAAA6OAAGAAAAOFAAD
AAAA6OAAGAAAAOFAAE
AAAA6OAAGAAAAOFAAF
AAAA6OAAGAAAAOFAAG
AAAA6OAAGAAAAOFAAH
AAAA6OAAGAAAAOFAAI
AAAA6OAAGAAAAOFAAJ
AAAA6OAAGAAAAOFAAK
AAAA6OAAGAAAAOFAAL
AAAA6OAAGAAAAOFAAM
AAAA6OAAGAAAAOFAAN
AAAA6OAAGAAAAOFAAN

PL/SQL procedure successfully completed.
```

In the previous example, the unusual looking ROWIDs are the result of running the test on an Oracle8 database. (Remember that ROWID formats have changed in Oracle8.)

NOTE   The numeric datatype identifiers in the ORA-06559 message do not match the item type values returned by the NEXT_ITEM_TYPE function.

The DBMS_PIPE.NEXT_ITEM_TYPE function

The NEXT_ITEM_TYPE function returns a number indicating the datatype of the next item in the user session's message buffer. The header for this function follows:

```
FUNCTION DBMS_PIPE.NEXT_ITEM_TYPE RETURN INTEGER;
```

The return value will be one of the following:

Item Type	Description
0	No more items in buffer
6	NUMBER
9	VARCHAR2
11	ROWID

Item Type	Description
12	DATE
23	RAW

The program does not raise any package exceptions.

Example. The following PL/SQL block contains an inline procedure called unpack_all_items, which can unpack any message and display its contents using DBMS_OUTPUT. The unpack_all_items procedure uses NEXT_ITEM_TYPE to determine which version of UNPACK_MESSAGE to call for each item.

```
/* Filename on companion disk: pipex2.sql */
set serveroutput on size 100000

DECLARE
    call_stat    INTEGER;

    PROCEDURE unpack_all_items
    IS
        /*
        || declare temp variables of all message item types
        */
        temp_varchar2   VARCHAR2(2000);
        temp_date       DATE;
        temp_number     NUMBER;
        temp_rowid      ROWID;
        temp_raw        RAW(2000);

        next_item       INTEGER:=0;

    BEGIN
        next_item := DBMS_PIPE.NEXT_ITEM_TYPE;

        /*
        || unpack by item type and convert to varchar2
        */
        WHILE next_item > 0
        LOOP
            IF next_item = 9
            THEN
                DBMS_PIPE.UNPACK_MESSAGE(temp_varchar2);

            ELSIF next_item = 6
            THEN
                DBMS_PIPE.UNPACK_MESSAGE(temp_number);
                temp_varchar2 := 'NUMBER: '||TO_CHAR(temp_number);

            ELSIF next_item = 11
            THEN
                DBMS_PIPE.UNPACK_MESSAGE_ROWID(temp_rowid);
```

```
                        temp_varchar2 := 'ROWID: '||ROWIDTOCHAR(temp_rowid);

                 ELSIF next_item = 12
                 THEN
                     DBMS_PIPE.UNPACK_MESSAGE(temp_date);
                     temp_varchar2 := 'DATE: '||
                                  TO_CHAR(temp_date,'YYYY:MM:DD:HH24:MI:SS');

                 ELSIF next_item = 23
                 THEN
                     DBMS_PIPE.UNPACK_MESSAGE_RAW(temp_raw);
                     temp_varchar2 := 'RAW: '||RAWTOHEX(temp_raw);

                 ELSE
                     temp_varchar2 := 'Invalid item type: '||TO_CHAR(next_item);
                 END IF;

                 /*
                 || display item and determine next item
                 */
                 DBMS_OUTPUT.PUT_LINE(temp_varchar2);
                 next_item := DBMS_PIPE.NEXT_ITEM_TYPE;

           END LOOP;
      END unpack_all_items;

   BEGIN
      /* empty pipe */
      DBMS_PIPE.PURGE('OPBIP_TEST_PIPE');

      /* initialize buffer  */
      DBMS_PIPE.RESET_BUFFER;

      /* pack in some data of different types */
      DBMS_PIPE.PACK_MESSAGE('HELLO THERE');
      DBMS_PIPE.PACK_MESSAGE(123456789);
      DBMS_PIPE.PACK_MESSAGE(SYSDATE);
      DBMS_PIPE.PACK_MESSAGE_RAW(HEXTORAW('FFDDEE2344AA'));

      /* send and receive the message */
      call_stat := DBMS_PIPE.SEND_MESSAGE('OPBIP_TEST_PIPE');
      call_stat := DBMS_PIPE.RECEIVE_MESSAGE('OPBIP_TEST_PIPE');

      /* call the generic unpack procedure */
      unpack_all_items;

   END;
```

Here is output from running the example script:

```
SQL> @pipex2.sql

HELLO THERE
NUMBER: 123456789
DATE: 1998:02:01:12:01:19
```

```
RAW: FFDDEE2344AA
```

```
PL/SQL procedure successfully completed.
```

The unpack_all_items inline procedure is a prototype for the procedure of the same name found in the dbpipe package, discussed in the "DBMS_PIPE Examples" section.

NOTE   The item type values returned by the NEXT_ITEM_TYPE function do not match the numeric datatype identifiers in the ORA-06559 message.

Sending and Receiving Messages

Use DBMS_PIPE's SEND_MESSAGE and RECEIVE_MESSAGE functions to send and receive messages on the pipe you have created.

The DBMS_PIPE.SEND_MESSAGE function

The SEND_MESSAGE function sends a message on the named pipe. The message sent is whatever has been packed into the user session's current message buffer. The header for this program follows:

```
FUNCTION DBMS_PIPE.SEND_MESSAGE
    (pipename IN VARCHAR2
    ,timeout IN INTEGER DEFAULT MAXWAIT
    ,maxpipesize IN INTEGER DEFAULT 8192)
    RETURN INTEGER;
```

Parameters are summarized in the following table.

Name	Description
pipename	Name of the database pipe
timeout	Time in seconds to wait for message to be sent
maxpipesize	Maximum size in bytes of the pipe

The value returned is one of the following:

Return Value	Description
0	Success
1	Timed out
3	Interrupted

Exceptions. The program does not raise any package exceptions. The following Oracle exceptions are raised if the user attempts to receive a message on a pipe belonging to another user or on a NULL pipename:

Number	Description
ORA-23322	Insufficient privileges to access pipe
ORA-23321	Pipename may not be NULL

Restrictions. Note the following restrictions on calling SEND_MESSAGE:

- Pipenames are limited to 128 bytes in length, are case-insensitive, and cannot contain NLS characters.

- Pipenames must not begin with "ORA$", as these names are reserved for use by Oracle Corporation.

Example. This example shows the use of SEND_MESSAGE to send a message based on a PL/SQL record out on a database pipe.

The pack_send_request procedure can be found in the pipesvr package discussed in the "DBMS_PIPE Examples" section.

```
/* Filename on companion disk: pipesvr.sql */
PROCEDURE pack_send_request
    (request_rec_IN IN request_rectype
    ,return_code_OUT OUT NUMBER)
IS
BEGIN
    /* discard any previous unsent message items */
    DBMS_PIPE.RESET_BUFFER;

    /* pack message in standard order */
    DBMS_PIPE.PACK_MESSAGE(request_protocol);
    DBMS_PIPE.PACK_MESSAGE(request_rec_IN.response_pipe);
    DBMS_PIPE.PACK_MESSAGE(request_rec_IN.service);

    /*
    || send message to request pipe nowait
    */
    return_code_OUT := DBMS_PIPE.SEND_MESSAGE
                        (pipename => request_pipe
                        ,timeout  => 0);
    END pack_send_request;
```

The SEND_MESSAGE function will implicitly create a public pipe if the pipe specified by the pipename parameter does not already exist. Be careful not to assume that the call to SEND_MESSAGE has been successful. Note that in this example, the value returned by the call to SEND_MESSAGE is passed out of the pack_send_request procedure to its caller, so it will be the caller's responsibility to handle a nonzero return value.

Calls to SEND_MESSAGE will wait for up to the value of the timeout parameter in seconds for the call to complete. Applications using database pipes that stay full of messages may incur lengthy wait times or timeouts. When using SEND_MES-SAGE under these circumstances, be careful to specify a timeout that users can tolerate.

Applications experiencing frequent timeouts or long waits when calling SEND_ MESSAGE may benefit by increasing the size of the database pipe. This can be done by specifying a value for the maxpipesize parameter that is greater than the current maximum size of the pipe.

The DBMS_PIPE.RECEIVE_MESSAGE function

The RECEIVE_MESSAGE function is used to fetch a message from the named pipe into the user session's message buffer. The header for this program follows:

```
FUNCTION DBMS_PIPE.RECEIVE_MESSAGE
    (pipename IN VARCHAR2
    ,timeout IN INTEGER DEFAULT MAXWAIT)
RETURN INTEGER;
```

Parameters are summarized in the following table.

Parameter	Description
pipename	Name of the database pipe
timeout	Time in seconds to wait for message to be received

The function returns one of the following values:

Return Value	Description
0	Success
1	Timed out
2	Message too big for buffer
3	Interrupted

Exceptions. The program does not raise any package exceptions. The following Oracle exceptions are raised if the user attempts to receive a message on a pipe belonging to another user or on a NULL pipename:

Number	Description
ORA-23322	Insufficient privileges to access pipe
ORA-23321	Pipename may not be NULL

Restrictions. Note the following restrictions on calling RECEIVE_MESSAGE:

- Pipenames are limited to 128 bytes in length, are case-insensitive, and cannot contain NLS characters.

- Pipenames must not begin with "ORA$", as these names are reserved for use by Oracle Corporation.

Example. This example shows the use of the RECEIVE_MESSAGE function to receive a message based on a PL/SQL record from a database pipe.

The receive_unpack_request procedure can be found in the pipesvr package discussed in the "DBMS_PIPE Examples" section.

```
/* Filename on companion disk: pipesvr.sql */
PROCEDURE receive_unpack_request
     (timeout_IN IN INTEGER
     ,request_rec_OUT OUT request_rectype
     ,return_code_OUT OUT NUMBER)
IS
     /* temp variables */
     temp_protocol  request_protocol%TYPE;
     temp_return_code  NUMBER;

BEGIN

     temp_return_code := DBMS_PIPE.RECEIVE_MESSAGE
              (pipename => request_pipe
              ,timeout  => timeout_IN);

     IF temp_return_code = 0
     THEN
          /* check if expected protocol */
          DBMS_PIPE.UNPACK_MESSAGE(temp_protocol);

          IF temp_protocol = request_protocol
          THEN
               DBMS_PIPE.UNPACK_MESSAGE(request_rec_OUT.response_pipe);
               DBMS_PIPE.UNPACK_MESSAGE(request_rec_OUT.service);
          ELSE
               /* pipe message has unexpected protocol */
               temp_return_code := -1;
               debug('UNKNOWN PROTOCOL: '||temp_protocol);
               DBMS_PIPE.RESET_BUFFER;
          END IF;
     END IF;

     return_code_OUT := temp_return_code;

EXCEPTION
     WHEN OTHERS THEN
          return_code_OUT := SQLCODE;
          debug('RECEIVE REQUEST EXCP: '||SQLERRM
```

```
                   ,force_TF_IN=>TRUE);
               DBMS_PIPE.RESET_BUFFER;

       END receive_unpack_request;
```

Calls to RECEIVE_MESSAGE will wait for up to the value of the timeout parameter in seconds for the call to complete. Applications accessing database pipes that are usually empty of messages can incur lengthy wait times or timeouts. When using RECEIVE_MESSAGE under these circumstances, be careful to specify a timeout that users can tolerate.

The RECEIVE_MESSAGE function will implicitly create a public pipe of the given name if one does not already exist.

Tips on Using DBMS_PIPE

Oracle does not provide detailed documentation of exactly how database pipes work, nor much in the way of how best to use them. The programs in DBMS_ PIPE are quite low-level utilities. Higher-level programs using DBMS_PIPE typically need to make numerous calls to these programs, which must be in the correct order, to handle communications. This can lead to complex and difficult code, unless a structured, modular, template-based approach is used.

Through research and experience, I have adopted a method for building safe, reliable, and extensible higher-level communications layers on top of DBMS_PIPE. The following items are the main elements of this method:

- Define message types using PL/SQL records
- Encapsulate pack/send and receive/unpack logic around record types
- Separate messages using session-specific pipes
- Use a well-defined protocol across applications
- Pay attention to timeout values
- Use RESET_BUFFER in exception handlers and pack/unpack routines
- Take the time to size pipes correctly
- Purge and remove pipes when finished

Defining message types and encapsulating communications logic

PL/SQL records and DBMS_PIPE messages both bundle related data items together, so there is a natural affinity between them. When implementing applications that use DBMS_PIPE, do the following:

1. Determine the kinds of message data that will be communicated between sessions.

2. Develop a PL/SQL record type corresponding to each different type of message.

3. Build two procedures around the record type. One procedure takes a PL/SQL record and pipename as IN parameters, packs the record into a message using PACK_MESSAGE, and sends it to the pipe using SEND_MESSAGE. This procedure is usually named pack_send_rectype. The second procedure, usually called receive_unpack_rectype, performs the inverse operation. It takes a pipename as an IN parameter and a record as an OUT parameter, retrieves a message on the pipe using RECEIVE_MESSAGE, and unbundles the message into the record using calls to UNPACK_MESSAGE.

4. Once these two procedures are built, I can send and receive PL/SQL records as messages on database pipes; using these procedure calls, all of the low-level calls to DBMS_PIPE programs are hidden. This approach also makes it easy to extend the messaging to add new data items: simply add a new field to the end of the record type, and new calls to PACK_MESSAGE and UNPACK_MESSAGE to the two procedures.

Examples of this record-to-pipe-message encapsulation technique can be seen in the examples for PACK_MESSAGE and UNPACK_MESSAGE, where procedures to pack/send and receive/unpack a record type called friend_rectype are defined. These examples are repeated here:

```
/* Filename on companion disk: pipex1.sql */
TYPE friend_rectype IS RECORD
     (name         VARCHAR2(60)
     ,birthdate   DATE
     ,weight_lbs NUMBER
     );

friend_rec  friend_rectype;

PROCEDURE pack_send_friend
     (friend_rec_IN IN friend_rectype
     ,pipename_IN IN VARCHAR2)
IS
     call_status    INTEGER;
BEGIN
     /*
     ||notice the PACK_MESSAGE overloading
     */
     DBMS_PIPE.PACK_MESSAGE(friend_rec_IN.name);
     DBMS_PIPE.PACK_MESSAGE(friend_rec_IN.birthdate);
     DBMS_PIPE.PACK_MESSAGE(friend_rec_IN.weight_lbs);

     call_status := DBMS_PIPE.SEND_MESSAGE
                    (pipename=>pipename_IN,timeout=>0);

     IF call_status != 0
```

```
        THEN
            DBMS_OUTPUT.PUT_LINE('Send message failed');
        END IF;

    END pack_send_friend;

    PROCEDURE receive_unpack_friend
        (friend_rec_OUT OUT friend_rectype
         ,pipename_IN IN VARCHAR2)
    IS
        call_status    INTEGER;
    BEGIN

        call_status := DBMS_PIPE.RECEIVE_MESSAGE
                    (pipename=>pipename_IN,timeout=>0);
        /*
        ||NOTE: UNPACK_MESSAGE overloaded but we must
        ||      call the correct version
        */
        DBMS_PIPE.UNPACK_MESSAGE(friend_rec_OUT.name);
        DBMS_PIPE.UNPACK_MESSAGE(friend_rec_OUT.birthdate);
        DBMS_PIPE.UNPACK_MESSAGE(friend_rec_OUT.weight_lbs);

    END receive_unpack_friend;
```

Separating messages

Once a reliable mechanism is established for sending and receiving a specific message type, the next step is to make sure that messages get to their expected recipients. Database pipes themselves can hold any message, so separating messages of different types is usually done by creating specific pipes to handle specific types of messages. Messages intended for a specific user will usually be placed on a pipe whose name is unique to the user session. Unique pipenames can be established using the UNIQUE_SESSION_NAME function. Common pipes—for example, those on which server programs listen for service requests—will have pipenames known to all sessions that use the service. These names are typically contained in private global variables embedded in the packages that handle the DBMS_PIPE communications for the server.

Establishing messaging protocols

Since any session with access to a database pipe can put a message there, it is good practice for programs that receive and unpack messages to establish a protocol to reliably identify the type of message received prior to unpacking. This protects against receiving ORA-06559 errors because the next item type in the message does not match the item parameter in the call to UNPACK_MESSAGE. It also protects against unpacking a message successfully, only to find out that the data itself was not really what was expected. Therefore, it is good practice for all messages to have a protocol identifier as the first item in the message. This item should always be a specific datatype. I use and recommend VARCHAR2, because safer and more meaningful protocol identifiers than numbers can be created this way.

Once protocol identifiers are established, receive/unpack routines will have code that looks like the following:

```
call_status := DBMS_PIPE.RECEIVE_MESSAGE(pipename_IN, timeout_value);

IF call_status = 0
THEN
    /* unpack protocol id */
    DBMS_PIPE.UNPACK_MESSAGE(protocol_id);

    IF protocol_id = 'EXPECTED ID FOR THIS ROUTINE'
    THEN
        /*
        || OK, we know what message type, unpack the rest here
        || using calls to DBMS_PIPE.UNPACK_MESSAGE
        */
    ELSE
        DBMS_PIPE.RESET_BUFFER;
        RAISE_APPLICATION_ERROR('Invalid protocol');
    END IF;
END IF;
```

Paying attention to timeouts

Note also in the previous code fragment that a timeout is specified in the call to RECEIVE_MESSAGE, which is another of my recommended best practices. Sessions will block and wait for up to the value of the timeout parameter for calls to SEND_MESSAGE or RECEIVE_MESSAGE to complete. The default for this parameter is the constant DBMS_PIPE.maxwait, which equates to 1000 days! Since most users are not quite this patient, it pays to spend some time determining and using acceptable timeout values.

Using RESET_BUFFER

The code fragment also illustrates one place where I use the RESET_BUFFER procedure: when a message has been received but the protocol is unrecognized. This effectively discards the message. Another place where the message buffer should be reset for safety is at the beginning of message packing routines. Resetting here ensures that the message packed does not include any items that may have been packed into the buffer prior to entering the routine (i.e., that the message is only what is intended). Finally, another good place to use RESET_BUFFER is in exception handlers for programs using DBMS_PIPE programs. Since exceptions indicate unexpected results, it is safe practice to make sure that the message buffer is initialized under these circumstances.

Sizing and removing pipes for good memory management

Finally, my best practices call for proper sizing, purging, and removal of database pipes. These all amount to observing good memory management in the Oracle shared pool. Pipes that are too large may interfere with other shared pool operations. Pipes that are too small for their traffic volume can result in long wait times or timeouts in calls to SEND_MESSAGE. Pipes that are no longer needed and that still contain messages effectively waste SGA memory because they will not be aged out of the shared pool. Thus, it pays to spend time making pipe sizes large enough to handle traffic with minimum wait times, yet as small as possible to conserve memory, and to remove pipes or at least purge them of messages when they are no longer needed.

DBMS_PIPE Examples

This section contains several longer examples of using DBMS_PIPE.

Communicating with the outside world

One of the primary advantages of DBMS_PIPE is that it facilitates the long-desired ability to communicate with the "outside world" from within Oracle. In this new situation, database pipes can provide users access to external services from within their Oracle sessions. Oracle's package specification script for DBMS_PIPE (*dbmspipe.sql*) presents a relatively complete example of how a "stock price request server" service could be implemented. Several examples of how to implement such external services using 3GL languages like C are available through online sources. In particular, Oracle Technical Support Bulletin 105688.158 gives a complete implementation of a daemon process written in C that listens on a database pipe and provides Oracle sessions with the ability to execute operating system commands from PL/SQL (similar to the HOST command in SQL*Plus).

Exploring DBMS_PIPE

I had several questions about database pipes and decided to explore the following:

- Can a message packed into the buffer be unpacked prior to sending?

- Do PACK_MESSAGE and RECEIVE_MESSAGE use a common buffer?

- Does the PACK_MESSAGE procedure do any data compression to conserve memory?

I developed several tests to help answer these questions. The first question seemed quite straightforward. This is the test I developed and the results:

```
DECLARE
    message_out    VARCHAR2(2000);
```

```
BEGIN
   /* try to pack and unpack */
   DBMS_PIPE.PACK_MESSAGE('This is my message');
   DBMS_PIPE.UNPACK_MESSAGE(message_out);
   DBMS_OUTPUT.PUT_LINE
      ('message unpacked: '||message_out);
END;
/

DECLARE
*
ERROR at line 1:
ORA-06556: the pipe is empty, cannot fulfill the unpack_message request
ORA-06512: at "SYS.DBMS_PIPE", line 71
ORA-06512: at line 11
```

Calling UNPACK_MESSAGE immediately following a call to PACK_MESSAGE generated an exception, so it appears that the first answer is no: the packed message buffer cannot be unpacked prior to sending. However, check out the results of the following test:

```
DECLARE
    message_out     VARCHAR2(2000);

BEGIN
   /* initialize buffer */
   DBMS_PIPE.RESET_BUFFER;

   /* try to pack and unpack */
   DBMS_PIPE.PACK_MESSAGE('This is my message');
   DBMS_PIPE.UNPACK_MESSAGE(message_out);
   DBMS_OUTPUT.PUT_LINE
      ('message unpacked: '||message_out);
END;
/

message unpacked: This is my message

PL/SQL procedure successfully completed.
```

The only difference in the second test was that RESET_BUFFER was called prior to packing and unpacking the message. Furthermore, subsequent executions of the first test block completed successfully even though RESET_BUFFER was not explicitly called. So the real answer to the first question appears to be that packed messages can be unpacked prior to sending as long as RESET_BUFFER has been previously called in the session. This confuses me, and I don't like the fact that Oracle does not expose more details about the inner workings of the local message buffer in relation to packing and unpacking messages.

The second question ("Do PACK_MESSAGE and UNPACK_MESSAGE use a common buffer?") is a little trickier. It actually occurred to me only after exploring the first question about unpacking a packed buffer before sending. I wondered whether packing and unpacking messages could happen independently of each other in the message buffer, or whether the session message buffer was essentially a single slot with room for only one message. I expanded my earlier test script into the following:

```
/* Filename on companion disk: pipe2.sql */
DECLARE
    test_pipename  VARCHAR2(30):='OPBIP_TEST_PIPE2';
    call_status    INTEGER;
    message1_out   VARCHAR2(2000);
    message2_out   VARCHAR2(2000);

BEGIN
    DBMS_PIPE.RESET_BUFFER;

    /* make sure pipe is empty */
    call_status := DBMS_PIPE.CREATE_PIPE(test_pipename);
    DBMS_PIPE.PURGE(test_pipename);

    /* pack and send first message */
    DBMS_PIPE.PACK_MESSAGE('This is message one');
    call_status := DBMS_PIPE.SEND_MESSAGE(test_pipename);
    DBMS_OUTPUT.PUT_LINE('call status send1: '||TO_CHAR(call_status));

    /* now pack second message without sending */
    DBMS_PIPE.PACK_MESSAGE('This is message two');

    /* receive, unpack and print message */
    call_status := DBMS_PIPE.RECEIVE_MESSAGE(test_pipename);
    DBMS_OUTPUT.PUT_LINE('call status receive1: '||TO_CHAR(call_status));
    DBMS_PIPE.UNPACK_MESSAGE(message1_out);
    DBMS_OUTPUT.PUT_LINE('message unpacked: '||message1_out);

    /* now send message two...is it still there? */
    call_status := DBMS_PIPE.SEND_MESSAGE(test_pipename);
    DBMS_OUTPUT.PUT_LINE('call status send2: '||TO_CHAR(call_status));

    /* receive, unpack and print message */
    call_status := DBMS_PIPE.RECEIVE_MESSAGE(test_pipename);
    DBMS_OUTPUT.PUT_LINE('call status receive2: '||TO_CHAR(call_status));
    DBMS_PIPE.UNPACK_MESSAGE(message2_out);
    DBMS_OUTPUT.PUT_LINE('message unpacked: '||message2_out);
END;
/
call status send1: 0
call status receive1: 0
message unpacked: This is message one
call status send2: 0
call status receive2: 0
message unpacked: This is message one

PL/SQL procedure successfully completed.
```

Notice that all calls to SEND_MESSAGE and RECEIVE_MESSAGE returned 0, indicating success. However, message two was never sent or received; instead, message one was sent and received twice. This indicates that the message buffer can contain only one message at a time for either sending or receiving. Receiving message one from the pipe overlaid message two in the buffer. It is interesting that the second call to SEND_MESSAGE sent the message that was just unpacked into the buffer, not the last message packed. It seems that a message that has been received and unpacked can also be sent without being repacked. As with the first question, this is somewhat confusing and counterintuitive, and again begs for more detailed documentation from Oracle on DBMS_PIPE.

One idea this second test gave me was forwarding messages from one pipe to another without consuming them. I developed a procedure to do just that; it's discussed later in "The dbpipe utility package."

The concept of "packing" message items into a buffer suggested that perhaps the items were also being compressed somehow. If this were true, then message items containing strings of repeating characters should pack tightly into the 4096-byte buffer, and the buffer could contain more than 4096 bytes worth of messages. In order to test this theory, I developed a procedure to stuff as many copies as possible of an input string into the message buffer and count exactly how big the resulting message is. Here is the source code for the pipe1 procedure:

```
/* Filename on companion disk: pipe1.sql */
CREATE OR REPLACE PROCEDURE pipe1
    (message_item_IN IN VARCHAR2)
    /*
    || Tests whether DBMS_PIPE compresses
    || string message items on packing by
    || stuffing buffer full and counting total
    || size of message.
    ||
    || Author:  John Beresniewicz, Savant Corp
    || Created: 09/16/97
    ||
    */
  IS
    test_pipename  VARCHAR2(30):='OPBIP_TEST_PIPE';
    call_status       INTEGER;

    item_counter   INTEGER :=0;
    total_msg_size  INTEGER :=0;

    buffer_full    EXCEPTION;
    PRAGMA EXCEPTION_INIT(buffer_full,-6558);

  BEGIN

    /* make sure pipe is empty and buffer initialized */
```

```
    call_status := DBMS_PIPE.CREATE_PIPE(test_pipename);
    DBMS_PIPE.PURGE(test_pipename);
    DBMS_PIPE.RESET_BUFFER;

BEGIN
    /* buffer_full exception ends the loop */
    LOOP
        DBMS_PIPE.PACK_MESSAGE(message_item_IN);

        /*
        || increment total size:  1 byte for datatype and
        || 2 bytes for item length
        */
        total_msg_size := total_msg_size+3+LENGTHB(message_item_IN);
        item_counter := item_counter +1;
    END LOOP;

EXCEPTION
    WHEN buffer_full
        THEN
            /* test if message can send OK on buffer_full */
            call_status := DBMS_PIPE.SEND_MESSAGE(test_pipename);

            IF call_status = 0
            THEN
                /* OK, display results for this message item */
                DBMS_OUTPUT.PUT_LINE
                    ('Items Packed: '||TO_CHAR(item_counter));
                DBMS_OUTPUT.PUT_LINE
                    ('Total Msg Size: '||TO_CHAR(total_msg_size+1));
            ELSE
                DBMS_OUTPUT.PUT_LINE
                    ('Pipe Send Error, return code: '||
                                    TO_CHAR(call_status));
            END IF;
        WHEN OTHERS
            THEN
                DBMS_OUTPUT.PUT_LINE('Oracle Error: '||TO_CHAR(SQLCODE));
    END;

END pipe1;
```

There are a couple of useful techniques demonstrated in pipe1. For one, the EXCEPTION_INIT pragma is used to define an exception to trap the buffer full condition. This exception is then used to exit the message packing loop, which is somewhat unusual but precisely what we need in this case. Also, the pipe is created and immediately purged to ensure that it is empty for the test. The purge is done because the DBMS_PIPE.CREATE_PIPE call will succeed if the pipe already exists, and it may contain messages, which could interfere with the test. Since the test is designed to measure how much can be packed into the local buffer, DBMS_PIPE.RESET_BUFFER is called to make sure that the buffer starts off completely empty.

The pipe1 procedure is not particularly useful, except to answer the question about whether message items are compressed. Well, here are the results from several calls to pipe1 using different message items:

```
SQL> execute pipe1('This is a long text message');

Items Packed: 136
Total Msg Size: 4081

PL/SQL procedure successfully completed.

SQL> execute pipe1(RPAD(' ',2000));

Items Packed: 2
Total Msg Size: 4007

PL/SQL procedure successfully completed.

SQL> execute pipe1('1');

Items Packed: 1023
Total Msg Size: 4093

PL/SQL procedure successfully completed.
```

The tests show there is no data compression taking place when message items are packed into the buffer. This is most clearly seen in the second test, where only two strings of 2000 blanks could be packed into the buffer. Also note the inefficiency of packing many small items into a message (third test) since the three bytes of per-item overhead account for most of the space used.

The conclusion I've drawn from all these tests: the inner workings of DBMS_PIPE are not at all intuitive or obvious. I'm still somewhat confused by some of the test results, and the lack of clear documentation by Oracle is frustrating. The good news is that reliable pipe-based communications can be achieved by following the simple guidelines and best practices discussed previously. Doing so will help avoid programs that enter those murky areas which my testing purposely explored.

The dbpipe utility package

While conducting my experiments on DBMS_PIPE, I had a couple of ideas for some utility programs. One thing I wanted was a kind of "sniffer" program that could show me the contents of any pipe. Since I was not following safe pipe programming practices (on purpose)—I kept stuffing all kinds of messages into all kinds of pipes—I often did not know what had gotten where. I needed a generic program that could show me the contents of any pipe without knowing message specifics such as number of items and their datatypes. Another idea was to forward a message from one pipe to another. This seemed potentially useful, perhaps as the basis for a kind of pipe-based broadcasting or chain-letter application.

It turns out that one key to both of these utilities was creating utility programs that could unpack and repack any message without knowing the form of its contents in advance.

These ideas became the dbpipe package. Here is the package specification:

```
/* Filename on companion disk: dbpipe.sql */
CREATE OR REPLACE PACKAGE dbpipe
   /*
   || Package of interesting utilities illustrating use of
   || DBMS_PIPE programs.  Includes a forwarding program to
   || pass pipe messages from one pipe to another, a peek
   || program to inspect and replace pipe messages, and
   || generic unpack and pack programs.
   ||
   || Author:  John Beresniewicz, Savant Corp
   ||
   || 10/10/97: added purge_all_pipes
   || 10/10/97: made cannot_use_pipe a public
   ||           exception
   || 10/05/97: added makepipe and closepipe
   || 09/28/97: added invalid_item_type exception to
   ||           unpack_to_tbl
   || 09/25/97: added safe or cool mode to forward
   || 09/21/97: created
   ||
   || Compilation Requirements:
   ||
   || EXECUTE on DBMS_PIPE
   || EXECUTE on DBMS_SESSION
   || SELECT  on SYS.V_$DB_PIPES
   ||
   || Execution Requirements:
   ||
   */
AS
   /*
   || declare exceptions raised by various DBMS_PIPE
   || programs when user cannot access a private pipe
   || or pipename is null
   */
   cannot_use_pipe   EXCEPTION;
   PRAGMA EXCEPTION_INIT(cannot_use_pipe,-23322);
   null_pipename   EXCEPTION;
   PRAGMA EXCEPTION_INIT(null_pipename,-23321);

   /*
   || message_rectype records can capture any single
   || item which can be packed into a DBMS_PIPE message
   */
   TYPE message_rectype IS RECORD
```

```
(item_type   INTEGER
,Mvarchar2   VARCHAR2(4093)
,Mdate       DATE
,Mnumber     NUMBER
,Mrowid      ROWID
,Mraw        RAW(4093)
);

/*
|| message_tbltype tables can hold an ordered list of
|| message items, thus any message can be captured
*/
TYPE message_tbltype IS TABLE OF message_rectype
   INDEX BY BINARY_INTEGER;

/*
|| unpacks message buffer into table,
|| optionally displays message to screen
*/
PROCEDURE unpack_to_tbl
   (message_tbl_OUT OUT message_tbltype
   ,display_TF IN BOOLEAN := FALSE);
/*
|| packs message buffer from message table
*/
PROCEDURE pack_from_tbl
   (message_tbl_IN IN message_tbltype);

/*
|| forward a message from one pipe to another,
|| supports two techniques (safe and cool)
*/
PROCEDURE forward
   (from_pipename_IN IN VARCHAR2
   ,to_pipename_IN IN VARCHAR2
   ,timeout_secs_IN IN INTEGER := 10
   ,safe_mode_IN IN BOOLEAN := FALSE);

/*
|| takes sample message from a pipe and displays the
|| contents, replaces message back into pipe if
|| boolean parameter is TRUE
*/
PROCEDURE peek
   (pipename_IN IN VARCHAR2
   ,timeout_secs_IN IN INTEGER := 60
   ,replace_message_TF IN BOOLEAN := TRUE);

/*
|| encapsulates DBMS_PIPE.CREATE_PIPE and returns
|| FALSE if ORA-23322 is raised, indicating
|| the pipename is already used and not accessible
|| to the caller
*/
```

```
FUNCTION makepipe
    (pipename_IN IN VARCHAR2
    ,maxsize_bytes_IN IN INTEGER DEFAULT 8192
    ,private_IN IN BOOLEAN DEFAULT TRUE)
RETURN BOOLEAN;

/*
|| encapsulates DBMS_PIPE.REMOVE_PIPE and returns
|| FALSE if ORA-23322 is raised, indicating
|| the pipename exists and is not removable
|| by the caller
*/
FUNCTION closepipe
    (pipename_IN IN VARCHAR2)
RETURN BOOLEAN;

/*
|| purges all pipes the caller can access
*/
PROCEDURE purge_all_pipes;

END dbpipe;
```

Unpack_to_tbl and pack_from_tbl procedures. The two procedures unpack_to_
tbl and pack_from_tbl implement the generic unpack and pack functionality.
They use PL/SQL tables of records based on message_tbltype, which is designed
to hold an ordered list of items of any datatype. Each row in a table of type
message_tbltype contains two data values: an entry in the item_type field indicating the type of this message item (as returned by DBMS_PIPE.NEXT_ITEM_TYPE)
and an entry in the field of the corresponding datatype with the value of this message item. The unpack_to_tbl procedure unpacks all items in a newly received
message into a message table, indexing them in the table by their unpack order.
The pack_from_tbl procedure takes a message table loaded in this fashion and
repacks the original message into the message buffer in index order. The unpack_
to_tbl procedure can also optionally use the DBMS_OUTPUT built-in package
(described in Chapter 6, *Generating Output from PL/SQL Programs*) to display the
message unpacked.

Here are the full package bodies for unpack_to_tbl and pack_from_tbl. Note how
unpack_to_tbl grew out of the example code for the DBMS.PIPE.NEXT_ITEM_
TYPE function.

```
/* Filename on companion disk: dbpipe.sql */
PROCEDURE unpack_to_tbl
    (message_tbl_OUT OUT message_tbltype
    ,display_TF IN BOOLEAN := FALSE)
IS
    /*
    || NOTE: this procedure should only be called after
    || a successful call to DBMS_PIPE.RECEIVE_MESSAGE
```

```
     */

     /* empty table to flush output table on exception */
     null_message_tbl message_tbltype;

     /*
     || temp display variable extra long to account
     || for RAWTOHEX conversion that can double size
     */
     temp_varchar2  VARCHAR2(8186);

     next_item      INTEGER;
     item_count     INTEGER := 0;

BEGIN

     next_item := DBMS_PIPE.NEXT_ITEM_TYPE;

     /*
     || loop through all items, unpacking each by item
     || type and convert to varchar2 for display
     */
     WHILE next_item > 0
     LOOP
        /*
        || increment item count and store item type
        */
        item_count := item_count + 1;
        message_tbl_OUT(item_count).item_type := next_item;

        /*
        || now use next_item to call correct unpack procedure,
        || saving item to message_tbl
        ||
        || also stuff temp_varchar2 with string conversion
        || of the item
        */
        IF next_item = 9
        THEN
           DBMS_PIPE.UNPACK_MESSAGE
              (message_tbl_OUT(item_count).Mvarchar2);

           temp_varchar2 := 'VARCHAR2: '||
                    message_tbl_OUT(item_count).Mvarchar2;
        ELSIF next_item = 6
        THEN
           DBMS_PIPE.UNPACK_MESSAGE
              (message_tbl_OUT(item_count).Mnumber);

           temp_varchar2 := 'NUMBER: '||
                    TO_CHAR(message_tbl_OUT(item_count).Mnumber);

        ELSIF next_item = 11
           THEN
```

```
            DBMS_PIPE.UNPACK_MESSAGE_ROWID
                (message_tbl_OUT(item_count).Mrowid);

            temp_varchar2 := 'ROWID: '||
                ROWIDTOCHAR(message_tbl_OUT(item_count).Mrowid);

        ELSIF next_item = 12
        THEN
            DBMS_PIPE.UNPACK_MESSAGE
                (message_tbl_OUT(item_count).Mdate);

            temp_varchar2 := 'DATE: '||
                TO_CHAR(message_tbl_OUT(item_count).Mdate,
                                'YYYY:MM:DD:HH24:MI:SS');

        ELSIF next_item = 23
        THEN
            DBMS_PIPE.UNPACK_MESSAGE_RAW
                (message_tbl_OUT(item_count).Mraw);

            temp_varchar2 := 'RAW: '||
                RAWTOHEX(message_tbl_OUT(item_count).Mraw);

        ELSE
            temp_varchar2 := 'Invalid item type: '||
                                TO_CHAR(next_item);

            RAISE invalid_item_type;
        END IF;

        /*
        || display results and get next item type
        */
        IF display_TF
        THEN
            DBMS_OUTPUT.PUT_LINE(temp_varchar2);
        END IF;

        next_item := DBMS_PIPE.NEXT_ITEM_TYPE;

    END LOOP;

EXCEPTION
    WHEN invalid_item_type
    THEN
        message_tbl_OUT := null_message_tbl;

END unpack_to_tbl;


PROCEDURE pack_from_tbl
    (message_tbl_IN IN message_tbltype)
IS
    /*
```

```
      || packs the session message buffer from a generic
      || message table
      */
   BEGIN
      FOR i IN message_tbl_IN.FIRST..message_tbl_IN.LAST
      LOOP
         IF message_tbl_IN(i).item_type = 9
         THEN
            DBMS_PIPE.PACK_MESSAGE(message_tbl_IN(i).Mvarchar2);

         ELSIF message_tbl_IN(i).item_type = 6
         THEN
            DBMS_PIPE.PACK_MESSAGE(message_tbl_IN(i).Mnumber);

         ELSIF message_tbl_IN(i).item_type = 12
         THEN
            DBMS_PIPE.PACK_MESSAGE(message_tbl_IN(i).Mdate);

         ELSIF message_tbl_IN(i).item_type = 11
         THEN
            DBMS_PIPE.PACK_MESSAGE_ROWID(message_tbl_IN(i).Mrowid);

         ELSIF message_tbl_IN(i).item_type = 23
         THEN
            DBMS_PIPE.PACK_MESSAGE_RAW(message_tbl_IN(i).Mraw);

         END IF;

      END LOOP;

   ENDpack_from_tbl;
```

I really like these utilities, but they suffer from a potentially serious limitation inherited from Oracle's rather poor memory management for PL/SQL tables of records. Basically, each row of a PL/SQL table of type message_tbltype consumes at least enough memory to fill out the variable-length columns, which is greater than eight kilobytes. Thus, unpacking a message with more than a few items in it can result in a very large PL/SQL table. This is demonstrated by the following test results, which use the my_session.memory procedure (see Chapter 11, *Managing Session Information*) to display user session memory before and after unpacking a message.

```
/* Filename on companion disk: pipemem.sql. */
set serveroutput on size 100000

DECLARE
   null_msg_tbl dbpipe.message_tbltype;
   msg_tbl dbpipe.message_tbltype;
   call_stat  INTEGER;

BEGIN

   /* pack a message with a number of items */
```

```
    FOR i in 1..50
    LOOP
        DBMS_PIPE.PACK_MESSAGE('message number: '||TO_CHAR(i));
    END LOOP;

    /* send and receive the message */
    call_stat :=DBMS_PIPE.SEND_MESSAGE('PIPEX');
    call_stat :=DBMS_PIPE.RECEIVE_MESSAGE('PIPEX');

    /* use the generic unpack and show memory */
    dbpipe.unpack_to_tbl(msg_tbl,FALSE);
    my_session.memory;

    /* now free, release and show memory */
    msg_tbl := null_msg_tbl;
    DBMS_SESSION.FREE_UNUSED_USER_MEMORY;
    my_session.memory;

END;
/
session UGA: 41160
session PGA: 987576
session UGA: 41160
session PGA: 137760

PL/SQL procedure successfully completed.
```

The test shows that using unpack_to_tbl on a message with 50 items results in session PGA memory exceeding 900 kilobytes in size, most of which is wasted. Clearly, this is not a good scenario for a real application with many users, so the general usefulness of unpack_to_tbl and pack_from_tbl will have to wait until Oracle fixes these PL/SQL memory management problems.

NOTE   The problem caused by unpacking messages with more than a few items in them can result in a very large PL/SQL table that has been fixed in Oracle PL/SQL8.

The peek procedure. Developers or DBAs working with and testing DBMS_PIPE applications may really like the peek procedure built on top of the generic pack and unpack procedures. The peek procedure lets you pull a message off any pipe (which you have permission to use), look at its content, and place it back into the pipe, if you desire. Note that using peek will change the message order in the pipe, since database pipes are FIFO queues.

```
    /* Filename on companion disk: dbpipe.sql */
PROCEDURE peek
    (pipename_IN IN VARCHAR2
    ,timeout_secs_IN IN INTEGER := 60
```

```
                ,replace_message_TF IN BOOLEAN := TRUE)
      IS
          /*
      || Takes a sample message from a pipe, unpacks and displays
          || contents using unpack_to_tbl procedure.
          ||
          || If replace_message_TF parameter is TRUE (the default),
          || then the message is replaced into the pipe.NOTE: this
          || will change message order in the pipe.
          */

          message_tblmessage_tbltype;
          call_statusINTEGER;

          /* empty table used to free and release memory */
          null_message_tblmessage_tbltype;

      BEGIN

          call_status := DBMS_PIPE.RECEIVE_MESSAGE
              (pipename=>pipename_IN, timeout=>timeout_secs_IN);

          IF call_status = 0
          THEN
              unpack_to_tbl(message_tbl, display_TF=>TRUE);

              IF replace_message_TF
              THEN
                  /*
                  || repack message into initialized buffer
                  */
                  DBMS_PIPE.RESET_BUFFER;
                  pack_from_tbl(message_tbl);

                  /*
                  || replace message on the pipe
                  */
                  call_status := DBMS_PIPE.SEND_MESSAGE
                      (pipename=>pipename_IN, timeout=>0);
              END IF;

              /*
              || empty message_tbl and free memory
              */
              message_tbl := null_message_tbl;
              DBMS_SESSION.FREE_UNUSED_USER_MEMORY;

          END IF;

      END peek;
```

The peek procedure takes the memory management limitations into account. It returns memory consumed by the unpack_to_tbl procedure to the operating sys-

tem by initializing message_tbl and calling DBMS_SESSION.FREE_UNUSED_USER_
MEMORY.

The forward procedure. The final fun utility from dbpipe to be discussed here is
the forward procedure, which lets you forward a message from one pipe to
another. The procedure has four IN parameters:

from_pipename_IN and to_pipename_IN
> Receiving and sending pipes for the message forwarding.

timeout_secs_IN
> Determines the number of seconds to wait for a message to forward (on the
> pipe from_pipename_IN).

safe_mode_IN
> A Boolean that determines which of two message forwarding techniques to
> use (which I call "safe" and "cool"). *Safe mode forwarding* uses unpack_to_tbl
> and pack_from_tbl to physically unbundle and recreate the message before
> sending it on to_pipename_IN. *Cool mode forwarding* is based on the idea
> that the best way to forward a message should be to execute DBMS_
> PIPE.RECEIVE_MESSAGE followed immediately by DBMS_PIPE.SEND_MES-
> SAGE. After all, forwarding should be fast—so why bother with the overhead
> of unpacking and repacking?

Well, it turns out that you cannot just receive and immediately send a message
using DBMS_PIPE unless you have previously called the DBMS_PIPE.PACK_MES-
SAGE procedure. Why? I have no idea; it just seems to be another one of those
mysteries of DBMS_PIPE that I happened to discover during my experimentation.
I don't like the fact that it's mysterious, but I do like the fact that it works, so I
used this "feature" to implement the cool forwarding mode.

```
    /* Filename on companion disk: dbpipe.sql. */
PROCEDURE forward
     (from_pipename_IN IN VARCHAR2
     ,to_pipename_IN IN VARCHAR2
     ,timeout_secs_IN IN INTEGER := 10
     ,safe_mode_IN IN BOOLEAN := FALSE)
IS
     call_status INTEGER;
     message_tbl message_tbltype;

BEGIN
     /* initialize buffer */
     DBMS_PIPE.RESET_BUFFER;

     IF NOT safe_mode_IN
     THEN
         /*
         || do an initial pack so COOL mode forwarding will work,
```

```
       || why this is necessary is unknown
       */
       DBMS_PIPE.PACK_MESSAGE('bogus message');
   END IF;

   /*
   || receive the message on from_pipename, if success
   || then forward on to_pipename
   */
   call_status := DBMS_PIPE.RECEIVE_MESSAGE
               (pipename=>from_pipename_IN
               ,timeout=>timeout_secs_IN);

   IF call_status = 0
   THEN
       /*
       || safe mode does full unpack and repack
       */
       IF safe_mode_IN
       THEN
       unpack_to_tbl(message_tbl);
       pack_from_tbl(message_tbl);
       END IF;

       /*
       || OK, now send on to_pipename
       */
       call_status := DBMS_PIPE.SEND_MESSAGE
               (pipename=>to_pipename_IN
               ,timeout=>timeout_secs_IN);
   END IF;

END forward;
```

Implementing a server program

One common application of DBMS_PIPE is to implement an external service interface, as mentioned previously. This interface allows Oracle users to communicate with host operating system programs and receive data from them into their session context. What about writing a service provider program internal to Oracle? That is, what about writing a PL/SQL program that will listen on a database pipe and provide certain Oracle-based services to client sessions connected to the same Oracle database?

There are a number of possible applications of such internal service programs, including:

* Complex calculation engines
* Debug message logging
* Audit message logging

- Transaction concentrators

- Batch program scheduling

The pipesvr package

I have written a package that demonstrates how to use DBMS_PIPE to implement a basic PL/SQL server program and associated client programs. The package implements basic client-server communications, as well as a simple server-side debugger. Here is the specification for the pipesvr package:

```
/* Filename on companion disk: pipesvr.sql */
CREATE OR REPLACE PACKAGE pipesvr
AS
   /*
   || Illustrates the use of DBMS_PIPE to implement
   || communications between a PL/SQL background server
   || program and client programs.
   ||
   || Clients communicate requests over a database pipe
   || on which the server listens and receive responses
   || on pipes unique to each session.
   ||
   || The server can be set to place debugging info into a
   || table.
   ||
   || Author:  John Beresniewicz, Savant Corp
   ||
   || 10/04/97: created
   ||
   || Compilation Requirements:
   ||
   || EXECUTE on DBMS_PIPE
   ||
   || Execution Requirements:
   ||
   */

   /*
   || simple server program which listens indefinitely on
   || database pipe for instructions
   */
   PROCEDURE server;

   /*
   || Client programs
   */

   /* stop the server */
   PROCEDURE server_stop;

   /* turn server debug mode toggle on or off */
   PROCEDURE server_debug_on;
```

```
PROCEDURE server_debug_off;

/* get and display server status using DBMS_OUTPUT */
PROCEDURE server_status;
```

```
END pipesvr;
```

Once the server is running, it listens on a database pipe for client service requests. When a request is received, the server processes the request and goes back to listening on the pipe. In the case of the server_status client procedure call, the server sends its current status back to the client over a pipename unique to the session. The following record types and variables, declared in the package body of pipesvr, are used to implement the client-server communications:

```
/* used as a tag for this application */
app_id   VARCHAR2(10) := 'OPBIP$';

/* identifiers for message protocols */
request_protocol VARCHAR2(20) := app_id||'REQUEST$';
status_protocol  VARCHAR2(20) := app_id||'STATUS$';

/* server listens on this pipe */
request_pipe VARCHAR2(30) := app_id||'SERVER$';

/* client responses come on this pipe, unique to each client */
my_response_pipe VARCHAR2(100) := app_id||
                              DBMS_PIPE.UNIQUE_SESSION_NAME;

/*
|| requests to server made in this format,
|| should never need to override response_pipe
*/
TYPE request_rectype IS RECORD
      (response_pipe VARCHAR2(100) := my_response_pipe
      ,service  stop_req%TYPE
      );

/*
|| server reports status in this format
*/
TYPE status_rectype IS RECORD
      (start_date     DATE
      ,total_requests   INTEGER := 0
      ,debug_status  VARCHAR2(5) := 'OFF'
      );

/* private global for server current status */
status_rec status_rectype;
```

Message types. Two record types have been declared for the two kinds of messages that will be handled: service request messages (sent from client to server) and server status messages (sent from server to client). Corresponding to each record (message) type is a protocol identifier to use when unpacking messages.

Pipenames. The following pipenames are established for proper message separation:

- request_pipe, into which all client requests are placed for receipt by the server

- my_response_pipe, from which each session receives its response from the server

Pack/send, receive/unpack encapsulation. In keeping with the best practices for safe pipe communications, the following four (package private) procedures are implemented in the body of pipesvr (only the specifications are shown below):

```
/* Filename on companion disk: pipesvr.sql */
/*
|| private program to put service request on pipe,
|| called by client programs
*/
PROCEDURE pack_send_request
(request_rec_IN IN request_rectype
  ,return_code_OUT OUT NUMBER);

/*
|| private program to receive request on the
|| request pipe
*/
PROCEDURE receive_unpack_request
(timeout_IN IN INTEGER
  ,request_rec_OUT OUT request_rectype
  ,return_code_OUT OUT NUMBER);

/*
|| private program to put request on pipe,
|| called by client programs
*/
PROCEDURE pack_send_status
  (status_rec_IN IN status_rectype
  ,response_pipe_IN IN my_response_pipe%TYPE
  ,return_code_OUT OUT NUMBER);

/*
|| private program to receive status on unique
|| session pipe
*/
PROCEDURE receive_unpack_status
(timeout_IN IN INTEGER
,status_rec_OUT OUT status_rectype
,return_code_OUT OUT NUMBER);
```

The server procedure. The server procedure itself is quite straightforward. It begins by creating the request pipe and initializing its private status record. Then it loops forever (or until the terminate_TF boolean is TRUE) on request_pipe for client requests using receive_unpack_request. Valid requests are passed on to the process_request procedure, which encapsulates the inelegant IF...THEN logic required to handle various types of requests. Finally, when the loop terminates, due to setting terminate_TF to TRUE, the pipe is removed and the program ends.

The code for the server is surprisingly simple.

```
/* Filename on companion disk: pipesvr.sql */
PROCEDURE server
IS
   request_rec   request_rectype;
   temp_return_code   NUMBER;

BEGIN
   /* create pipe */
   temp_return_code := DBMS_PIPE.CREATE_PIPE(request_pipe);

   /* initialize status rec */
   status_rec.start_date := SYSDATE;
   status_rec.total_requests := 0;
   status_rec.debug_status := 'OFF';

   /*
   || loop forever and process requests
   */
   WHILE NOT terminate_TF
   LOOP
       receive_unpack_request
           (timeout_IN => DBMS_PIPE.maxwait
           ,request_rec_OUT=> request_rec
           ,return_code_OUT => temp_return_code);

       IF temp_return_code != 0
       THEN
           DBMS_PIPE.PURGE(request_pipe);
           debug('REQUEST PIPE STAT: '||temp_return_code);
       ELSE
           process_request(request_rec);
           debug('REQUEST PROCESSED');
       END IF;
   END LOOP;

   /*
   || terminating: remove pipe and exit
   */
   temp_return_code := DBMS_PIPE.REMOVE_PIPE(request_pipe);

EXCEPTION
   WHEN OTHERS THEN
       debug('SERVER EXCP: '||SQLERRM, force_TF_IN=>TRUE);
```

```
                temp_return_code := DBMS_PIPE.REMOVE_PIPE(request_pipe);

        END server;
```

The process_request procedure. When the server procedure receives a valid service request, it calls the process_request procedure. This procedure has the
responsibility of interpreting the service request and performing the requested
action. Note that this procedure sets the terminate_TF Boolean, which stops the
server. You must always code a stop routine into this type of service program, or
you will have to kill the process running the procedure. Other services performed
by process_request include setting debugging to on or off, and sending the
server's current status_rec back to the requesting session on a database pipe using
pack_send_status.

```
/* Filename on companion disk: pipesvr.sql */
/*
|| private program to encapsulate request processing
|| logic (lots of IF...THEN stuff) of server
*/
PROCEDURE process_request
    (request_rec_IN IN request_rectype)
IS
    temp_return_code NUMBER;
BEGIN
    /* increment total */
    status_rec.total_requests := status_rec.total_requests +1;

    /* stop the server, this is a MUST have */
    IF request_rec_IN.service = stop_req
    THEN
        terminate_TF := TRUE;

    ELSIF request_rec_IN.service = debugon_req
    THEN
        debug_TF := TRUE;
        status_rec.debug_status := 'ON';

    ELSIF request_rec_IN.service = debugoff_req
    THEN
        debug_TF := FALSE;
        status_rec.debug_status := 'OFF';

    ELSIF request_rec_IN.service = status_req
    THEN
        pack_send_status
            (status_rec_IN=>status_rec
            ,response_pipe_IN=> request_rec_IN.response_pipe
            ,return_code_OUT=> temp_return_code);
        debug('SEND STATUS: '||temp_return_code);
    /* unrecognized request */

    ELSE
```

```
        DBMS_PIPE.RESET_BUFFER;
        debug('UNKNOWN REQUEST: '||request_rec_IN.service);
    END IF;

END process_request;
```

Debug procedure. Notice that the server procedure makes several calls to a procedure called debug. The debug procedure dumps informational messages into a
simple table to allow tracking of server-side events. This procedure usually inserts
data to the table only if the server is in debug mode, as determined by the debug_
TF global variable. This prevents too many debugging rows from being inserted
when the server is operating normally. The debug procedure can be forced to
write to the table by setting a parameter called force_TF_IN to TRUE. This is used
to guarantee that certain debugging information gets into the table regardless of
the server's current debug mode. Debugging messages are usually forced in
exception handlers, as in the server procedure. Here is the source code for debug:

```
/* Filename on companion disk: pipesvr.sql */
/*
|| private program to put debug messages into table
|| if boolean is TRUE, or if force_IN is TRUE
|| NOTE: commits after inserting row
*/
PROCEDURE debug
    (message_IN IN VARCHAR2
    ,force_TF_IN IN BOOLEAN := FALSE)
IS
BEGIN
    IF debug_TF OR force_TF_IN
    THEN
        INSERT INTO pipesvr_debug
        VALUES (SYSDATE, message_IN);
        COMMIT;
    END IF;
END debug;
```

Client side procedures. The four client-side procedures all have to send specific
request records to the server, and the request records they use vary only in the
contents of the service field. I reduced code redundancy by creating the client_
request procedure as follows:

```
/* Filename on companion disk: pipesvr.sql. */
/*
|| private program to make simple service requests,
|| if request_rectype gets more complex or need more
|| flexibility use pack_send_request instead
*/
PROCEDURE client_request(request_IN IN stop_req%TYPE)
IS
```

```
        request_rec request_rectype;
        temp_return_code  NUMBER;

   BEGIN
        request_rec.service := request_IN;

        pack_send_request
            (request_rec_IN => request_rec
            ,return_code_OUT => temp_return_code);

   END client_request;
```

The client_request procedure loads the service field of a request record and then calls pack_send_request. This procedure helps simplify client programs, as seen in server_stop:

```
   PROCEDURE server_stop
   IS
   BEGIN
        client_request(stop_req);
   END server_stop;
```

The server_status procedure calls client_request and then waits for up to a minute on the receive_unpack_status procedure. If a status record is successfully received from the server, it is displayed using the DBMS_OUTPUT package.

I hope the pipesvr package will serve as a useful template to those seeking to implement PL/SQL service programs. It works and it incorporates the best practices for using DBMS_PIPE, so it should be a good starting point.

DBMS_ALERT: Broadcasting Alerts to Users

The DBMS_ALERT package provides a facility to broadcast notification of database events (alerts) to multiple users who have previously registered their interest in receiving those alerts. You will use the DBMS_ALERT package to implement applications that respond immediately to data modifications of interest to the application. In this way, you can avoid the need to do regular polling on the data to determine if changes have taken place. This is typically accomplished by having the application register to receive an alert on the specific data of interest, querying the data to establish a baseline, and then waiting for the alert to be signaled, which indicates the need to requery the data. Alerts can be automatically signaled using database triggers on the tables of interest, so that all modifications to the data will signal the alert, regardless of which application or user modified the data. Alerts are asynchronous and transaction-based, meaning that users can wait for and receive notification after the signaling event and that only committed transactions (usually involving data changes) will signal the alert.

Here are two good examples of applications that could be implemented using DBMS_ALERT:

- Graphical displays of statistics that must be updated whenever the underlying data changes

- An online auction where bidders want to be notified when they have been outbid on an item

Getting Started with DBMS_ALERT

The DBMS_ALERT package is created when the Oracle database is installed. The *dbmsalrt.sql* script (found in the built-in packages source code directory, as described in Chapter 1) contains the source code for this package's specification. This script is called by *catproc.sql*, which is normally run immediately after database creation. Under Oracle7, no privileges are automatically granted on DBMS_ALERT. Under Oracle8, the EXECUTE_CATALOG_ROLE role is granted EXECUTE privilege on DBMS_ALERT. Thus the DBMS_ALERT programs are not generally available to users. Access to DBMS_ALERT is obtained by granting EXECUTE privilege explicitly to users or roles that require use of the package.

Note also that a public synonym for DBMS_ALERT is not created automatically by *dbmsalrt.sql*, so references to the package's programs must be qualified by the owning schema (SYS), unless synonyms have been created. To create a public synonym for DBMS_ALERT, issue the following SQL command:

```
CREATE PUBLIC SYNONYM DBMS_ALERT FOR SYS.DBMS_ALERT;
```

DBMS_ALERT programs

Table 3-2 lists the programs included in the DBMS_ALERT package.

Table 3-2. DBMS_ALERT Programs

Name	Description	Use in SQL?
REGISTER	Registers interest in notification of an alert	No
REMOVE	Unregisters interest in notification of an alert	No
REMOVEALL	Unregisters interest in all alert notification	No
SET_DEFAULTS	Sets polling loop interval	No
SIGNAL	Signals the occurrence of an alert	No
WAITANY	Waits for any registered alerts to occur	No
WAITONE	Waits for a specific registered alert to occur	No

DBMS_ALERT does not declare any package exceptions of its own. Many of the individual programs raise Oracle exceptions under certain circumstances, as described in the following sections.

DBMS_ALERT nonprogram elements

The DBMS_ALERT package contains one nonprogram element, maxwait. It is defined as follows:

```
maxwait CONSTANT INTEGER := 86400000;
```

The maxwait constant is the maximum time to wait for an alert. It is used as the default value for the timeout parameter in the WAITONE and WAITANY procedures. The value of 86400000 seconds corresponds to 1000 days.

The DBMS_ALERT Interface

This section describes the programs available through the DBMS_ALERT package.

The DBMS_ALERT.REGISTER procedure

The REGISTER procedure registers interest in a specific alert by a database session. Once registered, the session will be notified of any occurrences of the alert. The header for this procedure is,

```
PROCEDURE DBMS_ALERT.REGISTER
    (name IN VARCHAR2);
```

where name is the name of the alert to register for notification.

Exceptions. The REGISTER procedure does not raise any package exceptions. It will raise an ORA-20000 exception for specific error conditions, with message text indicating the error as follows:

ORU-10021
  Lock request error; status: n

ORU-10025
  Lock request error; status: n

Restrictions. Note the following restrictions on calling REGISTER:

* Alert names are limited to 30 bytes and are case-insensitive.

* Alert names beginning with "ORA$" are reserved for use by Oracle Corporation.

Example. In this example, the session will be registered to be notified of the EMP_ INSERT alert, which is raised whenever INSERTs are performed on the EMP table:

```
BEGIN
    DBMS_ALERT.REGISTER('EMP_INSERT');
END;
```

The DBMS_ALERT.REMOVE procedure

The REMOVE procedure unregisters a session's interest in receiving notification of a specific alert. It has the following header,

```
PROCEDURE DBMS_ALERT.REMOVE
    (name IN VARCHAR2);
```

where name is the name of the alert to unregister from notification.

The REMOVE procedure does not raise any package exceptions, nor does it assert a purity level with the RESTRICT_REFERENCES pragma.

Example. The following example unregisters for the EMP_INSERT alert:

```
BEGIN
    DBMS_ALERT.REMOVE('EMP_INSERT');
END;
```

The DBMS_ALERT.REMOVEALL procedure

The REMOVEALL procedure unregisters the session from receiving notification of any and all alerts that have been previously registered. Here's the header:

```
PROCEDURE DBMS_ALERT.REMOVEALL;
```

The REMOVEALL procedure does not raise package exceptions, nor does it assert a purity level with the RESTRICT_REFERENCES pragma.

Example. This example stops all alert notifications to the session:

```
SQL> execute DBMS_ALERT.REMOVALL;
```

The DBMS_ALERT.SET_DEFAULTS procedure

The SET_DEFAULTS procedure is used to set session configurable settings used by the DBMS_ALERT package. Currently, the polling loop interval sleep time is the only session setting that can be modified using this procedure. The header for this procedure is,

```
PROCEDURE DBMS_ALERT.SET_DEFAULTS
    (sensitivity IN NUMBER);
```

where sensitivity is the polling interval sleep time in seconds.

The SET_DEFAULTS procedure does not raise any package exceptions.

Example. The following example sets the polling interval to one second:

```
SQL>  execute DBMS_ALERT.SET_DEFAULTS(600);
```

Setting the polling interval is relevant primarily to users of DBMS_ALERT under Oracle Parallel Server (OPS), since under OPS a polling loop is required to check for alerts issued from another Oracle instance.

The DBMS_ALERT.SIGNAL procedure

The SIGNAL procedure posts notification of the occurrence of an alert, which is then propagated to all sessions registered for the alert. Alert notification happens only if and when the signaling transaction COMMITs. Here's the header:

```
PROCEDURE DBMS_ALERT.SIGNAL
    (name IN VARCHAR2
    ,message IN VARCHAR2);
```

Parameters are summarized in the following table.

Name	Description
name	Name of the alert to signal
message	Message to associate and pass on with the alert

When you are signaling alerts using SIGNAL, it is important to COMMIT (or ROLL-BACK) the signaling transaction as soon as possible. Several problems can develop when signaling transactions are held open too long, including the following:

- Other sessions signaling this alert will block and wait until the COMMIT.

- Under the multithreaded server, a shared server will be bound to the session until the COMMIT.

- The signaling session will receive an error if it waits on the alert prior to a COMMIT.

If the signaling transaction is rolled back, no sessions will be notified of the alert. Thus the alerts in DBMS_ALERT are strictly transaction-based.

Multiple sessions can signal the same alert. Note that this process is serialized using DBMS_LOCK (described in Chapter 4, *User Lock and Transaction Management*) and can add significant wait times unless transactions are closed quickly (as noted earlier).

Exceptions. This program does not raise any package exceptions. It will raise an ORA-20000 exception for specific error conditions, with message text indicating the error as follows:

ORU-10001
    Lock request error, status: n

ORU-10016

Error: n sending on pipe 'pipename'

ORU-10017

Error: n receiving on pipe 'pipename'

ORU-10022

Lock request error, status: n

Restrictions. Note the following restrictions on calling SIGNAL:

- Alert names are limited to 30 bytes and are case-insensitive.

- Alert names beginning with "ORA$" are reserved for use by Oracle Corporation.

- RESTRICT_REFERENCES cannot be called in SQL.

Example. This trigger will signal the EMP_INSERT alert when rows are inserted into the EMP table. The empid column is passed as the alert message for receivers of the alert to use:

```
CREATE OR REPLACE TRIGGER emp_ARI
AFTER INSERT ON emp
FOR EACH ROW
BEGIN
   /*
   || signal alert that emp has been inserted,
   || passing the empid as alert message
   */
   DBMS_ALERT.SIGNAL('EMP_INSERT', :NEW.empid);
   END IF;

END emp_ARI;
/
```

The DBMS_ALERT.WAITANY procedure

The WAITANY procedure waits for notification of any alerts for which the session is registered. The procedure call will complete when the first alert is signaled or when the wait timeout is reached. Here's the header:

```
PROCEDURE DBMS_ALERT.WAITANY
   (name OUT VARCHAR2
   ,message OUT VARCHAR2
   ,status OUT INTEGER
   ,timeout IN NUMBER DEFAULT MAXWAIT);
```

Parameters are summarized in the following table.

Name	Description
name	Name of the alert that occurred
message	Message attached to alert when signaled
status	Status of WAITANY call: 0 means alert; 1 means timeout
timeout	Time in seconds to wait for alerts

When multiple alerts for which the session is registered have been signaled, the call to WAITANY will return the most recent alert that has occurred.

If a session waits on an alert that it has also signaled, a lock request exception will occur unless a COMMIT has taken place between the calls to the SIGNAL and WAITANY procedures.

The WAITANY call uses a polling loop to detect alerts. This avoids notification problems that could otherwise occur when signaled, but uncommitted alerts mask notification of subsequent committed alerts. The polling loop begins with a 1-second interval that increases exponentially to 30 seconds.

Exceptions. The program does not raise any package exceptions. The program will raise an ORA-20000 exception for specific error conditions, with message text indicating the error as follows:

ORU-10002
> Lock request error, status: n

ORU-10015
> Error: n waiting for pipe status

ORU-10020
> Error: n waiting on lock request

ORU-10024
> No alerts registered

Restrictions. Note the following restrictions on WAITANY:

- The message parameter is limited to 1800 bytes in length.
- WAITANY cannot be called in SQL.

Example. This example waits five minutes to receive the next alert for which the session is registered. If an alert is received, it is displayed. If the EMP_INSERT alert is received, the employee id should be the message, and the employee status is changed without displaying the alert.

```
DECLARE
   alert_msg      VARCHAR2(1800);
   alert_status   INTEGER;
   alert_name;
BEGIN
   DBMS_ALERT.WAITANY(alert_name, alert_msg, alert_status, 300);

   IF alert_status = 1
   THEN
      DBMS_OUTPUT.PUT_LINE('timed out');

   ELSIF alert_name = 'EMP_INSERT'
   THEN
      UPDATE emp SET status = 'REGISTERED'
      WHERE empid := alert_msg;

   ELSE
      DBMS_OUTPUT.PUT_LINE('received alert: '||alert_name);
   END IF;
END;
/
```

The DBMS_ALERT.WAITONE procedure

The WAITONE procedure waits to be notified of an occurrence of the specified
alert. The procedure call will complete when the alert is signaled or when the
wait timeout is reached. Here's the header:

```
PROCEDURE DBMS_ALERT.WAITONE
   (name IN VARCHAR2
   ,message OUT VARCHAR2
   ,status OUT INTEGER
   ,timeout IN NUMBER DEFAULT MAXWAIT);
```

Parameters are summarized in the following table.

Name	Description
name	Name of the alert to wait for
message	Message attached to alert when signaled
status	Status of WAITONE call: 0 means alert; 1 means timeout
timeout	Time in seconds to wait for alerts

Note the following special cases:

- If the alert has been registered and signaled prior to the call to the WAITONE
  procedure, the call will return immediately with the most recent occurrence of
  the alert.

- When multiple instances of the alert have been signaled, the call to WAIT-
  ONE will return the most recent occurrence of the alert.

- If a session waits for and has also signaled the alert, a lock request exception will occur unless a COMMIT has taken place between the calls to the SIGNAL and WAITONE procedures.

Exceptions. This program does not raise any package exceptions. The program will raise an ORA-20000 exception for specific error conditions, with message text indicating the error as follows:

ORU-10019

> Error: n on lock request

ORU-10023

> Lock request error; status: n

ORU-10037

> Attempting to wait on uncommitted signal from same session

Restrictions. Note the following restrictions on WAITONE:

- The message parameter is limited to 1800 bytes in length.

- The WAITONE procedure cannot be called in SQL.

Example. This example waits specifically on the EMP_INSERT alert and updates the status when it is signaled:

```
DECLARE
    alert_msg       VARCHAR2(1800);
    alert_status    INTEGER;
BEGIN
    DBMS_ALERT.WAITONE('EMP_INSERT', alert_msg, alert_status, 300);

    IF alert_status = 1
    THEN
        DBMS_OUTPUT.PUT_LINE('timed out');

    ELSE
        UPDATE emp SET status = 'REGISTERED'
        WHERE empid := alert_msg;

        DBMS_OUTPUT.PUT_LINE('employee registered');
    END IF;
END;
/
```

DBMS_ALERT Examples

The DBMS_ALERT package is a good example of how you can build higher-level functionality out of lower-level built-ins. Both the DBMS_LOCK and DBMS_PIPE packages are used extensively in the implementation of DBMS_ALERT.

TIP   If you have an old Version 7.1 installation of Oracle, you can check
              out *dbmsalrt.sql* to see exactly how this is done, since the code is
              not wrapped.

An important feature of the alerting mechanism in DBMS_ALERT is that it is transaction-based. This means that alerts will be sent to registered sessions only if and
when the signaling session issues a COMMIT. If the signaler issues a ROLLBACK
instead, the alerts will not be sent. Applications that are interested only in real
changes to data in the database will benefit from using transaction-based alerts.
Applications that need to signal other sessions regardless of transaction boundaries or data modifications (like debuggers or auditing monitors) will probably
need to use DBMS_PIPE instead of DBMS_ALERT.

What kind of application might actually need to be alerted to changes in data?
The classic example given in the Oracle documentation is a continuous graphical
display of data extracted from some table. Pulling data from the table at set intervals using a polling mechanism can be very inefficient. For one thing, the data
may not have changed since the last pull, so a refresh is not really necessary.
Also, if the application is separated from the database by a network (as it most
likely would be), then the overhead of redundant data extraction is multiplied. In
this example, the application could use DBMS_ALERT to suspend itself and wait
for a signal to awaken and pull new data for the display. The signal will be
received only when data in the table has actually been modified (i.e., a new pull
is truly necessary).

The online auction

Well, I wanted to do something new and original. I spent some time thinking
about other examples for using DBMS_ALERT. Finally, I realized that I had partici-
pated in a perfect application for this technology many times already: an online
auction. During an auction (especially a virtual one over a computer network), it
is important to know when an item you have a bidding interest in has been bid
upon. In a traditional auction, this happens because items are auctioned off seri-
ally, so bids can only be placed on the current item. In an online auction, the participants are not in a room together, and the auction itself typically takes longer
than a traditional auction. Also, it is desirable to auction multiple items simultaneously, taking advantage of the virtual nature of the auction. An auction application that notifies participants of bidding activity relevant (to them) would relieve
them of having to constantly monitor their screens to stay abreast of the auction.
Bidding could take place simultaneously on multiple items since users interested
in those items would automatically be notified of new bids.

The auction schema

The online auction was perfect for DBMS_ALERT, so I set about to prove the concept. First, I needed a basic schema. Professional data modelers may wince, but I came up with the following:

Object	Type	Description
AUCTION_ITEMS	TABLE	Items up for auction
BIDS	TABLE	Bids on auction items
HIGH_BIDS	VIEW	High bids by item

These objects are created by the *auction.ddl* script, reproduced as follows:

```
/* Filename on companion disk:  auction.ddl */
rem ********************************************************
rem   AUCTION.DDL
rem
rem   Creates objects used in the "online auction" example
rem   for the DBMS_ALERT package.
rem
rem   Auction_items -- table of items being auctioned
rem   Bids -- table of bids placed on items
rem   High_bids -- view showing the current high bids on
rem                items and who placed them
rem
rem   Author:  John Beresniewicz, Savant Corp
rem
rem
rem   12/07/97: created
rem ********************************************************
DROP VIEW high_bids;
DROP TABLE bids;
DROP TABLE auction_items;

CREATE TABLE auction_items
    (id            VARCHAR2(20)   NOT NULL PRIMARY KEY
    ,description    VARCHAR2(200) NOT NULL
    ,min_bid        NUMBER        NOT NULL
    ,curr_bid       NUMBER
    ,status         VARCHAR2(10)
                    CONSTRAINT    valid_status
                    CHECK (status IN ('OPEN','CLOSED') )
    );

CREATE TABLE bids
    (bidder        VARCHAR2(30)
    ,item_id       VARCHAR2(20)
                   REFERENCES auction_items(id)
                   ON DELETE CASCADE
    ,bid           NUMBER         NOT NULL
    );
```

```
CREATE OR REPLACE VIEW high_bids
    (item_id
    ,item_desc
    ,bidder
    ,high_bid)
AS
SELECT
        BID.item_id
       ,AI.description
       ,BID.bidder
       ,BID.bid
   FROM
        bids            BID
       ,auction_items  AI
   WHERE
        BID.item_id    = AI.id
    AND BID.bid        = (SELECT  MAX(bid)
                            FROM  bids      B2
                           WHERE  BID.item_id = B2.item_id)
  /
```

The AUCTION_ITEMS table contains an identifier and a description of each auction item. There are also columns for the minimum bid, status, and current high bid. This latter is really redundant with information derived in the HIGH_BIDS view, but this denormalization makes for a more interesting example.

The BIDS table holds the bidding activity. Each bid is a bid on an auction_item by a user for a specified amount. Originally, I had a BIDDERS table to track the auction participants, and this would likely be necessary for a real-world application. However, to simplify the example I decided to use the Oracle session username to identify bidders. Thus, there is an assumption that the online auction users will all be connected using unique usernames. The BIDS table also has a complex integrity constraint, which states that all bids must exceed the previous high bid for the same item (this is, after all, how an auction works). An additional constraint is that no bids may be updated or deleted from the table. These constraints are enforced by database triggers discussed later.

The HIGH_BIDS view selects the highest bid for each item along with the item's description and the bidder who made the bid. The auction application's GUI component can make use of this view to display current bidding levels for all items.

Auction system requirements

Some basic requirements of the online auction application are as follows:

- Enforce the complex integrity constraint on the BIDS table.

- Enforce the no-update, no-delete rule on the BIDS table.

- Update the CURR_BID column of AUCTION_ITEMS for new bids.

- Inform bidders when they have been outbid on an item.

- Inform bidders when an item is closed from further bidding.

There is certainly more than one way to satisfy these requirements, especially the data integrity constraints on the two tables. I decided to implement a combination of database triggers and a package called auction. The database triggers enforce some data integrity constraints and signal changes to interested bidders using DBMS_ALERT.SIGNAL. A procedure called place_bid is responsible for placing bids on items, making sure that the complex integrity constraint is satisfied, and that the bidder is registered to receive notice of any bidding or status changes on the item. Another packaged procedure, called watch_bidding, demonstrates how an application might use DBMS_ALERT.WAITANY to be alerted for any bidding activity of interest to the user.

One immediate issue to address is what the alert names should be. The auction_items.id column seems a natural option since all alerts will concern a specific item.

Integrity constraint triggers

Here are the triggers for the auction_items and bids tables:

```
/* Filename on companion disk:  auction2.sql */
CREATE OR REPLACE TRIGGER auction_items_ARU
AFTER UPDATE ON auction_items
FOR EACH ROW
BEGIN
   /*
   || trigger enforces no update of item_id and also
   || signals an alert when status changes
   */
   IF UPDATING ('ITEM_ID')
   THEN
      RAISE_APPLICATION_ERROR(-20000, 'Cannot update item id');

   ELSIF UPDATING ('STATUS') AND (:NEW.status != :OLD.status)
   THEN
      /* send new status on as the alert message */
      DBMS_ALERT.SIGNAL(:NEW.id, :NEW.status);
   END IF;
END auction_items_ARU;
/

CREATE OR REPLACE TRIGGER bids_ARIUD
AFTER INSERT OR UPDATE OR DELETE ON bids
FOR EACH ROW
BEGIN
   /*
   || enforce all bids are final rule
   */
   IF UPDATING OR DELETING
   THEN
```

```
      RAISE_APPLICATION_ERROR
         (-20001, 'Cannot update or delete, all bids final!');
  ELSE
  /*
  || signal alert on item, send bidder name as message
  */
      DBMS_ALERT.SIGNAL(:NEW.item_id, :NEW.bidder);
  END IF;

END bids_ARIUD;
/
```

The triggers enforce the basic integrity rules that auction_items.id is a non-updatable column and that rows in the BIDS table cannot be updated or deleted. More importantly, they signal database alerts to registered sessions that auction data has changed using DBMS_ALERT.SIGNAL. The trigger on auction items signals status changes for items. Note the additional check requiring that :NEW.status be different from :OLD.status in order for the alert to be signaled. Also note that the item id is used as the alert name and that the new item status is passed as the alert's message. The trigger on BIDS signals the alert named by the item id and passes the bidder's name as the message. The use of the message parameter with the alerts allows the alert receiver to implement a context-sensitive response to the alert.

By the way, my naming convention for triggers has the table name suffixed by a string like [A|B][R|S][I|U|D] where:

- A or B indicates an AFTER or BEFORE trigger

- R or S indicates ROW or STATEMENT level trigger

- I and/or U and/or D indicates an INSERT or UPDATE or DELETE

The auction package

The rest of the online auction requirements are implemented in the auction package. Here is the package specification:

```
/* Filename on companion disk:  auction1.sql */
CREATE OR REPLACE PACKAGE auction
   /*
   || Implements a simple interactive bidding system
   || using DBMS_ALERT to keep bidders informed
   || of activity in items they are interested in.
   ||
   || The item_id is used as the ALERT name for the
   || item.
   ||
   || Author:  John Beresniewicz, Savant Corp
   ||
   || 12/07/97: created
   ||
```

```
        || Compilation Requirements:
        ||
        || EXECUTE on DBMS_ALERT
        || SELECT, UPDATE on AUCTION_ITEMS
        || INSERT on BIDS
        || SELECT on HIGH_BIDS
        ||
        || Execution Requirements:
        ||
        */
   AS
        /*
        || exceptions raised and handled in PLACE_BID
        || procedure
        */
        invalid_item    EXCEPTION;
        bid_too_low     EXCEPTION;
        item_is_closed EXCEPTION;

        /*
        || place a bid on an item, the bid must exceed any
        || other bids on the item (and the minimum bid)
        ||
        || bidding on an item registers interest in the
        || item using DBMS_ALERT.REGISTER
        ||
        || only this procedure should be used to add rows
        || to the bids table, since it also updates
        || auction_items.curr_bid column
        */
        PROCEDURE place_bid
           (item_id_IN IN VARCHAR2
           ,bid_IN IN NUMBER);

        /*
        || close bidding on an item
        */
        PROCEDURE close_item(item_id_IN IN VARCHAR2);

        /*
        || watch for any alerts on items bid by the user
        || indicating other users have raised the bid
        */
        PROCEDURE watch_bidding(timeout_secs_IN IN NUMBER:=300);

   END auction;
    /
```

Place_bid procedure. The place_bid procedure is intended to be used by the GUI application to place all bids in the auction. No INSERTS or UPDATES to the BIDS table should be allowed except through this procedure, as it maintains the complex integrity constraint on the table, updates the curr_bid column of AUCTION_

ITEMS, and registers the session for receiving alerts on the item. The body of place_bid looks like this:

```
/* Filename on companion disk: auction1.sql */
PROCEDURE place_bid
     (item_id_IN IN VARCHAR2
     ,bid_IN IN NUMBER)
  IS
     temp_curr_bid auction_items.curr_bid%TYPE;
     temp_statusauction_items.status%TYPE;

     CURSOR auction_item_cur
     IS
     SELECT NVL(curr_bid,min_bid), status
         FROM auction_items
         WHERE id = item_id_IN
         FOR UPDATE OF curr_bid;

  BEGIN
     /*
     || lock row in auction_items
     */
     OPEN auction_item_cur;
     FETCH auction_item_cur INTO temp_curr_bid, temp_status;

     /*
     || do some validity checks
     */
     IF auction_item_cur%NOTFOUND
     THEN
         RAISE invalid_item;

     ELSIF temp_status = 'CLOSED'
     THEN
         RAISE item_is_closed;

     ELSIF bid_IN <= temp_curr_bid
     THEN
         RAISE bid_too_low;

     ELSE
         /*
         || insert to bids AND update auction_items,
         || bidders identified by session username
         */
         INSERT INTO bids (bidder, item_id, bid)
         VALUES (USER, item_id_IN, bid_IN);

         UPDATE auction_items
         SET curr_bid = bid_IN
         WHERE CURRENT OF auction_item_cur;

         /*
```

```
                || commit is important because it will send
                || the alert notifications out on the item
                */
                COMMIT;

                /*
                || register for alerts on item since bidding,
                || register after commit to avoid ORU-10002
                */
                DBMS_ALERT.REGISTER(item_id_IN);

        END IF;

        CLOSE auction_item_cur;

EXCEPTION
     WHEN invalid_item
          THEN
               ROLLBACK WORK;
               RAISE_APPLICATION_ERROR
                    (-20002,'PLACE_BID ERR: invalid item');
     WHEN bid_too_low
          THEN
               ROLLBACK WORK;
               RAISE_APPLICATION_ERROR
                    (-20003,'PLACE_BID ERR: bid too low');
     WHEN item_is_closed
          THEN
               ROLLBACK WORK;
               RAISE_APPLICATION_ERROR
                    (-20004,'PLACE_BID ERR: item is closed');
     WHEN OTHERS
          THEN
               ROLLBACK WORK;
               RAISE;
END place_bid;
```

There are a few things to notice about place_bid. First, the row in AUCTION_ITEMS is locked FOR UPDATE to begin the transaction. I chose not to use NOWAIT in the cursor, because the transaction is small and should be quite fast, minimizing contention problems. The COMMIT immediately follows the INSERT and UPDATE and precedes the call to DBMS_ALERT.REGISTER. Originally I had it the other way around, but kept getting ORU-10002 errors when calling DBMS_ALERT.WAITANY immediately after place_bid. What was happening was that the call to DBMS_ALERT.REGISTER was holding a user lock that the insert trigger to BIDS was also trying to get. By doing the COMMIT first, the trigger is able to acquire and release the lock, which can then be acquired by DBMS_ALERT.REGISTER.

NOTE	To avoid the locking problems mentioned, be careful to code applications in such a way that a COMMIT will occur between calls to SIGNAL and REGISTER.

Exception handling. Exception handling in place_bid is inelegant but useful. The package defines named exceptions that place_bid detects, raises, and then handles using RAISE_APPLICATION_ERROR. In practice, it may be better to pass these out from the procedure to the calling application and let it handle them. Since I was prototyping in SQL*Plus and wanted to see the exception and an error message immediately, I used RAISE_APPLICATION_ERROR. When using DBMS_ALERT, note also that it is very important to terminate transactions to avoid the locking problems mentioned earlier, so the EXCEPTION section makes sure to include ROLLBACK WORK statements.

The watch_bidding procedure. With the triggers and the place_bid procedure in place, the online auction system is basically ready to go. Since a real application would involve a GUI, but I was prototyping in SQL*Plus, I needed a way to simulate what the GUI should do to receive DBMS_ALERT signals and inform the user of auction activity. This is basically what the watch_bidding procedure does. It could be modified and called directly from the GUI or its logic could be adapted and embedded into the GUI. The watch_bidding procedure uses DBMS_OUTPUT to display bidding alerts received. It also demonstrates the use of the alert message to implement a context-sensitive response to alerts.

Here is the source code for watch_bidding:

```
/* Filename on companion disk:auction1.sql */
PROCEDURE watch_bidding(timeout_secs_IN IN NUMBER:=300)
IS
     temp_nameVARCHAR2(30);
     temp_message VARCHAR2(1800);
     temp_statusINTEGER;
BEGIN
     /*
     || enter a loop which will be exited explicitly
     || when a new bid from another user received or
     || DBMS_ALERT.WAITANY call times out
     */
     LOOP
          /*
          || wait for up to timeout_secs_IN for any alert
          */
          DBMS_ALERT.WAITANY
               (temp_name, temp_message, temp_status, timeout_secs_IN);

          IF temp_status = 1
```

```
      THEN
            /*
            || timed out, return control to application
            || so it can do something here if necessary
            */
            EXIT;

      ELSIF temp_message = 'CLOSED'
      THEN
            /*
            || unregister closed item, re-enter loop
            */
            DBMS_ALERT.REMOVE(temp_name);
            DBMS_OUTPUT.PUT_LINE('Item '||temp_name||
                        ' has been closed.');

      ELSIF temp_message = USER OR temp_message = 'OPEN'
      THEN
            /*
            || bid was posted by this user (no need to alert)
            || re-enter loop and wait for another
            */
            NULL;

      ELSE
            /*
            || someone raised the bid on an item this user is bidding
            || on, application should refresh user's display with a
            || query on the high_bids view and/or alert visually
            || (we will just display a message)
            ||
            || exit loop and return control to user so they can bid
            */
            DBMS_OUTPUT.PUT_LINE
                ('Item '||temp_name||' has new bid: '||
                TO_CHAR(curr_bid(temp_name),'$999,999.00')||
                ' placed by: '||temp_message);
            EXIT;
      END IF;
    END LOOP;

  END watch_bidding;
```

The watch_bidding procedure uses DBMS_ALERT.WAITANY to wait for any alerts for which the session has registered. In the auction system, registering for alerts is done when a bid is placed using place_bid. When an alert is received, the name of the alert is the auction item that has been updated. The alert message is used to respond intelligently to the alert as follows:

* If the alert signals that bidding is closed on the item, the procedure unregisters the alert using DBMS_ALERT.REMOVE and waits for another alert.

* If the alert was raised by the current user placing a bid or indicates that bidding has been opened on the item, the procedure waits for another alert.

- If the DBMS_ALERT.WAITANY call times out, control is passed back to the caller.

- If the alert is raised by another user, a message is displayed and control is passed back to the caller (so the user can make a new bid).

Testing the system

So the question is, does it work? I inserted some rows into the AUCTION_ITEMS table as follows:

```
/* Filename on companion disk:  auction3.sql */
INSERT INTO auction_items
VALUES ('GB123','Antique gold bracelet',350.00,NULL,'OPEN');

INSERT INTO auction_items
VALUES ('PS447','Paul Stankard paperweight',550.00,NULL,'OPEN');

INSERT INTO auction_items
VALUES ('SC993','Schimmel print',750.00,NULL,'OPEN');

COMMIT;
```

I granted EXECUTE privilege on the AUCTION package to two users, USER01 and USER02, and connected two SQL*Plus sessions, one for each user. Then I initiated a bidding war using the following PL/SQL block:

```
/* Filename on companion disk:  auction4.sql */
set serveroutput on size 100000
set verify off
BEGIN
    opbip.auction.place_bid('GB123',&bid);
    opbip.auction.watch_bidding(300);
END;
/
```

On each execution of the previous block in each session, I raised the bid. Here are the results from the USER01 session:

```
SQL> @auction4
Enter value for bid: 1000
Item GB123 has new bid:    $1,100.00 placed by: USER02

PL/SQL procedure successfully completed.

SQL> /
Enter value for bid: 1200
Item GB123 has new bid:    $1,300.00 placed by: USER02

PL/SQL procedure successfully completed.
```

USER01 opened the bidding on GB123 with a $1000 bid, which was quickly upped by USER02 to $1100, so USER01 came back with $1200 only to be topped finally by the winning $1300 bid by USER02. USER02's log of events confirms this exciting back and forth bidding war:

```
SQL> @auction4
Enter value for bid: 1100
Item PS447 has been closed.
Item GB123 has new bid:    $1,200.00 placed by: USER01

PL/SQL procedure successfully completed.

SQL> /
Enter value for bid: 1300

PL/SQL procedure successfully completed.
```

Note that each user is informed only of bids placed by the other user, and not of their own bids. Note also that USER02 was alerted to the fact that item PS447 (the subject of the previous bidding by USER02) had been closed.

So the auction system really does work, and quite well, as a matter of fact!

4

User Lock and Transaction Management

Complex, multiuser applications that manage new types of resources (objects, BLOBs, etc.) require the ability to manage contention for those resources. The Oracle database manages concurrent, multiuser contention for data using sophisticated locking mechanisms. This chapter describes two packages that provide interfaces to the Oracle lock and transaction management facilities:

DBMS_LOCK

Oracle now provides developers with the "keys" to its locking mechanisms through the DBMS_LOCK package; watch out, though, this deceptively powerful package might also put your applications to "sleep!"

DBMS_TRANSACTION

Complements DBMS_LOCK by providing a programmatic interface to a number of transaction-oriented SQL statements.

DBMS_LOCK: Creating and Managing Resource Locks

The DBMS_LOCK package makes Oracle lock management services available to PL/SQL developers. User locks created and managed using DBMS_LOCK are functionally identical to native RDBMS locks, even down to the various sharing modes and the deadlock detection.

Locks are typically used to provide serialized access to some resource. Within the database, the most familiar use of locking is to prevent multiple users from updating the same row in a table at the same time. Using DBMS_LOCK, applications can be written that serialize and coordinate access or usage of nondata resources. For instance, user locks can be used to do the following:

- Provide exclusive access to an external device or service (e.g., a printer)
- Coordinate or synchronize parallelized applications
- Disable or enable execution of programs at specific times
- Detect whether a session has ended a transaction using COMMIT or ROLL-BACK

Getting Started with DBMS_LOCK

The DBMS_LOCK package is created when the Oracle database is installed. The *dbmslock.sql* script (found in the built-in packages source code directory, as described in Chapter 1, *Introduction*) contains the source code for this package's specification. This script is called by *catproc.sql*, which is normally run immediately after database creation. The script creates the public synonym DBMS_LOCK for the package. Under Oracle7, no privileges are automatically granted on DBMS_LOCK. Under Oracle8, the EXECUTE_CATALOG_ROLE role is granted EXECUTE privilege on DBMS_LOCK. Thus, the DBMS_LOCK programs are not generally available to users. Access to DBMS_LOCK is obtained by granting EXECUTE privilege explicitly to users or roles that require use of the package.

DBMS_LOCK programs

Table 4-1 lists the programs available in the DBMS_LOCK package.

Table 4-1. DBMS_LOCK Programs

Name	Description	Use in SQL?
ALLOCATE_UNIQUE	Generates a unique lock ID for a given lock name	No
CONVERT	Converts lock to specified mode	No
RELEASE	Releases previously acquired lock	No
REQUEST	Requests lock with specified mode	No
SLEEP	Suspends the session for a specified time	No

DBMS_LOCK does not declare any package exceptions, and none of its programs assert a purity level with the RESTRICT_REFERENCES pragma.

DBMS_LOCK nonprogram elements

DBMS_LOCK declares a number of constants, most of which identify specific locking modes. Table 4-2 describes these elements.

Table 4-2. DBMS_LOCK Declared Constants

Constant	Description
nl_mode CONSTANT INTEGER	Null lock mode
ss_mode CONSTANT INTEGER	Sub-shared lock mode
sx_mode CONSTANT INTEGER	Sub-exclusive lock mode
s_mode CONSTANT INTEGER	Shared lock mode
ssx_mode CONSTANT INTEGER	Sub-shared exclusive lock mode
x_mode CONSTANT INTEGER	Exclusive lock mode
maxwait CONSTANT INTEGER	Used as default for timeout parameters

Lock compatibility rules

A lock held by one user session in a certain mode may prevent another session from being able to obtain that lock in the same or another mode. There are lock compatibility rules determining the success or failure of acquiring and converting locks from one mode to another, depending on the modes in which the same lock is held by other sessions. Table 4-3 indicates the compatibility rules for the various lock modes. The HELD MODE column indicates the mode in which the lock is currently held by some session. The other columns indicate whether the lock can be obtained by other sessions in the mode specified by the column header.

Table 4-3. Lock Mode Compatibility

HELD MODE	GET NL	GET SS	GET SX	GET S	GET SSX	GET X
NL	Succeed	Succeed	Succeed	Succeed	Succeed	Succeed
SS	Succeed	Succeed	Succeed	Succeed	Succeed	Fail
SX	Succeed	Succeed	Succeed	Fail	Fail	Fail
S	Succeed	Succeed	Fail	Succeed	Fail	Fail
SSX	Succeed	Succeed	Fail	Fail	Fail	Fail
X	Succeed	Fail	Fail	Fail	Fail	Fail

The DBMS_LOCK Interface

This section contains descriptions of all of the procedures and functions available through DBMS_LOCK.

The DBMS_LOCK.ALLOCATE_UNIQUE procedure

The ALLOCATE_UNIQUE procedure returns a unique "handle" to a lock specified by the lockname parameter. The handle can be used to safely identify locks in calls to other DBMS_LOCK programs. Using lockhandles avoids the potential for lock identifier collisions that exists when identifiers are determined by applications. The header for this program follows:

```
PROCEDURE DBMS_LOCK.ALLOCATE_UNIQUE
    (lockname IN VARCHAR2
    ,lockhandle OUT VARCHAR2
    ,expiration_secs IN INTEGER DEFAULT 864000);
```

Parameters for this procedure are summarized in the following table.

Parameter	Description
lockname	Name of the lock
lockhandle	Unique handle to lock by name
expiration_secs	Length of time to leave lock allocated

The program does not raise any package exceptions.

Restrictions. Note the following restrictions on calling ALLOCATE_UNIQUE:

- Lock names can be up to 128 characters in length and are case-sensitive.

- Lock names must not begin with "ORA$", as these names are reserved for use by Oracle Corporation.

- The ALLOCATE_UNIQUE procedure always performs a COMMIT, so it cannot be called from a database trigger.

Example. The following function returns the lockhandle of a specific named lock. It calls ALLOCATE_UNIQUE only if the lockhandle has not already been determined, and avoid the COMMIT unless it is necessary. The function manipulates global variables and thus needs to be included in a PL/SQL package.

```
PACKAGE BODY printer_access
IS
    /* global variables for lock name and handle */
    printer_lockname  VARCHAR2(128) := 'printer_lock';
    printer_lockhandle  VARCHAR2(128);

    FUNCTION get_printer_lockhandle
    RETURN VARCHAR2
    IS
    BEGIN
       IF printer_lockhandle IS NULL
       THEN
          DBMS_LOCK.ALLOCATE_UNIQUE
```

```
                        (lockname => printer_lockname
                        ,lockhandle => printer_lockhandle);
             END IF;

             RETURN printer_lockhandle;
          END get_printer_lockhandle;

       END printer_access;
```

As illustrated in the example, it is a good idea to call ALLOCATE_UNIQUE only once for any given lockname per session. This is why the function stashes the lockhandle in the global variable, printer_lockhandle, and calls ALLOCATE_UNIQUE only if this global has not been initialized. There are two reasons for using this technique: efficiency and avoidance of extra COMMITs. Remember that ALLOCATE_UNIQUE will always return the same handle for a given lockname and that it always performs a COMMIT. Thus, best practice for using DBMS_LOCK includes calling ALLOCATE_UNIQUE only once per named lock.

Locks allocated using ALLOCATE_UNIQUE can be viewed in the Oracle data dictionary via the DBMS_LOCK_ALLOCATED view.

It is good practice to avoid the possibility of lockname conflicts between applications by adopting standard naming conventions for locknames. Just as Oracle reserves names that begin with "ORA$", you may want to prefix locknames with your own company and application identifier string.

The DBMS_LOCK.REQUEST function

The REQUEST function is used to acquire a lock in the mode specified by the lockmode parameter. If the lock cannot be acquired in the requested mode within the specified time, the function call completes with a nonzero return value (see the parameter table).

The REQUEST function is overloaded on the first parameter, which is used to identify the lock by either an INTEGER identifier or by a VARCHAR2 lockhandle. The release_on_commit parameter indicates whether the lock should persist across RDBMS transactions or be automatically released upon COMMIT or ROLL-BACK. The headers for this program, corresponding to each type, are as follows:

```
FUNCTION DBMS_LOCK.REQUEST
     (id IN INTEGER
     ,lockmode IN INTEGER DEFAULT X_MODE
     ,timeout IN INTEGER DEFAULT MAXWAIT
     ,release_on_commit IN BOOLEAN DEFAULT FALSE)
RETURN INTEGER;

FUNCTION DBMS_LOCK.REQUEST
     (lockhandle IN VARCHAR2
     ,lockmode IN INTEGER DEFAULT X_MODE
```

```
      ,timeout IN INTEGER DEFAULT MAXWAIT
      ,release_on_commit IN BOOLEAN DEFAULT FALSE)
   RETURN INTEGER;
```

Parameters for this function are summarized in the following table.

Parameter	Description
id	Numeric identifier of the lock
lockhandle	Handle for lock returned by DBMS_LOCK.ALLOCATE_UNIQUE
lockmode	Locking mode requested for lock
timeout	Time in seconds to wait for successful conversion
release_on_commit	If TRUE, release lock automatically on COMMIT or ROLLBACK

The following table summarizes the return values of the function.

Return Value	Description
0	Success
1	Timed out
2	Deadlock
3	Parameter error
4	Do not own lock; cannot convert
5	Illegal lockhandle

The program does not raise any package exceptions.

Restrictions. User-defined lock identifiers must be in the range 0 to 1073741823. Lock identifiers in the range 2000000000 to 2147483647 are reserved for use by Oracle Corporation.

Example. The following procedure calls the REQUEST function to get exclusive access to a lock designated to serialize access to a printer by Oracle sessions. It uses the get_printer_lockhandle function (see the example for the ALLOCATE_ UNIQUE procedure) to identify the correct value for the lockhandle parameter.

```
   PROCEDURE lock_printer
      (return_code_OUT OUT INTEGER)
   IS
      /* initialize variable with desired lockhandle */
      temp_lockhandle printer_lockhandle%TYPE := get_printer_lockhandle;

      call_status  INTEGER;
   BEGIN

      /*
      || lock in exclusive mode, wait for up to 5 seconds
      */
```

```
    call_status := DBMS_LOCK.REQUEST
                      (lockhandle => temp_lockhandle
                      ,lockmode => DBMS_LOCK.x_mode
                      ,timeout => 5
                      ,release_on_commit => TRUE);

    return_code_OUT := call_status;
  END lock_printer;
```

It is safest to use the form of REQUEST that identifies the lock by a lockhandle (returned by ALLOCATE_UNIQUE). This minimizes the potential for inadvertent use of the same lock by different applications for different purposes, which is possible when locks are identified by integer values chosen by the application.

Sessions connected to Oracle using the multithreaded server configuration will not be released from their shared server until all held locks are released. Thus, be careful of specifying FALSE for the release_on_commit parameter in MTS (multithreaded server) environments, as holding locks for long periods could have a negative impact on MTS efficiency.

Be sure that distributed transactions specify TRUE for the release_on_commit parameter. If a distributed transaction does not release locks after COMMIT, it is possible for a distributed deadlock to occur, which will be undetectable by either of the databases involved.

When two sessions request locks with modes resulting in a deadlock, this is detected by Oracle, and one of the sessions is notified of the deadlock status.

The DBMS_LOCK.CONVERT function

The CONVERT function is used to convert a previously acquired lock to the mode specified by the lockmode parameter. If the mode conversion cannot be granted within the specified time, the function call completes with a nonzero return value (see the following parameter table). CONVERT is overloaded on the first parameter, which is used to identify the lock by either an INTEGER identifier or a VARCHAR2 lockhandle. The headers for this program, corresponding to each type, follow:

```
FUNCTION DBMS_LOCK.CONVERT
    (id IN INTEGER
    ,lockmode IN INTEGER
    ,timeout IN NUMBER DEFAULT MAXWAIT)
RETURN INTEGER;

FUNCTION DBMS_LOCK.CONVERT
    (lockhandle IN VARCHAR2
    ,lockmode IN INTEGER
    ,timeout IN NUMBER DEFAULT MAXWAIT)
RETURN INTEGER;
```

Parameters for this program are summarized in the following table.

Parameter	Description
id	Numeric identifier of the lock
lockhandle	Handle for lock returned by ALLOCATE_UNIQUE
lockmode	Locking mode to which to convert the lock
timeout	Time in seconds to wait for successful conversion

The return values for this function are summarized in the following table.

Return Value	Description
0	Success
1	Timed out
2	Deadlock
3	Parameter error
4	Do not own lock, cannot convert
5	Illegal lockhandle

The program does not raise any package exceptions.

Restrictions. User-defined lock identifiers must be in the range 0 to 1073741823. Lock identifiers in the range 2000000000 to 2147483647 are reserved for use by Oracle Corporation.

Example. The following anonymous PL/SQL block converts a previously acquired lock to null mode, reporting success or failure to the screen:

```
DECLARE
    call_status INTEGER;
BEGIN
    /* convert lock 9999 down to null mode with no wait */
    call_status := DBMS_LOCK.CONVERT(9999,DBMS_LOCK.nl_mode,0);

    IF call_status = 0
    THEN
        DBMS_OUTPUT.PUT_LINE('SUCCESS');
    ELSE
        DBMS_OUTPUT.PUT_LINE('FAIL, RC = '||TO_CHAR(call_status));
    END IF;
END;
```

See the discussion in the "Example" section for the The DBMS_LOCK.REQUEST function; all of that discussion also applies to CONVERT.

The DBMS_LOCK.RELEASE function

The RELEASE function releases a previously acquired lock. RELEASE is overloaded on the first parameter, which is used to identify the lock by either an INTEGER identifier or a VARCHAR2 lockhandle. The program headers for each corresponding type follow:

```
FUNCTION DBMS_LOCK.RELEASE
    (id IN INTEGER)
RETURN INTEGER;

FUNCTION DBMS_LOCK.RELEASE
    (lockhandle IN VARCHAR2)
RETURN INTEGER;
```

Parameters are summarized in the following table.

Parameter	Description
id	Numeric identifier of the lock
lockhandle	Handle for lock returned by ALLOCATE_UNIQUE

The return values for this function are summarized in the following table.

Return Value	Description
0	Success
3	Parameter error
4	Do not own lock; cannot release
5	Illegal lockhandle

The program does not raise any package exceptions.

Restrictions. User-defined lock identifiers must be in the range 0 to 1073741823. Lock identifiers in the range 2000000000 to 2147483647 are reserved for use by Oracle Corporation.

Example. The following procedure calls the RELEASE function to relinquish control of the printer lock (see also the example for the REQUEST function):

```
PROCEDURE release_printer
    (return_code_OUT OUT INTEGER)
IS
    /* initialize variable with desired lockhandle */
    temp_lockhandle printer_lockhandle%TYPE := get_printer_lockhandle;

    call_status  INTEGER;
BEGIN

    /*
```

```
   || release the printer lock
   */
   call_status := DBMS_LOCK.RELEASE
                     (lockhandle => temp_lockhandle);

      return_code_OUT := call_status;
   END release_printer;
```

It is good practice to release locks as soon as possible. Doing so minimizes the potential for unnecessary wait times or deadlocks in applications where concurrent access to resources is serialized using DBMS_LOCK.

The DBMS_LOCK.SLEEP procedure

The SLEEP procedure suspends the session for the number of seconds specified in the seconds parameter. Sleep periods can be specified with accuracy down to the hundredth of a second (e.g., 1.35 and 1.29 are recognized as distinct sleep times). Here's the header for this program:

```
PROCEDURE DBMS_LOCK.SLEEP
     (seconds IN NUMBER);
```

Exceptions. This program does not raise any package exceptions.

WARNING   The following nasty Oracle exception was raised on Windows NT when the SLEEP procedure was called with a NULL value for seconds: ORA-00600: internal error code, arguments: [15454], [0], [], [], [], [], [], [].

Restrictions. Do not specify a null value for the seconds parameter; this may result in an ORA-00600 error, as noted previously.

Example. The following SQL*Plus script displays a screen message and pauses for ten seconds before continuing:

```
prompt ***********************************
prompt * This is a very important message
prompt * ***********************************

BEGIN
   DBMS_LOCK.SLEEP(10);
END;
/
```

Applications using resources to which concurrent access is restricted may need to try again later if the resource is busy. The SLEEP procedure provides a mechanism for including low-overhead wait times into PL/SQL programs. After waiting, an application can retry the operation that failed to acquire the busy resource.

Tips on Using DBMS_LOCK

In this section I've pulled together a number of best practices for using the DBMS_LOCK package.

Named locks or lock ids?

Oracle provides two methods of identifying and manipulating user locks: integer lock identifiers and handles for named locks. Using names and lockhandles to identify locks is considered safer than using integer identifiers directly because naming standards can be adopted to virtually guarantee that different applications will not use the same lock for different purposes. Therefore, best practices for using DBMS_LOCK include the use of named locks and lockhandles.

Issues with named locks

There are a couple of drawbacks to using named locks that are worth pointing out. In particular:

- Named locks are recorded in the catalog, and thus may be slower.

- The DBMS_LOCK.ALLOCATE_UNIQUE procedure issues a COMMIT.

- Applications need to keep track of lockhandles for each named lock used.

It is worth investigating these drawbacks and developing techniques to minimize their impact, thus further encouraging the use of named locks.

Performance of named locks

We can investigate the performance penalty for using named locks, and quantify that penalty in a relatively straightforward manner. Consider the following PL/SQL script:

```
/* Filename on companion disk:  lock1.sql */
set timing on
set serveroutput on size 100000

DECLARE

    lockname VARCHAR2(30) := 'OPBIP_TEST_LOCK_10';
    lockhandle VARCHAR2(128);
    lockid  INTEGER := 99999;

    call_status  INTEGER;
    timer NUMBER;

BEGIN

    /*
    || timed test using lockhandles
```

```
*/
timer := DBMS_UTILITY.GET_TIME;
DBMS_LOCK.ALLOCATE_UNIQUE(lockname,lockhandle);
FOR i IN 1..10000
LOOP
   call_status := DBMS_LOCK.REQUEST(lockhandle,timeout=>0);
   call_status := DBMS_LOCK.RELEASE(lockhandle);
END LOOP;
DBMS_OUTPUT.PUT_LINE('Using lockhandles: '||
   TO_CHAR(ROUND((DBMS_UTILITY.GET_TIME-timer)/100,2)) ||' secs');

/*
|| timed test using lockids
*/
timer := DBMS_UTILITY.GET_TIME;
FOR i IN 1..10000
LOOP
   call_status := DBMS_LOCK.REQUEST(lockid,timeout=>0);
   call_status := DBMS_LOCK.RELEASE(lockid);
END LOOP;
DBMS_OUTPUT.PUT_LINE('Using lockids: '||
   TO_CHAR(ROUND((DBMS_UTILITY.GET_TIME-timer)/100,2)) ||' secs');

END;
```

The PL/SQL block reports on the elapsed times to request and release a lock 10,000 times using either a lockhandle or an integer lock identifier. The test yielded the following results on a Personal Oracle7 database with no other activity:

```
SQL> @12
Using lockhandles: 9.57 secs
Using lockids: 3.02 secs

PL/SQL procedure successfully completed.

 real: 12740
SQL> spool off
```

These results confirm that use of lockhandles is significantly slower than use of lock identifiers. However, the results also indicate that the overhead of named locks was less than one-thousandth of a second per usage. Thus, the performance impact of using named locks is negligible and is probably not a legitimate concern for most applications.

ALLOCATE_UNIQUE drawbacks

The other issues mentioned with named locks are usage related. The ALLOCATE_ UNIQUE procedure needs to be called to identify a lockhandle for each named lock. This procedure issues a COMMIT, which presents some usability issues. For one, the procedure cannot be called from a database trigger, so using named locks from a database trigger requires that the lockhandle be acquired outside of the trigger and saved for use in the trigger. Another problem is the COMMIT itself: an application may want to utilize a named lock but not necessarily COMMIT the current transaction. Thus, it is desirable when using named locks to limit the number of calls to ALLOCATE_UNIQUE to exactly one call per named lock used.

Optimizing named locks

One way to achieve the objective of minimizing calls to ALLOCATE_UNIQUE is to use private package global variables to store lockhandles for each named lock. A function that will return the lockhandle can then be written, calling ALLOCATE_UNIQUE only if the lockhandle has not been previously identified. This technique is illustrated as follows:

```
PACKAGE BODY print_pkg
IS
    /* private globals for lock identification */
    printer_lockname  VARCHAR2(128) := 'printer_lock';
    printer_lockhandle  VARCHAR2(128);

    FUNCTION get_printer_lockhandle
    RETURN VARCHAR2
    IS
    BEGIN
       IF printer_lockhandle IS NULL
       THEN
          DBMS_LOCK.ALLOCATE_UNIQUE
             (lockname => printer_lockname
             ,lockhandle => printer_lockhandle);
       END IF;

       RETURN printer_lockhandle;
    END get_printer_lockhandle;

END print_pkg;
```

Using this technique ensures that the ALLOCATE_UNIQUE procedure is called only once per session requiring use of the printer lock. The lock can even be used in a database trigger if the function get_printer_lockhandle has been called prior to the triggering event.

One drawback to this technique is code redundancy: each named lock used by an application requires adding a specific package global variable for the lockhandle and an associated function to return it. Referencing a new named lock in an application involves adding a nontrivial amount of code before it can be used.

REQUEST or CONVERT?

Another usability issue with DBMS_LOCK (not specific to named locks): applications using multiple lock modes need to have intelligence about whether to call the REQUEST function or the CONVERT function. If the user has requested and

received a lock in a specific mode, then that mode can only be changed by calling CONVERT. On the other hand, a lock conversion can only take place if it is
preceded by a successful call to REQUEST. Getting it right can mean developing
code that checks and tracks return codes from the calls to these two procedures.

DBMS_LOCK Examples

In response to the usability issues described in the previous section, I have developed a utility package called dblock to simplify, and consequently encourage, the
use of named locks in PL/SQL applications.

The dblock package

The dblock package specification follows:

```
/* Filename on on companion disk: dblock.sql */
CREATE OR REPLACE PACKAGE dblock
   /*
   || Adds value to DBMS_LOCK by allowing easier manipulation
   || of named locks. Calling programs use lock names only,
   || corresponding lockhandles are automatically identified,
   || used and saved for subsequent use.
   ||
   ||
   || Author:  John Beresniewicz, Savant Corp
   ||
   || 10/26/97: added expiration_secs_IN to lockhandle
   || 10/21/97: added release
   || 10/21/97: added dump_lockhandle_tbl
   || 10/17/97: created
   ||
   || Compilation Requirements:
   ||
   || EXECUTE on DBMS_LOCK
   || EXECUTE on DBMS_SESSION
   ||
   || Execution Requirements:
   ||
   */
AS
   /* variables to anchor other variables */
   lockname_var  VARCHAR2(128);
   lockhandle_var VARCHAR2(128);

   /*
   || returns TRUE if a COMMIT has taken place between
   || subsequent calls to the function
   || NOTE: returns TRUE on first call in session
   */
   FUNCTION committed_TF RETURN BOOLEAN;

   /*
```

```
|| returns lockhandle for given lockname, only calls
|| DBMS_LOCK.ALLOCATE_UNIQUE if lockhandle has not been
|| previously determined
*/
FUNCTION lockhandle
    (lockname_IN IN lockname_var%TYPE
    ,expiration_secs_IN IN INTEGER := 864000)
RETURN lockhandle_var%TYPE;

/*
|| returns TRUE if named lock is acquired in mode
|| specified
*/
FUNCTION get_lock_TF
    (lockname_IN IN lockname_var%TYPE
    ,mode_IN IN INTEGER := DBMS_LOCK.x_mode
    ,timeout_IN IN INTEGER := 1
    ,release_on_commit_TF IN BOOLEAN := FALSE)
RETURN BOOLEAN;

/* releases named lock */
PROCEDURE release (lockname_IN IN lockname_var%TYPE);

/* print contents of lockhandle_tbl for debugging */
PROCEDURE dump_lockhandle_tbl;

END dblock;
```

The dblock programs allow the user to identify and acquire locks by name only. Lockhandles for each named lock are managed within the package, transparent to the application. The package associates locknames with lockhandles by using a private global PL/SQL table called lockhandle_tbl. The table is defined as follows:

```
/* rectype to pair handles with names */
TYPE handle_rectype IS RECORD
    (name    lockname_var%TYPE
    ,handle lockhandle_var%TYPE
    );

/* table to store lockhandles by name */
TYPE handle_tbltype IS TABLE OF handle_rectype
    INDEX BY BINARY_INTEGER;

lockhandle_tbl handle_tbltype;
```

The lockhandle function. The lockhandle function takes a lockname as an IN parameter and returns the associated lockhandle. If the lockhandle has already been identified and stored in the lockhandle_tbl table, it is returned directly. Otherwise, DBMS_LOCK.ALLOCATE_UNIQUE is called to determine the lockhandle, which is then stored in lockhandle_tbl and is also returned to the caller. Here is the body of lockhandle:

```
/* Filename on companion disk: dblock.sql */
    FUNCTION lockhandle
```

```
    (lockname_IN IN lockname_var%TYPE
    ,expiration_secs_IN IN INTEGER := 864000)
RETURN lockhandle_var%TYPE
IS
    call_status INTEGER;
    temp_lockhandle  lockhandle_var%TYPE;

    temp_index  BINARY_INTEGER;

BEGIN
    /*
    || if lockhandle_tbl empty must call ALLOCATE_UNIQUE
    */
    IF lockhandle_tbl.COUNT = 0
    THEN

        DBMS_LOCK.ALLOCATE_UNIQUE
            (lockname => lockname_IN
            ,lockhandle => temp_lockhandle
            ,expiration_secs => expiration_secs_IN);

        lockhandle_tbl(1).handle := temp_lockhandle;
        lockhandle_tbl(1).name := lockname_IN;

    /*
    || check lockhandle_tbl for matching lockname
    */
    ELSE
        FOR i IN lockhandle_tbl.FIRST..lockhandle_tbl.LAST
        LOOP
            IF lockhandle_tbl(i).name = lockname_IN
            THEN
                temp_lockhandle := lockhandle_tbl(i).handle;
            END IF;
        END LOOP;
    END IF;

    /*
    || if temp_lockhandle still null, call ALLOCATE_UNIQUE
    || and load entry into lockhandle_tbl
    */
    IF temp_lockhandle IS NULL
    THEN
        DBMS_LOCK.ALLOCATE_UNIQUE
            (lockname => lockname_IN
            ,lockhandle => temp_lockhandle);

        /*
        || add to end of lockhandle_tbl
        */
        temp_index := lockhandle_tbl.LAST+1;
        lockhandle_tbl(temp_index).handle := temp_lockhandle;
        lockhandle_tbl(temp_index).name := lockname_IN;

    END IF;
```

```
    RETURN temp_lockhandle;
END lockhandle;
```

The lockhandle function alone is enough to make using named locks much easier. It relieves the programmer of having to create lockhandle variables for each
named lock and also guarantees that the ALLOCATE_UNIQUE procedure is called
only once per named lock. New named locks can be used immediately without
coding supporting routines, as these are handled generically in the function. Furthermore, the lockhandle function can be invoked directly in calls to REQUEST or
CONVERT. In the following procedure, the printer_lockname variable holds the
name of a lock being used to serialize access to a printer:

```
PROCEDURE get_printer_lock
    (lock_status_OUT OUT INTEGER)
IS
BEGIN
    lock_status_OUT := DBMS_LOCK.REQUEST
                        (dblock.lockhandle(printer_lockname));
END get_printer_lock;
```

get_lock_TF function. Applications using DBMS_LOCK usually must check return
values from calls to the REQUEST or CONVERT functions to determine if access
to the locked resource has been acquired. The dblock package includes a function called get_lock_TF, which takes a lockname and lock mode as IN parameters
and returns the Boolean value TRUE if the named lock has been acquired in the
desired mode. Using get_lock_TF, we can write code like the following:

```
IF dblock.get_lock_TF
        (printer_lockname,DBMS_LOCK.x_mode)
THEN
    /* invoke print routine here */
ELSE
    /* cannot print, tell user to try later */
END IF;
```

Code like this is far easier to understand and maintain than code that calls DBMS_
LOCK programs directly. All the complexity of using DBMS_LOCK is eliminated;
the program merely calls get_lock_TF and proceeds directly to appropriate logic
based on the return value. Here is the body of get_lock_TF:

```
/* Filename on companion disk:  dblock.sql */
FUNCTION get_lock_TF
    (lockname_IN IN lockname_var%TYPE
    ,mode_IN IN INTEGER := DBMS_LOCK.x_mode
    ,timeout_IN IN INTEGER := 1
    ,release_on_commit_TF IN BOOLEAN := FALSE)
RETURN BOOLEAN
IS
    call_status INTEGER;

    /* handle for the named lock */
```

```
      temp_lockhandle lockhandle_var%TYPE := lockhandle(lockname_IN);

BEGIN
   call_status := DBMS_LOCK.REQUEST
                     (lockhandle => temp_lockhandle
                     ,lockmode => mode_IN
                     ,timeout => timeout_IN
                     ,release_on_commit => release_on_commit_TF
                     );
   /*
   || if lock already owned, convert to requested mode
   */
   IF call_status = 4
   THEN
      call_status := DBMS_LOCK.CONVERT
                        (lockhandle => temp_lockhandle
                        ,lockmode => mode_IN
                        ,timeout => timeout_IN
                        );
   END IF;

   RETURN (call_status = 0);
END get_lock_TF;
```

Notice that get_lock_TF first calls REQUEST and then CONVERT if the lock is already owned. This relieves the programmer of yet another bit of housekeeping, and the return value accurately reflects whether the lock is owned in the requested mode. The temp_lockhandle variable is used in the calls to DBMS_LOCK programs to avoid calling the lockhandle function more than once.

The committed_TF and release functions. The dblock package also includes a procedure called release, which releases a named lock, and a function called committed_TF. The latter demonstrates using the release_on_commit parameter of the REQUEST function to determine whether a COMMIT has taken place in the session. The body of committed_TF looks like this:

```
/* Filename on companion disk:  dblock.sql */
/* used by committed_TF, unique to each session */
   commit_lockname  lockname_var%TYPE :=
                     DBMS_SESSION.UNIQUE_SESSION_ID;

FUNCTION committed_TF RETURN BOOLEAN
IS
   call_status INTEGER;
BEGIN
   /* get unique lock, expire in one day */
   call_status := DBMS_LOCK.REQUEST
                     (lockhandle =>
                     lockhandle(commit_lockname,86400)
                     ,lockmode => DBMS_LOCK.x_mode
                     ,timeout => 0
```

```
                        ,release_on_commit => TRUE);

        RETURN (call_status = 0);
    END committed_TF;
```

The committed_TF function uses a named lock called commit_lockname that is
unique to each session, having been initialized by calling DBMS_SES-
SION.UNIQUE_SESSION_ID. It then calls DBMS_LOCK.REQUEST to acquire an
exclusive lock on commit_lockname, making sure to specify TRUE for the release_
on_commit parameter. Once the lock has been acquired initially, the success of
subsequent calls indicates that the lock has been released, and thus a COMMIT
(or ROLLBACK) has taken place. The function is probably not that useful in practice, but it makes a nice academic exercise.

Using locks to signal service availability

One way in which DBMS_LOCK can be usefully employed is to indicate the availability of service programs to database sessions. The basic steps are quite simple:

1. Assign specific locks to the server and/or each service provided.

2. The server process holds the lock(s) in exclusive mode when services are
   available.

3. Client programs request the lock to determine service availability.

To make this more concrete, the following code fragments might be part of a
package used to coordinate access to a computation server called calcman:

```
PACKAGE calcman
IS
    /* the actual service provider program */
    PROCEDURE calcman_driver;

    /* function called by clients to determine availability */
    FUNCTION calcman_available RETURN BOOLEAN;

END calcman;

PACKAGE BODY calcman
IS
    /* lock name used to flag service availability */
    calcman_lockname  VARCHAR2(100):= 'CALCMAN_LOCK';

    PROCEDURE calcman_driver
    IS
    BEGIN
        /*
        || get the special lock in exclusive mode
        */
        IF dblock.get_lock_TF
                (lockname_IN => calcman_lockname
```

```
                    ,mode_IN => DBMS_LOCK.x_mode
                    ,timeout_IN => 1
                    ,release_on_commit_TF => FALSE)
        THEN
            /*
            || execute the service loop here, which probably
            || involves listening on a database pipe for
            || service requests and sending responses on pipes
            */
            /*
            || loop forever and process calc requests
            */
            WHILE NOT terminate_TF
            LOOP
                receive_unpack_calc_request
                    (timeout_IN => DBMS_PIPE.maxwait
                    ,request_rec_OUT=> request_rec
                    ,return_code_OUT => temp_return_code);
                IF temp_return_code != 0
                THEN
                    DBMS_PIPE.PURGE(request_pipe);
                ELSE
                    process_request(request_rec);
                END IF;
            END LOOP;
        ELSE
            /* service is already running in another process, exit */
            RETURN;
        END IF:
    END calcman_driver;


    FUNCTION calcman_available RETURN BOOLEAN
    IS
        got_lock    BOOLEAN;
    BEGIN
        got_lock := dblock.get_lock_TF
                        (lockname => calcman_lockname
                        ,mode_IN => DBMS_LOCK.sx_mode
                        ,timeout_IN => 0
                        ,release_on_commit_TF => TRUE);

        /*
        || do not hold lock, this could conflict with
        || starting service
        */
        dblock.release(calcman_lockname);

        /* failure to get lock indicates server available */
        RETURN NOT got_lock;
    END calcman_available;

END calcman;
```

The calcman_driver procedure grabs and holds the lock as long as it is executing. If the lock is not available within one second, the procedure is already running in another session and exits silently in the current session. Thus, the lock ensures that only one calcman_driver will be executing at any time. Note the importance of not releasing the lock at COMMIT, ensuring that the lock is held as long as the service process is alive. The service can make itself unavailable at any time by simply releasing the lock.

The service that calcman_driver provides is not specified in the previous code fragments. It could be a complex calculation requiring large PL/SQL tables for which the overhead of having all users execute the calculation individually is too great. Or it could be connected to an external service routine of some kind. A fuller discussion of how to implement such service procedures using database pipes can be found in Chapter 3, *Intersession Communication.*

Client programs call the calcman_available function to determine whether the server is executing and providing its computation services. The function attempts to get the lock and, if it succeeds, this indicates that the service is not available. The lock is requested in shared mode exclusive; as a consequence, concurrent calls to the get_lock_TF function from different sessions may all succeed and indicate unavailability. If the lock is requested in exclusive mode, there is a chance that simultaneous execution of the function by two users could falsely indicate to one user that the service is available. The calcman_available function also releases the lock immediately to keep it from interfering with the calcman_driver program, which is attempting to secure the lock.

DBMS_TRANSACTION: Interfacing to SQL Transaction Statements

The DBMS_TRANSACTION package provides a programmatic interface to a number of the SQL transaction statements. The majority of the DBMS_TRANSACTION programs have SQL equivalents that you can utilize directly from within SQL. For this reason, developers and DBAs may choose to use the direct SQL equivalents rather than these procedures. A number of other procedures and functions have no equivalents, however, and nicely abstract the PL/SQL programmer or database administrator from the internal details managed by the database.

Getting Started with DBMS_TRANSACTION

The DBMS_TRANSACTION package is created when the Oracle database is installed. The *dbmsutil.sql* script (found in the built-in packages source code directory, as described in Chapter 1) contain the source code for this package's specification. This script is called by *catproc.sql*, which is normally run immediately after database creation. The script creates the public synonym DBMS_TRANSACTION for the package and grants EXECUTE privilege on the package to public. All Oracle users can reference and make use of this package.

DBMS_TRANSACTION programs

Table 4-4 lists the procedures and functions available through DBMS_TRANSACTION, along with their SQL equivalents (if applicable).

Table 4-4. DBMS_TRANSACTION Programs

Name	Description	Use in SQL?
ADVISE_COMMIT	Executes the equivalent of the ALTER SESSION ADVISE COMMIT command.	Yes
ADVISE_NOTHING	Executes the equivalent of the ALTER SESSION ADVISE NOTHING command.	Yes
ADVISE_ROLLBACK	Executes the equivalent of the ALTER SESSION ADVISE ROLLBACK command.	Yes
BEGIN_DISCRETE_TRANSACTION	Sets the discrete transaction mode.	No
COMMIT	Executes the equivalent of the COMMIT command.	Yes
COMMIT_COMMENT	Executes the equivalent of the COMMIT COMMENT command.	Yes
COMMIT_FORCE	Executes the equivalent of the COMMIT FORCE command.	Yes
LOCAL_TRANSACTION_ID	Returns a local (to instance) unique identfier for the current transaction.	No
PURGE_MIXED	Deletes information on a mixed outcome transaction (a possible scenario with two-phase commit).	No
PURGE_LOST_DB_ENTRY	Removes "lost database entries" otherwise used to control recovery in pending two-phase commit operations.	No
READ_ONLY	Executes the equivalent of the SET TRANSACTION READ ONLY command.	Yes
READ_WRITE	Executes the equivalent of the SET TRANSACTION READ WRITE command.	Yes
ROLLBACK	Executes the equivalent of the ROLLBACK command.	Yes
ROLLBACK_FORCE	Executes the equivalent of the ROLLBACK FORCE command.	Yes
ROLLBACK_SAVEPOINT	Executes the equivalent of the ROLLBACK TO command.	Yes
SAVEPOINT	Executes the equivalent of the SAVEPOINT command.	Yes

Table 4-4. DBMS_TRANSACTION Programs (continued)

Name	Description	Use in SQL?
STEP_ID	Returns a local (to local transaction) unique positive integer that orders the DML operations of a transaction.	No
USE_ROLLBACK_ SEGMENT	Executes the equivalent of the SET TRANSACTION USE ROLLBACK SEGMENT command.	Yes

DBMS_TRANSACTION exceptions

The DBMS_TRANSACTION package gives names (using the EXCEPTION_INIT pragma) to Oracle exceptions -8175 and -8176 as follows:

Name	Number	Description.
DISCRETE_TRANSACTION_FAILED	-8175	Discrete transaction restriction violated. An attempt was made to perform an action that is not currently supported in a discrete transaction. Roll back the transaction and retry it as a normal transaction.
CONSISTENT_READ_FAILURE	-8176	Cannot continue consistent read for the table/index—no undo records. Oracle encountered an operation that does not generate undo records. Retry the operation with a different snapshot time. If an index is involved, retry the operation without using the index.

These exceptions may be raised in calls to the BEGIN_DISCRETE_TRANSACTION procedure.

Advising Oracle About In-Doubt Transactions

The DBMS_TRANSACTION advise procedures (ADVISE_COMMIT, ADVISE_NOTHING, and ADVISE_ROLLBACK) specify what in-doubt transaction advice is sent to remote databases during distributed transactions. This advice appears on the remote database in the ADVICE column of the DBA_2PC_PENDING data dictionary view if the distributed transaction becomes in doubt (i.e., a network or machine failure occurs during the commit). The remote database administrator can then review the DBA_2PC_PENDING information and manually commit or roll back in-doubt transactions using the FORCE clause of the COMMIT or ROLLBACK commands.

Each call to an ADVISE procedure remains in effect for the duration of that connection or until a different ADVISE procedure call is made. This allows you to send different advice to various remote databases.

The DBMS_TRANSACTION.ADVISE_ROLLBACK, ADVISE_NOTHING, and ADVISE_COMMIT procedures

Here are the headers for the three advise procedures:

```
PROCEDURE DBMS_TRANSACTION.ADVISE_ROLLBACK;

PROCEDURE DBMS_TRANSACTION.ADVISE_NOTHING;

PROCEDURE DBMS_TRANSACTION.ADVISE_COMMIT;
```

Example. In the following example, we address a common data-warehousing scenario. We want to promote daily extract data from our legacy systems to each of our data marts and our corporate data warehouse. First, the extract data is summarized and loaded into a staging database copy of the fact table. Then, this fact table's data is promoted to each of the data marts and the data warehouse. The marketing department wants its data mart loaded very aggressively (i.e., ADVISE_ COMMIT). The accounting department, being more conservative, wants its data mart loaded with caution (i.e., ADVISE_ROLLBACK). Finally, management does not have a preference for loading the data warehouse. We could run the following PL/SQL locally from our staging database:

```
BEGIN
    FOR fact_rec IN (SELECT * FROM fact_load_table)
    LOOP
        DBMS_TRANSACTION.ADVISE_COMMIT;
        INSERT INTO fact_table@marketing_data_mart
            VALUES (fact_rec.product_id, fact_rec.location_id,
            fact_record.period_id, fact_rec.numeric_value1);

        DBMS_TRANSACTION.ADVISE_ROLLBACK;
        INSERT INTO fact_table@accounting_data_mart
            VALUES (fact_rec.product_id, fact_rec.location_id,
            fact_record.period_id, fact_rec.numeric_value1);

        DBMS_TRANSACTION.ADVISE_NOTHING;
        INSERT INTO fact_table@corp_data_warehouse
            VALUES (fact_rec.product_id, fact_rec.location_id,
            fact_record.period_id, fact_rec.numeric_value1);

        COMMIT;
    END LOOP;
END;
/
```

Committing Data

The DBMS_TRANSACTION package offers a number of programs you can use to issue COMMITs in your application.

The DBMS_TRANSACTION.COMMIT procedure

The COMMIT procedure is provided primarily for completeness. It is equivalent to the COMMIT command of PL/SQL. Here's the header for this procedure:

```
PROCEDURE DBMS_TRANSACTION.COMMIT;
```

There is no advantage to using this program instead of the COMMIT command.

The DBMS_TRANSACTION.COMMIT_COMMENT procedure

The COMMIT_COMMENT procedure specifies what in-doubt transaction comment is sent to remote databases during distributed transactions. The specification for the procedure follows:

```
PROCEDURE DBMS_TRANSACTION.COMMIT_COMMENT (cmnt IN VARCHAR2);
```

This comment (cmnt parameter) appears on the remote database in the TRAN_ COMMENT column of the DBA_2PC_PENDING data dictionary view if the distributed transaction becomes in doubt (i.e., a network or machine failure occurs during the commit). The remote database administrator can then review the DBA_ 2PC_PENDING information and manually commit or roll back in-doubt transactions using the FORCE clause of the COMMIT or ROLLBACK commands.

In the following example, we update our previous data mart and data warehouse promotion PL/SQL code to utilize the COMMIT_COMMENT procedure:

```
BEGIN
   FOR fact_rec IN (SELECT * FROM fact_load_table)
   LOOP
      DBMS_TRANSACTION.ADVISE_COMMIT;
      INSERT INTO fact_table@marketing_data_mart
         VALUES (fact_rec.product_id,
             fact_rec.location_id, fact_record.period_id,
             fact_record.numeric value1);

      DBMS_TRANSACTION.ADVISE_ROLLBACK;
      INSERT INTO fact_table@accounting_data_mart
         VALUES (fact_rec.product_id, fact_rec.location_id,
             fact_record.period_id,
             fact_rec.numeric_value1);

      DBMS_TRANSACTION.ADVISE_NOTHING;
       INSERT INTO fact_table@corp_data_warehouse
         VALUES (fact_rec.product_id,
             fact_rec.location_id, fact_record.period_id,
             fact_rec.numeric_value1);
```

```
            DBMS_TRANSACTION.COMMIT_COMMENT
                ('Fact Load for date: '||TO_CHAR(sysdate,'MON-DD-YYYY'));
        END LOOP;
    END;
    /
```

The DBMS_TRANSACTION.COMMIT_FORCE procedure

The COMMIT_FORCE procedure manually commits local in doubt, distributed transactions. Here's the specification for the procedure:

```
PROCEDURE DBMS_TRANSACTION.COMMIT_FORCE
        (xid IN VARCHAR2
        ,scn IN VARCHAR2 DEFAULT NULL);
```

Parameters are summarized in the following table.

Parameter	Description
xid	The transaction's local or global transaction ID. To find these transaction IDs, query the data dictionary view DBA_2PC_PENDING.
scn	System change number (SCN) under which to commit the transaction.

Specifying a system change number (scn parameter) allows you to commit an in-doubt transaction with the same SCN assigned by other nodes, thus maintaining the synchronized commit time of the distributed transaction. If the scn parameter is omitted, the transaction is committed using the current SCN.

Any decisions to force in-doubt transactions should be made after consulting with the database administrator(s) at the remote database location(s). If the decision is made to locally force any transactions, the database administrator should either commit or roll back such transactions (as was done by nodes that successfully resolved the transactions). Otherwise, the administrator should query the DBA_2PC_PENDING view's ADVICE and TRAN_COMMENT columns for further insight.

For more information on this topic, see "Manually Overriding In-Doubt Transactions" in the Oracle Corporation document *Oracle8 Server Distributed Systems*.

Rolling Back Changes

The DBMS_TRANSACTION package offers a number of programs you can use to issue rollbacks in your application.

The DBMS_TRANSACTION.ROLLBACK procedure

The ROLLBACK procedure is provided primarily for completeness. It is equivalent to the ROLLBACK command of PL/SQL. The header for this procedure follows:

```
PROCEDURE DBMS_TRANSACTION.ROLLBACK;
```

There is no advantage to using this program instead of the ROLLBACK command.

The DBMS_TRANSACTION.ROLLBACK_FORCE procedure

The ROLLBACK_FORCE procedure manually rolls back local in-doubt, distributed transactions. The specification for the procedure is,

```
PROCEDURE DBMS_TRANSACTION.ROLLBACK_FORCE (xid IN VARCHAR2);
```

where xid identifies the transaction's local or global transaction ID. To find these transaction IDs, query the data dictionary view DBA_2PC_PENDING.

Any decisions to force in-doubt transactions should be made after consulting with the database administrator(s) at the remote database location(s). If the decision is made to locally force any transactions, the database administrator should either commit or roll back such transactions (as was done by nodes that successfully resolved the transactions). Otherwise, the administrator should query the DBA_2PC_PENDING view's ADVICE and TRAN_COMMENT columns for further insight.

For more information on this topic, see "Manually Overriding In-Doubt Transactions" in the Oracle Corporation document *Oracle8 Server Distributed Systems*.

The DBMS_TRANSACTION.SAVEPOINT procedure

The SAVEPOINT procedure is equivalent to the SAVEPOINT command, which is already implemented as part of PL/SQL. The header for this procedure is,

```
PROCEDURE DBMS_TRANSACTION.SAVEPOINT (savept IN VARCHAR2);
```

where savept specifies the savepoint.

Why would you use this procedure and not simply rely on the SAVEPOINT command? When you use SAVEPOINT, you must use an "undeclared identifier" for the savepoint:

```
BEGIN
   SAVEPOINT right_here;
   do_my_stuff;
EXCEPTION
   WHEN OTHERS
   THEN
      ROLLBACK TO right_here;
END;
```

The "right_here" identifier is not declared anywhere; it is simply hard-coded into your application. With the DBMS_TRANSACTION programs, you can soft code these savepoint names, as you can see from the following block:

```
DECLARE
   v_sp VARCHAR2(30) := 'right_here';
```

```
BEGIN
    DBMS_TRANSACTION.SAVEPOINT (v_sp);
    do_my_stuff;

EXCEPTION
    WHEN OTHERS
    THEN
        /* Soft-coded rollback to, as well! */
        DBMS_TRANSACTION.ROLLBACK_SAVEPOINT (v_sp);
END;
/
```

The DBMS_TRANSACTION.ROLLBACK_SAVEPOINT procedure

The ROLLBACK_SAVEPOINT procedure is equivalent to the ROLLBACK TO command in PL/SQL. The header for this procedure is,

```
PROCEDURE DBMS_TRANSACTION.ROLLBACK_SAVEPOINT (savept IN VARCHAR2);
```

where savept specifies the savepoint.

You should use this program in coordination with the SAVEPOINT procedure, as illustrated in the example in the previous section. With this program, you can roll back to a savepoint that is not hard-coded into your application.

The DBMS_TRANSACTION.USE_ROLLBACK_SEGMENT procedure

The USE_ROLLBACK_SEGMENT procedure assigns the current transaction to the specified rollback segment. This option also establishes the transaction as a read-write transaction.

Here's the specification for the procedure:

```
PROCEDURE DBMS_TRANSACTION.USE_ROLLBACK_SEGMENT (rb_name IN VARCHAR2);
```

The specified rollback segment (rb_name) must be online. Often, the rollback specified is a large one that is kept offline during the day and is specifically enabled at night for large batch jobs. You cannot use both the DBMS_TRANSACTION.READ_ONLY (see next section) and the USE_ROLLBACK_SEGMENT procedures within the same transaction. Read-only transactions do not generate rollback information and thus cannot be assigned rollback segments.

In the following example, we have modified our data warehousing extract promotion program to reference the staging fact table remotely in order to load our local fact table—and to do so utilizing the big rollback segment. This version of the code has the advantage that it could be run without change from each remote database (assuming that each remote database had a big rollback segment named BIG_RBS).

```
BEGIN
    DBMS_TRANSACTION.USE_ROLLBACK_SEGMENT('BIG_RBS');
```

```
   INSERT INTO fact_table
      SELECT * FROM fact_table@staging;
   COMMIT;
 END;
 /
```

Setting Transaction Characteristics

DBMS_TRANSACTION offers several programs that set various characteristics of the transaction for your session.

The DBMS_TRANSACTION.READ_ONLY procedure

The READ_ONLY procedure establishes transaction-level read consistency (i.e., repeatable reads). Here's the header for this program:

```
PROCEDURE DBMS_TRANSACTION.READ_ONLY;
```

Once a transaction is designated as read-only, all queries within that transaction can see only changes committed prior to that transaction's start. Hence, read-only transactions permit you to issue two or more queries against tables that may be undergoing concurrent inserts or updates, and yet return results consistent as of the transaction's start. The READ_ONLY procedure is quite useful for reports. Long-running read-only transactions can receive a "snapshot too old" error (ORA-01555). If this occurs, increase rollback segment sizes.

In the following example, we can separately query the order and item tables successfully, regardless of other transactions. Even if someone deletes the item we are interested in while we query the order, a read-consistent image will be maintained in the rollback segments. So we will always be able to see the items for any order we look at.

```
DECLARE
   lv_order_count INTEGER := 0;
  lv_item_count INTEGER := 0;
BEGIN
   DBMS_TRANSACTION.READ_ONLY;
   SELECT COUNT(*) INTO lv_order_count FROM order WHERE order_number = 12345;
   SELECT COUNT(*) INTO lv_item_count FROM item WHERE order_number = 12345;
END;
/
```

The DBMS_TRANSACTION.READ_WRITE procedure

The READ_WRITE procedure establishes the current transaction as a read-write transaction. As this is the default transaction mode, you will not often need to use this procedure. The header for this program follows:

```
PROCEDURE DBMS_TRANSACTION.READ_WRITE;
```

The following example demonstrates using READ_WRITE in a transaction where we want to delete an order and its associated items. However, this example would execute in exactly the same way, even if the READ_WRITE procedure call were commented out.

```
BEGIN
    DBMS_TRANSACTION.READ_WRITE;
    DELETE FROM item WHERE order_number = 12345;
    DELETE FROM order WHERE order_number = 12345;
END;
/
```

The DBMS_TRANSACTION.BEGIN_DISCRETE_TRANSACTION procedure

The BEGIN_DISCRETE_TRANSACTION procedure streamlines transaction processing so that short transactions can execute more rapidly. The header for this program follows:

```
PROCEDURE DBMS_TRANSACTION.BEGIN_DISCRETE_TRANSACTION;
```

During discrete transactions, normal redo information is generated, although it is stored in a separate location in memory. When the discrete transaction commits, the redo information is written to the redo log file and data block changes are applied directly. As a result, there is no need for undo information in rollback segments. The block is then written to the database file in the usual manner. The call to this procedure is effective only until the transaction is committed or rolled back; the next transaction is processed as a standard transaction.

Restrictions. Although discrete transactions offer improved performance, there are numerous restrictions:

- The database initialization parameter DISCRETE_TRANSACTIONS_ENABLED must be set to TRUE; otherwise, calls to this procedure are ignored and transactions function normally.

- Discrete transactions cannot be distributed transactions.

- Discrete transactions can change each database block only once.

- Discrete transactions cannot see their own changes (since there are no rollback segments).

- Discrete transactions cannot perform inserts or updates on both tables involved in a referential integrity constraint.

- Discrete transactions cannot modify tables containing any LONG values.

Exceptions. This procedure may raise either of the following exceptions:

```
DBMS_TRANSACTION.DISCRETE_TRANSACTION_FAILED
DBMS_TRANSACTION.CONSISTENT_READ_FAILURE
```

Example. In the following example, we have modified the last version of our data
warehousing extract promotion program to utilize discrete transactions. The code
is written in such a way that it ensures that the transaction is attempted again in
the event of a discrete transaction failure. This coding practice should be followed
strictly.

```
BEGIN
    FOR fact_rec in (SELECT * FROM fact table@staging)
    LOOP
        DBMS_TRANSACTION. BEGIN_DISCRETE_TRANSACTION;
        FOR I in 1 .. 2
        LOOP
            BEGIN
                INSERT INTO fact_table
                    VALUES (fact_rec.product_id,
                        fact_rec.location_id,
                        fact_record.period_id,
                        fact_rec.numeric_value1,
                        fact_rec.numeric_value2);
                COMMIT;
                EXIT;
            EXCEPTION
                WHEN DBMS_TRANSACTION.DISCRETE_TRANSACTION_FAILED
                THEN
                    ROLLBACK;
            END;
        END LOOP;
    END LOOP;
END;
/
```

For more information on this topic, see "Using Discrete Transactions" in the Oracle Corporation document *Oracle8 Server Tuning*.

Cleaning Up Transaction Details

When performing two-phase commits, it is possible to "strand" information about
recovery or resolution steps. The two procedures PURGE_MIXED and PURGE_
LOST_DB_ENTRY are provided by Oracle to clean up that information.

The DBMS_TRANSACTION.PURGE_MIXED procedure

The PURGE_MIXED procedure deletes information about a given in-doubt, distributed transaction that has had mixed outcomes as the consequence of transaction
resolution mismatch. This occurs when an in-doubt, distributed transaction is
forced to commit or roll back on one node, and other nodes do the opposite. For
example, we may force commit on node 1 a distributed transaction that rolled
back on node 2. Oracle cannot automatically resolve such inconsistencies, but it
does flag entries in the DBA_2PC_PENDING view by setting the MIXED column

to "yes." When the database administrator is sure that any inconsistencies for a transaction have been resolved, he or she can call PURGE_MIXED procedure. The specification for the procedure is,

```
PROCEDURE DBMS_TRANSACTION.PURGE_MIXED (xid IN VARCHAR2);
```

where xid identifies the mixed transaction's local transaction ID, which can be found in the LOCAL_TRAN_ID column of the data dictionary view DBA_2PC_PENDING.

For more information on this topic, see "Manually Overriding In-Doubt Transactions" in the Oracle Corporation document *Oracle8 Server Distributed Systems.*

The DBMS_TRANSACTION.PURGE_LOST_DB_ENTRY procedure

The PURGE_LOST_DB_ENTRY procedure deletes information about a given indoubt, distributed transaction that has had mixed outcomes as the consequence of a lost database. This occurs when an in-doubt, distributed transaction is able to commit or roll back on one node and other nodes have either destroyed or recreated their databases. For example, we may successfully commit on node 1 a distributed transaction that is no longer represented in the recreation of the database now on node 2. Oracle cannot automatically resolve such inconsistencies. The information in DBA_2PC_PENDING will never be deleted, and Oracle will try periodically to recover (even though it can't).

When the database administrator is sure that any inconsistencies for a transaction have been resolved, he or she can call the PURGE_MIXED procedure.

The specification for the procedure is,

```
PROCEDURE DBMS_TRANSACTION.PURGE_LOST_DB_ENTRY (xid IN VARCHAR2);
```

where xid identifies the mixed transaction's local transaction ID, which can be found in the LOCAL_TRAN_ID column of the data dictionary view DBA_2PC_PENDING.

Oracle's *dbmsutil.sql* file, which contains the definition of the DBMS_TRANSACTION package, offers some insights into when and how you would use this program. According to that file, the DBMS_TRANSACTION.PURGE_LOST_DB_ENTRY procedure should only be used when the other database is lost or has been recreated. Any other use may leave that other database in an unrecoverable or inconsistent state.

Before you run automatic recovery, the transaction appears in the DBA_2PC_PENDING view in the state "collecting," "committed," or "prepared." If the DBA has forced an in-doubt transaction to have a particular result by using the COMMIT FORCE or ROLLBACK FORCE options, then the additional states FORCED COMMIT or FORCED ROLLBACK may also appear.

Automatic recovery will normally delete entries that are in any of these states. The only exception occurs when the recovery process finds a forced transaction that is in a state inconsistent with other sites in the transaction. In this case, the entry will be left in the table and the MIXED column will be given a value of "yes."

Under certain conditions, it may not be possible for an automatic recovery to execute without errors. For example, a remote database may have been permanently lost. In this case, even if it is recreated, it will be assigned a new database ID. As a result, recovery cannot identify it. (A possible symptom for this situation is when the ORA-02062 error is raised.)

In this case, the DBA may use the DBMS_TRANSACTION.PURGE_LOST_DB_ENTRY procedure to clean up any entries whose state is not "prepared."

The following table indicates what the various states indicate about the transaction and what the DBA actions should be.

State Column	State of Global Transaction	State of Local Transaction	Normal DBA Action	Alternative DBA Action
Collecting	Rolled back	Rolled back	None	PURGE_LOST_DB_ENTRY[a]
Committed	Committed	Committed	None	PURGE_LOST_DB_ENTRY
Prepared	Unknown	Unknown	None	COMMIT_FORCE or ROLLBACK_FORCE
Forced commit	Unknown	Committed	None	PURGE_LOST_DB_ENTRY
Forced rollback	Unknown	Rolled back	None	PURGE_LOST_DB_ENTRY
Forced commit (mixed)	Mixed	Committed	[b]	
Forced rollback (mixed)	Mixed	Rolled back	[b]	

[a] Use only if significant reconfiguration has occurred so that automatic recovery cannot resolve the transaction. Examples are total loss of the remote database, reconfiguration in software resulting in loss of two-phase commit capability, or loss of information from an external transaction coordinator such as a TP monitor.

[b] Examine manual action to remove inconsistencies, then use the PROCEDURE_PURGE_MIXED. The xid argument must be set to the value of the LOCAL_TRAN_ID column in the DBA_2PC_PENDING table.

For more information on this topic, see "Manually Overriding In-Doubt Transactions" in the Oracle Corporation document *Oracle8 Server Distributed Systems,* and the *dbmsutil* file under comments for PURGE_LOST_DB_ENTRY.

Returning Transaction Identifiers

The functions described in this section return indentifiers used by DBMS_TRANS-ACTION.

The DBMS_TRANSACTION.LOCAL_TRANSACTION_ID function

The LOCAL_TRANSACTION_ID function returns the unique identifier for the current transaction. The specification for the function follows:

```
FUNCTION DBMS_TRANSACTION.LOCAL_TRANSACTION_ID
    (create_transaction IN BOOLEAN := FALSE)
RETURN VARCHAR2;
```

The create_transaction parameter specifies whether to create a new transaction or use the current one. The function returns NULL if there is no current transaction.

So in your session, the transaction ID begins as NULL and is assigned a value upon first DML operation (transaction initiation). Transaction closure (COMMIT or ROLLBACK) nullifies the transaction ID. Explicit transaction initiation (passing TRUE for second argument to procedure call) assigns a new transaction ID value, regardless of whether you've actually started a transaction.

See an example of using this function in the next section (STEP_ID).

The DBMS_TRANSACTION.STEP_ID function

The STEP_ID function returns the unique positive integer that orders the DML operations of the current transaction. Here's the specification for the function:

```
FUNCTION DBMS_TRANSACTION.STEP_ID RETURN NUMBER;
```

If a transaction has not been initiated, then this function returns NULL. Values of step ID across transactions do not appear to have any guaranteed relationship to each other. Within a transaction, however, they will always be increasing.

The following script (written by John Beresniewicz) demonstrates the usage and output of the LOCAL_TRANSACTION_ID and STEP_ID functions:

```
/* Filename on companion disk: transid.sql */
set serveroutput on size 1000000
CREATE TABLE foo (col1 NUMBER);
DECLARE
    trx    VARCHAR2(200);
    step   NUMBER;

    PROCEDURE printem(message_IN IN VARCHAR2)
    IS
    BEGIN
        DBMS_OUTPUT.PUT_LINE(message_IN);
        DBMS_OUTPUT.PUT_LINE
            ('Trx id: '||RPAD(NVL(trx,'NULL'),30)||
```

```
                'Step: '||NVL(TO_CHAR(step),'NULL') );
        END printem;

        PROCEDURE getem
        IS
        BEGIN
            trx := DBMS_TRANSACTION.local_transaction_id;
            step := DBMS_TRANSACTION.step_id;
        END getem;

    BEGIN
        /* close any open transaction */
        COMMIT;
        /* how does it look at start of trx? */
        getem; printem('BEGIN');
        /*
        || do some DML and see  how step changes
        */
        INSERT INTO foo SELECT ROWNUM FROM dictionary;
        getem; printem('INSERT');
        UPDATE foo SET col1 = col1 + 1;
        getem; printem('UPDATE');
        DELETE FROM foo WHERE MOD(col1,2) = 0;
        getem; printem('DELETE');
        /*
        || now commit, they should be null
        */
        COMMIT;
        getem; printem('COMMIT');
        /*
        || now explicitly open a new transaction
        */
        trx := DBMS_TRANSACTION.local_transaction_id(TRUE);
        getem; printem('NEW TRX FORCED');
    END;
    /
```

The results of this script follow:

```
SQL> @transid.sql
Table created.
BEGIN
Trx id: NULL                        Step: NULL
INSERT
Trx id: 1.6.28680                   Step: 42802896748631309
UPDATE
Trx id: 1.6.28680                   Step: 42802896748632625
DELETE
Trx id: 1.6.28680                   Step: 42802896748633616
COMMIT
Trx id: NULL                        Step: NULL
NEW TRX FORCED
Trx id: 2.7.28508                   Step: 42045333236522790
```

5

Oracle Advanced Queuing

Oracle8 offers a facility (new to Oracle 8) called Oracle AQ (Oracle Advanced Queuing, referred to as AQ in this chapter) that will make it much easier for developers to build applications that require deferred execution of activity. Oracle is positioning Oracle AQ as an alternative to the queuing mechanisms of teleprocessing monitors and messaging interfaces. Oracle AQ will serve as a foundation technology for workflow management applications, both those delivered by Oracle Corporation itself and those implemented by third parties.

From a PL/SQL standpoint, Oracle AQ is made available through two packages: DBMS_AQADM and DBMS_AQ. The DBMS_AQADM package is the interface to the administrative tasks of Oracle AQ. These tasks include:

- Creating or dropping queue tables that contain one or more queues

- Creating, dropping, and altering queues, which are stored in a queue table

- Starting and stopping queues in accepting message creation or consumption

Most users of the Oracle AQ facility will not work with DBMS_AQADM. The DBA will most likely initialize all needed queue tables and queues. PL/SQL developers will instead work with the DBMS_AQ, whose tasks include:

- Creating a message to the specified queue

- Consuming a message from the specified queue

Most of the background information presented early in this chapter applies to both packages. Later, we'll provide individual discussions of the two packages and their programs.

Oracle AQ is full of features and offers tremendous flexibility in how you manipulate messages in queues. It also has only a handful of programs with which to administer and operate the queues. This relatively small number of procedures and functions can, nevertheless, be misleading. You will probably encounter lots of frustrating moments as you come up to speed on Oracle AQ (I know I did).

Some of the frustration will arise from the way that Oracle allows you to modify the characteristics of queues, queue tables, and specific enqueue and dequeue operations by setting individual fields of PL/SQL records, which are then passed to the appropriate programs as arguments. If you are not comfortable with declaring and manipulating record structures in PL/SQL, you should read through Chapter 9 of *Oracle PL/SQL Programming* (O'Reilly & Associates, 1997) before continuing with this chapter.

NOTE   Oracle AQ first became available with Oracle 8.0.3. A number of Oracle AQ features described in this chapter were added in Oracle 8.0.4. These additions will be noted, but it is generally assumed in this chapter that you have installed and are using Oracle 8.0.4, which should be widely available by the time this book is published.

Oracle AQ Concepts

Oracle AQ provides message queuing as an integrated part of the Oracle server. It provides this functionality by integrating the queuing system with the database itself. Oracle Corporation is therefore now beginning to describe Oracle8 not only as an object-relational database, but also as a "message-enabled" database. Its intention is to free application developers from having to construct a messaging infrastructure (or rely on a third-party tool such as a TP monitor). Instead they can use AQ and devote their efforts to implementing their own specific business rules.

General Features

The following list summarizes Oracle's perspective on the features of the AQ facility that it offers to developers:

SQL-based access and management

Messages are placed in normal rows in a database table. They can be queried using standard SQL. Thus, users can use SQL to access the message properties, the message history, and the payload. All available SQL technology, such as indexes, can be used to optimize the access to these messages.

Integrated database-level operational support

All standard database features, such as recovery, restart, and enterprise manager, are supported. Oracle AQ queues are implemented in database tables; thus, all the operational benefits of high availability, scalability, and reliability are applicable to queue data. In addition, database development and management tools can be used with queues. For instance, queue tables can be imported and exported.

Structured payload

Users can use object types to structure and manage the *payload* (i.e., content). RDBMSs in general have had a far richer typing system than messaging systems. Since Oracle8 is an object-relational DBMS, it supports traditional relational types and also user-defined types. Many powerful features are enabled as a result of having strongly typed content (i.e., content whose format is defined by an external type system). These include:

Content-based routing

An external agent can examine the content and route the message to another queue based on the content.

Content-based subscription

A publish and subscribe system built on top of a messaging system can offer content based on subscription.

Querying

The ability to execute queries on the content of the message enables message warehousing.

Retention and message history

Users can specify that messages be retained after consumption. The system administrator can specify the duration for which messages will be retained. Oracle AQ stores information about the history of each message. The information contains the enqueue/dequeue time and the identification of the transaction that executed each request. This allows users to keep a history of relevant messages. The history can be used for tracking, data warehouse, and data mining operations.

Tracking and event journals

If messages are retained they can be related to each other. For example, if a message m2 is produced as a result of the consumption of message m1, m1 is related to m2. This facility allows users to track sequences of related messages. These sequences represent "event journals" that are often constructed by applications. Oracle AQ is designed to let applications create event journals automatically.

NOTE   Oracle AQ does not automatically produce messages as a result of
            the consumption of other messages. You will do this programmatically. On the other hand, Oracle AQ does automatically track that
            these messages were processed in the same transaction.

Integrated transactions

The integration of control information with content (data payload) simplifies application development and management.

Enqueue Features

Oracle AQ offers a wide sweep of options for the way you enqueue messages.

Correlation identifier

Users can assign an identifier to each message, thus providing a means of retrieving specific messages at a later time.

Subscription and recipient lists

Multiple consumers can consume a single message. A queue administrator can specify the list of subscribers who can retrieve messages from a queue. Different queues can have different subscribers, and a consumer program can be a subscriber to more than one queue. Further, specific messages in a queue can be directed toward specific recipients who may or may not be subscribers to the queue, thereby overriding the subscriber list.

Prioritization and ordering of messages

It is possible to specify the priority of the enqueued message. An enqueued message can also have its exact position in the queue specified. This means that users have three options to specify the order in which messages are consumed: (a) a sort order specifies which properties are used to order all messages in a queue; (b) a priority can be assigned to each message; (c) a sequence deviation allows you to position a message in relation to other messages. Furthermore, if several consumers act on the same queue, a consumer will get the first message that is available for immediate consumption. A message that is in the process of being consumed by another consumer will be skipped.

Propagation

With Oracle 8.0.4 and later versions, applications can use AQ to communicate with one another without having to be connected to the same database instance or to the same queue. Instead, messages can be propagated from one Oracle AQ environment to another. These AQ instances can be local or remote. AQ propagation relies on database links and Net8.

Message grouping

Messages belonging to one queue can be grouped to form a set that can only be consumed by one user at a time. This requires the queue be created in a queue table that is enabled for message grouping. Messages belonging to a group must be created in the same transaction, and all messages created in one transaction belong to the same group. This feature allows users to segment complex messages into simple messages. For example, messages directed to a queue containing invoices could be constructed as a group of messages starting with the header, followed by messages representing details, followed by the trailer message.

Time specification and scheduling

Delay interval and/or expiration intervals can be specified for an enqueued message, thereby providing windows of execution. A message can be marked as available for processing only after a specified time elapses (a delay time) and has to be consumed before a specified time limit expires. Messages can also be scheduled for propagation from a queue to a local or remote destination (Oracle 8.0.4 only). AQ administrators have the option to specify the start time, propagation window, and a function that determines the next propagation window for scheduling on a periodic basis.

Dequeue Features

As you would expect, Oracle AQ also allows you to dequeue messages in a variety of methods.

Multiple recipients

A message in a queue can be retrieved by multiple recipients without the need to store multiple copies of that same message.

Navigation of messages for dequeuing

Users have several options for selecting a message from a queue. They can select the first message, or, once they have selected a message and established a position, they can retrieve the next. The selection is influenced by the ordering or can be limited by specifying a correlation identifier. Users can also retrieve a specific message using the message identifier.

Multiple dequeue modes

A dequeue request can either browse or remove a message. If a message is browsed, it remains available for further processing; if a message is removed, it is no longer available for dequeue requests. Depending on the queue properties, a removed message may be retained in the queue table.

Message-waiting optimization

A dequeue could be issued against an empty queue. To avoid polling for the arrival of a new message, a user can specify if and for how long the request is allowed to wait for the arrival of a message.

Retries with delays

A message must be consumed exactly once. If an attempt to dequeue a message fails and the transaction is rolled back, the message will be made available for reprocessing after some user-specified delay elapses. Reprocessing will be attempted up to the user-specified limit.

Optional transaction protection

Enqueue/dequeue requests are normally part of a transaction that contains the requests, thereby providing the desired transactional behavior. Users can, however, specify that a specific request is a transaction by itself, making the result of that request immediately visible to other transactions. This means that messages can be made visible to the external world either as soon as the ENQUEUE or DEQUEUE statement is issued, or only after the transaction is committed.

Exception handling

A message may not be consumed within given constraints—that is, within the window of execution or within the limits of the retries. If such a condition arises, the message will be moved to a user-specified exception queue.

Propagation Features

Oracle AQ with Oracle 8.0.4 supports propagation of messages, allowing automated coordination of enqueuing and dequeuing operations. The recipient of a message can be either in the same database as AQ (local) or in another database (remote). Since Oracle8 does not support distributed object types, it is not possible to rely on standard database links to perform remote AQ operations. Instead, Oracle AQ offers a special message propagation facility to allow an agent to enqueue to a remote queue.

You can configure AQ so that any messages enqueued in one (local) queue will be automatically propagated to another queue in either the local or remote database. AQ checks automatically that the type of the local queue to which the message is enqueued is the same as the type of the remote queue (same payload type). You can perform this same check by calling the DBMS_AQADM.VERIFY_QUEUE_TYPES procedure.

There are two useful ways to think about employing message propagation in Oracle AQ: *fanning out* and *funnelling in* messages.

Fanning out messages

Suppose you want to distribute a message to a large number of recipients without forcing those recipients to perform dequeue operations from a single queue. This is most important when working in a distributed database environment. You can accomplish this by defining another queue as a recipient of a message. When a queue is a recipient for a message, the actual recipients are the set of agents defined in the subscription list for that queue.

Consider the following scenario: an international human rights organization based in London has received news of the torture and imprisonment of a dissident. It needs to notify its branch organizations throughout the world as quickly as possible—using Oracle AQ, of course. The subscribers to its *urgent_alert* queue consist of each of its regional offices: *urgent_alert@new_york, urgent_alert@johannesburg,* and so on. Each of the regional urgent alert queues has as its subscribers the country offices. So the Johannesburg queue has the following subscribers: *urgent_alert@harare, urgent_alert@cairo,* and so on.

When the headquarters office enqueues the alert message to its *urgent_alert* queue, the message will be propagated out to each regional office queue. That message will then in turn be propagated to each country office. Figure 5-1 illustrates the fanning out technique.

Funnelling in messages

It is also very useful to concentrate messages from different queues back to a single queue. Examples of this technique, also called "compositing," include roll-up of monthly accounting figures from regional offices and confirmation messages in response to a broadcast.

If we use the same scenario as with the fanning out approach, each country office employs a *report_back* queue to confirm that urgent alerts have been received and responded to. The subscriber list for each office's *report_back* queue include the regional office as well as the international office. As a result, the London-based *report_back@london_hq* will automatically receive a copy of all confirmation reports without having to wait for those messages to be transferred back through the individual regional offices. Figure 5-2 illustrates the funneling in technique.

A Glossary of Terms

Before diving into the sometimes overwhelming details of configuring queue tables and queues and enqueuing and dequeuing messages, let's review some of the terms used throughout this chapter. Then we'll take a step back and look at the process flow for the queuing facility. At that point, you'll have a much easier job understanding and then deploying Oracle AQ.

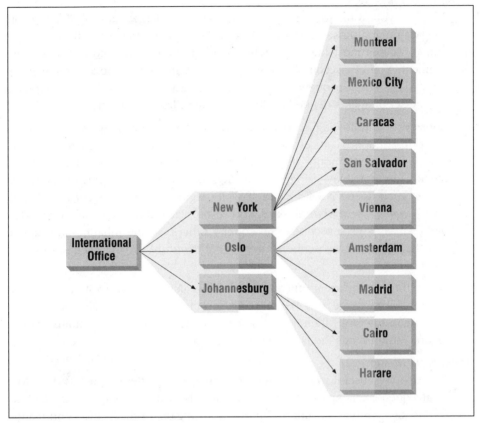

Figure 5-1. Fanning out messages

The basic elements of Oracle AQ follow:

Message

The smallest unit of work in the queue, consisting of information about how the message is to be treated (metadata) and the payload (the data supplied by the user). The metadata or control information is used by AQ to manage the messages. The payload information is stored in the queue and is transparent to AQ (that is, AQ does not try to *interpret* that information in any way). A message resides in only one queue. It is created by a call to the DBMS_AQ.ENQUEUE procedure and is dequeued by a call to the DBMS_AQ.DEQUEUE procedure.

Queue

A queue is a storage space for messages. You can create two different types of queues: *user queues*, also known as normal queues, and *exception queues*. The user queue is employed for standard message processing. The exception queue is used to hold messages if attempts to retrieve the message through a

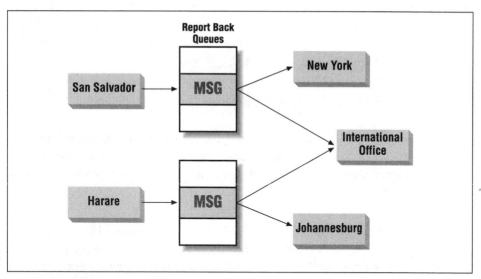

Figure 5-2. Funneling in messages

dequeue operation fail (this is done automatically by AQ) or if the message is not dequeued before its expiration time. You will use the AQ administrative interface, the DBMS_AQADM package, to create, start, stop, and drop queues.

Queue table

A queue table is a database table that holds one or more queues; this queue table is created when you create the queue table. Each queue table also contains a default exception queue. You will use the AQ administrative interface (the DBMS_AQADM package) to create and drop queue tables.

Agent

An agent is a user of a queue. There are two types of agents: *producers*, who place messages in a queue (enqueuing); and *consumers*, who retrieve messages (dequeuing). Any number of producers and consumers may be accessing the queue at a given time. An agent's name, address, and protocol identify that agent. The address field is a character field of up to 1024 bytes that is interpreted according to the protocol value (of which the only supported value is currently 0). A protocol of 0 indicates that the address is to be interpreted as a database link. The address will therefore have this form,

```
queue_name@dblink
```

where queue_name has the form [schema.]queue and dblink is either a fully-qualified database link name or a database link name that does not incorporate the domain name.

Agents insert messages into a queue and retrieve messages from the queue by using the Oracle AQ operational interfaces offered in the DBMS_AQ package.

Recipient list

> A list of one or more agents that you can construct to receive a message (through the dequeue operation). With Oracle 8.0.4., a recipient can be either an agent or a queue.

Producer

> An agent that places messages in a queue with the enqueue operation.

Consumer

> An agent that retrieves messages from a queue with the dequeue operation. Note that you can modify the characteristics of your dequeue operation so that the agent does not actually consume (i.e., read and then remove from the queue) its message.

Message ID

> The unique handle for a message. This value is generated by AQ. You can use it to retrieve a specific message from a queue (bypassing the default order of dequeuing associated with the queue and/or queue table). You can also use this message ID to find out about the status of a message from the underlying data dictionary views. These message IDs are long, complex values like "105E7A2EBFF11348E03400400B40F149."

Message group

> One or more messages can be joined together logically as a *group*. You do this by specifying a queue table as supporting message grouping. All messages queued in a single transaction must then be dequeued as a group for that set of messages to be considered completely dequeued.

Queue Monitor

> The Queue Monitor is an optional background process that monitors the status of messages in your queues. Use the Queue Monitor when you want to set expiration and delay intervals for messages.

Lots of concepts, lots of terminology. Let's see if we can obtain some additional clarity from the following figures.

Figure 5-3 illustrates how you create one or more queues within a queue table. Each queue can have one or more messages. Messages in different queues do not have any relation to each other. Each queue table has a single default exception queue, which contains messages that have expired or have otherwise failed to dequeue successfully

Figure 5-4 shows that producer agents place messages in a queue and consumer agents remove messages from a queue. The same Oracle process can be both a producer and a consumer; more commonly, you will use Oracle AQ to allow multiple Oracle connections to enqueue and dequeue messages. Some points to keep in mind:

- Messages do not have to be dequeued in the same order in which they were enqueued.

- Messages can be enqueued but never dequeued.

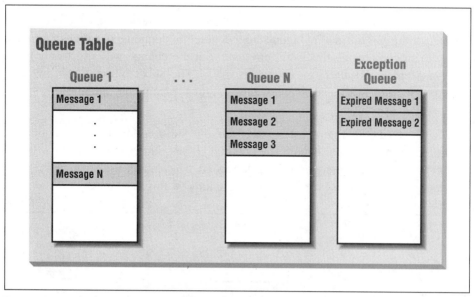

Figure 5-3. Multiple queues in a single queue table

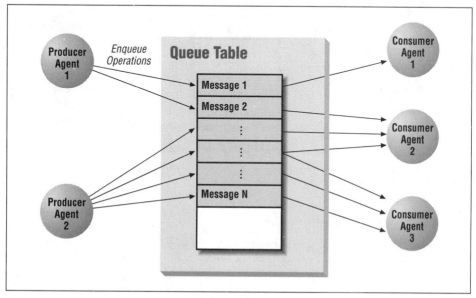

Figure 5-4. Producers enqueue, consumers dequeue

Figure 5-5 illustrates the "broadcast" feature of Oracle AQ. You can define a queue table to support "multiple consumers." In this configuration, a single message can be consumed by more than one agent, either through the default subscription list or with an override recipient list. Under this scenario, a message remains in the queue until it is consumed by all of its intended consumer agents.

When you set up a subscriber list for a queue, you are establishing that list of agents as the default set of agents to be able to dequeue messages from the queue. You can change this list at any time, but the change will affect only those messages enqueued after the change is made. The subscription list is, in other words, associated with a message at the time of the enqueue operation, not with the dequeue operation.

You will use the recipient list to override the subscription list for dequeuing. Under this scenario, at the time the message is enqueued, you specify a list of agents to which the message may be dequeued. The default list of subscribers for the queue is then ignored for dequeue operations on this message.

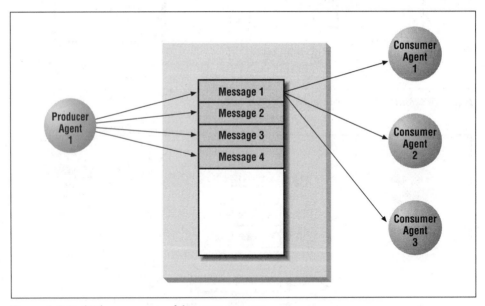

Figure 5-5. Multiple consumers of the same message

Components of Oracle AQ

Oracle AQ is composed of a number of different elements, not just a single built-in package. These elements follow:

The DBMS_AQADM package

An interface to the administrative tasks of Oracle AQ, such as creating and dropping queues and queue tables. This package and the programs it supports, are described in later sections.

The DBMS_AQ package

The package that offers access to the enqueue and dequeue operations (the "operational tasks") of Oracle AQ. This package, and the programs it supports are described in later sections.

The Queue Monitor

A background process that can be used to delay and expire messages for dequeuing (described in the "Queue Monitor" section following).

Data dictionary views

A set of views against the underlying AQ tables that allows users of AQ to view the results of administrative and operational tasks (described in the "Data Dictionary Views" section following).

Queue Monitor

The Queue Monitor is an Oracle process that runs in the background and monitors the status of messages in your queues. It is optional and is present only when you set the appropriate database initialization parameter, or you call the DBMS_AQADM.START_TIME_MANAGER procedure (see "Database Initialization," later in this chapter). You will need the Queue Monitor if you want to set expiration and delay intervals for messages.

Data Dictionary Views

Oracle AQ offers a set of data dictionary views that allows you to monitor the status of queuing operations. This section lists the different views. At the end of the chapter, you will find a section titled "Oracle AQ Database Objects," which offers more details on these views and other database objects created and used by Oracle AQ.

Queue table database table

The queue table in which message data is stored. This table is created automatically when you create a queue table. The name of this table is <queue_table>, where <queue_table> is the name of the queue table you specified.

Queue table view

A view of the queue table in which message data is stored. This view is created automatically when you create a queue table. The name of this view is aq$<queue_table>, where <queue_table> is the name of the queue table you specified.

DBA_QUEUE_TABLES

> This view describes the names and types of all queue tables created in the database. To see this view, you must have the DBA authority or the SELECT ANY TABLE privilege.

USER_QUEUE_TABLES

> This view describes the names and types of all queue tables created in your schema. It has the same structure as DBA_QUEUE_TABLES, except that it does not have an OWNER column.

DBA_QUEUES

> This view displays all operational characteristics for every queue in a database. Operational characteristics include whether the queue is enabled for queuing, the number of retries allowed for a dequeue operation, and so on. To see this view, you must have DBA authority or the SELECT ANY TABLE privilege.

USER_QUEUES

> This view displays all operational characteristics for every queue in your schema. It has the same structure as DBA_QUEUES, except that it does not have an OWNER column.

Getting Started with Oracle AQ

There are five basic steps involved in using Oracle AQ:

1. Install Oracle AQ for use in your database. For this, the underlying database objects must be created and the initialization file for the instance modified.

2. Authorize administrative and operational privileges on queues.

3. Set up the message queue tables and corresponding queues.

4. Enqueue messages to a queue.

5. Dequeue messages from a queue.

In many organizations, steps 1 through 3 will be performed by a database administrator. They require specific authorization and can be a complex process, depending on the type of queues you want to create. The fourth and fifth steps will be performed from within the PL/SQL programs that you have written to take advantage of this message queuing technology.

Steps 3, 4, and 5 are explained in detail later in this chapter. For now, let's take a look at the steps you must take to install AQ and to grant the proper privileges to Oracle accounts in order to perform AQ activities.

Installing the Oracle AQ Facility

Oracle Corporation has established the following guidelines for use of Oracle AQ:

- If you have a license to the Oracle8 Enterprise Edition with the Objects Option, then you will be able to take advantage of the full functionality of Oracle AQ.

- If you have a license to the Oracle8 Enterprise Edition without the Objects option, then you will be able to use Oracle AQ with queues of type RAW only.

- If you have a license to Oracle8 without the Enterprise Edition, you are not licensed to use Oracle AQ at all.

The DBMS_AQ and DBMS_AQADM packages (and the database object used by them) are created when the Oracle database is installed. You should not have to take any special steps to install Oracle AQ and make it available in your environment. (You will, as covered in a later section, need to grant access to Oracle AQ to specific users.)

Before you can execute any programs in the DBMS_AQADM or DBMS_AQ packages, you may need to grant EXECUTE privilege on those packages explicitly (role-based privileges do not take effect inside stored code). If you have trouble executing any program in these packages, connect to the SYS account and execute these commands,

```
GRANT EXECUTE ON DBMS_AQADM TO <user>;
GRANT EXECUTE ON DBMS_AQ TO <user>;
```

where <user> is the name of the account to which you want to grant EXECUTE privilege.

Database Initialization

You will need to set one or more initialization parameters in order to obtain the desired behavior from Oracle AQ.

Starting the Queue Monitor

One of the features of Oracle AQ is the ability to manage the time in which messages are available for dequeueing and the time after which messages are "expired." If you want to employ this "time management" feature, you need to add a parameter to your initialization file or INIT.ORA file for your database instance. The name of this parameter is AQ_TM_PROCESSES, and it can be assigned a nonzero integer value. If the parameter is set to any number between 1 and 10, that number of Queue Monitor background processes will be created to monitor messages in the various queues.

The name of the process created is,

```
ora_aqtm_<oracle_SID>
```

where oracle_SID is the System ID for the database instance being started. If the parameter is not specified or is set to 0, then the Queue Monitor background process will not be created.

Here is an example of a line in the INIT.ORA file that specifies that one Queue Monitor process be created:

```
AQ_TM_PROCESSES = 1
```

If the Queue Monitor process it not started, you will not be able to start and stop the Queue Monitor using the DBMS_AQADM.START_TIME_MANAGER and DBMS_AQADM.STOP_TIME_MANAGER procedures, respectively.

Starting propagation processes

Message propagation (an Oracle 8.0.4 AQ feature) is implemented by job queue processes. The number of these processes is defined with the JOB_QUEUE_PRO-CESSES parameter. The default value for this parameter is 0. If you want message propagation to take place, you must set this parameter to at least 1. If you plan to propagate messages from many queues in your instance or receive messages to many destination queues, you (or your DBA) should set this parameter to a higher value.

Here is an example of a setting of this parameter to three processes:

```
JOB_QUEUE_PROCESSES = 3
```

See Chapter 12, *Managing Server Resources*, for more information about DBMS_JOB and the setting of this parameter.

Setting Oracle AQ compatibility

If you want to use the Oracle AQ propagation feature, set your compatibility setting in the INIT.ORA file as follows:

```
COMPATIBLE = 8.0.4
```

This parameter will be checked under any of the following conditions:

- If a call to the DBMS_AQADM.ADD_SUBSCRIBER procedure includes an agent (defined with the SYS.AQ$_AGENT object type) whose address field is non-NULL.

- If an agent defined with the SYS.AQ$_AGENT object type whose address field is non-NULL is specified in the recipient list field of a message properties record in a call to the DBMS_AQ.ENQUEUE procedure.

- If you call the DBMS_AQADM.SCHEDULE_PROPAGATION procedure.

You can also downgrade to 8.0.3 after you have used the Oracle 8.0.4 features by using the following command:

```
ALTER DATABASE RESET COMPATIBILITY
```

Users will not be able to restart the database in 8.0.3 compatibility mode under the following conditions:

- If you have messages in queues that have not yet been propagated to their destination queues.

- If there are propagation schedules still pending for execution. If this is the case, then you will probably need to run DBMS_AQADM.UNSCHEDULE_ PROPAGATION to remove those schedules.

- If you have queues with subscribers that specify remote destination (with a non-NULL address field in the agent). In this scenario, you will want to run DBMS_AQADM.REMOVE_SUBSCRIBER to remove the remote subscribers.

If you have been using Oracle AQ in Oracle 8.0.3 and are now upgrading to 8.0.4, check the online Oracle documentation for upgrade steps you must take.

Authorizing Accounts to Use Oracle AQ

When working with AQ, you will perform either administrative or operational activities. Administrative tasks include creating queue tables and queues, and starting and stopping queues. Operational tasks include different aspects of using existing queues (i.e., queuing messages to them and dequeuing messages from them). Access to these operations is granted to users through database roles. There are two such roles:

AQ_ADMINISTRATOR_ROLE
> This role grants EXECUTE privileges for all programs in DBMS_AQ and DBMA_AQADM. The user SYS must grant this role to the account(s) defined to be AQ administrators.

AQ_USER_ROLE
> This role grants EXECUTE privileges for all programs in DBMS_AQ. The AQ administrator (an account to which the AQ_ADMINISTRATOR_ROLE privilege has been previously granted) must grant this role to the account(s) defined to be AQ users.

> *NOTE*   Administrator and user privileges are granted at the database level, and not on specific objects or within schemas. As a result, any Oracle account with the AQ_USER_ROLE can perform enqueue and dequeue operations on *any* queue in the database instance. Given this situation, how can you minimize the chance of messages being incorrectly queued or dequeued? You are always best off building a package around your AQ usage that hides the names of your queue tables and queues. See the "Oracle AQ Examples" section for many illustrations of this technique.

Here is an example of the steps you might perform from SQL*Plus to set up an AQ administrator:

```
SQL> CONNECT SYS/CHANGE_ON_INSTALL
SQL> GRANT AQ_ADMINISTRATOR_ROLE TO AQADMIN;
```

The AQADMIN account can now set up that old standby SCOTT as an AQ user account as follows:

```
SQL> CONNECT aqadmin/top_secret
SQL> GRANT AQ_USER_ROLE TO scott;
```

If you further wish to create and manipulate queue tables that are enabled for multiple dequeuing (in other words, queues that use subscriber lists to dequeue a message to multiple consumers), you must also execute the GRANT_TYPE_ACCESS procedure of the DBMS_AQADM package. The SYS account must do this for the AQ administrator account; that administrator can then do the same for AQ user accounts. Here are the steps:

1. Enable AQADMIN for multiple dequeues from SYS:

```
SQL> CONNECT SYS/CHANGE_ON_INSTALL
SQL> exec DBMS_AQADM.GRANT_TYPE_ACCESS ('aqadmin');
```

2. Enable SCOTT for multiple dequeues from AQADMIN:

```
SQL> CONNECT aqadmin/top_secret
SQL> exec DBMS_AQADM.GRANT_TYPE_ACCESS ('scott');
```

Now we have two accounts that are ready, willing, and able to do some queuing! These steps are also performed for you by the files *aqadmset.sql* (for AQ administrators) and *aqfor.sql* (for AQ users).

> *TIP*   If you are running Oracle 8.0.3, you might encounter problems with this approach. Under this first production release of Oracle8, you should instead perform all grant operations from the SYS or SYSTEM accounts.

Oracle AQ Nonprogram Elements

Oracle AQ defines a number of data structures, exceptions, and other nonprogram elements you'll use when creating and manipulating queues. In addition, there are several data structures you will create and pass to Oracle AQ programs. In many cases, you will find yourself creating and manipulating objects, index-by tables (formerly known as PL/SQL tables), and records. If you are not familiar with these programming constructs, you should review the appropriate chapters in the second edition of *Oracle PL/SQL Programming.*

Constants

Oracle AQ predefines a set of constants that you then use in various calls to procedures and functions. The following two lists break out these constants into those that are used for administrative tasks and those that figure into operational actions. In both cases, I intentionally do not show the values assigned to these constants. You should never hard-code those values into your code. Instead, always rely on the constants.

Administrative tasks

When you are performing administrative tasks in AQ (such as creating queue tables and queues), you may need to use one of the following constants:

Task	Constant
Specify the type of payload	DBMS_AQADM.OBJECT_TYPE_PAYLOAD DBMS_AQADM.RAW_TYPE
Enable or disable a queue for multiple consumers	DBMS_AQADM.SINGLE DBMS_AQADM.MULTIPLE
Request that messages on a queue never expire	DBMS_AQADM.INFINITE
Specify type of message grouping for a queue table	DBMS_AQADM.TRANSACTIONAL DBMS_AQADM.NONE
Specify type of queue	DBMS_AQADM.NORMAL_QUEUE DBMS_AQADM.EXCEPTION_QUEUE

Operational tasks

When you are enqueuing and dequeuing messages (the operational tasks in AQ), you may need to use one of the following constants:

Description	Constant
Specify visibility of the queue message	DBMS_AQ.IMMEDIATE DBMS_AQ.ON_COMMIT

Description	Constant
Specify dequeuing mode	DBMS_AQ.BROWSE DBMS_AQ.LOCKED DBMS_AQ.REMOVE
Specify method of inter-message navigation	DBMS_AQ.FIRST_MESSAGE DBMS_AQ.NEXT_MESSAGE DBMS_AQ.NEXT_TRANSACTION
Specify state of the message	DBMS_AQ.WAITING DBMS_AQ.READY DBMS_AQ.PROCESSED DBMS_AQ.EXPIRED
Specify deviation from normal dequeuing sequence	DBMS_AQ.BEFORE DBMS_AQ.TOP
Specify amount of time to wait for a dequeue operation to succeed	DBMS_AQ.FOREVER DBMS_AQ.NO_WAIT
Specify amount of time to delay before making a message available for dequeuing	DBMS_AQ.NO_DELAY
Specify amount of time to elapse before a message expires	DBMS_AQ.NEVER

Object Names

You will specify the name of an Oracle AQ object (queue, queue table, or object type) in many different program calls. An AQ object name can be up to 24 characters long, and can be qualified by an optional schema name (also a maximum of 24 characters in length). If you do not specify a schema, then the current schema is used.

In the following block I create a RAW queue table for use with my own schema:

```
DECLARE
    v_queuetable VARCHAR2(24) := 'myqueue';
BEGIN
    DBMS_AQADM.CREATE_QUEUE_TABLE (
        queue_table => v_queuetable,
        queue_payload_type => 'RAW');
```

But in the next call to the same built-in procedure, I create a queue table in another schema:

```
DECLARE
    v_queuetable VARCHAR2(49) := 'scott.myqueue';
BEGIN
    DBMS_AQADM.CREATE_QUEUE_TABLE (
        queue_table => v_queuetable,
        queue_payload_type => 'RAW');
```

I specified 49 characters, since I needed room (potentially) for the period.

Now you know the rules for object names. However, you should never hard-code those rules into your programs as shown in the previous examples. What if Oracle decides to increase the allowable size for these names? Your programs will be stuck using the old limitations. Instead, you should define subtypes that you can then use to declare queue-related variables without any hard-coded restraints.

My aq package (*aq.spp*) demonstrates this technique. Here are the first few lines of that package's specification:

```
/* Filename on companion disk: aq.spp */
CREATE OR REPLACE PACKAGE aq
   IS
      v_msgid RAW(16);
      SUBTYPE msgid_type IS v_msgid%TYPE;

      v_name VARCHAR2(49);
      SUBTYPE name_type IS v_name%TYPE;
```

With the aq package defined in my schema, I would set up my raw queue table as follows:

```
DECLARE
   v_queuetable aq.name_type := 'myqueue';
BEGIN
   DBMS_AQADM.CREATE_QUEUE_TABLE (
      queue_table => v_queuetable,
      queue_payload_type => 'RAW');
```

No more literal value in the datatype of my declaration!

Queue Type Names

When you specify the name of a queue type (also referred to as "payload type"), you provide either the name of an object type (previously defined in the database) or you specify the constant "RAW" (as shown in the previous section).

If you specify a payload type of RAW, AQ creates a queue table with a LOB column as the repository for any messages in its queues. The LOB value is limited to a maximum of 32K bytes of data. In addition, since LOB columns are used, the AQ administrator can specify the LOB tablespace and configure the LOB storage by providing a storage string in the storage_clause parameter in the call to the DBMS_AQADM.CREATE_QUEUE_TABLE procedure.

Agents Object Type

An agent is an object that produces or consumes a message. You will create agents in order to specify subscribers for queues and also to create recipient lists for the dissemination of messages. You define an agent as an instance of the following object type,

```
TYPE SYS.AQ$_AGENT IS OBJECT
   (name VARCHAR2(30),
    address VARCHAR2(1024),
    protocol NUMBER);
```

where the name is the name of the agent, and address is a character field of up to 1024 bytes that is interpreted according to the protocol value (of which the only supported value is currently 0). A protocol of 0 indicates that the address is to be interpreted as a database link. The address will therefore have this form: queue_name@dblink, where queue_name has the form [schema.]queue and dblink is either a fully qualified database link name or a database link name that does not incorporate the domain name.

Here is an example of defining an agent to be used with AQ:

```
DECLARE
   consumer_agent SYS.AQ$_AGENT;
BEGIN
   /* And now I use the constructor method to give
      a name to that object. */
   consumer_agent := SYS.AQ$_AGENT ('CLERK');
```

Recipient and Subscriber List Table Types

The subscriber and recipient lists are lists of agents, each of which is an instance of one of the following two index-by table types:

```
TYPE DBMS_AQ.AQ$_RECIPIENT_LIST_T IS TABLE OF SYS.AQ$_AGENT
   INDEX BY BINARY_INTEGER;

TYPE DBMS_AQADM.AQ$_SUBSCRIBER_LIST_T IS TABLE OF SYS.AQ$_AGENT
   INDEX BY BINARY_INTEGER;
```

The recipient list is used when enqueuing a message to establish a specific list of agents who can dequeue or consume a message. It is therefore defined in the DBMS_AQ package.

The subscriber list is used to enqueue a message to a list of subscribers for a given queue. You will call the DBMS_AQADM.QUEUE_SUBSCRIBERS function to obtain the subscript list for a queue. The subscripter list table type is therefore defined in the DBMS_AQADM package. As you can see, these table types are identical in structure; only their names differ.

The following block of code demonstrates the creation of a recipient list:

```
DECLARE
   recipients DBMS_AQ.AQ$_RECIPIENT _LIST_T;
BEGIN
```

```
recipients(1) := SYS.AQ$_AGENT ('DBA');
recipients(2) := SYS.AQ$_AGENT ('DESIGNER');
recipients(3) := SYS.AQ$_AGENT ('DEVELOPER');
```

See the "Oracle AQ Examples" section entitled "Working with Multiple Consumers" for a complete example of the creation of recipient lists and the association of those lists with a queued message.

Message Properties Record Type

When you enqueue a message, you can associate a set of properties with that message. You can then also receive these properties (or most of them) when you dequeue the message. You define the properties of a message by declaring and populating a PL/SQL record based on the following record type:

```
TYPE DBMS_AQ.MESSAGE_PROPERTIES_T IS RECORD
    (priority        BINARY_INTEGER DEFAULT 1,
     delay           BINARY_INTEGER DEFAULT DBMS_AQ.NO_DELAY,
     expiration      BINARY_INTEGER DEFAULT DBMS_AQ.NEVER,
     correlation     VARCHAR2(128) DEFAULT NULL,
     attempts        BINARY_INTEGER,
     recipient_list  DBMS_AQ.AQ$_RECIPIENT_LIST_T,
     exception_queue VARCHAR2(51) DEFAULT NULL,
     enqueue_time    DATE,
     state           BINARY_INTEGER);
```

Here is an explanation of the various fields of this record type:

priority

Specifies the priority of the message you are queueing. A smaller number indicates a higher priority. The priority can be any number, including negative numbers. The default is 1.

delay

Specifies the delay of the enqueued message. This value indicates the number of seconds after which a message becomes available for dequeuing. If you specify DBMS_AQ.NO_DELAY (the default), then the message is available for immediate dequeueing. A message enqueued with a delay set will be placed in the WAITING state. When the delay time expires, the message changes to the READY state. Delay processing requires that the Queue Monitor be started.

NOTE   Dequeuing by the message ID overrides the delay specification. In addition, the delay is set by the producer, who enqueues the message, not the consumer, who dequeues the message.

---

expiration

Specifies the time in seconds after which the message expires. This value
determines the number of seconds a message will remain in the READY state,
available for dequeuing. If you specify DBMS_AQ.NEVER, then the message
will never expire (the default behavior). If the message is not dequeued
before it expires, it will be moved to the exception queue in the EXPIRED
state.

This parameter is an offset from the delay value specified (see earlier). Expiration processing requires that the Queue Monitor be running.

correlation

Specifies identification supplied by the producer for a message at enqueuing.
This is a free-form text field. Place whatever value you would like to use to
later identify this message for dequeuing.

attempts

Specifies the number of attempts that have been made to dequeue this message. This parameter cannot be set at enqueue time. Instead, it is maintained
automatically by AQ and is available when you have dequeued the message.

recipient_list

A table containing a list of agents. This parameter is valid only for queues that
allow multiple consumers. If you do not specify a recipient list, then the
default recipients of this message are the agents identified as subscribers to
the queue (with a call to DBMS_AQADM.ADD_SUBSCRIBER). This parameter
is not returned to a consumer at dequeue time.

exception_queue

Specifies the name of the queue to which the message is moved if it cannot
be processed successfully. You specify this value at enqueue time.

Messages are moved in two cases: the number of unsuccessful dequeue
attempts has exceeded the maximum number of retries, or the message has
expired. All messages in the exception queue are set to the EXPIRED state. If
you do not specify an exception queue, the exception queue associated with
the queue table is used. If the exception queue specified does not exist at the
time of the move, the message will be moved to the default exception queue
associated with the queue table. A warning will then be logged in the Oracle
alert file. If the default exception queue is used, the parameter will return a
NULL value at dequeue time.

You will find an example of using a non-default exception queue in the "Oracle AQ Examples" section entitled "Using Time Delay and Expiration."

enqueue_time

> Specifies the time the message was enqueued. This value is determined by the system and cannot be set by the user. This parameter cannot be set at enqueue time. It is available only when the message is dequeued.

state

> Specifies the state of the message at the time of the dequeue. This parameter cannot be set at enqueue time. Instead, this state is maintained automatically by AQ and can be one of the following values:

> *DBMS_AQ.WAITING*

> > The message delay has not yet been reached (value = 1).

> *DBMS_AQ.READY*

> > The message is ready to be processed (value = 0).

> *DBMS_AQ.PROCESSED*

> > The message has been processed and is retained (value = 3).

> *DBMS_AQ.EXPIRED*

> > The message has been moved to the exception queue (value = 4).

The following block of code demonstrates how to define a message properties record and set several of the fields:

```
DECLARE
    msgprop DBMS_AQ.MESSAGE_PROPERTIES_T;
BEGIN
    msgprop.priority := -100; /* high priority */
    msgprop.delay := 60*60*24 /* delay for one day */
    msgprop.expiration := 60*60; /* expire one hour after delay */
```

Enqueue Options Record Type

When you enqueue a message, you can specify the options you want associated with that message. You do this by declaring and populating a record based on the following record type:

```
TYPE DBMS_AQ.ENQUEUE_OPTIONS_T IS RECORD
    (visibility          BINARY_INTEGER DEFAULT DBMS_AQ.ON_COMMIT,
     relative_msgid      RAW(16) DEFAULT NULL,
     sequence_deviation  BINARY_INTEGER DEFAULT NULL);
```

Fields have the following meanings:

visibility

> Specifies the transactional behavior of the enqueue request. There are two possible values:

> *DBMS_AQ.ON_COMMIT*

> > The enqueue is treated as part of the current transaction. The enqueue

operation completes only when the transaction commits. This is the default case.

DBMS_AQ.IMMEDIATE

The enqueue is not treated as part of the current transaction. Instead, the enqueue operation acts as its own transaction. The queued message is then immediately available for dequeuing by other Oracle sessions.

relative_msgid

Specifies the message identifier of the message referenced in the sequence deviation operation. This field is valid if, and only if, BEFORE is specified in the sequence_deviation field (see the next field description). This parameter will be ignored if sequence deviation is not specified (i.e., if the default of NULL is used for the sequence_deviation field).

sequence_deviation

Specifies whether the message being enqueued should be dequeued before other message(s) already in the queue. There are three valid options:

DBMS_AQ.BEFORE

The message is enqueued ahead of the message specified by relative_ msgid.

DBMS_AQ.TOP

The message is enqueued ahead of any other messages.

NULL

The default value, specifying that there is no deviation from the normal sequence for dequeueing.

The following block of code sets up the enqueue properties such that the queued message goes to the top of the queue and is made immediately visible to other sessions:

```
DECLARE
    queueopts DBMS_AQ.ENQUEUE_OPTIONS_T;
BEGIN
    queueopts.visibility := DBMS_AQ.IMMEDIATE;
    queueopts.sequence_deviation := DBMS_AQ.TOP;
```

Dequeue Options Record Type

When you dequeue a message, you can specify the options you want associated with that message by declaring and populating a record based on the following record type:

```
TYPE DBMS_AQ.DEQUEUE_OPTIONS_T IS RECORD
    (consumer_name   VARCHAR2(30) DEFAULT NULL,
     dequeue_mode    BINARY_INTEGER DEFAULT DBMS_AQ.REMOVE,
     navigation      BINARY_INTEGER DEFAULT DBMS_AQ.NEXT_MESSAGE,
```

```
visibility      BINARY_INTEGER DEFAULT DBMS_AQ.ON_COMMIT,
wait            BINARY_INTEGER DEFAULT DBMS_AQ.FOREVER
msgid           RAW(16) DEFAULT NULL,
correlation     VARCHAR2(128) DEFAULT NULL);
```

Fields have the following meanings:

consumer_name

Specifies the name of the consumer of this message. Only those messages matching the consumer name are accessed. If a queue is not set up for multiple consumers (either subscribers to the queue as a whole or the recipient list specified at the time of queuing), this field should be set to NULL (the default).

dequeue_mode

Specifies the locking behavior associated with the dequeue operation. These are the valid options:

DBMS_AQ.BROWSE

Read the message without acquiring any lock on the message. This is equivalent to a query: "readers never block writers or readers."

DBMS_AQ.LOCKED

Read and obtain a write lock on the message. The lock lasts for the duration of the transaction. This is equivalent to a SELECT FOR UPDATE statement.

DBMS_AQ.REMOVE

Read the message and update or delete it. This is the default behavior. When you read from the queue, the message is removed from the queue. Note that the message can be retained in the queue table based on its retention properties.

navigation

Specifies the position of the message that will be retrieved next. When you perform a dequeue, the following steps are taken: (a) the position in the queue is determined; (b) the search criterion specified by this and other fields is applied; and (c) the appropriate message is retrieved. These are the valid options for this field:

DBMS_AQ.NEXT_MESSAGE

Retrieve the next message that is available and matches all the search criteria. If the previous message belongs to a message group, AQ will retrieve the next available message that matches the search criteria and belongs to the message group. This is the default behavior.

DBMS_AQ.NEXT_TRANSACTION

Skip the remainder of the current transaction group (if any) and retrieve the first message of the next transaction group. This option can be used only if message grouping is enabled for the current queue.

DBMS_AQ.FIRST_MESSAGE

Retrieve the first message that is available and matches the search criteria. This will reset the current position to the beginning of the queue.

visibility

Specifies whether the new message is dequeued as part of the current transaction. This parameter is ignored when you have specified the BROWSE mode to read the queue. The following options are valid:

DBMS_AQ.ON_COMMIT

The dequeue is treated as part of the current transaction. The dequeue operation completes only when the transaction commits. This is the default case.

DBMS_AQ.IMMEDIATE

The dequeue is not treated as part of the current transaction. Instead, the dequeue operation acts as its own transaction. The queued message is then immediately available for dequeuing by other Oracle sessions.

wait

Specifies the number of seconds to wait if there is currently no message available matching the search criteria. If the queue table for this queue specified message grouping, then this value is applied only after the last message in a group has been dequeued. You can specify a number of seconds or one of the following named constants:

DBMS_AQ.FOREVER

Wait forever. This is the default.

DBMS_AQ.NO_WAIT

Do not wait at all. If there is no matching message, then return to the calling program immediately.

msgid

Specifies the message identifier of the message to be dequeued. If you specify the message ID, then you can bypass other criteria establishing the next message for dequeuing.

correlation

Specifies the correlation identifier of the message to be dequeued. If you provided a correlation string when you enqueued this message, that string will be used as part of the criteria to establish the next message. You can perform pattern matching by including the percent sign (%) or the underscore (_) in your correlation identifier. These characters follow the standard SQL wildcard rules. If more than one message matches the pattern, the order of dequeuing is not determined.

Oracle AQ Exceptions

There are no named exceptions defined in either of the AQ packages. Instead, Oracle has set aside error messages for Oracle AQ in the following ranges:

–24099 through –24000
–25299 through –25200

Here are some of the more common exceptions you will encounter:

ORA-24010: QUEUE <queue> does not exist
You have tried to perform an operation on a queue that does not yet exist.

ORA-24001: cannot create QUEUE_TABLE, <queue_table> already exists
You have tried to create a queue table, but there is already one by that name.

ORA-24011: cannot drop QUEUE, <queue> should be stopped first
You have tried to drop a queue that has not been stopped.

ORA-24012: cannot drop QUEUE_TABLE, some queues in <queue_table> have not been dropped
You must stop and drop all queues in a queue table before the queue table itself can be dropped.

ORA-24034: application <agent_name> is already a subscriber for queue <queue>
You tried to add an agent to a subscriber list that is already present. Note that agent names are not case-sensitive.

ORA-25215: user_data type and queue type do not match
The object type specified in an enqueue operation does not match the object type used to define the queue table.

ORA-25228: timeout in dequeue from <queue> while waiting for a message
This error usually occurs when you try to dequeue a message from an empty queue.

ORA-25235: fetched all messages in current transaction
You have dequeued the last message in the current message group. You must now specify NEXT_TRANSACTION navigation in order to start dequeuing messages from the next available group.

ORA-25237: navigation option used out of sequence
The NEXT_MESSAGE or NEXT_TRANSACTION option was specified after dequeuing all the messages. You must reset the dequeuing position using the FIRST_MESSAGE navigation option and then specify the NEXT_MESSAGE or NEXT_TRANSACTION option.

DBMS_AQ: Interfacing to Oracle AQ (Oracle8 only)

The DBMS_AQ package provides an interface to the operational tasks of Oracle AQ as performed by the programs listed in Table 5-1. To use these programs, you must have been granted the new role AQ_USER_ROLE.

Table 5-1. DBMS_AQ Programs

Name	Description	Use in SQL?
ENQUEUE	Adds a message to the specified queue.	No
DEQUEUE	Retrieves a message from the specified queue.	No

The following sections describe how to call these programs.

Enqueuing Messages

The ENQUEUE procedure allows you to add a message to a specified queue.

The DBMS_AQ.ENQUEUE procedure

Use the ENQUEUE procedure to add a message to a particular queue. Here's the header for the procedure:

```
PROCEDURE DBMS_AQ.ENQUEUE
    (queue_name IN VARCHAR2,
     enqueue_options IN DBMS_AQ.ENQUEUE_OPTIONS_T,
     message_properties IN DBMS_AQ.MESSAGE_PROPERTIES_T,
     payload IN <type_name>,
     msgid OUT RAW);
```

Parameters are summarized in the following table.

Name	Description
queue_name	Specifies the name of the queue to which this message should be enqueued. The queue cannot be an exception queue and must have been previously defined by a call to DBMS_AQADM.CREATE_QUEUE.
enqueue_options	A record containing the enqueuing options, defined using the specified record type. See "Enqueue Options Record Type" for more details.
message_properties	A record containing the message properties, defined using the specified record type. See "Message Properties Record Type" for more details.

Name	Description
payload	The data or payload that is placed on the queue. This is either an object (an instance of an object type), a RAW value, or NULL. The payload must match the specification in the associated queue table. This value is not interpreted by Oracle AQ, so any object type can be passed into the procedure.
msgid	This is the ID number of the message generated by AQ. It is a globally unique identifier that can be used to identify the message at dequeue time. In other words, you can specifically request that the message with this message ID be dequeued next.

Examples

The "Oracle AQ Examples" section at the end of this chapter offers many different illustrations of using DBMS_AQ.ENQUEUE to send messages through a queue. In this section, I offer some initial examples to get you familiar with the kind of code you would write when enqueuing messages. In all these cases, assume that I have defined an object type as follows:

```
CREATE TYPE message_type AS OBJECT
    (title VARCHAR2(30),
     text VARCHAR2(2000));
```

My AQ administrator created a queue table and a message queue as follows:

```
EXEC DBMS_AQADM.CREATE_QUEUE_TABLE
    (queue_table => 'msg',
     queue_payload_type => 'message_type');

EXEC DBMS_AQADM.CREATE_QUEUE
    (queue_name => 'msgqueue',
     queue_table => 'msg');

EXEC DBMS_AQADM.START_QUEUE (queue_name => 'msgqueue');
```

So now I can enqueue a message to this queue as follows:

```
/* Filename on companion disk: aqenq1.sql */
DECLARE
    queueopts DBMS_AQ.ENQUEUE_OPTIONS_T;
    msgprops DBMS_AQ.MESSAGE_PROPERTIES_T;
    msgid RAW(16);
    my_msg message_type;
BEGIN
    my_msg := message_type ('First Enqueue', 'May there be many more...');

    DBMS_AQ.ENQUEUE ('msgqueue',
        queueopts,
        msgprops,
        my_msg,
        msgid);
END;
/
```

This is the simplest usage possible of DBMS_AQ.ENQUEUE. I declare my two record structures, because I *must* pass them in as arguments. I do not, however, modify any of the values in the fields; all have the default values documented in the "Oracle AQ Nonprogram Elements" section for the message properties record type.

As you can see, the message ID is a RAW of length 16. Rather than hard-coding that declaration again and again in your application, I suggest that you instead declare a subtype that hides that information. My aq package (*aq.spp*), for example, offers this predefined type:

```
v_msgid RAW(16);
SUBTYPE msgid_type IS v_msgid%TYPE;
```

So when you want to declare a variable to store AQ message IDs, you can do the following:

```
DECLARE
    mymsgid aq.msgid_type;
```

Are you curious about those message IDs? When I ran the previous script, I also asked PL/SQL to display the msgid value with the following statement,

```
DBMS_OUTPUT.PUT_LINE (RAWTOHEX (msgid));
```

and this is what I saw:

```
E2CEA14B51F411D1B977E59CD6EE8E46
```

That is certainly a mouthful. When would you use this ID? Well, I can go right back to the data dictionary and ask to see all the information about this message. Every time you create a queue table, Oracle AQ creates an underlying database view with the name aq$<queue_table_name>. So if I created a queue table named "msg," I should be able to examine the contents of a table called aq$msg in my own schema.

I put together a little SQL*Plus script to show the status and user data for a message:

```
/* Filename on companion disk: aqshomsg.sql */
SELECT msg_state, user_data
   FROM aq$&1
  WHERE msg_id = HEXTORAW ('&2');
```

I can then call this script in SQL*Plus to show me the information about the just-queued message as follows:

```
SQL> @aqshomsg msg E2CEA14B51F411D1B977E59CD6EE8E46

MSG_STATE USER_DATA(TITLE, TEXT)
--------- ----------------------------------------------------------------
READY     MESSAGE_TYPE('First Enqueue', 'May there be many more...')
```

Notice that the query automatically detected the fact that my user_data is in fact an object, and showed me the full contents of that object quite neatly. You can, of course, also see other attributes of the message; see the later section entitled "Oracle AQ Database Objects" for more details on this table and how best to retrieve information from it.

Of course, you will sometimes want to modify the message properties or enqueue options before performing your enqueue. To do this, simply change the values of the fields in the record. The following example shows how you can delay the availability of a message for dequeuing by three days and also request that one message be dequeued before another:

```
/* Filename on companion disk: aqenq2.sql */
DECLARE
    queueopts DBMS_AQ.ENQUEUE_OPTIONS_T;
    msgprops DBMS_AQ.MESSAGE_PROPERTIES_T;
    msgid1 aq.msgid_type;
    msgid2 aq.msgid_type;
    my_msg message_type;
BEGIN
    my_msg := message_type ('First Enqueue', 'May there be many more...');

    /* Delay first message by three days, but otherwise rely on defaults. */

    msgprops.delay := 3 * 60 * 60  * 24;

    DBMS_AQ.ENQUEUE ('msgqueue', queueopts, msgprops, my_msg, msgid1);

    /* Now use the same properties record, but modify the enqueue options
       to deviate from the normal sequence. */

    my_msg := message_type ('Second Enqueue', 'And this one goes first...');

    queueopts.sequence_deviation := DBMS_AQ.BEFORE;
    queueopts.relative_msgid := msgid1;

    DBMS_AQ.ENQUEUE ('msgqueue', queueopts, msgprops, my_msg, msgid2);
END;
/
```

Dequeuing Messages

Once you have placed a message on a queue, you need to extract that message from the queue. This is done with the DEQUEUE procedure.

The DBMS_AQ.DEQUEUE procedure

Use the DEQUEUE procedure to extract a message from a particular queue. Here's the header for this procedure:

```
PROCEDURE DBMS_AQ.DEQUEUE
    (queue_name IN VARCHAR2,
```

```
dequeue_options IN DBMS_AQ.DEQUEUE_OPTIONS_T,
message_properties OUT DBMS_AQ.MESSAGE_PROPERTIES_T,
payload OUT <type_name>,
msgid OUT RAW)
```

Parameters are summarized in the following table.

Name	Description
queue_name	Name of the queue from which the message should be dequeued. The queue cannot be an exception queue and must have been previously defined by a call to DBMS_AQADM.CREATE_QUEUE.
dequeue_options	Record containing the dequeuing options, defined using the specified record type. See "Dequeue Options Record Type" for more details.
message_properties	Record containing the message properties supplied when the message was enqueued. See "Message Properties Record Type" for more details.
payload	Data or "payload" that is associated with this message on the queue. This is an object (an instance of an object type), a RAW value, or NULL. The payload must match the specification in the associated queue table.
msgid	ID number of the message generated by AQ.

Examples

The "Oracle AQ Examples" section at the end of this chapter offers many different illustrations of using DBMS_AQ.DEQUEUE to retrieve messages from a queue. In the remainder of this section, though, I offer some examples to get you familiar with the kind of code you would write when dequeuing messages. In all of these cases, assume that I have defined an object type as follows:

```
CREATE TYPE message_type AS OBJECT
    (title VARCHAR2(30),
     text VARCHAR2(2000));
```

Assume further that my AQ administrator has created a queue table and a message queue as follows:

```
EXEC DBMS_AQADM.CREATE_QUEUE_TABLE
    (queue_table => 'msg',
     queue_payload_type => 'message_type');

EXEC DBMS_AQADM.CREATE_QUEUE
    (queue_name => 'msgqueue',
     queue_table => 'msg');

EXEC DBMS_AQADM.START_QUEUE (queue_name => 'msgqueue');
```

Now I can dequeue a message that has previously been placed in this queue as follows:

```
/* Filename on companion disk: aqdeq1.sql */
DECLARE
    queueopts DBMS_AQ.DEQUEUE_OPTIONS_T;
    msgprops DBMS_AQ.MESSAGE_PROPERTIES_T;
    msgid aq.msgid_type; /* defined in aq.spp */
    my_msg message_type;
BEGIN
    DBMS_AQ.DEQUEUE ('msgqueue',
        queueopts,
        msgprops,
        my_msg,
        msgid);

    /* Now display some of the information. */
    DBMS_OUTPUT.PUT_LINE ('Dequeued message id is ' || RAWTOHEX (msgid));
    DBMS_OUTPUT.PUT_LINE ('Dequeued title is ' || my_msg.title);
    DBMS_OUTPUT.PUT_LINE ('Dequeued text is ' || my_msg.text);
END;
/
```

Here is an example of output from this script:

```
SQL> @aqdeq1
Dequeued message id is E2CEA14C51F411D1B977E59CD6EE8E46
Dequeued title is First Enqueue
Dequeued text is May there be many more...
```

This is the simplest possible usage of DBMS_AQ.DEQUEUE. I declare my two record structures, because I *must* pass them in as arguments. However, I do not modify any of the values in the fields; all have the default values documented in the "Oracle AQ Nonprogram Elements" section for the message properties record type.

You can also modify the dequeue properties to change the behavior of the dequeue operation. The full set of options is explained in the "Dequeue Options Record Type" section under "Oracle AQ Nonprogram Elements." The following script demonstrates how you can request that messages not be removed from the queue after they are dequeued. You would do this when you want to search through a queue for a specific message, leaving all the others in place.

The following script dequeues a message once in BROWSE mode, then dequeues the same message in the default REMOVE mode, and then dequeues with REMOVE again:

```
/* Filename on companion disk: aqdeq2.sql */
DECLARE
    queueopts DBMS_AQ.DEQUEUE_OPTIONS_T;
    msgprops DBMS_AQ.MESSAGE_PROPERTIES_T;
    msgid aq.msgid_type; /* defined in aq.spp */
    my_msg message_type;

    /* A nested procedure to minimize code redundancy! */
```

```
    PROCEDURE getmsg (mode_in IN INTEGER)
    IS
    BEGIN
        queueopts.dequeue_mode := mode_in;

        DBMS_AQ.DEQUEUE ('msgqueue', queueopts, msgprops, my_msg, msgid);

        /* Now display some of the information. */
        DBMS_OUTPUT.PUT_LINE ('Dequeued msg id is ' || RAWTOHEX (msgid));
        DBMS_OUTPUT.PUT_LINE ('Dequeued title is ' || my_msg.title);
    END;
BEGIN
    /* Request browse, not remove, for dequeue operation. */
    getmsg (DBMS_AQ.BROWSE);

    /* Do the same thing again, this time with remove. You will dequeue
       the same entry as before. */
    getmsg (DBMS_AQ.REMOVE);

    /* Dequeue a third time, again with remove, and notice the different
       message ID. The previous message was, in fact, removed. */
    getmsg (DBMS_AQ.REMOVE);
END;
/
```

Here is the output from running the *aqdeq2.sql* script:

```
SQL> @aqdeq2
Dequeued msg id is E2CEA15251F411D1B977E59CD6EE8E46
Dequeued title is TWO EGGS OVER MEDIUM
Dequeued msg id is E2CEA15251F411D1B977E59CD6EE8E46
Dequeued title is TWO EGGS OVER MEDIUM
Dequeued msg id is E2CEA15351F411D1B977E59CD6EE8E46
Dequeued title is TWO EGGS OVER EASY
```

Dequeue search criteria

When you request a dequeue operation, you can specify search criteria. These criteria are used to determine which message is dequeued. The search criteria are established by the following fields in the dequeue options record: consumer_name, msgid, and correlation.

- If you specify a message ID in the dequeue options record, the message with that ID will be dequeued, regardless of its place in the queue.

- If you specify a correlation value, only those messages that have a correlation value matching the one you specify will be candidates for dequeuing. A match can be specified as an exact match or a pattern match.

- If you provide a value for the consumer_name field, only those messages that were enqueued for that consumer (a subscriber either to the queue as a whole or specified in the recipient list at enqueue time) are considered for dequeuing.

The "Oracle AQ Examples" section shows you the kind of code you need to write to support these different kinds of search criteria.

Dequeue order

The order in which messages are generally dequeued is determined by the characteristics of the queue table, established at the time of creation. For example, you can define a queue table in which the messages are ordered by the priority associated with the message.

You can override the default order by specifying the message ID or a correlation value in the dequeue options record. Remember that a message must be in the READY state to be dequeued—unless you specify the message ID explicitly. When you use that ID, you override any other search criteria and restrictions.

Here is an example of dequeuing a message from the msg queue by specifying a message ID number (passed in as an argument to the procedure):

```
/* Filename on companion disk: aqdeq3.sql */
CREATE OR REPLACE PROCEDURE getmsg (msgid_in IN RAW)
IS
    queueopts DBMS_AQ.DEQUEUE_OPTIONS_T;
    msgprops DBMS_AQ.MESSAGE_PROPERTIES_T;
    msgid aq.msgid_type; /* defined in aq.spp */
    my_msg message_type;
BEGIN
    queueopts.msgid := msgid_in;

    DBMS_AQ.DEQUEUE ('msgqueue',
        queueopts, msgprops, my_msg, msgid);

    /* Now display some of the information. */
    DBMS_OUTPUT.PUT_LINE
        ('Requested message id is ' || RAWTOHEX (msgid_in));
    DBMS_OUTPUT.PUT_LINE
        ('Dequeued message id is  ' || RAWTOHEX (msgid));
    DBMS_OUTPUT.PUT_LINE ('Dequeued title is ' || my_msg.title);
END;
/
```

Here is an example of using this procedure:

```
/* Filename on companion disk: aqdeq4.sql */
DECLARE
    enqueue_opts DBMS_AQ.ENQUEUE_OPTIONS_T;
    dequeue_opts DBMS_AQ.DEQUEUE_OPTIONS_T;
    msgprops DBMS_AQ.MESSAGE_PROPERTIES_T;
    msgid1 aq.msgid_type;
    msgid2 aq.msgid_type;
    my_msg message_type;
BEGIN
    /* Enqueue two messages */
```

```
my_msg := message_type
    ('Joy of Cooking', 'Classic Recipes for Oral Delight');
DBMS_AQ.ENQUEUE ('msgqueue', enqueue_opts, msgprops, my_msg, msgid1);

my_msg := message_type ('Joy of Sex', 'Classic Recipes for Delight');
DBMS_AQ.ENQUEUE ('msgqueue', enqueue_opts, msgprops, my_msg, msgid2);

/* Now dequeue the first by its message ID explicitly. */
getmsg (msgid1);
END;
/
```

And the results from executing *aqdeq4.sql*:

```
SQL> @aqdeq4
Requested message id is E2CEA16351F411D1B977E59CD6EE8E46
Dequeued message id is  E2CEA16351F411D1B977E59CD6EE8E46
Dequeued title is Joy of Cooking
```

Dequeue navigation

You specify the navigation method by setting a value in the navigation field of the dequeue options record.

The default navigation through a queue for dequeuing is "next message." This means that each subsequent dequeue retrieves messages from the queue based on the snapshot or view of the queue as it appeared when the first dequeue was performed. This approach offers a read consistency model similar to that of the Oracle RDBMS. For example, if you enqueue a message after you have issued a dequeue command, that message will not be dequeued (or even checked for availability for dequeuing) until all messages already in the queue have been processed.

Specifying DBMS_AQ.NEXT_MESSAGE for message navigation (the default) is often sufficient for dequeue operations. If either of the following conditions occur, however, you may need to change the navigation:

- You enqueue messages after dequeues have occurred, and you want those newly enqueued messages to be immediately considered for a dequeue.

- You have a nondefault (i.e., priority-based) ordering in your queue. In this case, if a higher-priority message enters the queue at any time, you want to consider that message for dequeuing immediately.

In either of these situations you should set the navigation method as follows:

```
DECLARE
    queueopts DBMS_AQ.DEQUEUE_OPTIONS_T;
BEGIN
    queueopts.navigation := DBMS_AQ.FIRST_MESSAGE;
```

When you use "first message" navigation, you tell Oracle AQ that you want it to consider the entire set of messages in the queue for every dequeue command. Internally, this means that AQ will create a new "snapshot" view of the queue whenever you request a dequeue.

You will find many illustrations of the use of "first message" navigation in the "Oracle AQ Examples" section.

Dequeuing with message grouping

When you create a queue table specifying DBMS_AQADM.TRANSACTIONAL for the message_ grouping argument, any messages enqueued in the same transaction are considered part of a *group* of messages. This group may consist of only one message; there is also no upper limit on the number of messages allowed in a group.

When you work with queues that are not enabled for message grouping, a dequeue operation that specified LOCKED or REMOVE mode will only affect a single message. In a message grouping queue, on the other hand, a dequeue operation on one message in a group will lock the entire group. This allows you to treat all the messages in a group as a single unit or transaction.

When you are dequeuing against a message group, keep the following rules in mind:

- When you dequeue the last message in the current message group, Oracle AQ will raise the ORA-25235 exception.

- When you dequeue the last message in a message group, you must specify NEXT_TRANSACTION navigation in a dequeue options record in order to start dequeuing messages from the next available group.

- If there aren't any more message groups available in the queue, then the dequeue operation will time out after the period of time specified in the WAIT field of the dequeue options record.

DBMS_AQADM: Performing AQ Administrative Tasks (Oracle8 only)

Before AQ users can enqueue and dequeue, they must have queues with which to work. The AQ administrator must create queue tables and queues within those tables and then start the queues. Additional administrative tasks include stopping queues and removing queue tables, managing lists of subscribers, and starting and stopping the Queue Monitor.

The DBMS_AQADM package provides an interface to the administrative tasks of Oracle AQ. The DBMS_AQADM programs are listed in Table 5-2. In order to use these procedures, a DBMS_AQADM user must have been granted the role AQ_ADMINISTRATOR_ROLE from the SYS account.

NOTE   None of the DBMS_AQADM programs may be used inside SQL, directly or indirectly. The reason for this restriction is that many of these programs perform a COMMIT (unless you have set the auto_commit parameter to FALSE).

Table 5-2. DBMS_AQADM Programs

Name	Description	Use in SQL?
ADD_SUBSCRIBER	Adds a subscriber to a queue.	No
ALTER_QUEUE	Alters limited set of properties of an existing queue.	No
CREATE_QUEUE	Creates a queue within the specified queue table.	No
CREATE_QUEUE_TABLE	Creates a queue table in which queues can be defined.	No
DROP_QUEUE	Drops an existing queue table.	No
DROP_QUEUE_TABLE	Drops an existing queue from a queue table.	No
GRANT_TYPE_ACCESS	Grants access to multiple consumer tasks.	No
QUEUE_SUBSCRIBERS	Retrieves the list of subscribers associated with a queue.	No
REMOVE_SUBSCRIBER	Removes a subscriber from a queue.	No
SCHEDULE_PROPAGATION	Schedules propagation of messages from a source queue to a destination queue (either in the same or a remote database).	No
START_QUEUE	Enables the queue (i.e., permits enqueue and/or dequeue operations).	No
START_TIME_MANAGER	Starts the Queue Monitor process.	No
STOP_QUEUE	Disables the queue for enqueuing, dequeuing, or both.	No
STOP_TIME_MANAGER	Stops the Queue Monitor process.	No
UNSCHEDULE_PROPAGA-TION	Unschedules the propagation of messages from a source queue to a destination queue.	No
VERIFY_QUEUE_TYPES	Determines whether two different queues have the same payload type. You can perform this verification for two local queues or for a local and a remote queue.	No

The following sections describe these programs in a number of categories.

Creating Queue Tables

First, you need to create your queue tables and grant the necessary capabilities.

The DBMS_AQADM.GRANT_TYPE_ACCESS procedure

If you would like to support multiple consumers with your queue (that is, so that the same or different messages can be dequeued by more than one agent), call the GRANT_TYPE_ACCESS program to grant that capability,

```
PROCEDURE DBMS_AQADM.GRANT_TYPE_ACCESS (user_name IN VARCHAR2);
```

where user_name is the name of the user who needs to perform multiple consumer queue activities.

The SYS account must call this procedure to grant the privilege to the AQ administrator. The AQ administrator then runs this program to grant the privilege to AQ users. Here is an example of granting multiple consumer capabilities to the SCOTT account:

```
SQL> exec DBMS_AQADM.GRANT_TYPE_ACCESS ('scott');
```

The DBMS_AQADM.CREATE_QUEUE_TABLE procedure

The CREATE_QUEUE_TABLE procedure creates a queue table. A queue table is the named repository for a set of queues and their messages. A queue table may contain numerous queues, each of which may have many messages. But a given queue and its messages may exist in only one queue table. The specification for the procedure follows:

```
PROCEDURE DBMS_AQADM.CREATE_QUEUE_TABLE
      (queue_table IN VARCHAR2
      ,queue_payload_type IN VARCHAR2
      ,storage_clause IN VARCHAR2 DEFAULT NULL
      ,sort_list IN VARCHAR2 DEFAULT NULL
      ,multiple_consumers IN BOOLEAN DEFAULT FALSE
      ,message_grouping IN BINARY_INTEGER DEFAULT NONE
      ,comment IN VARCHAR2 DEFAULT NULL
      ,auto_commit IN BOOLEAN DEFAULT TRUE);
```

Parameters are summarized in the following table.

Name	Description
queue_table	Name of a queue table to be created. Maximum of 24 characters in length, unless you have combined the schema and the table name, as in 'SCOTT.MSG_TABLE', in which case the maximum length of the argument is 49 characters.
queue_payload_type	Type of the user data stored. This is either the name of an already defined object type or it is the string "RAW," indicating that the payload for this queue table will consist of a single LOB column.

Name	Description
storage_clause	Storage parameter, which will be included in the CREATE TABLE statement when the queue table is created. The storage parameter can be made up of any combination of the following parameters: PCTFREE, PCTUSED, INITRANS, MAXTRANS, TABLEPSACE, LOB, and a table storage clause. Refer to the *Oracle SQL Reference Guide* for more information about defining a storage parameter.
sort_list	Columns to be used as the sort key in ascending order; see the following discussion.
multiple_consumers	Specifies whether queues created in this table can have more than one consumer per message. The default is FALSE (only one consumer per message). If a value of TRUE is passed for this argument, the user must have been granted type access by executing the DBMS_AQADM.GRANT_TYPE_ACCESS procedure.
message_grouping	Message grouping behavior for queues created in the table. Valid arguments for this parameter: *DBMS_AQADM.NONE* Each message is treated individually (this is the default). *DBMS_AQADM.TRANSACTIONAL* Messages enqueued as part of one transaction are considered part of the same group and must be dequeued as a group of related messages.
comment	User-specified description of the queue table. This user comment will be added to the queue catalog.
auto_commit	Specifies the transaction behavior for queues associated with this table. Valid arguments: *TRUE* Causes the current transaction, if any, to commit before the operation is carried out. The operation becomes persistent when the call returns. This is the default. *FALSE* Any administrative operation on a queue is part of the current transaction and will become persistent only when the caller issues a commit. In other words, this argument does not apply to enqueue/dequeue operations performed on the queue.

The sort_list has the following format,

```
'<sort_column_1>,<sort_column_2>'
```

where each sort_column_N is either PRIORITY or ENQ_TIME. If both columns are specified, then <sort_column_1> defines the most significant order. In other words, these are the only valid values for sort_list besides NULL:

```
'PRIORITY'
'PRIORITY,ENQ_TIME'
'ENQ_TIME' (this is the default)
'ENQ_TIME,PRIORITY'
```

Once a queue table is created with a specific ordering mechanism, all queues in the queue table inherit the same default ordering. This order cannot be altered once the queue table has been created. If no sort list is specified, all the queues in this queue table will be sorted by the enqueue time in ascending order. This order is equivalent to FIFO (first-in-first-out)' order.

Even with the default ordering defined, a consumer can override this order by specifying the msgid or correlation value for a specific message. The msgid, correlation, and sequence_deviation take precedence over the default dequeueing order if they are specified.

When you create a queue table, the following objects are created:

- The default exception queue associated with the queue table. It is named,

  aq$_<queue_table_name>_e

  where <queue_table_name> is the name of the queue table just created. So if my queue table is named msg, then my exception queue table is named aq$_msg_e (and now you can see why the maximum length name for a queue table is 24 characters!).

- A read-only view that is used by AQ applications for querying queue data called:

  aq$<queue_table_name>.

- An index for the Queue Monitor operations called:

  aq$_<queue_table_name>_t.

- An index (or an index organized table [IOT] in the case of multiple consumer queues) for dequeue operations. It is named:

  aq$_<queue_table_name>_i

Example. In the following example, I construct a basic queue table in the current schema with a comment as to when it was created:

```
BEGIN
    DBMS_AQADM.CREATE_QUEUE_TABLE
        (queue_table => 'msg',
         queue_payload_type => 'message_type',
         comment => 'General message queue table created on ' ||
            TO_CHAR(SYSDATE, 'MON-DD-YYYY HH24:MI:SS'));
END;
/
```

Notice that I pass the payload type as a string: the name of the object type I defined in the section explaining how to enqueue messages. I can verify the creation of this queue table by querying the USER_QUEUE_TABLES.

```
SQL> SELECT queue_table, user_comment FROM USER_QUEUE_TABLES;
QUEUETABLEUSER_COMMENT
MSG              General message queue table created on JUN-08-1997 14:22:01
```

The following request to create a queue table specifies support for multiple consumers of a single message and also enables message grouping:

```
BEGIN
    DBMS_AQADM.CREATE_QUEUE_TABLE
        (queue_table => 'msg',
         queue_payload_type => 'message_type',
         multiple_consumers => TRUE,
         message_grouping => DBMS_AQADM.TRANSACTIONAL,
         comment => 'Specialized queue table created on ' ||
             TO_CHAR(SYSDATE, 'MON-DD-YYYY HH24:MI:SS'));
END;
/
```

Notice the extensive use of named notation (the "=>" symbols). This feature of PL/SQL comes in very handy when working with programs that have long lists of parameters, or with programs that are used infrequently. The named notation approach, which explicitly associates a parameter with an argument value, documents more clearly how the program is being used.

See the "Oracle AQ Examples" section for a more thorough explanation of the message grouping and multiple consumers feature.

Notes on usage. Note the following about using the CREATE_QUEUE_TABLE procedure:

- If you specify a schema for your queue table, then the payload type (if an object type) must also be defined in that schema.

- You do not need to specify the schema for the payload type, but you can. If you do specify the object type schema for the payload type, it must be the same schema as that of the queue table or you will receive an ORA-00902: invalid datatype error.

- If you are going to create your queue tables from one (administrator) account and manage those queues from another (user) account, then you will need to grant EXECUTE privilege to the administrator account on the queue message types from the user account.

Creating and Starting Queues

Once a queue table has been created, you can create and then start individual queues in that queue table.

The DBMS_AQADM.CREATE_QUEUE procedure

Call the CREATE_QUEUE to create a queue in the specified queue table. All queue names must be unique within a schema. Once a queue is created, it can be enabled by calling DBMS_AQADM.START_QUEUE. By default, the queue is created with both enqueue and dequeue disabled.

```
PROCEDURE DBMS_AQADM.CREATE_QUEUE
    (queue_name IN VARCHAR2,
    queue_table IN VARCHAR2,
    queue_type IN BINARY_INTEGER default DBMS_AQADM.NORMAL_QUEUE,
    max_retries IN NUMBER default 0,
    retry_delay IN NUMBER default 0,
    retention_time IN NUMBER default 0,
    dependency_tracking IN BOOLEAN default FALSE,
    comment IN VARCHAR2 default NULL,
    auto_commit IN BOOLEAN default TRUE);
```

Parameters are summarized in the following table.

Name	Description
queue_name	Name of the queue to be created. All queue names must be unique within a schema.
queue_table	Name of the queue table in which this queue is to be created.

queue_type	Specifies the type of queue. Valid options for this parameter:
	DBMS_AQADM.NORMAL_QUEUE
	    The default, a normal queue.
	DBMS_AQADM.EXCEPTION_QUEUE
	    An exception queue. Only dequeue operations are valid on an exception queue.

max_retries	Maximum number of times a dequeue with the REMOVE mode can be attempted on a message. The count is incremented when the application issues a rollback after executing a dequeue (but before a commit is performed). The message is moved to the exception queue when the number of failed attempts reaches its max_retries. Specify 0, the default, to indicate that no retries are allowed.
retry_delay	Delay in seconds to wait after an application rollback before the message is scheduled for processing again. The default of 0 means that the dequeue operation should be retried as soon as possible. The retry parameters in effect allow you to control the fault tolerance of the message queue. This value is ignored if max_retries is set to 0 (the default). This value may not be specified if this is a multiple consumer queue table.
retention_ time	Number of seconds for which a message will be retained in the queue table after being dequeued from the queue. The default is 0, meaning no retention. You can also specify the DBMS_AQADM.INFINITE packaged constant to request that the message be retained forever.
dependency_ tracking	Reserved for future use by Oracle Corporation. FALSE is the default, and TRUE is not permitted.

Name	Description
comment	User comment to associate with the message queue in the queue catalog.
auto_commit	Specify TRUE (the default) to cause the current transaction, if any, to commit before the operation is carried out. The operation becomes persistent when the call returns. Specify FALSE to make this operation part of the current transaction. In this case, it will become persistent only when the caller issues a commit.

Example. In the following example, I create a new message queue within the previously created message queue table. I want it to allow for up to ten retries at hourly delays and keep ten days worth of history before deleting processed messages.

```
BEGIN
  DBMS_AQADM.CREATE_QUEUE(
      queue_name => 'never_give_up_queue',
      queue_table => 'msg',
      max_retries => 10,
      retry_delay => 3600,
      retention_time => 10 * 24 * 60 * 60,
      comment => 'Test Queue Number 1');
END;
/
```

The DBMS_AQADM.START_QUEUE procedure

It is not enough to simply create a queue inside a queue table. You must also enable it for enqueuing and/or dequeuing operation, with the START_QUEUE procedure:

```
PROCEDURE DBMS_AQADM.START_QUEUE
    (queue_name IN VARCHAR2,
     enqueue IN BOOLEAN DEFAULT TRUE,
     dequeue  IN BOOLEAN DEFAULT TRUE);
```

Parameters are summarized in the following table.

Name	Description
queue_name	Name of the queue to be started.
enqueue	Flag indicating whether the queue should be enabled for enqueuing (TRUE means enable, the default; FALSE means do not alter the current setting.)
dequeue	Flag indicating whether the queue should be enabled for dequeuing (TRUE means enable, the default; FALSE means do not alter the current setting.)

Notice that a value of FALSE for either of the Boolean parameters does not disable a queue for the respective operation. It simply does not change the current status of that operation on the specified queue. To disable queuing or enqueuing on a queue, you must call the DBMS_AQADM.STOP_QUEUE procedure.

Example. The following block starts a queue for enqueuing actions only:

```
BEGIN
VP   DBMS_AQADM.START_QUEUE ('number_stack', dequeue=>FALSE);

END;VPU
/
```

You will often want to perform the following steps in sequence:
DBMS_AQADMP.CREATE_QUEUE_TABLE
DBMS_AQADM.CREATE_QUEUE
DBMS_AQADM.START_QUEUE

The following files on the companion disk provide various examples of these steps:

aqcrepq.sql

aqcreq.sql

aqcref.sql

The DBMS_AQADM.ALTER_QUEUE procedure

The ALTER_QUEUE procedure of the DBMS_AQADM package modifies an existing message queue. An error is returned if the message queue does not exist. The specification for the procedure follows:

```
PROCEDURE DBMS_AQADM.ALTER_QUEUE
    queue_name IN VARCHAR2,
    max_retries IN NUMBER default NULL,
    retry_delay IN NUMBER default NULL,
    retention_time IN NUMBER default NULL,
    auto_commit IN BOOLEAN default TRUE);
```

Parameters are summarized in the following table.

Name	Description
queue_name	Name of the message queue to be altered.
max_retries	Specifies the maximum number of times a dequeue with the REMOVE mode can be attempted on a message. The count is incremented when the application issues a rollback after executing a dequeue (but before a commit is performed). The message is moved to the exception queue when the number of failed attempts reach its max_retries. Specify 0, the default, to indicate that no retries are allowed.

Name	Description
retry_delay	Specifies the delay in seconds to wait after an application rollback before the message is scheduled for processing again. The default of 0 means that the dequeue operation should be retried as soon as possible. The retry parameters in effect allow you to control the fault tolerance of the message queue. This value is ignored if max_retries is set to 0 (the default). This value may not be specified if this is a multiple consumer queue table.
retention_time	Specifies the number of seconds for which a message will be retained in the queue table after being dequeued from the queue. The default is 0, meaning no retention. You can also specify the DBMS_AQADM.INFI-NITE packaged constant to request that the message be retained forever.
auto_commit	Specifies the transaction behavior for queues associated with this table. Specify TRUE (the default) to cause the current transaction, if any, to commit before the operation is carried out. The operation becomes persistent when the call returns. If you specify FALSE, any administrative operation on a queue is part of the current transaction and will become persistent only when the caller issues a commit. In other words, this argument does not apply to enqueue/dequeue operations performed on the queue.

Example. In the following example, I modify the properties of the queue created under CREATE_QUEUE. I now want it to allow for up to 20 retries at hourly delays and to keep 30 days worth of history before deleting processed messages.

```
BEGIN
   DBMS_AQADM.ALTER_QUEUE(
        queue_name => 'never_give_up_queue',
        max_retries => 20,
        retention_time => 30 * 24 * 60 * 60);
   END;
   /
```

I can verify the impact of this call by querying the USER_QUEUES data dictionary view.

```
SQL> SELECT name, max_retries, retention FROM USER_QUEUES;

NAME                               MAX_RETRIES       RETENTION
------------------------------     -----------       ----------
AQ$_MSG_E                          0                 0
MSGQUEUE                           0                 0
NEVER_GIVE_UP_QUEUE                20                2592000
```

The first line in the listing is the exception queue for the "msg" queue table. The "msgqueue" queue in the "msg" queue table is a previously defined queue. The third line displays the information for the queue modified by the call to DBMS_AQADM.ALTER_QUEUE.

Managing Queue Subscribers

A program can enqueue messages to a specific list of recipients or to the default list of subscribers. A subscriber to a queue is an agent that is registered to dequeue messages from a queue.

You can add and remove subscribers, as well as retrieve the current set of subscribers for a queue. These operations will work only with queues that allow multiple consumers (i.e., the multiple_consumers parameter is set to TRUE when you called DBMS_AQADM.CREATE_QUEUE_TABLE). The command takes effect immediately, and the containing transaction is committed. Enqueue requests executed after the completion of this call will reflect the new behavior. Users attempting to modify the subscriber list of a queue must have been granted type access by executing the DBMS_AQADM.GRANT_TYPE_ACCESS procedure.

The DBMS_AQADM.ADD_SUBSCRIBER procedure

To add a subscriber to a queue, call the ADD_SUBSCRIBER procedure:

```
PROCEDURE DBMS_AQADM.ADD_SUBSCRIBER
    (queue_name IN VARCHAR2, subscriber IN SYS.AQ$_AGENT);
```

Parameters are summarized in the following table.

Name	Description
queue_table	Name of the queue to which the subscriber is being added.
subscriber	Subscriber to be added. Not the actual name of the subscriber, but an object of type SYS.AQ$_AGENT. If you try to add a subscriber that is already on the list, AQ will raise the ORA-24034 exception. Agent names are case-insensitive.

Example. Here is an example of adding a subscriber to a queue:

```
BEGIN
    DBMS_AQADM.ADD_SUBSCRIBER
        ('msgqueue', SYS.AQ$_AGENT ('multiconsqueue', NULL, NULL));
```

In this case, I have embedded the call to the object constructor method to convert a name to an agent. You can also perform this task in two steps as follows:

```
DECLARE
    v_agent SYS.AQ$_AGENT;
BEGIN
    v_agent := SYS.AQ$_AGENT ('Danielle', NULL, NULL);
    DBMS_AQADM.ADD_SUBSCRIBER ('multiconsqueue', v_agent);
```

The DBMS_AQADM.REMOVE_SUBSCRIBER procedure

To remove a default subscriber from a queue, call the REMOVE_SUBSCRIBER procedure:

```
PROCEDURE DBMS_AQADM.REMOVE_SUBSCRIBER
    (queue_name IN VARCHAR2, subscriber IN SYS.AQ$_AGENT);
```

Parameters are summarized in the following table.

Name	Description
queue_table	Name of the queue from which the subscriber is being removed.
subscriber	Subscriber to be removed. Not the actual name of the subscriber, but an object of type SYS.AQ$_AGENT. Agent names are case-insensitive.

Example. Here is an example of removing a subscriber from a queue:

```
BEGIN
    DBMS_AQADM.REMOVE_SUBSCRIBER
        ('multiconsqueue', SYS.AQ$_AGENT ('CEO', NULL, NULL));
```

In this case I have embedded the call to the object constructor method to convert a name to an agent. You can also perform this task in two steps as follows:

```
DECLARE
    v_agent SYS.AQ$_AGENT;
BEGIN
    v_agent := SYS.AQ$_AGENT ('CEO', NULL, NULL);
    DBMS_AQADM.REMOVE_SUBSCRIBER ('multiconsqueue', v_agent);
```

All references to the subscriber in existing messages are removed as part of the operation.

If you try to remove a subscriber that does not exist for this queue, you will receive this error message:

```
ORA-24035: application <subscriber> is not a subscriber for queue <queue>
```

The DBMS_AQADM.QUEUE_SUBSCRIBERS procedure

The QUEUE_SUBSCRIBERS function returns the list of subscribers associated with the specified queue. This list is an index-by table, as shown in the header,

```
FUNCTION DBMS_AQADM.QUEUE_SUBSCRIBERS
    (queue_name IN VARCHAR2)
RETURN DBMS_AQADM.AQ$_SUBSCRIBER_LIST_T;
```

where queue_name is the name of the queue.

Example. The following procedure encapsulates the steps needed to obtain this list and then to display it:

```
/* Filename on companion disk: showsubs.sp */
CREATE OR REPLACE PROCEDURE showsubs (qname IN VARCHAR2)
IS
    sublist DBMS_AQADM.AQ$_SUBSCRIBER_LIST_T;
    v_row PLS_INTEGER;
BEGIN
    /* Retrieve the list. */
    sublist := DBMS_AQADM.QUEUE_SUBSCRIBERS (qname);

    v_row := sublist.FIRST;
    LOOP
        EXIT WHEN v_row IS NULL;
        DBMS_OUTPUT.PUT_LINE (v_row);
        DBMS_OUTPUT.PUT_LINE (sublist(v_row).name);
        v_row := sublist.NEXT (v_row);
    END LOOP;
END;
/
```

Now let's put the procedure to use. First of all, you can associate a set of subscribers only with a queue that supports multiple consumers. Here are the steps:

```
/* Filename on companion disk: aqcremq.sql */
BEGIN
    DBMS_AQADM.CREATE_QUEUE_TABLE
        (queue_table => 'multicons',
         queue_payload_type => 'message_type',
         multiple_consumers => TRUE);

    DBMS_AQADM.CREATE_QUEUE
        (queue_name => 'multiconsqueue',
         queue_table => 'multicons');

    DBMS_AQADM.START_QUEUE (queue_name => 'multiconsqueue');

END;
/
```

You can then add subscribers to the multicons queue and display the results:

```
/* Filename on companion disk: showsubs.sql */
DECLARE
    v_queue VARCHAR2(10) := 'multiconsqueue';
BEGIN
    DBMS_AQADM.ADD_SUBSCRIBER
        (v_queue, SYS.AQ$_AGENT ('Danielle', NULL, NULL));
    DBMS_AQADM.ADD_SUBSCRIBER
        (v_queue, SYS.AQ$_AGENT ('Benjamin', NULL, NULL));
    DBMS_AQADM.ADD_SUBSCRIBER
        (v_queue, SYS.AQ$_AGENT ('Masada', NULL, NULL));
    DBMS_AQADM.ADD_SUBSCRIBER
        (v_queue, SYS.AQ$_AGENT ('Timnah', NULL, NULL));

    showsubs (v_queue);
END;
/
```

Stopping and Dropping Queues

DBMS_AQADM offers two programs to clean up queues: STOP_QUEUE and DROP_QUEUE. The stop program disables activity on the queue. The drop program actually removes that queue from the queue table.

The DBMS_AQADM.STOP_QUEUE procedure

To disable enqueuing and/or dequeuing on a particular queue, call the STOP_QUEUE procedure:

```
PROCEDURE DBMS_AQADM.STOP_QUEUE
    (queue_name IN VARCHAR2,
     enqueue IN BOOLEAN DEFAULT TRUE,
     dequeue IN BOOLEAN DEFAULT TRUE,
     wait IN BOOLEAN DEFAULT TRUE);
```

Parameters are summarized in the following table.

Name	Description
queue_name	Name of the queue to be stopped.
enqueue	Specify TRUE (the default) if you want to disable enqueuing on this queue. FALSE means that the current setting will not be altered.
dequeue	Specify TRUE (the default) if you want to disable dequeuing on this queue. FALSE means that the current setting will not be altered.
wait	If you specify TRUE (the default), then your program will wait for any outstanding transactions to complete. While waiting, no new transactions are allowed to enqueue to or dequeue from this queue. If you specify FALSE, then the program will return immediately and raise ORA–24023 if it was unable to stop the queue.

Example. The following example shows the disabling of a queue for enqueuing purposes only. I also request that the program wait until all outstanding transactions are completed. You might take these steps in order to allow consumers to empty the queue, while not allowing any new messages to be placed on the queue.

```
BEGIN
    DBMS_AQADM.STOP_QUEUE
        ('msgqueue', enqueue=>TRUE, dequeue=>FALSE, wait=>TRUE);
END;
```

You can check the status of your queue by querying the USER_QUEUES data dictionary view:

```
SQL> SELECT name, enqueue, dequeue FROM USER_QUEUES
  2    WHERE name = 'MSGQUEUE';

NAME        ENQUEUE   DEQUEUE
MSGQUEUE    NO        YES
```

The DBMS_AQADM.DROP_QUEUE procedure

The DROP_QUEUE procedure drops an existing message queue. An error is returned if the message queue does not exist. In addition, this operation is not allowed unless DBMS_AQADM.STOP_QUEUE has been called to disable both enqueuing and dequeuing. If the message queue has not been stopped, then DROP_QUEUE returns an error of queue resource (ORA-24023). Here's the header for the procedure:

```
PROCEDURE DBMS_AQADM.DROP_QUEUE
    (queue_name  IN VARCHAR2,
     auto_commit IN BOOLEAN DEFAULT TRUE);
```

Parameters are summarized in the following table.

Name	Description
queue_name	Name of the queue to be dropped.
auto_commit	Specify TRUE (the default) to cause the current transaction, if any, to commit before the operation is carried out. The operation becomes persistent when the call returns. Specify FALSE if you want the drop action to be part of the current transaction, thereby taking effect only when the calling session issues a commit.

The DBMS_AQADM.DROP_QUEUE_TABLE procedure

Once you have stopped and dropped all queues in a queue table, you can remove that entire queue table with the DROP_QUEUE_TABLE procedure:

```
PROCEDURE DBMS_AQADM.DROP_QUEUE_TABLE
    (queue_table IN VARCHAR2,
     force IN BOOLEAN default FALSE,
     auto_commit IN BOOLEAN default TRUE);
```

Parameters are summarized in the following table.

Name	Description
queue_table	Name of the queue table to be dropped.
force	Specify FALSE (the default) to ensure that the drop action will not succeed unless all queues have been dropped. Specify TRUE if you want to force the dropping of this queue table. In this case, any remaining queues will be automatically stopped and dropped.
auto_commit	Specify TRUE (the default) to cause the current transaction, if any, to commit before the operation is carried out. The operation becomes persistent when the call returns. Specify FALSE if you want the drop action to be part of the current transaction, thereby taking effect only when the calling session issues a commit.

Example. The following example forces the dropping of the msg queue table, stopping and dropping all queues along the way.

```
BEGIN
   DBMS_AQADM.DROP_QUEUE_TABLE ('msg', force => TRUE);
END;
/
```

Managing Propagation of Messages

In order to propagate messages from one queue to another (an Oracle 8.0.4 and later feature), you need to schedule propagation between queues. You can also unschedule propagation of those messages.

The DBMS_AQADM.SCHEDULE_PROPAGATION procedure

Call the SCHEDULE_PROPAGATION procedure to schedule propagation of messages. The header for this procedure follows:

```
PROCEDURE DBMS_AQADM.SCHEDULE_PROPAGATION
   (src_queue_name IN VARCHAR2,
    destination IN VARCHAR2 DEFAULT NULL,
    start_time IN DATE DEFAULT SYSDATE,
    duration IN NUMBER DEFAULT NULL,
    next_time IN VARCHAR2 DEFAULT NULL,
    latency IN NUMBER DEFAULT 60);
```

Parameters are summarized in the following table.

Name	Description
src_queue_name	Name of the source queue whose messages are to be propagated. This name should include the schema name, if the queue is not located in the default schema, which is the schema name of the Oracle AQ administrator.
destination	Database link for the destination. If this argument is NULL, then the destination is the local database; messages will be propagated to other queues in the local database as determined by the subscription or recipient lists. The maximum length for the destination is currently 128 bytes. If the name is not fully qualified, then the default domain named will be used.
start_time	Initial start date-time for the window of time in which messages are propagated from the source queue to the destination queue.
duration	Length of time in seconds that the propagation window will be open. If you supply a NULL value (the default), then the propagation window is open continually, or at least until the propagation is unscheduled through a call to DBMS_AQ.UNSCHEDULE_PROPAGATION.

Name	Description
next_time	An expression returning a date value that is used to compute the start of the next propagation window. If you supply a NULL value (the default), then propagation will stop when the current (initial) window closes. As an example, suppose you want to make sure the next propagation doesn't start until 24 hours after the last propagation window closed. You would then set next_time to SYSDATE + 1 − duration/ 86400. If you want to make sure the next propagation starts 24 hours after the last propagation window closed, provide a next_time value of 'SYSDATE + 1'.
latency	The maximum wait in seconds that a message may sit in a queue after the start of a propagation window before it is propagated. The default amount of time is 60 seconds. This would mean, for example, that when the propagation window opens, the Queue Monitor propagates any messages present. It would then wait 60 seconds (or until the window closes due to the duration setting) before checking for the presence of and propagating any other messages.

To summarize that relatively complex set of parameters and their interactions, when you schedule propagation you identify an initial start date/time and a span of time (number of seconds) in which messages are available to be propagated out of the queue to other queues. You can request that this window of time be opened on a regular basis (every day, once a week, every morning at 10 a.m., etc.). Finally, you can specify that the Queue Monitor check no less frequently than every N seconds (latency) during the time the propagation window is open to see if there are messages to propagate.

Example. In this example, I schedule the propagation of a queue to the Boston brokerage office to occur every two hours. The propagation window is five minutes, and during that period of time, I want messages to be flushed out at least every 30 seconds.

```
BEGIN
    DBMS_AQADM.SCHEDULE_PROPAGATION
       ('sell_orders',
        'broker@boston',
        SYSDATE,
        5 * 60,
        'SYSDATE + 2/24',
        30);
    END;
    /
```

If I do not specify a destination, then propagation occurs to the same database in which the source queue is defined. The following call to DBMS_ AQADM.SCHEDULE_PROPAGATION takes all default values (including a local destination database), except that it requests a latency of ten minutes by using named notation:

```
BEGIN
    DBMS_AQADM.SCHEDULE_PROPAGATION
```

```
        ('share_the_blame',
         latency => 60 * 10);
END;
/
```

The DBMS_AQADM.UNSCHEDULE_PROPAGATION procedure

You can stop or unschedule propagation of a queue with the UNSCHEDULE_
PROPAGATION procedure:

```
PROCEDURE DBMS_AQADM.UNSCHEDULE_PROPAGATION
    (src_queue_name IN VARCHAR2,
     destination IN VARCHAR2 DEFAULT NULL);
```

Parameters are summarized in the following table:

Name	Description
src_queue_name	Name of the source queue whose messages are no longer to be propagated. This name should include the schema name if the queue is not located in the default schema, which is the schema name of the Oracle AQ administrator.
destination	Database link for the destination for which propagation will be terminated. If this argument is NULL, then the destination is the local database; messages will no longer be propagated to other queues in the local database as determined by the subscription or recipient lists. The maximum length for destination is currently 128 bytes. If the name is not fully qualified, then the default domain named will be used.

Verifying Queue Types

The DBMS_AQADM.VERIFY_QUEUE_TYPES procedure

The VERIFY_QUEUE_TYPES procedure allows you to determine whether two different queues have the same payload type. Here's the header:

```
PROCEDURE DBMS_AQADM.VERIFY_QUEUE_TYPES
    (src_queue_name IN VARCHAR2,
     dest_queue_name IN VARCHAR2
     destination IN VARCHAR2 DEFAULT NULL,
     rc OUT BINARY_INTEGER);
```

Parameters are summarized in the following table.

Name	Description
src_queue_name	Name of the source queue, usually one from which messages are to be propagated. This name should include the schema name if the queue is not located in the default schema, which is the schema name of the user.
dest_queue_name	Name of the destination queue, usually one to which messages are to be propagated. This name should include the schema name if the queue is not located in the default schema, which is the schema name of the user.
destination	Database link for the destination queue. If this argument is NULL, then the destination queue is located in the same database as the source queue. The maximum length for destination is currently 128 bytes. If the name is not fully qualified, then the default domain named will be used.
rc	Status code returned by the procedure. If there is no problem verifying the queue types and if the source and destination queue types match, then the result code is 0. If the queue types do not match (and there is no error), then the result code is 1. If an Oracle exception is raised, the SQLCODE is returned in rc.

Whenever this program is run (either by Oracle AQ itself or by an AQ administrator), it updates the SYS.AQ$_MESSAGE_TYPES table. You can access this table (to verify the success of the type match after propagation has taken place) using the OID (Object ID) of the source queue and the address of the destination queue.

Starting and Stopping the Queue Monitor

If you want to use the delay and expiration features of AQ, you must have the Queue Monitor process running in the background. Before you can do this, you must add an AQ_TM_PROCESS parameter to your database initialization file (see "Getting Started with Oracle AQ" at the beginning of this chapter for more information).

The DBMS_AQADM.START_TIME_MANAGER procedure

To start the Queue Monitor process, call the START_TIME_MANAGER procedure:

```
PROCEDURE DBMS_AQADM.START_TIME_MANAGER;
```

The operation takes effect when the call completes; there are no transactional dependencies.

You can use the START_TIME_MANAGER to restart the Queue Monitor after you stopped it with a call to STOP_TIME_MANAGER. You can also use it to start the Queue Monitor process if the database initialization parameter was set to 0. In other words, you can override the default state of the database with this program-matic call.

The DBMS_AQADM.STOP_TIME_MANAGER procedure

To stop the Queue Monitor process, call the STOP_TIME_MANAGER procedure:

```
PROCEDURE DBMS_AQADM.STOP_TIME_MANAGER;
```

The operation takes effect when the call completes; there are no transactional dependencies.

The STOP_TIME_MANAGER procedure does not actually stop the physical process running in the background. This process is started when the database is initialized. The procedure simply disables the time management features of Oracle AQ in that database instance.

Oracle AQ Database Objects

Oracle AQ relies on a variety of database objects to get its job done. Some objects are created for each queue table established. Other objects are created at the time that Oracle AQ is installed.

Objects Per Queue Table

When a queue table is created, Oracle AQ defines a database table to hold all the messages for all queues in that queue table, as well as a view that allows a user to both query from and change (with caution and the guidance of Oracle Support) messages stored in queues of the queue table.

The database table for queue data

The name of the database table has the following form,

```
<queue_table>
```

where queue_table is the name of the queue table created. Table 5-3 shows the columns of this view.

Table 5-3. Columns in the Database Table for Queue Data

Name	Description	Datatype
Q_NAME	Name of the queue (remember that you can have more than one queue in a queue table)	VARCHAR2(30)
MSGID	Unique identifier of the message	RAW(16)
CORRID	Optional correlation identifier value provided by the user	VARCHAR2(30)

Table 5-3. Columns in the Database Table for Queue Data (continued)

Name	Description	Datatype
PRIORITY	Message priority	NUMBER
STATE	Message state	NUMBER
DELAY	The point in time to which the message is delayed for dequeuing	DATE
EXPIRATION	Number of seconds in which the message will expire after its message state is set to READY	NUMBER
TIME_MANAGER_INFO	For internal use only	DATE
LOCAL_ORDER_NO	For internal use only	NUMBER
CHAIN_NO	For internal use only	NUMBER
CSCN	For internal use only	NUMBER
DSCN	For internal use only	NUMBER
ENQ_TIME	Date-time at which the message was enqueued	DATE
ENQ_UID	User ID of the session that enqueued the message	NUMBER
ENQ_TID	ID number of the transaction that enqueued this message	VARCHAR2(30)
DEQ_TIME	Date-time at which the message was dequeued	DATE
DEQ_UID	User ID of the session that dequeued the message	NUMBER
DEQ_TID	ID number of the transaction that dequeued this message	VARCHAR2(30)
RETRY_COUNT	Number of retries at dequeuing the message	NUMBER
EXCEPTION_QSCHEMA	Name of the schema containing the exception queue for this message	VARCHAR2(30)
EXCEPTION_QUEUE	Name of the exception queue for this message	VARCHAR2(30)
STEP_NO	For internal use only	NUMBER
RECIPIENT_KEY	For internal use only	NUMBER
DEQUEUE_MSGID	Message ID for the dequeue operation	RAW(16)
USER_DATA	Payload of the queue (<user_data>); this might be a RAW value or the contents of the object that was placed in the queue	RAW or <object_type>

You will find it useful to execute queries directly against this base table when you need to examine dequeue status information for messages that reside in a multiple consumer queue.

Here, for example, is the kind of query you might write to view the list of the agents that consumed a message with the following ID,

```
452F77CD652E11D1B999B14141A17646.


SELECT consumer, transaction_id, deq_time, deq_user
   FROM THE
      (SELECT CAST (history AS SYS.AQ$_DEQUEUE_HISTORY_T)
         FROM msg_qtable
         WHERE msgid = 452F77CD652E11D1B999B14141A17646).
```

where SYS.AQ$_DEQUEUE_HISTORY_T is a nested table of type SYS.AQ$_DEQUEUE_HISTORY. This dequeue history object type is defined in *catqueue.sql* as follows:

```
CREATE TYPE sys.aq$_dequeue_history_t
AS OBJECT
( consumer  VARCHAR2(30),          -- identifies dequeuer
  transaction_id VARCHAR2(22),     -- M_LTID, transaction id of dequeuer
  deq_time  DATE,                  -- time of dequeue
  deq_user  NUMBER,                -- user id of client performing dequeue
  remote_apps  VARCHAR2(4000),     -- string repn. of remote agents
  agent_naming NUMBER,             -- how the message was sent to agent
  propagated_msgid RAW(16));
```

The queue table view

The name of the view for a queue table has the following form,

```
AQ$<queue_table>
```

where queue_table is the name of the queue table created. Table 5-4 shows the columns of this view. Notes about this view and its usage are included after the table.

Table 5-4. Columns in the Queue Table View

Name	Description	Type
QUEUE	Name of the queue (remember you can have more than one queue in a queue table)	VARCHAR2(30)
MSG_ID	Unique identifier of the message	RAW(16)
CORR_ID	Optional correlation identifier value provided by the user	VARCHAR2(128)
MSG_PRIORITY	Message priority	NUMBER

Table 5-4. Columns in the Queue Table View (continued)

Name	Description	Type
MSG_STATE	Message state	VARCHAR2(9)
DELAY	Point in time to which the message is delayed for dequeuing	DATE
EXPIRATION	Number of seconds in which the message will expire after its message state is set to READY	NUMBER
ENQ_TIME	Date-time at which the message was enqueued	DATE
ENQ_USER_ID	User ID of the enqueuing process	NUMBER
ENQ_TXN_ID	Transaction ID of the enqueue action	VARCHAR2(30)
DEQ_TIME	Date-time at which the message was dequeued	DATE
DEQ_USER_ID	User ID of the dequeuing process	NUMBER
DEQ_TXN_ID	Transaction ID of the dequeue action	VARCHAR2(30)
RETRY_COUNT	Number of attempts to dequeue the message	NUMBER
EXCEPTION_QUEUE_OWNER	Owner of exception queue	VARCHAR2(30)
EXCEPTION_QUEUE	Name of exception queue for this message	VARCHAR2(30)
USER_DATA	Payload of the queue (<user_data>); this might be a RAW value or the contents of the object which was placed in the queue	RAW or <object_type>

Note the following about using the queue table view:

- The AQ administrator can use the SQL language to examine the contents of any queue or queue table.
- The dequeue columns are relevant only for single consumer queues. If you want to examine the dequeue history of messages in a multiple consumer queue, you will need to examine the underlying database table owned by SYS that contains the message data (see the next section).

Data Dictionary Objects

This section documents the database objects in the data dictionary that contain information for all queue tables and queues to which you have access.

The DBA_QUEUE_TABLES view

You can obtain information about all the queue tables created in your instance by examining the DBA_QUEUE_TABLES data dictionary view. The USER_QUEUE_TABLES view will show you all information about queue tables defined in your schema. Its columns are identical to the DBA version, except that there is no OWNER column. Table 5-5 lists the columns of the DBA_QUEUE_TABLES view.

Table 5-5. Columns in DBA_QUEUE_TABLES View

Name	Description	Type
OWNER	The schema owning the queue table	VARCHAR2(30)
QUEUE_TABLE	Name of the queue table	VARCHAR2(30)
TYPE	Type of payload in the queue table (either 'RAW' or 'OBJECT')	VARCHAR2(7)
OBJECT_TYPE	Name of the object type if the type of the queue table is OBJECT	VARCHAR2(61)
SORT_ORDER	A sort order for queues in the queue table, if specified	VARCHAR2(22)
RECIPIENTS	A value indicating whether it is a single consumer queue table (DBMS_AQADM.SINGLE) or a multiple consumer queue table (DBMS_AQADM.MULTIPLE)	VARCHAR2(8)
MESSAGE_GROUPING	The type of message grouping, either DBMS_AQADM.NONE or DBMS_AQADM.TRANSACTION	VARCHAR2(13)
USER_COMMENT	Comment provided by the user to associate with the queue table	VARCHAR2(50)

The DBA_QUEUES view

You can obtain information about all the queues created in your instance by examining the DBA_QUEUES data dictionary view. The USER_QUEUES view will show you all information about queues defined in your schema. Its columns are identical to the DBA version except that there is no OWNER column. Table 5-6 lists the columns of the DBA_QUEUES view.

Table 5-6. Columns in DBA_QUEUES View

Name	Description	Type
OWNER	The schema owning the queue	VARCHAR2(30)
NAME	Name of the queue	VARCHAR2(30)

Table 5-6. Columns in DBA_QUEUES View (continued)

Name	Description	Type
QUEUE_TABLE	Name of the queue table that contains this queue	VARCHAR2(30)
QID	Unique identifier for queue	NUMBER
QUEUE_TYPE	Type of the queue, either DBMS_AQADM.NORMAL_QUEUE or DBMS_AQADM.EXCEPTION_QUEUE	VARCHAR2(5)
MAX_RETRIES	Maximum number of dequeue attempts that are allowed on messages in this queue	NUMBER
RETRY_DELAY	Number of seconds before a dequeue retry can be attempted	NUMBER
ENQUEUE_ENABLED	Flag indicating whether or not (YES or NO) the enqueue operation is enabled for this queue	VARCHAR2(7)
DEQUEUE_ENABLED	Flag indicating whether or not (YES or NO) the dequeue operation is enabled for this queue	VARCHAR2(7)
RETENTION	Number of seconds a message is retained in the queue after dequeuing	NUMBER
USER_COMMENT	Comment provided by the user to associate with the queue table	VARCHAR2(50)

The DBA_JOBS view

For Oracle 8.0.4 and later, AQ provides a view to the schedules currently defined for propagating messages. Table 5-7 shows the columns of the DBA_JOBS view.

Table 5-7. Columns in the DBA_JOBS View

Name	Description	Type
SCHEMA	Schema owning the queue	VARCHAR2(30)
QNAME	Name of the source queue	VARCHAR2(30)
DESTINATION	Name of the destination; currently limited to being a database link (dblink) name	VARCHAR2(128)
START_DATE	Date at which propagation will be started	DATE
START_TIME	Time of day at which propagation will be started; this is stored in a string of format HH:MM:SS	VARCHAR2(8)
PROPAGATION_WINDOW	Duration of the propagation window in seconds	NUMBER
NEXT_TIME	String containing a date expression that evaluates to the starting date/time of the next propagation window	VARCHAR2(128)
LATENCY	Maximum number of seconds AQ will wait before it attempts to propagate messages during a propagation window	NUMBER

Check this view to see if a particular combination of source queue and destination have been scheduled for propagation. If so, you can determine the job ID or job number for the propagation by examining the SYS.AQ$_SCHEDULES table. Apply this job number to the DBA_JOBS view to find out:

- The last time that propagation was scheduled.

- The next time that propagation will occur.

- The status of the job. If the job is marked as broken, you can check for errors in the trace files generated by the job queue processes in the *$ORACLE_HOME/log* directory.

The GV$AQ and V$AQ dynamic statistics views

Oracle AQ provides two views for retrieving dynamic statistics for AQ operations: GV$AQ and V$AQ. The columns for these views are exactly the same, but they contain different data:

GV$AQ view

Provides information about the numbers of messages in various states for the entire database. It consolidates information from all instances when it is queried in an Oracle parallel server environment.

V$AQ view

Contains information about the messages in a specific database instance. It does this by examining AQ statistics stored in the System Global Area (SGA) of the instance.

Table 5-8 lists the columns of the GV$AQ and V$AQ views.

Table 5-8. Columns in GV$AQ and V$AQ Views

Name	Description	Type
QID	Unique identifier of a queue; its value matches the same column in DBA_QUEUES and USER_QUEUES	NUMBER
WAITING	Number of messages in the WAITING state	NUMBER
READY	Number of messages in the READY state	NUMBER
EXPIRED	Number of messages in the EXPIRED state	NUMBER
TOTAL_WAIT	Number of seconds for which messages in the queue have been waiting in the READY state	NUMBER
AVERAGE_WAIT	Average number of seconds for which messages in the queue have been waiting in the READY state to be dequeued	NUMBER

Oracle AQ Examples

This section offers numerous examples of using AQ, including packages you can install and reuse in your environment. In all these examples, unless otherwise noted, assume that I have (a) defined an Oracle account named AQADMIN to perform administrative tasks and (b) assigned the AQ_USER_ROLE to SCOTT to perform operational tasks. I then connect to AQADMIN.

After setting up the queue tables and queues, I connect to SCOTT and create this object type:

```
CREATE TYPE message_type AS OBJECT
   (title VARCHAR2(30),
    text VARCHAR2(2000));
```

I also grant EXECUTE privilege on this object to my AQ administrator:

```
GRANT EXECUTE ON message_type TO AQADMIN;
```

My AQ administrator then can create a queue table and a message queue as follows:

```
BEGIN
   DBMS_AQADM.CREATE_QUEUE_TABLE
      (queue_table => 'scott.msg',
       queue_payload_type => 'message_type');

   DBMS_AQADM.CREATE_QUEUE
      (queue_name => 'msgqueue',
       queue_table => 'scott.msg');

   DBMS_AQADM.START_QUEUE (queue_name => 'msgqueue');
END;
/
```

Notice that I do not need to specify the schema for the payload type. AQ assumes the same schema as specified for the queue table.

I will make use of these objects throughout the following examples; I will also at times supplement these queue objects with other, more specialized queue table and queues.

Oracle also provides a set of examples scripts for AQ. In Oracle 8.0.3, the following files were located in *$ORACLE_HOME/rdbms80/admin/aq/demo*:

aqdemo00.sql

   The driver program for the demonstration

aqdemo01.sql

   Create queue tables and queues

aqdemo02.sql
> Load the demo package

aqdemo03.sql
> Submit the event handler as a job to the job queue

aqdemo04.sql
> Enqueue messages

Improving AQ Ease of Use

Let's start by constructing a package to make it easier to work with AQ objects. I am always looking for ways to shortcut steps I must perform to get things done. The complexity of AQ, along with all of the different records and structures, begs for a wrapper of code to perform common steps more easily.

I describe the program elements defined in the aq package later. To save a few trees, I will leave the reader to examine the package body to see how I constructed these programs. In most cases they are very straightforward.

First off, I define two subtypes so that you can declare variables using names instead of hard-coded declarations like RAW(16). These subtypes are as follows:

```
v_msgid RAW(16);
SUBTYPE msgid_type IS v_msgid%TYPE;

v_name VARCHAR2(49);
SUBTYPE name_type IS v_name%TYPE;
```

I also predefined two common exceptions so that you can trap these by name through a WHEN OTHERS clause and a hard-coding of the error number (see the *aqbrowse.sp* file for an example of using this named exception):

```
dequeue_timeout EXCEPTION
PRAGMA EXCEPTION_INIT (dequeue_timeout, -25228);

dequeue_disabled EXCEPTION;
PRAGMA EXCEPTION_INIT (dequeue_disabled, -25226);
```

Now let's run through the different procedures and functions in the packages. The aq.create_queue procedure combines the create table queue, create queue, and start queue steps into a single procedure call:

```
PROCEDURE aq.create_queue
    (qtable IN VARCHAR2,
     payload_type IN VARCHAR2,
     qname IN VARCHAR2,
     prioritize IN VARCHAR2 := NULL);
```

If the queue table already exists, it is not created. You can also provide a prioritization string if you want to override the default.

The aq.create_priority_queue procedure has the same interface as aq.create_queue, but the default value for the prioritize parameter is the most common non-standard string: order by the priority number, and within the same priority number, by the enqueue time.

```
PROCEDURE create_priority_queue
   (qtable IN VARCHAR2,
    payload_type IN VARCHAR2,
    qname IN VARCHAR2,
    prioritize IN VARCHAR2 := 'PRIORITY,ENQ_TIME');
```

The aq.stop_and_drop procedure is a neat little program. It combines the following operations: stop queue, drop queue, and drop queue table. But it also figures out when it is appropriate to execute each of those steps.

```
PROCEDURE aq.stop_and_drop (
   qtable IN VARCHAR2,
   qname IN VARCHAR2 := '%',
   enqueue IN BOOLEAN := TRUE,
   dequeue IN BOOLEAN := TRUE,
   wait IN BOOLEAN := TRUE);
```

Here are the rules followed by aq.stop_and_drop:

- Stop all queues within the specified queue table that match the queue name you provide. Notice that the default is '%', so if you do not provide a queue name, then all queues in the queue table are stopped.

- If you specify that you want to stop both enqueue and dequeue operations on queues, then those queues will also be dropped.

- If you stop and drop all queues in the queue table, then the queue table itself will be dropped.

The default values for this program specify that all queues in the specified queue table should be stopped and dropped, but only after any outstanding transactions on those queues are completed.

The rest of the aq programs retrieve information about queues and queue tables from the data dictionary views. You could write many more programs along these lines to make it easier to view the contents of the AQ views. In fact, the aq package will contain more programs by the time this book is printed, so check out the *aq.spp* file to see the latest set of functionality.

The aq.queue_exists function returns TRUE if a queue of the specified name exists:

```
FUNCTION aq.queue_exists (qname IN VARCHAR2) RETURN BOOLEAN;
```

The aq.qtable_exists function returns TRUE if a queue table of the specified name exists:

```
FUNCTION aq.qtable_exists (qtable IN VARCHAR2) RETURN BOOLEAN;
```

The aq.msgcount function returns the number of messages in the specified queue:

```
FUNCTION aq.msgcount (qtable IN VARCHAR2, qname IN VARCHAR2)
     RETURN INTEGER
```

You have to specify both the queue table and the queue name so that the function can construct the name of the database table holding the queue messages. You could enhance this function so that you provide only the queue name and the function looks up the queue table name for you.

The aq.msgdata function returns the specified piece of information (the data_in argument) for a specific message ID in the queue table:

```
FUNCTION aq.msgdata (qtable_in IN VARCHAR2,
    msgid_in IN RAW,
    data_in IN VARCHAR2) RETURN VARCHAR2;
```

The data_in argument must be one of the columns in the aq$<qtable_in> database table, which contains all the messages for queues in that queue table.

For example, to obtain the correlation ID for a message in the "msg" queue table, you could call aq.msgdata as follows:

```
CREATE OR REPLACE FUNCTION corr_id (msg_id IN aq.msgid_type)
    RETURN VARCHAR2
IS
    v_corr_id := aq.msgdata ('msg', msgid_in, 'corr_id');
END;
/
```

Call the aq.showmsgs procedure to show some of the message information for the specified queue:

```
PROCEDURE showmsgs (qtable IN VARCHAR2, qname IN VARCHAR2);
```

This procedure currently shows the priority, message state, number of retries, and correlation ID of messages in the queue. You can easily modify the procedure to show different pieces of information about the message. Remember that it is probably impossible to create a generic program like this that will display the *contents* of the message, since that is either a RAW or an instance of an object type. For this same reason, there is no generic enqueue or dequeue procedure.

I hope these programs will get you started on encapsulating commonly needed tasks at your site for performing queueing operations. There is much more to be done, particularly in the area of building queries (which can then be placed behind functions and in mini-report generator procedures) against the various data dictionary views.

Working with Prioritized Queues

The normal priority order for dequeuing is by enqueue time: in other words, "first in, first out" or FIFO. You can modify this priority order when you create a different value for the sort_list argument when you create a queue table. Since this value is specified for a queue table, you will be setting the default sorting for any queue defined in this queue table.

The only other option for the default sorting of queue messages is by the priority number. In the world of AQ, the lower the priority number, the higher the priority.

Suppose that I want to create a queue that manages messages of three different priorities: low, medium, and high. The rule is very simple: dequeue high-priority messages before medium-priority messages, and medium-priority messages before low-priority messages.

As you might expect, I would strongly urge that when faced with a task like this one, you immediately think in terms of building a package to encapsulate your different actions and make your code easier to use. In this scenario, for example, I don't really want users of my prioritized queue to have to know about specific priority numbers. Instead, I want to provide them with programs that hide the details and let them concentrate on their tasks.

The following specification for a package offers an interface to a three-level prioritization queue. The payload type for this queue is the same message_type described at the beginning of the example section.

```
/* Filename on companion disk: priority.spp */
CREATE OR REPLACE PACKAGE priority
IS
     PROCEDURE enqueue_low (item IN VARCHAR2);

     PROCEDURE enqueue_medium (item IN VARCHAR2);

     PROCEDURE enqueue_high (item IN VARCHAR2);

     PROCEDURE dequeue (item OUT VARCHAR2);
END;
/
```

This is a very simple package specification. You can enqueue messages with one of three priorities, and you can dequeue messages. Here is a script that tests this package by helping me prioritize my chores for the evening:

```
/* Filename on companion disk: priority.tst */
DECLARE
   str varchar2(100);
BEGIN
   priority.enqueue_low ('Cleaning the basement');
   priority.enqueue_high ('Cleaning the bathroom');
   priority.enqueue_high ('Helping Eli with his non-French homework');
```

```
    priority.enqueue_medium ('Washing the dishes');

    LOOP
        priority.dequeue (str);
        EXIT WHEN str IS NULL;
        DBMS_OUTPUT.PUT_LINE (str);
    END LOOP;
END;
/
```

I place four messages with different priorities in my queue. Notice that the order in which I enqueue does not correspond to the priorities. Let's run this script and see what I get:

```
SQL> @priority.tst
HIGH: Cleaning the bathroom
HIGH: Helping Eli with his non-French homework
MEDIUM: Washing the dishes
LOW: Cleaning the basement
```

As you can see, my messages have been dequeued in priority order.

You can view the entire package body in the *priority.spp* file. Let's take a look at the individual components I used to build this package. First, I define a set of constants as follows:

```
CREATE OR REPLACE PACKAGE BODY priority
IS
    c_qtable CONSTANT aq.name_type := 'hi_med_lo_q_table';
    c_queue CONSTANT aq.name_type := 'hi_med_lo_q';

    c_high CONSTANT    PLS_INTEGER := 1;
    c_medium CONSTANT PLS_INTEGER := 500000;
    c_low CONSTANT     PLS_INTEGER := 1000000;
```

I don't want to hard-code the names of my queue table and queue throughout my body, so I use constants instead. I also define constants for my three different priority levels. (Notice the space between these values; I will come back to that later.)

I have three different enqueue procedures to implement. Each of them performs the same basic steps. Here, for example, is the way I first implemented enqueue_ low:

```
PROCEDURE enqueue_low (item IN VARCHAR2)
IS
    queueopts DBMS_AQ.ENQUEUE_OPTIONS_T;
    msgprops DBMS_AQ.MESSAGE_PROPERTIES_T;
    item_obj message_type;
BEGIN
    item_obj := message_type (priority, item);
    queueopts.visibility := DBMS_AQ.IMMEDIATE;
    msgprops.priority := c_low;
```

```
        DBMS_AQ.ENQUEUE (c_queue, queueopts, msgprops, item_obj, g_msgid);
    END;
```

I declare my records to hold the queue options and message properties. I construct the object to be placed in the queue. I request that the operation be immediately visible (no commit required) and set the priority. Once these steps are complete, I enqueue the message.

I finished this procedure and then embarked on enqueue_medium. I quickly discovered that the only difference between the two was the assignment to the msgprops.priority field. I just as quickly put the kibosh on this approach. It made no sense at all to me to write (or cut-and-paste) three different procedures with all that code when there was virtually no difference between them. Instead I wrote a single, generic enqueue as follows:

```
    PROCEDURE enqueue (item IN VARCHAR2, priority IN PLS_INTEGER)
    IS
        queueopts DBMS_AQ.ENQUEUE_OPTIONS_T;
        msgprops DBMS_AQ.MESSAGE_PROPERTIES_T;
        item_obj message_type;
    BEGIN
        item_obj := message_type (priority, item);
        queueopts.visibility := DBMS_AQ.IMMEDIATE;
        msgprops.priority := priority;
        DBMS_AQ.ENQUEUE (c_queue, queueopts, msgprops, item_obj, g_msgid);
    END;
```

And then I implemented the priority-specific enqueue procedures on top of this one:

```
    PROCEDURE enqueue_low (item IN VARCHAR2)
    IS
    BEGIN
        enqueue (item, c_low);
    END;

    PROCEDURE enqueue_medium (item IN VARCHAR2)
    IS
    BEGIN
        enqueue (item, c_medium);
    END;

    PROCEDURE enqueue_high (item IN VARCHAR2)
    IS
    BEGIN
        enqueue (item, c_high);
    END;
```

It is extremely important that you always consolidate your code and modularize within package bodies as much as possible. You will then find it much easier to maintain and enhance your programs.

My enqueue procedures are now done. I have only a single dequeue and it is fairly straightforward:

```
PROCEDURE dequeue (item OUT VARCHAR2)
IS
    queueopts DBMS_AQ.DEQUEUE_OPTIONS_T;
    msgprops DBMS_AQ.MESSAGE_PROPERTIES_T;
    item_obj message_type;
BEGIN
    queueopts.wait := DBMS_AQ.NO_WAIT;
    queueopts.visibility := DBMS_AQ.IMMEDIATE;
    DBMS_AQ.DEQUEUE (c_queue, queueopts, msgprops, item_obj, g_msgid);
    item := priority_name (item_obj.title) || ': ' || item_obj.text;
EXCEPTION
    WHEN OTHERS
    THEN
        IF SQLCODE = -25228 /* Timeout; queue is likely empty... */
        THEN
            item := NULL;
        ELSE
            RAISE;
        END IF;
END;
```

Most of the code is taken up with the basic steps necessary for any dequeue operation: create the records, specify that I want the action to be immediately visible, and specify that AQ should not wait for messages to be queued. I then dequeue, and, if successful, construct the string to be passed back.

If the dequeue fails, I trap for a specific error that indicates that the queue was empty (ORA-025228). In this case, I set the item to NULL and return. Otherwise, I reraise the same error.

Notice that I call a function called priority_name as a part of my message passed back in dequeue. This function converts a priority number to a string or name as follows:

```
FUNCTION priority_name (priority IN PLS_INTEGER) RETURN VARCHAR2
IS
    retval VARCHAR2(30);
BEGIN
    IF    priority = c_high THEN retval := 'HIGH';
    ELSIF priority = c_low THEN retval := 'LOW';
    ELSIF priority = c_medium THEN retval := 'MEDIUM';
    ELSE
        retval := 'Priority ' || TO_CHAR (priority);
    END IF;
    RETURN retval;
END;
```

This function offers some consistency in how the priorities are named.

This package contains the following initialization section:

```
BEGIN
   /* Create the queue table and queue as necessary. */
   aq.create_priority_queue (c_qtable, 'message_type', c_queue);
END priority;
```

This line of code is run the first time any of your code references a program in this package. This aq procedure (see the earlier section, "Improving AQ Ease of Use") makes sure that all elements of the priority queue infrastructure are ready to go. If the queue table and queue are already in place, it will not do anything, including raise any errors.

Remember the comment I made about the big gaps between the priority numbers? Take a look at the body for the priority package. If you add the header of the generic enqueue procedure to the specification, this package will support not only high, low, and medium priorities, but also any priority number you want to pass to the enqueue procedure.

More complex prioritization approaches

In many situations, the priority may be established by relatively fluid database information. In this case, you should create a function that returns the priority for a record in a table. Suppose, for example, that you are building a student registration system and that priority is given to students according to their seniority: if a senior wants to get into a class, she gets priority over a freshman.

If I have a student object type as follows (much simplified from a real student registration system),

```
CREATE TYPE student_t IS OBJECT
   (name VARCHAR2 (100),
    enrolled_on DATE);
```

and a table built upon that object type as follows:

```
CREATE TABLE student OF student_t;
```

I might create a function as follows to return the priority for a student:

```
CREATE OR REPLACE FUNCTION reg_priority (student_in IN student_t)
   RETURN PLS_INTEGER
IS
BEGIN
   RETURN -1 * TRUNC (SYSDATE - student_in.enrolled_on);
END;
/
```

Why did I multiply by -1 the difference between today's date and the enrolled date? Because the lower the number, the higher the priority.

Of course, this function could also be defined as a member of the object type itself.

Building a Stack with AQ Using Sequence Deviation

A queue is just one example of a "controlled access list." The usual definition of a queue is a FIFO list (first-in, first-out). Another type of list is a stack, which follows the LIFO rule: last-in, first-out. You can use AQ to build and manage persistent stacks with ease (its contents persist between connections to the database).

The files *aqstk.spp* and *aqstk2.spp* offer two different implementations of a stack using Oracle AQ. The package specifications in both cases are exactly the same and should be familiar to anyone who has worked with a stack:

```
CREATE OR REPLACE PACKAGE aqstk
IS
    PROCEDURE push (item IN VARCHAR2);
    PROCEDURE pop (item OUT VARCHAR2);
END;
/
```

You push an item onto the stack and pop an item off the stack. The differences between *aqstk.spp* and *aqstk2.spp* lie in the package body. A comparison of the two approaches will help you see how to take advantage of the many different flavors of queuing available.

The *aqstk.spp* file represents my first try at a stack implementation. I decided to create a prioritized queue. I then needed to come up with a way to make sure that the last item added to the queue always had the lowest priority. This is done by maintaining a global variable inside the package body (g_priority) to keep track of the priority of the most-recently enqueued message.

Every time I enqueue a new message, that global counter is decremented (lower number = higher priority) as shown in the following push procedure (bold lines show priority-related code):

```
PROCEDURE push (item IN VARCHAR2)
IS
    queueopts DBMS_AQ.ENQUEUE_OPTIONS_T;
    msgprops DBMS_AQ.MESSAGE_PROPERTIES_T;
    msgid aq.msgid_type;
    item_obj aqstk_objtype;
BEGIN
    item_obj := aqstk_objtype (item);
    msgprops.priority := g_priority;
    queueopts.visibility := DBMS_AQ.IMMEDIATE;
    g_priority := g_priority - 1;
    DBMS_AQ.ENQUEUE (c_queue, queueopts, msgprops, item_obj, msgid);
END;
```

The problem with this approach is that each time you started anew using the stack package in your session, the global counter would be set at its initial value: 2^{30}. (I wanted to make sure that you didn't exhaust your priority values in a single session.) Why is that a problem? Because AQ queues are based in database tables and are persistent between connections. So if my stack still held a few items, it would be possible to end up with multiple items with the same priority.

To avoid this problem, I set up the initialization section of my stack package in *aqstk.spp* as follows:

```
BEGIN
   /* Drop the existing queue if present. */
   aq.stop_and_drop (c_queue_table);

   /* Create the queue table and queue as necessary. */
   aq.create_priority_queue (c_queue_table, 'aqstk_objtype', c_queue);
END aqstk;
```

In other words: wipe out the existing stack queue table, and queue and recreate it. Any leftover items in the stack will be discarded.

That approach makes sense if I don't want my stack to stick around. But why build a stack on Oracle AQ if you don't want to take advantage of the persistence? I decided to go back to the drawing board and see if there was a way to always dequeue from the top without relying on some external (to AQ) counter.

I soon discovered the sequence deviation field of the enqueue options record. This field allows you to request a deviation from the normal sequencing for a message in a queue. The following values can be assigned to this field:

DBMS_AQ.BEFORE

    The message is enqueued ahead of the message specified by relative_msgid.

DBMS_AQ.TOP

    The message is enqueued ahead of any other messages.

NULL (the default)

    There is no deviation from the normal sequence.

So it seemed that if I wanted my queue to act like a stack, I simply had to specify "top" for each new message coming into the queue. With this in mind, I created my push procedure as follows:

```
PROCEDURE push (item IN VARCHAR2)
IS
   queueopts DBMS_AQ.ENQUEUE_OPTIONS_T;
   msgprops DBMS_AQ.MESSAGE_PROPERTIES_T;
   item_obj aqstk_objtype;
BEGIN
   item_obj := aqstk_objtype (item);
   queueopts.sequence_deviation := DBMS_AQ.TOP;
   queueopts.visibility := DBMS_AQ.IMMEDIATE;
   DBMS_AQ.ENQUEUE (c_queue, queueopts, msgprops, item_obj, g_msgid);
END;
```

My pop procedure could now perform an almost-normal dequeue as follows:

```
PROCEDURE pop (item OUT VARCHAR2)
IS
    queueopts DBMS_AQ.DEQUEUE_OPTIONS_T;
    msgprops DBMS_AQ.MESSAGE_PROPERTIES_T;
    msgid aq.msgid_type;
    item_obj aqstk_objtype;
BEGIN
    /* Workaround for 8.0.3 bug; insist on dequeuing of first message. */
    queueopts.navigation := DBMS_AQ.FIRST_MESSAGE;

    queueopts.wait := DBMS_AQ.NO_WAIT;
    queueopts.visibility := DBMS_AQ.IMMEDIATE;
    DBMS_AQ.DEQUEUE (c_queue, queueopts, msgprops, item_obj, g_msgid);
    item := item_obj.item;
END;
```

Notice that the first line of this procedure contains a workaround. A bug in Oracle 8.0.3 requires that I insist on dequeuing of the first message (which is always the last-enqueued message, since I used sequence deviation) to avoid raising an error. I was not able to confirm by the time of this book's printing whether this was necessary in Oracle 8.0.4.

With this second implementation of a stack, I no longer need or want to destroy the queue table and queue for each new connection. As a consequence, my package initialization section simply makes sure that all the necessary AQ objects are in place:

```
BEGIN
    /* Create the queue table and queue as necessary. */
    aq.create_queue ('aqstk_table', 'aqstk_objtype', c_queue);
END aqstk;
```

 So you have two choices with a stack implementation (and probably more, but this is all I am going to offer):

aqstk.spp
    A stack that is refreshed each time you reconnnect to Oracle.

aqstk2.spp
    A stack whose contents persist between connections to the Oracle database.

Browsing a Queue's Contents

One very handy feature of Oracle AQ is the ability to retrieve messages from a queue in a nondestructive fashion. In other words, you can read a message from the queue without *removing* it from the queue at the same time. Removing on dequeue is the default mode of AQ (at least for messages that are not part of a message group). However, you can override that default by requesting BROWSE mode when dequeuing.

Suppose that I am building a student registration system. Students make requests for one or more classes and their requests go into a queue. Another program dequeues these requests (destructively) and fills the classes. But what if a student drops out? All of their requests must be removed from the queue. To perform this task, I must scan through the queue contents, but remove destructively only when I find a match on the student social security number. To illustrate these steps, I create an object type for a student's request to enroll in a class:

```
/* Filename on companion disk: aqbrowse.sp */
CREATE TYPE student_reg_t IS OBJECT
   (ssn VARCHAR2(11),
    class_requested VARCHAR2(100));
/
```

I then build a drop_student procedure, which scans the contents of a queue of previous objects of the type. The algorithm used is quite simple: within a simple LOOP, dequeue messages in BROWSE mode. If a match is found, dequeue in REMOVE mode for that specific message by its unique message identifier. Then continue in BROWSE mode until there aren't any more messages to be checked.

```
/* Filename on companion disk: aqbrowse.sp */
CREATE OR REPLACE PROCEDURE drop_student (queue IN VARCHAR2, ssn_in IN
VARCHAR2)
IS
    student student_reg_t;
    v_msgid aq.msgid_type;
    queue_changed BOOLEAN := FALSE;

    queueopts DBMS_AQ.DEQUEUE_OPTIONS_T;
    msgprops DBMS_AQ.MESSAGE_PROPERTIES_T;

    /* Translate mode number to a name. */
    FUNCTION mode_name (mode_in IN INTEGER) RETURN VARCHAR2
    IS
    BEGIN
        IF    mode_in = DBMS_AQ.REMOVE THEN RETURN 'REMOVE';
        ELSIF mode_in = DBMS_AQ.BROWSE THEN RETURN 'BROWSE';
        END IF;
    END;

    /* Avoid any redundancy; doing two dequeues, only difference is the
       dequeue mode and possibly the message ID to be dequeued. */
    PROCEDURE dequeue (mode_in IN INTEGER)
    IS
    BEGIN
        queueopts.dequeue_mode := mode_in;
        queueopts.wait := DBMS_AQ.NO_WAIT;
        queueopts.visibility := DBMS_AQ.IMMEDIATE;

        IF mode_in = DBMS_AQ.REMOVE
```

```
         THEN
            queueopts.msgid := v_msgid;
            queue_changed := TRUE;
         ELSE
            queueopts.msgid := NULL;
         END IF;

         DBMS_AQ.DEQUEUE (queue_name => queue,
            dequeue_options => queueopts,
            message_properties => msgprops,
            payload => student,
            msgid => v_msgid);

         DBMS_OUTPUT.PUT_LINE
            ('Dequeued-' || mode_name (mode_in) || ' ' || student.ssn ||
             ' class ' || student.class_requested);
      END;
BEGIN
   LOOP
      /* Non-destructive dequeue */
      dequeue (DBMS_AQ.BROWSE);

      /* Is this the student I am dropping? */
      IF student.ssn = ssn_in
      THEN
         /* Shift to destructive mode and remove from queue.
            In this case I request the dequeue by msg ID.
            This approach completely bypasses the normal order
            for dequeuing. */
         dequeue (DBMS_AQ.REMOVE);
      END IF;
   END LOOP;

EXCEPTION
   WHEN aq.dequeue_timeout
   THEN
      IF queue_changed
      THEN
         COMMIT;
      END IF;
END;
/
```

Notice that even in this relatively small program, I still create a local or nested procedure to avoid writing all of the dequeue code twice. It also makes the main body of the program more readable. I also keep track of whether any messages have been removed, in which case queue_changed is TRUE. I also perform a commit to save those changes as a single transaction.

Here is a script I wrote to test the functionality of the drop_student procedure:

```
/* Filename on companion disk: aqbrowse.tst */
DECLARE
   queueopts DBMS_AQ.ENQUEUE_OPTIONS_T;
   msgprops DBMS_AQ.MESSAGE_PROPERTIES_T;
```

```
      student student_reg_t;
      v_msgid aq.msgid_type;
   BEGIN
      aq.stop_and_drop ('reg_queue_table');

      aq.create_queue ('reg_queue_table', 'student_reg_t', 'reg_queue');

      queueopts.visibility := DBMS_AQ.IMMEDIATE;

      student := student_reg_t ('123-46-8888', 'Politics 101');
      DBMS_AQ.ENQUEUE ('reg_queue', queueopts, msgprops, student, v_msgid);

      student := student_reg_t ('555-09-1798', 'Politics 101');
      DBMS_AQ.ENQUEUE ('reg_queue', queueopts, msgprops, student, v_msgid);

      student := student_reg_t ('987-65-4321', 'Politics 101');
      DBMS_AQ.ENQUEUE ('reg_queue', queueopts, msgprops, student, v_msgid);

      student := student_reg_t ('123-46-8888', 'Philosophy 101');
      DBMS_AQ.ENQUEUE ('reg_queue', queueopts, msgprops, student, v_msgid);

      DBMS_OUTPUT.PUT_LINE ('Messages in queue: ' ||
         aq.msgcount ('reg_queue_table', 'reg_queue'));

      drop_student ('reg_queue', '123-46-8888');

      DBMS_OUTPUT.PUT_LINE ('Messages in queue: ' ||
         aq.msgcount ('reg_queue_table', 'reg_queue'));
   END;
   /
```

Here is an explanation of the different elements of the test script:

- Since this is a test, I first get rid of any existing queue elements and recreate them. This guarantees that my queue is empty when I start the test.

- I then perform four enqueues to the registration queue. In each case, I use the constructor method for the object type to construct an object. I then place that object on the queue. Notice that there are two requests for class enrollments for 123-46-8888 (the first and fourth enqueues).

- Next, I call my handy aq.msgcount function to verify that there are four messages in the queue.

- Time to scan and remove! I request that all class requests for the student with the 123-46-8888 social security number be dropped.

- Finally, I check the number of messages remaining in the queue (should be just two).

Here is the output from execution of the test script:

```
SQL> @aqbrowse.tst
stopping AQ$_REG_QUEUE_TABLE_E
dropping AQ$_REG_QUEUE_TABLE_E
```

```
stopping REG_QUEUE
dropping REG_QUEUE
dropping reg_queue_table
Messages in queue: 4
Dequeued-BROWSE 123-46-8888   class Politics 101
Dequeued-REMOVE 123-46-8888   class Politics 101
Dequeued-BROWSE 555-09-1798   class Politics 101
Dequeued-BROWSE 987-65-4321   class Politics 101
Dequeued-BROWSE 123-46-8888   class Philosophy 101
Dequeued-REMOVE 123-46-8888   class Philosophy 101
Messages in queue: 2
```

The first five lines of output show the drop-and-create phase of the script. It then verifies four messages in the queue. Next, you can see the loop processing. It browses the first entry, finds a match, and then dequeues in REMOVE mode. Three browsing dequeues later, it finds another match, does the remove dequeue, and is then done.

A template for a show_queue procedure

You can also take advantage of BROWSE mode to display the current contents of a queue. The following code offers a template for the kind of procedure you would write. (It is only a template because you will need to modify it for each different object type (or RAW data) you are queueing.)

```
/* Filename on companion disk: aqshowq.sp */
CREATE OR REPLACE PROCEDURE show_queue (queue IN VARCHAR2)
IS
/* A generic program to dequeue in browse mode from a queue to
   display its current contents.

   YOU MUST MODIFY THIS FOR YOUR SPECIFIC OBJECT TYPE.
*/
   obj <YOUR OBJECT TYPE>;
   v_msgid aq.msgid_type;

   queueopts DBMS_AQ.DEQUEUE_OPTIONS_T;
   msgprops DBMS_AQ.MESSAGE_PROPERTIES_T;

   first_dequeue BOOLEAN := TRUE;
BEGIN
   LOOP
      /* Non-destructive dequeue */
      queueopts.dequeue_mode := DBMS_AQ.BROWSE;
      queueopts.wait := DBMS_AQ.NO_WAIT;
      queueopts.visibility := DBMS_AQ.IMMEDIATE;

      DBMS_AQ.DEQUEUE (queue_name => queue,
         dequeue_options => queueopts,
         message_properties => msgprops,
         payload => obj,
         msgid => v_msgid);

      /* Now display whatever you want here. */
```

```
        IF first_dequeue
        THEN
           DBMS_OUTPUT.PUT_LINE ('YOUR HEADER HERE');
           first_dequeue := FALSE;
        END IF;

        DBMS_OUTPUT.PUT_LINE ('YOUR DATA HERE');
     END LOOP;

   EXCEPTION
      WHEN aq.dequeue_timeout
      THEN
         NULL;
   END;
   /
```

Check out the *aqcorrid.spp* file (and the layaway.display procedure), described in the next section, for an example of the way I took this template file and modified it for a specific queue.

Searching by Correlation Identifier

You don't have to rely on message identifiers in order to dequeue a specific message from a queue. You can also use application-specific data by setting the correlation identifier.

Suppose that I maintain a queue for holiday shopping layaways. All year long, shoppers have been giving me money towards the purchase of their favorite bean-bag stuffed animal. I keep track of the requested animal and the balance remaining in a queue of the following object type (found in *aqcorrid.spp*):

```
CREATE TYPE layaway_t IS OBJECT
   (animal VARCHAR2(30),
    held_for VARCHAR2(100),
    balance NUMBER
   );
/
```

When a person has fully paid for his or her animal, I will remove the message from the queue and store it in a separate database table. Therefore, I need to be able to identify that message by the customer and the animal for which they have paid. I can use the correlation identifier to accomplish this task.

Here is the package specification I have built to manage my layaway queue:

```
/* Filename on companion disk: aqcorrid.spp */
CREATE OR REPLACE PACKAGE BODY layaway
IS
   FUNCTION one_animal (customer_in IN VARCHAR2, animal_in IN VARCHAR2)
      RETURN layaway_t;

   PROCEDURE make_payment
```

```
                (customer_in IN VARCHAR2,
                 animal_in IN VARCHAR2,
                 payment_in IN NUMBER);

           PROCEDURE display
                (customer_in IN VARCHAR2 := '%', animal_in IN VARCHAR2 := '%');
        END layaway;
        /
```

The layaway.one_animal function retrieves the specified animal from the queue
utilizing the correlation identifier. The layaway.make_payment procedure records
a payment for that stuffed animal (and decrements the remaining balance). The
layaway.display procedure displays the contents of the queue by dequeuing in
BROWSE mode.

I built a script to test this package as follows:

```
/* Filename on companion disk: aqcorrid.tst */
DECLARE
    obj layaway_t;
BEGIN
    layaway.make_payment ('Eli', 'Unicorn', 10);

    layaway.make_payment ('Steven', 'Dragon', 5);

    layaway.make_payment ('Veva', 'Sun Conure', 12);

    layaway.make_payment ('Chris', 'Big Fat Cat', 8);

    layaway.display;

    obj := layaway.one_animal ('Veva', 'Sun Conure');

    DBMS_OUTPUT.PUT_LINE ('** Retrieved ' || obj.animal);
END;
/
```

Notice that I do not have to deal with the layaway object type unless I am retrieving an animal for final processing (i.e., the customer has paid the full amount and
it is time to hand that adorable little pretend animal over the counter).

Here is the output from my test script:

```
SQL> @aqcorrid.tst
Customer              Animal              Balance
Eli                   Unicorn             39.95
Steven                Dragon              44.95
Veva                  Sun Conure          37.95
Chris                 Big Fat Cat         41.95
** Retrieved Sun Conure
```

And if I run the same script twice more, I see the following:

```
SQL> @aqcorrid.tst
Input truncated to 1 characters
```

```
Customer              Animal                 Balance
Steven                Dragon                 39.95
Veva                  Sun Conure             37.95
Eli                   Unicorn                29.95
Chris                 Big Fat Cat            33.95
** Retrieved Sun Conure

PL/SQL procedure successfully completed.

SQL> @aqcorrid.tst
Input truncated to 1 characters
Customer              Animal                 Balance
Veva                  Sun Conure             37.95
Eli                   Unicorn                19.95
Steven                Dragon                 34.95
Chris                 Big Fat Cat            25.95
** Retrieved Sun Conure
```

Notice that the order of messages in the queue changes each time (as well as the balance remaining). That happens because I am dequeuing and enqueuing back into the queue. Since I have not specified any priority for the queue table, it always dequeues (for purposes of display) those messages most recently enqueued.

Let's now take a look at the implementation of this package (also found in *aqcorrid.spp*). Let's start with the one_animal function:

```
FUNCTION one_animal (customer_in IN VARCHAR2, animal_in IN VARCHAR2)
   RETURN layaway_t
IS
   queueopts DBMS_AQ.DEQUEUE_OPTIONS_T;
   msgprops DBMS_AQ.MESSAGE_PROPERTIES_T;

   retval layaway_t;
BEGIN
   /* Take immediate effect; no commit required. */
   queueopts.wait := DBMS_AQ.NO_WAIT;
   queueopts.visibility := DBMS_AQ.IMMEDIATE;

   /* Retrieve only the message for this correlation identifier. */
   queueopts.correlation := corr_id (customer_in, animal_in);

   /* Reset the navigation location to the first message. */
   queueopts.navigation := DBMS_AQ.FIRST_MESSAGE;

   /* Locate the entry by correlation identifier and return the object. */
   DBMS_AQ.DEQUEUE (c_queue, queueopts, msgprops, retval, g_msgid);

   RETURN retval;

EXCEPTION
   WHEN aq.dequeue_timeout
   THEN
```

```
        /* Return a NULL object. */
        RETURN layaway_t (NULL, NULL, 0);
    END;
```

Most of this is standard enqueue processing. The lines that are pertinent to using the correlation ID are in boldface. I set the correlation field of the dequeue options to the string returned by the corr_id function (shown next). I also set the navigation for the dequeue operation to the *first message* in the queue. I do this to make sure that Oracle AQ starts from the beginning of the queue to search for a match. If I do not take this step, then I raise the following exception when running my *aqcorrid.tst* script more than once in a session:

```
ORA-25237: navigation option used out of sequence
```

This behavior may be related to bugs in the Oracle 8.0.3 release, but the inclusion of the navigation field setting definitely takes care of the problem.

So when I dequeue from the layaway queue, I always specify that I want the first message with a matching correlation string. I have hidden away the construction of that string behind the following function:

```
    FUNCTION corr_id  (customer_in IN VARCHAR2, animal_in IN VARCHAR2)
        RETURN VARCHAR2
    IS
    BEGIN
        RETURN UPPER (customer_in || '.' || animal_in);
    END;
```

I have taken this step because I also need to create a correlation string when I enqueue (shown in the following make_payment procedure). In order to minimize maintenance and reduce the chance of introducing bugs into my code, I do not want this concatenation logic to appear more than once in my package.

Here is the make_payment procedure:

```
    PROCEDURE make_payment
        (customer_in IN VARCHAR2, animal_in IN VARCHAR2, payment_in IN NUMBER)
    IS
        queueopts DBMS_AQ.ENQUEUE_OPTIONS_T;
        msgprops DBMS_AQ.MESSAGE_PROPERTIES_T;
        layaway_obj layaway_t;
    BEGIN
        /* Locate this entry in the queue by calling the function.
           If found, decrement the balance and reinsert into the queue.
           If not found, enqueue a new message to the queue. For example
           purposes, the price of all my bean-bag animals is $49.95. */

        layaway_obj := one_animal (customer_in, animal_in);

        /* Adjust the balance. We SHOULD check for 0 or negative values,
           and not requeue if finished. I will leave that to the reader. */

        IF layaway_obj.animal IS NOT NULL
```

```
THEN
    layaway_obj.balance := layaway_obj.balance - payment_in;
ELSE
    /* Construct new object for enqueue, setting up initial balance. */
    layaway_obj := layaway_t (animal_in, customer_in, 49.95 - payment_in);
END IF;

/* Don't wait for a commit. */
queueopts.visibility := DBMS_AQ.IMMEDIATE;

/* Set the correlation identifier for this message. */
msgprops.correlation := corr_id (customer_in, animal_in);

DBMS_AQ.ENQUEUE (c_queue, queueopts, msgprops, layaway_obj, g_msgid);
END;
```

The first thing that make_payment does is attempt to retrieve an existing queue entry for this customer-animal combination by calling one_animal. Again, notice that I do *not* repeat the dequeue logic in make_payment. I am always careful to reuse existing code elements whenever possible. If I find a match (the animal field is not NULL; see the exception section in one_animal to understand how I set the "message not found" values in the returned object), then I update the remaining balance. If no match is found, then I construct an object to be placed in the queue.

Once my layaway object has been updated or created, I set the correlation identifier by calling the same corr_id function. Notice that when I enqueue, I set the correlation field of the message properties record. When I dequeue, on the other hand, I set the correlation field of the dequeue options record. Finally, I enqueue my object.

Wildcarded correlation identifiers

You can also specify wildcard comparisons with the correlation identifier, using the standard SQL wildcarding characters _ (single-character substitution) and % (multiple-character substitution).

For example, if I set the value of "S%" for my queue options correlation field, as follows, then AQ will find a correlation for any message whose correlation identifier starts with an upper-case "S."

```
queueopts.correlation := "S%";
```

Tips for using the correlation identifier. When you are using the correlation identifier, remember these tips:

- When you enqueue, set the correlation field of the message properties record.

- When you dequeue, set the correlation field of the dequeue options record.

- Before you dequeue, set the navigation field of the dequeue options record to DBMS_AQ.FIRST_MESSAGE to avoid out-of-sequence errors.

Using Time Delay and Expiration

If you have started the Queue Monitor process, you can set up queues so that messages cannot be dequeued for a period of time. You can also specify that a message will expire after a certain amount of time has passed. These features come in handy when messages in your queue have a "window of applicability" (in other words, when there is a specific period of time in which a message should or should not be available for dequeuing).

If a message is not dequeued before it expires, that message is automatically moved to the exception queue (either the default exception queue associated with the underlying queue table or the exception queue specified at enqueue time). Remember that the time of expiration is calculated from the earlier dequeuing time. So if you specify a delay of one week (and you do this in seconds, as in $7 \times 24 \times 60 \times 60$) and an expiration of two weeks, the message would expire (if not dequeued) in three weeks.

To delay the time when a message can be dequeued, modify the delay field of the message properties record. Modify the expiration time by setting a value for the expiration field of the message properties record.

Now let's see how to use the expiration feature on messages to manage sales for products in my store. I created the following object type:

```
CREATE TYPE sale_t IS OBJECT
   (product VARCHAR2(30),
    sales_price NUMBER
   );
/
```

Here are the rules I want to follow:

- A product goes on sale for a specific price in a given period (between start and end dates).

- Every product that is on sale goes into my sales queue. When a message is enqueued, I compute the delay and expiration values based on the start and end dates.

- I can then check to see if a product is on sale by checking my sales queue: if I can dequeue it (nondestructively: that is, in BROWSE mode) successfully, then it is on sale.

- I never dequeue in REMOVE mode from the sales queue. Instead, I simply let the Queue Monitor automatically move the product from the sales queue to the exception queue when that message expires.

To hide all of these details from my application developers (who in turn will hide all programmatic details from *their* users, the people pushing buttons on a screen), I will construct a package. Here's the specification for this sale package:

```
/* Filename on companion disk: aqtiming.spp */
CREATE OR REPLACE PACKAGE sale
IS
    FUNCTION onsale (product_in IN VARCHAR2) RETURN BOOLEAN;

    PROCEDURE mark_for_sale
        (product_in IN VARCHAR2,
         price_in IN NUMBER,
         starts_on IN DATE,
         ends_on IN DATE);

    PROCEDURE show_expired_sales;

END sale;
/
```

So I can check to see if the Captain Planet game is on sale as follows:

```
IF sale.onsale ('captain planet')
THEN
    ...
END IF;
```

I can mark Captain Planet for a special sales price of $15.95 during the month of December as follows:

```
sale.mark_for_sale (
    'captain planet',
    15.95,
    TO_DATE ('01-DEC-97'),
    TO_DATE ('31-DEC-97'));
```

Finally, I can at any time display those products whose sales windows have expired as follows:

```
SQL> exec sale.show_expired_sales;
```

To test this code, I put together the following scripts. First, I create the queue table, queue for sales, and exception queue for sale items that expire in the original sales queue.

```
/* Filename on companion disk: aqtiming.ins */
DECLARE
    c_qtable CONSTANT aq.name_type := 'sale_qtable';
    c_queue CONSTANT aq.name_type := 'sale_queue';
```

```
      c_exc_queue CONSTANT aq.name_type := 'sale_exc_queue';

   BEGIN
      /* Create the queue table and queue as necessary. */
      aq.create_queue (c_qtable, 'sale_t', c_queue);

      /* Create a special exception queue for expired sales listings. */
      aq.create_queue (c_qtable, 'sale_t', c_exc_queue,
         qtype => DBMS_AQADM.EXCEPTION_QUEUE);
   END sale;
   /
```

I then combine a number of sales-related operations into a single script:

NOTE   To run this script, you must have EXECUTE privilege on DBMS_
              LOCK. If you do not will see this error:

                  `PLS-00201: identifier 'SYS.DBMS_LOCK' must be declared`

              You or your DBA must connect to SYS and issue this command:

                  `GRANT EXECUTE ON DBMS_LOCK TO PUBLIC;`

```
/* Filename on companion disk: aqtiming.tst */
DECLARE
   FUNCTION seconds_from_now (num IN INTEGER) RETURN DATE
   IS
   BEGIN
      RETURN SYSDATE + num / (24 * 60 * 60);
   END;

   PROCEDURE show_sales_status (product_in IN VARCHAR2)
   IS
      v_onsale BOOLEAN := sale.onsale (product_in);
      v_qualifier VARCHAR2(5) := NULL;
   BEGIN
      IF NOT v_onsale
      THEN
         v_qualifier := ' not';
      END IF;

      DBMS_OUTPUT.PUT_LINE (product_in ||
         ' is' || v_qualifier || ' on sale at ' ||
         TO_CHAR (SYSDATE, 'HH:MI:SS'));
   END;
BEGIN
   DBMS_OUTPUT.PUT_LINE ('Start test at ' || TO_CHAR (SYSDATE, 'HH:MI:SS'));

   sale.mark_for_sale ('Captain Planet', 15.95,
      seconds_from_now (30), seconds_from_now (50));

   sale.mark_for_sale ('Mr. Math', 12.95,
```

```
            seconds_from_now (120), seconds_from_now (180));

      show_sales_status ('Captain Planet');
      show_sales_status ('Mr. Math');

      DBMS_LOCK.SLEEP (30);
      DBMS_OUTPUT.PUT_LINE ('Slept for 30 seconds.');
      show_sales_status ('Captain Planet');
      show_sales_status ('Mr. Math');

      sale.show_expired_sales;

      DBMS_LOCK.SLEEP (100);
      DBMS_OUTPUT.PUT_LINE ('Slept for 100 seconds.');
      show_sales_status ('Captain Planet');
      show_sales_status ('Mr. Math');

      sale.show_expired_sales;

      DBMS_LOCK.SLEEP (70);
      DBMS_OUTPUT.PUT_LINE ('Slept for 70 seconds.');
      show_sales_status ('Captain Planet');
      show_sales_status ('Mr. Math');
   END;
   /
```

Here is the output from this test script (I insert my comments between chunks of output to explain their significance):

```
Start test at 12:42:57
```

The next four lines come from sale.mark_for_sale and show how the start and end dates were converted to seconds for delay and expiration. As you start using this technology, I strongly suggest that you encapsulate your date-time computations inside a wrapper like seconds_from_now so that you can keep it all straight.

```
Delayed for 30 seconds.
Expires after 20 seconds.
Delayed for 120 seconds.
Expires after 60 seconds.
```

I check the status of my sale items immediately, and neither is yet available at their sale price. The delay time is still in effect.

```
Captain Planet is not on sale at 12:42:58
Mr. Math is not on sale at 12:42:58
```

I put the program to sleep for 30 seconds and then check again. Now Captain Planet is on sale (the delay was only 30 seconds), but smart shoppers cannot pick up Mr. Math for that special deal.

```
Slept for 30 seconds.
Captain Planet is on sale at 12:43:28
Mr. Math is not on sale at 12:43:28
```

After another 100 seconds, Captain Planet is no longer on sale, but look at those copies of Mr. Math fly out the door!

```
Slept for 100 seconds.
Captain Planet is not on sale at 12:45:08
Mr. Math is on sale at 12:45:08
```

Why isn't Captain Planet on sale? The output from a call to sale.show_expired_ sales makes it clear: the window of opportunity for that sale has closed, and the message has been "expired" into the exception queue.

```
Product             Price             Expired on
Captain Planet      $15.95            11/14/1997 12:42:57
```

After another 70 seconds, neither Captain Planet nor Mr. Math are on sale, and as you might expect, both appear on the exception queue:

```
Slept for 70 seconds.
Captain Planet is not on sale at 12:46:18
Mr. Math is not on sale at 12:46:18
```

```
Product             Price             Expired on
Captain Planet      $15.95            11/14/1997 12:42:57
Mr. Math            $12.95            11/14/1997 12:42:58
```

Yes, dear readers, these nifty Oracle AQ features do seem to work as documented!

Now let's examine the implementation of the programs in the sale package. Rather than reproduce the entire body in these pages, I will focus on the individual programs. You can find the full set of code in the *aqtiming.spp* file.

First, we have the sale.onsale function. This program returns TRUE if the specified product is currently available for dequeuing. Here is the code:

```
/* Filename on companion disk: aqtiming.spp */
FUNCTION onsale (product_in IN VARCHAR2) RETURN BOOLEAN
IS
    queueopts DBMS_AQ.DEQUEUE_OPTIONS_T;
    msgprops DBMS_AQ.MESSAGE_PROPERTIES_T;
    obj sale_t;
BEGIN
   /* Take immediate effect; no commit required. */
   queueopts.wait := DBMS_AQ.NO_WAIT;
   queueopts.visibility := DBMS_AQ.IMMEDIATE;

   /* Reset the navigation location to the first message. */
   queueopts.navigation := DBMS_AQ.FIRST_MESSAGE;

   /* Dequeue in BROWSE. You never dequeue destructively. You let
      the Queue Monitor automatically expire messages and move them
      to the exception queue. */
   queueopts.dequeue_mode := DBMS_AQ.BROWSE;

   /* Retrieve only the message for this product. */
```

```
        queueopts.correlation := UPPER (product_in);

        /* Locate the entry by correlation identifier and return the object. */
        DBMS_AQ.DEQUEUE (c_queue, queueopts, msgprops, obj, g_msgid);

        RETURN obj.product IS NOT NULL;

    EXCEPTION
        WHEN aq.dequeue_timeout
        THEN
            RETURN FALSE;
    END;
```

This is a standard nondestructive dequeue operation. Notice that I use the correlation identifier to make sure that I attempt to dequeue a message only for this particular product. I also set navigation to "first message" to make sure I get the first message (in enqueue time) for the product. In this case, I do not return any of the sale information. Instead, I return TRUE if I found a non-NULL product in the dequeued object. If I timeout trying to retrieve a message, I return FALSE.

Of course, I need to be able to put a product on sale. I do that with the sale.mark_for_sale procedure.

```
/* Filename on companion disk: aqtiming.spp */
PROCEDURE mark_for_sale
    (product_in IN VARCHAR2,
     price_in IN NUMBER,
     starts_on IN DATE,
     ends_on IN DATE)
IS
    queueopts DBMS_AQ.ENQUEUE_OPTIONS_T;
    msgprops DBMS_AQ.MESSAGE_PROPERTIES_T;
    sale_obj sale_t;

BEGIN
    /* Calculate the delay number of seconds and the expiration in same terms */
    msgprops.delay := GREATEST (0, starts_on - SYSDATE) * 24 * 60 * 60;
    msgprops.expiration := GREATEST (0, ends_on - starts_on) * 24 * 60 * 60;

    DBMS_OUTPUT.PUT_LINE
        ('Delayed for ' || msgprops.delay || ' seconds.');
    DBMS_OUTPUT.PUT_LINE
        ('Expires after ' || msgprops.expiration || ' seconds.');

    /* Don't wait for a commit. */
    queueopts.visibility := DBMS_AQ.IMMEDIATE;

    /* Set the correlation identifier for this message to the product. */
    msgprops.correlation := UPPER (product_in);

    /* Specify a non-default exception queue. */
```

```
        msgprops.exception_queue := c_exc_queue;

        /* Set up the object. */
        sale_obj := sale_t (product_in, price_in);

        DBMS_AQ.ENQUEUE (c_queue, queueopts, msgprops, sale_obj, g_msgid);
    END;
```

This procedure is a wrapper around the enqueue operation. First I convert the start and end dates to numbers of seconds for the delay and expiration field values, and I display those values for debugging purposes.

Then I set the other characteristics of the enqueue. Most importantly, I set the correlation ID so that I can look just for this product later in my dequeue operation (shown in the sale.onsale function), and I specify an alternate exception queue just for expired sales messages.

Finally, I include a program to show me the contents of my exception queue. The sale.show_expired_sales is interesting because it combines two different elements of Oracle AQ: use of the operational interface (the dequeue program) and direct access against the data dictionary view. I execute a cursor FOR loop against AQ$sale_qtable, which is the underlying database table created by Oracle AQ to hold messages for all queues in this queue table. Notice that I request only those rows in the exception queue I specified in sale.mark_for_sale. I retrieve the message ID and then I dequeue explicitly for that message ID. Why do I do this? When a message is moved to the exception queue, its message state is set to EXPIRED. I cannot dequeue a message in this state using normal navigation.

```
    /* Filename on companion disk: aqtiming.spp */
    PROCEDURE show_expired_sales
    IS
        obj sale_t;

        v_msgid aq.msgid_type;

        CURSOR exp_cur
        IS
            SELECT msg_id
              FROM AQ$sale_qtable
             WHERE queue = c_exc_queue
             ORDER BY enq_time;

        queueopts DBMS_AQ.DEQUEUE_OPTIONS_T;
        msgprops DBMS_AQ.MESSAGE_PROPERTIES_T;
    BEGIN
        FOR exp_rec IN exp_cur
        LOOP
            /* Non-destructive dequeue by explicit message ID. */
            queueopts.dequeue_mode := DBMS_AQ.BROWSE;
            queueopts.wait := DBMS_AQ.NO_WAIT;
            queueopts.visibility := DBMS_AQ.IMMEDIATE;
```

```
        queueopts.msgid := exp_rec.msg_id;

        DBMS_AQ.DEQUEUE (c_exc_queue, queueopts, msgprops, obj, v_msgid);

        IF exp_cur%ROWCOUNT = 1
        THEN
            DBMS_OUTPUT.PUT_LINE (
                RPAD ('Product', 21) || RPAD ('Price', 21) || 'Expired on');
        END IF;

        DBMS_OUTPUT.PUT_LINE (
            RPAD (obj.product, 21) ||
            RPAD (TO_CHAR (obj.sales_price, '$999.99'), 21) ||
            TO_CHAR (msgprops.enqueue_time, 'MM/DD/YYYY HH:MI:SS'));
    END LOOP;

EXCEPTION
    WHEN aq.dequeue_timeout
    THEN
        NULL;
END;
```

The range of possible behaviors for enqueue and dequeue operations is truly remarkable. However, this flexibility has its dark side: it can take a lot of experimentation and playing around to get your code to work just the way you want it to. It took me several hours, for example, to put together, debug, test, and think about the sale package in *aqtiming.spp* before it all came together. Try not to get too frustrated, and take things a step at a time, so you are always working from sure footing in terms of your understanding of AQ and your program's behavior.

Working with Message Groups

In some cases, you may wish to combine multiple messages into a single "logical" message. For example, suppose that you were using AQ to manage workflow on invoices. An invoice is a complex data structure with a header row (or object), multiple line item rows (or objects), and so forth. If you were up and running on a fully object-oriented implementation in Oracle8, you might easily have a single object type to encapsulate that information. On the other hand, what if your invoice information is spread over numerous objects and you just don't want to have to restructure them or create a single object type to hold that information for purposes of queueing? And on yet another hand, what if you want to make sure that when a consumer process dequeues the header invoice information, it also must dequeue all of the related information?

Simply set up your queue to treat all messages queued in your own logical transaction as a single message group. Once you have done this, a message is not considered by AQ to be dequeued until all the messages contained in the same group have been dequeued.

Enqueuing messages as a group

Let's walk through the different steps necessary to group messages logically, and then we'll explore the consequences in the way that the dequeue operation works. This section will cover these steps:

- Creating a queue table that will support message grouping
- Enqueuing messages within the same transaction boundary

Step 1. Create a queue table that will support message grouping. To do this, you simply override the default value for the message_grouping argument in the call to DBMS_AQADM.CREATE_QUEUE_TABLE with the appropriate packaged constant as follows:

```
BEGIN
    DBMS_AQADM.CREATE_QUEUE_TABLE
        (queue_table => 'msg_with_grouping',
         queue_payload_type => 'message_type',
         message_grouping => DBMS_AQADM.TRANSACTIONAL);

    /* Now I will create and start a queue to use in the next example. */
    DBMS_AQ.CREATE_QUEUE ('classes_queue', 'msg_with_grouping');
    DBMS_AQ.START_QUEUE ('classes_queue');
END;
/
```

One thing to note immediately is that all of the different messages in the queue must be of the same type, even though they may potentially hold different kinds, or levels, of information.

Step 2. Enqueue messages within the same transaction boundary. However, your queue table is enabled to store and treat messages as a group. You must still make sure that when you perform the enqueue operation, all messages you want in a group are committed at the same time.

This means that you should *never* specify DBMS_AQ.IMMEDIATE for the visibility of your enqueue operation in a message group-enabled queue. Instead, you should rely on the DBMS_AQ.ON_COMMIT visibility mode. This mode ensures that all messages will be processed as a single transaction, giving AQ the opportunity to assign the same transaction ID to all the messages in that group.

Here is an example of an enqueue operation loading up all the classes for a student as a single message group:

```
PROCEDURE semester_to_queue (student_in IN VARCHAR2)
IS
    CURSOR classes_cur
    IS
        SELECT classyear, semester, class
```

```
        FROM semester_class
        WHERE student = student_in;

    queueopts DBMS_AQ.ENQUEUE_OPTIONS_T;
    msgprops DBMS_AQ.MESSAGE_PROPERTIES_T;

    v_msgid aq.msgid_type;
    class_obj semester_class_t;

BEGIN
    /* This is the default, but let's make sure! */
    queueopts.visibility := DBMS_AQ.ON_COMMIT;

    FOR rec IN classes_cur
    LOOP
        class_obj := semester_class_t (student_in, rec.class, rec.semester);
        DBMS_AQ.ENQUEUE
            ('classes_queue', queueopts, msgprops, class_obj, v_msgid);
    END LOOP;

    /* Now commit as a batch to get the message grouping. */
    COMMIT;
END;
```

And that's all it takes to make sure that messages are treated as a group: enable the queue when you create the queue table, and make sure that all messages are committed together.

When you work with message groups, you'll find that you will almost always be using PL/SQL loops to either enqueue the set of messages as a group or dequeue all related messages.

Now let's take a look at the dequeuing side of message group operations.

Dequeuing messages when part of a group

To give you a full sense of the code involved, I will shift from individual programs to a package. Suppose that I want to place in a queue (as a single group) all of the classes for which a student is enrolled (that is, the semester_to_queue procedure shown in the previous section). But I also want to display (and simultaneously dequeue) the contents of that queue for each student. I can take advantage of the message grouping feature to do this.

Here is the specification of the package:

```
/* Filename on companion disk: aqgroup.spp */
CREATE OR REPLACE PACKAGE schedule_pkg
IS
    PROCEDURE semester_to_queue (student_in IN VARCHAR2);
```

```
        PROCEDURE show_by_group;
    END;
    /
```

The *aqgroup.ins* file creates the data needed to demonstrate the functionality of the schedule_pkg package. I will not repeat the implementation of semester_to_queue; instead, let's focus on the code you have to write to *dequeue* grouped messages in the show_by_group procedure.

```
PROCEDURE show_by_group
IS
    obj semester_class_t;
    v_msgid aq.msgid_type;
    first_in_group BOOLEAN := TRUE;

    queueopts DBMS_AQ.DEQUEUE_OPTIONS_T;
    msgprops DBMS_AQ.MESSAGE_PROPERTIES_T;
BEGIN
    /* Just dumping out whatever is in the queue, so no waiting. */
    queueopts.wait := DBMS_AQ.NO_WAIT;

    /* Start at the beginning of the queue, incorporating all enqueues. */
    queueopts.navigation := DBMS_AQ.FIRST_MESSAGE;

    LOOP
        /* Local block to trap exception: end of group. */
        BEGIN
            DBMS_AQ.DEQUEUE (c_queue, queueopts, msgprops, obj, v_msgid);

            IF first_in_group
            THEN
                first_in_group := FALSE;

                DBMS_OUTPUT.PUT_LINE
                    ('Schedule for ' || obj.student ||
                     ' in semester ' || obj.semester);
            END IF;

            DBMS_OUTPUT.PUT_LINE ('*   ' || obj.class);

            /* Navigate to the next message in the group. */
            queueopts.navigation := DBMS_AQ.NEXT_MESSAGE;

        EXCEPTION
            WHEN aq.end_of_message_group
            THEN
                /* Throw out a break line. */
                DBMS_OUTPUT.PUT_LINE ('*****');

                /* Move to the next student. */
                queueopts.navigation := DBMS_AQ.NEXT_TRANSACTION;

                /* Set header flag for new student. */
```

```
                first_in_group := FALSE;
        END;
    END LOOP;
EXCEPTION
    WHEN aq.dequeue_timeout
    THEN
        /* No more students, no more message groups. */
        NULL;
END;
```

Working with Multiple Consumers

In the simpler schemes of queueing, one producer puts a message on a queue and another agent, a consumer, retrieves that single message from a queue. A common variant of this process follows a broadcasting model, where a producer enqueues a message with the intention of distributing that message to many consumers. Oracle AQ allows you to perform this kind of broadcast in two different ways:[*]

- Define a default subscriber list for a queue. Then any message that is placed on that queue is available for dequeuing by any of the agents in that subscriber list.

- Specify an "override" recipient list when you enqueue a specific message to the queue, by assigning a list (index-by table) of recipients to the recipient_list field of the message properties record.

In both of these cases, you must have defined the queue table in which your queue is defined to support multiple consumers. Here is an example of the creation of a queue table that supports multiple consumers:

```
BEGIN
    DBMS_AQADM.CREATE_QUEUE_TABLE
        (queue_table => 'msg',
         queue_payload_type => 'message_type',
         multiple_consumers => TRUE);
END;
/
```

Let's take a look at the different steps involved in using both the default subscriber list and the override recipient list. Suppose that in my student registration and management system, I want to define a default set of subscribers who are to receive notification of a student's change in major_pkg. When the student

---

[*] Prior to Oracle AQ, the DBMS_ALERT package already supported this broadcast mechanism; I would not be surprised to find that DBMS_ALERT is redesigned to use AQ in a future release.

changes his or her major from mathematics or philosophy to business, however, notification is sent to the school psychologist and the professor of ethics.

I will demonstrate these techniques by constructing incrementally a package that supports the change-major operation.

Using the subscriber list

The default application behavior is to send out the major change notification to the president of the school and the single guidance counselor (it's a small place). I could just hard-code this logic into my programs, but instead, I will build a more flexible, encapsulated interface for this action and then deploy it for those two people.

First, I must create an object type to use in my queue. (All the elements of these initialization steps, including the creation of the queue table, can be found in the file *aqmult.ins*.)

```
CREATE TYPE student_major_t IS OBJECT
   (student VARCHAR2(30),
    major VARCHAR2(100));
/
```

I then create a queue table and queue based on this object type. Notice the specification of a multiple consumers queue:

```
/* Filename on companion disk: aqmult.ins */
BEGIN
   /* Create the queue table and queue for multiple consumers. */
   DBMS_AQADM.CREATE_QUEUE_TABLE
      (queue_table => 'major_qtable',
       queue_payload_type => 'student_major_t',
       multiple_consumers => TRUE);

   DBMS_AQADM.CREATE_QUEUE ('major_queue', 'major_qtable');

   DBMS_AQADM.START_QUEUE ('major_queue');
END;
/
```

Now I can construct my package. Here is the specification:

```
/* Filename on companion disk: aqmult1.spp */
CREATE OR REPLACE PACKAGE major_pkg
IS
   PROCEDURE add_reviewer (name_in IN VARCHAR2);

   PROCEDURE change_it_again
      (student_in IN VARCHAR2, new_major_in IN VARCHAR2);
END major_pkg;
/
```

So at this point, I can add a reviewer to the queue; this is a person who is to be notified *by default* of any major changes. I can also change the major of a student. Let's look at how I would use these programs. First of all, I need to specify the default reviewers:

```
/*Filename on companion disk: aqmult2.ins */
BEGIN
    major_pkg.add_reviewer ('President Runtheshow');
    major_pkg.add_reviewer ('Counselor Twocents');
END;
/
```

Now that my main subscribers are in place, I can change the major of a student and rest assured that entries will be made in the queue for all the people who need to know.

```
SQL> exec major_pkg.change_it_again ('Steven Feuerstein', 'Biology');
```

Wait a minute! That's not what I want—I want to study the English language!

```
SQL> exec major_pkg.change_it_again ('Steven Feuerstein', 'English');
```

And so on. We're about to get into more detailed scenarios for both construction and testing, so I added the following steps to my installation script, *aqmult.ins*:

```
CREATE TABLE student_intention
    (name VARCHAR2(30),
    ssn CHAR(11),
    major_study VARCHAR2(100));

BEGIN
    INSERT INTO student_intention VALUES
        ('Steven Feuerstein', '123-45-6789', 'Mathematics');
    INSERT INTO student_intention VALUES
        ('Eli Feuerstein', '123-45-6780', 'Philosophy');
    INSERT INTO student_intention VALUES
        ('Veva Feuerstein', '123-45-6781', 'Pottery');
    INSERT INTO student_intention VALUES
        ('Chris Feuerstein', '123-45-6782', 'Art');
    COMMIT;
END;
/
```

You should run this script before playing around with *aqmult2.spp* or *aqmult3.spp* (the last two iterations in this exercise), described in the following code examples.

Now, each time I change my major (or someone else's), a message is written to the queue. By default, each message is read by two subscribers, the president and the guidance counselor. The way Oracle AQ works is that a message is not considered dequeued (and therefore *removed*, assuming that you are dequeuing in the

default destructive mode) until all consumers specified by the subscriber list or
the override recipients list have dequeued that message. You request messages
for which you are a subscriber or a recipient by setting the appropriate value in
the dequeue options consumer name field.

Here is how the process might work for our ever-changing student majors: each
morning, the executive assistant of the president connects to the system and pulls
out a report of any students who changed their major yesterday. Here is a procedure that might do this:

```
/* Filename on companion disk: aqmult2.spp */
PROCEDURE show_changers_to (curious_in IN VARCHAR2)
IS
    obj student_major_t;
    v_msgid aq.msgid_type;

    queueopts DBMS_AQ.DEQUEUE_OPTIONS_T;
    msgprops DBMS_AQ.MESSAGE_PROPERTIES_T;

    first_dequeue BOOLEAN := TRUE;
BEGIN
    queueopts.consumer_name := curious_in;

    /* Loop through the contents of the queue looking for
       matches on the specified recipient name. */
    LOOP
        /* Non-destructive dequeue */
        queueopts.wait := DBMS_AQ.NO_WAIT;
        queueopts.navigation := DBMS_AQ.FIRST_MESSAGE;
        queueopts.visibility := DBMS_AQ.IMMEDIATE;

        DBMS_AQ.DEQUEUE (queue_name => c_queue,
            dequeue_options => queueopts,
            message_properties => msgprops,
            payload => obj,
            msgid => v_msgid);

        IF first_dequeue
        THEN
            DBMS_OUTPUT.PUT_LINE
                ('Changed Majors on ' || TO_CHAR (SYSDATE-1));
            first_dequeue := FALSE;
        END IF;

        DBMS_OUTPUT.PUT_LINE (
            obj.student || ' changed major to ' || obj.major);
    END LOOP;

EXCEPTION
    WHEN aq.dequeue_timeout
    THEN
        NULL;
END;
```

This is a typical destructive dequeue operation, except that it will dequeue the message only if the specified curious person is in the default subscription list or is specified in a recipient list an enqueue time.

The following script demonstrates how this technology all works together:

```
/* Filename on companion disk: aqmult2.tst */
BEGIN
    major_pkg.change_it_again ('Steven Feuerstein', 'Philosophy');
    major_pkg.change_it_again ('Veva Feuerstein', 'English');
    major_pkg.change_it_again ('Eli Feuerstein', 'Strategic Analysis');

    COMMIT;

    major_pkg.show_changers_to ('President Runtheshow');
END;
/
```

And here is the output from that script:

```
SQL> @aqmult2.tst
Changed Majors on 23-NOV-97
Steven Feuerstein changed major to Philosophy
Veva Feuerstein changed major to English
Eli Feuerstein changed major to Strategic Analysis
```

Overriding with a recipient list

Now let's add some code to the package to support the special logic for changing from math or philosophy to a business degree. (Surely we have enough MBAs in the world already!) I need to make changes to the change_it_again procedure. You will find this third iteration in the *aqmult3.spp* file.

In this final version, I need to find out what the current major is for my student, so that I can compare it to the new choice and see if it triggers my rule to notify two different nosey-bodies at the school. I could simply drop that query into the change_it_again procedure, but that practice leads to redundant coding of SQL statements in my application—a serious no-no. I will surely want to fetch the major of a student in more than one place, so I should put that specific action inside a standard lookup function, which is shown here as a fragment of the major package:

```
/* Filename on companion disk: aqmult3.spp */
CREATE OR REPLACE package body major_pkg
IS
    /* Just showing this new part of the package. */
    FUNCTION current_choice (student_in IN VARCHAR2) RETURN VARCHAR2
    IS
        CURSOR maj_cur
        IS
            SELECT major_study
              FROM student_intention
```

```
              WHERE name = student_in;
       maj_rec maj_cur%ROWTYPE;
    BEGIN
       OPEN maj_cur;
       FETCH maj_cur INTO maj_rec;
       RETURN maj_rec.major_study;
    END;


    END major_pkg;
    /
```

The sharp reader will no doubt also point out that I have embedded an UPDATE statement inside the change_it_again procedure as well. True. That should be converted into a procedure with a name like major_pkg.upd_major_study. I will leave that exercise for the reader.

Now I can use this current_choice function inside my upgraded change_it_again, as shown in the next code listing. First, an explanation: I declare a recipient list (which is actually an index-by table) to hold the school psychologist and the professor of ethics—if needed. Then before I update the major, I retrieve the current choice using that function. After the update, I see if the condition is met. If so, I define two rows in the recipient list and assign that list to the recipient_list field of the message properties record. I then perform the same enqueue operation as before.

```
PROCEDURE change_it_again
    (student_in IN VARCHAR2, new_major_in IN VARCHAR2)
IS
    queueopts DBMS_AQ.ENQUEUE_OPTIONS_T;
    msgprops DBMS_AQ.MESSAGE_PROPERTIES_T;
    major_obj major_t;
    those_who_need_to_know DBMS_AQ.AQ$_RECIPIENT_LIST_T;
BEGIN
    /* What is the current major? */
    v_major := current_choice (student_in);

    /* Update the database table. */
    UPDATE student_intention
       SET major_study = new_major_in
     WHERE name = student_in;

    /* IF changing from math or philosophy to business,
       build a special recipient list and add that to
       the enqueue operation. */
    IF v_major IN (c_philosophy, c_mathematics) AND
       new_major_in = c_business
    THEN
       /* Notify the school psychologist and professor of ethics. */
       those_who_need_to_know (1) := SYS.AQ$_AGENT ('Doctor Baddreams');
       those_who_need_to_know (1) := SYS.AQ$_AGENT ('Doctor Whatswrong');

       msgprops.recipient_list := those_who_need_to_know;
```

```
           END IF;

           /* Put a message on the queue so that everyone is
              properly notified. Notice I will coordinate visibility
              of this message with a COMMIT of the entire transaction.*/
           queueopts.visibility := DBMS_AQ.ON_COMMIT;

           /* Populate the object. */
           major_obj := student_major_t (student_in, new_major_in);

           DBMS_AQ.ENQUEUE (c_queue, queueopts, msgprops, major_obj, g_msgid);
        END;
```

The following script shows how the package now will automatically notify all of the right parties:

```
/* Filename on companion disk: aqmult3.tst */
DECLARE
    prez VARCHAR2(100) := 'President Runtheshow';
    counselor VARCHAR2(100) := 'Counselor Twocents';
    psych_dr VARCHAR2(100) := 'Doctor Baddreams';
    ethics_prof VARCHAR2(100) := 'Professor Whatswrong';
BEGIN
    major_pkg.change_it_again ('Steven Feuerstein', 'Philosophy');
    major_pkg.change_it_again ('Veva Feuerstein', 'English');

    major_pkg.show_changes_to (prez);
    major_pkg.show_changes_to (psych_dr);

    major_pkg.change_it_again ('Steven Feuerstein', major_pkg.c_business);
    major_pkg.change_it_again ('Veva Feuerstein', major_pkg.c_philosphy);

    major_pkg.show_changes_to (counselor);
    major_pkg.show_changes_to (ethics_prof);
END;
/
```

Here is the output from the execution of this script:

```
SQL> @aqmult3.tst
Showing to President Runtheshow Majors Changed on 23-NOV-97
Steven Feuerstein changed major to Philosophy
Veva Feuerstein changed major to English

Showing to Counselor Twocents Majors Changed on 23-NOV-97
Steven Feuerstein changed major to Philosophy
Veva Feuerstein changed major to English
Veva Feuerstein changed major to Philosophy

Showing to Professor Whatswrong Majors Changed on 23-NOV-97
Steven Feuerstein changed major to Business
```

As you *should* be able to tell from this section's examples, it's not terribly difficult to set up a queue table for multiple consumers. Nor is it hard to define lists of subscribers and recipients. You must remember, however, to set the message properties consumer name field to retrieve a message for a given agent. And you should remember that the message will stay queued until all agents who have access to that message have performed their dequeue (or, for some reason, the message is moved to the exception queue).

In this chapter:
- DBMS_OUTPUT:
  Displaying Output
- UTL_FILE: Reading
  and Writing Server-
  side Files

6

Generating Output from PL/SQL Programs

The built-in packages offer a number of ways to generate output from within your PL/SQL program. While updating a database table is, of course, a form of "output" from PL/SQL, this chapter shows you how to use two packages that explicitly generate output. UTL_FILE reads and writes information in server-side files, and DBMS_OUTPUT displays information to your screen.

DBMS_OUTPUT: Displaying Output

DBMS_OUTPUT provides a mechanism for displaying information from your PL/SQL program on your screen (your session's output device, to be more specific). As such, it serves as just about the only immediately accessible (meaning "free with PL/SQL") means of debugging your PL/SQL stored code.* It is certainly your "lowest common denominator" debugger, similar to the used-and-abused MESSAGE built-in of Oracle Forms. DBMS_OUTPUT is also the package you are most likely to use to generate reports from PL/SQL scripts run in SQL*Plus.

Of all the built-in packages, the DBMS_OUTPUT package (and its PUT_LINE procedure, in particular) is likely to be the one you will find yourself using most frequently. You may therefore find it strange that I never call DBMS_OUTPUT.PUT_LINE. I find the design and functionality of DBMS_OUTPUT to be substandard and very frustrating.

---

* As this book is going to press, the following PL/SQL debuggers are now available: SQL-Station Debugger from Platinum Technology; SQL Navigator from Quest; Xpediter/SQL from Compuware; and Procedure Builder from Oracle Corporation.

In fact, I recommend that you never use this package—at least, not directly. You should instead encapsulate calls to DBMS_OUTPUT (and the PUT_LINE procedure, in particular) inside a package of your own construction. This technique is discussed in the "DBMS_OUTPUT Examples" section later in this chapter.

Getting Started with DBMS_OUTPUT

The DBMS_OUTPUT package is created when the Oracle database is installed. The *dbmsoutp.sql* script (found in the built-in packages source code directory, as described in Chapter 1, *Introduction*) contains the source code for this package's specification. This script is called by the *catproc.sql* script, which is normally run immediately after database creation. The script creates the public synonym DBMS_OUTPUT for the package. Instance-wise access to this package is provided on installation, so no additional steps should be necessary in order to use DBMS_OUTPUT. As far as package usage is concerned, you will almost always be using only the DBMS_OUTPUT.PUT_LINE procedure and only in SQL*Plus. The section "Enabling and Disabling Output" later in this chapter shows how you set up DBMS_OUTPUT for use in SQL*Plus.

DBMS_OUTPUT programs

Table 6-1 shows the DBMS_OUTPUT program names and descriptions.

Table 6-1. DBMS_OUTPUT Programs

Name	Description	Use in SQL?
DISABLE	Disables output from the package; the DBMS_OUTPUT buffer will not be flushed to the screen	Yes
ENABLE	Enables output from the package	Yes
GET_LINE	Gets a single line from the buffer	Yes
GET_LINES	Gets specified number of lines from the buffer and passes them into a PL/SQL table	Yes
NEW_LINE	Inserts an end-of-line mark in the buffer	Yes
PUT	Puts information into the buffer	Yes
PUT_LINE	Puts information into the buffer and appends an end-of-line marker after that data	Yes

NOTE   All procedures in DBMS_OUTPUT have been enabled for indirect usage in SQL (that is, they can be called by a function that is then executed in a SQL statement), but only for Oracle 7.3 and later.

DBMS_OUTPUT concepts

Each user has a DBMS_OUTPUT buffer of up to 1,000,000 bytes in size. Write information to this buffer by calling the DBMS_OUTPUT.PUT and DBMS_OUTPUT.PUT_LINE programs. If you are using DBMS_OUTPUT from within SQL*Plus, this information will be displayed automatically when your program terminates. You can (optionally) explicitly retrieve information from the buffer with calls to DBMS_OUTPUT.GET and DBMS_OUTPUT.GET_LINE.

The DBMS_OUTPUT buffer can be set to a size between 2,000 and 1,000,000 bytes with the DBMS_OUTPUT.ENABLE procedure. If you do not enable the package, no information will be displayed or be retrievable from the buffer.

The buffer stores three different types of data—VARCHAR2, NUMBER, and DATE—in their internal representations. These types match the overloading available with the PUT and PUT_LINE procedures. Note that DBMS_OUTPUT does *not* support Boolean data in either its buffer or its overloading of the PUT procedures.

The following anonymous PL/SQL block uses DBMS_OUTPUT to display the name and salary of each employee in department 10:

```
DECLARE
    CURSOR emp_cur
    IS
        SELECT ename, sal
          FROM emp
         WHERE deptno = 10
         ORDER BY sal DESC;
BEGIN
    FOR emp_rec IN emp_cur
    LOOP
        DBMS_OUTPUT.PUT_LINE
            ('Employee ' || emp_rec.ename || ' earns ' ||
             TO_CHAR (emp_rec.sal) || ' dollars.');
    END LOOP;
END;
/
```

This program generates the following output when executed in SQL*Plus:

```
Employee KING earns 5000 dollars.
Employee SCOTT earns 3000 dollars.
Employee JONES earns 2975 dollars.
Employee ADAMS earns 1100 dollars.
Employee JAMES earns 950 dollars.
```

DBMS_OUTPUT exceptions

DBMS_OUTPUT does not contain any declared exceptions. Instead, Oracle designed the package to rely on two error numbers in the −20 NNN range (usually reserved for Oracle customers). You may, therefore, encounter one of these two exceptions when using the DBMS_OUTPUT package (no names are associated with these exceptions).

The −20000 error number indicates that these package-specific exceptions were raised by a call to RAISE_APPLICATION_ERROR, which is in the DBMS_STANDARD package.

−20000

> ORU-10027: buffer overflow, limit of <buf_limit> bytes.

> If you receive the −10027 error, you should see if you can increase the size of your buffer with another call to DBMS_OUTPUT.ENABLE.

−20000

> ORU-10028: line length overflow, limit of 255 bytes per line.

> If you receive the −10028 error, you should restrict the amount of data you are passing to the buffer in a single call to PUT_LINE, or in a batch of calls to PUT followed by NEW_LINE.

You may also receive the ORA-06502 error:

ORA-06502

> Numeric or value error.

> If you receive the −06502 error, you have tried to pass more than 255 bytes of data to DBMS_OUTPUT.PUT_LINE. You must break up the line into more than one string.

DBMS_OUTPUT nonprogram elements

The DBMS_OUTPUT package defines a PL/SQL table TYPE as follows:

```
TYPE chararr IS TABLE OF VARCHAR2(255) INDEX BY BINARY_INTEGER;
```

The DBMS_OUTPUT.GET_LINES procedure returns its lines in a PL/SQL table of this type.

Drawbacks of DBMS_OUTPUT

Before learning all about this package, and rushing to use it, you should be aware of several drawbacks with the implementation of this functionality:

* The "put" procedures that place information in the buffer are overloaded only for strings, dates, and numbers. You cannot request the display of Booleans or any other types of data. You cannot display combinations of data (a string and a number, for instance), without performing the conversions and concatenations yourself.

- You will see output from this package only after your program completes its execution. You *cannot* use DBMS_OUTPUT to examine the results of a program while it is running. And if your program terminates with an unhandled exception, you may not see anything at all!

- If you try to display strings longer than 255 bytes, DBMS_OUTPUT will raise a VALUE_ERROR exception.

- DBMS_OUTPUT is not a strong choice as a report generator, because it can handle a maximum of only 1,000,000 bytes of data in a session before it raises an exception.

- If you use DBMS_OUTPUT in SQL*Plus, you may find that any leading blanks are automatically truncated. Also, attempts to display blank or NULL lines are completely ignored.

There are workarounds for almost every one of these drawbacks. The solution invariably requires the construction of a package that encapsulates and hides DBMS_OUTPUT. This technique is explained in the "DBMS_OUTPUT Examples" section.

Enabling and Disabling Output

The ENABLE and DISABLE procedures enable and disable output from the DBMS_OUTPUT.PUT_LINE (and PUT and PUTF) procedure.

The DBMS_OUTPUT.ENABLE procedure

The ENABLE procedure enables calls to the other DBMS_OUTPUT modules. If you do not first call ENABLE, then any other calls to the package modules are ignored. The specification for the procedure is,

```
PROCEDURE DBMS_OUTPUT.ENABLE  (buffer_size IN INTEGER DEFAULT 20000);
```

where buffer_size is the size of the buffer that will contain the information stored by calls to PUT and PUT_LINE. The buffer size can be as large as 1,000,000 bytes. You can pass larger values to this procedure without raising an error, but doing so will have no effect besides setting the buffer size to its maximum.

You can call ENABLE more than once in a session. The buffer size will be set to the largest size passed in any call to ENABLE. In other words, the buffer size is not necessarily set to the size specified in the last call.

If you want to make sure that the DBMS_OUTPUT package is enabled in a program you are testing, add a statement like this one to the start of the program:

```
DECLARE
   ... declarations ...
BEGIN
```

```
    DBMS_OUTPUT.ENABLE (1000000);
    ...
  END;
```

The DBMS_OUTPUT.DISABLE procedure

The DISABLE procedure disables all calls to the DBMS_OUTPUT package (except for ENABLE). It also purges the buffer of any remaining lines of information. Here's the specification for the procedure:

```
    PROCEDURE DBMS_OUTPUT.DISABLE;
```

SQL*Plus and SQL*DBA offer a native command, SET SERVEROUTPUT, with which you can disable the package without having to execute the DISABLE procedure directly. You can use the command as follows:

```
    SQL> SET SERVEROUTPUT OFF
```

This command is equivalent to the following PL/SQL statement:

```
    DBMS_OUTPUT.DISABLE;
```

After you execute this command, any calls to PUT_LINE and other modules will be ignored, and you will not see any output.

Enabling output in SQL*Plus

Most developers use DBMS_OUTPUT almost exclusively in the SQL*Plus environment. To enable output from calls to PUT_LINE in SQL*Plus, you will use the SET SERVEROUTPUT command,

```
    SET SERVEROUTPUT ON SIZE 1000000
```

or:

```
    SET SERVEROUTPUT ON
```

Each of these calls the DBMS_OUTPUT.ENABLE procedure.

I have found it useful to add SET SERVEROUTPUT ON SIZE 1000000 to my *login.sql* file, so that the package is automatically enabled whenever I go into SQL*Plus. (I guess that tells you how often I have to debug my code!)

You should also check the Oracle documentation for SQL*Plus to find out about the latest set of options for the SET SERVEROUTPUT command. As of Oracle8, the documentation shows the following syntax for this SET command:

```
    SET SERVEROUT[PUT] {OFF|ON}
       [SIZE n] [FOR[MAT] {WRA[PPED]| WOR[D_WRAPPED]|TRU[NCATED]}]
```

In other words, you have these options when you enable DBMS_OUTPUT in SQL*Plus:

SET SERVEROUTPUT OFF
    Turns off the display of text from DBMS_OUTPUT.

SET SERVEROUTPUT ON

Turns on the display of text from DBMS_OUTPUT with the default 2000-byte buffer. This is a very small size for the buffer; I recommend that you always specify a size when you call this command.

SET SERVEROUTPUT ON SIZE NNNN

Turns on the display of text from DBMS_OUTPUT with the specified buffer size (maximum of 1,000,000 bytes).

SET SERVEROUTPUT ON FORMAT WRAPPED

(Available in Oracle 7.3 and later only.) Specifies that you want the text displayed by DBMS_OUTPUT wrapped at the SQL*Plus line length. The wrapping occurs regardless of word separation. This will also stop SQL*Plus from stripping leading blanks from your text. You can also specify a SIZE value with this variation.

SET SERVEROUTPUT ON FORMAT WORD_WRAPPED

(Available in Oracle 7.3 and later only.) Specifies that you want the text displayed by DBMS_OUTPUT wrapped at the SQL*Plus line length. This version respects integrity of "words." As a result, lines will be broken in a way that keeps separate tokens intact. This will also stop SQL*Plus from stripping leading blanks from your text. You can also specify a SIZE value with this variation.

SET SERVEROUTPUT ON FORMAT TRUNCATED

(Available in Oracle 7.3 and later only.) Specifies that you want the text displayed by DBMS_OUTPUT to be truncated at the SQL*Plus line length; the rest of the text will not be displayed. This will also stop SQL*Plus from stripping leading blanks from your text. You can also specify a SIZE value with this variation.

Writing to the DBMS_OUTPUT Buffer

You can write information to the buffer with calls to the PUT, NEW_LINE, and PUT_LINE procedures.

The DBMS_OUTPUT.PUT procedure

The PUT procedure puts information into the buffer, but does not append a newline marker into the buffer. Use PUT if you want to place information in the buffer (usually with more than one call to PUT), but not also automatically issue a newline marker. The specification for PUT is overloaded, so that you can pass data in its native format to the package without having to perform conversions,

```
PROCEDURE DBMS_OUTPUT.PUT (A VARCHAR2);
PROCEDURE DBMS_OUTPUT.PUT (A NUMBER);
PROCEDURE DBMS_OUTPUT.PUT (A DATE);
```

where A is the data being passed.

Example. In the following example, three simultaneous calls to PUT place the employee name, department ID number, and hire date into a single line in the DBMS_OUTPUT buffer:

```
DBMS_OUTPUT.PUT (:employee.lname || ', ' || :employee.fname);
DBMS_OUTPUT.PUT (:employee.department_id);
DBMS_OUTPUT.PUT (:employee.hiredate);
```

If you follow these PUT calls with a NEW_LINE call, that information can then be retrieved with a single call to GET_LINE.

The DBMS_OUTPUT.PUT_LINE procedure

The PUT_LINE procedure puts information into the buffer and then appends a newline marker into the buffer. The specification for PUT_LINE is overloaded, so that you can pass data in its native format to the package without having to perform conversions:

```
PROCEDURE DBMS_OUTPUT.PUT_LINE (A VARCHAR2);
PROCEDURE DBMS_OUTPUT.PUT_LINE (A NUMBER);
PROCEDURE DBMS_OUTPUT.PUT_LINE (A DATE);
```

The PUT_LINE procedure is the one most commonly used in SQL*Plus to debug PL/SQL programs. When you use PUT_LINE in these situations, you do not need to call GET_LINE to extract the information from the buffer. Instead, SQL*Plus will automatically dump out the DBMS_OUTPUT buffer when your PL/SQL block finishes executing. (You will not see any output until the program ends.)

Of course, you can also call DBMS_OUTPUT programs directly from the SQL*Plus command prompt, and not from inside a PL/SQL block, as shown in the following example.

Example. Suppose that you execute the following three statements in SQL*Plus:

```
SQL> exec DBMS_OUTPUT.PUT ('I am');
SQL> exec DBMS_OUTPUT.PUT (' writing ');
SQL> exec DBMS_OUTPUT.PUT ('a ');
```

You will not see anything, because PUT will place the information in the buffer, but will not append the newline marker. When you issue this next PUT_LINE command,

```
SQL> exec DBMS_OUTPUT.PUT_LINE ('book!');
```

you will then see the following output:

```
I am writing a book!
```

All of the information added to the buffer with the calls to PUT waited patiently to be flushed out with the call to PUT_LINE. This is the behavior you will see when you execute individual calls at the SQL*Plus command prompt to the put programs.

If you place these same commands in a PL/SQL block,

```
BEGIN
    DBMS_OUTPUT.PUT ('I am');
    DBMS_OUTPUT.PUT (' writing ');
    DBMS_OUTPUT.PUT ('a ');
    DBMS_OUTPUT.PUT_LINE ('book');
END;
/
```

the output from this script will be exactly the same as that generated by this single call:

```
SQL> exec DBMS_OUTPUT.PUT_LINE ('I am writing a book!');
```

The DBMS_OUTPUT.NEW_LINE procedure

The NEW_LINE procedure inserts an end-of-line marker in the buffer. Use NEW_LINE after one or more calls to PUT in order to terminate those entries in the buffer with a newline marker. Here's the specification for NEW_LINE:

```
PROCEDURE DBMS_OUTPUT.NEW_LINE;
```

Retrieving Data from the DBMS_OUTPUT Buffer

You can use the GET_LINE and GET_LINES procedures to extract information from the DBMS_OUTPUT buffer. If you are using DBMS_OUTPUT from within SQL*Plus, however, you will never need to call either of these procedures. Instead, SQL*Plus will automatically extract the information and display it on the screen for you.

The DBMS_OUTPUT.GET_LINE procedure

The GET_LINE procedure retrieves one line of information from the buffer. Here's the specification for the procedure:

```
PROCEDURE DBMS_OUTPUT.GET_LINE
    (line OUT VARCHAR2,
     status OUT INTEGER);
```

The parameters are summarized in the following table.

Parameter	Description
line	Retrieved line of text
status	GET request status

The line can have up to 255 bytes in it, which is not very long. If GET_LINE completes successfully, then status is set to 0. Otherwise, GET_LINE returns a status of 1.

Notice that even though the PUT and PUT_LINE procedures allow you to place information into the buffer in their native representations (dates as dates, numbers and numbers, and so forth), GET_LINE always retrieves the information into a character string. The information returned by GET_LINE is everything in the buffer up to the next newline character. This information might be the data from a single PUT_LINE or from multiple calls to PUT.

Example. The following call to GET_LINE extracts the next line of information into a local PL/SQL variable:

```
FUNCTION get_next_line RETURN VARCHAR2
IS
    return_value VARCHAR2(255);
    get_status INTEGER;
BEGIN
    DBMS_OUTPUT.GET_LINE (return_value, get_status);
    IF get_status = 0
    THEN
        RETURN return_value;
    ELSE
        RETURN NULL;
    END IF;
END;
```

The DBMS_OUTPUT.GET_LINES procedure

The GET_LINES procedure retrieves multiple lines from the buffer with one call. It reads the buffer into a PL/SQL string table. Here's the specification for the procedure:

```
PROCEDURE DBMS_OUTPUT.GET_LINES
    (lines OUT DBMS_OUTPUT.CHARARR,
     numlines IN OUT INTEGER);
```

The parameters for this procedure are summarized in the following table.

Parameter	Description
lines	PL/SQL array where retrieved lines are placed
numlines	Number of individual lines retrieved from the buffer and placed into the array

The lines parameter is a PL/SQL table TYPE declared in the specification of the package. It is described at the beginning of this chapter.

The values retrieved by GET_LINES are placed in the first numlines rows in the table, starting from row one. As indicated in the PL/SQL table structure, each line (row in the table) may contain up to 255 bytes.

Notice that numlines is an IN OUT parameter. The IN aspect of the parameter specifies the number of lines to retrieve. Once GET_LINES is done retrieving data, however, it sets numlines to the number of lines actually placed in the table. If you ask for ten rows and there are only six in the buffer, then you need to know that only the first six rows of the table are defined.

Notice also that even though the PUT and PUT_LINE procedures allow you to place information into the buffer in their native representations (dates as dates, numbers and numbers, and so forth), GET_LINES always retrieves the information into a character string. The information in each line returned by GET_LINES is everything in the buffer up to the next newline character. This information might be the data from a single PUT_LINE or from multiple calls to PUT.

While GET_LINES is provided with the DBMS_OUTPUT package, it is not needed to retrieve information from the DBMS_OUTPUT buffer—at least when used inside SQL*Plus. In this interactive query tool, you simply execute calls to PUT_LINE, and when the PL/SQL block terminates, SQL*Plus will automatically dump the buffer to the screen.

Example. The following script demonstrates both the kind of code you would write when using the GET_LINES procedure, and also the way in which the PL/SQL table is filled:

```
/* Filename on companion disk: getlines.tst */
DECLARE
   output_table DBMS_OUTPUT.CHARARR;  /* output_buf_tab */
   a_line VARCHAR2(10) := RPAD('*',10,'*');
   status INTEGER;
   max_lines CONSTANT NUMBER := 15;
BEGIN
   output_table (0) := 'ABC';
   output_table (12) := 'DEF';

   /* Output 10 lines */
   FOR linenum IN 1..10
   LOOP
      DBMS_OUTPUT.PUT_LINE (a_line ||  TO_CHAR (linenum);
   END LOOP;
   /* retrieve 15 lines, status will receive the line count */
   status := max_lines;
   DBMS_OUTPUT.GET_LINES ( output_table, status);
   DBMS_OUTPUT.PUT_LINE ('lines retrieved= ' || status));

   FOR linenum in 0..max_lines
   LOOP
```

```
      BEGIN
         DBMS_OUTPUT.PUT_LINE
            (linenum || ':' || NVL (output_table(linenum),'<null>') );
      EXCEPTION
         WHEN OTHERS
         THEN
            DBMS_OUTPUT.PUT_LINE (linenum || ':' || sqlerrm );
      END;
   END LOOP;
EXCEPTION
   WHEN OTHERS
   THEN
      DBMS_OUTPUT.PUT_LINE ('Exception, status=' || status);
      DBMS_OUTPUT.PUT_LINE (SQLERRM );
END;
/
```

Here is the output from the execution of this script:

```
lines retrieved= 10
0:ORA-01403: no data found
1:**********1
2:**********2
3:**********3
4:**********4
5:**********5
6:**********6
7:**********7
8:**********8
9:**********9
10:**********10
11:<null>
12:ORA-01403: no data found
13:ORA-01403: no data found
14:ORA-01403: no data found
15:ORA-01403: no data found
```

You can therefore deduce the following rules:

1. The PL/SQL table is filled starting with row 1.

2. If DBMS_OUTPUT.GET_LINES finds N lines of data to pass to the PL/SQL table, it sets row N+1 in that table to NULL.

3. All other rows in the PL/SQL table are set to "undefined." In other words, any other rows that might have been defined before the call to GET_LINES are deleted.

Tips on Using DBMS_OUTPUT

As noted at the beginning of the chapter, DBMS_OUTPUT comes with several handicaps. The best way to overcome these handicaps is to create your own layer of code over the built-in package. This technique is explored in the "DBMS_OUTPUT Examples" section.

Regardless of the use of an encapsulation package, you should keep the following complications in mind as you work with DBMS_OUTPUT:

1. If your program raises an unhandled exception, you may not see any executed output from PUT_LINE, even if you enabled the package for output.

    This can happen because the DBMS_OUTPUT buffer will not be flushed until it is full or until the current PL/SQL block completes its execution. If a raised exception never gets handled, the buffer will not be flushed. As a result, calls to the DBMS_OUTPUT.PUT_LINE module might never show their data. So if you are working with DBMS_OUTPUT.PUT_LINE and are frustrated because you are not seeing the output you would expect, make sure that you have:

    a. Enabled output from the package by calling SET SERVEROUTPUT ON in SQL*Plus.

    b. Placed an exception section with a WHEN OTHERS handler in the outer block of your code (usually some sort of test script) so that your output can be flushed to your terminal by SQL*Plus.

2. When package state has been reinitialized in your session, DBMS_OUTPUT is reset to "not enabled."

    Packages can be reset to their initial state with a call to DBMS_SESSION.RESET_PACKAGE. (See Chapter 11, *Managing Session Information*, for more information about this program.) You might call this procedure yourself, but that is unlikely. A more common scenario for resetting package states is when an error is raised in your session that *causes* packages to be reset to their initial state. Here is the error for which you need to beware:

    ```
    ERROR at line 1:
    ORA-04068: existing state of packages has been discarded
    ORA-04061: existing state of package "PKG.PROC" has been invalidated
    ORA-04065: not executed, altered or dropped package "PKG.PROC"
    ORA-06508: PL/SQL: could not find program unit being called
    ```

If you get this error and simply continue with your testing, you may be surprised to find that you are not getting any output. If you remember that DBMS_OUTPUT relies on package variables for its settings, this makes perfect sense. So when you get the preceding error, you should immediately "re-enable" DBMS_OUTPUT with a command such as the following:

```
SQL> set serveroutput on size 1000000 format wrapped
```

I usually just re-execute my *login.sql* script, since I may be initializing several different packages:

```
SQL> @login.sql
```

When will you get this error? I have found that it occurs when I have multiple sessions connected to Oracle. Suppose that I am testing program A in session USER1.

I run it and find a bug. I fix the bug and recompile program A in session USER2 (the owner of the code). When I try to execute program A from session USER1 again, it raises the ORA-04068 error.

If you do encounter this error, don't panic. Just reset your package variables and run the program again. It will now work fine; the error is simply the result of a quirk in Oracle's automatic recompilation feature.

DBMS_OUTPUT Examples

This section contains several longer examples of DBMS_OUTPUT operations.

Encapsulating DBMS_OUTPUT

Sure, it was nice of Oracle Corporation to give us the DBMS_OUTPUT package. Without it, as users of PL/SQL 1.0 found, we are running blind when we execute our code. As is the case with many of the developer-oriented utilities from Oracle, however, the DBMS_OUTPUT package is not a polished and well-planned tool. It offers nothing more than the most basic functionality, and even then it is crippled in some important ways. When I started to use it in real life (or whatever you might call the rarified atmosphere of authoring a book on software development), I found DBMS_OUTPUT.PUT_LINE to be cumbersome and limiting in ways.

I hated having to type "DBMS_OUTPUT.PUT_LINE" whenever I simply wanted to display some information. That's a mouthful and a keyboardful. I felt insulted that they hadn't even taken the time to overload for Booleans, requiring me to write silly IF logic just to see the value of a Boolean variable or function. I also found myself growing incensed that DBMS_OUTPUT would actually raise a VALUE_ERROR exception if I tried to pass it a string with more than 255 characters. I had enough errors in my code without having to worry about DBMS_OUTPUT adding to my troubles.

I decided that all this anger and frustration was not good for me. I needed to move past this nonconstructive lashing out at Oracle. I needed, in short, to *fix* my problem. So I did—with a package of my own. I am not going to provide a comprehensive explanation of my replacement package, but you can read about it (there are actually two of them) in my other books as follows:

Oracle PL/SQL Programming

The Companion Disk section on "Package Examples" introduces you to the do package, which contains the do.pl procedure, a substitute for DBMS_OUTPUT.PUT_LINE. The *do.sps* and *do.spb* files in the book you are reading also contain the source code for this package.

Advanced Oracle PL/SQL Programming with Packages

Chapter 7, *p: A Powerful Substitute for DMBS_OUTPUT,* presents the p package and the p.l procedure (I told you I didn't like typing those long program names!), a component of the PL/Vision library.[*]

The following section shows you the basic elements involved in constructing an encapsulation around DBMS_OUTPUT.PUT_LINE, which compensates for many of its problems. You can pursue building one of these for yourself, but I would strongly suggest that you check out the PL/Vision p package. That will leave you more time to build your own application-specific code.

Package specification for a DBMS_OUTPUT encapsulator

The absolute minimum you need for such an encapsulator package is an overloading of the "print" procedure for dates, strings, and numbers. Let's at least add Booleans to the mix in this prototype:

```
/* Filename on companion disk: prt.spp */
CREATE OR REPLACE PACKAGE prt
IS
    c_prefix CONSTANT CHAR(1) := '*';
    c_linelen CONSTANT INTEGER := 80;

    PROCEDURE ln (val IN VARCHAR2);
    PROCEDURE ln (val IN DATE);
    PROCEDURE ln (val IN NUMBER);
    PROCEDURE ln (val IN BOOLEAN);
END;
/
```

The prefix constant is concatenated to the beginning of any string to be displayed to avoid the problem of truncated spaces and ignored lines in SQL*Plus. The line length constant is used when the string is longer than 255 bytes. Finally, each of the prt.ln procedures prints a different type of data.

A complete implementation of this package would allow you to change the line length and the prefix, specify a date format for conversion, and so on. Again, check out the p package of PL/Vision for such a package.

Here is the body of the prt package:

```
/* Filename on companion disk: prt.spp */
CREATE OR REPLACE PACKAGE BODY prt
IS
    PROCEDURE ln (val IN VARCHAR2)
    IS
    BEGIN
        IF LENGTH (val) > 255
```

---

[*] A version of PL/Vision is available through a free download from the *www.revealnet.com* site.

```
        THEN
            PLVprs.display_wrap (val, c_linelen);
        ELSE
            DBMS_OUTPUT.PUT_LINE (c_prefix || val);
        END IF;
    EXCEPTION
        WHEN OTHERS
        THEN
            DBMS_OUTPUT.ENABLE (1000000);
            DBMS_OUTPUT.PUT_LINE (c_prefix || val);
    END;
    PROCEDURE ln (val IN DATE)
    IS
    BEGIN
        ln (TO_CHAR (val));
    END;
    PROCEDURE ln (val IN NUMBER)
    IS
    BEGIN
        ln (TO_CHAR (val));
    END;
    PROCEDURE ln (val IN BOOLEAN)
    IS
    BEGIN
        IF val
        THEN
            ln ('TRUE');
        ELSIF NOT val
        THEN
            ln ('FALSE');
        ELSE
            ln ('NULL BOOLEAN');
        END IF;
    END;
END;
/
```

Here are a few things to notice about the package implementation:

- The string version of prt.ln is the "core" print procedure. The other three programs all call that one, after they have formatted the string appropriately.

- The Boolean version of prt.ln simply performs the same IF logic you would have to write if you were using DBMS_OUTPUT. By hiding it inside the prt procedure, though, nobody else has to write that kind of code again. Plus, it handles NULL values.

- The string version of prt.ln contains all the complex logic. For long strings, it relies on the PL/Vision display wrap procedure of the PLVprs package.[*] For strings with fewer than 256 characters, it calls DBMS_OUTPUT.PUT_LINE.

---

[*] Available through a free download from the *www.revealnet.com* site.

- As an added feature, if the attempt to display using DBMS_OUTPUT.PUT_ LINE raises an exception, prt.ln assumes that the problem might be that the buffer is too small. So it increases the buffer to the maximum possible value and then tries again. I believe that it is very important for developers to make the extra effort to increase the usefulness of our code.

The prt package should give you a solid idea about the way to encapsulate a built-in package inside a package of your own construction.

UTL_FILE: Reading and Writing Server-side Files

UTL_FILE is a package that has been welcomed warmly by PL/SQL developers. It allows PL/SQL programs to both read from and write to any operating system files that are accessible from the server on which your database instance is running. File I/O was a feature long desired in PL/SQL, but available only with PL/SQL Release 2.3 and later (Oracle 7.3 or Oracle 8.0). You can now read *ini* files and interact with the operating system a *little* more easily than has been possible in the past. You can load data from files directly into database tables while applying the full power and flexibility of PL/SQL programming. You can generate reports directly from within PL/SQL without worrying about the maximum buffer restrictions of DBMS_OUTPUT

Getting Started with UTL_FILE

The UTL_FILE package is created when the Oracle database is installed. The utlfile.sql script (found in the built-in packages source code directory, as described in Chapter 1) contains the source code for this package's specification. This script is called by *catproc.sql*, which is normally run immediately after database creation. The script creates the public synonym UTL_FILE for the package and grants EXECUTE privilege on the package to public. All Oracle users can reference and make use of this package.

UTL_FILE programs

Table 6-2 shows the UTL_FILE program names and descriptions.

Table 6-2. UTL_FILE Programs

Name	Description	Use in SQL
FCLOSE	Closes the specified files	No
FCLOSE_ALL	Closes all open files	No

Table 6-2. UTL_FILE Programs (continued)

Name	Description	Use in SQL
FFLUSH	Flushes all the data from the UTL_FILE buffer	No
FOPEN	Opens the specified file	No
GET_LINE	Gets the next line from the file	No
IS_OPEN	Returns TRUE if the file is already open	No
NEW_LINE	Inserts a newline mark in the file at the end of the current line	No
PUT	Puts text into the buffer	No
PUT_LINE	Puts a line of text into the file	No
PUTF	Puts formatted text into the buffer	No

Trying out UTL_FILE

Just getting to the point where your first call to UTL_FILE's FOPEN function works can actually be a pretty frustrating experience. Here's how it usually goes.

You read about UTL_FILE and you are excited. So you dash headlong into writing some code like this,

```
DECLARE
    config_file UTL_FILE.FILE_TYPE;
BEGIN
    config_file := UTL_FILE.FOPEN ('/tmp', 'newdata.txt', 'W');

    ... lots of write operations ...

    ... and no exception section ...
END;
/
```

and then this is all you get from your "quick and dirty script" in SQL*Plus:

```
SQL> @writefile.sql
DECLARE
*
ERROR at line 1:
ORA-06510: PL/SQL: unhandled user-defined exception
ORA-06512: at "SYS.UTL_FILE", line 91
ORA-06512: at "SYS.UTL_FILE", line 146
ORA-06512: at line 4
```

What is going wrong? This error message certainly provides little or no useful information. So you go back to the documentation, thoroughly chastened, and (over time) discover the following:

- You need to modify the INIT.ORA parameter initialization file of your instance. You will have to contact your database administrator and have him or her make the changes (if willing) and then "bounce" the database.

- You need to get the format of the parameter entries correct. That alone used to take me days!

- You need to add exception sections to your programs to give yourself a fighting chance at figuring out what is going on.

I hope that the information in this chapter will help you avoid most, if not all, of these frustrations and gotchas. But don't give up! This package is well worth the effort.

File security

UTL_FILE lets you read and write files accessible from the server on which your database is running. So you could theoretically use UTL_FILE to write right over your tablespace data files, control files, and so on. That is of course a very bad idea. Server security requires the ability to place restrictions on where you can read and write your files.

UTL_FILE implements this security by limiting access to files that reside in one of the directories specified in the INIT.ORA file for the database instance on which UTL_FILE is running.

When you call FOPEN to open a file, you must specify both the location and the name of the file, in separate arguments. This file location is then checked against the list of accessible directories.

Here's the format of the parameter for file access in the INIT.ORA file:

```
utl_file_dir = <directory>
```

Include a parameter for utl_file_dir for each directory you want to make accessible for UTL_FILE operations. The following entries, for example, enable four different directories in UNIX:

```
utl_file_dir = /tmp
utl_file_dir = /ora_apps/hr/time_reporting
utl_file_dir = /ora_apps/hr/time_reporting/log
utl_file_dir = /users/test_area
```

To bypass server security and allow read/write access to all directories, you can use this special syntax:

```
utl_file_dir = *
```

You should not use this option on production systems. In a development system, this entry certainly makes it easier for developers to get up and running on UTL_FILE and test their code. However, you should allow access to only a few specific directories when you move the application to production.

Some observations on working with and setting up accessible directories with UTL_FILE follow:

- Access is not recursive through subdirectories. If the following lines were in your INIT.ORA file, for example,

  ```
  utl_file_dir = c:\group\dev1
  utl_file_dir = c:\group\prod\oe
  utl_file_dir = c:\group\prod\ar
  ```

  then you would not be able to open a file in the *c:\group\prod\oe\reports* subdirectory.

- Do not include the following entry in UNIX systems:

  ```
  utl_file_dir = .
  ```

  This would allow you to read/write on the current directory in the operating system.

- Do not enclose the directory names within single or double quotes.

- In the UNIX environment, a file created by FOPEN has as its owner the shadow process running the Oracle instance. This is usually the "oracle" owner. If you try to access these files outside of UTL_FILE, you will need the correct privileges (or be logged in as "oracle") to access or change these files.

- You should not end your directory name with a delimiter, such as the forward slash in UNIX. The following specification of a directory will result in problems when trying to read from or write to the directory:

  ```
  utl_file_dir = /tmp/orafiles/
  ```

Specifying file locations

The location of the file is an operating system-specific string that specifies the directory or area in which to open the file. The location you provide must have been listed as an accessible directory in the INIT.ORA file for the database instance.

The INIT.ORA location is a valid directory or area specification, as shown in these examples:

- In Windows NT:

  ```
  'k:\common\debug'
  ```

- In UNIX:

  ```
  '/usr/od2000/admin'
  ```

Notice that in Windows NT, the backslash character (\) is used as a delimiter. In UNIX, the forward slash (/) is the delimiter. When you pass the location in the call to UTL_FILE.FOPEN, you provide the location specification as it appears in the INIT.ORA file (unless you just provided * for all directories in the initialization file). And remember that in case-sensitive operating systems, the case of the location specification in the initialization file must match that used in the call to UTL_FILE.FOPEN.

Here are some examples:

- In Windows NT:

  ```
  file_id := UTL_FILE.FOPEN ('k:\common\debug', 'trace.lis', 'R');
  ```

- In UNIX:

  ```
  file_id := UTL_FILE.FOPEN ('/usr/od2000/admin', 'trace.lis', 'W');
  ```

Your location must be an explicit, complete path to the file. You cannot use operating system-specific parameters such as environment variables in UNIX to specify file locations.

UTL_FILE exceptions

The package specification of UTL_FILE defines seven exceptions. The cause behind a UTL_FILE exception can often be difficult to understand. Here are the explanations Oracle provides for each of the exceptions:

NOTE   As a result of the way these exceptions are declared (as "user-defined exceptions"), there is no error number associated with any of the exceptions. Thus you must include explicit exception handlers in programs that call UTL_FILE if you wish to find out which error was raised. See the section "Handling file I/O errors" for more details on this process.

INVALID_PATH
The file location or the filename is invalid. Perhaps the directory is not listed as a utl_file_dir parameter in the INIT.ORA file (or doesn't exist as all), or you are trying to read a file and it does not exist.

INVALID_MODE
The value you provided for the open_mode parameter in UTL_FILE.FOPEN was invalid. It must be "A," "R," or "W."

INVALID_FILEHANDLE
The file handle you passed to a UTL_FILE program was invalid. You must call UTL_FILE.FOPEN to obtain a valid file handle.

INVALID_OPERATION
UTL_FILE could not open or operate on the file as requested. For example, if you try to write to a read-only file, you will raise this exception.

READ_ERROR

> The operating system returned an error when you tried to read from the file. (This does not occur very often.)

WRITE_ERROR

> The operating system returned an error when you tried to write to the file. (This does not occur very often.)

INTERNAL_ERROR

> Uh-oh. Something went wrong and the PL/SQL runtime engine couldn't assign blame to any of the previous exceptions. Better call Oracle Support!

Programs in UTL_FILE may also raise the following standard system exceptions:

NO_DATA_FOUND

> Raised when you read past the end of the file with UTL_FILE.GET_LINE.

VALUE_ERROR

> Raised when you try to read or write lines in the file which are too long. The current implementation of UTL_FILE limits the size of a line read by UTL_FILE.GET_LINE to 1022 bytes.

In the following descriptions of the UTL_FILE programs, I list the exceptions that can be raised by each individual program.

UTL_FILE nonprogram elements

When you open a file, PL/SQL returns a handle to that file for use within your program. This handle has a datatype of UTL_FILE.FILE_TYPE currently defined as the following:

```
TYPE UTL_FILE.FILE_TYPE IS RECORD (id BINARY_INTEGER);
```

As you can see, UTL_FILE.FILE_TYPE is actually a PL/SQL record whose fields contain all the information about the file needed by UTL_FILE. However, this information is for use only by the UTL_FILE package. You will reference the handle, but not any of the individual fields of the handle. (The fields of this record may expand over time as UTL_FILE becomes more sophisticated.)

Here is an example of how to declare a local file handle based on this type:

```
DECLARE
    file_handle UTL_FILE.FILE_TYPE;
BEGIN
    . . .
```

UTL_FILE restrictions and limitations

While UTL_FILE certainly extends the usefulness of PL/SQL, it does have its drawbacks, including:

- You cannot read or write a line of text that has more than 1022 bytes. I hope this limitation will be increased in a future release of PL/SQL8, but no commitments have yet been made by Oracle.

- You cannot delete files through UTL_FILE. The best you can do is *empty* a file, but it will still be present on the disk.

- You cannot rename files. The best you can do is copy the contents of the file to another file with that new name.

- You do not have random access to lines in a file. If you want to read the 55th line, you must read through the first 54 lines. If you want to insert a line of text between the 1,267th and 1,268th lines, you will have to (a) read those 1,267 lines, (b) write them to a new file, (c) write the inserted line of text, and (d) read/write the remainder of the file. Ugh.

- You cannot change the security on files through UTL_FILE.

- You cannot access mapped files. Generally, you will need to supply real directory locations for files if you want to read from or write to them.

You are probably getting the idea. UTL_FILE is a basic facility for reading and writing server-side files. Working with UTL_FILE is not always pretty, but you can usually get what you need done with a little or a lot of code.

The UTL_FILE process flow

The following sections describe each of the UTL_FILE programs, following the process flow for working with files. That flow is described for both writing and reading files.

In order to write to a file you will (in most cases) perform the following steps:

1. Declare a file handle. This handle serves as a pointer to the file for subsequent calls to programs in the UTL_FILE package to manipulate the contents of this file.

2. Open the file with a call to FOPEN, which returns a file handle to the file. You can open a file to read, replace, or append text.

3. Write data to the file using the PUT, PUTF, or PUT_LINE procedures.

4. Close the file with a call to FCLOSE. This releases resources associated with the file.

To read data from a file you will (in most cases) perform the following steps:

1. Declare a file handle.

2. Declare a VARCHAR2 string buffer that will receive the line of data from the file. You can also read directly from a file into a numeric or date buffer. In this case, the data in the file will be converted implicitly, and so it must be compatible with the datatype of the buffer.

3. Open the file using FOPEN in read mode.

4. Use the GET_LINE procedure to read data from the file and into the buffer. To read all the lines from a file, you would execute GET_LINE in a loop.

5. Close the file with a call to FCLOSE.

Opening Files

Use the FOPEN and IS_OPEN functions when you open files via UTL_FILE.

NOTE   Using the UTL-FILE package, you can only open a maximum of ten files for each Oracle session.

The UTL_FILE.FOPEN function

The FOPEN function opens the specified file and returns a file handle that you can then use to manipulate the file. Here's the header for the function:

```
FUNCTION UTL_FILE.FOPEN
    (location IN VARCHAR2,
     filename IN VARCHAR2,
     openmode IN VARCHAR2)
    RETURN UTL_FILE.FILE_TYPE;
```

Parameters are summarized in the following table.

Parameter	Description
location	Location of the file
filename	Name of the file
openmode	Mode in which the file is to be opened (see the following modes)

You can open the file in one of three modes:

R   Open the file read-only. If you use this mode, use UTL_FILE's GET_LINE procedure to read from the file.

W   Open the file to read and write in replace mode. When you open in replace mode, all existing lines in the file are removed. If you use this mode, then you can use any of the following UTL_FILE programs to modify the file: PUT, PUT_LINE, NEW_LINE, PUTF, and FFLUSH.

A   Open the file to read and write in append mode. When you open in append mode, all existing lines in the file are kept intact. New lines will be appended after the last line in the file. If you use this mode, then you can use any of the following UTL_FILE programs to modify the file: PUT, PUT_LINE, NEW_LINE, PUTF, and fFFLUSH.

Keep the following points in mind as you attempt to open files:

- The file location and the filename joined together must represent a legal file-name on your operating system.

- The file location specified must be accessible and must already exist; FOPEN will not create a directory or subdirectory for you in order to write a new file, for example.

- If you want to open a file for read access, the file must already exist. If you want to open a file for write access, the file will either be created, if it does not exist, or emptied of all its contents, if it does exist.

- If you try to open with append, the file must already exist. UTL_FILE will not treat your append request like a write access request. If the file is not present, UTL_FILE will raise the INVALID_OPERATION exception.

Exceptions. FOPEN may raise any of the following exceptions, described earlier:

```
UTL_FILE.INVALID_MODE
UTL_FILE.INVALID_OPERATION
UTL_FILE.INVALID_PATH
```

Example. The following example shows how to declare a file handle and then open a configuration file for that handle in read-only mode:

```
DECLARE
    config_file UTL_FILE.FILE_TYPE;
BEGIN
    config_file := UTL_FILE.FOPEN ('/maint/admin', 'config.txt', 'R');
    ...
```

The UTL_FILE.IS_OPEN function

The IS_OPEN function returns TRUE if the specified handle points to a file that is already open. Otherwise, it returns false. The header for the function is,

```
FUNCTION UTL_FILE.IS_OPEN (file IN UTL_FILE.FILE_TYPE) RETURN BOOLEAN;
```

where file is the file to be checked.

Within the context of UTL_FILE, it is important to know what this means. The IS_ OPEN function does not perform any operating system checks on the status of the file. In actuality, it merely checks to see if the id field of the file handle record is not NULL. If you don't play around with these records and their contents, then this id field is only set to a non-NULL value when you call FOPEN. It is set back to NULL when you call FCLOSE.

Reading from Files

UTL_FILE provides only one program to retrieve data from a file: the GET_LINE procedure.

The UTL_FILE.GET_LINE procedure

The GET_LINE procedure reads a line of data from the specified file, if it is open, into the provided line buffer. Here's the header for the procedure:

```
PROCEDURE UTL_FILE.GET_LINE
    (file IN UTL_FILE.FILE_TYPE,
     buffer OUT VARCHAR2);
```

Parameters are summarized in the following table.

Parameter	Description
file	The file handle returned by a call to FOPEN
buffer	The buffer into which the line of data is read

The variable specified for the buffer parameter must be large enough to hold all the data up to the next carriage return or end-of-file condition in the file. If not, PL/SQL will raise the VALUE_ERROR exception. The line terminator character is not included in the string passed into the buffer.

Exceptions. GET_LINE may raise any of the following exceptions:

```
NO_DATA_FOUND
VALUE_ERROR
UTL_FILE.INVALID_FILEHANDLE
UTL_FILE.INVALID_OPERATION
UTL_FILE.READ_ERROR
```

Example. Since GET_LINE reads data only into a string variable, you will have to perform your own conversions to local variables of the appropriate datatype if your file holds numbers or dates. Of course, you could call this procedure and read data directly into string and numeric variables as well. In this case, PL/SQL will be performing a runtime, implicit conversion for you. In many situations, this is fine. I generally recommend that you avoid implicit conversions and perform your own conversion instead. This approach more clearly documents the steps and dependencies. Here is an example:

```
DECLARE
    fileID UTL_FILE.FILE_TYPE;
    strbuffer VARCHAR2(100);
    mynum NUMBER;
BEGIN
    fileID := UTL_FILE.FOPEN ('/tmp', 'numlist.txt', 'R');
    UTL_FILE.GET_LINE (fileID, strbuffer);
    mynum := TO_NUMBER (strbuffer);
END;
/
```

When GET_LINE attempts to read past the end of the file, the NO_DATA_FOUND exception is raised. This is the same exception that is raised when you (a) execute an implicit (SELECT INTO) cursor that returns no rows or (b) reference an undefined row of a PL/SQL (nested in PL/SQL8) table. If you are performing more than one of these operations in the same PL/SQL block, remember that this same exception can be caused by very different parts of your program.

Writing to Files

In contrast to the simplicity of reading from a file, UTL_FILE offers a number of different procedures you can use to write to a file:

UTL_FILE.PUT

Puts a piece of data (string, number, or date) into a file in the current line.

UTL_FILE.NEW_LINE

Puts a newline or line termination character into the file at the current position.

UTL_FILE.PUT_LINE

Puts a string into a file, followed by a platform-specific line termination character.

UTL_FILE.PUTF

Puts up to five strings out to the file in a format based on a template string, similar to the printf function in C.

You can use these procedures only if you have opened your file with modes W or A; if you opened the file for read-only, the runtime engine will raise the UTL_FILE.INVALID_OPERATION exception.

Starting with Oracle 8.0.3, the maximum size of a file string is 32K; the limit for earlier versions is 1023 bytes. If you have longer strings, you must break them up into individual lines, perhaps using a special continuation character to notify a post-processor to recombine those lines.

The UTL_FILE.PUT procedure

The PUT procedure puts data out to the specified open file. Here's the header for this procedure:

```
PROCEDURE UTL_FILE.PUT
      (file IN UTL_FILE.FILE_TYPE,
       buffer OUT VARCHAR2);
```

Parameters are summarized in the following table.

Parameter	Description
file	The file handle returned by a call to FOPEN
buffer	The buffer containing the text to be written to the file; maximum size allowed is 32K for Oracle 8.0.3 and above; for earlier versions, it is 1023 bytes

The PUT procedure adds the data to the current line in the opened file, but does not append a line terminator. You must use the NEW_LINE procedure to terminate the current line or use PUT_LINE to write out a complete line with a line termination character.

Exceptions. PUT may raise any of the following exceptions:

```
UTL_FILE.INVALID_FILEHANDLE
UTL_FILE.INVALID_OPERATION
UTL_FILE.WRITE_ERROR
```

The UTL_FILE.NEW_LINE procedure

The NEW_LINE procedure inserts one or more newline characters in the specified file. Here's the header for the procedure:

```
PROCEDURE UTL_FILE.NEW_LINE
      (file IN UTL_FILE.FILE_TYPE,
       lines IN NATURAL := 1);
```

Parameters are summarized in the following table.

Parameter	Description
file	The file handle returned by a call to FOPEN
lines	Number of lines to be inserted into the file

If you do not specify a number of lines, NEW_LINE uses the default value of 1, which places a newline character (carriage return) at the end of the current line. So if you want to insert a blank line in your file, execute the following call to NEW_LINE:

```
UTL_FILE.NEW_LINE (my_file, 2);
```

If you pass 0 or a negative number for lines, nothing is written into the file.

Exceptions. NEW_LINE may raise any of the following exceptions:

```
VALUE_ERROR
UTL_FILE.INVALID_FILEHANDLE
UTL_FILE.INVALID_OPERATION
UTL_FILE.WRITE_ERROR
```

Example. If you frequently wish to add an end-of-line marker after you PUT data out to the file (see the PUT procedure information), you might bundle two calls to UTL_FILE modules together, as follows:

```
PROCEDURE add_line (file_in IN UTL_FILE.FILE_TYPE, line_in IN VARCHAR2)
IS
BEGIN
   UTL_FILE.PUT (file_in, line_in);
   UTL_FILE.NEW_LINE (file_in);
END;
```

By using add_line instead of PUT, you will not have to worry about remembering to call NEW_LINE to finish off the line. Of course, you could also simply call the PUT_LINE procedure.

The UTL_FILE.PUT_LINE procedure

This procedure writes data to a file and then immediately appends a newline character after the text. Here's the header for PUT_LINE:

```
PROCEDURE UTL_FILE.PUT_LINE
    (file IN UTL_FILE.FILE_TYPE,
    buffer IN VARCHAR2);
```

Parameters are summarized in the following table.

Parameter	Description
file	The file handle returned by a call to FOPEN
buffer	Text to be written to the file; maximum size allowed is 32K for Oracle 8.0. 3 and above; for earlier versions, it is 1023 bytes

Before you can call UTL_FILE.PUT_LINE, you must have already opened the file.

Exceptions. PUT_LINE may raise any of the following exceptions:

```
UTL_FILE.INVALID_FILEHANDLE
UTL_FILE.INVALID_OPERATION
UTL_FILE.WRITE_ERROR
```

Example. Here is an example of using PUT_LINE to dump the contents of the emp table to a file:

```
PROCEDURE emp2file
IS
```

```
       fileID UTL_FILE.FILE_TYPE;
   BEGIN
       fileID := UTL_FILE.FOPEN ('/tmp', 'emp.dat', 'W');

       /* Quick and dirty construction here! */
       FOR emprec IN (SELECT * FROM emp)
       LOOP
          UTL_FILE.PUT_LINE
             (TO_CHAR (emprec.empno) || ',' ||
              emprec.ename || ',' ||
              ...
              TO_CHAR (emprec.deptno));
       END LOOP;

       UTL_FILE.FCLOSE (fileID);
   END;
```

A call to PUT_LINE is equivalent to a call to PUT followed by a call to NEW_LINE. It is also equivalent to a call to PUTF with a format string of "%s\n" (see the description of PUTF in the next section).

The UTL_FILE.PUTF procedure

Like PUT, PUTF puts data into a file, but it uses a message format (hence, the "F" in "PUTF") to interpret the different elements to be placed in the file. You can pass between one and five different items of data to PUTF. Here's the specification:

```
PROCEDURE UTL_FILE.PUTF
      (file IN FILE_TYPE
      ,format IN VARCHAR2
      ,arg1 IN VARCHAR2 DEFAULT NULL
      ,arg2 IN VARCHAR2 DEFAULT NULL
      ,arg3 IN VARCHAR2 DEFAULT NULL
      ,arg4 IN VARCHAR2 DEFAULT NULL
      ,arg5 IN VARCHAR2 DEFAULT NULL);
```

Parameters are summarized in the following table.

Parameter	Description
file	The file handle returned by a call to FOPEN
format	The string that determines the format of the items in the file; see the following options
argN	An optional argument string; up to five may be specified

The format string allows you to substitute the argN values directly into the text written to the file. In addition to "boilerplate" or literal text, the format string may contain the following patterns:

%s

Directs PUTF to put the corresponding item in the file. You can have up to five %s patterns in the format string, since PUTF will take up to five items.

n

> Directs PUTF to put a newline character in the file. There is no limit to the number of \n patterns you may include in a format string.

The %s formatters are replaced by the argument strings in the order provided. If you do not pass in enough values to replace all of the formatters, then the %s is simply removed from the string before writing it to the file.

Exceptions. UTL_FILE.PUTF may raise any of the following exceptions:

```
UTL_FILE.INVALID_FILEHANDLE
UTL_FILE.INVALID_OPERATION
UTL_FILE.WRITE_ERROR
```

Example. The following example illustrates how to use the format string. Suppose you want the contents of the file to look like this:

```
Employee: Steven Feuerstein
Soc Sec #: 123-45-5678
Salary: $1000
```

This single call to PUTF will accomplish the task:

```
UTL_FILE.PUTF
   (file_handle, 'Employee: %s\nSoc Sec #: %s\nSalary: %s',
    'Steven Feuerstein',
    '123-45-5678',
    TO_CHAR (:employee.salary, '$9999'));
```

If you need to write out more than five items of data, you can simply call PUTF twice consecutively to finish the job, as shown here:

```
UTL_FILE.PUTF
   (file_handle, '%s\n%s\n%s\n%s\n%s\n',
    TO_DATE (SYSDATE, 'MM/DD/YYYY'),
    TO_CHAR (:pet.pet_id),
    :pet.name,
    TO_DATE (:pet.birth_date, 'MM/DD/YYYY'),
    :pet.owner);

UTL_FILE.PUTF
   (file_handle, '%s\n%s\n',
    :pet.bites_mailperson,
    :pet.does_tricks);
```

The UTL_FILE.FFLUSH procedure

This procedure makes sure that all pending data for the specified file is written physically out to a file. The header for FFLUSH is,

```
PROCEDURE UTL_FILE.FFLUSH (file IN UTL_FILE.FILE_TYPE);
```

where file is the file handle.

Your operating system probably buffers physical I/O to improve performance. As a consequence, your program may have called one of the "put" procedures, but when you look at the file, you won't see your data. UTL_FILE.FFLUSH comes in handy when you want to read the contents of a file before you have closed that file. Typical scenarios include analyzing execution trace and debugging logs.

Exceptions. FFLUSH may raise any of the following exceptions:

```
UTL_FILE.INVALID_FILEHANDLE
UTL_FILE.INVALID_OPERATION
UTL_FILE.WRITE_ERROR
```

Closing Files

Use the FCLOSE and FCLOSE_ALL procedures in closing files.

The UTL_FILE.FCLOSE procedure

Use FCLOSE to close an open file. The header for this procedure is,

```
PROCEDURE UTL_FILE.FCLOSE (file IN OUT FILE_TYPE);
```

where file is the file handle.

Notice that the argument to UTL_FILE.FCLOSE is an IN OUT parameter, because the procedure sets the id field of the record to NULL after the file is closed.

If there is buffered data that has not yet been written to the file when you try to close it, UTL_FILE will raise the WRITE_ERROR exception.

Exceptions. FCLOSE may raise any of the following exceptions:

```
UTL_FILE.INVALID_FILEHANDLE
UTL_FILE.WRITE_ERROR
```

The UTL_FILE.FCLOSE_ALL procedure

FCLOSE_ALL closes all of the opened files. The header for this procedure follows:

```
PROCEDURE UTL_FILE.FCLOSE_ALL;
```

This procedure will come in handy when you have opened a variety of files and want to make sure that none of them are left open when your program terminates.

In programs in which files have been opened, you should also call FCLOSE_ALL in exception handlers in programs. If there is an abnormal termination of the program, files will then still be closed.

```
EXCEPTION
   WHEN OTHERS
```

```
THEN
     UTL_FILE.FCLOSE_ALL;
     ... other clean up activities ...
END;
```

NOTE   When you close your files with the FCLOSE_ALL procedure, none of
         your file handles will be marked as closed (the id field, in other
         words, will still be non-NULL). The result is that any calls to IS_
         OPEN for those file handles will *still* return TRUE. You will not,
         however, be able to perform any read or write operations on those
         files (unless you reopen them).

Exceptions. FCLOSE_ALL may raise the following exception:

```
UTL_FILE.WRITE_ERROR
```

Tips on Using UTL_FILE

This section contains a variety of tips on using UTL_FILE to its full potential.

Handling file I/O errors

You may encounter a number of difficulties (and therefore raise exceptions)
when working with operating system files. The good news is that Oracle has predefined a set of exceptions specific to the UTL_FILE package, such as UTL_
FILE.INVALID_FILEHANDLE. The bad news is that these are all "user-defined
exceptions," meaning that if you call SQLCODE to see what the error is, you get a
value of 1, regardless of the exception. And a call to SQLERRM returns the less-
than-useful string "User-Defined Exception."

To understand the problems this causes, consider the following program:

```
PROCEDURE file_action
IS
   fileID UTL_FILE.FILE_TYPE;
BEGIN
   fileID := UTL_FILE.FOPEN ('c:/tmp', 'lotsa.stf', 'R');
   UTL_FILE.PUT_LINE (fileID, 'just the beginning');
   UTL_FILE.FCLOSE (fileID);
END;
```

It is filled with errors, as you can see when I try to execute the program:

```
SQL> exec file_action
declare
*
ERROR at line 1:
ORA-06510: PL/SQL: unhandled user-defined exception
ORA-06512: at "SYS.UTL_FILE", line 91
```

```
ORA-06512: at "SYS.UTL_FILE", line 146
ORA-06512: at line 4
```

But what error or errors? Notice that the only information you get is that it was an
"unhandled user-defined exception"—even though Oracle defined the exception!

The bottom line is that if you want to get more information out of the UTL_FILE-
related errors in your code, you need to add exception handlers designed explicitly to trap UTL_FILE exceptions and *tell you* which one was raised. The following
template exception section offers that capability. It includes an exception handler
for each UTL_FILE exception. The handler writes out the name of the exception
and then reraises the exception.

```
/* Filename on companion disk: fileexc.sql */
EXCEPTION
    WHEN UTL_FILE.INVALID_PATH
    THEN
        DBMS_OUTPUT.PUT_LINE ('invalid_path'); RAISE;

    WHEN UTL_FILE.INVALID_MODE
    THEN
        DBMS_OUTPUT.PUT_LINE ('invalid_mode'); RAISE;

    WHEN UTL_FILE.INVALID_FILEHANDLE
    THEN
        DBMS_OUTPUT.PUT_LINE ('invalid_filehandle'); RAISE;

    WHEN UTL_FILE.INVALID_OPERATION
    THEN
        DBMS_OUTPUT.PUT_LINE ('invalid_operation'); RAISE;

    WHEN UTL_FILE.READ_ERROR
    THEN
        DBMS_OUTPUT.PUT_LINE ('read_error'); RAISE;

    WHEN UTL_FILE.WRITE_ERROR
    THEN
        DBMS_OUTPUT.PUT_LINE ('write_error'); RAISE;

    WHEN UTL_FILE.INTERNAL_ERROR
    THEN
        DBMS_OUTPUT.PUT_LINE ('internal_error'); RAISE;
END;
```

If I add this exception section to my file_action procedure, I get this message,

```
SQL> @temp
invalid_operation
declare
*
ERROR at line 1:
ORA-06510: PL/SQL: unhandled user-defined exception
```

which helps me realize that I am trying to write to a read-only file. So I change the file mode to "W" and try again, only to receive the same error again! Additional analysis reveals that my file location is not valid. It should be "C:\temp" instead of "C:/tmp". So why didn't I get a UTL_FILE.INVALID_PATH exception? Who is to say? With those two changes made, file_action then ran without error.

I suggest that whenever you work with UTL_FILE programs, you include either all or the relevant part of *fileexc.sql*. (See each program description earlier in this chapter to find out which exceptions each program might raise.) Of course, you might want to change my template. You may not want to reraise the exception. You may want to display other information. Change whatever you need to change—just remember the basic rule that if you don't handle the UTL_FILE exception by name in the block in which the error was raised, you won't be able to tell what went wrong.

Closing unclosed files

As a corollary to the last section on handling I/O errors, you must be very careful to close files when you are done working with them, or when errors occur in your program. If not, you may sometimes have to resort to UTL_FILE.FCLOSE_ALL to close *all* your files before you can get your programs to work properly.

Suppose you open a file (and get a handle to that file) and then your program hits an error and fails. Suppose further that you do *not* have an exception section, so the program simply fails. So let's say that you fix the bug and rerun the program. Now it fails with UTL_FILE.INVALID_OPERATION. The problem is that your file is still open—and you have lost the handle to the file, so you cannot explicitly close just that one file.

Instead, you must now issue this command (here, from SQL*Plus):

```
SQL> exec UTL_FILE.FCLOSE_ALL
```

With any luck, you won't close files that you wanted to be left open in your session. As a consequence, I recommend that you always include calls to UTL_FILE.FCLOSE in each of your exception sections to avoid the need to call FCLOSE_ALL and to minimize extraneous INVALID_OPERATION exceptions.

Here is the kind of exception section you should consider including in your programs. (I use the PLVexc.recNstop handler from PL/Vision as an example of a high-level program to handle exceptions, in this case requesting that the program "record and then stop.")

```
EXCEPTION
   WHEN OTHRES
   THEN
      UTL_FILE.FCLOSE (ini_fileID);
```

```
    UTL_FILE.FCLOSE (new_fileID);
    PLVexc.recNstop;
END;
```

In other words, I close the two files I've been working with, and then handle the exception.

Combining locations and filenames

I wonder if anyone else out there in the PL/SQL world finds UTL_FILE as frustrating as I do. I am happy that Oracle built the package, but I sure wish they'd given us more to work with. I am bothered by these things:

- The need to separate my filename from the location. Most of the time when I work with files, those two pieces are stuck together. With UTL_FILE, I have to split them apart.

- The lack of support for paths. It would be nice to not have to provide a file location and just let UTL_FILE *find* my file for me.

This section shows you how to enhance UTL_FILE to allow you to pass in a "combo" filename: location and name joined together, as we so often encounter them. The next section explains the steps for adding path support to your manipulation of files with UTL_FILE.

If you are going to specify your file specification (location and name) in one string, what is the minimum information needed in order to separate these two elements to pass to FOPEN? The delimiter used to separate directories from filenames. In DOS (and Windows) that delimiter is "\". In UNIX it is "/". In VAX/VMS it is "]". Seems to me that I just have to find the *last* occurrence of this delimiter in your string and that will tell me where to break apart the string.

So to allow you to get around splitting up your file specification in your call to FOPEN, I can do the following:

- Give you a way to tell me in advance the operating system delimiter for directories—and store that value for use in future attempts to open files.

- Offer you a substitute FOPEN procedure that uses that delimiter.

Since I want to store that value for your entire session, I will need a package. (You can also use a database table so that you do not have to specify this value each time you start up your application.) Here is the specification:

```
/* Filename on companion disk: onestring.spp */
CREATE OR REPLACE PACKAGE fileIO
IS
    PROCEDURE setsepchar (str IN VARCHAR2);
    FUNCTION sepchar RETURN VARCHAR2;

    FUNCTION open (file IN VARCHAR2, filemode IN VARCHAR2)
```

```
        RETURN UTL_FILE.FILE_TYPE;
   END;
   /
```

In other words, I set the separation character or delimiter with a call to fileIO.set-sepchar, and I can retrieve the current value with a call to the fileIO.sepchar function. Once I have that value, I can call fileIO.open to open a file without having to split apart the location and name. I show an example of this program in use here:

```
DECLARE
    fid UTL_FILE.FILE_TYPE;
BEGIN
    fileIO.setsepchar ('\');
    fid := fileio.open ('c:\temp\newone.txt', 'w'));
END;
/
```

The body of this package is quite straightforward:

```
CREATE OR REPLACE PACKAGE BODY fileIO
IS
    g_sepchar CHAR(1) := '/'; /* Unix is, after all, dominant. */

    PROCEDURE setsepchar (str IN VARCHAR2)
    IS
    BEGIN
        g_sepchar := NVL (str, '/');
    END;

    FUNCTION sepchar RETURN VARCHAR2
    IS
    BEGIN
        RETURN g_sepchar;
    END;

    FUNCTION open (file IN VARCHAR2, filemode IN VARCHAR2)
        RETURN UTL_FILE.FILE_TYPE
    IS
        v_loc PLS_INTEGER := INSTR (file, g_sepchar, -1);
        retval UTL_FILE.FILE_TYPE;
    BEGIN
        RETURN UTL_FILE.FOPEN
            (SUBSTR (file, 1, v_loc-1),
             SUBSTR (file, v_loc+1),
             filemode);
    END;
END;
/
```

Notice that when I call INSTR I pass −1 for the third argument. This negative value tells the built-in to scan from the end of string backwards to the *first* occurrence of the specified character.

Adding support for paths

Why should I have to provide the directory name for my file each time I call
FOPEN to read that file? It would be so much easier to specify a path, a list of possible directories, and then just let UTL_FILE scan the different directories in the
specified order until the file is found.

Even though the notion of a path is not built into UTL_FILE, it is easy to add this
feature. The structure of the implementation is very similar to the package built to
combine file locations and names. I will need a package to receive and store the
path, or list of directories. I will need an alternative open procedure that uses the
path instead of a provided location. Here is the package specification:

```
/* Filename on companion disk: filepath.spp */
CREATE OR REPLACE PACKAGE fileIO
IS
    c_delim CHAR(1) := ';';

    PROCEDURE setpath (str IN VARCHAR2);
    FUNCTION path RETURN VARCHAR2;

    FUNCTION open (file IN VARCHAR2, filemode IN VARCHAR2)
        RETURN UTL_FILE.FILE_TYPE;
END;
/
```

I define the path delimiter as a constant so that a user of the package can see
what he should use to separate different directories in his path. I provide a procedure to set the path and a function to get the path—but the variable containing
the path is hidden away in the package body to protect its integrity.

Before exploring the implementation of this package, let's see how you would
use these programs. The following test script sets a path with two directories and
then displays the first line of code in the file containing the previous package:

```
/* Filename on companion disk: filepath.tst */
DECLARE
    fID UTL_FILE.FILE_TYPE;
    v_line VARCHAR2(2000);
BEGIN
    fileio.setpath ('c:\temp;d:\oreilly\builtins\code');
    fID := fileIO.open ('filepath.spp');
    UTL_FILE.GET_LINE (fID, v_line);
    DBMS_OUTPUT.PUT_LINE (v_line);
    UTL_FILE.FCLOSE (fID);
END;
/
```

I include a trace message in the package (commented out on the companion
disk) so that we can watch the path-based open doing its work:

```
SQL> @filepath.tst
...looking in c:\temp
...looking in d:\oreilly\builtins\code
CREATE OR REPLACE PACKAGE fileIO
```

It's nice having programs do your work for you, isn't it? Here is the implementation of the fileIO package with path usage:

```
/* Filename on companion disk: filepath.spp */
CREATE OR REPLACE PACKAGE BODY fileIO
IS
   g_path VARCHAR2(2000);

   PROCEDURE setpath (str IN VARCHAR2)
   IS
   BEGIN
      g_path := str;
   END;


   FUNCTION path RETURN VARCHAR2
   IS
   BEGIN
      RETURN g_path;
   END;


   FUNCTION open (file IN VARCHAR2, filemode IN VARCHAR2)
      RETURN UTL_FILE.FILE_TYPE
   IS
      /* Location of next path separator */
      v_lastsep PLS_INTEGER := 1;
      v_sep PLS_INTEGER := INSTR (g_path, c_delim);
      v_dir VARCHAR2(500);
      retval UTL_FILE.FILE_TYPE;
   BEGIN
      /* For each directory in the path, attempt to open the file. */
      LOOP
         BEGIN
            IF v_sep = 0
            THEN
               v_dir := SUBSTR (g_path, v_lastsep);
            ELSE
               v_dir := SUBSTR (g_path, v_lastsep, v_sep - v_lastsep);
            END IF;
            retval := UTL_FILE.FOPEN (v_dir, file, 'R');
            EXIT;
         EXCEPTION
            WHEN OTHERS
            THEN
               IF v_sep = 0
               THEN
                  RAISE;
               ELSE
                  v_lastsep := v_sep + 1;
                  v_sep := INSTR (g_path, c_delim, v_sep+1);
```

```
            END IF;
         END;
      END LOOP;
      RETURN retval;
   END;
END;
/
```

The logic in this fileio.open is a little bit complicated, because I need to parse the semicolon-delimited list. The v_sep variable contains the location in the path of the next delimiter. The v_lastsep variable contains the location of the last delimiter. I have to include special handling for recognizing when I am at the last directory in the path (v_sep equals 0). Notice that I do not hard-code the semi-colon into this program. Instead, I reference the c_delim constant.

The most important implementation detail is that I place the call to FOPEN inside a *loop*. With each iteration of the loop body, I extract a directory from the path. Once I have the next directory to search, I call the FOPEN function to see if I can read the file. If I am able to do so successfully, I will reach the next line of code inside my loop, which is an EXIT statement: I am done and can leave. This drops me down to the RETURN statement to send back the handle to the file.

If I am unable to read the file in that directory, UTL_FILE raises an exception. Notice that I have placed the entire body of my loop inside its own anonymous block. This allows me to trap the open failure and process it. If I am on my last directory (no more delimiters, as in v_sep equals 0), I will simply reraise the exception from UTL_FILE. This will cause the loop to terminate, and then end the function execution as well. Since the fileIO.open does not have its own exception section, the error will be propagated out of the function unhandled. Even with a path, I was unable to locate the file. If, however, there are more directories, I set my start and end points for the next SUBSTR from the path and go back to the top of the loop so that FOPEN can try again.

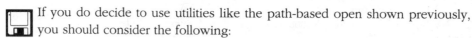 If you do decide to use utilities like the path-based open shown previously, you should consider the following:

- Combine the logic in *filepath.spp* with *onestring.spp* (a version of open that lets you pass the location and name in a single string). I should be able to *override* the path by providing a location; the version shown in this section assumes that the filename never has a location in it.

- Allow users to add a directory to the path without having to concatenate it to a string with a semicolon between them. Why not build a procedure called fileIO.adddir that does the work for the user and allows an application to modify the path at runtime?

You closed what?

You might run into some interesting behavior with the IS_OPEN function if you treat your file handles as variables. You are not likely to do this, but I did, so I thought I would pass on my findings to you.

In the following script, I define two file handles. I then open a file, assigning the handle record generated by FOPEN to fileID1. I immediately assign that record to fileID2. They now both have the same record contents. I then close the file by passing fileID2 to FCLOSE and check the status of the file afterwards. Finally, I assign a value of NULL to the id field of fileID1 and call IS_OPEN again.

```
DECLARE
   fileID1 UTL_FILE.FILE_TYPE;
   fileID2 UTL_FILE.FILE_TYPE;
BEGIN
   fileID1 := UTL_FILE.FOPEN ('c:\temp', 'newdata.txt', 'W');
   fileID2 := fileID1;
   UTL_FILE.FCLOSE (fileID2);

   IF UTL_FILE.IS_OPEN (fileid1)
   THEN
      DBMS_OUTPUT.PUT_LINE ('still open');
   END IF;

   fileid1.id := NULL;
   IF NOT UTL_FILE.IS_OPEN (fileid1)
   THEN
      DBMS_OUTPUT.PUT_LINE ('now closed');
   END IF;
END;
/
```

Let's run the script and check out the results:

```
SQL> @temp
still open
now closed
```

We can conclude from this test that the IS_OPEN function returns TRUE if the id field of a UTL_FILE.FILE_TYPE record is NULL. It doesn't check the status of the file with the operating system. It is a check totally internal to UTL_FILE.

This will not cause any problems as long as (a) you don't muck around with the id field of your file handle records and (b) you are consistent with your use of file handles. In other words, if you assign one file record to another, use that new record for all operations. Don't go back to using the original.

UTL_FILE Examples

So you've got a file (or a dozen files) out on disk, filled with all sorts of good information you want to access from your PL/SQL-based application. You will find yourself performing the same kinds of operations against those files over and over again.

After you work your way through this book, I hope that you will recognize almost without conscious thought that you do not want to repeatedly build the open, read, and close operations for each of these files, for each of the various recurring operations. Instead, you will instantly say to yourself, "Hot diggity! This is an opportunity to build a set of standard, generic modules that will help manage my files."

This section contains a few of my candidates for the first contributions to a UTL_ FILE toolbox of utilities. I recommend that you consider building a single package to contain all of these utilities.*

Enhancing UTL_FILE.GET_LINE

The GET_LINE procedure is simple and straightforward. It gets the next line from the file. If the pointer to the file is already located at the last line of the file, UTL_ FILE.GET_LINE does not return data, but instead raises the NO_DATA_FOUND exception. Whenever you write programs using GET_LINE, you will therefore need to handle this exception. Let's explore the different ways you can do this.

The following example uses a loop to read the contents of a file into a PL/SQL table (whose type definition, tabpkg.names_tabtype, has been declared previously):

```
/* Filename on companion disk: file2tab.sp */
CREATE OR REPLACE PACKAGE tabpkg
   IS
      TYPE names_tabtype IS TABLE OF VARCHAR2(100)
         INDEX BY BINARY_INTEGER;
   END;
/
CREATE OR REPLACE PROCEDURE file_to_table
      (loc_in IN VARCHAR2, file_in IN VARCHAR2,
       table_in IN OUT tabpkg.names_tabtype)
   IS
      /* Open file and get handle right in declaration */
      names_file UTL_FILE.FILE_TYPE := UTL_FILE.FOPEN (loc_in, file_in, 'R');
      /* Counter used to store the Nth name. */
      line_counter INTEGER := 1;
```

---

* You will find an example of such a package in Chapter 13 of *Advanced Oracle PL/SQL Programming with Packages.*

```
BEGIN
    LOOP
        UTL_FILE.GET_LINE (names_file, table_in(line_counter));
        line_counter := line_counter + 1;
    END LOOP;
EXCEPTION
    WHEN NO_DATA_FOUND
    THEN
        UTL_FILE.FCLOSE (names_file);
END;
/
```

The file_to_table procedure uses an infinite loop to read through the contents of the file. Notice that there is no EXIT statement within the loop to cause the loop to terminate. Instead I rely on the fact that the UTL_FILE package raises a NO_DATA_FOUND exception once it goes past the end-of-file marker and short-circuits the loop by transferring control to the exception section. The exception handler then traps that exception and closes the file.

I am not entirely comfortable with this approach. I don't like to code infinite loops without an EXIT statement; the termination condition is not structured into the loop itself. Furthermore, the end-of-file condition is not really an exception; every file, after all, must end at some point.

I believe that a better approach to handling the end-of-file condition is to build a layer of code around GET_LINE that immediately checks for end-of-file and returns a Boolean value (TRUE or FALSE). The get_nextline procedure shown here embodies this principle.

```
/* Filename on companion disk: getnext.sp */
PROCEDURE get_nextline
    (file_in IN UTL_FILE.FILE_TYPE,
     line_out OUT VARCHAR2,
     eof_out OUT BOOLEAN)
IS
BEGIN
    UTL_FILE.GET_LINE (file_in, line_out);
    eof_out := FALSE;
EXCEPTION
    WHEN NO_DATA_FOUND
    THEN
        line_out := NULL;
        eof_out  := TRUE;
END;
```

The get_nextline procedure accepts an already assigned file handle and returns two pieces of information: the line of text (if there is one) and a Boolean flag (set to TRUE if the end-of-file is reached, FALSE otherwise). Using get_nextline, I can now read through a file with a loop that has an EXIT statement.

My file_to_table procedure will look like the following after adding get_nextline:

```
/* Filename on companion disk: fil2tab2.sp */
PROCEDURE file_to_table
   (loc_in IN VARCHAR2, file_in IN VARCHAR2,
    table_in IN OUT names_tabtype)
IS
   /* Open file and get handle right in declaration */
   names_file CONSTANT UTL_FILE.FILE_TYPE :=
      UTL_FILE.FOPEN (loc_in, file_in, 'R');

   /* counter used to create the Nth name. */
   line_counter INTEGER := 1;

   end_of_file BOOLEAN := FALSE;
BEGIN
   WHILE NOT end_of_file
   LOOP
      get_nextline (names_file, table_in(line_counter), end_of_file);
      line_counter := line_counter + 1;
   END LOOP;
   UTL_FILE.FCLOSE (names_file);
END;
```

With get_nextline, I no longer treat end-of-file as an exception. I read a line from the file until I am done, and then I close the file and exit. This is, I believe, a more straightforward and easily understood program.

Creating a file

A common way to use files does not involve the contents of the file as much as a confirmation that the file does in fact exist. You can use the two modules defined next to create a file and then check to see if that file exists. Notice that when I create a file in this type of situation, I do not even bother to return the handle to the file. The purpose of the first program, create_file, is simply to make sure that a file with the specified name (and optional line of text) is out there on disk.

```
/* Filename on companion disk: crefile.sp */
PROCEDURE create_file
   (loc_in IN VARCHAR2, file_in IN VARCHAR2, line_in IN VARCHAR2 := NULL)
IS
   file_handle UTL_FILE.FILE_TYPE;
BEGIN
   /*
   || Open the file, write a single line and close the file.
   */
   file_handle := UTL_FILE.FOPEN (loc_in, file_in, 'W');
   IF line_in IS NOT NULL
   THEN
      UTL_FILE.PUT_LINE (file_handle, line_in);
   ELSE
      UTL_FILE.PUT_LINE
```

```
                (file_handle, 'I make my disk light blink, therefore I am.');
      END IF;
      UTL_FILE.FCLOSE (file_handle);
   END;
```

Testing for a file's existence

The second program checks to see if a file exists. Notice that it creates a local procedure to handle the close logic (which is called both in the body of the function and in the exception section).

```
/* Filename on companon disk: filexist.sf */
CCREATE OR REPLACE FUNCTION file_exists
    (loc_in IN VARCHAR2,
     file_in IN VARCHAR2,
     close_in IN BOOLEAN := FALSE)
    RETURN BOOLEAN
IS
    file_handle UTL_FILE.FILE_TYPE;
    retval BOOLEAN;

    PROCEDURE closeif IS
    BEGIN
       IF close_in AND UTL_FILE.IS_OPEN (file_handle)
       THEN
           UTL_FILE.FCLOSE (file_handle);
       END IF;
    END;
BEGIN
    /* Open the file. */
    file_handle := UTL_FILE.FOPEN (loc_in, file_in, 'R');

    /* Return the result of a check with IS_OPEN. */
    retval := UTL_FILE.IS_OPEN (file_handle);

    closeif;

    RETURN retval;
EXCEPTION
    WHEN OTHERS
    THEN
        closeif;
        RETURN FALSE;
 END;
 /
```

Searching a file for a string

Because I found the INSTR function to be so useful, I figured that this same kind of operation would also really come in handy with operating system files. The line_with_text function coming up shortly returns the line number in a file containing the specified text. The simplest version of such a function would have a specification like this:

```
FUNCTION line_with_text
    (loc_in IN VARCHAR2, file_in IN VARCHAR2, text_in IN VARCHAR2)
RETURN INTEGER
```

In other words, given a location, a filename, and a chunk of text, find the first line in the file that contains the text. You could call this function as follows:

```
IF line_with_text ('h:\pers', 'names.vp', 'Hanubi') > 0
THEN
    MESSAGE ('Josephine Hanubi is a vice president!');
END IF;
```

The problem with this version of line_with_text is its total lack of vision. What if I want to find the second occurrence in the file? What if I need to start my search from the tenth line? What if I want to perform a case-insensitive search? None of these variations are supported.

I urge you strongly to think through all the different ways a utility like line_with_text might be used before you build it. Don't just build for today's requirement. Anticipate what you will need tomorrow and next week as well.

For line_with_text, a broader vision would yield a specification like this:

```
FUNCTION line_with_text
    (loc_in IN VARCHAR2,
     file_in IN VARCHAR2,
     text_in IN VARCHAR2,
     occurrence_in IN INTEGER := 1,
     start_line_in IN INTEGER := 1,
     end_line_in IN INTEGER := 0,
     ignore_case_in IN BOOLEAN := TRUE)
RETURN INTEGER
```

Wow! That's a lot more parameter passing. Let's take a look at the kind of flexibility we gain from these additional arguments. First, the following table provides a description of each parameter.

Parameter	Description
loc_in	The location of the file on the operating system
file_in	The name of the file to be opened
text_in	The chunk of text to be searched for in each line of the file
occurrence_in	The number of times the text should be found in distinct lines in the file before the function returns the line number
srart_line_in	The first line in the file from which the function should start its search

Parameter	Description
end_line_in	The last line in the file to which the function should continue its search; if zero, then search through end of file
ignore_case_in	Indicates whether the case of the file contents and text_in should be ignored when checking for its presence in the line

Notice that all the new parameters, occurrence_in through ignore_case_in, have default values, so I can call this function in precisely the same way and with the same results as the first, limited version:

```
IF line_with_text ('names.vp', 'Hanubi') > 0
THEN
    MESSAGE ('Josephine Hanubi is a vice president!');
END IF;
```

Now, however, I can also do so much more:

- Confirm that the role assigned to this user is SUPERVISOR:

    ```
    line_with_text ('c:\temp', 'config.usr', 'ROLE=SUPERVISOR')
    ```

- Find the second occurrence of DELETE starting with the fifth line:

    ```
    line_with_text ('/tmp', 'commands.dat', 'delete', 2, 5)
    ```

- Verify that the third line contains a terminal type specification:

    ```
    line_with_text ('g:\apps\user\', 'setup.cfg', 'termtype=', 1, 3, 3)
    ```

Here is the code for the line_with_text function:

```
/* Filename on companion disk: linetext.sf */
CREATE OR REPLACE FUNCTION line_with_text
    (loc_in IN VARCHAR2,
     file_in IN VARCHAR2,
     text_in IN VARCHAR2,
     occurrence_in IN INTEGER := 1,
     start_line_in IN INTEGER := 1,
     end_line_in IN INTEGER := 0,
     ignore_case_in IN BOOLEAN := TRUE)
RETURN INTEGER
/*
|| An "INSTR" for operating system files. Returns the line number of
|| a file in which a text string was found.
*/
IS
    /* Handle to the file. Only will open if arguments are valid. */
    file_handle UTL_FILE.FILE_TYPE;

    /* Holds a line of text from the file. */
    line_of_text VARCHAR2(1000);

    text_loc INTEGER;
    found_count INTEGER := 0;

    /* Boolean to determine if there are more values to read */
```

```
      no_more_lines BOOLEAN := FALSE;

   /* Function return value */
   return_value INTEGER := 0;
BEGIN
   /* Assert valid arguments. If any fail, return NULL. */
   IF loc_in IS NULL OR
      file_in IS NULL OR
      text_in IS NULL OR
      occurrence_in <= 0 OR
      start_line_in < 1 OR
      end_line_in < 0
   THEN
      return_value := NULL;
   ELSE
      /* All arguments are fine. Open and read through the file. */
      file_handle := UTL_FILE.FOPEN (loc_in, file_in, 'R');
      LOOP
         /* Get next line and exit if at end of file. */
         get_nextline (file_handle, line_of_text, no_more_lines);
         EXIT WHEN no_more_lines;

         /* Have another line from file. */
         return_value := return_value + 1;

         /* If this line is between the search range... */
         IF (return_value BETWEEN start_line_in AND end_line_in) OR
            (return_value >= start_line_in AND end_line_in = 0)
         THEN
            /* Use INSTR to see if text is present. */
            IF NOT ignore_case_in
            THEN
               text_loc := INSTR (line_of_text, text_in);
            ELSE
               text_loc := INSTR (UPPER (line_of_text), UPPER (text_in));
            END IF;

            /* If text location is positive, have a match. */
            IF text_loc > 0
            THEN
               /* Increment found counter. Exit if matches request. */
               found_count := found_count + 1;
               EXIT WHEN found_count = occurrence_in;
            END IF;
         END IF;
      END LOOP;
      UTL_FILE.FCLOSE (file_handle);
   END IF;

   IF no_more_lines
   THEN
      /* read through whole file without success. */
      return_value := NULL;
```

```
      END IF;

      RETURN return_value;
   END;
```

Getting the nth line from a file

What if you want to get a specific line from a file? The following function takes a filename and a line number and returns the text found on that line:

```
/* Filename on companion disk: nthline.sf */
CREATE OR REPLACE FUNCTION get_nth_line
   (loc_in IN VARCHAR2, file_in IN VARCHAR2, line_num_in IN INTEGER)
IS
   /* Handle to the file. Only will open if arguments are valid. */
   file_handle UTL_FILE.FILE_TYPE;

   /* Count of lines read from the file. */
   line_count INTEGER := 0;

   /* Boolean to determine if there are more values to read */
   no_more_lines BOOLEAN := FALSE;

   /* Function return value */
   return_value VARCHAR2(1000) := NULL;
BEGIN
   /* Need a file name and a positive line number. */
   IF file_in IS NOT NULL AND line_num_in > 0
   THEN
      /* All arguments are fine. Open and read through the file. */
      file_handle := UTL_FILE.FOPEN (loc_in, file_in, 'R');
      LOOP
         /* Get next line from file. */
         get_nextline (file_handle, return_value, no_more_lines);

         /* Done if no more lines or if at the requested line. */
         EXIT WHEN no_more_lines OR line_count = line_num_in - 1;

         /* Otherwise, increment counter and read another line. */
         line_count := line_count + 1;
      END LOOP;
      UTL_FILE.FCLOSE (file_handle);
   END IF;

   /* Either NULL or contains last line read from file. */
   RETURN return_value;
END;
```

7

Defining an Application Profile

The DBMS_APPLICATION_INFO package provides procedures that allow applications to "register" their current execution status with the Oracle database. Once registered, information about the status of an application can be monitored externally through several of the V$ virtual tables.

DBMS_APPLICATION_INFO is used to develop applications that can be monitored in various ways, including the following:

- Module usage (where do users spend their time in the application?)
- Resource accounting by transaction and module
- End-user tracking and resource accounting in three-tier architectures
- Incremental recording of long-running process statistics

When applications register themselves using DBMS_APPLICATION_INFO, DBAs and developers are able to analyze their performance and resource consumption much more closely. This facilitates better application tuning and enables more accurate usage-based cost accounting.

WARNING   Oracle explicitly warns that DBMS_APPLICATION_INFO should not be used in Trusted Oracle databases.

Getting Started with DBMS_ APPLICATION_INFO

In Oracle 7.3, the DBMS_APPLICATION_INFO package is created when the Oracle database is installed. The *dbmsutil.sql* script found in the built-in packages source code directory (as described in Chapter 1, *Introduction*) contains the source code for this package's specification. In Oracle 8.0, the script *dbmsapin.sql* (also found in the source code directory) creates the package. In either case, the scripts are called by *catproc.sql*, which is normally run immediately after database creation. The script creates the public synonym DBMS_APPLICATION_INFO for the package and grants EXECUTE privilege on the package to public. All Oracle users can reference and make use of this package.

DBMS_APPLICATION_INFO Programs

Table 7-1 lists the programs available from DBMS_APPLICATION_INFO.

Table 7-1. DBMS_APPLICATION_INFO Programs

Name	Description	Use in SQL?
READ_CLIENT_INFO	Reads client information for session	No
READ_MODULE	Reads module and action for current session	No
SET_ACTION	Sets action within module	No
SET_CLIENT_INFO	Sets client information for session	No
SET_MODULE	Sets name of module executing	No
SET_SESSION_LONGOPS	Sets row in LONGOPS table (Oracle 8.0 only)	No

DBMS_APPLICATION_INFO does not declare any exceptions.

The V$ Virtual Tables

Most of the programs in DBMS_APPLICATION_INFO modify the V$ virtual tables to register application status. Table 7-2 lists the V$ tables and columns that each program modifies.

Table 7-2. V$ Tables and Columns Modified by DBMS_APPLICATION_INFO

Program	V$ Table.Column
SET_ACTION	V$SESSION.ACTION V$SQLAREA.ACTION
SET_CLIENT_INFO	V$SESSION.CLIENT_INFO
SET_MODULE	V$SESSION.MODULE V$SQLAREA.MODULE V$SESSION.ACTION V$SQLAREA.ACTION

Table 7-2. V$ Tables and Columns Modified by DBMS_APPLICATION_INFO (continued)

Program	V$ Table.Column
SET_SESSION_LONGOPS	V$SESSION_LONGOPS.CONTEXT
	V$SESSION_LONGOPS.STEPID
	V$SESSION_LONGOPS.STEPSOFAR
	V$SESSION_LONGOPS.STEPTOTAL
	V$SESSION_LONGOPS.SOFAR
	V$SESSION_LONGOPS.TOTALWORK
	V$SESSION_LONGOPS.APPLICATION_DATA_1
	V$SESSION_LONGOPS.APPLICATION_DATA_2
	V$SESSION_LONGOPS.APPLICATION_DATA_3

DBMS_APPLICATION_INFO Nonprogram Elements

The DBMS_APPLICATION_INFO package contains a single constant: set_session_longops_nohint. This constant is defined like this:

```
set_session_longops_nohint CONSTANT BINARY_INTEGER := -1;
```

This constant is used as a special value for the hint parameter of the SET_SESSION_LONGOPS procedure. When this value is passed, a new row in the V$SESSION_LONGOPS virtual table is acquired for tracking long operations. (See the example in the section, "The DBMS_APPLICATION_INFO.SET_SESSION_LONGOPS procedure.")

DBMS_APPLICATION_INFO Interface

This section describes all the programs available in the DBMS_APPLICATION_INFO package.

The DBMS_APPLICATION_INFO.READ_CLIENT_INFO procedure

The READ_CLIENT_INFO procedure returns the currently registered client information for the session. The program header is,

```
PROCEDURE DBMS_APPLICATION_INFO.READ_CLIENT_INFO
    (client_info OUT VARCHAR2);
```

where the client_info parameter contains the client information currently registered in V$SESSION.

The program does not raise any exceptions, nor does it assert a purity level with the RESTRICT_REFERENCES pragma.

Example. The following function calls DBMS_APPLICATION_INFO.READ_CLIENT_ INFO and returns the client information. This function is part of the register_app package discussed in "DBMS_APPLICATION_INFO Examples" later in this chapter.

```
FUNCTION current_client_info RETURN VARCHAR2
IS
    /*
    || calls DBMS_APPLICATION_INFO.READ_CLIENT_INFO
    || and returns the client info
    */
temp_client_info VARCHAR2(64);

BEGIN
    SYS.DBMS_APPLICATION_INFO.READ_CLIENT_INFO
        (temp_client_info);

    RETURN temp_client_info;
END current_client_info;
```

In this example, I have fully qualified the package name with the package owner (SYS), insuring that the SYS version of the package is called. This is not normally necessary, as there is (usually) a public synonym pointing to SYS.DBMS_ APPLICATION_INFO. The reason for using a fully qualified reference in this specific case is discussed in "Covering DBMS_APPLICATION_INFO."

The DBMS_APPLICATION_INFO.READ_MODULE procedure

The READ_MODULE procedure returns the currently registered module and action names for the session. Here's the program header:

```
PROCEDURE DBMS_APPLICATION_INFO.READ_MODULE
    (module_name OUT VARCHAR2
    ,action_name OUT VARCHAR2);
```

Parameters are summarized in the following table.

Parameter	Description
module_name	Name of the module currently registered in V$SESSION
action_name	Name of the action currently registered in V$SESSION

The READ_MODULE procedure does not raise any exceptions, nor does it assert a purity level with the RESTRICT_REFERENCES pragma.

Example. The following function calls DBMS_APPLICATION_INFO.READ_MOD- ULE and returns the value of the current action. This function is part of the register_app package discussed in "DBMS_APPLICATION_INFO Examples."

```
FUNCTION current_action RETURN VARCHAR2
IS
    /*
```

```
   || calls DBMS_APPLICATION_INFO.READ_MODULE
   || and returns the action name
   */
   temp_module_name VARCHAR2(64);
   temp_action_name VARCHAR2(64);

BEGIN
   SYS.DBMS_APPLICATION_INFO.READ_MODULE
      (temp_module_name, temp_action_name);

   RETURN temp_action_name;
END current_action;
```

See the section "Covering DBMS_APPLICATION_INFO" for an explanation of why the procedure call is qualified by SYS, the package owner's name.

The DBMS_APPLICATION_INFO.SET_ACTION procedure

The SET_ACTION procedure is used to set, or register, the current transaction or logical unit of work currently executing within the module. The registered action name appears in the ACTION column of the V$SESSION and V$SQLAREA virtual tables. The program header is,

```
PROCEDURE DBMS_APPLICATION_INFO.SET_ACTION
   (action_name IN VARCHAR2);
```

where the action_name parameter provides the name of the action to register into V$SESSION.

The SET_ACTION procedure does not raise any exceptions.

Restrictions. Note the following restrictions on calling SET_ACTION:

- The action_name parameter is limited to 32 bytes. Longer values will be truncated to this maximum size.

- The program does not assert a purity level with the RESTRICT_REFERENCES pragma.

Example. The following procedure could be part of an application that maintains corporate departmental information:

```
/* Filename on companion disk: apinex1.sql  */
CREATE OR REPLACE PROCEDURE drop_dept
   (deptno_IN IN NUMBER
   ,reassign_deptno_IN IN NUMBER)
IS
   temp_emp_count  NUMBER;
BEGIN
   DBMS_APPLICATION_INFO.SET_MODULE
      (module_name => 'DEPARTMENT FIXES'
```

```
        ,action_name => null);

    -- first check dept for employees

    DBMS_APPLICATION_INFO.SET_ACTION
        (action_name => 'CHECK EMP');

    SELECT COUNT(*)
      INTO temp_emp_count
      FROM emp
     WHERE deptno = deptno_IN;

    -- reassign any employees

    IF temp_emp_count >0
    THEN
        DBMS_APPLICATION_INFO.SET_ACTION
            (action_name => 'REASSIGN EMPLOYEES');

        UPDATE emp
           SET deptno = reassign_deptno_IN
         WHERE deptno = deptno_IN;
    END IF;

    -- OK, now drop the department

    DBMS_APPLICATION_INFO.SET_ACTION
        (action_name => 'DROP DEPT');

    DELETE FROM dept WHERE deptno = deptno_IN;

    COMMIT;

    DBMS_APPLICATION_INFO.SET_MODULE(null,null);

EXCEPTION
    WHEN OTHERS THEN
        DBMS_APPLICATION_INFO.SET_MODULE(null,null);
END drop_dept;
```

Notice in this example that DBMS_APPLICATION_INFO is called three times to distinguish between the three steps involved in the process of dropping the department. This gives a very fine granularity to the level at which the application can be tracked.

Recommendations for usage. Note the following recommendations for using the SET_ACTION procedure:

- Set the action name to a name that can identify the current transaction or logical unit of work within the module.

- When the transaction terminates, call SET_ACTION and pass a NULL value for the action_name parameter. In case subsequent transactions do not register using DBMS_APPLICATION_INFO, passing the NULL value ensures that they are not incorrectly counted as part of the current action. As in the example, if the program handles exceptions, the exception handler should reset the action information.

The DBMS_APPLICATION_INFO.SET_CLIENT_INFO procedure

The SET_CLIENT_INFO procedure is used to set, or register, additional client information about the user session. The registered client information appears in the CLIENT_INFO column of the V$SESSION virtual table. The header for this program is,

```
PROCEDURE DBMS_APPLICATION_INFO.SET_CLIENT_INFO
    (client_info IN VARCHAR2);
```

where the client_info parameter specifies the client information to register into V$SESSION.

The program does not raise any exceptions.

Restrictions. Note the following restrictions on calling SET_CLIENT_INFO:

- The client_info parameter is limited to 64 bytes. Longer values will be truncated to this maximum size.

- The program does not assert a purity level with the RESTRICT_REFERENCES pragma.

Example. The following procedure could be utilized by an application in which all sessions connect to a common Oracle username and security is handled within the application. This would allow the DBA to externally distinguish between user sessions in V$SESSION by examining the CLIENT_INFO column.

```
/* Filename on companion disk: apinex1.sql  */
CREATE OR REPLACE PROCEDURE set_user(app_user_IN IN VARCHAR2)
IS
BEGIN
    DBMS_APPLICATION_INFO.SET_CLIENT_INFO(app_user_IN);
END set_user;
```

Suppose that users JOE SMITH and SALLY DALLY log into the application, which connects to Oracle as the user OPBIP. If the application calls the set_user procedure at login, we can distinguish between the database sessions for Joe and Sally in V$SESSION as follows:

```
SQL> SELECT sid, username, client_info
  2    FROM v$session
```

```
3   WHERE username='OPBIP';

    SID USERNAME    CLIENT_INFO
--------- ---------- --------------------
     14 OPBIP       JOE SMITH
     24 OPBIP       SALLY DALLY
```

The DBMS_APPLICATION_INFO.SET_MODULE procedure

The SET_MODULE procedure is used to set, or register, a name for the program that the user is currently executing and, optionally, an action name for the current transaction within the program. Registered module and action names appear in the MODULE and ACTION columns of the V$SESSION and V$SQLAREA virtual tables. Here's the header for this procedure:

```
PROCEDURE DBMS_APPLICATION_INFO.SET_MODULE
    (module_name IN VARCHAR2
    ,action_name IN VARCHAR2);
```

Parameters are summarized in the following table.

Parameter	Description
module_name	Name of the module to register into V$SESSION
action_name	Name of the action to register into V$SESSION

The SET_MODULE procedure does not raise any exceptions.

Restrictions. Note the following restrictions on calling SET_MODULE:

- The module_name parameter is limited to 48 bytes, and action_name is limited to 32 bytes. Longer values for either parameter will be truncated to their respective maximum sizes.

- The program does not assert a purity level with the RESTRICT_REFERENCES pragma.

Example. The following procedure could be part of an application that maintains employee data:

```
/* Filename on companion disk: apinex1.sql  */
CREATE OR REPLACE PROCEDURE award_bonus
    (empno_IN IN NUMBER
    ,pct_IN IN NUMBER)
IS
BEGIN
    DBMS_APPLICATION_INFO.SET_MODULE
        (module_name => 'EMPLOYEE UPDATE'
        ,action_name => 'AWARD BONUS');

    UPDATE emp
```

```
        SET sal = sal*(1+pct_IN/100)
    WHERE empno = empno_IN;

    COMMIT;

    DBMS_APPLICATION_INFO.SET_MODULE(null,null);
EXCEPTION
    WHEN OTHERS THEN
        DBMS_APPLICATION_INFO.SET_MODULE(null,null);
END award_bonus;
```

Oracle recommends that the module name correspond to a recognizable name for the program or logical application unit that is currently executing. Examples Oracle provides include the name of the form executing in a Forms application and the name of a SQL script executing under SQL*Plus.

Recommendations for usage. Note the following recommendations for using the SET_MODULE procedure:

- Set the action name to one that can identify the current transaction or logical unit of work within the module.

- When the module terminates, call the SET_MODULE procedure and pass in NULL values for both parameters. In the event that subsequent transactions and programs do not register using DBMS_APPLICATION_INFO, they won't be incorrectly counted as part of the current module. As in the example, if the program handles exceptions, the exception handler should reset the module and action information.

The DBMS_APPLICATION_INFO.SET_SESSION_LONGOPS procedure

The SET_SESSION_LONGOPS procedure is used to track the progress of long-running operations by allowing the entry and modification of data in the V$SESSION_LONGOPS virtual table. Here's the header for the program:

```
PROCEDURE DBMS_APPLICATION_INFO.SET_SESSION_LONGOPS
        (hint IN OUT BINARY_INTEGER
        ,context IN NUMBER DEFAULT 0
        ,stepid IN NUMBER DEFAULT 0
        ,stepsofar IN NUMBER DEFAULT 0
        ,steptotal IN NUMBER DEFAULT 0
        ,sofar IN NUMBER DEFAULT 0
        ,totalwork IN NUMBER DEFAULT 0
        ,application_data_1 IN NUMBER DEFAULT 0
        ,application_data_2 IN NUMBER DEFAULT 0
        ,application_data_3 IN NUMBER DEFAULT 0);
```

The parameters are summarized in the following table.

Parameter	Description
hint	Token representing the row to update
context	Any number representing the context
stepid	Any number representing the stepid
stepsofar	Any number
steptotal	Any number
sofar	Any number
totalwork	Any number
application_data_1	Any number
application_data_2	Any number
application_data_3	Any number

The program does not raise any exceptions, nor does it assert a purity level with the RESTRICT_REFERENCES pragma.

Example. The following script loops 1000 times and sets values in the V$SESSION_ LONGOPS table as follows:

- The totalwork value is set to 1000.

- The sofar column is incremented for every iteration.

- The stepsofar column is incremented every 100 iterations.

```
/* Filename on companion disk: apinex2.sql  */
DECLARE
    longops_row BINARY_INTEGER:=
        DBMS_APPLICATION_INFO.set_session_longops_nohint;
    step_number  NUMBER:=0;
BEGIN
    -- get new row in V$SESSION_LONGOPS
    DBMS_APPLICATION_INFO.SET_SESSION_LONGOPS
        (hint => longops_row);

    -- Do operation 1000 times and record
    FOR i IN 1..1000
    LOOP
        DBMS_APPLICATION_INFO.SET_SESSION_LONGOPS
            (hint => longops_row
            ,sofar => i
            ,totalwork => 1000
            ,stepsofar => step_number);

        -- increment step every 100 iterations
        IF MOD(i,100) = 0
        THEN
            step_number := i/100;
```

```
        END IF;
    END LOOP;
END;
/
```

After executing the previous PL/SQL block, the following SQL shows the results recorded in V$SESSION_LONGOPS. Notice that the COMPNAM column has been updated by Oracle to indicate that DBMS_APPLICATION_INFO was used to set the row. Also notice that Oracle sets rows in V$SESSION_LONGOPS for internal operations like table scans, and sorts.

```
SELECT sid
     , compnam
     , stepsofar
     , sofar
     , totalwork
  FROM v$session_longops
 WHERE sid = my_session.sid;
```

SID	COMPNAM	STEPSOFAR	SOFAR	TOTALWORK
16	Table Scan	0	0	1
16	Sort Progression	0	1	1
16	dbms_application_info	9	1000	1000

3 rows selected.

Each session is allocated a maximum of four rows in the V$SESSION_LONGOPS virtual table for tracking long operations. Rows are identified by the combination of context and stepid. If calls to DBMS_APPLICATION_INFO.SET_SESSION_LON-GOPS are made with more than four distinct combinations of context and stepid, rows will be re-used in least-recently-used order.

All of the parameters except hint correspond directly to like-named columns in the V$SESSION_LONGOPS virtual table. While there are no restrictions on values stored in these columns, Oracle makes the following suggestions as a way of organizing information about the progress of long running operations:

stepsofar
> If the long-running operation consists of distinct individual steps, the amount of work which has been done so far for this step.

steptotal
> If the long-running operation consists of distinct individual steps, the total amount of work expected to be done in this step.

sofar
> The amount of work that has been done so far.

totalwork

The total amount of work expected to be done in this long-running operation.

application_data_1, application_data_2, application_data_3

Any numbers the client wishes to store.

Also note that all parameters to SET_SESSION_LONGOPS (except hint) default to zero. This means that calls to the procedure need not specify values for all parameters, which is convenient in the case of such a long parameter list. However, it also means that any unspecified parameters in a call to SET_SESSION_LONGOPS will have their corresponding columns in V$SESSION_LONGOPS set to zero for that row after the call, which may not be the desired behavior.

DBMS_APPLICATION_INFO Examples

Oracle suggests that one way to extend DBMS_APPLICATION_INFO is to capture session performance statistics as part of the process of registering modules and actions. To demonstrate how this might be done, I have created a package called register_app.

About the register_app Package

The programs in register_app are very similar to those in DBMS_APPLICATION_INFO. Here is the package specification:

```
/* Filename on companion disk: register.sql */
CREATE OR REPLACE PACKAGE register_app
IS
   /*
   || Enhances DBMS_APPLICATION_INFO by capturing performance
   || statistics when module, action, or client_info are set.
   ||
   || Statistics may be displayed in SQL*Plus for tracking and
   || debugging purposes.  A useful enhancement would be to
   || extend this idea to a logging feature, so stats are logged
   || to a table for analysis.
   ||
   || Also enforces requirement that a module be registered before
   || an action can be registered.
   ||
   || Author:  John Beresniewicz, Savant Corp
   || Created: 09/01/97
   ||
   || Compilation Requirements:
   ||
   || SELECT on SYS.V_$MYSTAT
   || SELECT on SYS.V_$STATNAME
   ||
   || Execution Requirements:
```

```
    ||
    ||
    */

    /* registers the application module */
    PROCEDURE module
       (module_name_IN IN VARCHAR2
       ,action_name_IN IN VARCHAR2 DEFAULT 'BEGIN');

    /* registers the action within module */
    PROCEDURE action(action_name_IN IN VARCHAR2);

    /* registers additional application client information */
    PROCEDURE client_info(client_info_IN IN VARCHAR2);

    /* returns the currently registered module */
    FUNCTION current_module RETURN VARCHAR2;

    /* returns the currently registered action */
    FUNCTION current_action RETURN VARCHAR2;

    /* returns the currently registered client info */
    FUNCTION current_client_info RETURN VARCHAR2;

    /* sets stat display for SQL*Plus ON (TRUE) or OFF (FALSE) */
    PROCEDURE set_display_TF(display_ON_TF_IN IN BOOLEAN);

  END register_app;
```

The module, action, and client_info programs of register_app correspond directly
to the SET_MODULE, SET_ACTION, and SET_CLIENT_INFO programs of DBMS_
APPLICATION_INFO; indeed, each of these programs eventually calls its counterpart. The difference is that the programs in register_app first collect session performance information and store it in a private package global record, before calling
the appropriate DBMS_APPLICATION_INFO program.

The action Procedure

Here is the body of the action procedure:

```
/* Filename on companion disk: register.sql */
PROCEDURE action(action_name_IN IN VARCHAR2)
IS
BEGIN
   /*
   || raise error if trying to register an action when module
   || has not been registered
   */
   IF current_module IS NULL AND action_name_IN IS NOT NULL
   THEN
      RAISE_APPLICATION_ERROR(-20001, 'Module not registered');
   ELSE
```

```
      set_stats;
      SYS.DBMS_APPLICATION_INFO.SET_ACTION(action_name_IN);
   END IF;

END action;
```

Note that the action procedure is written to enforce the rule that an action can be registered only if a module has previously been registered. The action procedure also calls a procedure called set_stats. This procedure is private to the package, and does the work of collecting and saving resource statistics whenever new module, action, or client information is registered.

The set_stats Procedure

The set_stats procedure loads session performance information into a private global record named stat_rec. Here are the definitions of stat_rec and the PL/SQL record type on which it is based:

```
/* record type to hold performance stats */
TYPE stat_rectype IS RECORD
   (timer_hsecs   NUMBER := 0
   ,logical_rds   NUMBER := 0
   ,physical_rds  NUMBER := 0
   );
/* private global to hold stats at begin of each module/action */
stat_rec stat_rectype;
```

Now let's take a look at the set_stats procedure:

```
/* Filename on companion disk: register.sql
|| Gets current performance stats from V$MYSTAT and
|| sets the global record stat_rec.  If display_TF_ is TRUE
|| then uses DBMS_OUTPUT to display the stat differences
|| since last call to set_stats.
*/
PROCEDURE set_stats
IS

   temp_statrec   stat_rectype;
   diff_statrec   stat_rectype;

   /*
   || Embedded inline function to retrieve stats by name
   || from V$MYSTAT.
   */
   FUNCTION get_stat(statname_IN IN VARCHAR2)
      RETURN NUMBER
   IS
      /* return value -9999 indicates problem */
      temp_stat_value  NUMBER := -9999;

      /* cursor retrieves stat value by name */
      CURSOR stat_val_cur(statname VARCHAR2)
```

```
   IS
      SELECT value
         FROM sys.v_$mystat      S
             ,sys.v_$statname    N
      WHERE
             S.statistic# = N.statistic#
         AND N.name = statname;

   BEGIN
      OPEN stat_val_cur(statname_IN);
      FETCH stat_val_cur INTO temp_stat_value;
      CLOSE stat_val_cur;
      RETURN temp_stat_value;

   EXCEPTION
      WHEN OTHERS THEN
         IF stat_val_cur%ISOPEN
         THEN
            CLOSE stat_val_cur;
         END IF;
         RETURN temp_stat_value;
   END get_stat;

BEGIN
   /*
   || load current values for performance statistics
   */
   temp_statrec.timer_hsecs := DBMS_UTILITY.GET_TIME;
   temp_statrec.logical_rds := get_stat('session logical reads');
   temp_statrec.physical_rds := get_stat('physical reads');

   /*
   || calculate diffs between current and previous stats
   */
   diff_statrec.timer_hsecs :=
           temp_statrec.timer_hsecs - stat_rec.timer_hsecs;
   diff_statrec.logical_rds :=
           temp_statrec.logical_rds - stat_rec.logical_rds;
   diff_statrec.physical_rds :=
           temp_statrec.physical_rds - stat_rec.physical_rds;

   /*
   || Both current module AND client info NULL indicates
   || initialization for session and stats should not be displayed.
   */
   IF display_TF AND
      (current_module IS NOT NULL OR current_client_info IS NOT NULL)
   THEN
      DBMS_OUTPUT.PUT_LINE('Module: '||current_module);
      DBMS_OUTPUT.PUT_LINE('Action: '||current_action);
      DBMS_OUTPUT.PUT_LINE('Client Info: '||current_client_info);
      DBMS_OUTPUT.PUT_LINE('Stats:  '||
         'elapsed secs:'||
                 TO_CHAR(ROUND(diff_statrec.timer_hsecs/100,2))||
```

```
                    ', physical reads: '||TO_CHAR(diff_statrec.physical_rds)||
                    ', logical reads: '||TO_CHAR(diff_statrec.logical_rds)
                   );

        END IF;

        /* OK, now initialize stat_rec to current values */
        stat_rec := temp_statrec;

    END set_stats;
```

The set_stats procedure logic is relatively straightforward:

1. Current values for the session performance statistics are gathered and the previous values (stored in the private global record stat_rec) are subtracted from them. These differences represent the changes in statistics since the last call to set_stats and are held in the record diff_statrec. Note that this works even for the initial call to set_stats because the declaration of stat_rectype assigns a default value of zero to all fields. Thus, on the first call, stat_rec will be initialized with zeros and diff_statrec will contain the current statistics.

2. The difference performance statistics are displayed using DBMS_OUTPUT if the display flag is set and this is not the first call to register application information.

3. Current values of the session performance statistics are saved in stat_rec for the next call to set_stats.

Exercise for the reader: Enhance the register_app package to log module and action performance statistics to a table for resource accounting. Be sure to allow for tracking by username and session.

The Information Procedures

The register_app package also contains three functions that return the currently registered information for the session. These functions invoke the DBMS_APPLICATION_INFO procedures READ_MODULE and READ_CLIENT_INFO and return the respective information. Procedures that return data in OUT parameters can often be encapsulated usefully with functions in this way. This promotes more terse and readable code, as illustrated by the following code excerpts from the register_app package:

```
    /* Filename on companion disk: register.sql */
    /* returns the currently registered module */
    FUNCTION current_module RETURN VARCHAR2;

    /* returns the currently registered client info */
    FUNCTION current_client_info RETURN VARCHAR2;

    PROCEDURE set_stats
```

```
IS
...
IF display_TF AND
        (current_module IS NOT NULL OR current_client_info IS NOT NULL)
THEN
...
END set_stats;
```

Using the register_app Package

The following SQL*Plus script demonstrates how the register_app package can be used to register each step of a multistep batch process. The script displays the resource utilization statistics that have been collected for each step. While the script is executing, DBAs can monitor which step is currently running by querying V$SESSION for the session executing the script.

```
/* Filename on companion disk: regtest.sql  */
rem ========================================================
rem REGTEST.SQL
rem
rem  SQL*Plus script to demonstrate the use of package
rem  REGISTER_APP for tracking performance statistics
rem
rem ========================================================

set serveroutput on size 100000

set feedback off
rem ========================================================
rem   register module first with display OFF to
rem   initialize stats, then set display ON
rem ========================================================
execute register_app.set_display_TF(FALSE);
execute register_app.module('REGTEST.SQL');
execute register_app.set_display_TF(TRUE);

set feedback on

rem ========================================================
rem   create a table my_dictionary copied from dictionary
rem ========================================================
execute register_app.action('CREATE');

CREATE TABLE my_dictionary
    (id, table_name, comments)
TABLESPACE user_data2
AS
    SELECT rownum,A.*
      FROM dictionary A;

rem ========================================================
rem   update one third of my_dictionary rows
rem ========================================================
```

```
execute register_app.action('UPDATE');

UPDATE my_dictionary
   SET comments = RPAD(comments,2000,'*')
 WHERE MOD(id,3) = 0;

rem =====================================================
rem  delete one third of my_dictionary rows
rem =====================================================
execute register_app.action('DELETE');

DELETE FROM my_dictionary
 WHERE MOD(id,3) = 1;

rem =====================================================
rem  drop table my_dictionary
rem =====================================================
execute register_app.action('DROP');

DROP TABLE my_dictionary;

rem =====================================================
rem  unregister and display previous step stats
rem =====================================================
execute register_app.module(null,null);
```

Here is sample output generated by the script:

```
SQL> @regtest
Module: REGTEST.SQL
Action: BEGIN
Client Info:
Stats: elapsed secs: .15, physical reads: 0, logical reads: 0

PL/SQL procedure successfully completed.

Table created.

Module: REGTEST.SQL
Action: CREATE
Client Info:
Stats: elapsed secs: 15.93, physical reads: 137, logical reads: 8407

PL/SQL procedure successfully completed.

92 rows updated.

Module: REGTEST.SQL
Action: UPDATE
Client Info:
Stats: elapsed secs: 9.32, physical reads: 8, logical reads: 2075

PL/SQL procedure successfully completed.

93 rows deleted.
```

```
Module: REGTEST.SQL
Action: DELETE
Client Info:
Stats: elapsed secs: .6, physical reads: 0, logical reads: 296

PL/SQL procedure successfully completed.


Table dropped.

Module: REGTEST.SQL
Action: DROP
Client Info:
Stats: elapsed secs: 5.36, physical reads: 35, logical reads: 356

PL/SQL procedure successfully completed.
```

Covering DBMS_APPLICATION_INFO

Oracle suggests in the DBMS_APPLICATION_INFO package documentation that DBAs may want to develop a cover package called DBMS_APPLICATION_INFO in a schema other than SYS. By redirecting the public synonym DBMS_APPLICATION_INFO to point at this version of the package, any programs referencing DBMS_APPLICATION_INFO programs will use the new package. Any functional extensions to DBMS_APPLICATION_INFO in the cover package will be immediately picked up by programs using DBMS_APPLICATION_INFO. In this way, resource tracking like that demonstrated by the register_app package can be implemented globally for programs using DBMS_APPLICATION_INFO.

Instead of directly covering DBMS_APPLICATION_INFO with a package of the same name, I chose to create the register_app package. One reason for this: I prefer the shorter and more meaningful name register_app. New applications can call register_app directly and avoid the painfully long DBMS_APPLICATION_INFO package name. Another reason was that I wanted to extend the functionality of DBMS_APPLICATION_INFO with new programs, and thus the new package would not look identical to DBMS_APPLICATION_INFO. When covering an Oracle built-in package, it is good practice to create a package with an identical specification (or API) to that of the built-in.

We can actually cover DBMS_APPLICATION_INFO with a package that calls the register_app programs. In this way, the functionality of register_app is extended to programs that reference DBMS_APPLICATION_INFO directly, and we still have our new package to use for new programs.

The following code shows how DBMS_APPLICATION_INFO.SET_MODULE can be covered in this way:

```
CREATE OR REPLACE PACKAGE BODY DBMS_APPLICATION_INFO
IS
PROCEDURE set_module
    (module_name IN VARCHAR2
    ,action_name IN VARCHAR2)
IS
    register_app.module(module_name, action_name);
END set_module;
```

Notice that the SET_MODULE cover procedure is identical in signature to the program of the same name in the SYS version of the DBMS_APPLICATION_INFO package.

Q: Why must the cover package for DBMS_APPLICATION_INFO match all program signatures identically, including parameter names?

A: The program signatures in the cover package to DBMS_APPLICATION_INFO must match those in the SYS version of the package because existing calls to DBMS_APPLICATION_INFO could otherwise be compromised. It is necessary to match not only the number of parameters and their datatypes and modes (IN or OUT) but also the parameter names. The parameter names must match in order to preserve functionality in existing programs calling DBMS_APPLICATION_INFO using named notation. The following fragment illustrates code that will not work if the cover package does not preserve parameter names in the signature for the SET_MODULE procedure:

```
DECLARE
    module_var  VARCHAR2(64) := 'Program 1';
    action_var  VARCHAR2(64) := 'Transaction A';
BEGIN
    DBMS_APPLICATION_INFO.SET_MODULE
        (module_name=>module_var
        ,action=>action_var);
END;
```

Q: What necessary precaution was taken in the register_app package to ensure that it could be used as part of a cover package for DBMS_APPLICATION_INFO?

A: All calls to DBMS_APPLICATION_INFO in the register_app package are fully qualified with the schema name (SYS). This way, when the public synonym DBMS_APPLICATION_INFO is redirected to point at the cover package, an infinite loop is avoided and the SYS version of the package is ultimately called.

Exercise for the reader: Create the full cover package for DBMS_APPLICATION_INFO using the register_app package.

Monitoring Application SQL Resource Consumption

When applications make use of DBMS_APPLICATION_INFO to register themselves, DBAs can monitor application usage and resource consumption through
the V$SESSION and V$SQLAREA virtual tables. The following is a simple report
summarizing SQL resource consumption data by application module and action.
Such reports can serve a number of useful purposes, including the following:

- Identifying tuning opportunities

- Quantifying utilization levels by application component

- Implementing chargeback schemes

```
/* Filename on companion disk: sqlarea.sql  */
rem ======================================================
rem SQLAREA.SQL
rem Simple report from V$SQLAREA on SQL resource
rem utilization by module and action
rem ======================================================

col module format a15
col action format a15

SELECT  module
       ,action
       ,SUM(buffer_gets) buffer_gets
       ,SUM(rows_processed) rows_processed
       ,SUM(disk_reads) disk_reads
   FROM sys.v_$sqlarea
  WHERE module IS NOT NULL
    AND action IS NOT NULL
GROUP BY module, action;
```

The following output was generated by the script after *regtest.sql* had been executed several times:

```
SQL> @sqlarea

MODULE          ACTION          BUFFER_GETS ROWS_PROCESSED DISK_READS
--------------- --------------- ----------- -------------- ----------
REGTEST.SQL     BEGIN                     0              7          0
REGTEST.SQL     CREATE                    0              7          0
REGTEST.SQL     DELETE                 1014            313          0
REGTEST.SQL     DROP                      0              7          0
REGTEST.SQL     UPDATE                 6721            308         33

5 rows selected.
```

Session Monitoring and Three-Tier Architectures

While writing this section on DBMS_APPLICATION_INFO, I had occasion to recommend the use of this package to help solve two real-world issues that came to

my attention. In one case, an application had been written to call DBMS_SES-SION.SET_SQL_TRACE and thus turn SQL tracing on for a session running the application.* The DBA wanted to know which sessions were being traced at any given time. I suggested the use of DBMS_APPLICATION_INFO.SET_CLIENT_INFO to put a message into the V$SESSION table indicating a tracing session. The procedure to set tracing could look something like this:

```
PROCEDURE set_trace (on_TF IN BOOLEAN)
IS
BEGIN
   IF on_TF
      THEN
         DBMS_APPLICATION_INFO.SET_CLIENT_INFO('TRACE ON');
      ELSE
         DBMS_APPLICATION_INFO.SET_CLIENT_INFO('');
   END IF;

   DBMS_SESSION.SET_SQL_TRACE(on_TF);
END set_trace;
```

In the second example, I was discussing with another DBA the difficult issue of tracking down specific users in the following types of applications:

- Three-tier applications like Oracle WebServer where users do not connect to Oracle directly, but through proxy connections held by the application server.

- Applications where all users connect to Oracle under a common username, and security and user-differentiation are maintained entirely within the application at runtime.

Both of these architectures make it difficult for the DBA to correlate specific end users with the database sessions they are currently using. In the first case, sessions are persistent and serve different users at different times—and sometimes no user at all. In the second case, all user sessions connect to a common username and thus are indistinguishable (by username) in V$SESSION. Interestingly enough, these are both perfect opportunities to use DBMS_APPLICATION_INFO.SET_CLIENT_INFO. When users connect to the application, call a procedure like the set_user procedure in the example for DBMS_APPLICATION_INFO.SET_CLIENT_INFO. A better version of set_user would call register_app.client_info to enable performance statistics tracking for the application users.

Tracking Long-Running Processes

The SET_SESSION_LONGOPS procedure is an interesting addition to DBMS_APPLICATION_INFO first found in the Oracle8 version of the package. Oracle documentation makes it clear that the intended use of the procedure is to enable

---

* Coding applications with the ability to set SQL tracing on and off is very good practice, as it can greatly assist in the detection of post-deployment runtime performance problems.

external tracking of the progress of long-duration operations through the new virtual table, V$SESSION_LONGOPS. However, I found SET_SESSION_LONGOPS rather nonintuitive and unwieldy to use.

One difficult concept is the reuse of the four rows in V$SESSION_LONGOPS based on unique combinations of context and stepid, and how this relates to the hint parameter, which is used to identify the row to modify. Context and stepid do not have to be unique among the rows in V$SESSION_LONGOPS, but setting a new context/stepid combination will always cause acquisition of a new row. Because multiple rows can be identical in context/stepid, they do not really form a key (along with the session SID) to the virtual table. The hint parameter to DBMS_APPLICATION_INFO.SET_SESSION_LONGOPS seems to be the only way to identify which row is currently being set, but there is no column in V$SESSION_ LONGOPS corresponding to the hint. Thus it is actually impossible to externally identify with accuracy the row modified by the last call to the procedure. This defeated my efforts to write a READ_SESSION_LONGOPS procedure that takes a hint value in and reports the values for the row identified by that hint value.

Another usability issue with SET_SESSION_LONGOPS is that any values not set in the procedure call will be set to zero. Thus, if you want to increment different counter columns at different times in an application (for the same row in V$SESSION_LONGOPS), you must keep track of all counter values and pass them all in each time the procedure is called. Adding to the cumbersome nature of the long parameter list are the extremely long names of the package and procedure themselves. You really have to want, or, as is more likely, *need* to call SET_ SESSION_LONGOPS in order to use it!

These usability issues seemed to provide an opportunity to improve ease-of-use through encapsulation. I decided to build a package called longops to offer some relief. Here is the package specification for longops:

```
/* Filename on companion disk: longops.sql */
CREATE OR REPLACE PACKAGE longops
IS
   /*
   || Enhances DBMS_APPLICATION_INFO.SET_SESSION_LONGOPS
   || by allowing individual columns to be updated without
   || passing all parameter values.
   ||
   || Author:  John Beresniewicz, Savant Corp
   || Created: 09/08/97
   ||
   || Compilation Requirements:
   || SELECT on SYS.V_$SESSION_LONGOPS
   ||
   || Execution Requirements:
   ||
   ||
```

```
*/

/* returns a new V$SESSION_LONGOPS row index */
FUNCTION new_row RETURN BINARY_INTEGER;

/* returns the last row index used */
FUNCTION current_row RETURN BINARY_INTEGER;

/* makes a new row the current row */
PROCEDURE set_current_row
    (row_idx_IN IN BINARY_INTEGER);

/*
|| Covers DBMS_APPLICATION_INFO.SET_SESSION_LONGOPS
*/
PROCEDURE set_row
    (hint_IN IN BINARY_INTEGER
    ,context_IN IN NUMBER DEFAULT 0
    ,stepid_IN IN NUMBER DEFAULT 0
    ,stepsofar_IN IN NUMBER DEFAULT 0
    ,steptotal_IN IN NUMBER DEFAULT 0
    ,sofar_IN IN NUMBER DEFAULT 0
    ,totalwork_IN IN NUMBER DEFAULT 0
    ,appdata1_IN IN NUMBER DEFAULT 0
    ,appdata2_IN IN NUMBER DEFAULT 0
    ,appdata3_IN IN NUMBER DEFAULT 0);

/*
|| Updates a single row in V$SESSION_LONGOPS
|| preserving values in columns corresponding
|| to parameters passed as NULL.
*/
PROCEDURE update_row
    (hint_IN IN BINARY_INTEGER DEFAULT current_row
    ,context_IN IN NUMBER DEFAULT NULL
    ,stepid_IN IN NUMBER DEFAULT NULL
    ,stepsofar_IN IN NUMBER DEFAULT NULL
    ,steptotal_IN IN NUMBER DEFAULT NULL
    ,sofar_IN IN NUMBER DEFAULT NULL
    ,totalwork_IN IN NUMBER DEFAULT NULL
    ,appdata1_IN IN NUMBER DEFAULT NULL
    ,appdata2_IN IN NUMBER DEFAULT NULL
    ,appdata3_IN IN NUMBER DEFAULT NULL);

END longops;
```

The real key to the package is the update_row procedure. This procedure allows the user to update individual columns in V$SESSION_LONGOPS for a given row without zeroing out the other columns. It does this by keeping a copy of the V$SESSION_LONGOPS rows that have been modified in a private PL/SQL table called my_longops_tab. Here is the definition of my_longops_tab:

```
TYPE longops_tabtype IS TABLE OF sys.v_$session_longops%ROWTYPE
    INDEX BY BINARY_INTEGER;
my_longops_tab longops_tabtype;
```

The current_row function and set_current_row procedure are used to maintain a context of which row is currently being modified. The presumption is that most users of SET_SESSION_LONGOPS will concentrate on a single row in V$SESSION_LONGOPS at a time. The set_row procedure covers SET_SESSION_LONGOPS but additionally saves the data to my_longops_tab.

The body of the update_row procedure looks like this:

```
PROCEDURE update_row
        (hint_IN IN BINARY_INTEGER DEFAULT current_row
        ,context_IN IN NUMBER DEFAULT NULL
        ,stepid_IN IN NUMBER DEFAULT NULL
        ,stepsofar_IN IN NUMBER DEFAULT NULL
        ,steptotal_IN IN NUMBER DEFAULT NULL
        ,sofar_IN IN NUMBER DEFAULT NULL
        ,totalwork_IN IN NUMBER DEFAULT NULL
        ,appdata1_IN IN NUMBER DEFAULT NULL
        ,appdata2_IN IN NUMBER DEFAULT NULL
        ,appdata3_IN IN NUMBER DEFAULT NULL)
    IS
        temp_hint_IN BINARY_INTEGER := hint_IN;
    BEGIN
        /*
        || First update saved row in my_longops_tab, any
        || parameters which are NULL will not change the
        || saved row.
        */
        my_longops_tab(hint_IN).context := NVL(context_IN,
                my_longops_tab(hint_IN).context);
        my_longops_tab(hint_IN).stepid := NVL(stepid_IN,
                my_longops_tab(hint_IN).stepid);
        my_longops_tab(hint_IN).stepsofar := NVL(stepsofar_IN,
                my_longops_tab(hint_IN).stepsofar);
        my_longops_tab(hint_IN).steptotal := NVL(steptotal_IN,
                my_longops_tab(hint_IN).steptotal);
        my_longops_tab(hint_IN).sofar := NVL(sofar_IN,
                my_longops_tab(hint_IN).sofar);
        my_longops_tab(hint_IN).totalwork := NVL(totalwork_IN,
                my_longops_tab(hint_IN).totalwork);
        my_longops_tab(hint_IN).application_data_1 := NVL(appdata1_IN,
                my_longops_tab(hint_IN).application_data_1);
        my_longops_tab(hint_IN).application_data_2 := NVL(appdata2_IN,
                my_longops_tab(hint_IN).application_data_2);
        my_longops_tab(hint_IN).application_data_3 := NVL(appdata3_IN,
                my_longops_tab(hint_IN).application_data_3);

        /*
        || Now call DBMS_APPLICATION_INFO.SET_SESSION_LONGOPS
        || passing all parameters from the row in my_longops_tab.
        */
        DBMS_APPLICATION_INFO.SET_SESSION_LONGOPS
            (hint=>temp_hint_IN
            ,context=>my_longops_tab(hint_IN).context
```

```
        ,stepid=>my_longops_tab(hint_IN).stepid
        ,stepsofar=>my_longops_tab(hint_IN).stepsofar
        ,steptotal=>my_longops_tab(hint_IN).steptotal
        ,sofar=>my_longops_tab(hint_IN).sofar
        ,totalwork=>my_longops_tab(hint_IN).totalwork
        ,application_data_1=>
                my_longops_tab(hint_IN).application_data_1
        ,application_data_2=>
                my_longops_tab(hint_IN).application_data_2
        ,application_data_3=>
                my_longops_tab(hint_IN).application_data_3
        );

    /* set the current row */
    set_current_row(hint_IN);

  END update_row;
```

The update_row procedure is pretty straightforward. One subtlety is that the hint_IN parameter defaults to the function current_row. This allows us to call update_row without even passing in a row identifier as long as we want to modify the same row as last time. Using the longops package, the example for DBMS_APPLICATION_INFO.SET_SESSION_LONGOPS can be rewritten as follows:

```
/* Filename on companion disk: apinex3.sql  */
BEGIN
    -- get new row in V$SESSION_LONGOPS and set totalwork
    longops.set_row(longops.new_row,totalwork_IN=>1000);

    -- Do operation 1000 times and record
    FOR i IN 1..1000
    LOOP
        -- update sofar each time
        longops.update_row(sofar_IN=>i);

        -- update stepsofar every 100 iterations
        IF MOD(i,100) = 0
        THEN
            longops.update_row(stepsofar_IN=>i/100);
        END IF;
    END LOOP;
END;
```

This code is much more readable than the earlier example. The calls are shorter in length, yet easier to understand. Overall readability is also improved by being able to update columns individually and not being forced to overload each call with a long list of saved parameter values.

8

In this chapter:
- *Getting Started with
  DBMS_LOB*
- *LOB Concepts*
- *DBMS_LOB Interface*

Managing Large
Objects

Oracle8 and PL/SQL8 support the storage and manipulation of large objects (a.k.a. LOBs). A LOB, which can be a column in a table or an attribute of an object type, may store up to four gigabytes of data, such as character text, graphic images, video, or "raw" data. The DBMS_LOB package (new to Oracle8) provides a set of procedures and functions to access and manipulate LOBs from within PL/SQL programs.

You can also manipulate LOBs from within SQL; refer to the Oracle documentation for these SQL-specific aspects of LOB management.

Getting Started with DBMS_LOB

The DBMS_LOB package is created when the Oracle8 database is installed. The *dbmslob.sql* script (found in the built-in packages source directory, as described in Chapter 1, *Introduction*) contains the source code for this package's specification. This script is called by *catproc.sql*, which is normally run immediately after database creation. The script creates the public synonym DBMS_LOB for the package and grants EXECUTE privilege on the package to public. All Oracle users can reference and make use of this package.

DBMS_LOB Programs

Table 8-1 summarizes the programs available in DBMS_LOB.

Table 8-1. DBMS_LOB Programs

Name	Description	Use in SQL
APPEND	Appends the contents of a source internal LOB to a destination internal LOB	No
COMPARE	Compares two LOBs of the same type; parts of LOBs can also be compared	Yes
COPY	Copies all or part of the contents of a source internal LOB to a destination internal LOB	No
ERASE	Erases all or part of an internal LOB	No
FILECLOSE	Closes an open BFILE	No
FILECLOSEALL	Closes all open BFILEs	No
FILEEXISTS	Checks if a given file exists	Yes
FILEGETNAME	Returns directory alias and file-name of given file locator	No
FILEOPEN	Opens a BFILE for read-only access	No
FILEISOPEN	Determines if a BFILE was opened with the given file locator	Yes
GETLENGTH	Returns the length of the input LOB; length is in bytes for BFILEs and BLOBs; length is in characters for CLOBs and NCLOBs	Yes
INSTR	Returns matching offset location in the input LOB of the Nth occurrence of a given pattern	Yes
LOADFROMFILE	Loads all or part of external LOB to internal LOB	No
READ	Provides piece-wise read access to a LOB	No
SUBSTR	Provides piece-wise read access to a LOB	Yes
TRIM	Trims the contents of an internal LOB to the length specified by the newlen parameter	No
WRITE	Writes a given number of bytes or characters to an internal LOB at a specified offset	No

Table 8-2 shows which LOB types you can manipulate with the individual DBMS_ LOB programs. For an explanation of these LOB types, see the section "LOB Concepts" later in this chapter.

Table 8-2. DBMS_LOB Programs Can Manipulate These LOB Types

Program	BFILE	BLOB	CLOB	NCLOB
APPEND		X	X	X
COMPARE	X	X	X	X
COPY		X	X	X
ERASE		X	X	X
FILECLOSE	X			
FILECLOSEALL	X			
FILEEXISTS	X			
FILEGETNAME	X			
FILEISOPEN	X			
FILEOPEN	X			
GETLENGTH	X	X	X	X
INSTR	X	X	X	X
LOADFROMFILE	X	X	X	X
READ	X	X	X	X
SUBSTR	X	X	X	X
TRIM		X	X	X
WRITE		X	X	X

DBMS_LOB Exceptions

Table 8-3 summarizes the exceptions declared by DBMS_LOB.

Table 8-3. DBMS_LOB Exceptions

Exception	SQLCODE	Cause
INVALID_ARGVAL	–21560	DBMS_LOB expects a valid argument to be passed, but the argument was NULL or invalid. Example: FILEOPEN is passed an invalid open mode. Example: a positional or size argument is outside of the range 1 through (4 gigabytes–1).
ACCESS_ERROR	–22925	An attempt to read or write beyond maximum LOB size has occurred.
NOEXIST_DIRECTORY	–22285	The directory specified does not exist in the data dictionary.

Table 8-3. DBMS_LOB Exceptions (continued)

Exception	SQLCODE	Cause
NOPRIV_DIRECTORY	−22286	The user does not have the required privileges on either the specified directory object or the specified file.
INVALID_DIRECTORY	−22287	The directory specified is not valid or has been modified by the database administrator since the last access.
OPERATION_FAILED	−22288	An operation attempted on a file failed.
UNOPENED_FILE	−22289	An operation was performed on a file that was not open.
OPEN_TOOMANY	−22290	The maximum number of open files has been reached. This maximum is set via the SESSION_MAX_OPEN_FILES database initialization parameter. The maximum applies to many kinds of files, not only BFILES; for example, it applies to files opened using the UTL_FILE package.

DBMS_LOB Nonprogram Elements

Table 8-4 summarizes the constants declared by the DBMS_LOB package.

Table 8-4. DBMS_LOB Constants

Element Name	Type	Value
FILE_READONLY	CONSTANT BINARY_INTEGER	Zero. Mode used to open files.
LOBMAXSIZE	CONSTANT INTEGER	4,294,967,295 (4 gigabytes–1). Positional and size arguments cannot exceed this value.

About the Examples

This chapter contains many examples of DBMS_LOB usage. For my examples, I use tables called my_book_files and my_book_text, which contain (or point to) large volumes of text for a book. The structures of these tables follow:

```
/* Filename on companion disk: lobtabs.sql */
CREATE TABLE my_book_files (
    file_descr VARCHAR2(100),
    book_file BFILE);

CREATE TABLE my_book_text (
    chapter_descr VARCHAR2(100),
    chapter_text CLOB);
```

Often, I'll query one of the fields from the table for a given chapter (chapter_
desc) value. To avoid repetition of code, here are the implementations of functions that will be used throughout the examples:

```
/* Filename on companion disk: lobfuncs.sql */
CREATE OR REPLACE FUNCTION book_file (chapter_in IN VARCHAR2)
   RETURN CLOB
IS
   CURSOR book_cur
   IS
      SELECT chapter_file
        FROM my_book_files
       WHERE file_descr = chapter_in;
   book_rec book_cur%ROWTYPE;
BEGIN
   OPEN book_cur;
   FETCH book_cur INTO book_rec;
   CLOSE book_cur;
   RETURN book_rec.chapter_file;
END;
/
CREATE OR REPLACE FUNCTION book_text (chapter_in IN VARCHAR2)
   RETURN CLOB
IS
   CURSOR book_cur
   IS
      SELECT chapter_text
        FROM my_book_text
       WHERE chapter_descr = chapter_in;
   book_rec book_cur%ROWTYPE;
BEGIN
   OPEN book_cur;
   FETCH book_cur INTO book_rec;
   CLOSE book_cur;
   RETURN book_rec.chapter_text;
END;
/
CREATE OR REPLACE FUNCTION book_text_forupdate (chapter_in IN VARCHAR2)
   RETURN CLOB
IS
   CURSOR book_cur
   IS
      SELECT chapter_text
        FROM my_book_text
       WHERE chapter_descr = chapter_in
         FOR UPDATE;
   book_rec book_cur%ROWTYPE;
BEGIN
   OPEN book_cur;
   FETCH book_cur INTO book_rec;
   CLOSE book_cur;
   RETURN book_rec.chapter_text;
END;
/
```

In several of the examples, I'll compare before and after "images" of LOB content using the following procedure:

```
CREATE OR REPLACE PROCEDURE compare_text (descr IN VARCHAR2)
IS
BEGIN
   SELECT chapter_descr, chapter_text
     FROM my_book_text
    WHERE chapter_descr = descr;
   ROLLBACK;

   DBMS_OUTPUT.PUT_LINE ('Rollback completed');

   SELECT chapter_descr, chapter_text
     FROM my_book_text
    WHERE chapter_descr = descr;
END;
/
```

TIP   It's a good practice to include exception handlers in any program working with LOBs to trap and deal with LOB-related errors. Not all of the programs and anonymous blocks shown in this chapter include exception handlers, but that is done only to reduce overall code volume.

LOB Concepts

This section describes some basic LOB concepts you'll need to understand when you work with large objects.

LOB Datatypes

Oracle8 provides four LOB datatypes:

BFILE

Large binary objects stored in operating system files outside of the database; for example, a bitmap image file.

BLOB

Large objects consisting of unstructured binary data.

CLOB

Large objects consisting of single-byte fixed-width character data.

NCLOB

Large binary objects consisting of single-byte or multiple-byte fixed-width character data.

Internal and external LOBs

There are two categories of LOBs, depending upon their location with respect to the physical database:

- *Internal LOBs* (of datatypes BLOB, CLOB, and NCLOB) are stored in the database and can participate in transactions. Changes to internal LOB values can be rolled back or committed. A cursor can select an internal LOB FOR UPDATE. Uncommitted changes to an internal LOB are not seen by a separate session.

- *External LOBs* (of datatype BFILE) are stored outside of the database in operating system files and cannot participate in transactions. Instead, the underlying operating system provides the data integrity. Access to external LOBs is read-only.

The BFILE datatype

The BFILE datatype is used to store large binary objects (up to four gigabytes) in files outside of the database.

A BFILE could be a PL/SQL variable,

```
DECLARE
    my_book_file BFILE;
```

or a column in a table,

```
CREATE TABLE my_book_files
    ( file_descr VARCHAR2(40),  book_file BFILE  );
```

or an attribute in a TYPE,

```
CREATE OR REPLACE PACKAGE blobby
IS
    TYPE adpage_rectype IS RECORD (
        customer_id NUMBER,
        persuasive_picture BFILE
        ),
```

or a parameter/RETURN type in a PL/SQL procedure or function:

```
CREATE OR REPLACE FUNCTION blended_image (
    old_image IN BFILE, new_image IN BFILE)
    RETURN BFILE
IS
BEGIN
    ...
END;
```

In each case, the BFILE value points to an operating-system file residing on the server and outside of the database.

The BLOB datatype

The BLOB datatype is used to store large binary objects within the database; the objects can be up to four gigabytes and may consist of unstructured raw data. A BLOB could be a PL/SQL variable,

```
DECLARE
    corporate_logo BLOB;
```

or a column in a table,

```
CREATE TABLE my_book_diagrams
    ( chapter_descr VARCHAR2(40),
      diagram_no INTEGER,
      diagram BLOB );
```

or an attribute in a TYPE,

```
CREATE OR REPLACE PACKAGE chapter
IS
    TYPE diagram_rectype IS RECORD (
        chapter_num NUMBER,
        diagram BLOB
        ),
```

or a parameter/RETURN type in a PL/SQL procedure or function:

```
CREATE OR REPLACE PROCEDURE show_blob (
    blob_in IN BLOB)
IS
BEGIN
    ...
END;
```

A BLOB is an internal LOB, and therefore can participate in database transactions. In other words, changes made to a BLOB can be rolled back or committed along with other changes during a transaction. BLOBs cannot span transactions.

The CLOB datatype

The CLOB datatype is used to store large blocks within the database. The blocks can be up to four gigabytes of single-byte character data. A CLOB could be a PL/SQL variable,

```
DECLARE
    gettysburg_address_text   CLOB;
```

or a column in a table,

```
CREATE TABLE my_book_text
    ( chapter_descr VARCHAR2(40), chapter_text CLOB );
```

or an attribute in a TYPE,

```
CREATE OR REPLACE PACKAGE speechifying
```

```
IS
    TYPE poll_results_rectype IS RECORD (
        speech_num NUMBER,
        speech_txt CLOB
        ),
```

or a parameter/RETURN type in a PL/SQL procedure or function:

```
CREATE OR REPLACE PROCEDURE edit_speech  (
    text_in IN CLOB)
IS
BEGIN
    ...
END;
```

A CLOB is an internal LOB and therefore can participate in database transactions. In other words, changes made to a CLOB can be rolled back or committed along with other changes during a transaction. CLOBs cannot span transactions, and do not support variable-width character sets.

The NCLOB datatype

The NCLOB datatype is used to store large blocks within the database. The blocks can be up to four gigabytes of single-byte or multiple-byte fixed-width character data. A NCLOB could be a PL/SQL variable,

```
DECLARE
    gettysburg_address_in_japanese NCLOB;
```

or a column in a table:

```
CREATE TABLE my_book_in_japanese
    ( chapter_no INTEGER,
        chapter_in_japanese NCLOB );
```

You may also use the NCLOB datatype in the parameter of a PL/SQL program or the RETURN type for a function. However, you may not use NCLOB as the datatype of an attribute in a TYPE statement.

A NCLOB is an internal LOB, and therefore can participate in database transactions. In other words, changes made to a NCLOB can be rolled back or committed along with other changes during a transaction. NCLOBs cannot span transactions, and do not support variable-width character sets.

The LOB locator

The value held in a LOB column or variable is not the actual binary data, but a "locator" or pointer to the physical location of the large object.

For internal LOBs, since one LOB value can be up to four gigabytes in size, the binary data will be stored "out of line" (i.e., physically separate) from the other column values of a row (unless otherwise specified; see the next paragraph). This allows the physical size of an individual row to be minimized for improved performance (the LOB column contains only a pointer to the large object). Operations involving multiple rows, such as full table scans, can be performed more efficiently.

A user can specify that the LOB value be stored in the row itself. This is usually done when working with small LOB values. This approach decreases the time needed to obtain the LOB value. However, the LOB data is migrated out of the row when it gets too big.

For external LOBs, the BFILE value represents a filename and an operating system directory, which is also a pointer to the location of the large object.

BFILE Considerations

There are some special considerations you should be aware of when you work with BFILEs.

The DIRECTORY object

A BFILE locator consists of a directory alias and a filename. The directory alias is an Oracle8 database object that allows references to operating system directories without hard-coding directory pathnames. This statement creates a directory:

```
CREATE DIRECTORY IMAGES AS 'c:\images';
```

To refer to the *c:\images* directory within SQL, you can use the IMAGES alias, rather than hard-coding the actual directory pathname.

To create a directory, you need the CREATE DIRECTORY or CREATE ANY DIRECTORY privilege. To reference a directory, you must be granted the READ privilege, as in:

```
GRANT READ ON DIRECTORY IMAGES TO SCOTT;
```

Populating a BFILE locator

The Oracle8 built-in function BFILENAME can be used to populate a BFILE locator. BFILENAME is passed a directory alias and filename and returns a locator to the file. In the following block, the BFILE variable corporate_logo is assigned a locator for the file named *ourlogo.bmp* located in the IMAGES directory:

```
DECLARE
   corporate_logo     BFILE;
BEGIN
   corporate_logo := BFILENAME ( 'IMAGES', 'ourlogo.bmp' );
END;
```

The following statements populate the my_book_files table; each row is associated with a file in the BOOK_TEXT directory:

```
INSERT INTO my_book_files ( file_descr, book_file )
    VALUES ( 'Chapter 1', BFILENAME('BOOK_TEXT', 'chapter01.txt') );
UPDATE  my_book_files
   SET  book_file = BFILENAME( 'BOOK_TEXT', 'chapter02rev.txt' )
   WHERE  file_descr = 'Chapter 2';
```

Once a BFILE column or variable is associated with a physical file, read operations on the BFILE can be performed using the DBMS_LOB package. Remember that access to physical files via BFILEs is read-only, and that the BFILE value is a pointer. The contents of the file remain outside of the database, but on the same server on which the database resides.

Internal LOB Considerations

There are also some special considerations you need to be aware of when you work with internal LOBs.

Retaining the LOB locator

The following statement populates the my_book_text table, which contains CLOB column chapter_text:

```
INSERT INTO my_book_text ( chapter_descr, chapter_text )
    VALUES ( 'Chapter 1', 'It was a dark and stormy night.' );
```

Programs within the DBMS_LOB package require a LOB locator to be passed as input. If you want to insert the preceding row and then call a DBMS_LOB program using the row's CLOB value, you must retain the LOB locator created by your INSERT statement. You could do this as in the following block, which inserts a row, selects the inserted LOB locator, and then calls the DBMS_LOB.GETLENGTH program to get the size of the CLOB chapter_text column. Note that the GETLENGTH program expects a LOB locator.

```
DECLARE
    chapter_loc         CLOB;
    chapter_length      INTEGER;
BEGIN
    INSERT INTO my_book_text ( chapter_descr, chapter_text )
        VALUES ( 'Chapter 1', 'It was a dark and stormy night.' );
    SELECT  chapter_text
      INTO  chapter_loc
      FROM  my_book_text
     WHERE  chapter_descr = 'Chapter 1';
    chapter_length := DBMS_LOB.GETLENGTH( chapter_loc );
    DBMS_OUTPUT.PUT_LINE( 'Length of Chapter 1: ' || chapter_length );
END;
/
```

This is the output of the script:

```
Length of Chapter 1: 31
```

The RETURNING clause

You can avoid the second trip to the database (i.e., the SELECT of the LOB locator after the INSERT) by using a RETURNING clause in the INSERT statement. Using this feature, perform the INSERT operation and the LOB locator value for the new row in a single operation.

```
DECLARE
    chapter_loc         CLOB;
    chapter_length      INTEGER;
BEGIN

    INSERT INTO my_book_text ( chapter_descr, chapter_text )
        VALUES ( 'Chapter 1', 'It was a dark and stormy night.' )
      RETURNING chapter_text INTO chapter_loc;

    chapter_length := DBMS_LOB.GETLENGTH( chapter_loc );

    DBMS_OUTPUT.PUT_LINE( 'Length of Chapter 1: ' || chapter_length );

END;
/
```

This is the output of the script:

```
Length of Chapter 1: 31
```

The RETURNING clause can be used in both INSERT and UPDATE statements.

NULL LOB locators can be a problem

Programs in the DBMS_LOB package expect to be passed a LOB locator that is not NULL. For example, the GETLENGTH program raises an exception when passed a LOB locator that is NULL.

```
DECLARE
    chapter_loc         CLOB;
    chapter_length      INTEGER;

BEGIN
        UPDATE  my_book_text
           SET  chapter_text = NULL
         WHERE  chapter_descr = 'Chapter 1'
     RETURNING  chapter_text INTO chapter_loc;

    chapter_length := DBMS_LOB.GETLENGTH( chapter_loc );

    DBMS_OUTPUT.PUT_LINE( 'Length of Chapter 1: ' || chapter_length );

EXCEPTION
```

```
        WHEN OTHERS
        THEN
            DBMS_OUTPUT.PUT_LINE('OTHERS Exception ' || sqlerrm);

    END;
    /
```

This is the output of the script:

```
OTHERS Exception ORA-00600: internal error code, arguments: ...
```

When a BLOB, CLOB, or NCLOB column is set to NULL, *both* the LOB binary data *and* its LOB locator are NULL; this NULL LOB locator should not be passed to a program in the DBMS_LOB package.

NULL versus "empty" LOB locators

Oracle8 provides the built-in functions EMPTY_BLOB and EMPTY_CLOB to set BLOB, CLOB, and NCLOB columns to "empty." For example:

```
INSERT INTO my_book_text ( chapter_descr, chapter_text )
    VALUES ( 'Table of Contents', EMPTY_CLOB() );
```

The LOB data is set to NULL. However, the associated LOB locator is assigned a valid locator value, which points to the NULL data. This LOB locator can then be passed to DBMS_LOB programs.

```
DECLARE
    chapter_loc        CLOB;
    chapter_length     INTEGER;

BEGIN
    INSERT INTO my_book_text (chapter_descr, chapter_text)
        VALUES ( 'Table of Contents', EMPTY_CLOB() )
        RETURNING chapter_text INTO chapter_loc;

    chapter_length := DBMS_LOB.GETLENGTH( chapter_loc );

    DBMS_OUTPUT.PUT_LINE
        ('Length of Table of Contents: ' || chapter_length);

EXCEPTION
    WHEN OTHERS
    THEN
        DBMS_OUTPUT.PUT_LINE( 'OTHERS Exception ' || sqlerrm);

END;
/
```

This is the output of the script:

```
Length of Table of Contents: 0
```

Note that EMPTY_CLOB can be used to populate both CLOB and NCLOB columns. EMPTY_BLOB and EMPTY_CLOB can be called with or without empty parentheses.

| TIP | Do not populate BLOB, CLOB, or NCLOB columns with NULL values. Instead, use the EMPTY_BLOB or EMPTY_CLOB functions, which will populate the columns with a valid LOB locator and set the associated data to NULL. |

DBMS_LOB Interface

This section describes the programs available through the DBMS_LOB packages in several categories.

Working with BFILEs

The following sections describe the programs in the DBMS_LOB package that perform operations on BFILE objects.

The DBMS_LOB.FILEEXISTS function

The FILEEXISTS function indicates whether the given BFILE locator points to a file that exists in the operating system. Here's the specification for this program:

```
FUNCTION DBMS_LOB.FILEEXISTS
    ( file_loc IN BFILE )
    RETURN INTEGER;
```

The file_loc parameter is the name of the file locator. The function returns one of the following values:

Value	Description
0	The specified file does not exist
1	The specified file exists

Exceptions. One of the following exceptions may be raised if the file_loc parameter contains an improper value (e.g., NULL):

```
DBMSLOB.NOEXIST_DIRECTORY
DBMSLOB.NOPRIV_DIRECTORY
DBMSLOB.INVALID_DIRECTORY
```

Restrictions. The FILEEXISTS function asserts a purity level with the RESTRICT_ REFERENCES pragma.

```
PRAGMA RESTRICT_REFERENCES (fileexists, WNDS, RNDS, WNPS, RNPS);
```

Examples. This block uses the FILEEXISTS function to see if *chapter01.txt* exists in the BOOK_TEXT directory:

```
DECLARE
    book_file_loc       BFILE := NULL;
    book_file_exists    BOOLEAN := FALSE;

BEGIN
    book_file_loc := BFILENAME( 'BOOK_TEXT', 'chapter01.txt' );
    book_file_exists := DBMS_LOB.FILEEXISTS( book_file_loc ) = 1;

    IF book_file_exists
    THEN
        DBMS_OUTPUT.PUT_LINE
            ('chapter01.txt exists in BOOK_TEXT directory');
    ELSE
        DBMS_OUTPUT.PUT_LINE
            ('chapter01.txt does not exist in BOOK_TEXT directory');
    END IF;
END;
/
```

This is the output of the script:

```
chapter01.txt exists in BOOK_TEXT directory
```

The following example selects the file locator for *chapter01.txt* from the my_ book_files table and checks to see if the file exists:

```
INSERT INTO my_book_files ( file_descr, book_file )
    VALUES ('Chapter 1', BFILENAME('BOOK_TEXT', 'chapter01.txt') );

DECLARE
    book_file_loc       BFILE := NULL;
    book_file_exists    BOOLEAN := FALSE;
BEGIN
    book_file_loc := book_file ('Chapter 1');
    IF book_file_loc IS NOT NULL
    THEN
        book_file_exists := DBMS_LOB.FILEEXISTS( book_file_loc ) = 1;
    END IF;
    IF book_file_exists
    THEN
        DBMS_OUTPUT.PUT_LINE('Chapter 1 exists');
    ELSE
        DBMS_OUTPUT.PUT_LINE('Chapter 1 does not exist');
    END IF;
END;
/
```

This is the output of the script:

```
Chapter 1 exists
```

FILEEXISTS raises a VALUE_ERROR exception when passed a NULL file locator, so you should always include conditional logic and an exception section.

The next example raises the NOEXIST_DIRECTORY exception. This can occur if the directory alias does not exist, or if the user has not been granted READ privilege on the directory.

```
DECLARE
    book_file_loc BFILE := NULL;
    book_file_exists    BOOLEAN := FALSE;
BEGIN
    book_file_loc :=  BFILENAME( 'NON_EXISTENT_DIRECTORY', 'chapter01.txt' );
    book_file_exists := DBMS_LOB.FILEEXISTS( book_file_loc ) = 1;
    IF book_file_exists
    THEN
        DBMS_OUTPUT.PUT_LINE('chapter01.txt exists');
    ELSE
        DBMS_OUTPUT.PUT_LINE('chapter01.txt does not exist');
    END IF;
END;
/
```

Running this script results in this unhandled exception:

```
ORA-22285: non-existent directory or file for FILEEXISTS operation
```

If the directory exists and READ privileges have been granted to the user, but the specified file does not exist, FILEEXISTS returns zero.

```
DECLARE
    book_file_loc BFILE := NULL;

BEGIN
    book_file_loc := BFILENAME( 'BOOK_TEXT', 'non_existent_file.txt');

    IF DBMS_LOB.FILEEXISTS( book_file_loc ) = 0
    THEN
        DBMS_OUTPUT.PUT_LINE('non_existent_file.txt does not exist');
    END IF;

END;
/
```

This script produces the following:

```
non_existent_file.txt does not exist
```

FILEEXISTS can be called from SQL, for example:

```
SELECT DBMS_LOB.FILEEXISTS  ( BFILENAME ('BOOK_TEXT','chapter01.txt') )
fileexists
    FROM DUAL;

    FILEEXISTS
    ----------------
                  1
```

Calls to FILEEXISTS should trap and handle the NOEXIST_DIRECTORY exception (directory alias does not exist) and the VALUE_ERROR exception (input file locator is NULL).

The DBMS_LOB.FILEGETNAME procedure

Given a file locator, the FILEGETNAME procedure determines its associated directory alias and filename. The specification for this program follows:

```
PROCEDURE DBMS_LOB.FILEGETNAME
    ( file_loc IN BFILE,
      dir_alias OUT VARCHAR2,
      filename OUT VARCHAR2 );
```

Parameters are summarized in the following table.

Parameter	Description
file_loc	File locator
dir_alias	Directory alias for the file locator
filename	File name for the file locator

Exceptions. The following VALUE_ERROR exception is raised if the file_loc parameter contains an improper value (e.g., NULL):

```
INVALID_ARGVAL
```

Examples. The following example uses FILEGETNAME to get the directory alias and filename for the "Chapter 1" row in the my_book_files table:

```
INSERT INTO my_book_files (file_descr, book_file)
    VALUES ( 'Chapter 1', BFILENAME('BOOK_TEXT', 'chapter01.txt') );
DECLARE
   book_file_exists    BOOLEAN := FALSE;
   book_file_loc       BFILE := NULL;
   book_file_dir       VARCHAR2(30) := NULL;
   book_file_name      VARCHAR2(2000) := NULL;
BEGIN
   book_file_loc := book_file ('Chapter 1');
   IF book_file_loc IS NOT NULL
   THEN
      book_file_exists := DBMS_LOB.FILEEXISTS( book_file_loc ) = 1;
   END IF;
   IF book_file_exists
   THEN
      DBMS_LOB.FILEGETNAME
          (book_file_loc, book_file_dir, book_file_name);
      DBMS_OUTPUT.PUT_LINE ('File name is: ' || book_file_name);
      DBMS_OUTPUT.PUT_LINE
          ('File is in Oracle directory: ' || book_file_dir);
   ELSE
      DBMS_OUTPUT.PUT_LINE('Chapter 1 does not exist');
```

```
      END IF;
   EXCEPTION
      WHEN OTHERS
      THEN
         DBMS_OUTPUT.PUT_LINE('OTHERS Exception ' || sqlerrm );
   END;
   /
```

This is the output of the script:

```
File name is: chapter01.txt
File is in Oracle directory: BOOK_TEXT
```

FILEGETNAME raises a VALUE_ERROR exception when passed a NULL file locator, so be sure to check the value of the file locator and/or include an exception handler.

Note that FILEGETNAME does not actually confirm that the *physical* file and directory alias exist. This can be done via FILEEXISTS.

The DBMS_LOB.FILEOPEN procedure

Given a file locator, the FILEOPEN procedure opens the BFILE for read-only access. Here's the header for this program:

```
PROCEDURE DBMS_LOB.FILEOPEN
   ( file_loc IN OUT BFILE,
     open_mode IN BINARY_INTEGER := FILE_READONLY   )
```

Parameters are summarized in the following table.

Parameter	Purpose
file_loc	File locator for the file to be opened
open_mode	Indicates that file access will be read-only; this parameter can be omitted from calls to FILEOPEN because the program assigns a default value of FILE_READONLY

Exceptions. The following types of exceptions can be raised by the the FILEOPEN procedure:

NOEXIST_DIRECTORY
   The directory alias associated with file_loc does not exist.

OPEN_TOOMANY
   The number of open files exceeds the SESSION_MAX_OPEN_FILES limit.

INVALID_ARGVAL
   The open_mode value is not FILE_READONLY.

INVALID_OPERATION

The file does not exist or the user does not have privileges to access the file.

VALUE_ERROR

The file_loc parameter contains an improper value (e.g., NULL).

Examples. This example uses the FILEOPEN procedure to check whether *chapter01.txt* exists in the BOOK_TEXT directory, then opens and closes the file:

```
DECLARE
    book_file_loc      BFILE := NULL;
    book_file_exists   BOOLEAN := FALSE;

BEGIN
    book_file_loc := BFILENAME('BOOK_TEXT','chapter01.txt');
    book_file_exists := DBMS_LOB.FILEEXISTS( book_file_loc ) = 1;

    IF book_file_exists
    THEN
       DBMS_OUTPUT.PUT_LINE('chapter01.txt exists');

       DBMS_OUTPUT.PUT_LINE('opening the file');
       DBMS_LOB.FILEOPEN( book_file_loc );

       DBMS_OUTPUT.PUT_LINE('closing the file');
       DBMS_LOB.FILECLOSE( book_file_loc );
    END IF;
END;
/
```

This is the output of the script:

```
chapter01.txt exists
opening the file
closing the file
```

The FILEOPEN procedure raises a VALUE_ERROR exception when passed to a NULL file. The procedure raises a NOEXIST_DIRECTORY exception when passed to a file locator associated with a nonexistent directory alias.

Note that it is possible to open the same file using two different file locators, for example:

```
DECLARE
    book_file_loc_1    BFILE := NULL;
    book_file_loc_2    BFILE := NULL;
    book_file_exists   BOOLEAN := FALSE;

BEGIN
    book_file_loc_1 := BFILENAME('BOOK_TEXT','chapter01.txt');
    book_file_loc_2 := BFILENAME('BOOK_TEXT','chapter01.txt');
    book_file_exists := DBMS_LOB.FILEEXISTS( book_file_loc_1 ) = 1;

    IF book_file_exists
```

```
      THEN
          DBMS_OUTPUT.PUT_LINE('chapter01.txt exists');

          DBMS_OUTPUT.PUT_LINE('opening the file via loc_1');
          DBMS_LOB.FILEOPEN( book_file_loc_1 );

          DBMS_OUTPUT.PUT_LINE('opening the file via loc_2');
          DBMS_LOB.FILEOPEN( book_file_loc_2 );

          DBMS_OUTPUT.PUT_LINE('closing the file via loc_1');
          DBMS_LOB.FILECLOSE( book_file_loc_1 );

          DBMS_OUTPUT.PUT_LINE('closing the file via loc_2');
          DBMS_LOB.FILECLOSE( book_file_loc_2 );

      END IF;
  END;
  /
```

This is the output of the script:

```
  chapter01.txt exists
  opening the file via loc_1
  opening the file via loc_2
  closing the file via loc_1
  closing the file via loc_2
```

To avoid exceeding the SESSION_MAX_OPEN_FILES limit, include a matching call to the FILECLOSE procedure for each BFILE that is opened. When an exception occurs *after* opening a file, it is possible that execution continues without closing the file (i.e., the matching call to FILECLOSE is not executed due to abnormal termination). In this case, the file remains open, and we run the risk of exceeding the SESSION_MAX_OPEN_FILES limit. It is good practice to include a call to the FILECLOSEALL procedure within an exception handler whenever FILEOPEN is used. See the "The DBMS_LOB.FILECLOSEALL procedure" section for details.

The DBMS_LOB.FILEISOPEN function

The FILEISOPEN function indicates whether the file was opened via the input file locator given by file_loc. The header for this program is,

```
  FUNCTION DBMS_LOB.FILEISOPEN
      ( file_loc IN BFILE )
      RETURN INTEGER;
```

where file_loc is the file locator for the file to be opened. The function returns one of the following values:

Value	Description
0	The file is not open via the given file locator.
1	The file is open via the given file locator.

Exceptions. The FILEISOPEN function will raise the VALUE_ERROR exception if the file_loc parameter contains an improper value (e.g., NULL).

Restrictions. The program asserts a purity level with the RESTRICT_REFERENCES pragma.

```
PRAGMA RESTRICT_REFERENCES (fileisopen, WNDS, RNDS, WNPS, RNPS);
```

Examples. The following example uses the FILEISOPEN function to check whether *chapter01.txt* in the *BOOK_TEXT* directory is open. It opens the file if it is not already open.

```
DECLARE
    book_file_loc       BFILE := NULL;
    book_file_exists    BOOLEAN := FALSE;

BEGIN
    book_file_loc := BFILENAME('BOOK_TEXT','chapter01.txt');
    book_file_exists := DBMS_LOB.FILEEXISTS( book_file_loc ) = 1;

    IF book_file_exists
    THEN
        DBMS_OUTPUT.PUT_LINE('chapter01.txt exists');

        IF DBMS_LOB.FILEISOPEN( book_file_loc) = 1
        THEN
            DBMS_OUTPUT.PUT_LINE('file is open');

        ELSE
            DBMS_OUTPUT.PUT_LINE('file is not open');

            DBMS_OUTPUT.PUT_LINE('opening the file');
            DBMS_LOB.FILEOPEN( book_file_loc );

            IF DBMS_LOB.FILEISOPEN( book_file_loc) = 1
            THEN
                DBMS_OUTPUT.PUT_LINE('file is open');
                DBMS_OUTPUT.PUT_LINE('closing the file');
                DBMS_LOB.FILECLOSE( book_file_loc );
            END IF;
        END IF;

    END IF;

EXCEPTION
    WHEN OTHERS
    THEN
        DBMS_OUTPUT.PUT_LINE('OTHERS Exception ' || sqlerrm );
END;
/
```

This is the output of the script:

```
chapter01.txt exists
file is not open
opening the file
file is open
closing the file
```

The next example assigns two file locators to the same file, *chapter01.txt,* in the *BOOK_TEXT* directory. It opens the file using the first locator. When called with the first locator, FILEISOPEN indicates that the file is open. However, FILEISOPEN indicates that the file is *not* open when called with the second locator. Hence, FILEISOPEN indicates whether a file is open *with respect to a specific locator.*

```
DECLARE
    book_file_loc_1     BFILE := NULL;
    book_file_loc_2     BFILE := NULL;
    book_file_exists    BOOLEAN := FALSE;
    PROCEDURE check_open (loc IN BFILE, descr IN VARCHAR2)
    IS
BEGIN
    IF DBMS_LOB.FILEISOPEN (loc) = 1
    THEN
        DBMS_OUTPUT.PUT_LINE ('file is open via ' || descr);
    ELSE
        DBMS_OUTPUT.PUT_LINE ('file is not open via ' || descr);
    END IF;
END
BEGIN
    book_file_loc_1 := BFILENAME ('BOOK_TEXT', 'chapter01.txt');
    book_file_loc_2 := BFILENAME ('BOOK_TEXT', 'chapter01.txt');
    book_file_exists := DBMS_LOB.FILEEXISTS( book_file_loc_1 ) = 1;
    IF book_file_exists
    THEN
        DBMS_OUTPUT.PUT_LINE('chapter01.txt exists');
        IF DBMS_LOB.FILEISOPEN( book_file_loc_1 ) = 1
        THEN
            DBMS_OUTPUT.PUT_LINE('file is open via loc_1');
        ELSE
            DBMS_OUTPUT.PUT_LINE('file is not open via loc_1');
            DBMS_OUTPUT.PUT_LINE('opening the file via loc_1');
            DBMS_LOB.FILEOPEN( book_file_loc_1 );
            check_open (book_file_loc_1, 'loc_1');
            check_open (book_file_loc_2, 'loc_2');
            DBMS_OUTPUT.PUT_LINE('closing the file via loc_1');
            DBMS_LOB.FILECLOSE( book_file_loc_1 );
        END IF;
    END IF;
END;
/
```

This is the output of the script:

```
chapter01.txt exists
file is not open via loc_1
```

```
opening the file via loc_1
file is open via loc_1
file is not open via loc_2
closing the file via loc_1
```

FILEISOPEN raises a VALUE_ERROR exception when passed a NULL file locator. On the other hand, FILEISOPEN does not raise an exception when passed a file locator having a nonexistent directory alias or nonexistent file.

The DBMS_LOB.FILECLOSE procedure

The FILECLOSE procedure is used to close a file that has been opened via the input file locator indicated by the file_loc parameter. The header for this program is,

```
PROCEDURE DBMS_LOB.FILECLOSE ( file_loc IN OUT BFILE );
```

where file_loc is the file locator for the file to be opened.

Exceptions. The FILECLOSE procedure may raise a VALUE_ERROR exception if the file_loc parameter contains an improper value (e.g., NULL).

Examples. The following example demonstrates that FILECLOSE can be called with a locator for a file that has *not* been opened:

```
DECLARE
    book_file_loc      BFILE := NULL;
    book_file_exists   BOOLEAN := FALSE;
BEGIN
    book_file_loc := BFILENAME('BOOK_TEXT','chapter01.txt');
    book_file_exists := DBMS_LOB.FILEEXISTS( book_file_loc ) = 1;

    IF book_file_exists
    THEN
       DBMS_OUTPUT.PUT_LINE('chapter01.txt exists');

       IF DBMS_LOB.FILEISOPEN( book_file_loc ) = 1
       THEN
          DBMS_OUTPUT.PUT_LINE('file is open');
       ELSE
          DBMS_OUTPUT.PUT_LINE('file is not open');
       END IF;

       DBMS_OUTPUT.PUT_LINE('closing the file');
       DBMS_LOB.FILECLOSE( book_file_loc );

    END IF;
END;
/
```

This is the output of the script:

```
chapter01.txt exists
file is not open
closing the file
```

The FILECLOSE procedure can be called with a locator for a nonexistent file or directory, for example:

```
DECLARE
    book_file_loc       BFILE := NULL;
BEGIN
    book_file_loc :=
        BFILENAME('NON_EXISTENT_DIRECTORY','non_existent_file.txt');

    DBMS_OUTPUT.PUT_LINE
        ('closing non_existent_file.txt in NON_EXISTENT_DIRECTORY');
    DBMS_LOB.FILECLOSE( book_file_loc );
EXCEPTION
    WHEN OTHERS
    THEN
        DBMS_OUTPUT.PUT_LINE('OTHERS Exception ' || sqlerrm );
END;
/
```

This is the output of the script:

```
closing non_existent_file.txt in NON_EXISTENT_DIRECTORY
```

FILECLOSE raises a VALUE_ERROR exception when passed a NULL file locator.

See the FILEOPEN and FILECLOSEALL sections for other examples of FILECLOSE usage.

The DBMS_LOB.FILECLOSEALL procedure

The FILECLOSEALL procedure is used to close all BFILEs that are open within a session. Here's the header for this program:

```
PROCEDURE DBMS_LOB.FILECLOSEALL;
```

Exceptions. The FILECLOSEALL procedure raises an UNOPENED_FILE exception if no files are open.

Examples. When an exception occurs *after* opening a file, it is possible that execution continues without closing the file (i.e., a matching call to FILECLOSE is not executed due to abnormal termination of a block). In this case, the file remains open, and we run the risk of exceeding the SESSION_MAX_OPEN_FILES limit. It is good practice to include a call to FILECLOSEALL within an exception handler whenever FILEOPEN is used.

The following anonymous block shows how you might construct an exception
section that will close any open files:

```
DECLARE
    book_file_loc      BFILE := NULL;
    book_file_exists   BOOLEAN := FALSE;
    x NUMBER;
BEGIN
    book_file_loc := BFILENAME('BOOK_TEXT','chapter01.txt');
    book_file_exists := DBMS_LOB.FILEEXISTS( book_file_loc ) = 1;
    IF book_file_exists
    THEN
        DBMS_OUTPUT.PUT_LINE ('opening chapter01.txt');
        DBMS_LOB.FILEOPEN (book_file_loc);
        /* Intentionally raise a ZERO_DIVIDE exception */
        x := 1 / 0;
        DBMS_LOB.FILECLOSE( book_file_loc );
    END IF;
EXCEPTION
    WHEN OTHERS
    THEN
        BEGIN
            DBMS_OUTPUT.PUT_LINE ('Clean up using FILECLOSEALL');
            DBMS_LOB.FILECLOSEALL;
        EXCEPTION
            WHEN DBMS_LOB.UNOPENED_FILE
            THEN
                DBMS_OUTPUT.PUT_LINE
                    ('No files to close, raising the UNOPENED_FILE exception.');
            WHEN OTHERS
            THEN
                DBMS_OUTPUT.PUT_LINE ('OTHERS Exception ' || sqlerrm );
        END;
END;
/
```

This is the output of the script:

```
opening   chapter01.txt
Clean up using FILECLOSEALL
```

The DBMS_LOB.LOADFROMFILE procedure

The LOADFROMFILE procedure is used to load all or part of a external LOB
(source BFILE) to a destination internal LOB. This is the procedure used to load
binary data stored in operating system files into internal LOBs, which reside in the
database. The specification for this program is overloaded as follows:

```
PROCEDURE DBMS_LOB.LOADFROMFILE
    (dest_lob IN OUT BLOB | CLOB CHARACTER SET ANY_CS,
     src_lob IN BFILE,
     amount IN INTEGER,
     dest_offset IN INTEGER := 1,
     src_offset IN INTEGER := 1);
```

The overloaded specification allows LOADFROMFILE to be used with BLOBs or CLOBs. The clause ANY_CS in the second specification allows acceptance of either CLOB or NCLOB locators as input.

Parameters are summarized in the following table.

Parameter	Description
dest_lob	Locator for the destination internal LOB
src_lob	File locator for the source external LOB
amount	Number of bytes to copy from the source BFILE
dest_offset	Location of the byte (BLOB) or character (CLOB, NCLOB) in the destination LOB at which the copy operation begins; the default value is 1
src_offset	Location of the byte in the source BFILE at which the load operation begins; the default value is 1

Exceptions. The LOADFROMFILE procedure raises a VALUE_ERROR exception if dest_lob, src_lob, or amount are NULL or invalid.

An INVALID_ARGVAL exception is raised if any of the following conditions are true:

- src_offset < 1 or src_offset > LOBMAXSIZE

- dest_offset < 1 or dest_offset > LOBMAXSIZE

- amount < 1 or amount > LOBMAXSIZE

LOADFROMFILE raises the ORA-22993 exception (specified input amount is greater than actual source amount) if the end of the source BFILE is reached before the specified amount of bytes has been copied.

Examples. The following example loads the CLOB chapter_text column of the my_book_text table with the contents of the first 100 bytes of the file *chapter01.txt* in the *BOOK_TEXT* directory.

Note that the update of the chapter_text column occurs without the issue of an UPDATE statement. LOADFROMFILE accomplishes this via the chapter_text locator, which has been selected FOR UPDATE. LOB locators and DBMS_LOB allow changes to LOB columns in Oracle tables without issuing INSERT or UPDATE statements.

If you want to take this approach, you *must* lock the row that contains the LOB prior to modification. The best way to obtain this lock is to use the FOR UPDATE clause in the SELECT statement (in this example, this translates to calling the book_text_forupdate function):

```
INSERT INTO my_book_text (chapter_descr, chapter_text)
    VALUES ('Chapter 1', EMPTY_CLOB());
```

```
COMMIT;

DECLARE
    v_text_loc    CLOB;
    v_file_loc    BFILE;
BEGIN
    v_text_loc := book_text_forupdate ('Chapter 1');
    v_file_loc := BFILENAME('BOOK_TEXT','chapter01.txt');
    DBMS_LOB.LOADFROMFILE (v_text_loc, v_file_loc, 100);
    COMMIT;
END;
/
SET LONG 100
COL chapter_descr FOR A15
COL chapter_text FOR A40 WORD_WRAPPED
SELECT chapter_descr, chapter_text
  FROM my_book_text
 WHERE chapter_descr = 'Chapter 1';
```

This is the output of the script:

```
CHAPTER_DESCR    CHAPTER_TEXT
---------------  ----------------------------------------
Chapter 1        It was a dark and stormy night.
                 Suddenly a scream rang out.  An
                 EXCEPTION had not been handled.
```

The next example also loads the CLOB chapter_text column of the my_book_text table with the contents of the first 100 bytes of the file *chapter01.txt* in the *BOOK_ TEXT* directory. This time, the LOB locator is not selected FOR UPDATE, but has been returned via the RETURNING clause.

```
DECLARE
    v_text_loc    CLOB;
    v_file_loc    BFILE;
BEGIN
    INSERT INTO my_book_text (chapter_descr, chapter_text)
        VALUES ('Chapter 1', EMPTY_CLOB )
      RETURNING chapter_text INTO v_text_loc;

    v_file_loc := BFILENAME('BOOK_TEXT','chapter01.txt');

    DBMS_LOB.LOADFROMFILE(v_text_loc, v_file_loc, 100);

    COMMIT;
END;
/

SET LONG 100

COL chapter_descr FOR A15
COL chapter_text FOR A40 WORD_WRAPPED

SELECT chapter_descr, chapter_text
```

```
      FROM my_book_text
      WHERE chapter_descr = 'Chapter 1';
```

This is the output of the script:

```
CHAPTER_DESCR    CHAPTER_TEXT
---------------  ----------------------------------------
Chapter 1        It was a dark and stormy night.
                 Suddenly a scream rang out.  An
                 EXCEPTION had not been handled.
```

This example loads the BLOB diagram column of the by_book_diagrams table with the contents of the file *ch01_01.bmp* in the *IMAGES* directory. The LOB locator has been returned via the RETURNING clause.

Note that the update of the diagram column occurs without the issue of an UPDATE statement. LOADFROMFILE accomplishes this via the diagram locator, which has been returned by the RETURNING clause. LOB locators and DBMS_LOB allow changes to LOB columns in Oracle tables without issuing INSERT or UPDATE statements.

```
DECLARE
    v_file_loc        BFILE;

    v_diagram_loc     BLOB;
    v_diagram_size    INTEGER;
BEGIN
    v_file_loc := BFILENAME('IMAGES','ch01_01.bmp');

    v_diagram_size := DBMS_LOB.GETLENGTH(v_file_loc);
    DBMS_OUTPUT.PUT_LINE('Diagram size: ' || v_diagram_size);

    DBMS_OUTPUT.PUT_LINE('Inserting Empty Diagram Row');
    INSERT INTO my_book_diagrams (chapter_descr, diagram_no, diagram)
        VALUES ( 'Chapter 1', 1, EMPTY_BLOB )
      RETURNING diagram INTO v_diagram_loc;

    DBMS_OUTPUT.PUT_LINE('Loading Diagram From File');
    DBMS_LOB.LOADFROMFILE(v_diagram_loc, v_file_loc, v_diagram_size);

    COMMIT;
EXCEPTION
    WHEN OTHERS
    THEN
        DBMS_OUTPUT.PUT_LINE('OTHERS Exception ' || sqlerrm);

END;
/

SELECT chapter_descr,
       diagram_no,
       dbms_lob.getlength(diagram) diagram_size
  FROM my_book_diagrams
 WHERE chapter_descr = 'Chapter 1';
```

This script produces the following:

```
Diagram size: 481078
Inserting Empty Diagram Row
Loading Diagram From File


CHAPTER_DESCR   DIAGRAM_NO DIAGRAM_SIZE
--------------- ---------- ------------
Chapter 1                1       481078
```

Reading and Examining LOBs

The following sections describe the programs in the DBMS_LOB package that are used to read and examine LOBs.

The DBMS_LOB.COMPARE function

The COMPARE function is used to compare two LOBs that are of the same type. Parts of LOBs can also be compared. The specification for this program takes the following forms for each LOB type that may be compared:

```
FUNCTION DBMS_LOB.COMPARE
     (lob_1 IN BLOB | CLOB CHARACTER SET ANY_CS,
     lob_2 IN BLOB | CLOB CHARACTER SET ANY_CS,
     amount IN INTEGER := 4294967295,
     offset_1 IN INTEGER := 1,
     offset_2 IN INTEGER := 1)
     RETURN INTEGER;

FUNCTION DBMS_LOB.COMPARE
     (lob_1 IN BFILE,
     lob_2 IN BFILE,
     amount IN INTEGER,
     offset_1 IN INTEGER := 1,
     offset_2 IN INTEGER := 1)
     RETURN INTEGER;
```

The overloaded specification allows COMPARE to be used with all types of LOBs. The clause ANY_CS in the specification allows either CLOB or NCLOB locators as input.

Parameters are summarized in the following table.

Parameter	Description
lob_1	Locator for the first LOB to be compared
lob_2	Locator for the second LOB to be compared
amount	Number of bytes (BFILE, BLOB) or characters (CLOB, NCLOB) to compare
offset_1	Location of the byte (BFILE, BLOB) or character (CLOB, NCLOB) in the first LOB at which the comparison begins; the default value is 1
offset_2	Location of the byte (BFILE, BLOB) or character (CLOB, NCLOB) in the second LOB at which the comparison begins; the default value is 1

The function returns one of the following values:

Value	Description
Zero	LOBs match exactly over the offsets and amount specified.
Not Zero	LOBs do not match exactly over the offsets and amount specified.
NULL	Either amount, offset_1 or offset_2, is less than 1, or amount, offset_1, or offset_2 is greater than LOBMAXSIZE.

Exceptions. The COMPARE function may raise the following exceptions:

NOEXIST_DIRECTORY
> For BFILEs.

UNOPENED_FILE
> For BFILES. Files must be open before comparison.

NOPRIV_DIRECTORY
> For BFILEs.

INVALID_DIRECTORY
> For BFILEs.

INVALID_OPERATION
> For BFILEs.

Restrictions. The program asserts a purity level with the RESTRICT_REFERENCES pragma.

```
PRAGMA RESTRICT_REFERENCES (compare, WNDS, RNDS, WNPS, RNPS);
```

Examples. The following example compares two BFILE locators that are pointing to the same file. Note that for BFILEs we must provide a number of bytes (in the amount parameter) to compare, which is determined via the GETLENGTH function. Note also that for BFILES we must first open the files.

```
DECLARE
    v_file_loc_1      BFILE;
    v_file_1_length   INTEGER;

    v_file_loc_2      BFILE;
BEGIN
    v_file_loc_1 := BFILENAME ('IMAGES', 'ourlogo.bmp');
    v_file_loc_2 := BFILENAME ('IMAGES', 'ourlogo.bmp');

    DBMS_LOB.FILEOPEN(v_file_loc_1);
    DBMS_LOB.FILEOPEN(v_file_loc_2);

    v_file_1_length := DBMS_LOB.GETLENGTH( v_file_loc_1);

    IF DBMS_LOB.COMPARE
```

```
              ( v_file_loc_1, v_file_loc_2, v_file_1_length) = 0
        THEN
           DBMS_OUTPUT.PUT_LINE('file_loc_1 equals file_loc_2');
        ELSE
           DBMS_OUTPUT.PUT_LINE('file_loc_1 is not equal to file_loc_2');
        END IF;

        DBMS_LOB.FILECLOSEALL;
     END;
     /
```

This is the output of the script:

```
     file_loc_1 equals file_loc_2
```

This example compares two diagrams from the my_book_diagrams table:

```
     DECLARE
        CURSOR diagram_cur (num IN INTEGER)
        IS
        SELECT diagram
          FROM my_book_diagrams
         WHERE chapter_descr = 'Chapter 1'
           AND diagram_no = num;
        v_diagram_1_loc    BLOB;
        v_diagram_2_loc    BLOB;
     BEGIN
        OPEN diagram_cur (1);
        FETCH diagram_cur INTO v_diagram_1_loc;
        CLOSE diagram_cur;

        OPEN diagram_cur (2);
        FETCH diagram_cur INTO v_diagram_1_loc;
        CLOSE diagram_cur;

        IF DBMS_LOB.COMPARE (v_diagram_1_loc, v_diagram_2_loc) = 0
        THEN
           DBMS_OUTPUT.PUT_LINE ('diagrams are equal');
        ELSE
           DBMS_OUTPUT.PUT_LINE ('diagrams are different');
        END IF;
     END;
     /
```

This is the output of the script:

```
     diagrams are different
```

The DBMS_LOB.GETLENGTH function

The GETLENGTH function returns the length of the input LOB. The length is in bytes for BFILEs and BLOBs, and in characters for CLOBs and NCLOBs. The headers for this program, for each corresponding LOB type, are the following:

```
     FUNCTION DBMS_LOB.GETLENGTH (lob_loc IN BLOB) RETURN INTEGER;
```

```
FUNCTION DBMS_LOB.GETLENGTH (lob_loc IN CLOB CHARACTER SET ANY_CS)
    RETURN INTEGER;

FUNCTION DBMS_LOB.GETLENGTH (lob_loc IN BFILE) RETURN INTEGER;
```

The lob_loc parameter is the locator of the LOB whose length is to be determined.

The overloaded specification allows GETLENGTH to be used with all types of LOBs. The clause ANY_CS in the specification allows either CLOB or NCLOB locators as input.

The function returns the length (in bytes or characters) of the input LOB, or it returns NULL if the input LOB is NULL or invalid.

Restrictions. The program asserts a purity level with the RESTRICT_REFERENCES pragma.

```
PRAGMA RESTRICT_REFERENCES (getlength, WNDS, RNDS, WNPS, RNPS);
```

Examples. The following example gets the size in bytes of the file *ch01_01.bmp* in the *IMAGES* directory:

```
DECLARE
    v_file_loc        BFILE;
    v_diagram_size    INTEGER;

BEGIN
    v_file_loc := BFILENAME('IMAGES','ch01_01.bmp');

    v_diagram_size := DBMS_LOB.GETLENGTH(v_file_loc);
    DBMS_OUTPUT.PUT_LINE('Diagram size: ' || v_diagram_size);
END;
/
```

This is the output of the script:

```
Diagram size: 481078
```

This example gets the size in characters of "Chapter 1" from the my_book_text table:

```
DECLARE
    v_text_loc        CLOB;
BEGIN
    v_text_loc := book_text ('Chapter 1');
    DBMS_OUTPUT.PUT_LINE
        ('Length of Chapter 1: ' || DBMS_LOB.GETLENGTH(v_text_loc));
END;
/
```

This is the output of the script:

```
Length of Chapter 1: 100
```

The DBMS_LOB.READ procedure

The READ procedure provides piece-wise read access to a LOB. A specified number of bytes (BFILE, BLOB) or characters (CLOB, NCLOB) is read into the buffer, starting from a specified location. The number of bytes or characters actually read by the operation is returned. The headers for this program, corresponding to each type, are the following:

```
PROCEDURE DBMS_LOB.READ
    (lob_loc IN BLOB | BFILE,
     amount IN OUT BINARY_INTEGER,
     offset IN INTEGER,
     buffer OUT RAW);

PROCEDURE DBMS_LOB.READ
    (lob_loc IN CLOB CHARACTER SET ANY_CS,
     amount IN OUT BINARY_INTEGER,
     offset IN INTEGER,
     buffer OUT VARCHAR2 CHARACTER SET lob_loc%CHARSET);
```

The overloaded specification allows READ to be used with all types of LOBs. The term ANY_CS in the specification allows either CLOB or NCLOB locators as input.

The READ procedure and the DBMS_LOB.SUBSTR function provide similar functionality. READ is a procedure, while SUBSTR is a function. However, READ will raise NO_DATA_FOUND and INVALID_ARGVAL exceptions, while SUBSTR will ignore these exceptions and return NULL when they occur. DBMS_LOB.SUBSTR can also be called from within a SQL statement, but READ cannot be, since it is a procedure.

Parameters are summarized in the following table.

Parameter	Description
lob_loc	A locator for the LOB to be read
amount	Number of bytes (BFILE, BLOB) or characters (CLOB, NCLOB) to read; the number of bytes or characters actually read by the operation is returned in amount
offset	Location of the byte (BFILE, BLOB) or character (CLOB, NCLOB) in the LOB at which the read begins
buffer	Buffer where the results of the read operation are placed

Exceptions. The READ procedure may raise any of the following exceptions:

VALUE_ERROR
    lob_loc, amount, or offset is NULL.

INVALID_ARGVAL
    One of the following conditions exists:

— amount < 1 or amount > 32767

— offset < 1 or offset > LOBMAXSIZE

— size of amount > size of buffer

NO_DATA_FOUND

The end of the LOB is reached.

UNOPENED_FILE

For BFILEs, files must be open before the read.

NOEXIST_DIRECTORY

For BFILEs.

NOPRIV_DIRECTORY

For BFILEs.

INVALID_DIRECTORY

For BFILEs.

INVALID_OPERATION

For BFILEs.

Examples. The following example reads the first 60 characters of the CLOB chapter_text column of the my_book_text table using the "Chapter 1" row:

```
DECLARE
    v_text_loc      CLOB;
    v_text_amt      BINARY_INTEGER := 60;
    v_text_buffer   VARCHAR2(60);
BEGIN
    v_text_loc := book_text ('Chapter 1');
    DBMS_LOB.READ (v_text_loc, v_text_amt, 1, v_text_buffer);
    DBMS_OUTPUT.PUT_LINE('Chapter 1: ' || v_text_buffer);
END;
/
```

This is the output of the script:

```
Chapter 1: It was a dark and stormy night.  Suddenly a scream rang out.
```

The next example reads sixty characters at a time from the CLOB chapter_text column of the my_book_text table using the "Chapter 1" row. Note that the loop continues until READ raises the NO_DATA_FOUND exception.

```
DECLARE
    v_text_loc      CLOB;
    v_text_amt      BINARY_INTEGER := 60;
    v_text_pos      INTEGER := 1;
    v_text_buffer   VARCHAR2(60);
BEGIN
    v_text_loc := book_text ('Chapter 1');
    LOOP
```

```
            DBMS_LOB.READ
                (v_text_loc, v_text_amt, v_text_pos, v_text_buffer);
            /* process the text and prepare to read again */
            DBMS_OUTPUT.PUT_LINE('Chapter 1: ' || v_text_buffer);
            v_text_pos := v_text_pos + v_text_amt;
        END LOOP;
    EXCEPTION
        WHEN NO_DATA_FOUND
        THEN
            DBMS_OUTPUT.PUT_LINE('End of Chapter Reached.');
    END;
    /
```

This script produces the following:

```
Chapter 1: It was a dark and stormy night.  Suddenly a scream rang out.
Chapter 1:   An EXCEPTION had not been handled.
End of Chapter Reached.
```

Note that the maximum size of a VARCHAR2 or RAW variable is 32767 bytes. This is the size limit of the buffer to be used with READ.

The DBMS_LOB.SUBSTR function

The SUBSTR function provides piece-wise access to a LOB. The specified number of bytes (BFILE, BLOB) or characters (CLOB, NCLOB) is returned, starting from the specified location. The headers for this program, corresponding to each LOB type, are the following:

```
FUNCTION DBMS_LOB.SUBSTR
    (lob_loc IN BLOB | BFILE,
     amount IN INTEGER := 32767,
     offset IN INTEGER := 1)
    RETURN RAW;

FUNCTION DBMS_LOB.SUBSTR
    (lob_loc IN CLOB CHARACTER SET ANY_CS,
     amount IN INTEGER := 32767,
     offset IN INTEGER := 1)
    RETURN VARCHAR2 CHARACTER SET lob_loc%CHARSET;
```

The overloaded specification allows SUBSTR to be used with all types of LOBs. The term ANY_CS in the specification allows either CLOB or NCLOB locators as input.

The SUBSTR function and DBMS_LOB.READ procedure provide similar functionality. READ is a procedure, while SUBSTR is a function. However, READ will raise NO_DATA_FOUND and INVALID_ARGVAL exceptions, while SUBSTR will ignore these exceptions when they occur and will return NULL. SUBSTR can also be called from within a SQL statement, but DBMS_LOB.READ cannot, since it is a procedure.

Parameters are summarized in the following table.

Parameter	Description
lob_loc	Locator for the LOB to be read
amount	Number of bytes (BFILE, BLOB) or characters (CLOB, NCLOB) to read
offset	Location of the byte (BFILE, BLOB) or character (CLOB, NCLOB) in the LOB at which the read begins

The SUBSTR function returns a NULL value for any of the following conditions:

- One of the parameters is NULL or invalid

- amount < 1 or amount > 32767

- offset < 1 or offset > LOBMAXSIZE

Exceptions. The SUBSTR function may raise one of the following exceptions:

UNOPENED_FILE
   For BFILEs. Files must be open before the SUBSTR operation.

NOEXIST_DIRECTORY
   For BFILEs.

NOPRIV_DIRECTORY
   For BFILEs.

INVALID_DIRECTORY
   For BFILEs.

INVALID_OPERATION
   For BFILEs.

Restrictions. The program asserts a purity level with the RESTRICT_REFERENCES pragma.

```
PRAGMA RESTRICT_REFERENCES (substr, WNDS, RNDS, WNPS, RNPS);
```

Examples. The following example reads the first 60 characters of the CLOB chapter_text column of the my_book_text table using the "Chapter 1" row:

```
DECLARE
    v_text_loc      CLOB;
    v_text_amt      BINARY_INTEGER := 60;
    v_text_buffer   VARCHAR2(60);
BEGIN
    v_text_loc := book_text ('Chapter 1');

    v_text_buffer := DBMS_LOB.SUBSTR (v_text_loc, v_text_amt, 1);
    DBMS_OUTPUT.PUT_LINE ('Chapter 1: ' || v_text_buffer);
END;
/
```

This is the output of the script:

```
Chapter 1: It was a dark and stormy night.   Suddenly a scream rang out.
```

The next example reads 60 characters at a time from the CLOB chapter_text column of the my_book_text table using the "Chapter 1" row. Note that the loop continues until SUBSTR returns NULL (i.e., SUBSTR does not raise the NO_DATA_FOUND exception).

```
DECLARE
    v_text_loc        CLOB;
    v_text_amt        BINARY_INTEGER := 60;
    v_text_pos        INTEGER := 1;
    v_buffer    VARCHAR2(60);
BEGIN
    v_text_loc := book_text ('Chapter 1');

    LOOP
        v_buffer := DBMS_LOB.SUBSTR (v_text_loc, v_text_amt, v_text_pos);
        EXIT WHEN v_buffer IS NULL;

        /* process the text and prepare to read again */
        DBMS_OUTPUT.PUT_LINE('Chapter 1: ' || v_buffer);
        v_text_pos := v_text_pos + v_text_amt;
    END LOOP;
END;
/
```

This is the output of the script:

```
Chapter 1: It was a dark and stormy night.   Suddenly a scream rang out.
Chapter 1:   An EXCEPTION had not been handled.
```

The DBMS_LOB.INSTR function

The INSTR function returns the matching offset location of the Nth occurrence of the given pattern in the LOB. It returns zero if the pattern is not found. The headers for this program, corresponding to each LOB type, are the following:

```
FUNCTION DBMS_LOB.INSTR
    (lob_loc IN BLOB | BFILE,
     pattern IN RAW,
     offset IN INTEGER := 1,
     nth IN INTEGER := 1)
    RETURN INTEGER;

FUNCTION DBMS_LOB.INSTR
    (lob_loc IN CLOB CHARACTER SET ANY_CS,
     pattern IN VARCHAR2 CHARACTER SET lob_loc%CHARSET,
     offset IN INTEGER := 1,
     nth IN INTEGER := 1)
    RETURN INTEGER;
```

The overloaded specification allows INSTR to be used with all types of LOBs. The clause ANY_CS in the specification allows either CLOB or NCLOB locators as input.

Parameters are summarized in the following table.

Parameter	Description
lob_loc	A locator for the LOB to be searched
pattern	The pattern to search for in the LOB
offset	Location of the byte (BFILE, BLOB) or character (CLOB, NCLOB) in the LOB at which the search begins
nth	Search for the Nth occurrence of the given pattern in the LOB

The INSTR function returns NULL for any of the following conditions:

- file_loc or pattern is NULL

- one of the parameters is invalid

- offset < 1 or offset > LOBMAXSIZE

- nth < 1 or nth > LOBMAXSIZE

Exceptions. The INSTR function may raise any of the following exceptions:

UNOPENED_FILE
　　For BFILEs. Files must be open before the INSTR operation.

NOEXIST_DIRECTORY
　　For BFILEs.

NOPRIV_DIRECTORY
　　For BFILEs.

INVALID_DIRECTORY
　　For BFILEs.

INVALID_OPERATION
　　For BFILEs.

Restrictions. The program asserts a purity level with the RESTRICT_REFERENCES pragma.

```
PRAGMA RESTRICT_REFERENCES (instr, WNDS, RNDS, WNPS, RNPS);
```

Example. The following example searches for the first occurrence of the string "dark" in the first sixty characters of the CLOB chapter_text column of the "Chapter 1" row of the my_book_text table:

```
DECLARE
     v_text_loc      CLOB;
```

```
      v_text_buffer    VARCHAR2(60);
      v_text_pattern   VARCHAR2(60) := 'dark';
BEGIN
      v_text_loc := book_text ('Chapter 1');
      v_text_buffer := DBMS_LOB.SUBSTR (v_text_loc, 60, 1);

      DBMS_OUTPUT.PUT_LINE ('buffer: ' || v_text_buffer);
      DBMS_OUTPUT.PUT_LINE
          ('location of "' || v_text_pattern || '": ' ||
          DBMS_LOB.INSTR(v_text_loc, v_text_pattern));
END;
/
```

This is the output of the script:

```
buffer: It was a dark and stormy night.   Suddenly a scream rang out.
location of "dark": 10
```

Updating BLOBs, CLOBs, and NCLOBs

The following sections describe the programs in the DBMS_LOB package that are used to update or alter BLOB, CLOB, and NCLOB object types.

The DBMS_LOB.APPEND procedure

The APPEND procedure appends the contents of a source internal LOB to a destination internal LOB. The headers for this program, corresponding to each LOB type, are the following:

```
PROCEDURE DBMS_LOB.APPEND
    (dest_lob IN OUT BLOB,
     src_lob IN BLOB);

PROCEDURE DBMS_LOB.APPEND
    (dest_lob IN OUT CLOB CHARACTER SET ANY_CS,
     src_lob IN CLOB CHARACTER SET dest_lob%CHARSET);
```

The overloaded specification allows APPEND to be used with BLOBs, CLOBs, and NCLOBs. The term ANY_CS in the specification allows either CLOB or NCLOB locators as input. APPEND cannot be used with BFILEs because access to BFILEs is read-only.

Parameters are summarized in the following table.

Parameter	Description
dest_lob	A locator for the destination LOB
src_lob	A locator for the source LOB

Exceptions. The program may raise any of the following exceptions:

VALUE_ERROR

    Either of the LOBs is NULL.

ORA-22920

    dest_lob is not locked for update.

Examples. The following example shows that the destination LOB must be selected FOR UPDATE before calling APPEND. We attempt to append the chapter_text for "Chapter 2" to the chapter_text for "Chapter 1."

```
DECLARE
    v_text_loc      CLOB;
    v_text_buffer   VARCHAR2(60);
    v_text_pattern  VARCHAR2(60) := 'dark';
BEGIN
    v_dest_loc := book_text ('Chapter 1');
    v_src_loc  := book_text ('Chapter 2');
    DBMS_LOB.APPEND (v_dest_loc, v_src_loc);
EXCEPTION
    WHEN OTHERS
    THEN
        DBMS_OUTPUT.PUT_LINE('OTHERS Exception ' || sqlerrm);
END;
/
```

This is the output of the script:

```
OTHERS Exception ORA-22920: row containing the LOB value is not locked
```

In the next example we append the chapter_text for "Chapter" to the chapter_text for "Chapter 1." We display the appended text, roll back the changes, and display the original text. Internal LOBs *can* participate in database transactions.

```
DECLARE
    v_text_loc      CLOB;
    v_text_buffer   VARCHAR2(60);
    v_text_pattern  VARCHAR2(60) := 'dark';
BEGIN
    v_dest_loc := book_text_forupdate ('Chapter 1');
    v_src_loc  := book_text ('Chapter 2');
    DBMS_LOB.APPEND (v_dest_loc, v_src_loc);
END;
/

    SET LONG 200
    COL chapter_descr FOR A15
    COL chapter_text FOR A40 WORD_WRAPPED

exec compare_text ('Chapter 1');
```

This is the output of the script:

```
CHAPTER_DESCR    CHAPTER_TEXT
---------------  ----------------------------------------
Chapter 1        It was a dark and stormy night.
                 Suddenly a scream rang out.  An
                 EXCEPTION had not been handled.  The sun
                 shone brightly the following morning.
                 All traces of the storm had disappeared.


Rollback complete.

CHAPTER_DESCR    CHAPTER_TEXT
---------------  ----------------------------------------
Chapter 1        It was a dark and stormy night.
                 Suddenly a scream rang out.  An
                 EXCEPTION had not been handled.
```

The DBMS_LOB.COPY procedure

The COPY procedure copies all or part of the contents of a source internal LOB to a destination internal LOB. An offset location in each LOB can be specified. The headers for this program, corresponding to each LOB type, are the following:

```
PROCEDURE DBMS_LOB.COPY
   (dest_lob IN OUT BLOB,
    src_lob IN BLOB,
    amount IN INTEGER,
    dest_offset IN INTEGER := 1,
    src_offset IN INTEGER := 1);

PROCEDURE DBMS_LOB.COPY
   (dest_lob IN OUT CLOB CHARACTER SET ANY_CS,
    src_lob IN CLOB CHARACTER SET dest_lob%CHARSET,
    amount IN INTEGER,
    dest_offset IN INTEGER := 1,
    src_offset IN INTEGER := 1);
```

The overloaded specification allows COPY to be used with BLOBs, CLOBs, and NCLOBs. The term ANY_CS in the specification allows either CLOB or NCLOB locators as input. COPY cannot be used with BFILEs, because access to BFILEs is read-only.

Parameters are summarized in the following table.

Parameter	Description
dest_lob	Locator for the destination LOB
src_lob	Locator for the source LOB
amount	Number of bytes (BLOB) or characters (CLOB, NCLOB) to copy

Parameter	Description
dest_offset	Location of the byte (BLOB) or character (CLOB, NCLOB) in the destination LOB at which the copy operation begins; the default value is 1
src_offset	Location of the byte (BLOB) or character (CLOB, NCLOB) in the source LOB at which the copy operation begins; the default value is 1

Exceptions. The COPY procedure may raise one of the following exceptions:

VALUE_ERROR

One or both LOBs are NULL or invalid.

INVALID_ARGVAL

One of the following conditions exists:

— src_offset < 1 or src_offset > LOBMAXSIZE

— dest_offset <1 or dest_offset > LOBMAXSIZE

— amount < 1 or amount > LOBMAXSIZE

ORA-22920

dest_lob is not locked for update.

Example. In the following example, the text "Suddenly a scream rang out..." is copied from the "Chapter 1" row of the my_book_text table to the "Chapter 2" row. Note that the COPY operation replaces (i.e., does not append) existing text. We display the copied text, roll back the changes, and display the original text. Internal LOBs *can* participate in database transactions.

```
SET LONG 200
COL chapter_descr FOR A15
COL chapter_text FOR A40 WORD_WRAPPED

SELECT chapter_descr, chapter_text
  FROM my_book_text;

DECLARE
    v_text_loc      CLOB;
    v_text_buffer   VARCHAR2(60);
    v_text_pattern  VARCHAR2(60) := 'dark';
BEGIN
    v_dest_loc := book_text_forupdate ('Chapter 2');
    v_src_loc  := book_text ('Chapter 1');
    DBMS_LOB.COPY(v_dest_loc, v_src_loc, 63, 47 ,34);
END;
/
exec compare_text ('Chapter 2');
```

This is the output of the script:

```
CHAPTER_DESCR    CHAPTER_TEXT
---------------  ----------------------------------------
Chapter 1        It was a dark and stormy night.
                 Suddenly a scream rang out.  An
                 EXCEPTION had not been handled.

Chapter 2        The sun shone brightly the following
                 morning.  All traces of the storm had
                 disappeared.

PL/SQL procedure successfully completed.

CHAPTER_DESCR    CHAPTER_TEXT
---------------  ----------------------------------------
Chapter 2        The sun shone brightly the following
                 morning. Suddenly a scream rang out.  An
                 EXCEPTION had not been handled.

Rollback complete.

CHAPTER_DESCR    CHAPTER_TEXT
---------------  ----------------------------------------
Chapter 2        The sun shone brightly the following
                 morning.  All traces of the storm had
                 disappeared.
```

The DBMS_LOB.ERASE procedure

The ERASE procedure removes all or part of the contents of an internal LOB. An offset location in the LOB can be specified. In the middle of a LOB, spaces are written for CLOBs and NCLOBs, and zero-byte filler is written for BLOBs.

```
PROCEDURE DBMS_LOB.ERASE
    (lob_loc IN OUT BLOB | CLOB CHARACTER SET ANY_CS,
     amount IN OUT INTEGER,
     offset IN INTEGER := 1);
```

The overloaded specification allows ERASE to be used with BLOBs, CLOBs, and NCLOBs. The term ANY_CS in the specification allows either CLOB or NCLOB locators as input. ERASE cannot be used with BFILEs because access to BFILEs is read-only.

Parameters are summarized in the following table.

Parameter	Description
lob_loc	Locator for the LOB to be erased
amount	Number of bytes (BLOB) or characters (CLOB, NCLOB) to erase
offset	Location of the byte (BLOB) or character (CLOB, NCLOB) in the LOB at which the erase operation begins; the default value is 1

Exceptions

The ERASE procedure may raise any of the following exceptions:

VALUE_ERROR

　　lob_loc or amount is NULL or invalid.

INVALID_ARGVAL

　　One of the following conditions exists:

　　— amount < 1 or amount > LOBMAXSIZE

　　— offset < 1 or offset > LOBMAXSIZE

ORA-22920

　　dest_lob is not locked for update.

Example. In the following example, we erase the string "brightly" from the "Chapter 2" chapter_text column in the my_book_text table. Note that the string is replaced with spaces. We display the erased text, roll back the changes, and display the original text. Internal LOBs *can* participate in database transactions.

```
SET LONG 200
COL chapter_descr FOR A15
COL chapter_text FOR A40 WORD_WRAPPED

SELECT chapter_descr, chapter_text
  FROM my_book_text
 WHERE chapter_descr = 'Chapter 2';

DECLARE
   v_dest_loc      CLOB;
   v_erase_amt     INTEGER;
BEGIN
   v_dest_loc := book_text_forupdate ('Chapter 2');
   v_erase_amt := 9;
   DBMS_LOB.ERASE(v_dest_loc, v_erase_amt, 15);
END;
/

exec compare_text ('Chapter 2');
```

This is the output of the script:

```
CHAPTER_DESCR    CHAPTER_TEXT
---------------  ----------------------------------------
Chapter 2        The sun shone brightly the following
                 morning.  All traces of the storm had
                 disappeared.


PL/SQL procedure successfully completed.


CHAPTER_DESCR    CHAPTER_TEXT
---------------  ----------------------------------------
Chapter 2        The sun shone          the following
                 morning.  All traces of the storm had
                 disappeared.


Rollback complete.


CHAPTER_DESCR    CHAPTER_TEXT
---------------  ----------------------------------------
Chapter 2        The sun shone brightly the following
                 morning.  All traces of the storm had
                 disappeared.
```

The DBMS_LOB.TRIM procedure

The TRIM procedure trims the contents of an internal LOB to a specified length. The headers for this program, corresponding to each LOB type, are the following:

```
PROCEDURE DBMS_LOB.TRIM
    (lob_loc IN OUT BLOB|CLOB CHARACTER SET ANY_CS,
     newlen IN INTEGER);
```

The overloaded specification allows TRIM to be used with BLOBs, CLOBs, and NCLOBs. The term ANY_CS in the specification allows either CLOB or NCLOB locators as input. TRIM cannot be used with BFILEs because access to BFILEs is read-only.

The parameters for this program are summarized in the following table.

Parameter	Description
lob_loc	Locator for the LOB to be erased
newlen	Number of bytes (BLOB) or characters (CLOB, NCLOB) to remain in the LOB

Exceptions. The TRIM procedure may raise any of the following exceptions:

VALUE_ERROR
    lob_loc or newlen is NULL or invalid.

INVALID_ARGVAL
    newlen < 0 or newlen > LOBMAXSIZE.

ORA-22920

dest_lob is not locked for update.

Example. In the following example, we trim the "Chapter 1" chapter_text column in the my_book_text table to 31 characters. We display the trimmed text, roll back the changes, and display the original text. Internal LOBs *can* participate in database transactions.

```
SET LONG 200
COL chapter_descr FOR A15
COL chapter_text FOR A40 WORD_WRAPPED

SELECT chapter_descr, chapter_text
  FROM my_book_text
 WHERE chapter_descr = 'Chapter 1';
DECLARE
   v_text_loc CLOB;
BEGIN
   v_text_loc := book_text ('Chapter 1');
   DBMS_LOB.TRIM (v_text_loc, 31);
END;
/
exec compare_text ('Chapter 1');
```

This is the output of the script:

```
CHAPTER_DESCR   CHAPTER_TEXT
--------------- ---------------------------------------
Chapter 1       It was a dark and stormy night.
                Suddenly a scream rang out.  An
                EXCEPTION had not been handled.

PL/SQL procedure successfully completed.

CHAPTER_DESCR   CHAPTER_TEXT
--------------- ---------------------------------------
Chapter 1       It was a dark and stormy night.

Rollback complete.

CHAPTER_DESCR   CHAPTER_TEXT
--------------- ---------------------------------------
Chapter 1       It was a dark and stormy night.
                Suddenly a scream rang out.  An
                EXCEPTION had not been handled.
```

The DBMS_LOB.WRITE procedure

The WRITE procedure writes a given number of bytes (BLOB) or characters (CLOB, NCLOB) to an internal LOB, beginning at a specified offset. The contents of the write operation are taken from the buffer. WRITE replaces (overlays) any data that exists in the LOB at the offset. The headers for this program, for each corresponding LOB type, are the following:

```
PROCEDURE DBMS_LOB.WRITE
    (lob_loc IN OUT BLOB,
     amount IN BINARY_INTEGER,
     offset IN INTEGER,
     buffer IN RAW);

PROCEDURE DBMS_LOB.WRITE
    (lob_loc IN OUT CLOB CHARACTER SET ANY_CS,
     amount IN BINARY_INTEGER,
     offset IN INTEGER,
     buffer IN VARCHAR2 CHARACTER SET lob_loc%CHARSET);
```

The overloaded specification allows WRITE to be used with BLOBs, CLOBs, and NCLOBs. The term ANY_CS in the specification allows either CLOB or NCLOB locators as input. WRITE cannot be used with BFILEs, because access to BFILEs is read-only.

Parameters are summarized in the following table.

Parameter	Description
lob_loc	A locator for the target LOB
amount	Number of bytes (BLOB) or characters (CLOB, NCLOB) to be written
offset	The location of the byte (BLOB) or character (CLOB, NCLOB) in the LOB at which the write begins
buffer	Buffer holding the contents of the write operation

Exceptions

The WRITE procedure may raise any of the following exceptions:

VALUE_ERROR
  lob_loc, amount, or offset is NULL or invalid.

INVALID_ARGVAL
  One of the following conditions exists:

  — amount < 1 or amount > 32767

  — offset < 1 or offset > LOBMAXSIZE

Example. In the following example, we write the string "The End" to the end of the "Chapter 2" chapter_text column in the my_book_text table. We display the new text, roll back the changes, and display the original text. Internal LOBs *can* participate in database transactions.

```
    SET LONG 200
    COL chapter_descr FOR A15
    COL chapter_text FOR A40 WORD_WRAPPED

    SELECT chapter_descr, chapter_text
      FROM my_book_text
     WHERE chapter_descr = 'Chapter 2';

DECLARE
    v_text_loc CLOB;
    v_offset   INTEGER;
    v_buffer   VARCHAR2(100);
BEGIN
    v_text_loc := book_text_forupdate ('Chapter 1');
    v_offset := DBMS_LOB.GETLENGTH (v_text_loc) + 3;
    v_buffer := 'The End.';
    DBMS_LOB.WRITE (v_text_loc, 8, v_offset, v_buffer);
END;
/

exec compare_text ('Chapter 2');
```

This is the output of the script:

```
CHAPTER_DESCR   CHAPTER_TEXT
--------------- ----------------------------------------
Chapter 2       The sun shone brightly the following
                morning.  All traces of the storm had
                disappeared.


PL/SQL procedure successfully completed.

CHAPTER_DESCR   CHAPTER_TEXT
--------------- ----------------------------------------
Chapter 2       The sun shone brightly the following
                morning.  All traces of the storm had
                disappeared.  The End.


Rollback complete.

CHAPTER_DESCR   CHAPTER_TEXT
--------------- ----------------------------------------
Chapter 2       The sun shone brightly the following
                morning.  All traces of the storm had
                disappeared.
```

9

Datatype Packages

In this chapter:
- *DBMS_ROWID: Working with the ROWID Pseudo-Column (Oracle8 only)*
- *UTL_RAW: Manipulating Raw Data*
- *UTL_REF: Referencing Objects (Oracle8.1 Only)*

This chapter introduces you to several packages that let you work effectively with particular types of Oracle data:

DBMS_ROWID

New in Oracle8, allows you to work with the two different ROWID formats: extended (new to Oracle8) and restricted (traditional Oracle7 ROWIDs).

UTL_RAW

Offers a set of functions allowing you to perform concatenation, substring, bit-wise logical analysis, byte translation, and length operations on RAW data.

UTL_REF

New in Oracle8 Release 8.1; provides a PL/SQL interface to select and modify objects (instances of an object type) in an object table without having to specify or know about the underlying database table.

DBMS_ROWID: Working with the ROWID Pseudo-Column (Oracle8 only)

The DBMS_ROWID package lets you work with ROWIDs from within PL/SQL programs and SQL statements. You can use the programs in this package to both create and manipulate ROWIDs. You can determine the data block number, the object number, and other components of the ROWID without having to write code to translate the base-64 character external ROWID.

NOTE   With Oracle8, there are two types of ROWIDs: extended and restricted. Restricted ROWIDs are the ROWIDs available with Oracle Version 7 and earlier. Extended ROWIDs are used only in Oracle8.

Getting Started with DBMS_ROWID

The DBMS_ROWID package is created when the Oracle8 database is installed. The *dbmsutil.sql* script (found in the built-in packages source code directory, as described in Chapter 1, *Introduction*), contains the source code for this package's specification. This script is called by *catproc.sql*, which is normally run immediately after database creation. The script creates the public synonym DBMS_ROWID for the package and grants EXECUTE privilege on the package to public. All Oracle users can reference and make use of this package.

All of the programs in DBMS_ROWID run as invoker, meaning that the privileges of the programs are taken from the session running the DBMS_ROWID programs and not from the owner of that package.

DBMS_ROWID programs

Table 9-1 lists the programs defined for the DBMS_ROWID package. For a dicussion of some of the concepts underlying these program operations, see the next section, "ROWID Concepts."

Table 9-1. DBMS_ROWID Programs

Name	Description	Use in SQL
ROWID_BLOCK_NUMBER	Returns the database block number of the ROWID.	Yes
ROWID_CREATE	Creates a ROWID (either restricted or extended as you request) based on the individual ROWID component values you specify. Use this function for test purposes only.	Yes
ROWID_INFO	Returns information about the specified ROWID. This procedure essentially "parses" the ROWID.	Yes
ROWID_OBJECT	Returns the data object number for an extended ROWID. Returns 0 if the specified ROWID is restricted.	Yes
ROWID_RELATIVE_FNO	Returns the relative file number (relative to the tablespace) of the ROWID.	Yes
ROWID_ROW_NUMBER	Returns the row number of the ROWID.	Yes
ROWID_TO_ABSOLUTE_FNO	Returns the absolute file number (for a row in a given schema and table) from the ROWID.	Yes
ROWID_TO_EXTENDED	Converts a restricted ROWID to an extended ROWID.	Yes
ROWID_TO_RESTRICTED	Converts an extended ROWID to a restricted ROWID.	Yes

Table 9-1. DBMS_ROWID Programs (continued)

Name	Description	Use in SQL
ROWID_TYPE	Returns 0 if the ROWID is restricted, 1 if the ROWID is extended.	Yes
ROWID_VERIFY	Returns 0 if the restricted ROWID provided can be converted to an extended format, and 1 otherwise.	Yes

DBMS_ROWID exceptions

Table 9-2 lists the named exceptions defined in the DBMS_ROWID package; they are associated with the error number listed beside the name.

Table 9-2. DBMS_ROWID Exceptions

Name	Number	Description
ROWID_INVALID	−1410	The value entered is larger than the maximum width defined for the column.
ROWID_BAD_BLOCK	−28516	The block number specified in the ROWID is invalid.

DBMS_ROWID nonprogram elements

Table 9-3 lists the named constants defined by the DBMS_ROWID package for use with its programs.

Table 9-3. DBMS_ROWID Constants

Name/Type	Description
ROWID_TYPE_RESTRICTED	A ROWID type: integer constant assigned the value of 0.
ROWID_TYPE_EXTENDED	A ROWID type: integer constant assigned the value of 1.
ROWID_IS_VALID	A ROWID verification result: integer constant assigned the value of 0.
ROWID_IS_INVALID	A ROWID verification result: integer constant assigned the value of 1.
ROWID_OBJECT_UNDEFINED	An object type indicating that the object number is not defined (for restricted ROWIDs): integer constant assigned the value of 0.
ROWID_CONVERT_INTERNAL	A ROWID conversion type: integer constant assigned the value of 0.
ROWID_CONVERT_EXTERNAL	A ROWID conversion type: integer constant assigned the value of 1.

ROWID Concepts

This section offers a quick overview of the Oracle ROWID. You can get much more extensive information on ROWIDs from the Oracle documentation.

In the Oracle RDBMS, ROWID is a pseudocolumn that is a part of every table you create. The ROWID is an internally generated and maintained binary value that identifies a row of data in your table. It is called a pseudocolumn because a SQL statement includes it in places where you would normally use a column. However, it is not a column that you create for the table. Instead, the RDBMS generates the ROWID for each row as it is inserted into the database. The information in the ROWID provides the exact physical location of the row in the database. You cannot change the value of a ROWID.

You can use the ROWID datatype to store ROWIDs from the database in your PL/ SQL program. You can SELECT or FETCH the ROWID for a row into a ROWID variable. To manipulate ROWIDs in Oracle8, you will want to use the DBMS_ ROWID package described in this chapter. In Oracle7, you will use the ROWID-TOCHAR function to convert the ROWID to a fixed-length string and then perform operations against that string.

In Oracle7, the format of the fixed-length ROWID is,

> *BBBBBBB.RRRR.FFFFF*

where components of this format have the following meanings:

BBBBBBB
> The block in the database file.

RRRR
> The row in the block (where the first row is zero, not one).

FFFFF
> The database file.

All these numbers are hexadecimal; the database file is a number that you would then use to look up the actual name of the database file through the data dictionary.

In Oracle8, ROWIDs have been "extended" to support partitioned tables and indexes. The new, extended ROWIDs include a data object number, identifying the database segment. Any schema object found in the same segment, such as a cluster of tables, will have the same object number. In Oracle8, then, a ROWID contains the following information:

- The data object number
- The data file (where the first file is 1)

- The data block within the data file

- The row in the data block (where the first row is 0)

Usually (and always in Oracle7), a ROWID will uniquely identify a row of data. Within Oracle8, however, rows in different tables stored in the same cluster can have the same ROWID value.

The DBMS_ROWID Interface

The following sections describe the procedures and functions available through DBMS_ROWID.

The DBMS_ROWID.ROWID_BLOCK_NUMBER function

The ROWID_BLOCK_NUMBER function returns the block number of a ROWID. Its header is,

```
FUNCTION DBMS_ROWID.ROWID_BLOCK_NUMBER (row_id IN ROWID)
RETURN NUMBER;
```

where the ROWID parameter is the ROWID from which the value is extracted.

Restrictions. The DBMS_ROWID package supplies the following pragma for ROWID_BLOCK_NUMBER:

```
PRAGMA RESTRICT_REFERENCES (ROWID_BLOCK_NUMBER, WNDS, RNDS, WNPS, RNPS);
```

The DBMS_ROWID.CREATE_ROWID function

The CREATE_ROWID function creates and returns a ROWID (either restricted or extended, as you request) based on the individual ROWID component values you specify. Use this function for test purposes only. Here is its header:

```
FUNCTION DBMS_ROWID.ROWID_CREATE
    (rowid_type IN NUMBER
    ,object_number IN NUMBER
    ,relative_fno IN NUMBER
    ,block_number IN NUMBER
    ,row_number IN NUMBER)
RETURN ROWID;
```

Parameters are summarized in the following table.

Parameter	Description
rowid_type	The type of ROWID to be created. Specify either of the named constants ROWID_TYPE_RESTRICTED or ROWID_TYPE_EXTENDED.
object_number	The data object number for the ROWID. For a restricted ROWID (Oracle7), use the ROWID_OBJECT_UNDEFINED constant.
relative_fno	The relative file number for the ROWID.

Parameter	Description
block_number	The block number for the ROWID.
row_number	The row number for the ROWID.

Restrictions. The DBMS_ROWID package supplies the following pragma for CREATE_ROWID:

```
PRAGMA RESTRICT_REFERENCES (CREATE_ROWID, WNDS, RNDS, WNPS, RNPS);
```

Example. Here is an example of a call to the ROWID_CREATE procedure:

```
DECLARE
   my_rowid ROWID;
BEGIN
   my_rowid := DBMS_ROWID.ROWID_CREATE
      (DBMS_ROWID.ROWID_TYPE_EXTENDED, 100, 15, 103, 345);
END;
/
```

The DBMS_ROWID.ROWID_INFO procedure

The ROWID_INFO procedure parses out and returns the individual components of the specified ROWID. Here is its header:

```
PROCEDURE DBMS_ROWID.ROWID_INFO
      (rowid_in IN ROWID
      ,rowid_type OUT NUMBER
      ,object_number OUT NUMBER
      ,relative_fno OUT NUMBER
      ,block_number OUT NUMBER
      ,row_number OUT NUMBER);
```

Parameters are summarized in the following table.

Parameter	Description
rowid_in	The ROWID value to be parsed into components.
rowid_type	The type of ROWID. The value returned will be either of the named constants ROWID_TYPE_RESTRICTED or ROWID_TYPE_EXTENDED.
object_number	The data object number for the ROWID. For a restricted ROWID (Oracle7), the ROWID_OBJECT_UNDEFINED constant is returned.
relative_fno	The relative file number for the ROWID.
block_number	The block number for the ROWID in the file.
row_number	The row number for the ROWID.

Restrictions. The DBMS_ROWID package supplies the following pragma for ROWID_INFO:

```
PRAGMA RESTRICT_REFERENCES (ROWID_INFO, WNDS, RNDS, WNPS, RNPS);
```

The DBMS_ROWID.ROWID_OBJECT function

The ROWID_OBJECT function returns the object number of a ROWID. The ROWID_OBJECT_UNDEFINED constant is returned for restricted ROWIDs. Its header is,

```
FUNCTION DBMS_ROWID.ROWID_OBJECT (row_id IN ROWID)
RETURN NUMBER;
```

where the row_id parameter is the ROWID from which the value is extracted.

Restrictions. The DBMS_ROWID package supplies the following pragma for ROWID_OBJECT:

```
PRAGMA RESTRICT_REFERENCES (ROWID_OBJECT, WNDS, RNDS, WNPS, RNPS);
```

Example. You will want to obtain a ROWID's object number only if the ROWID type is extended. You would write code like this to perform that check:

```
IF DBMS_ROWID.ROWID_TYPE (v_rowid) = DBMS_ROWID.ROWID_TYPE_EXTENDED
THEN
    v_objnum := DBMS_ROWID.ROWID_OBJECT (v_rowid);
END IF;
```

The DBMS_ROWID.ROWID_RELATIVE_FNO function

The ROWID_RELATIVE_FNO function returns the relative file number of a ROWID. Its header is,

```
FUNCTION DBMS_ROWID.ROWID_RELATIVE_FNO
    (row_id IN ROWID)
RETURN NUMBER;
```

where the row_id parameter is the ROWID from which the value is extracted.

Restrictions. The DBMS_ROWID package supplies the following pragma for ROWID_RELATIVE_FNO:

```
PRAGMA RESTRICT_REFERENCES (ROWID_RELATIVE_FNO, WNDS, RNDS, WNPS, RNPS);
```

The DBMS_ROWID.ROWID_ROW_NUMBER function

The ROWID_ROW_NUMBER function returns the row number of a ROWID. Its header is,

```
FUNCTION DBMS_ROWID.ROWID_RELATIVE_FNO (row_id IN ROWID)
RETURN NUMBER;
```

where the row_id parameter is the ROWID from which the value is extracted.

Restrictions. The DBMS_ROWID package supplies the following pragma for ROWID_ROW_NUMBER:

```
PRAGMA RESTRICT_REFERENCES (ROWID_ROW_NUMBER, WNDS, RNDS, WNPS, RNPS);
```

The DBMS_ROWID.ROWID_TO_ABSOLUTE_FNO function

The ROWID_TO_ABSOLUTE_FNO function returns the absolute file number of a ROWID. Here is its header:

```
FUNCTION DBMS_ROWID.ROWID_TO_ABSOLUTE_FNO
     (row_id IN ROWID
     ,schema_name IN VARCHAR2
     ,object_name IN VARCHAR2)
     RETURN NUMBER;
```

Parameters are summarized in the following table.

Parameter	Description
row_id	The ROWID from which the value is extracted.
schema_name	The name of the schema contains the table.
object_name	The table name.

Restrictions. The DBMS_ROWID package supplies the following pragma for ROWID_RELATIVE_FNO:

```
PRAGMA RESTRICT_REFERENCES (ROWID_RELATIVE_FNO, WNDS, WNPS, RNPS);
```

The DBMS_ROWID.ROWID_TO_EXTENDED function

The ROWID_TO_EXTENDED function converts a restricted ROWID, addressing a specific row in a table, to an extended ROWID. Here is its header:

```
FUNCTION DBMS_ROWID.ROWID_TO_EXTENDED
     (old_rowid IN ROWID
     ,schema_name IN VARCHAR2
     ,object_name IN VARCHAR2
     ,conversion_type IN INTEGER)
     RETURN ROWID;
```

Parameters are summarized in the following table.

Parameter	Description
old_rowid	The ROWID to be converted.
schema_name	The name of the schema that contains the table.
object_name	The table name.
conversion_type	The type of conversion. Pass either the ROWID_CONVERT_INTERNAL constant (if old_ROWID was stored in a column of type ROWID) or ROWID_CONVERT_EXTERNAL (if old_ROWID was stored as a character string).

Restrictions. Note the following restrictions on calling ROWID_TO_EXTENDED:

- The ROWID_TO_EXTENDED function returns a ROWID in the extended character format. If you provide a NULL ROWID, the function will return NULL. If a zero-valued ROWID is supplied (00000000.0000.0000), a zero-valued restricted ROWID is returned.

- The DBMS_ROWID package supplies the following pragma for ROWID_TO_EXTENDED:

  ```
  PRAGMA RESTRICT_REFERENCES (ROWID_TO_EXTENDED, WNDS, WNPS, RNPS);
  ```

- If the schema and object names are provided as IN parameters, this function first verifies that you have SELECT privilege on the table named. It then converts the restricted ROWID provided to an extended ROWID, using the data object number of the specified table. Even if ROWID_TO_EXTENDED returns a value, however, that does not guarantee that the converted ROWID actually references a valid row in the table, either at the time that the function is called, or when the extended ROWID is actually used. It is only performing a conversion.

- If the schema and object name are not provided (i.e., are passed as NULL), then this function attempts to fetch the page specified by the restricted ROWID provided. It treats the file number stored in this ROWID as the absolute file number. This may cause problems if the file has been dropped, and its number has been reused prior to the data migration. If the fetched page belongs to a valid table, the data object number of this table is used in converting to an extended ROWID value.

  This approach is very inefficient. Oracle recommends doing this only as a last resort, when the target table is not known. Note that the user must still be aware of the correct table name when using the converted ROWID.

- If an extended ROWID value is supplied, that ROWID's data object is verified against the data object number calculated from the table name argument. If the two numbers do not match, DBMS_ROWID raises the INVALID_ROWID exception. If there is a match, then the input ROWID is returned.

Example. Suppose that I have a table in my APP schema called ROWID_conversion. This table contains two columns: ROWID_value and table_name. The ROWID_value column contains the restricted-format ROWIDs for rows in the table specifed by the table_name column. I can then convert all of my restricted ROWID values to extended ones with the following UPDATE statement:

```
UPDATE app.rowid_conversion
    SET rowid_value =
        DBMS_ROWID.ROWID_TO_EXTENDED
            (rowid_value,
```

```
        'APP',
        table_name,
        DBMS_ROWID.ROWID_CONVERT_INTERNAL);.
```

The DBMS_ROWID.ROWID_TO_RESTRICTED function

The ROWID_TO_RESTRICTED function converts an extended ROWID to a restricted ROWID. Here is its header:

```
FUNCTION DBMS_ROWID.ROWID_TO_RESTRICTED
    (old_rowid IN ROWID
    ,conversion_type IN INTEGER)
    RETURN ROWID;
```

Parameters are summarized in the following table.

Parameter	Description
old_rowid	The ROWID to be converted.
conversion_type	The format of the returned ROWID. Pass either the ROWID_CONVERT_INTERNAL constant (if the returned ROWID is to be stored in a column of type ROWID) or the ROWID_CONVERT_EXTERNAL constant (if the returned ROWID is to be stored as a character string).

Restrictions. The DBMS_ROWID package supplies the following pragma for ROWID_TO_RESTRICTED:

```
PRAGMA RESTRICT_REFERENCES
    (ROWID_TO_RESTRICTED, WNDS, RNDS, WNPS, RNPS);
```

The DBMS_ROWID.ROWID_TYPE function

The ROWID_TYPE function returns the type of a ROWID via one of the following package constants: ROWID_TYPE_RESTRICTED or ROWID_TYPE_EXTENDED. Its header is,

```
FUNCTION DBMS_ROWID.ROWID_TYPE (row_id IN ROWID)
    RETURN NUMBER;
```

where the row_id parameter is the ROWID from which the value is extracted.

Restrictions. The DBMS_ROWID package supplies the following pragma for ROWID_TYPE:

```
PRAGMA RESTRICT_REFERENCES (ROWID_TYPE, WNDS, RNDS, WNPS, RNPS);
```

Example. In the following query, I determine the ROWID types in the emp table:

```
SELECT DISTINCT (DBMS_ROWID.ROWID_TYPE(ROWID))
    FROM emp;
```

This returns the value of 1, that is: DBMS_ROWID.ROWID_TYPE_EXTENDED. The emp table was created under Oracle8 and therefore uses the Oracle8 type of ROWID.

The DBMS_ROWID.ROWID_VERIFY function

The ROWID_VERIFY function verifies a ROWID. It returns either the ROWID_ VALID or ROWID_INVALID constants. Here is its header:

```
FUNCTION DBMS_ROWID.ROWID_VERIFY
     (rowid_in IN ROWID
     ,schema_name IN VARCHAR2
     ,object_name IN VARCHAR2
     ,conversion_type IN INTEGER)
   RETURN NUMBER;
```

Parameters are summarized in the following table.

Parameter	Description
rowid_in	The ROWID to be verified.
schema_name	The name of the schema containing the table.
object_name	The name of the table.
conversion_type	The type of conversion to be used for the verification. You should pass either the ROWID_CONVERT_INTERNAL constant (if ROWID_in is stored in a column of type ROWID) or the ROWID_CONVERT_ EXTERNAL constant (if ROWID_in is stored as a character string).

Restrictions. The DBMS_ROWID package supplies the following pragma for ROWID_VERIFY:

```
PRAGMA RESTRICT_REFERENCES (ROWID_VERIFY, WNDS, WNPS, RNPS);
```

Example. Interestingly, you can call this numeric function as a kind of Boolean function within SQL. Suppose that I want to find all the invalid ROWIDs prior to converting them from restricted to extended. I could write the following query (using the same tables used in the example for the ROWID_TO_EXTENDED function):

```
SELECT ROWID, rowid_value
   FROM app.rowid_conversion
   WHERE DBMS_ROWID.ROWID_VERIFY (rowid_value, NULL, NULL);
```

UTL_RAW: Manipulating Raw Data

The UTL_RAW package contains a set of programs that allow you to manipulate raw data. This package was originally written as a component of the Oracle Server's advanced replication option, and it supported procedural replication of data across different NLS (National Language Support) language databases. By converting data to RAW, the remote procedure calls would not perform NLS conversion, thus preserving the nature of some special data. The functions included in this package actually go beyond this original functionality and provide a toolkit for the manipulation of raw data that is not otherwise available in the Oracle Server product. These functions perform a number of special operations: conversion and coercion, slicing and dicing of raw data, and bit-fiddling, all described in the next section.

Other than replication support, there are a number of advantages Oracle can offer in storing raw data in the database, such as tighter integration with the rest of the application, transaction-level consistency, concurrency, and recoverability. One of the difficulties in the use of raw data in an Oracle database has been in the poor support for manipulation of this data. The UTL_RAW package provides this support.

Getting Started with UTL_RAW

The UTL_RAW package is created when the Oracle database is installed. The *utl-raw.sql* script (found in the built-in packages source code directory, as described in Chapter 1) contains the source code for this package's specification and body. This script is called by *catrep.sql*, which is run when the advanced replication option of the Oracle database is installed. If this package is not already installed, check to see if these files are in your *admin* subdirectory. If so, you can connect as SYS and install this package by running the two scripts in the following order:

```
SQL> @utlraw.sql
SQL> @prvtrawb.plb
```

UTL_RAW programs

Table 9-4 lists the programs provided by the UTL_RAW package. For a discussion of some of the concepts underlying the operations performed by these programs, see the next section, "Raw Data Manipulation Concepts."

Table 9-4. UTL_RAW Programs

Name	Description	Use In SQL
BIT_AND	Performs bitwise logical AND of the values in raw r1 with raw r2 and returns the ANDed result raw.	Yes
BIT_COMPLEMENT	Performs bitwise logical "complement" of the values in raw r and returns the "complemented" result raw.	Yes
BIT_OR	Performs bitwise logical OR of the values in raw r1 with raw r2 and returns the ORed result raw.	Yes
BIT_XOR	Performs bitwise logical "exclusive or" (XOR) of the values in raw r1 with raw r2 and returns the XORed result raw.	Yes
CAST_TO_RAW	Converts a VARCHAR2 string represented using N data bytes into a raw with N data bytes.	Yes
CAST_TO_VARCHAR2	Converts a raw represented using N data bytes into a VARCHAR2 string with N data bytes.	Yes

Table 9-4. UTL_RAW Programs (continued)

Name	Description	Use In SQL
COMPARE	Compares raw r1 against raw r2. Returns 0 if r1 and r2 are identical; otherwise, returns the position of the first byte from r1 that does not match r2.	Yes
CONCAT	Concatenates a set of up to 12 raws into a single raw.	Yes
CONVERT	Converts a raw from one character set to another character set.	Yes
COPIES	Returns N copies of the original raw concatenated together.	Yes
LENGTH	Returns the length in bytes of a raw.	Yes
OVERLAY	Overlays the specified portion of a raw with a different raw value.	Yes
REVERSE	Reverses the byte sequence in the raw from end to end.	Yes
SUBSTR	Returns the specified sub-portion of a raw.	Yes
TRANSLATE	Translates original bytes in the raw with the specified replacement set.	Yes
TRANSLITERATE	Translates original bytes in the raw with the specified replacement set following rules, which result in the transliterated raw always being the same length as the original raw.	Yes
XRANGE	Returns a raw containing all valid 1-byte encodings in succession beginning with the value start_byte and ending with the value end_byte.	Yes

UTL_RAW does not declare any exceptions or nonprogram elements.

Raw Data Manipulation Concepts

This section provides an overview of the types of data manipulation you might perform on raw data.

Conversion and coercion

Conversion refers to functions that convert raw byte strings to other values. *Coercion* is a specialized conversion that changes the datatype but not the data itself. UTL_RAW has functions that convert from one NLS language set to another, from one set of raw byte strings to another, and from raw datatypes to VARCHAR2 datatypes (as well as from VARCHAR2 to raw). The coercion operations supported by Oracle involving raw datatypes via the standard SQL functions are raw-to-hex and hex-to-raw; via UTL_RAW functions, they are raw-to-VARCHAR2 and VARCHAR2-to-raw. Notably unsupported are raw-to/from-numeric datatypes and raw-to/from-date datatypes.

Slicing and dicing

Slicing and dicing refers to functions that divide and combine raw byte strings in various ways. These functions include COMPARE, CONCATENATE, COPY, LENGTH, OVERLAY, REVERSE, and SUBSTRING.

Bit-fiddling

Bit-fiddling refers to the manipulation of individual bits. Because bits are the smallest possible unit of storage, bit-fiddling provides a highly efficient storage mechanism. Bitmap indexes take advantage of this and offer substantial disk savings over traditional Btree indexes. The Oracle kernel supports the bitwise AND function natively via the undocumented function BITAND(x,x),[*] but the other bitwise operations needed to support bitmasks are supported only via the UTL_RAW package.

Bitmasks are commonly used to combine a number of flags or semaphores into a single object as follows:

- To see if a bit/flag/semaphore is set, use the bitwise AND function.
- To turn a bit on or combine bitmasks, use the bitwise OR function.
- To turn a bit off, use the bitwise OR and NOT functions together.
- To toggle a bit, use the bitwise XOR function.

Other bitwise functions, such as shift left and shift right, are supported in C and other languages, but not in PL/SQL or UTL_RAW.

To better understand bitmasks and what these functions do, let's look at some examples of their use. A mask is a bit that represents some data; for example, each day of the month can be represented by one bit as follows.

The first of the month is the bit mask:

```
0000 0000 0000 0000 0000 0000 0000 0001 or hex 0000 0001
```

---

[*] See the definitions of some V$ tables, such as V$session_wait, in the V$fixed_view_definition view.

The second of the month is the bit mask:

```
0000 0000 0000 0000 0000 0000 0000 0010 or hex 0000 0002
....
```

The 26th of the month is the bit mask:

```
0000 0010 0000 0000 0000 0000 0000 0000 or hex 0200 0000
```

And so on. In a single 32-bit string (4 bytes), any combination of days of the month can be set. In a scheduling application, we may want to find out if the variable DayInQuestion has the bit set for the 26th. We can perform a bitwise AND on the variable and the mask like this:

```
DayInQuestion      0000 0111 1111 1000 0000 0000 0000 0000  Bits 20-27 set
                                    AND
Mask for the 26th  0000 0010 0000 0000 0000 0000 0000 0000
------------------------------------------------------------------------------
Result             0000 0010 0000 0000 0000 0000 0000 0000  True
```

Likewise, if the variable needs to be checked for any of the bits 14th through 21st, then the masks for the 14th through 21st can be combined (via bitwise OR) and compared to the variable.

```
DayInQuestion      0000 0111 1111 1000 0000 0000 0000 0000  Bits 20-27 set
                                    AND
Mask               0000 0000 0001 1111 1110 0000 0000 0000  Bits 14-21 set
------------------------------------------------------------------------------
Result             0000 0000 0001 1000 0000 0000 0000 0000  True
```

The UTL_RAW package can also be used separately from replication, and offers facilities for manipulating raw data types that are not found elsewhere in the Oracle Server product. Oracle has a robust set of functions available for the structured datatypes RAW, CHARACTER, NUMERIC, and DATE.

The UTL_RAW Interface

This section describes the programs available through the UTL_RAW package.

The UTL_RAW.BIT_AND function

The BIT_AND function performs a bitwise logical AND of two input raw strings. If input strings are different lengths, the return value is the same length as the longer input string. The return value is the bitwise AND of the two inputs up to the length of the shorter input string, with the remaining length filled from the unprocessed data in the longer input string. If either input string is NULL, the return value is NULL. Here's the specification for this function:

```
FUNCTION UTL_RAW.BIT_AND
   (r1 IN RAW
   ,r2 IN RAW)
RETURN RAW;
```

Parameters are summarized in the following table.

Parameter	Description
r1	Raw string to AND with r2
r2	Raw string to AND with r1

Restrictions. This program asserts the following purity level with the RESTRICT_ REFERENCES pragma:

```
PRAGMA RESTRICT_REFERENCES(BIT_AND, WNDS, RNDS, WNPS, RNPS);
```

Example. To check if a bit is turned on in a bit flag variable using a bitmask, you can use the BIT_AND function. This section of example code also uses the BIT_ OR function to merge bitmasks:

```
DECLARE
   fourteenth      VARCHAR2(8);
   fifteenth       VARCHAR2(8);
   twentieth       VARCHAR2(8);
   mask            RAW(4);
   bitfield1       VARCHAR2(8);
   bitfield2       VARCHAR2(8);
BEGIN
  /* set bitfield1 for the 15th through 18th */
  bitfield1 := '0003C000';

  /* set bitfield2 for the 26st */
  bitfield2 := '02000000';

  /* set the mask for the 14th */
  fourteenth := '00002000';

  /* set the mask for the 15th */
  fifteenth := '00004000';

  /* set the mask for the 20th */
  twentieth := '00080000';

  /* merge the masks for the 14th, 15th and 20th */
  mask := UTL_RAW.BIT_OR(hextoraw(fourteenth),hextoraw(fifteenth));
  mask := UTL_RAW.BIT_OR(mask,hextoraw(twentieth));

  /* check to see if the bitfields have the 14th, 15th, or 20th set */
  if UTL_RAW.BIT_AND(mask,hextoraw(bitfield1)) = '00000000' then
    dbms_output.put_line('bitfield1 is not set');
  else
    dbms_output.put_line('bitfield1 is set');
  end if;

  if UTL_RAW.BIT_AND(mask,hextoraw(bitfield2)) = '00000000' then
    dbms_output.put_line('bitfield2 is not set');
  else
```

```
        dbms_output.put_line('bitfield2 is set');
    end if;

END;
```

This is the output from this code:

```
Bitfield1 is set
Bitfield2 is Anot set
```

The UTL_RAW.BIT_COMPLEMENT function

The BIT_COMPLEMENT function performs a logical NOT, or one's complement, of the raw input string r1. The complement of a raw string flips all 0 bits to 1 and all 1 bits to 0,

```
FUNCTION UTL_RAW.COMPLEMENT
    (r1 IN RAW)
RETURN RAW;
```

where r1 is the raw input string.

Restrictions. This program asserts the following purity level with the RESTRICT_ REFERENCES pragma:

```
PRAGMA RESTRICT_REFERENCES(BIT_COMPLEMENT, WNDS, RNDS, WNPS, RNPS);
```

Example. To turn off a bit, regardless of its original state, in a bit flag variable using a bitmap, you can use the BIT_COMPLEMENT function together with the BIT_AND function.

```
DECLARE
    fourteenth      VARCHAR2(8);
    fifteenth       VARCHAR2(8);
    twentieth       VARCHAR2(8);
    mask            RAW(4);
    bitfield1       VARCHAR2(8);
    bitfield2       VARCHAR2(8);
BEGIN
    /* set the bitfield for the 15th through 18th */
    bitfield1 := '0003C000';

    /* set the bitfield for the 26st */
    bitfield2 := '02000000';

    /* set the mask for the 14th */
    fourteenth := '00002000';

    /* set the mask for the 15th */
    fifteenth := '00004000';

    /* set the mask for the 20th */
    twentieth := '00080000';
```

```
/* merge the masks for the 14th, 15th and 20th */
mask := UTL_RAW.BIT_OR(hextoraw(fourteenth),hextoraw(fifteenth));
mask := UTL_RAW.BIT_OR(mask,hextoraw(twentieth));
mask := UTL_RAW.BIT_OR(mask,hextoraw(twentieth));

/* check to see if the bitfields have the 14th, 15th, or 20th set */
if UTL_RAW.BIT_AND(mask,hextoraw(bitfield1)) = '00000000' then
  dbms_output.put_line('bitfield1 is not set');
else
  dbms_output.put_line('bitfield1 is set');
end if;

if UTL_RAW.BIT_AND(mask,hextoraw(bitfield2)) = '00000000' then
  dbms_output.put_line('bitfield2 is not set');
else
  dbms_output.put_line('bitfield2 is set');
end if;

/* turn off bit 15 in the mask */
mask := UTL_RAW.BIT_AND(mask,UTL_RAW.BIT_COMPLEMENT(hextoraw(fifteenth)));

/* check to see if the bitfield1 has the 14th, 15th, or 20th set */
if UTL_RAW.BIT_AND(mask,hextoraw(bitfield1)) = '00000000' then
  dbms_output.put_line('bitfield1 is not set');
else
  dbms_output.put_line('bitfield1 is set');
end if;
END;
```

This is the output from the above code:

```
bitfield1 is set
bitfield2 is not set
bitfield1 is not set
```

The UTL_RAW.BIT_OR function

The BIT_OR function performs a bitwise logical OR of the two input raw strings r1 and r2. If r1 and r2 are of different length, the return value is the same length as the longer input string. The return value is the bitwise OR of the two inputs up to the length of the shorter input string, with the remaining length filled from the unprocessed data in the longer input string. If either input string is NULL, the return value is NULL.

```
FUNCTION UTL_RAW.BIT_OR
   (r1 IN RAW
   ,r2 IN RAW)
RETURN RAW;
```

Parameters are summarized in the following table.

Parameter	Description
r1	Raw string to OR with r2
r2	Raw string to OR with r1

Restrictions. This program asserts the following purity level with the RESTRICT_REFERENCES pragma:

```
PRAGMA RESTRICT_REFERENCES(BIT_OR, WNDS, RNDS, WNPS, RNPS);
```

Example. To turn on a bit in a bit flag variable using a bitmask, or to merge bitmasks, you can use the BIT_OR function, as shown in the example from BIT_AND.

The UTL_RAW.BIT_XOR function

The BIT_XOR function performs a bitwise logical XOR of the two input raw strings r1 and r2. If r1 and r2 are of different lengths, the return value is the same length as the longer input string. The return value is the bitwise XOR of the two inputs, up to the length of the shorter input string with the remaining length filled from the unprocessed data in the longer input string. If either input string is NULL, the return value is NULL. Here's the specification:

```
FUNCTION UTL_RAW.BIT_XOR
    (r1 IN RAW
    ,r2 IN RAW)
RETURN RAW;
```

Parameters are summarized in the following table.

Parameter	Description
r1	Raw string to XOR with r2
r2	Raw string to XOR with r1

Restrictions. This program asserts the following purity level with the RESTRICT_REFERENCES pragma:

```
PRAGMA RESTRICT_REFERENCES(BIT_XOR, WNDS, RNDS, WNPS, RNPS);
```

Example. To toggle a bit (if it is off, turn it on, and if it is on, turn it off) in a bit flag variable using a bitmask, use the BIT_XOR function as follows:

```
DECLARE
    fourteenth    VARCHAR2(8);
    fifteenth     VARCHAR2(8);
    twentieth     VARCHAR2(8);
    mask          RAW(4);
```

```
  bitfield1        VARCHAR2(8);
  bitfield2        VARCHAR2(8);
BEGIN
  /* set the bitfield for the 15th through 18th */
  bitfield1 := '0003C000';
  /* set the bitfield for the 26st */
  bitfield2 := '02000000';
  /* set the mask for the 14th */
  fourteenth := '00002000';
  /* set the mask for the 15th */
  fifteenth := '00004000';
  /* set the mask for the 20th */
  twentieth := '00080000';
  /* merge the masks for the 14th, 15th and 20th */
  mask := UTL_RAW.BIT_OR (HEXTORAW (fourteenth),HEXTORAW (fifteenth));
  mask := UTL_RAW.BIT_OR (mask, HEXTORAW (twentieth));
  /* check to see IF the bitfields have the 14th  or 20th set */
  IF UTL_RAW.BIT_AND (mask, HEXTORAW (bitfield1)) = '00000000' THEN
    DBMS_OUTPUT.PUT_LINE ('bitfield1 is not set');
  ELSE
    DBMS_OUTPUT.PUT_LINE ('bitfield1 is set');
  END IF;
  IF UTL_RAW.BIT_AND (mask, HEXTORAW (bitfield2)) = '00000000' THEN
    DBMS_OUTPUT.PUT_LINE ('bitfield2 is not set');
  ELSE
    DBMS_OUTPUT.PUT_LINE ('bitfield2 is set');
  END IF;
  /* toggle bit 15 in the mask */
  mask := UTL_RAW.BIT_XOR (mask, HEXTORAW (fifteenth));
  /* check to see IF the bitfield1 has the 14th, 15th, or 20th set */
  IF UTL_RAW.BIT_AND (mask, HEXTORAW (bitfield1)) = '00000000' THEN
    DBMS_OUTPUT.PUT_LINE ('bitfield1 is not set');
  ELSE
    DBMS_OUTPUT.PUT_LINE ('bitfield1 is set');
  END IF;
END;
/
```

This is the output from the previous example:

```
bitfield1 is set
bitfield2 is not set
bitfield1 is not set
```

The UTL_RAW.CAST_TO_RAW function

The CAST_TO_RAW function converts the VARCHAR2 input string into a raw datatype. The data is not altered; only the data type is changed. This is essentially a VARCHAR2_to_RAW function,

```
FUNCTION UTL_RAW.CAST_TO_RAW
   (c IN VARCHAR2)
RETURN RAW;
```

where c is the text string that should be converted to a raw datatype.

Restrictions. This program asserts the following purity level with the RESTRICT_
REFERENCES pragma:

```
PRAGMA RESTRICT_REFERENCES(CAST_TO_RAW, WNDS, RNDS, WNPS, RNPS);
```

Example. For an example of CAST_TO_RAW, see "The UTL_RAW.TRANSLATE
function" later in this chapter.

The UTL_RAW.CAST_TO_VARCHAR2 function

The CAST_TO_VARCHAR2 function converts the raw input string into a
VARCHAR2 datatype. The data is not altered; only the data type is changed. The
current NLS language is used. The specification is,

```
FUNCTION UTL_RAW.CAST_TO_VARCHAR2
    (r IN RAW)
  RETURN VARCHAR2;
```

where r is the raw string that should be converted into a VARCHAR2.

Restrictions. This program asserts the following purity level with the RESTRICT_
REFERENCES pragma:

```
PRAGMA RESTRICT_REFERENCES(CAST_TO_VARCHAR2, WNDS, RNDS, WNPS, RNPS);
```

Example. The data dictionary views USER_TAB_COLUMNS, ALL_TAB_COLUMNS,
and DBA_TAB_COLUMNS have the first 32 bytes of the lowest and highest data
values for each column in analyzed tables. Unfortunately, this data is of data type
RAW and not very readable by humans. The CAST_TO_VARCHAR2 function can
be used on character datatype columns to see these data in more readable form.

```
SELECT column_name, UTL_RAW.CAST_TO_VARCHAR2(low_value)
       ,UTL_RAW.CAST_TO_VARCHAR2(high_value)
FROM   user_tab_columns
WHERE  table_name = 'FOO_TAB'
  AND  column_name = 'VCHAR1'
```

The UTL_RAW.COMPARE function

The COMPARE function does a binary compare of the two raw input strings and
returns the number of the first byte position where the two strings differ. If the
two strings are identical, a zero is returned. If the two input strings are different
lengths, then the pad character is repeatedly appended to the shorter string,
extending it to the length of the longer string. The default pad character is 0x00
(binary zero).

```
FUNCTION UTL_RAW.COMPARE
    (r1 IN RAW
    ,r2 IN RAW
    ,pad IN RAW DEFAULT NULL)
  RETURN NUMBER;
```

The parameters for this program are summarized in this table.

Parameter	Description
r1	The first input string to compare
r2	The second input string to compare
pad	The single character used to right pad the shorter of two unequal length strings

Restrictions. This program asserts the following purity level with the RESTRICT_ REFERENCES pragma:

```
PRAGMA RESTRICT_REFERENCES(COMPARE, WNDS, RNDS, WNPS, RNPS);
```

Example. Here is an example of the COMPARE function:

```
DECLARE
    r_string1      RAW(16);
    r_string2      RAW(16);
    diff_position  INTEGER;

BEGIN
    r_string1 := UTL_RAW.CAST_TO_RAW('test string1');
    r_string2 := UTL_RAW.CAST_TO_RAW('test string2');
    diff_position := UTL_RAW.COMPARE(r_string1,r_string2);
    DBMS_OUTPUT.PUT_LINE (
        'r_string1='|| UTL_RAW.CAST_TO_VARCHAR2(r_string1));
    DBMS_OUTPUT.PUT_LINE (
        'r_string2='|| UTL_RAW.CAST_TO_VARCHAR2(r_string2));
    DBMS_OUTPUT.PUT_LINE ('diff_position='|| diff_position);
END;
/
```

Sample output follows:

```
r_string1=test string1
r_string2=test string2
diff_position=12
```

The UTL_RAW.CONCAT function

The CONCAT function is used to concatenate a set of 12 raw strings into a single raw string. The size of the concatenated result must not exceed 32K or the procedure will raise the ORA-6502 exception.

```
FUNCTION UTL_RAW.CONCAT
    (r1 IN RAW DEFAULT NULL
    ,r2 IN RAW DEFAULT NULL
    ,r3 IN RAW DEFAULT NULL
    ,r4 IN RAW DEFAULT NULL
    ,r5 IN RAW DEFAULT NULL
    ,r6 IN RAW DEFAULT NULL
    ,r7 IN RAW DEFAULT NULL
```

```
       ,r8 IN RAW DEFAULT NULL
       ,r9 IN RAW DEFAULT NULL
       ,r10 IN RAW DEFAULT NULL
       ,r11 IN RAW DEFAULT NULL
       ,r12 IN RAW DEFAULT NULL)
    RETURN RAW;
```

The parameters for this program are summarized in this table.

Parameter	Description
r1	First piece of raw data to be concatenated
r2	Second piece of raw data to be concatenated
r3	Third piece of raw data to be concatenated
r4	Fourth piece of raw data to be concatenated
r5	Fifth piece of raw data to be concatenated
r6	Sixth piece of raw data to be concatenated
r7	Seventh piece of raw data to be concatenated
r8	Eighth piece of raw data to be concatenated
r9	Ninth piece of raw data to be concatenated
r10	Tenth piece of raw data to be concatenated
r11	Eleventh piece of raw data to be concatenated
r12	Twelfth piece of raw data to be concatenated

Exceptions. The VALUE_ERROR exception (ORA-6502) is raised if the returned raw string exceeds 32K. The documentation from Oracle 7.3 and 8.0 indicates that this *is to be revised in a future release*, so don't count on this exception to remain unchanged.

Restrictions. This program asserts the following purity level with the RESTRICT_ REFERENCES pragma:

```
    PRAGMA RESTRICT_REFERENCES(CONCAT, WNDS, RNDS, WNPS, RNPS);
```

Example. For an example of CONCAT, see the example for TRANSLATE.

The UTL_RAW.CONVERT function

The CONVERT function converts the input raw string r from one installed NLS character set to another installed NLS character set. Here's the specification:

```
    FUNCTION UTL_RAW.CONVERT
       (r IN RAW
       ,to_charset IN VARCHAR2
       ,from_charset IN VARCHAR2)
    RETURN RAW;
```

Parameters are summarized in the following table.

Parameter	Description
r	The raw string to be converted
to_charset	The name of the output NLS character set
from_charset	The name of the input NLS character set

Exceptions. The VALUE_ERROR exception (ORA-6502) is raised if the input raw string is missing, NULL, or has zero length. This exception is also raised if the from_charset or to_charset parameters are missing, NULL, zero length, or name an invalid character set. The documentation from both Oracle 7.3 and 8.0 indicates that this *is to be revised in a future release*, so don't count on this exception to remain unchanged.

Restrictions. This program asserts the following purity level with the RESTRICT_ REFERENCES pragma:

```
PRAGMA RESTRICT_REFERENCES(CONVERT, WNDS, RNDS, WNPS, RNPS);
```

The UTL_RAW.COPIES function

The COPIES function concatenates the input raw string r, n number of times. Here's the specification:

```
FUNCTION UTL_RAW.COPIES
    (r IN RAW
    ,n IN NUMBER)
RETURN RAW;
```

The parameters for this program are summarized in this table.

Parameter	Description
r	The input raw string that is to be copied
n	The number of copies of the input string to make (must be positive)

Exceptions. The VALUE_ERROR exception (ORA-6502) is raised if the input raw string r is missing, NULL, or has zero length. This exception is also raised if the input number of copies n is less than 1 (n<1). The documentation from both Oracle 7.3 and 8.0 indicates that this *is to be revised in a future release*, so don't count on this exception to remain unchanged.

Restrictions. This program asserts the following purity level with the RESTRICT_ REFERENCES pragma:

```
PRAGMA RESTRICT_REFERENCES(COPIES, WNDS, RNDS, WNPS, RNPS);
```

Example. Here is an example of the COPIES function:

```
DECLARE
  r_string1       RAW(64);
  r_repeat        RAW(16);

BEGIN
  r_repeat := UTL_RAW.CAST_TO_RAW('Test ');
  r_string1 := UTL_RAW.COPIES(r_repeat,4);
  DBMS_OUTPUT.PUT_LINE (
    'r_string1='||UTL_RAW.CAST_TO_VARCHAR2(r_string1));
END;
/
```

Sample output follows:

```
r_string1=Test Test Test Test
```

The UTL_RAW.LENGTH function

The LENGTH function returns the number of bytes in the raw input string given by the r parameter,

```
FUNCTION UTL_RAW.LENGTH
    (r IN RAW)
RETURN NUMBER;
```

where r is the raw input string.

Restrictions. This program asserts the following purity level with the RESTRICT_ REFERENCES pragma:

```
PRAGMA RESTRICT_REFERENCES(LENGTH, WNDS, RNDS, WNPS, RNPS);
```

Exanple. Here is an example of the LENGTH function:

```
    r_1             RAW(32000);
    r_2             RAW(32000);
    r_3             RAW(32000);
BEGIN
  r_1 := UTL_RAW.XRANGE (hextoraw('00'),hextoraw('FF'));
  r_2 := UTL_RAW.CONCAT (r_1,r_1,r_1,r_1,r_1,r_1,r_1,r_1);
  r_3 := UTL_RAW.CONCAT (r_2,r_2,r_2,r_2,r_2,r_2,r_2,r_2);
  DB<S_OUTPUT.PUT_LINE ('Length of r_1='||UTL_RAW.LENGTH(r_1));
  DBMS_OUTPUT.PUT_LINE ('Length of r_2='||UTL_RAW.LENGTH(r_2));
  DBMS_OUTPUT.PUT_LINE ('Length of r_3='||UTL_RAW.LENGTH(r_3));
END;
/
```

Sample output follows:

```
Length of r_1=256
Length of r_2=2048
Length of r_3=16384
```

The UTL_RAW.OVERLAY function

The OVERLAY function overwrites the specified section of the target raw string with the string specified in the overlay_str parameter and returns the overwritten raw string. The overwriting starts pos bytes into the target string and continues for len bytes, right-padding the target with the pad parameter as needed to extend the target, if necessary. The len parameter must be greater than 0 and pos must be greater than 1. If pos is greater than the length of the target string, then the target is right-padded with pad before the overlaying begins. Here's the specification:

```
FUNCTION UTL_RAW.OVERLAY
    (overlay_str IN RAW
    ,target IN RAW
    ,pos IN BINARY_INTEGER DEFAULT 1
    ,len IN BINARY_INTEGER DEFAULT NULL
    pad IN RAW DEFAULT NULL)
RETURN RAW;
```

The parameters for this program are summarized in the following table.

Parameter	Description
overlay_str	The raw string used to overwrite to target
target	The raw string that is to be overlaid/overwritten
pos	The byte position in the target to begin overlaying; the default is 1
len	The number of bytes to overwrite; the default is the length of overlay_str
pad	The pad character to fill in extra space if needed; the default is 0x00

Exceptions. The VALUE_ERROR exception (ORA-6502) is raised if one of the folowing occurs:

- The input raw string overlay is NULL or has zero length

- The input target is missing or undefined

- The length of the target exceeds the maximum length of a raw, len < 0, or pos < 1

The documentation from both version 7.3 and 8.0 indicates that this *is to be revised in a future release,* so don't count on this exception to remain unchanged.

Restrictions. This program asserts the following purity level with the RESTRICT_REFERENCES pragma:

```
PRAGMA RESTRICT_REFERENCES(OVERLAY, WNDS, RNDS, WNPS, RNPS);
```

Example. Here is an example of the OVERLAY function:

```
DECLARE
    r_input        RAW(40);
```

```
    r_overlay        RAW(40);
    start_position INTEGER;
    overlay_length INTEGER;
    r_pad            RAW(2);
    r_output         RAW(40);

BEGIN
    -- set the parameters
    r_input := UTL_RAW.CAST_TO_RAW (
        'This is the full length text string');
    r_overlay := UTL_RAW.CAST_TO_RAW ('overlaid part');
    start_position := 13;
    overlay_length := 8;
    r_pad := UTL_RAW.CAST_TO_RAW ('.');
    r_output := UTL_RAW.OVERLAY (
        r_overlay, r_input, start_position, overlay_length,r_pad);

    DBMS_OUTPUT.PUT_LINE (
        'r_input          ='|| utl_raw.cast_to_varchar2(r_input));
    DBMS_OUTPUT.PUT_LINE (
        'r_output(len 8)='|| UTL_RAW.CAST_TO_VARCHAR2(r_output));
    overlay_length := 16;
    r_output := UTL_RAW.OVERLAY (
        r_overlay, r_input, start_position , overlay_length, r_pad);
    DBMS_OUTPUT.PUT_LINE (
        'r_output(len16)='|| UTL_RAW.CAST_TO_VARCHAR2(r_output));
END;
/
```

Sample output follows:

```
r_input          =This is the full length text string
r_output(len 8)=This is the overlaidgth text string
r_output(len16)=This is the overlaid part... string
```

The UTL_RAW.REVERSE function

The REVERSE function reverses the input raw string and returns this reversed string.

```
FUNCTION UTL_RAW.REVERSE
    (r IN RAW)
RETURN RAW;
```

Exceptions. The VALUE_ERROR exception (ORA-6502) is raised if the input raw string (r) is null or has zero length. The documentation from both Oracle 7.3 and 8.0 indicates that this *is to be revised in a future release*, so don't count on this exception to remain unchanged.

Restrictions. This program asserts the following purity level with the RESTRICT_REFERENCES pragma:

```
PRAGMA RESTRICT_REFERENCES(REVERSE, WNDS, RNDS, WNPS, RNPS);
```

Example. Here is an example of the REVERSE function:

```
DECLARE
  r_string      RAW(16);
  r_reverse     RAW(16);

BEGIN
  r_string := UTL_RAW.CAST_TO_RAW('Java Beans');
  r_reverse := UTL_RAW.REVERSE(r_string);
  DBMS_OUTPUT.PUT_LINE (
    'r_string='|| UTL_RAW.CAST_TO_VARCHAR2(r_string));
  DBMS_OUTPUT.PUT_LINE (
    'r_reverse='|| UTL_RAW.CAST_TO_VARCHAR2(r_reverse));
END;
```

Sample output follows:

```
r_string=Java Beans
r_reverse=snaeB avaJ
```

The UTL_RAW.SUBSTR function

The SUBSTR function returns a substring of the input raw string r beginning at pos and extending for len bytes. If pos is positive, the substring extends len bytes from the left; if pos is negative, the substring extends len bytes from the right (the end backwards). The value of pos cannot be 0. The default for len is to the end of the string r. If r is NULL, then NULL is returned. Here's the specification:

```
FUNCTION UTL_RAW.SUBSTR
    (r IN RAW
    ,pos IN BINARY_INTEGER
    ,len IN BINARY_INTEGER DEFAULT NULL)
  RETURN RAW;
```

Parameters are summarized in the following table.

Parameter	Description
r	The input raw string, from which the substring is extracted
pos	The starting position for the substring extraction
len	The length of the substring to extract; the default is to the end of the input string r

Exceptions. The VALUE_ERROR exception (ORA-6502) is raised if pos is 0 or len is less than 0. The documentation from both Oracle 7.3 and 8.0 indicates that this *is to be revised in a future release*, so don't count on this exception to remain unchanged.

Restrictions. This program asserts the following purity level with the RESTRICT_ REFERENCES pragma:

```
PRAGMA RESTRICT_REFERENCES(SUBSTR, WNDS, RNDS, WNPS, RNPS);
```

Example. Here is an example of the SUBSTR function:

```
DECLARE
  r_string        RAW(32);
  r_substring     RAW(16);

BEGIN
  r_string := UTL_RAW.CAST_TO_RAW('This is the test string');
  r_substring := UTL_RAW.SUBSTR(r_string,9,8);
  DBS_OUTPUT.PUT_LINE (
      'r_string='|| UTL_RAW.CAST_TO_VARCHAR2(r_string));
  DBMS_OUTPUT,PUT_LINE (
      'r_substring='|| UTL_RAW.CAST_TO_VARCHAR2(r_substring));
END;
```

Sample output follows:

```
r_string=This is the test string
r_substring=the test
```

The UTL_RAW.TRANSLATE function

The TRANSLATE function translates bytes in the input raw sting r, substituting bytes found in from_set with positionally corresponding bytes in to_set. The translated string is returned. Bytes in r that do not appear in from_set are not modified. If from_set is longer than to_set, then the unmatched bytes in from_set are removed from the return string. Here's the specification:

```
FUNCTION UTL_RAW.TRANSLATE
    (r IN RAW
    ,from_set IN RAW
    ,to_set IN RAW)
  RETURN RAW;
```

Parameters are summarized in the following table.

Parameter	Description
r	The input raw string to be translated
from_set	The list of bytes to translate
to_set	The list of bytes that from_set bytes are translated to

TRANSLATE is similar to TRANSLITERATE; however, with TRANSLATE, the return string can be shorter than the input string r. TRANSLITERATE return strings are always the same length as the input string r. Also, TRANSLATE requires values for from_set, and to_set while TRANSLITERATE has defaults for these inputs.

Exceptions. The VALUE_ERROR exception (ORA-6502) is raised if the r, from_set, or to_set parameters are NULL or have zero length. The documentation from both

Oracle 7.3 and 8.0 indicates that this *is to be revised in a future release*, so don't count on this exception to remain unchanged.

Restrictions. This program asserts the following purity level with the RESTRICT_ REFERENCES pragma:

```
PRAGMA RESTRICT_REFERENCES(TRANSLATE, WNDS, RNDS, WNPS, RNPS);
```

Example. An example use of TRANSLATE is a switch case function that switches the case of every character in a text string, swapping upper and lowercase characters. This function also makes use of other UTL_RAW functions: CAST_TO_RAW, XRANGE, and CONCAT. This method may not be the most efficient case-switching technique, but it serves to demonstrate the functions nicely.

```
CREATE OR REPLACE FUNCTION switch_case(c_in IN VARCHAR2)
RETURN VARCHAR2
IS
   r_in           RAW(2000);
   r_out          RAW(2000);
   r_upper        RAW(32);
   r_lower        RAW(32);
   r_upper_lower  RAW(64);
   r_lower_upper  RAW(64);

BEGIN
   /* Convert input to raw */
   r_in := UTL_RAW.CAST_TO_RAW(c_in);

   /* Get raw string of uppercase letters from 'A' to 'Z' */
   r_upper := UTL_RAW.XRANGE(UTL_RAW.CAST_TO_RAW('A'),
      UTL_RAW.CAST_TO_RAW('Z'));

   /* Get raw string of lowercase letters from 'a' to 'z' */
   r_lower := UTL_RAW.XRANGE(UTL_RAW.CAST_TO_RAW('a'),
      UTL_RAW.CAST_TO_RAW('z'));

  /* Create a raw string of uppercase followed by lowercase letters */
   r_upper_lower := UTL_RAW.CONCAT(r_upper , r_lower);

   /* Create a raw string of lowercase followed by uppercase letters */
   r_lower_upper := UTL_RAW.CONCAT(r_lower , r_upper);

   /* Translate upper to lower and lower to upper for the input string */
   r_out := UTL_RAW.TRANSLATE(r_in , r_upper_lower , r_lower_upper );

   /* Convert the result back to varchar2 and return the result */
   return(UTL_RAW.CAST_TO_VARCHAR2(r_out));
END;
/
```

Sample output follows:

```
SQL> select switch_case('This Is A Test') from dual;

SWITCH_CASE('THISISATEST')
--------------------------------------------------------
tHIS iS a tEST
```

The UTL_RAW.TRANSLITERATE function

The TRANSLITERATE function translates bytes in the input raw sting r, substituting bytes found in from_set with positionally corresponding bytes in to_set. The translated string is returned. Bytes in r that do not appear in from_set are not modified. If from_set is longer than to_set, then the unmatched bytes in from_set are right-padded with the pad byte. The return string is always the same length as the input string r. The specification follows:

```
FUNCTION UTL_RAW.TRANSLITERATE
    (r IN RAW
    ,to_set IN RAW DEFAULT NULL
    ,from_set IN RAW DEFAULT NULL
    ,pad IN RAW DEFAULT NULL)
RETURN RAW;
```

TRANSLITERATE is similar to TRANSLATE, but it differs in that the return string is always the same length as the input string (r). TRANSLITERATE is just like TRANSLATE if to_set and from_set are the same length. If from_set is longer than to_set, then to_set is right-padded with the pad byte. TRANSLITERATE allows NULL from_set, to_set, and pad parameters.

Parameters are summarized in the following table.

Parameter	Description
r	Input string to be translated
from_set	The list of bytes to be translated; the default is 0x00 through 0xFF
to_set	The list of bytes that from_set bytes are translated to; the default is NULL
pad	If from_set is shorter than to_set, then this pad byte is the translation character for any unmatched bytes in from_set; the default is 0x00

Exceptions. The VALUE_ERROR exception (ORA-6502) is raised if r is null or has 0 length. The documentation from both Oracle 7.3 and 8.0 indicates that this *is to be revised in a future release*, so don't count on this exception to remain unchanged.

Restrictions. This program asserts the following purity level with the RESTRICT_REFERENCES pragma:

```
PRAGMA RESTRICT_REFERENCES(TRANSLITERATE, WNDS, RNDS, WNPS, RNPS);
```

Example. An example use of TRANSLITERATE is a make_lower function that switches uppercase characters in a text string to lowercase characters, converting spaces, dashes, and dots to underscores. This function also makes use of other UTL_RAW functions: CAST_TO_RAW, XRANGE, and CONCAT. This method may not be the most efficient technique for this conversion, but it serves to demonstrate some UTL_RAW functions in an easily understandable context.

```
CREATE OR REPLACE FUNCTION make_lower(c_in IN VARCHAR2)
RETURN VARCHAR2
IS
   r_in          RAW(2000);
   r_out         RAW(2000);
   r_upper       RAW(48);
   r_lower       RAW(32);
   r_underscore  RAW(1);
BEGIN
   -- convert the input to raw
   r_in := UTL_RAW.CAST_TO_RAW(c_in);
   r_underscore := UTL_RAW.CAST_TO_RAW('_');
   -- start the from characters with the uppercase letters
   r_upper :=
UTL_RAW.XRANGE(UTL_RAW.CAST_TO_RAW('A'),UTL_RAW.CAST_TO_RAW('Z'));
   -- space, dash and dot to the from list of characters
   r_upper := UTL_RAW.CONCAT(r_upper,UTL_RAW.CAST_TO_RAW(' ')
             ,UTL_RAW.CAST_TO_RAW('-'),UTL_RAW.CAST_TO_RAW('.'));
   -- set the to characters to be lowercase letters
   r_lower :=
UTL_RAW.XRANGE(UTL_RAW.CAST_TO_RAW('a'),UTL_RAW.CAST_TO_RAW('z'));
   -- convert the uppercase to lowercase and punctuation marks to underscores
   r_out := UTL_RAW.TRANSLITERATE(r_in , r_lower , r_upper, r_underscore);
   -- return the character version
   return(UTL_RAW.CAST_TO_VARCHAR2(r_out));
END;
```

Sample output follows:

```
SQL> exec DBMS_OUTPUT.PUT_LINE (make_lower('This.is-A tEst'));
this_is_a_test
```

The UTL_RAW.XRANGE function

The XRANGE function returns a raw string containing all bytes in order beginning with the start_byte parameter and ending with end_byte. If start_byte is greater than end_byte, then the return string wraps from 0XFF to 0X00.

```
FUNCTION UTL_RAW.XRANGE
    (start_byte IN RAW DEFAULT 0x00
    ,end_byte IN RAW DEFAULT 0xFF)
RETURN RAW;
```

The parameters for this program are summarized in the following table.

Parameter	Description
start_byte	Start byte; the default is 0x00.
end_byte	End byte; the default is 0xFF.

Restrictions. This program asserts the following purity level with the RESTRICT_ REFERENCES pragma:

```
PRAGMA RESTRICT_REFERENCES(XRANGE, WNDS, RNDS, WNPS, RNPS);
```

Example. For an example of XRANGE, see the example for TRANSLATE or TRANS-LITERATE.

UTL_REF: Referencing Objects (Oracle8.1 Only)

The UTL_REF package provides a PL/SQL interface that allows you to select and modify objects (instances of an object type) in an object table without having to specify or know about the underlying database table. With UTL_REF, you only need a *reference* to the object in order to identify it in the database and perform the desired operations. With UTL_REF, you can do any of the following:

- Select or retrieve an object from the database
- Lock an object so that no other session can make changes to the object
- Select and lock an object in a single operation (similar to SELECT FOR UPDATE)
- Update the contents of an object
- Delete an object

You will typically use UTL_REF programs when you have references to an object and one of the following is true:

- You do not want to have to resort to an SQL statement to perform the needed action.
- You do not even *know* the name of the table that contains the object, and therefore cannot rely on SQL to get your job done.

Before getting into the details, let's start with an initial example of how you might use the UTL_REF packages.

You will be able to use UTL_REF programs only to select or modify objects in an object table. An object table is a table in which each row of the table is an object. Here are the steps one might take to create an object table.

First, create an object type:

```
CREATE TYPE hazardous_site_t IS OBJECT (
    name VARCHAR2(100),
    location VARCHAR2(100),
    dixoin_level NUMBER,
    pcb_level NUMBER,
    METHOD FUNCTION cleanup_time RETURN NUMBER);
```

Now you can create a table of these objects:

```
CREATE TABLE hazardous_sites OF hazardous_site_t;
```

As you will see in the headers for the UTL_REF programs, Oracle has provided a special parameter-passing syntax called ANY. This syntax allows us to pass references and objects of any object type in and out of the programs. This behavior is not otherwise available in Oracle8 built-in packages or the code that you yourself can write using object types.

Getting Started with UTL_REF

The UTL_REF package is created when the Oracle8.1 (or later) database is installed. The *utlref.sql* script (found in the built-in packages source code directory, as described in Chapter 1) contains the source code for this package's specification. The script is called by *catproc.sql*, which is normally run immediately after the database is created. The script creates the public synonym UTL_REF for the package and grants EXECUTE privilege on the package to public. All Oracle users can reference and make use of the package.

Every program in this package runs as "owner." This means that programs in the UTL_REF package operate within the privileges of the session running those programs. You will be able to select and modify only objects to which your session has been granted the necessary privileges.

UTL_REF programs

Table 9-5 lists the programs defined for the UTL_REF packages.

Table 9-5. UTL_REF Programs

Name	Description	Use in SQL
DELETE_OBJECT	Deletes an object from the underlying object table	No
LOCK_OBJECT	Locks an object so that another session cannot change the object	No
SELECT_OBJECT	Selects an object based on its reference, returning that object as an OUT argument	No
UPDATE_OBJECT	Updates the object specified by the reference by replacing it with the object you pass to the program	No

UTL_REF does not declare any nonprogram elements.

UTL_REF exceptions

UTL_REF does not declare any exceptions. However, you may encounter any of the following Oracle exceptions when running the UTL_REF programs:

ORA-00942

> Insufficient privileges. You must have the appropriate privileges on the underlying database table.

ORA-01031

> Insufficient privileges. You attempted to update an object table on which you have only SELECT privileges. You must have the appropriate privileges on the underlying database table.

ORA-08177

> Cannot serialize access for this transaction. You have tried to change data after the start of a serialized transaction.

ORA-00060

> Deadlock detected while waiting for resource. Your session and another session are waiting for a resource locked by the other. You will need to wait or ROLLBACK.

ORA-01403

> No data found. The REF is NULL or otherwise not associated with an object in the database.

UTL_REF Interface

This section describes the programs available through the UTL_REF package. A single, extended example at the end of the chapter shows how you might be able to take advantage of the UTL_REF programs in your own applications.

The UTL_REF.DELETE_OBJECT procedure

Use the DELETE_OBJECT procedure to delete an object (actually, the row containing that object) specified by the given reference. The header is,

```
PROCEDURE UTL_REF.DELETE_(reference IN REF ANY);
```

where reference identifies the object.

This program effectively substitutes for the following kind of SQL statement:

```
DELETE FROM the_underlying_object_table t
  WHERE REF (t) = reference;
```

In contrast to this SQL statement, with DELETE_OBJECT you will not need to specify the name of the underlying database object table to retrieve the object.

Restrictions. Note the following restrictions on calling DELETE_OBJECT:

- The program does not assert a purity level with the RESTRICT_REFERENCES pragma.

- You cannot call this program from within an SQL statement, either directly or indirectly.

The UTL_REF.LOCK_OBJECT procedure

Use the LOCK_OBJECT procedure to lock or lock and retrieve an object for a given reference. The header is overloaded as follows:

```
PROCEDURE UTL_REF.LOCK_OBJECT (reference IN REF ANY);

PROCEDURE UTL_REF.LOCK_OBJECT
   (reference IN REF ANY
   ,object IN OUT ANY);
```

Parameters are summarized in the following table.

Parameter	Description
reference	The reference to the object
object	The value of the object selected from the database (if supplied)

If you call LOCK_OBJECT and do not provide a second argument, then the object will be locked, but that object will not be returned to the calling program.

This program effectively substitutes for the following type of SQL statement:

```
SELECT VALUE (t)
   INTO object
   FROM the_underlying_object_table t
  WHERE REF (t) = reference
    FOR UPDATE;
```

In contrast to this SQL statement, with LOCK_OBJECT you will not need to specify the name of the underlying database object table to retrieve the object.

NOTE It is not necessary to lock an object before you update or delete it. By requesting a lock, however, you ensure that another session cannot even attempt to make changes to that same object until you commit or roll back.

Restrictions. Note the following restrictions on calling LOCK_OBJECT:

- The program does not assert a purity level with the RESTRICT_REFERENCES pragma.

- You cannot call this program from within an SQL statement, either directly or indirectly.

The UTL_REF.SELECT_OBJECT procedure

Use the SELECT_OBJECT procedure to retrieve an object for a given reference. The header follows:

```
PROCEDURE UTL_REF.SELECT_OBJECT
    (reference IN REF ANY
    ,object IN OUT ANY);
```

Parameters are summarized in the following table.

Parameter	Description
reference	The reference to the object
object	The value of the object selected from the database

This program effectively substitutes for the following type of SQL statement:

```
SELECT VALUE (t)
   INTO object
   FROM the_underlying_object_table t
  WHERE REF (t) = reference;
```

In contrast to this SQL statement, with SELECT_OBJECT you will not need to specify the name of the underlying database object table to retrieve the object.

Restrictions. Note the following restrictions on calling SELECT_OBJECT:

- The program does not assert a purity level with the RESTRICT_REFERENCES pragma.

- You cannot call this program from within an SQL statement, either directly or indirectly.

Example. In the following procedure, I use the SELECT_OBJECT built-in to retrieve the object based on the passed-in reference:

```
CREATE OR REPLACE PROCEDURE show_emp (emp_in IN REF employee_t)
IS
    emp_obj employee_t
BEGIN
    UTL_REF.SELECT_OBJECT (emp_in, emp_obj);
    DBMS_OUTPUT.PUT_LINE (emp_obj.name);
END;.
```

The UTL_REF.UPDATE_OBJECT procedure

Use the UPDATE_OBJECT procedure to replace an object in the database specified by a given reference with your "replacement" object. Here's the header:

```
PROCEDURE UTL_REF.UPDATE_OBJECT
    (reference IN REF ANY
    ,object IN ANY);
```

Parameters are summarized in the following table.

Parameter	Description
reference	The reference to the object
object	The object that is to be placed in the row of the object table specified by the reference

This program effectively substitutes for the following type of SQL statement:

```
UPDATE the_underlying_object_table t
   SET VALUE (t) = object
 WHERE REF (t) = reference;
```

In contrast to this SQL statement, with UPDATE_OBJECT you will not need to specify the name of the underlying database object table to retrieve the object.

Restrictions. Note the following restrictions on calling UPDATE_OBJECT:

- The program does not assert a purity level with the RESTRICT_REFERENCES pragma.

- You cannot call this program from within an SQL statement, either directly or indirectly.

UTL_REF Example

Let's start with an object type that can hold various types of documents

```
CREATE OR REPLACE TYPE Document_t AS OBJECT (
    doc_id NUMBER,
    author VARCHAR2(65),
    created DATE,
    revised DATE,
    body BLOB,
    MEMBER PROCEDURE update_revised
);
/
```

To keep this example simple, we'll implement only a single object method:

```
CREATE OR REPLACE TYPE BODY Document_t
AS
    MEMBER PROCEDURE update_revised
```

```
      IS
      BEGIN
         revised := SYSDATE;
      END;
   END;
   /
```

Here's a table that will hold any kind of document:

```
CREATE TABLE documents OF Document_t;
```

We might have a requisition type that has a special type of document. Each requisition contains a REF to a particular document.

```
CREATE OR REPLACE TYPE Requisition_t AS OBJECT (
   doc_ref REF Document_t,
   needed DATE,
   approved DATE,
   MEMBER PROCEDURE update_revision_date,
   MEMBER FUNCTION has_valid_need_date RETURN BOOLEAN
);
/
```

In a moment, we're going to look at an example of UTL_REF that implements the type body of Requisition_t. But let's first look at life without UTL_REF. Not only do we have to write SQL, we also have to know the table name in each statement where we need access to a persistent object. In fact, the following methods are hard-coded to work with only one particular table implementation (not good):

```
CREATE OR REPLACE TYPE BODY Requisition_t
AS
   MEMBER FUNCTION has_valid_need_date RETURN BOOLEAN
   IS
      document Document_t;
      CURSOR doc_cur IS                  /* Ugly! */
         SELECT VALUE(d)
            FROM documents d
           WHERE REF(d) = SELF.doc_ref;
   BEGIN
      OPEN doc_cur;
      FETCH doc_cur INTO document;    /* Ditto */
      CLOSE doc_cur;
      IF document.created > SELF.approved
      THEN
         RETURN FALSE;
      ELSE
         RETURN TRUE;
      END IF;
   END;
   MEMBER PROCEDURE update_revision_date
   IS
   BEGIN
      UPDATE documents d                 /* Even uglier */
         SET revised = SYSDATE
```

```
            WHERE REF(d) = SELF.doc_ref;
      END;
   END;
   /
```

Let's turn now to see what UTL_REF can do for us:

```
CREATE OR REPLACE TYPE BODY Requisition_t
AS
   MEMBER FUNCTION has_valid_need_date RETURN BOOLEAN
   IS
      document Document_t;
   BEGIN
      /* UTL_REF.SELECT_OBJECT allows us to retrieve the document object
      || from persistent database storage into a local variable.  No muss,
      || no fetch, no bother!  SELECT_OBJECT finds the table and object
      || for us.
      */
      UTL_REF.SELECT_OBJECT (SELF.doc_ref, document);
      /* Now that we have retrieved the document object, we can
      || easily gain access to its attributes:
      */
      IF document.created > SELF.approved
      THEN
         RETURN FALSE;
      ELSE
         RETURN TRUE;
      END IF;
   END;
   MEMBER PROCEDURE update_revision_date
   IS
      document Document_t;
   BEGIN
      /* To update the revision date of the requisition object,
      || we'll simply "delegate" to the referenced document.
      || First we retrieve it...
      */
      UTL_REF.SELECT_OBJECT (SELF.doc_ref, document);
      /* ...then we can invoke a method on the newly retrieved
      || (but transient) object.  Notice that we do NOT update
      || the attribute directly, but rely instead on the public
      || method supplied for this purpose.
      */
      document.update_revised;
      /* ...and now we easily update the data in the underlying table
      || (whatever table it is...we don't know or care!)
      */
      UTL_REF.UPDATE_OBJECT(SELF.doc_ref, document);
   END;
END;
/
```

Since UTL_REF frees us from dependence on the specific underlying table, it allows us to achieve greater reuse, portability, modularity, and resilience to change.

10

Miscellaneous Packages

You can't find a neat category for everything, can you? This chapter brings together a variety of useful packages you are sure to dip into on a regular basis:

DBMS_UTILITY

> The actual "miscellaneous" package. It offers programs to free unused user memory, parse comma-delimited lists, calculate the elapsed time of PL/SQL programs, and much more. You never know what you'll find popping up next in DBMS_UTILITY!

DBMS_DESCRIBE

> Contains a single procedure, DESCRIBE_PROCEDURE, which you can use to get information about the parameters of a stored program.

DBMS_DDL

> Contains programs to recompile stored code, analyze objects in your schema, and modify the referenceability of object identifiers in Oracle8.

DBMS_RANDOM

> New to Oracle8, supplies PL/SQL developers with a random number generator.

DBMS_UTILITY: Performing Miscellaneous Operations

The DBMS_UTILITY package is the "miscellaneous package" for PL/SQL. It contains programs that perform a wide variety of operations (listed in Table 10-1).

| *TIP* | I recommend that whenever you install a new version of the Oracle database, you scan the contents of the *dbmsutil.sql* file. Check to see if Oracle has added any new programs or changed the functionality of existing programs. |

Getting Started with DBMS_UTILITY

The DBMS_UTILITY package is created when the Oracle database is installed. The *dbmsutil.sql* script (found in the built-in packages source code directory, as described in Chapter 1, *Introduction*) contains the source code for this package's specification. This script is called by *catproc.sql*, which is normally run immediately after database creation. The script creates the public synonym DBMS_UTILITY for the package and grants EXECUTE privilege on the package to public. All Oracle users can reference and make use of this package.

Table 10-1 summarizes the programs available with DBMS_UTILITY.

Table 10-1. DBMS_UTILITY Programs

Name	Description	Use in SQL
ANALYZE_DATABASE	Analyzes all the tables, clusters, and indexes in a database	No
ANALYZE_PART_OBJECT	Runs the equivalent of the SQL ANALYZE TABLE or ANALYZE INDEX command for each partition of the object, using parallel job queues (PL/SQL8 only)	No
ANALYZE_SCHEMA	Analyzes all the tables, clusters, and indexes in the specified schema	No
COMMA_TO_TABLE	Parses a comma-delimited list into a PL/SQL table (PL/SQL Release 2.1 and later)	No
COMPILE_SCHEMA	Compiles all procedures, functions, and packages in the specified schema	No
DATA_BLOCK_ADDRESS_BLOCK	Gets the block number part of a data block address	Yes
DATA_BLOCK_ADDRESS_FILE	Gets the file number part of a data block address	Yes
DB_VERSION	Returns the database version and compatibility information for the current instance (PL/SQL8 only)	No
EXEC_DDL_STATEMENT	Executes the provided DDL statement (PL/SQL8 only)	No
FORMAT_CALL_STACK	Returns the current module call stack in a formatted display	No

Table 10-1. DBMS_UTILITY Programs (continued)

Name	Description	Use in SQL
FORMAT_ERROR_STACK	Returns the current error stack in a formatted display	No
GET_HASH_VALUE	Returns a hash value for a string; used to obtain unique (it is hoped) integer values for strings	No
GET_PARAMETER_VALUE	Retrieves information about a parameter in the database parameter file, otherwise known as the INIT.ORA file (PL/SQL8 only)	Yes
GET_TIME	Returns the elapsed time since an arbitrary time in 100ths of seconds	No
IS_PARALLEL_SERVER	Returns TRUE if the database instance was started in parallel server mode	No
MAKE_DATA_BLOCK_ADDRESS	Creates a data block address given a file number and a block number	Yes
NAME_RESOLVE	Resolves the name of an object into its component parts	No
NAME_TOKENIZE	Returns the individual components or tokens in a string	No
PORT_STRING	Returns a string describing the platform and version of the current database	Yes
TABLE_TO_COMMA	Moves the names in a PL/SQL table into a comma-delimited list	No

DBMS_UTILITY nonprogram elements

In addition to the functions and procedures defined in the package, DBMS_UTIL-
ITY also declares five PL/SQL tables that are used either as input into or output
from the package's built-in modules. By the way, these tables are also used by
other built-in packages, such as DBMS_DEFER. See Chapter 10 of *Oracle PL/SQL
Programming* for more information about PL/SQL tables (also called index-by
tables as of Oracle8).

DBMS_UTILITY.UNCL_ARRAY

This PL/SQL table type is used to store lists of strings in the format:

```
"USER"."NAME."COLUMN"@LINK
```

You can use the array to store any strings you want up to the length determined in the following TABLE type statement:

```
TYPE DBMS_UTILITY.UNCL_ARRAY IS
    TABLE OF VARCHAR2(227) INDEX BY BINARY_INTEGER;
```

DBMS_UTILITY.NAME_ARRAY

This PL/SQL table type is used to store names of identifiers and is defined as follows:

```
TYPE DBMS_UTILITY.NAME_ARRAY IS
TABLE OF VARCHAR2(30) INDEX BY BINARY_INTEGER;
```

DBMS_UTILITY.DBLINK_ARRAY

This PL/SQL table type is used to store database links and is defined as follows:

```
TYPE DBMS_UTILITY.DBLINK_ARRAY IS
TABLE OF VARCHAR2(128) INDEX BY BINARY_INTEGER;
```

DBMS_UTILITY.INDEX_TABLE_TYPE

This PL/SQL table type is declared within the package, but is not otherwise used. It is made available for use by other packages and programs.

```
TYPE DBMS_UTILITY.INDEX_TABLE_TYPE IS
TABLE OF BINARY_INTEGER INDEX BY BINARY_INTEGER;
```

DBMS_UTILITY.NUMBER_ARRAY

This PL/SQL table type is declared within the package, but is not otherwise used. It is made available for use by other packages and programs.

```
TYPE DBMS_UTILITY.NUMBER_ARRAY IS
TABLE OF NUMBER INDEX BY BINARY_INTEGER;
```

You can declare PL/SQL tables based on these TABLE type statements as shown below:

```
DECLARE
    short_name_list DBMS_UTILITY.NAME_ARRAY;
    long_name_list DBMS_UTILITY.INDEX_TABLE_TYPE;
BEGIN
...
```

Of course, if you do declare PL/SQL tables based on DBMS_UTILITY data structures, then those declarations will change with any changes in the package.

The DBMS_UTILITY Interface

This section describes each of the programs in the DBMS_UTILITY package; because of the miscellaneous nature of these programs, they are simply listed in alphabetical order.

The DBMS_UTILITY.ANALYZE_DATABASE procedure

This procedure analyzes all the tables, clusters, and indexes in the entire database. The header for the procedure follows:

```
PROCEDURE DBMS_UTILITY.ANALYZE_DATABASE
    (method IN VARCHAR2
    ,estimate_rows IN NUMBER DEFAULT NULL
    ,estimate_percent IN NUMBER DEFAULT NULL
    ,method_opt IN VARCHAR2 DEFAULT NULL);
```

Parameters are summarized in this table.

Parameter	Description
method	Action to be taken by the program. ESTIMATE, DELETE, and NULL are accepted values and are explained later.
estimate_rows	The number of rows to be used to perform the statistics estimate. Cannot be less than 1. Used only if method is ESTIMATE.
estimate_percent	The percentage of rows to be used to perform the statistics estimate. Ignored if estimate_rows is non-NULL. Must be between 1 and 99. Used only if method is ESTIMATE.
method_opt	The method option, indicating which elements of the object will be analyzed.

Here are the valid entries for the method argument, and the resulting activity (when you pass one of these values, they must be enclosed in single quotes):

NULL

Exact statistics are computed based on the entire contents of the objects. These values are then placed in the data dictionary.

ESTIMATE

Statistics are estimated. With this option, either estimate_rows or estimate_percent must be non-NULL. These values are then placed in the data dictionary.

DELETE

The statistics for this object are deleted from the data dictionary.

Here are the valid method_opt entries and the resulting impact (when you pass one of these values, they must be enclosed in single quotes):

FOR TABLE

Collects statistics for the table.

FOR ALL COLUMNS [SIZE N]

Collects column statistics for all columns and scalar attributes. The size is the maximum number of partitions in the histogram, with a default of 75 and a maximum of 254.

FOR ALL INDEXED COLUMNS [SIZE N]

Collects column statistics for all indexed columns in the table. The size is the maximum number of partitions in the histogram, with a default of 75 and a maximum of 254.

FOR ALL INDEXES

Collects statistics for all indexes associated with the table.

Example. Here is an example of a request to this program to analyze all columns in my database:

```
BEGIN
    DBMS_UTILITY.ANALYZE_DATABASE (
        'ESTIMATE',
        100,
        50,
        'FOR ALL COLUMNS SIZE 200');
END;
```

The DBMS_UTILITY.ANALYZE_SCHEMA procedure

This procedure analyzes all of the tables, clusters, and indexes in the specified schema. The header for the procedure follows:

```
PROCEDURE DBMS_UTILITY.ANALYZE_SCHEMA
    (schema IN VARCHAR2
    ,method IN VARCHAR2
    ,estimate_rows IN NUMBER DEFAULT NULL
    ,estimate_percent IN NUMBER DEFAULT NULL
    ,method_opt IN VARCHAR2 DEFAULT NULL);
```

Parameters are summarized in this table.

Parameters	Description
schema	The name of the schema containing the object for which you wish to compute statistics. If NULL, then the current schema is used. This argument is case-sensitive.
method	Action to be taken by the program. ESTIMATE, DELETE, and NULL are accepted values (explained later).
estimate_rows	The number of rows to be used to perform the statistics estimate. Cannot be less than 1. Used only if method is ESTIMATE.
estimate_percent	The percentage of rows to be used to perform the statistics estimate. Ignored if estimate_rows is non-NULL. Must be between 1 and 99. Used only if method is ESTIMATE.
method_opt	The method option, indicating which elements of the object will be analyzed.

Here are the valid entries for the method argument, and the resulting activity (when you pass one of these values, they must be enclosed in single quotes):

NULL

  Exact statistics are computed based on the entire contents of the objects. These values are then placed in the data dictionary.

ESTIMATE

  Statistics are estimated. With this option, either estimate_rows or estimate_percent must be non-NULL. These values are then placed in the data dictionary.

DELETE

The statistics for this object are deleted from the data dictionary.

Here are the valid method_opt entries and the resulting impact (when you pass one of these values, they must be enclosed in single quotes):

FOR TABLE

Collects statistics for the table.

FOR ALL COLUMNS [SIZE N]

Collects column statistics for all columns and scalar attributes. The size is the maximum number of partitions in the histogram, with a default of 75 and a maximum of 254.

FOR ALL INDEXED COLUMNS [SIZE N]

Collects column statistics for all indexed columns in the table. The size is the maximum number of partitions in the histogram, with a default of 75 and a maximum of 254.

FOR ALL INDEXES

Collects statistics for all indexes associated with the table.

Example. Here is an example of a request to this program to analyze all indexes in my current schema:

```
BEGIN
    DBMS_UTILITY.ANALYZE_SCHEMA (
        USER,
        'ESTIMATE',
        100,
        50,
        'FOR ALL INDEXES');
END;
/
```

The DBMS_UTILITY.ANALYZE_PART_OBJECT procedure (Oracle8 Only)

This procedure analyzes the specified, partitioned object. Here's the header for the procedure:

```
PROCEDURE DBMS_UTILITY.ANALYZE_PART_OBJECT
    (schema IN VARCHAR2 DEFAULT NULL
    ,object_name IN VARCHAR2 DEFAULT NULL
    ,object_type IN CHAR DEFAULT 'T'
    ,command_type IN CHAR DEFAULT 'E'
    ,command_opt IN VARCHAR2 DEFAULT NULL
    ,sample_clause IN VARCHAR2 DEFAULT 'SAMPLE 5 PERCENT');
```

Parameters are summarized in the following table.

Parameter	Description
schema	The schema containing the specified object.
object_name	The name of the object to be analyzed. It must be partitioned.
object_type	The type of the object. Must be either T for TABLE or I for INDEX.
command_type	A code indicating the type of analysis to perform. Valid values: C for COMPUTE STATISTICS, E for ESTIMATE STATISTICS, D for DELETE STATISTICS, and V for VALIDATE STRUCTURE.
command_opt	Options for the different command types. If command type is C or E, then command_opt can be any of the following: FOR TABLE, FOR ALL LOCAL INDEXES, FOR ALL COLUMNS, or a combination of some of the FOR options of the ANALYZE STATISTICS command. If command_type is V, then command_opt can be CAS-CADE if the object_type is T for TABLE.
sample_clause	Specifies the sample clause to use when command_type is E for ESTI-MATE.

Running this program is equivalent to executing this SQL command,

```
ANALYZE TABLE|INDEX [<schema>.]<object_name>
    PARTITION <pname> [<command_type>] [<command_opt>] [<sample_clause>]
```

for each partition of the specified object. DBMS_UTILITY will submit a job for each partition, so that the analysis can run in parallel using job queues. It is up to the user to control the number of concurrent jobs that will be started by setting correctly the initialization parameter JOB_QUEUE_PROCESSES.

Any syntax errors encountered for the object specification will be reported in SNP trace files.

Example. Here is an example of a request to this program to delete the statistics associated with the columns of the emp table:

```
BEGIN
    DBMS_UTILITY.ANALYZE_PART_OBJECT (
        USER,
        'EMP',
        'T',
        'DELETE STATISTICS',
        'FOR ALL COLUMNS');
END;
/
```

The DBMS_UTILITY.COMMA_TO_TABLE procedure

The COMMA_TO_TABLE procedure parses a comma-delimited list and places each name into a PL/SQL table. Here's the header for the procedure:

```
PROCEDURE DBMS_UTILITY.COMMA_TO_TABLE
    (list IN VARCHAR2
```

```
,tablen OUT BINARY_INTEGER
,tab OUT UNCL_ARRAY);
```

Parameters are summarized in the following table.

Parameter	Description
list	Comma-delimited string
tablen	Number of names found in the list and placed in the PL/SQL table
tab	The PL/SQL table declared using one of the package's predeclared TABLE types

This procedure uses the NAME_TOKENIZE procedure to determine which of the string's characters are names and which are commas.

Example. COMMA_TO_TABLE is a handy utility if you happen to have a comma-delimited string; otherwise, it does you no good. Just think: with a tiny bit more effort, Oracle could have provided us with a much more general-purpose and useful string parsing engine.

In any case, here is a sample use of DBMS_UTILITY.COMMA_TO_TABLE. It takes two different lists of correlated information, parses them into rows in two different tables, and then uses that data in a series of UPDATE statements.

```
/* Filename on companion disk: upddelist.sp */
CREATE OR REPLACE PROCEDURE upd_from_list (
    empno_list IN VARCHAR2,
    sal_list IN VARCHAR2)
IS
    empnos DBMS_UTILITY.UNCL_ARRAY;
    sals DBMS_UTILITY.UNCL_ARRAY;
    numemps INTEGER;
BEGIN
    DBMS_UTILITY.COMMA_TO_TABLE (empno_list, numemps, empnos);
    DBMS_UTILITY.COMMA_TO_TABLE (sal_list, numemps, sals);
    FOR rownum IN 1 .. numemps
    LOOP
        UPDATE emp SET sal = TO_NUMBER (sals(rownum))
         WHERE empno = TO_NUMBER (empnos(rownum));
    END LOOP;
END;
/
```

NOTE   If you are running Oracle8, you could even rewrite this program to use array processing in DBMS_SQL and replace this loop with a single, dynamic UPDATE statement. See Chapter 2, *Executing Dynamic SQL and PL/SQL*, for more information.

The DBMS_UTILITY.COMPILE_SCHEMA procedure

This procedure compiles all procedures, functions, and packages in the specified schema. The header for the procedure is,

```
PROCEDURE DBMS_UTILITY.COMPILE_SCHEMA (schema VARCHAR2);
```

where schema is the name of the schema.

I have heard reports from developers that it sometimes seems as though they run this program and it does not do anything at all. As I write this, though, I have requested that DBMS_UTILITY recompile my PL/Vision schema, and the buzzing of the hard drive light, as well as the delay in the resurfacing of my SQL*Plus prompt, attests to the fact that it is indeed recompiling the scores of packages in this schema.

Example. I execute the following command in SQL*Plus to recompile all programs in my current schema. Notice that before the recompilation, I had a single invalid package. Afterwards, all objects are valid.

```
SQL> select object_name from user_objects where status='INVALID';
OBJECT_NAME
----------------------------------------------------------------
PLGTE

SQL> exec DBMS_UTILITY.COMPILE_SCHEMA(user)
PL/SQL procedure successfully completed.

SQL> select object_name from user_objects where status='INVALID';
no rows selected
```

The DBMS_UTILITY.DATA_BLOCK_ADDRESS_BLOCK function

This function extracts and returns the block number of a data block address. The header for this function is,

```
FUNCTION DBMS_UTILITY.DATA_BLOCK_ADDRESS_BLOCK (dba IN NUMBER)
   RETURN NUMBER;
```

where dba is the data block address.

The DBMS_UTILITY.DATA_BLOCK_ADDRESS_FILE function

This function extracts and returns the file number of a data block address. The header for this function is,

```
FUNCTION DBMS_UTILITY.DATA_BLOCK_ADDRESS_FILE (dba IN NUMBER)
RETURN NUMBER;
```

where dba is the data block address.

The DBMS_UTILITY.DB_VERSION procedure

This procedure (PL/SQL8 only) returns version information for the current database instance. Here's the header for this procedure:

```
PROCEDURE DBMS_UTILITY.DB_VERSION
    (version OUT VARCHAR2
    ,compatibility OUT VARCHAR2);
```

Parameters are summarized in the following table.

Parameter	Description
version	A string that represents the internal software version of the database. The length of this string is variable and is determined by the database version.
compatibility	The compatibility setting of the database determined by the INIT.ORA parameter, COMPATIBLE. If the parameter is not specified in the INIT.ORA file, NULL is returned.

Example. Before this function was available, you had to build a query against a V$ table in order to obtain this information. Now it is easy to obtain your database version from within PL/SQL. In fact, you can make it even *easier* to get this information by building a wrapper around DBMS_UTILITY.DB_VERSION, as shown here:

```
/* Filename on companion disk: dbver.spp */
CREATE OR REPLACE PACKAGE db
IS
    FUNCTION version RETURN VARCHAR2;
    FUNCTION compatibility RETURN VARCHAR2;
END;
/
CREATE OR REPLACE PACKAGE BODY db
IS
    v VARCHAR2(100);
    c VARCHAR2(100);

    PROCEDURE init_info
    IS
    BEGIN
       IF v IS NULL
       THEN
           DBMS_UTILITY.DB_VERSION (v, c);
       END IF;
    END;

    FUNCTION version RETURN VARCHAR2
    IS
    BEGIN
       init_info;
       RETURN v;
    END;

    FUNCTION compatibility RETURN VARCHAR2
```

```
      IS
      BEGIN
         init_info;
         RETURN c;
      END;
   END;
   /
```

Notice that this very simple package also optimizes lookups against the DBMS_ UTILITY package. The first time you call either the DB.VERSION or the DB.COM-PATILITY functions, the private init_info procedure will detect that the v variable is NULL, and so it will call the built-in procedure. From that point on, however, whenever you call either of the DB functions, they will simply return the current value. After all, the version of the database is *not* going to change during your connection to that database.

Here is the output I received from db.version on Oracle8:

```
SQL> exec DBMS_UTILITY.PUT_LINE (db.version)
8.0.3.0.0
```

The DBMS_UTILITY.EXEC_DDL_STATEMENT procedure

Oracle has added a procedure to the DBMS_UTILITY package that allows you to execute a DDL statement easily. The header for this procedure follows:

```
PROCEDURE DBMS_UTILITY.EXEC_DDL_STATEMENT
   (parse_string IN VARCHAR2);
```

Here, for example, is all the code I need to write to create an index from within PL/SQL:

```
BEGIN
   DBMS_UTILITY.EXEC_DDL_STATEMENT
      ('create index so_easy on emp (hiredate, mgr, sal)');
END;
/
```

You can also use the DBMS_SQL package to perform the same functionality.

The DBMS_UTILITY.FORMAT_CALL_STACK function

This function formats and returns the current call stack. You can use this function to access the call stack in your program. The header for the function follows:

```
FUNCTION DBMS_UTILITY.FORMAT_CALL_STACK RETURN VARCHAR2;
```

Example. I generated the information in this next example with the following statement:

```
DBMS_OUTPUT.PUT_LINE (DBMS_UTILITY.FORMAT_CALL_STACK);
```

The code shows sample output from a call to FORMAT_CALL_STACK.

```
----- PL/SQL Call Stack -----
  object      line   object
  handle     number  name
817efc90        3    procedure BOOK.CALC_TOTALS
817d99ec        3    function BOOK.NET_PROFIT
817d101c        4    anonymous block
```

The output from this function can be up to 2000 bytes in length.

The DBMS_UTILITY.FORMAT_ERROR_STACK function

The FORMAT_ERROR_STACK function formats and returns the current error stack. You might use this function in an exception handler to examine the sequence of errors raised. The header for the function follows:

```
FUNCTION DBMS_UTILITY.FORMAT_ERROR_STACK RETURN VARCHAR2;
```

The output from this function can be up to 2000 bytes in length.

Example. The script file *errstk.sql* creates three procedures, each of which raises a different exception, and then kicks off the nested execution of those programs.

```
/* Filename on companion disk: errstk.sql */
CREATE OR REPLACE PROCEDURE proc1
IS
BEGIN
   RAISE NO_DATA_FOUND;
END;
/
CREATE OR REPLACE PROCEDURE proc2 S
BEGIN
   proc1;
EXCEPTION
   WHEN OTHERS THEN RAISE VALUE_ERROR;
END;
/
CREATE OR REPLACE PROCEDURE proc2 IS
BEGIN
   proc1;
EXCEPTION
   WHEN OTHERS THEN RAISE VALUE_ERROR;
END;
/
CREATE OR REPLACE PROCEDURE proc3 IS
BEGIN
   proc2;
EXCEPTION
   WHEN OTHERS THEN RAISE DUP_VAL_ON_INDEX;
END;
/
BEGIN /* Now execute the top-level procedure. */
   proc3;
EXCEPTION
   WHEN OTHERS
```

```
        THEN
            DBMS_OUTPUT.PUT_LINE (DBMS_UTILITY.FORMAT_ERROR_STACK);
        END;
        /
```

Here is the output from this script:

```
ORA-00001: unique constraint (.) violated
ORA-06502: PL/SQL: numeric or value error
ORA-01403: no data found
```

Here is my conclusion from this test: the DBMS_UTILITY.FORMAT_ERROR_ STACK is of limited use in PL/SQL programs. You don't see the name of the program in which the error was raised, and you don't see the line number on which the error occurred.

The DBMS_UTILITY.GET_HASH_VALUE function

This function gives PL/SQL developers access to a hashing algorithm. You will generally use hashing to generate a unique (or at least likely to be unique) integer value for a string. Here's the header for this function:

```
FUNCTION DBMS_UTILITY.GET_HASH_VALUE
        (name IN VARCHAR2
        ,base IN NUMBER
        ,hash_size IN NUMBER)
    RETURN NUMBER;
```

Parameters are summarized in the following table.

Parameter	Description
name	The string to be converted or hashed into an integer
base	The base or starting value of integer values for the hashing algorithm
hash_size	The size of the "hash table," meaning the total number of values that are available to the hashing algorithm as conversions from the string inputs

The values of base and hash_size determine the range of integers that can be used as converted values. Clearly, the larger the hash size, the more likely it is that you will be able to obtain a unique integer for every string you pass to the program.

Here are some points to keep in mind when working with the GET_HASH_ VALUE function:

- Use a small prime number for the base parameter. This establishes the low point of the range of values for the hash table.

- Use a very large number, and, at Oracle's suggestion, a power of 2, for the hash size to obtain best results. I usually employ a number like 2^{30}.

- You can never be sure that the function will actually return an integer value that is unique across the different strings you are converting or have already converted. You must always check to ensure that the value is unique.

- If you hit a conflict, you must rebuild your entire hash table (the list of integer values you have generated so far).

- Since you want to make sure that your base and hash_size values are applied consistently to all hashings for a particular application, you should never call the GET_HASH_VALUE function directly. Instead, you should build a "wrapper" around it that presets all of the arguments *except* the string that you are hashing. This technique is shown in the following example.

Example. The following example demonstrates how to use the hash function. It also shows how to use the function to build an alternative index on a PL/SQL table. Finally, it compares the performance of hash-based lookups versus a "full table scan" of a PL/SQL table. Comments in the program should make it easy to follow the algorithm.

NOTE   The demohash procedure makes use of the p.l procedure, the PL/
                Vision replacement for the much more awkward and limited DBMS_
                OUTPUT.PUT_LINE, as well as the PLVtmr package.*

```
/* Filename on companion disk: hashdemo.sp */
CREATE OR REPLACE PROCEDURE demohash (counter IN INTEGER)
IS
    v_row PLS_INTEGER;
    v_name VARCHAR2(30);
    hashing_failure EXCEPTION;

    /* Define the PL/SQL table */
    TYPE string_tabtype IS TABLE OF VARCHAR2(60)
        INDEX BY BINARY_INTEGER;
    names string_tabtype;

    /* A function which returns the hashed value. */
    FUNCTION hashval (value IN VARCHAR2) RETURN NUMBER
    IS
    BEGIN
        RETURN DBMS_UTILITY.GET_HASH_VALUE
            (value, 37, 1073741824);   /* POWER (2, 30) */
    END hashval;

    /* Add a name to the table, using the hash function to
```

---

* You can download a trial edition of PL/Vision Professional from *www.revealnet.com*. See the Preface ("About PL/Vision") for more information.

```
        determine the row in which the value is placed. Ah,
        the beauty of sparse PL/SQL tables! */
   PROCEDURE addname (nm IN VARCHAR2) IS
   BEGIN
        v_row := hashval (nm);
        names (v_row) := nm;
   END;


   /* Obtain the row for a name by scanning the table. */
   FUNCTION rowbyscan (nm IN VARCHAR2) RETURN PLS_INTEGER
   IS
        v_row PLS_INTEGER := names.FIRST;
        retval PLS_INTEGER;
   BEGIN
      LOOP
         EXIT WHEN v_row IS NULL;
         IF names(v_row) = nm
         THEN
            retval := v_row;
            EXIT;
         ELSE
            v_row := names.NEXT (v_row);
         END IF;
      END LOOP;
      RETURN retval;
   END;


   /* Obtain the row for a name by hashing the string. */
   FUNCTION rowbyhash (nm IN VARCHAR2) RETURN PLS_INTEGER
   IS
   BEGIN
      RETURN hashval (nm);
   END;
BEGIN
   /* Load up the table with a set of strings based on the number
      of iterations requested. This allows us to easily test the
      scalability of the two algorithms. */
   FOR i IN 1 .. counter
   LOOP
       addname ('Steven' || i);
       addname ('Veva' || i);
       addname ('Eli' || i);
       addname ('Chris' || i);
   END LOOP;


   /* Verify that there were no hashing conflicts (the COUNT should
      be 4 x counter. */
   p.l ('Count in names', names.COUNT);


   IF names.COUNT != 4 * counter
   THEN
       p.l ('Hashing conflict! Test suspended...');
       RAISE hashing_failure;
```

```
      END IF;

      /* Verify that the two scans return matching values. */
      v_name := 'Eli' || TRUNC (counter/2);
      p.l ('scan',rowbyscan (v_name));
      p.l ('hash',rowbyhash (v_name));
      IF rowbyscan (v_name) != rowbyhash (v_name)
      THEN
          p.l ('Scanned row differs from hashed row. Test suspended...');
          RAISE hashing_failure;
      END IF;

      /* Time performance of retrieval via scan. */
      plvtmr.capture;
      FOR i IN 1 .. counter
      LOOP
          v_row := rowbyscan (v_name);
      END LOOP;
      plvtmr.show_elapsed ('scan');

      /* Time performance of retrieval via hashed value. */
      plvtmr.capture;
      FOR i IN 1 .. counter
      LOOP
          v_row := rowbyhash (v_name);
      END LOOP;
      plvtmr.show_elapsed ('hash');
   EXCEPTION
      WHEN hashing_failure
      THEN
          NULL;
   END;
   /
```

The DBMS_UTILITY.GET_PARAMETER_VALUE function

Available first in PL/SQL8, this function allows you to retrieve the value of a database initialization parameter (set in the *INIT.ORA* initialization file). Here's the header:

```
FUNCTION DBMS_UTILITY.GET_PARAMETER_VALUE
      (parnam IN VARCHAR2
      ,intval IN OUT BINARY_INTEGER
      ,strval IN OUT VARCHAR2)
RETURN BINARY_INTEGER;
```

The value returned by the function is either of the following:

0   Indicating a numeric or Boolean parameter value

1   Indicating a string parameter value

Parameters are summarized in the following table.

Parameter	Description
parnam	The name of the initialization parameter (case-insensitive).
intval	The parameter value if that value is numeric. If the value is a Boolean (i.e., the value in the initialization file is TRUE or FALSE), then intval is set to 0 for FALSE and 1 for TRUE. If the value is a string, then this argument contains the length of that string value.
strval	The parameter value if that value is a string. Otherwise it is NULL.

Long desired by Oracle developers, the GET_PARAMETER_VALUE function now allows you to get critical information about the current database instance, including the default date format and lots of information about the way shared memory is configured. And you don't have to use UTL_FILE to read the initialization file. (Chances are your DBA would not enable the database directory holding this file for UTL_FILE access anyway!). Note that if you have more than one entry for the same parameter (certainly a possibility with a parameter such as UTL_FILE_DIR), then this built-in will retrieve only the value associated with the *first* occurrence of the parameter.

You will probably want to build a wrapper around GET_PARAMETER_VALUE to make it easier to retrieve and interpret the results. Why? Whenever you call this built-in function, you must declare two variables to retrieve the OUT arguments. You must then interpret the results. Rather than write all this code and have to remember all these rules, you can build it into a package once and then simply call the appropriate program as needed. A prototype of such a package is shown later in this section.

My package specification contains these three sections:

- Generic interfaces to the built-in, by datatype: return a string value, integer value, or Boolean value. You have to know which type of value *should* be returned for the name you provide.

- Functions returning the values of specific named (by the name of the function) entries in the initialization file. You should expand this section to make it easy to retrieve values for parameters you work with.

- A display procedure to show the different values returned by the built-in for a particular parameter.

```
/* Filename on companion disk: dbparm.spp */
CREATE OR REPLACE PACKAGE dbparm
IS
    /* Generic (by datatype) interfaces to built-in. */
    FUNCTION strval (nm IN VARCHAR2) RETURN VARCHAR2;
    FUNCTION intval (nm IN VARCHAR2) RETURN INTEGER;
```

```
FUNCTION boolval (nm IN VARCHAR2) RETURN BOOLEAN;

/* Encapsulation for specific parameter retrieval */
FUNCTION nls_date_format RETURN VARCHAR2;
FUNCTION utl_file_dir RETURN VARCHAR2;
FUNCTION db_block_buffers RETURN INTEGER;

PROCEDURE showval (nm IN VARCHAR2);
END;
/
```

Rather than show the entire package body (also found in *dbparm.spp*), I will show you the two levels of encapsulation around DBMS_UTILITY.GET_PARAMETER_VALUE found in the package. You can then apply that technique to other parameters of interest.

Here is the dbparm.intval function. It calls the built-in procedure and then returns the integer value. You might want to enhance this procedure to check the datatype of the parameter and only return a value if it is in fact a numeric (or Boolean) type.

```
FUNCTION intval (nm IN VARCHAR2) RETURN INTEGER
IS
    valtype PLS_INTEGER;
    ival PLS_INTEGER;
    sval VARCHAR2(2000);
BEGIN
    valtype := DBMS_UTILITY.GET_PARAMETER_VALUE (nm, ival, sval);
    RETURN ival;
END;
```

Now I build my dbparm.db_block_buffers package on top of that one as follows:

```
FUNCTION db_block_buffers RETURN INTEGER
IS
BEGIN
    RETURN intval ('db_block_buffers');
END;
```

The DBMS_UTILITY.GET_TIME function

This function returns the number of 100ths of seconds that have elapsed from an arbitrary time. The header for the function follows:

```
FUNCTION DBMS_UTILITY.GET_TIME RETURN NUMBER;
```

You are probably wondering what this "arbitrary time" is and why I don't tell you about what that starting point is. Two reasons: I don't know and it doesn't matter. You should not use GET_TIME to establish the current time, but only to calculate the elapsed time *between* two events.

The following example calculates the number of 100ths of elapsed seconds since the calc_totals procedure was executed:

```
DECLARE
    time_before BINARY_INTEGER;
    time_after BINARY_INTEGER;
BEGIN
    time_before := DBMS_UTILITY.GET_TIME;
    calc_totals;
    time_after := DBMS_UTILITY.GET_TIME;
    DBMS_OUTPUT.PUT_LINE (time_after - time_before);
END;
```

Without GET_TIME, Oracle functions can only record and provide elapsed time in second intervals, which is a very coarse granularity in today's world of computing. With GET_TIME, you can get a much finer understanding of the processing times of lines in your program.

Notice that in my anonymous block I had to declare two local variables, make my calls to GET_TIME, and then compute the difference. I will probably need to perform those actions over and over again in my programs. I might even want to perform timings that cross product lines (e.g., start my timing in a form and then check elapsed time from inside a report module). To make it easier to use GET_TIME in these various ways, I built a package called sptimer ("stored package timer" mechanism), which you can find in the *sptimer.sps* and *sptimer.spb* files on the companion disk.*

The DBMS_UTILITY.IS_PARALLEL_SERVER function

This function helps determine whether the database is running in parallel server mode. The specification follows:

```
FUNCTION DBMS_UTILITY.IS_PARALLEL_SERVER  RETURN BOOLEAN;
```

The function returns TRUE if the database is running in parallel server mode; otherwise, it returns FALSE.

The DBMS_UTILITY.MAKE_DATA_BLOCK_ADDRESS function

Use this function to obtain a valid data block address from a file number and block number. The header follows:

```
FUNCTION DBMS_UTILITY.MAKE_DATA_BLOCK_ADDRESS
    (file IN NUMBER
    ,block IN NUMBER)
    RETURN NUMBER;
```

---

* PL/Vision also offers the PLVtmr package, a much more fully-realized timing utility. See the Preface ("About PL/Vision") for more information.

Example. Here is an example of calling this function and displaying the resulting value:

```
SQL> BEGIN
  2    DBMS_OUTPUT.PUT_LINE
  3       (DBMS_UTILITY.MAKE_DATA_BLOCK_ADDRESS (10000, 20000));
  4  END;
  5  /

268455456
```

The DBMS_UTILITY.NAME_RESOLVE procedure

This procedure resolves the name of an object into its component parts, performing synonym translations as necessary. Here's the header for the procedure:

```
PROCEDURE DBMS_UTILITY.NAME_RESOLVE
    (name IN VARCHAR2,
     context IN NUMBER,
     schema OUT VARCHAR2,
     part1 OUT VARCHAR2,
     part2 OUT VARCHAR2,
     dblink OUT VARCHAR2,
     part1_type OUT NUMBER,
     object_number OUT NUMBER);
```

Parameters are summarized in the following table.

Parameter	Description
name	The name of the object to be resolved.
context	Present for future compatibility; must be set to the value 1.
schema	Name of the object's schema.
part1	The first part of the object's name.
part2	The second part of the object's name (NULL unless the object is a package module, and then part1 is the package name).
dblink	Name of the database link for the object, if any.
part1_type	Indicates the type of object returned in part1.
object_number	The object number for the named object. When object_number is returned NOT NULL, the name was successfully resolved.

An object type may have one of the following values:

5   Synonym

7   Standalone procedure

8   Standalone function

9   Package

The NAME_RESOLVE procedure has six OUT parameters, which means that in order to use this module you will have to declare six variables—an annoying task that creates an obstacle to casual use of the procedure.

I built a procedure called show_name_components precisely to make it easier to take advantage of NAME_RESOLVE. The show_name_components accepts an object name, and then calls DBMS_OUTPUT.PUT_LINE to display the different components of the name. It shows information only if it is relevant; in other words, if there is no part2, then part2 is not displayed. The name of the database link is displayed only if there is a database link associated with that object.

Here are some examples of calls to show_name_components:

```
SQL> execute show_name_components('do.pl');
Schema: BOOK
Package: DO
Name: PL

SQL> execute show_name_components('do');
Schema: BOOK
Package: DO

SQL> execute show_name_components('show_name_components');
Schema: BOOK
Procedure: SHOW_NAME_COMPONENTS
```

Here is the show_name_components procedure in its entirety:

```
/* Filename on companion disk: showcomp.sp */
CREATE OR REPLACE PROCEDURE show_name_components (name_in IN VARCHAR2)
IS
    /* variables to hold components of the name */
    schema VARCHAR2(100);
    part1 VARCHAR2(100);
    part2 VARCHAR2(100);
    dblink VARCHAR2(100);
    part1_type NUMBER;
    object_number NUMBER;

    /*-------------------- Local Module ----------------------*/
    FUNCTION object_type (type_in IN INTEGER)
        RETURN VARCHAR2
    /* Return name for integer type */
    IS
        synonym_type CONSTANT INTEGER := 5;
        procedure_type CONSTANT INTEGER := 7;
        function_type CONSTANT INTEGER := 8;
        package_type CONSTANT INTEGER := 9;
    BEGIN
        IF type_in = synonym_type
        THEN
            RETURN 'Synonym';
        ELSIF type_in = procedure_type
```

```
      THEN
          RETURN 'Procedure';
      ELSIF type_in = function_type
      THEN
          RETURN 'Function';
      ELSIF type_in = package_type
      THEN
          RETURN 'Package';
      END IF;
   END;
BEGIN
   /* Break down the name into its components */
   DBMS_UTILITY.NAME_RESOLVE
      (name_in, 1,
       schema, part1, part2,
       dblink , part1_type, object_number);

   /* If the object number is NULL, name resolution failed. */
   IF object_number IS NULL
   THEN
      DBMS_OUTPUT.PUT_LINE
         ('Name "' || name_in ||
          '" does not identify a valid object.');
   ELSE
      /* Display the schema, which is always available. */
      DBMS_OUTPUT.PUT_LINE ('Schema: ' || schema);

      /* If there is a first part to name, have a package module */
      IF part1 IS NOT NULL
      THEN
         /* Display the first part of the name */
         DBMS_OUTPUT.PUT_LINE
            (object_type (part1_type) || ': ' || part1);

         /* If there is a second part, display that. */
         IF part2 IS NOT NULL
         THEN
            DBMS_OUTPUT.PUT_LINE ('Name: ' || part2);
         END IF;
      ELSE
         /* No first part of name. Just display second part. */
         DBMS_OUTPUT.PUT_LINE
            (object_type (part1_type) || ': ' || part2);
      END IF;

      /* Display the database link if it is present. */
      IF dblink IS NOT NULL
      THEN
         DBMS_OUTPUT.PUT_LINE ('Database Link:' || dblink);
      END IF;
   END IF;
END;
/
```

The DBMS_UTILITY.NAME_TOKENIZE procedure

This procedure calls the PL/SQL parser to parse the given name that is in the following format,

```
a [ . b [. c]] [@dblink ]
```

where dblink is the name of a database link. Here's the header for the procedure:

```
PROCEDURE DBMS_UTILITY.NAME_TOKENIZE
     (name   IN VARCHAR2,
      a OUT VARCHAR2,
      b OUT VARCHAR2,
      c OUT VARCHAR2,
      dblink OUT VARCHAR2,
      nextpos OUT BINARY_INTEGER);
```

Parameters are summarized in the following table.

Parameter	Description
name	Name being parsed
a, b, c	Components of name, if present
dblink	Name of database link
nextpos	Position where next token starts

NAME_TOKENIZE follows these rules:

- Strips off all double quotes

- Converts to uppercase if there are no quotes

- Ignores any inline comments

- Does no semantic analysis

- Leaves any missing values as NULL

The DBMS_UTILITY.PORT_STRING function

The PORT_STRING function returns a string that uniquely identifies the version of Oracle Server and the platform or operating system of the current database instance. The specification for this function follows:

```
FUNCTION DBMS_UTILITY.PORT_STRING RETURN VARCHAR2;
```

Running the PORT_STRING function in Oracle8 on Windows NT, for example, returns the following string:

```
IBMPC/WINNT-8.0.0
```

The maximum length of the string returned by this function is operating system-specific.

The DBMS_UTILITY.TABLE_TO_COMMA procedure

The TABLE_TO_COMMA procedure converts a PL/SQL table into a comma-delimited list. Here's the header for this procedure:

```
PROCEDURE DBMS_UTILITY.TABLE_TO_COMMA
  (tab IN UNCL_ARRAY,
   tablen OUT BINARY_INTEGER,
   list OUT VARCHAR2);
```

Parameters are summarized in the following table.

Parameter	Description
tab	A PL/SQL table declared using the package's TABLE type
tablen	The number of rows defined in the PL/SQL table (assumed to be densely packed, all rows contiguously defined)
list	The string that will contain a comma-delimited list of the names for the PL/SQL table

DBMS_DESCRIBE: Describing PL/SQL Program Headers

The DBMS_DESCRIBE package contains a single procedure used to describe the arguments of a stored PL/SQL object.

Getting Started with DBMS_DESCRIBE

The DBMS_DESCRIBE package is created when the Oracle database is installed. The *dbmsdesc.sql* script (found in the built-in packages source code directory, as described in Chapter 1) contains the source code for this package's specification. This script is called by *catproc.sql*, which is normally run immediately after database creation. The script creates the public synonym DMS_DESCRIBE for the package and grants EXECUTE privilege on the package to public. All Oracle users can reference and make use of this package.

DBMS_DESCRIBE program

Table 10-2 summarizes the single procedure available through DBMS_DESCRIBE.

Table 10-2. DBMS_DESCRIBE Program

Name	Description	Use in SQL
DESCRIBE_PROCEDURE	Describes the specified PL/SQL object by returning all of the information for the object in a set of scalar and PL/SQL table parameters.	No

DBMS_DESCRIBE nonprogram elements

In addition to the DESCRIBE_PROCEDURE procedure, DBMS_DESCRIBE defines two PL/SQL table types you can use when calling or describing a PL/SQL object. These are described in the following table.

Name/Type	Description
DBMS_DESCRIBE.VARCHAR2_TABLE	Table TYPE of 30-character strings; used to declare PL/SQL tables to hold string information returned by DBMS_DESCRIBE.DESCRIBE_PRO-CEDURE.
DBMS_DESCRIBE.NUMBER_TABLE	Table TYPE of numbers; used to declare PL/SQL tables to hold numeric information returned by DBMS_DESCRIBE.DESCRIBE_PRO-CEDURE.

The two table TYPES are defined as follows:

```
TYPE DBMS_DESCRIBE.VARCHAR2_TABLE IS
    TABLE OF VARCHAR2(30) INDEX BY BINARY_INTEGER;

TYPE DBMS_DESCRIBE.NUMBER_TABLE
    IS TABLE OF NUMBER INDEX BY BINARY_INTEGER;
```

The DBMS_DESCRIBE.DESCRIBE_PROCEDURE procedure

The DESCRIBE_PROCEDURE procedure describes the specified PL/SQL object (currently only procedures and functions are supported). It returns information about the parameters of the program in a series of PL/SQL tables. The header for this procedure follows:

```
PROCEDURE DBMS_DESCRIBE.DESCRIBE_PROCEDURE
        (object_name IN VARCHAR2
        ,reserved1 IN VARCHAR2
        ,reserved2 IN VARCHAR2
        ,overload OUT NUMBER_TABLE
        ,position OUT NUMBER_TABLE
        ,level OUT NUMBER_TABLE
        ,argument_name OUT VARCHAR2_TABLE
        ,datatype OUT NUMBER_TABLE
        ,default_value OUT NUMBER_TABLE
        ,in_out OUT NUMBER_TABLE
        ,length OUT NUMBER_TABLE
        ,precision OUT NUMBER_TABLE
        ,scale OUT NUMBER_TABLE
        ,radix OUT NUMBER_TABLE
        ,spare OUT NUMBER_TABLE);
```

Paremeters are summarized in the following table.

Parameter	Description
object_name	The name of the program being described. The form of the name is [[part1.]part2.]part3. The syntax for this name follows the rules for identifiers in SQL. This name can be a synonym and may also contain delimited identifiers (double-quoted strings). This parameter is required and may not be NULL. The total length of the name is limited to 197 bytes.
reserved1	Reserved for future use. Must be set to NULL or an empty string, as in ` ` .
reserved2	Reserved for future use. Must be set to NULL or an empty string, as in ` ` .
overload	An array of integers containing the unique number assigned to the program "signature." If the program is overloaded, the value in this array will indicate the specific overloading to which the argument belongs.
position	An array of integers showing the position of the argument in the parameter list. The first argument is always in position 1. A value of 0 indicates that the "argument" is actually the RETURN value of the function.
level	An array of integers describing the level of the argument. This is relevant when describing a procedure with a composite datatype, such as a record or PL/SQL table. For specific level values, see "The DESCRIBE level" later in this chapter.
argument_name	An array of strings containing the names of the arguments. This entry is NULL if the argument is the RETURN value of a function.
datatype	An array of integers describing the datatypes of the arguments. For specific datatype values, see the next table.
default_value	An array of integers indicating whether the argument has a default value. If 1, then a default value is present; if 0, then no default value.
in_out	An array of integers indicating the parameter mode: 0 = IN mode 1 = OUT mode 2 = IN OUT mode
length	An array of integers indicating the length of the argument. For string types, the length is the "N" in CHAR(N) or VARCHAR2(N). Currently, this value represents the number of bytes (not characters) on the server-side. (For a multibyte datatype, this may be different from the number of bytes on the client side.)
precision	An array of integers containing the precisions of the arguments. Relevant only for numeric arguments.
scale	An array of integers containing the scales of the arguments. Relevant only for numeric arguments.
radix	An array of integers containing the radixes of the arguments. Relevant only for numeric arguments.
spare	Reserved for future usage (but you still have to declare a PL/SQl table to hold it!).

The values for parameter datatypes are listed in the following table.

Datatype	Number
VARCHAR2	1
NVARCHAR2	1
NUMBER	2
INTEGER	2
BINARY_INTEGER	3
PLS_INTEGER	3
LONG	8
ROWID	11
DATE	12
RAW	23
LONGRAW	24
CHAR	96
NCHAR	96
MLSLABEL	106
CLOB	112
NCLOB	112
BLOB	113
BFILE	114
Object type (Oracle8)	121
Nested table type (Oracle8)	122
Variable array (Oracle8)	123
Record type	250
Index-by (PL/SQL) table type	251
BOOLEAN	252

Exceptions

DBMS_DESCRIBE.DESCRIBE_PROCEDURE may raise any of the exceptions listed in the following table.

Error Code	Description
ORA-20000	A package was specified. DESCRIBE_PROCEDURE currently allows you to request only describes for top-level ("standalone") programs (procedure and functions) or programs within a package.
ORA-20001	You requested a describe of a procedure or function that does not exist within the package.
ORA-20002	You requested a describe of a procedure or function that is remote (either by including a database link or by passing a program name that is actually a synonym for a program defined using a database link). DESCRIBE_PRO-CEDURE is currently unable to describe remote objects.

Error Code	Description
ORA-20003	You requested describe of an object that is marked invalid. You can describe only valid objects. Recompile the object and then describe it.
ORA-20004	There was a syntax error in the specification of the object's name.

Notice that these exceptions are not defined in the specification of the package. Instead, DESCRIBE_PROCEDURE simply calls RAISE_APPLICATION_ERROR with the error numbers listed earlier. These error numbers may therefore conflict with your own –20NNN error number usages (this is a very bad design decision on Oracle's part). If you embed calls to DESCRIBE_PROCEDURE inside your application or utility, watch out for the confusion such conflicts can cause.

Restrictions

There are several limitations on using DESCRIBE_PROCEDURE:

- You cannot describe remote objects (i.e., PL/SQL program elements that are defined in another database instance).

- You cannot get a describe or a listing of all elements defined in a package specification. You need to know the name of the procedure or function within the package in other to get a describe of it.

- DBMS_DESCRIBE.DESCRIBE_PROCEDURE will not show you the internal structure (attributes) of Oracle8 elements such as object types, variable arrays, and nested tables.

Explaining DBMS_DESCRIBE Results

In the following sections and in subsequent examples I will demonstrate different ways of using DBMS_DESCRIBE.DESCRIBE_PROCEDURE. I will be working with the following objects:

```
CREATE TABLE account
    (account_no number,
     person_id number,
     balance number(7,2));

CREATE TABLE person
    (person_id number(4),
     person_nm varchar2(10));
```

I will also describe objects in a package called desctest, which is defined in the *psdesc.tst* file on the companion disk. The output I display from the DESCRIBE_PROCEDURE is generated by the psdesc (PL/SQL DESCribe) package, which is explained in the "DBMS_DESCRIBE Example" section and is defined in the *psdesc.spp* file.

Specifying a program name

The valid syntax for a PL/SQL object to be described follows:

```
[[part1.]part2.]part3
```

Here are various valid object specifications for DBMS_DESCRIBE.DESCRIBE_PRO-
CEDURE:

Object Specification	Description
showemps	Standalone procedure or synonym to same
emppkg.employee_name	Function inside a package
scott.delete_dept	Standalone procedure in the SCOTT schema
scott.emppkg.update_salary	Procedure inside a package in the SCOTT schema

You can also describe procedures and functions in the STANDARD and DBMS_
STANDARD packages (the default packages of PL/SQL, containing the core elements of the language). To do this, you must prefix the name of the built-in with
its package name, as in:

```
'STANDARD.TO_CHAR'
```

The DESCRIBE level

The level array discloses the hierarchy of the elements in a program's arguments.
The level applies only to the following subset of composite datatypes: records
and PL/SQL tables. The default level of 0 means that it is the top level. For scalars, that is the only level. For composites, 0 indicates that you are pointing to the
actual composite argument. Each successive value of level (positive integers: 1, 2,
etc.) indicates that the argument attribute or field is a child of the previous level.

The following example demonstrates how DESCRIBE_PROCEDURE generates its
levels. Suppose that I have the following elements defined inside a package:

```
/* Filename on companion disk: psdesc.tst */
CREATE OR REPLACE PACKAGE desctest
IS
    TYPE number_table IS TABLE OF NUMBER INDEX BY BINARY_INTEGER;

    TYPE myrec1 IS RECORD (empno NUMBER, indsal NUMBER);
    TYPE myrec2 IS RECORD
        (ename VARCHAR2(20), hiredate DATE, empno_info myrec1);
    TYPE myrec3 IS RECORD
        (deptno NUMBER, totsal NUMBER, all_emp_info myrec2);

    TYPE myrec_table IS TABLE OF myrec1 INDEX BY BINARY_INTEGER;

    PROCEDURE composites (account_in NUMBER,
        person person%ROWTYPE,
        multirec myrec3,
```

```
        num_table number_table,
        recs_table myrec_table);
    END;
    /
```

I have double-nested a record (myrec1 inside myrec2 inside myrec3), a table based on a record (myrec_table), and a "simple" table-based record (person%ROWTYPE). Here are the results from DBMS_DESCRIBE.DESCRIBE_PROCEDURE:

```
SQL>  exec psdesc.showargs ('desctest.composites')
OvLd Pos Lev Type            Name
---- --- --- --------------- -----------------------

     0   1   0 NUMBER          ACCOUNT_IN
     0   2   0 RECORD          PERSON
     0   1   1 NUMBER          PERSON_ID
     0   2   1 VARCHAR2        PERSON_NM
     0   3   0 RECORD          MULTIREC
     0   1   1 NUMBER          DEPTNO
     0   2   1 NUMBER          TOTSAL
     0   3   1 RECORD          ALL_EMP_INFO
     0   1   2 VARCHAR2        ENAME
     0   2   2 DATE            HIREDATE
     0   3   2 RECORD          EMPNO_INFO
     0   1   3 NUMBER          EMPNO
     0   2   3 NUMBER          INDSAL
     0   4   0 INDEX-BY TABLE  NUM_TABLE
     0   1   1 NUMBER          RETURN Value
     0   5   0 INDEX-BY TABLE  RECS_TABLE
     0   1   1 RECORD          RETURN Value
     0   1   2 NUMBER          EMPNO
     0   2   2 NUMBER          INDSAL
```

How overloading is handled

When you overload, you define more than one program with the same name. You will usually do this in packages. DESCRIBE_PROCEDURE creates a set of rows in the arrays for each overloading of a program. It then generates a unique, sequential number in the overload array to indicate that (a) the program is overloaded (a value of 0 indicates no overloading), and (b) to which overloading the arguments belong.

Suppose that the desctest package has two overloaded versions of the upd function (the only difference is in the datatype of the last parameter, NUMBER vs. DATE).

```
    CREATE OR REPLACE PACKAGE desctest
    IS
        FUNCTION upd (account_in NUMBER,
          person person%ROWTYPE,
          amounts number_table,
```

```
        trans_date DATE) RETURN account.balance%TYPE;

    FUNCTION upd (account_in NUMBER,
        person person%ROWTYPE,
        amounts number_table,
        trans_no NUMBER) RETURN account.balance%TYPE;
END;
/
```

Then the output from DBMS_DESCRIBE.DESCRIBE_PROCEDURE would be as follows:

```
SQL> exec psdesc.showargs ('desctest.upd')
OvLd Pos Lev Type            Name
---- --- --- --------------- --------------------

   1   0   0 NUMBER          RETURN Value
   1   1   0 NUMBER          ACCOUNT_IN
   1   2   0 RECORD          PERSON
   1   1   1 NUMBER          PERSON_ID
   1   2   1 VARCHAR2        PERSON_NM
   1   3   0 INDEX-BY TABLE  AMOUNTS
   1   1   1 NUMBER          RETURN Value
   1   4   0 DATE            TRANS_DATE
---- --- --- --------------- --------------------
   2   0   0 NUMBER          RETURN Value
   2   1   0 NUMBER          ACCOUNT_IN
   2   2   0 RECORD          PERSON
   2   1   1 NUMBER          PERSON_ID
   2   2   1 VARCHAR2        PERSON_NM
   2   3   0 INDEX-BY TABLE  AMOUNTS
   2   1   1 NUMBER          RETURN Value
   2   4   0 NUMBER          TRANS_NO
```

DBMS_DESCRIBE Example

The most important example I can think of for DBMS_DESCRIBE.DESCRIBE_PRO-
CEDURE is the construction of a utility that makes it easier to *use* this procedure.
Without such a utility, you must declare a set of PL/SQL tables every time you
want to call the DESCRIBE_PROCEDURE. You must then also interpret the results.
By encapsulating all of this information and these data structures inside the package, you can take advantage of DBMS_DESCRIBE.DESCRIBE_PROCEDURE much
more easily, and also interpret the results with greater accuracy and understanding.

Features of the psdesc package

The psdesc package offers those features (PL/SQL Release 2.3 or later is needed to compile and use this package). Found in the *psdesc.spp* file, it contains the following elements:

- A set of constants that give names to each of the different datatype values. These constants allow you to write code without having to remember specific hard-coded values. Here are a few lines from that code:

```
c_varchar2      CONSTANT PLS_INTEGER := 1;
c_number        CONSTANT PLS_INTEGER := 2;
c_object_type   CONSTANT PLS_INTEGER := 121;
```

- A PL/SQL table containing names to go along with those datatype constants (numbers). The psdesc.showargs program uses this table to display more descriptive information about the argument (for example, more than simply saying that it is type 121).

- A set of constants that give names to the values for the different parameter modes. These are defined as follows:

```
c_in CONSTANT PLS_INTEGER := 0;
c_out CONSTANT PLS_INTEGER := 1;
c_inout CONSTANT PLS_INTEGER := 2;
```

- A user-defined record type that parallels the set of PL/SQL tables populated by the DESCRIBE_PROCEDURE procedure. This record type is defined as follows:

```
TYPE arglist_rt IS RECORD (
   overload NUMBER,
   position NUMBER
 ,level NUMBER
 ,argument_name VARCHAR2 (30)
 ,datatype NUMBER
 ,default_value NUMBER
 ,in_out NUMBER
 ,length NUMBER
 ,precision NUMBER
 ,scale NUMBER
 ,radix NUMBER);
```

  This record type is the RETURN value for the psdesc.arg function.

- A procedure that acts as a wrapper around the DESCRIBE_PROCEDURE procedure. The psdesc.args procedure has a much simpler interface.

```
PROCEDURE psdesc.args (obj IN VARCHAR2);
```

  When you call it, you don't need to provide a set of predeclared PL/SQL tables. Those arrays are already defined in the psdesc package specification.

- A procedure that displays all of the argument information in a very readable format. You have seen the output (or part of it) in a number of earlier sections in this chapter.

  ```
  PROCEDURE psdesc.showargs (obj IN VARCHAR2 := NULL);
  ```

  Notice that this procedure has an optional object name; if you don't provide one, it will show you the arguments for whatever program was last processed in a call to psdesc.args. In other words, it will examine whatever is sitting in the individual arrays.

- A procedure that returns information about a specified argument (by position in the arrays).

  ```
  FUNCTION psdesc.arg (pos IN INTEGER) RETURN arglist_rt;
  ```

For reasons of space, I will not show the entire package specification and body. You can examine both of those in the *psdesc.spp* file. You will notice that I have placed all of the predefined PL/SQL tables in the package specification, even though the programs of psdesc offer a programmatic interface to those tables. I did that to make it easier to examine and manipulate the contents of the argument information.

Just to give you a sense of how psdesc does its job, here is the implementation of psdesc.args (my "substitute" for the original DESCRIBE_PROCEDURE):

```
/* Filename on companion disk: psdesc.spp */
PROCEDURE args (obj IN VARCHAR2)
   IS
   BEGIN
      g_object_name := obj;

      DBMS_DESCRIBE.DESCRIBE_PROCEDURE (obj, NULL, NULL,
         g_overload,
         g_position,
         g_level,
         g_argument_name,
         g_datatype,
         g_default_value,
         g_in_out,
         g_length,
         g_precision,
         g_scale,
         g_radix,
         g_spare);
   END;
```

I save the object name you specify in a package variable. I then call DESCRIBE_PROCEDURE, dumping all of the retrieved information into the predeclared PL/SQL tables.

To display all of the argument information for a program, you would call psdesc.showargs. Here is a simplified presentation of this procedure:

```
PROCEDURE showargs (obj IN VARCHAR2 := NULL)
IS
    v_onearg arglist_rt;
BEGIN
    IF obj IS NOT NULL
    THEN
        args (obj);
    END IF;

    IF g_position.COUNT > 0
    THEN
        display_header;

        FOR argrow IN g_position.FIRST .. g_position.LAST
        LOOP
            v_onearg := arg (argrow);

            display_argument_info (v_onearg);
        END LOOP;
    END IF;
END;
```

In other words, if the object name is specified, call psdesc.args to fill up the pre-defined arrays. Then, if there is anything in those arrays (g_position.COUNT is greater than 0), proceed from the first to the last argument and (a) call psdesc.arg to retrieve all the information for the Nth argument, and (b) display that informa-tion—all the details of which are left to the *psdesc.spp* file. That was easy enough!

Here are some other aspects of psdesc you might find interesting:

- Use of the package initialization section to fill g_datatype_names and g_mode_names, which are lists of "translations" for the numeric codes.

- The use of a local function, strval, defined inside psdesc.showargs, which con-solidates otherwise redundant logic used to format output for display.

- The check for a non-NULL g_object_name in the psdesc.arg function to make sure that you have used psdesc.args or psdesc.showargs to fill up the pre-defined PL/SQL tables. This is a sure-fire validation step, since the g_object_name variable is defined in the package *body*. It is private data and is only modified by a call to psdesc.arg.

Using psdesc.args as a quality assurance tool

Rather than spend any more space on the implementation of psdesc, I will show you how you might put it to use.

Suppose that you want to perform quality assurance checks on your code (what a concept, eh?). One rule that you have established for all your developers is that no function should have OUT or IN OUT parameters. The only way that data is to be returned from a function is through the RETURN clause. This guideline improves the reusability and maintainability of the function. It also makes that function a candidate for execution within SQL.

How can you make sure that everyone is following this rule?

Sure, you could run some queries against ALL_SOURCE, which contains all the source code, but what would you look for? "IN OUT" and "OUT" are good candidates, but only when they are inside the parameter lists of functions. Hmmm. That actually involves some parsing. What's a software manager interested in code quality to do?

Let's see if DESCRIBE_PROCEDURE and the psdesc package can help. The following hasout function satisfies the request by obtaining all arguments with a call to psdesc.args and then scanning the PL/SQL table filled from DBMS_DESCRIBE.DESCRIBE_PROCEDURE for the offending parameter mode. This function returns TRUE if the program named by the string that I pass to it contains an OUT or IN OUT argument.

```
/* Filename on companion disk: hasout.sf */
CREATE OR REPLACE FUNCTION hasout (obj IN VARCHAR2) RETURN BOOLEAN
IS
   v_onearg psdesc.arglist_rt;
   v_argrow PLS_INTEGER;
   retval BOOLEAN := NULL;
BEGIN
   psdesc.args (obj);

   v_argrow := psdesc.numargs;

   IF v_argrow = 0
   THEN
      retval := NULL;
   ELSE
      retval := FALSE;
      LOOP
         v_onearg := psdesc.arg (v_argrow);
         IF v_onearg.argument_name IS NOT NULL
         THEN
            retval := v_onearg.in_out IN (psdesc.c_out, psdesc.c_inout);
         END IF;
         EXIT WHEN retval OR v_argrow = 1;
         v_argrow := v_argrow - 1;
      END LOOP;
   END IF;
   RETURN retval;
END;
/
```

This function works as advertised, even for overloaded programs. Suppose, for example, that I run this function against the desctst.upd function (overloaded earlier in two versions). These functions do not contain an OUT or IN OUT parameter. I run the following script:

```
/* Filename on companion disk: hasout.tst */
BEGIN
    /* I need to call hasout with an IF statement if I am going to use
       DBMS_OUTPUT.PUT_LINE to show the results; that built-in is very
       sadly not overloaded for Booleans... */
    IF hasout ('&1')
    THEN
        DBMS_OUTPUT.PUT_LINE ('&1 contains OUT or IN OUT argument(s).');
    ELSE
        DBMS_OUTPUT.PUT_LINE ('&1 contains only IN argument(s).');
    END IF;
END;
/
```

Calling this function, I get the following results:

```
SQL> @hasout.tst desctest.upd
desctest.upd contains only IN argument(s).
```

If I now add an additional overloading of the desctest.upd function as follows,

```
CREATE OR REPLACE PACKAGE desctest
IS
    FUNCTION upd (account_in NUMBER,
        person person%ROWTYPE,
        amounts number_table,
        trans_no NUMBER,
        maxsal OUT NUMBER) RETURN account.balance%TYPE;
END;
/
```

I then get this result from running the hasout function:

```
SQL> @hasout.tst desctest.upd
desctest.upd contains OUT or IN OUT argument(s).
```

And I bet you thought you wouldn't ever find any reason to use DESCRIBE_PROCEDURE! This handy little utility points the way to many other kinds of analyses you can perform on your code. Once you have the psdesc package in place, it becomes easy to construct these higher-level programs.

Now all you have to do is come up with a way to feed your full list of functions (both standalone and packaged) into the hasout function for its quality check. This sounds easier than it actually is. Why? Because Oracle does not offer any utilities that provide you with the list of programs defined inside of a package.

You cannot, in other words, do a describe on a package and see the list of elements defined in that package's specification. I hope that this is a shortcoming

Oracle will correct, both through the provision of an API (perhaps by adding another procedure to the DBMS_DESCRIBE package) and the extension of the DESCRIBE command in SQL*Plus.

In the meantime, though, you have some options. You can get all of the stand-alone functions from ALL_OBJECTS, and that will be a start. Furthermore, if you are using PL/Vision from RevealNet (see the Preface, "About PL/Vision"), you can use the PLVcat utility to catalog your package specifications. This process will extract the names of all procedures and functions and deposit them in the plvctlg table. If that is not available, you will have to come up with a list by performing a code review on all your packages. Then put those function names (with their package names prefixed) into a database table or file. Once you have that, you can easily construct a script to read those names and pass them to hasout.

DBMS_DDL: Compiling and Analyzing Objects

The DBMS_DDL package provides access from within PL/SQL to two DDL (Data Definition Language) statements. It also offers special administrative services that are not available through DDL syntax (Oracle8 only).

Getting Started with DBMS_DDL

This DBMS_DESCRIBE package is created when the Oracle database is installed. The *dbmsdesc.sql* script (found in the built-in packages source code directory, as described in Chapter 1) contains the source code for this package's specification. This script is called by *catproc.sql*, which is normally run immediately after data-base creation. The script creates the public synonym DBMS.DDL for the package and grants EXECUTE privilege on the package to public. All Oracle users can reference and make use of this package.

DBMS_DDL programs "run as user," which means that they execute with the privileges of the user who calls that program.

NOTE   All programs in DBMS_DDL first commit the current transaction, then perform the specified operation. When the operation is completed, another commit is performed.

DBMS_DDL programs

Table 10-3 shows the programs defined in DBMS_DDL.

Table 10-3. DBMS_DDL Programs

Name	Description	Use in SQL
ALTER_COMPILE	Compiles the specified PL/SQL object.	No
ANALYZE_OBJECT	Computes statistics for the specified database object.	No
ALTER_TABLE_REFERENCEABLE	Makes the specified table referenceable for object identifiers (OIDs) in existing data structures. Available in Oracle8 only.	No
ALTER_TABLE_NOT_REFERENCEABLE	Undoes the action of the previous procedure, ALTER_TABLE_REFERENCEABLE. Available in Oracle8 only.	No

DBMS_DDL does not define any exceptions or nonprogram elements.

Compiling PL/SQL Objects

You can recompile PL/SQL objects that are already stored in the database by calling the ALTER_COMPILE procedure.

The DBMS_DDL.ALTER_COMPILE procedure

Here's the header for this procedure:

```
PROCEDURE DBMS_DDL.ALTER_COMPILE
    (type IN VARCHAR2
    ,schema IN VARCHAR2
    ,name IN VARCHAR2);
```

Parameters are summarized in the following table.

Parameter	Description
type	The type of the database object. Legal values are shown following.
schema	The name of the schema containing the object you wish to compile.
name	The name of the object you wish to compile.

Here are the possible values you can provide for the type parameter (enclosed in single quotes when you pass them to the procedure) and the actions that result:

Type	Action
PROCEDURE	Recompiles the specified procedure
FUNCTION	Recompiles the specified function
PACKAGE	Recompiles the specified package specification and body

Type	Action
PACKAGE BODY	Recompiles the specified package body
PACKAGE SPECIFICATION	Recompiles the specified package specification

The schema and name arguments are case-sensitive. In almost every instance, the names of your PL/SQL objects are stored in uppercase (you must enclose those names in double quotes when creating the objects if you want mixed case). You will therefore need to specify the names in uppercase when you call ALTER_COMPILE.

Note the following about using this package:

- If you pass NULL for the schema, then the current schema (the same value returned by a call to the built-in function USER) will be used.

- If you try to recompile DBMS_DDL, STANDARD, or DBMS_STANDARD (assuming that you have the privileges to do so), this procedure will return without taking any action.

- When you request recompilation of a program, Oracle will first recompile any objects upon which that program depends, and which are marked invalid.

In order to compile a program, you must own that program (in other words, the schema you specify is the owner of the program for which you request compilation) or your schema must have been granted the ALTER ANY PROCEDURE privilege to compile another schema's programs.

The following command from a DBA account in SQL*Plus enables the SCOTT account to compile the programs of other schemas:

```
SQL> GRANT ALTER ANY PROCEDURE TO SCOTT;
```

Here are a few examples of usage, assuming that SCOTT has been granted the ALTER ANY PROCEDURE privilege:

1. Recompile the procedure in the SCOTT schema that shows employees.

    ```
    SQL> exec DBMS_DDL.ALTER_COMPILE ('PROCEDURE', USER, 'SHOWEMPS');
    ```

    Notice that I pass in all arguments in uppercase to ensure a match.

2. Recompile the body of the empmaint package in the SALLY schema.

    ```
    SQL> exec DBMS_DDL.ALTER_COMPILE ('PACKAGE BODY', 'SALLY', 'EMPMAINT');
    ```

    Here too, I pass in all arguments in uppercase to ensure a match.

3. Suppose that I had created a procedure as follows:

    ```
    CREATE OR REPLACE PROCEDURE "%$^abc" IS
    BEGIN
        ...
    ```

```
    END;
    /
```

(Try it! You will discover that this syntax will be acceptable to the compiler! It turns out that if you enclose your identifier—be it a table name, column name, program name or variable name—in double quotes, *all* of the normal rules are suspended.)

Then I can recompile this program with the following command:

```
SQL> exec DBMS_DDL.ALTER_COMPILE ('PROCEDURE', USER, '%$^abc');
```

Strange, but true!

Exceptions. The ALTER_COMPILE procedure may raise any of the following exceptions:

ORA-20000

Insufficient privileges or object does not exist. You must either own the specified object or be granted the CREATE ANY PROCEDURE privilege.

ORA-20001

Remote object, cannot compile. You can only recompile objects on the local database instance.

ORA-20002

Bad value for object type. You need to provide one of the values listed in the previous section.

Notice that these exceptions are not defined in the specification of the package. Instead, ALTER_COMPILE simply calls RAISE_APPLICATION_ERROR with one of the above error numbers. These error numbers may therefore conflict with your own –20NNN error number usages. If you embed calls to ALTER_COMPILE inside your application or utility, watch out for the confusion such conflicts can cause.

Example. At first glance, you might say this of the ALTER_COMPILE procedure: "Why bother? The command is available in SQL*Plus. I'll just execute the ALTER PROCEDURE XXX COMPILE command when I need to recompile."

The big difference between that command and the ALTER_COMPILE procedure, of course, is that you can run the latter within a PL/SQL block or program. This allows you to apply the full power and flexibility of a procedural language to make the utility more useful. This technique is demonstrated by my recompile procedure, which follows. This program recompiles all stored PL/SQL objects that are identified by the parameters you provide to it.

```
/* Filename on companion disk: recmpile.sp */
CREATE OR REPLACE PROCEDURE recompile
    (status_in IN VARCHAR2 := 'INVALID',
     name_in IN VARCHAR2 := '%',
```

```
            type_in IN VARCHAR2 := '%',
            schema_in IN VARCHAR2 := USER)
   IS
      v_objtype VARCHAR2(100);

      CURSOR obj_cur IS
         SELECT owner, object_name, object_type
           FROM ALL_OBJECTS
          WHERE status LIKE UPPER (status_in)
            AND object_name LIKE UPPER (name_in)
            AND object_type LIKE UPPER (type_in)
            AND owner LIKE UPPER (schema_in)
          ORDER BY
             DECODE (object_type,
                'PACKAGE', 1,
                'FUNCTION', 2,
                'PROCEDURE', 3,
                'PACKAGE BODY', 4);
   BEGIN
      FOR rec IN obj_cur
      LOOP
         IF rec.object_type = 'PACKAGE'
         THEN
            v_objtype := 'PACKAGE SPECIFICATION';
         ELSE
            v_objtype := rec.object_type;
         END IF;

         DBMS_DDL.ALTER_COMPILE (v_objtype, rec.owner, rec.object_name);

         DBMS_OUTPUT.PUT_LINE
            ('Compiled ' || v_objtype || ' of ' ||
             rec.owner || '.' || rec.object_name);
      END LOOP;
   END;
   /
```

Here are a few interesting aspects to this procedure:

- The default values are set up so that if you call recompile without any arguments, it will recompile all objects marked INVALID in your own schema. That seemed to be the most common usage for this utility, so why not design the interface to make that the easiest usage as well?

- I translate the PACKAGE type to PACKAGE SPECIFICATION. I also order the objects retrieved so that they are compiled in the following order: package, function, procedure, and finally package body. I do this so that package specifications are compiled first, putting in place as many of the *interfaces* as possible, before moving on to the implementations of standalone programs and then package bodies.

- It was necessary to declare a local variable for the object type because the definition of the OBJECT_TYPE column in ALL_OBJECTS is as VARCHAR2(12). When I combine PACKAGE and SPECIFICATION into a single "type" for purposes of the recompilation, the new type is too big for the record-based field.

- I call DBMS_OUTPUT.PUT_LINE to provide a "trace" of the recompilations that have taken place.

- You can use wildcarded values in just about all of the arguments (name, type, owner) in order to perform just those recompilations that you need to perform.

- I apply the UPPER function to all arguments. This will work (and make it easier to specify objects for recompilation) unless you use mixed case in your object names.

So to recompile all invalid programs in my schema, I would enter this command:

```
SQL> exec recompile
```

To recompile only package bodies that are invalid, I would execute the following:

```
SQL> exec recompile (type_in => 'PACKAGE BODY')
```

Computing Statistics for an Object

Use the ANALYZE_OBJECT procedure to compute statistics for the specified table, index, or cluster.

The DBMS_DDL.ANALYZE_OBJECT procedure

Here is the header for this procedure:

```
PROCEDURE DBMS_DDL.ANALYZE_OBJECT
    (type IN VARCHAR2
    ,schema IN VARCHAR2
    ,name IN VARCHAR2
    ,method IN VARCHAR2
    ,estimate_rows IN NUMBER DEFAULT NULL
    ,estimate_percent IN NUMBER DEFAULT NULL
    ,method_opt IN VARCHAR2 DEFAULT NULL);
```

Parameters are summarized in the following table.

Parameter	Description
type	The type of the database object. Legal values are TABLE, CLUSTER, or INDEX.
schema	The name of the schema containing the object for which you wish to compute statistics. If NULL, then the current schema is used.
name	The name of the object for which you wish to compute statistics.

Parameter	Description
method	Action to be taken by the program. ESTIMATE, DELETE, and NULL are accepted values and are explained following.
estimate_rows	The number of rows to be used to perform the statistics estimate. Cannot be less than 1. Used only if method is ESTIMATE.
estimate_percent	The percentage of rows to be used to perform the statistics estimate. Ignored if estimate_rows is non-NULL. Must be between 1 and 99. Used only if method is ESTIMATE.
method_opt	The method option, indicating which elements of the object will be analyzed.

The schema and name arguments are case-sensitive. In almost every instance, the names of your PL/SQL objects are stored in uppercase. (Enclose those names in double quotes when creating the objects if you want mixed case). You will therefore need to specify the names in uppercase when you call COMPUTE_STATISTICS.

This procedure offers a procedural equivalent to the SQL DDL statement:

```
ANALYZE TABLE|CLUSTER|INDEX [<schema>.]<name>
    [<method>] STATISTICS [SAMPLE <n> [ROWS|PERCENT]]
```

If the type you specify is not one of TABLE, CLUSTER, or INDEX, the procedure returns without taking action.

NOTE   The type is *not* case-sensitive; it is always converted to uppercase.

Here are the valid entries for the method argument, and the resulting activity. (Remember that when you pass one of these values, they must be enclosed in single quotes.)

NULL

Exact statistics are computed based on the entire contents of the specified object. These values are then placed in the data dictionary.

ESTIMATE

Statistics are estimated. With this option, either estimate_rows or estimate_percent must be non-NULL. These values are then placed in the data dictionary.

DELETE

The statistics for this object are deleted from the data dictionary.

Here are the valid method_opt entries and the resulting impact:

FOR TABLE

Collects statistics for the table.

FOR ALL COLUMNS [SIZE N]

Collects column statistics for all columns and scalar attributes. The size is the maximum number of partitions in the histogram, with a default of 75 and a maximum of 254.

FOR ALL INDEXED COLUMNS [SIZE N]

Collects column statistics for all indexed columns in the table. The size is the maximum number of partitions in the histogram, with a default of 75 and a maximum of 254.

FOR ALL INDEXES

Collects statistics for all indexes associated with the table.

Exceptions. DBMS_DDL.ANALYZE_OBJECT may raise any of the following exceptions:

ORA-20000

Insufficient privileges or object does not exist. You must either own the specified object or be granted the CREATE ANY PROCEDURE privilege.

ORA-20001

Bad value for object type. You must specify TABLE, INDEX, or CLUSTER.

Notice that these exceptions are not defined in the specification of the package. Instead, ANALYZE_OBJECT simply calls RAISE_APPLICATION_ERROR with one of the above error numbers. These error numbers may therefore conflict with your own –20NNN error number usages. If you embed calls to ANALYZE_OBJECT inside your application or utility, watch out for the confusion such conflicts can cause.

Setting Referenceability of Tables

When you create an object table, it automatically becomes referenceable, unless you use the OID AS clause when creating the table. The OID AS clause allows you to create an object table and to assign to the new table the same embedded object ID (EOID) as another object table of the same type. After you create a new table using the OID AS clause, you end up with two object tables with the same EOID; the new table is not referenceable, the original one is. All references that previously pointed to the objects in the original table still reference the same objects in the same original table. If you execute the ALTER_TABLE_REFERENCE-ABLE procedure of the DBMS_DDL package on the new table, it will make that table the referenceable table replacing the original one. Any references will then point to the objects in the new table instead of to the objects in the original table.

With DBMS_DDL, available only in Oracle8, you can both make a table referenceable and reverse that step.

The DBMS_DDL. ALTER_TABLE_REFERENCEABLE procedure (Oracle8 only)

To make a table referenceable, call the following procedure:

```
PROCEDURE DBMS_DDL.ALTER_TABLE_REFERENCEABLE
    (table_name IN VARCHAR2
    ,table_schema IN VARCHAR2 DEFAULT NULL
    ,affected_schema IN VARCHAR2 DEFAULT NULL);
```

Parameters are summarized in the following table.

Parameter	Description
table_name	The name of the table to be made referenceable. You cannot use a synonym. The argument is case-sensitive.
table_schema	The schema containing the table to be made referenceable. If NULL, then the current schema is used. The argument is case-sensitive.
affected_schema	The schema that is to be affected by this change. If NULL, then the PUBLIC schema is used. In other words, the change takes effect in all schemas. The argument is case-sensitive.

This program alters the specified object table, table_schema.table_name, so it becomes the referenceable table for the specified schema, affected_schema. This program is the equivalent of the following SQL statement,

```
ALTER TABLE [<table_schema>.]<table_name>
    REFERENCEABLE FOR <affected_schema>
```

which is currently neither supported nor available as a DDL statement. You can obtain this effect only through a call to the ALTER_TABLE_REFERENCEABLE built-in package.

Notice that each argument to this program is case-sensitive. ALTER_TABLE_REFER-ENCEABLE will *not* automatically convert to uppercase the table name you pass to it. You must make sure that the table and schema names you provide match exactly the case of the objects found inside the database.

You will be able to execute this procedure successfully only if you have the appropriate privileges. Here are some rules to keep in mind:

- The user who executes this procedure must own the new table, and the affected schema must be the same as the user or PUBLIC; alternatively, the user must have ALTER ANY TABLE, SELECT ANY TABLE, and DROP ANY TABLE privileges.

- If the affected schema is PUBLIC (and the user does *not* have ALTER ANY TABLE, SELECT ANY TABLE, and DROP ANY TABLE privileges), then the user must own the old mapping table (the table upon which the new table is based) for PUBLIC as well.

One tricky aspect to the way this built-in is defined: the default affected_schema is PUBLIC. Combine this fact with the previous rules, and you discover that the simplest form of calling the built-in (providing only the table name),

```
EXECUTE DBMS_DDL.ALTER_TABLE_REFERENCEABLE ('EMPOBJTAB');
```

will quite often fail with this error:

```
ORA-20000: insufficient privileges, invalid schema name or
           table does not exist
```

You will say to yourself, "But I own the table!" And then you will realize, "Oh, if I don't specify the affected schema, then PUBLIC is used and I do *not* have ALTER ANY TABLE or any of the other privileges needed." So all I can really do is this,

```
EXECUTE DBMS_DDL.ALTER_TABLE_REFERENCEABLE ('EMPOBJTAB', USER, USER);
```

and make sure that the command is applied only to my schema.

Example. Generally, you will use the ALTER_TABLE_REFERENCEABLE procedure when you want to replace an existing object table with a new table of the same structure. In this scenario, you will want to make sure that all EOIDS point to this new table.

Here are the steps you would take to use ALTER_TABLE_REFERENCEABLE to make this "switch." (These steps are collected together using an employee table as an example in *tabref.sql* on the companion disk.)

1. First, you must have an object table already in place. Here is the code to create an employee object and then an object table for that object:

   ```
   CREATE TYPE empobj AS OBJECT (ename VARCHAR2(100), empno INTEGER);
   /
   CREATE TABLE emp OF empobj
   /
   ```

2. Now I will create a new object table based on the same object as the original table like this:

   ```
   CREATE TABLE empNew OF empobj OID AS emp
   /
   ```

3. Next, I transfer the contents of the original emp table to the empNew table. In Oracle8, unique object identifiers are automatically assigned to objects when they are stored as "table objects." It turns out that this identifier is stored in a hidden 16-byte RAW field, SYS_NC_OID$. This ID or OID can be referenced from columns in other tables, much like a foreign key. I use this in my INSERT to make sure the new table has the same identifier as the old. I also must use aliases for my table names for this process to work correctly.

   ```
   INSERT INTO empNew en (SYS_NC_OID$, en)
      SELECT SYS_NC_OID$, VALUE (eo) FROM emp eo
   /
   ```

4. Now I make the new table referenceable. Notice that the name of the table is passed in upper case and I explicitly pass USER as the schema to avoid the inadvertent usage of PUBLIC.

```
EXECUTE DBMS_DDL.ALTER_TABLE_REFERENCEABLE ('EMPNEW', USER, USER);
```

5. For my final trick, I swap the names of the tables so that I end up with a new emp table.

```
RENAME emp TO empOld;
RENAME empNew TO emp;
```

Exceptions. The ALTER_TABLE_REFERENCEABLE procedure may raise the following exception:

ORA-20000

Insufficient privileges; invalid schema name, or table does not exist.

Notice that this exception is not defined in the specification of the package. Instead, this program simply calls RAISE_APPLICATION_ERROR with the previous error number. This error number may therefore conflict with your own –20NNN error number usages. If you embed calls to this procedure inside your application or utility, watch out for the confusion such a conflict can cause.

The DBMS_DDL.ALTER_TABLE_NOT_REFERENCEABLE procedure (Oracle8 only)

For the affected schema, this procedure simply reverts to the default table referenceable for PUBLIC; that is, it simply undoes the previous ALTER_TABLE_REFERCEABLE call for this specific schema. The header follows:

```
PROCEDURE DBMS_DDL.ALTER_TABLE_NOT_REFERENCEABLE
    (table_name IN VARCHAR2
    ,table_schema IN VARCHAR2 DEFAULT NULL
    ,affected_schema IN VARCHAR2 DEFAULT NULL);
```

Parameters are summarized in the following table.

Parameter	Description
table_name	The name of the table to be made nonreferenceable. You cannot use a synonym. The argument is case-sensitive.
table_schema	The schema containing the table to be made nonreferenceable. If NULL, then the current schema is used. The argument is case-sensitive.
affected_schema	The schema that is to be affected by this change. If NULL, then the current schema is used. PUBLIC may not be specified. The argument is case-sensitive.

This procedure is equivalent to the following SQL statement,

```
ALTER TABLE [<table_schema>.]<table_name>
   NOT REFERENCEABLE FOR <affected_schema>
```

which is currently neither supported nor available as a DDL statement.

Exceptions. The ALTER_TABLE_NOT_REFERENCEABLE procedure may raise the following exception:

ORA-20000

Insufficient privileges; invalid schema name or table does not exist.

Notice that this exception is not defined in the specification of the package. Instead, this program simply calls RAISE_APPLICATION_ERROR with the preceding error number. This error number may therefore conflict with your own – 20NNN error number usages. If you embed calls to this procedure inside your application or utility, watch out for the confusion such conflicts can cause.

DBMS_RANDOM: Generating Random Numbers (Oracle8 Only)

The DBMS_RANDOM package provides a built-in random number generator utility. Oracle Corporation suggests that this package will run faster than generators written in PL/SQL itself because DBMS_RANDOM calls Oracle's internal random number generator.

Oracle describes this package as a relatively simple interface for a random number generator, limited to returning an 8-digit number. They recommend that you use the DBMS_CRYPTO_TOOLKIT package if you need a more sophisticated engine with more options. This package is available with Trusted Oracle.*

As with any random number generator, before you can obtain any random numbers from DBMS_RANDOM, you must first initialize the package by providing a seed number with DBMS_RANDOM's INITIALIZE procedure. You can later reseed the random number generator via RANDOM_SEED. When you need a random number, issue a call to the RANDOM, which returns a random number for your use. Finally, when you no longer need to use the random number generator, terminate DBMS_RANDOM via the TERMINATE procedure.

---

* I must point out that DBMS_RANDOM is built on top of DBMS_CRYPTO_TOOLKIT, which is not documented in this book.

Getting Started with DBMS_RANDOM

The DBMS_RANDOM package is created when the Oracle database is first installed. The *dbmsrand.sql* script found in the built-in packages source code directory (described in Chapter 1) contains the source code for this package's specification. This script is called by *catoctk.sql*, which contains the scripts needed to use the PL/SQL Cryptographic Toolkit Interface. The scripts create the public synonym DBMS_RANDOM for the package and grant EXECUTE privilege on the package to public. All Oracle users can reference and make use of this package.

NOTE If you are running Oracle8 Release 8.0.3, DBMS_RANDOM may not have been installed in your database. In this case, you need to execute the following scripts in the specified order from within your SYS account: *dbmsoctk.sql*, *prvtoctk.plb*, and finally *dbmsrand.sql* (it contains both the package specification and body for DBMS_RANDOM).

Table 10-4 summarizes the DBMS_RANDOM programs.

Table 10-4. DBMS_RANDOM Programs

Name	Description	Use in SQL
INITIALIZE	Initializes the random number generator with a seed value	No
RANDOM	Returns a random number	No
SEED	Resets the seed number used to generate the random number	No
TERMINATE	Terminates the random number generator mechanism	No

DBMS_RANDOM does not declare any exceptions or nonprogram elements.

DBMS_RANDOM Interface

This section describes the DBMS_RANDOM programs in the order in which they are typically used.

The DBMS_RANDOM.INITIALIZE procedure

Before you can use the DBMS_RANDOM package, you must initialize it with this program,

```
PROCEDURE DBMS_RANDOM.INITIALIZE (seed IN BINARY_INTEGER);
```

where seed is the seed number used in the algorithm to generate a random number. You should provide a number with at least five digits to ensure that the value returned by the DBMS_RANDOM.RANDOM function will be sufficiently, well, random.

The INITIALIZE procedure does not assert a purity level with the RESTRICT_REFERENCES pragma.

Example. Here is an example of a call to initialize the DBMS_RANDOM package:

```
SQL> exec DBMS_RANDOM.INITIALIZE (309666789);
```

The DBMS_RANDOM.SEED procedure (Oracle8 only)

Once the random number generator has been initialized, you can change the seed value used by DBMS_RANDOM with the SEED procedure. The specification is,

```
PROCEDURE DBMS_RANDOM.SEED(seed IN BINARY_INTEGER);
```

where seed is the seed number used in the algorithm to generate a random number. As with INITIALIZE, you should provide a number with at least five digits to ensure that the value returned by the DBMS_RANDOM.RANDOM function will be sufficiently random.

The SEED procedure does not assert a purity level with the RESTRICT_REFERENCES pragma.

Example. Here is an example of a call to reseed the DBMS_RANDOM package:

```
SQL> exec DBMS_RANDOM.SEED (455663349);
```

The DBMS_RANDOM.RANDOM function (Oracle8 only)

Call the RANDOM function to retrieve a random number.

```
FUNCTION DBMS_RANDOM.RANDOM RETURN BINARY_INTEGER;
```

The RANDOM runction does not assert a purity level with the RESTRICT_REFERENCES pragma.

Example. Here is an example of a call to RANDOM to obtain a random number:

```
DECLARE
    my_random BINARY_INTEGER;
BEGIN
    my_random := DBMS_RANDOM.RANDOM;
```

The DBMS_RANDOM.TERMINATE procedure (Oracle8 only)

When you are done with DBMS_RANDOM, you should terminate the program. This will release any memory used by the package.

```
PROCEDURE DBMS_RANDOM.TERMINATE;
```

The TERMINATE procedure does not assert a purity level with the RESTRICT_REF-ERENCES pragma.

Here is an example of a call to terminate the DBMS_RANDOM package:

```
SQL> exec DBMS_RANDOM.TERMINATE;
```

III

Server Management Packages

This part of the book describes the built-in server management packages:

- Chapter 11, *Managing Session Information*, introduces you to DBMS_ SESSION and DBMS_SYSTEM; these two packages help you analyze and manage information about your current session.

- Chapter 12, *Managing Server Resources*, presents DBMS_SPACE and DBMS_SHARED_POOL, which contain handy tools for database administrators to help them manage database-related resources on the server.

- Chapter 13, *Job Scheduling in the Database*, shows you how to use DBMS_ JOB to schedule the execution of stored procedures without the use of operating sytem-specific schedulers such as UNIX's *cron*.

11

Managing Session Information

Oracle technologies allow for a great deal of user customization and security. Language preferences can be specified at the session level using the NLS (National Language Support) options of the ALTER SESSION command. Roles can be used to distinguish groups of users from each other and to modify application behavior accordingly. This chapter describes the following two packages that allow you to perform these operations:

DBMS_SESSION

Contains programs that can modify and inspect session roles and settings from within PL/SQL. This package also contains programs for manipulating session memory and package states; even if they aren't used very often, these programs are very instructive to understand.

DBMS_SYSTEM

Lets administrators set various trace events in other users' sessions. Setting these events can be invaluable when tracking down difficult application performance or database issues.

DBMS_SESSION: Managing Session Information

The DBMS_SESSION package lets you access and alter session-level settings, including features of the ALTER SESSION and SET ROLE commands in SQL. Some of the session modifications that can be made using DBMS_SESSION include the following:

- Enabling and disabling roles

- Setting National Language Support (NLS) characteristics

- Resetting package states and releasing session package memory

- Setting Trusted Oracle label characteristics

DBMS_SESSION is used primarily to set preferences and security levels for a user's current database session. For instance, if an application requires specific roles to be set prior to performing specific tasks, this can be done using DBMS_SESSION's SET_ROLE procedure.

Most of the programs in DBMS_SESSION would not likely be called deep in the processing layers of application code, but rather invoked early in the application to establish a necessary, appropriate, or preferred context for the user of the application.

Getting Started with DBMS_SESSION

The DBMS_SESSION package is created when the Oracle database is installed. The *dbmsutil.sql* script (found in the built-in packages source code directory, as described in Chapter 1, *Introduction*), contains the source code for this package's specification. This script is called by *catproc.sql*, which is normally run immediately after database creation. The script creates the public synonym DBMS_SESSION for the package and grants EXECUTE privilege on the package to public. This way, all Oracle users can reference and make use of this package.

DBMS_SESSION programs

Table 11-1 lists the programs found in the DBMS_SESSION package.

Table 11-1. DBMS_SESSION Programs

Name	Description	Use in SQL?
CLOSE_DATABASE_LINK	Closes an inactive but open database link	No
FREE_UNUSED_USER_MEMORY	Releases unused session memory	No
IS_ROLE_ENABLED	Returns TRUE if role enabled	No
RESET_PACKAGE	Clears all persistent package state	No
SET_CLOSE_CACHED_OPEN_CURSORS	Turns automatic closing of cached cursors on or off	No
SET_LABEL	Sets Trusted Oracle label	No
SET_MLS_LABEL_FORMAT	Sets Trusted Oracle MLS label format	No
SET_NLS	Sets National Language Support characteristics for the session	No
SET_ROLE	Enables or disables roles for the session	No
SET_SQL_TRACE	Turns session SQL tracing on or off	No
UNIQUE_SESSION_ID	Returns a unique character string for the session	Yes

DBMS_SESSION does not declare any exceptions of its own or any nonprogram elements.

Modifying Session Settings

This section describes the procedures you can use to modify various session settings: SET_LABEL, SET_MLS_LABEL_FORMAT, SET_NLS, and SET_ROLE.

The DBMS_SESSION.SET_LABEL procedure

The SET_LABEL procedure sets the session's label used by Trusted Oracle databases. The header looks like this:

```
PROCEDURE DBMS_SESSION.SET_LABEL
    (lbl IN VARCHAR2);
```

The lbl parameter contains the label for the session.

Exceptions. The SET_LABEL procedure does not raise any package exceptions. If Trusted Oracle is not installed, calling SET_LABEL results in the following Oracle exception:

ORA-02248
    Invalid option for ALTER SESSION.

Restrictions. Note the following restrictions on calling SET_LABEL:

* DBMS_SESSION.SET_LABEL is not allowed in remote sessions.

* The program does not assert a purity level with the RESTRICT_REFERENCES pragma.

Example. This example uses the SET_LABEL procedure to set the session label to DBHIGH:

```
BEGIN
    DBMS_SESSION.SET_LABEL('DBHIGH');
END;
```

For more information on SET_LABEL parameters, see the *Trusted Oracle7 Server Administrator's Guide*.

DBMS_SESSION.SET_MLS_LABEL_FORMAT

The SET_MLS_LABEL_FORMAT procedure sets the session's default format for the labels used by Trusted Oracle databases.

```
PROCEDURE DBMS_SESSION.SET_MLS_LABEL_FORMAT
    (fmt IN VARCHAR2);
```

The fmt parameter is a VARCHAR2 that contains the label format for the session.

The program does not raise any exceptions.

Restrictions. Note the following restrictions on calling SET_MLS_LABEL_FORMAT:

- DBMS_SESSION.SET_MLS_LABEL_FORMAT is not allowed in remote sessions.

- The program does not assert a purity level with the RESTRICT_REFERENCES pragma.

Example. For more information on MLS label formats, see the *Trusted Oracle7 Server Administrator's Guide.*

The DBMS_SESSION.SET_NLS procedure

The SET_NLS procedure sets or alters National Language Support characteristics for the current session. The SET_NLS header looks like this:

```
PROCEDURE DBMS_SESSION.SET_NLS
   (param IN VARCHAR2
   ,value IN VARCHAR2);
```

Parameters are summarized in the following table.

Parameter	Description
param	NLS parameter being set for the session (see following list of values)
value	Value of the specified parameter

The following session NLS characteristics can be set via this procedure; specify the desired one as the value of the param parameter:

```
NLS_CALENDAR
NLS_CURRENCY
NLS_DATE_FORMAT
NLS_DATE_LANGUAGE
NLS_ISO_CURRENCY
NLS_LANGUAGE
NLS_NUMERIC_CHARACTERS
NLS_SORT
NLS_SPECIAL_CHARS
NLS_TERRITORY
```

Exceptions. The DBMS_SESSION.SET_NLS procedure does not raise any exceptions. However, if the value parameter represents a format mask (which would be double-quoted in the ALTER SESSION command) it needs to be enclosed in triple quotes. Otherwise, the following Oracle error will be raised:

ORA-00922

Missing or invalid option.

Restrictions. Note the following restrictions on calling this procedure:

- SET_NLS cannot be called from triggers.

- SET_NLS is not allowed in remote sessions.

- The procedure does not assert a purity level with the RESTRICT_REFERENCES pragma.

Examples. To change the default date format for the current session, as used by the TO_CHAR and TO_DATE functions, specify the following:

```
BEGIN
    DBMS_SESSION.SET_NLS('NLS_DATE_FORMAT','''YYYY:MM:DD''');
    DBMS_OUTPUT.PUT_LINE(TO_CHAR(SYSDATE));
END;
```

The above PL/SQL block produces a result similar to this:

```
1997:07:26
```

Enclose the NLS parameter name in single quotes if it is passed as a string literal. Another option is to initialize a VARCHAR2 variable to the parameter value and pass the variable name for the param parameter. In this case, the variable name is not quoted in the call to SET_NLS.

As mentioned previously, if the value parameter represents a format mask (which would be double-quoted in the ALTER SESSION command) it needs to be enclosed in triple quotes. Otherwise, the ORA-00092 Oracle error will be raised.

WARNING   The following sample code and output reveals a problem with the Oracle7.3 DBMS_SESSION.SET_NLS procedure. The NLS_DATE_ FORMAT being passed in is valid, yet the procedure will generate an unhandled exception. This problem appears to have been fixed in the Oracle 8.0 package.

```
SQL> ALTER SESSION SET NLS_DATE_FORMAT='YYYY:MM:DD:HH24:MI:SS';
Session altered.

SQL> BEGIN
  2  DBMS_SESSION.SET_NLS('NLS_DATE_FORMAT','"YYYY:MM:DD:HH24:MI:SS"');
  3  END;
  4  /
BEGIN
*
ORA-06510: PL/SQL: unhandled user-defined exception
ORA-06512: at "SYS.DBMS_SESSION", line 46
ORA-06512: at line 2
```

You can query the NLS settings for the current session from the V$NLS_PARAME-TERS virtual table as follows:

```
SELECT parameter, value
  FROM v$nls_parameters;
```

See the *Oracle7 Server Reference Manual* for information on the possible meanings and values for the various NLS settings.

The DBMS_SESSION.SET_ROLE procedure

The SET_ROLE procedure enables and disables roles for the current session. It is equivalent to executing the SET ROLE command in SQL. The procedure call simply appends the text of the single parameter, role_cmd, to the string "SET ROLE" and executes the resulting SQL command. The SET_ROLE header looks like this:

```
PROCEDURE DBMS_SESSION.SET_ROLE
   (role_cmd IN VARCHAR2);
```

Exceptions. The program does not raise any package exceptions. It can raise the following Oracle exceptions due to improper data in the role_cmd parameter:

ORA-01919
   Role "rolename" does not exist.

ORA-01979
   Missing or invalid password for role "rolename."

ORA-01924
   Role "rolename" not granted or does not exist.

Restrictions. Note the following restrictions on calling the SET_ROLE procedure:

* SET_ROLE cannot be called from triggers.

* SET_ROLE cannot be called from PL/SQL stored procedures or functions.

* SET_ROLE does not assert a purity level with the RESTRICT_REFERENCES pragma.

To successfully enable a role, the user must already have been granted the role. After executing the SET_ROLE procedure, only the roles specified in the procedure call will be enabled.

Examples. Set the password-protected role SPECIAL_ROLE in the current session like this:

```
BEGIN
   DBMS_SESSION.SET_ROLE('SPECIAL_ROLE IDENTIFIED BY password');
END;
```

Disable all roles in the current session like this:

```
BEGIN
    DBMS_SESSION.SET_ROLE('NONE');
END;
```

Set multiple roles for the current session like this:

```
BEGIN
    DBMS_SESSION.SET_ROLE('ROLE1, ROLE2, ROLE3');
END;
```

The role_cmd parameter is case-insensitive, which is the default behavior for role names in the Oracle catalog. To set a case-sensitive role, the role name must be double-quoted in the role_cmd parameter. For example:

```
BEGIN
    DBMS_SESSION.SET_ROLE('"special_role"');
END;
```

Notice that the lowercase role name special_role is double-quoted and also contained in a string literal delimited by single quotes.

See the *Oracle7 Server SQL Reference* for more details about the SET ROLE command.

Obtaining Session Information

This section describes the functions you can use to obtain information about a session: IS_ROLE_ENABLED and UNIQUE_SESSION_ID.

The DBMS_SESSION.IS_ROLE_ENABLED function

The IS_ROLE_ENABLED function returns TRUE or FALSE depending on whether the role specified in the rolename parameter is enabled. The header for this function follows:

```
FUNCTION DBMS_SESSION.IS_ROLE_ENABLED
    (rolename IN VARCHAR2)
RETURN BOOLEAN;
```

The rolename parameter specifies the name of the role.

The IS_ROLE_ENABLED function does not raise any declared exceptions and does not assert a purity level with the RESTRICT_REFERENCES pragma.

Example. The following PL/SQL block will detect whether the user's session currently has the CONNECT role enabled:

```
BEGIN
    IF DBMS_SESSION.IS_ROLE_ENABLED('CONNECT');
    THEN
        DBMS_OUTPUT.PUT_LINE('CONNECT IS ENABLED');
```

```
        END IF;
    END;
```

An application might use this function to implement role-dependent behavior as in the following code fragment:

```
IF DBMS_SESSION.IS_ROLE_ENABLED('APP_ADMIN')
THEN
    /*
    || do special administrative logic here
    */
    app_admin_setup;
ELSE
    /*
    || do the normal user logic here
    */
    user_setup;
END IF;
```

NOTE   The IS_ROLE_ENABLED function is case-sensitive on the rolename parameter, so beware of unexpected results. The default behavior is for role names to be uppercase in the Oracle catalog, so it is probably best to cast the rolename to uppercase prior to calling this function.

For example, in the following block, the variable return_TF will be set to FALSE when CONNECT is enabled for the session because the CONNECT role is uppercase in the catalog:

```
DECLARE
    return_TF    BOOLEAN;
BEGIN
    return_TF := DBMS_SESSION.IS_ROLE_ENABLED('connect');
END;
```

The DBMS_SESSION.UNIQUE_SESSION_ID function

The UNIQUE_SESSION_ID function returns a character string unique to the session among all sessions currently connected to the database. The return string can be up to 24 bytes in length. Multiple calls to the function from the same session will always return the same string. The program header follows:

```
FUNCTION DBMS_SESSION.UNIQUE_SESSION_ID
RETURN VARCHAR2;
```

The UNIQUE_SESSION_ID function does not raise any exceptions.

Restrictions. Prior to Oracle 7.3.3, this function did not assert a purity level with the RESTRICT_REFERENCES pragma. In Oracle 7.3.3 and above, the program asserts the following purity:

```
PRAGMA RESTRICT_REFERENCES(UNIQUE_SESSION_ID,WNDS,RNDS,WNPS);
```

Thus, you can call the UNIQUE_SESSION_ID function directly in SQL for Oracle databases at release 7.3.3 and later.

Example. To display the value of the unique id for the current session, specify the following:

```
DECLARE
    my_unique_id    VARCHAR2(30);
BEGIN
    my_unique_id := DBMS_SESSION.UNIQUE_SESSION_ID;
    DBMS_OUTPUT.PUT_LINE('UNIQUE ID: '||my_unique_id);
END;
```

An example of output from executing the preceding PL/SQL block follows:

```
UNIQUE ID: F000E4020000
```

UNIQUE_SESSION_ID is functionally identical to the DBMS_PIPE.UNIQUE_ SESSION_NAME function; however, their return values are *not* identical. Be very careful not to write code that assumes that these two functions are equivalent.

NOTE   Ace technical reviewer Phil Pitha points out that the two functions may be related. He writes that it appears that DBMS_PIPE.UNIQUE_ SESSION_NAME returns an id of the format: 'ORA$PIPE$' || DBMS_ SESSION.UNIQUE_SESSION_ID.

Managing Session Resources

This section describes the procedures you can use to manage your session resources: CLOSE_DATABASE_LINK, FREE_UNUSED_USER_MEMORY, RESET_ PACKAGE, SET_CLOSE_CACHED_OPEN_CURSORS, and SET_SQL_TRACE.

The DBMS_SESSION.CLOSE_DATABASE_LINK procedure

The CLOSE_DATABASE_LINK procedure is used to close an open but inactive database link in the session. The header for the program is,

```
PROCEDURE DBMS_SESSION.CLOSE_DATABASE_LINK
    (dblink IN VARCHAR2);
```

where dblink specifies the name of the database link.

Exceptions. The CLOSE_DATABASE_LINK procedure does not raise any package exceptions. It can raise the following Oracle exceptions when the referenced database link cannot be closed:

ORA-02080

> Database link is in use.

ORA-02081

> Database link is not open.

Restrictions. Note the following restrictions on calling CLOSE_DATABASE_LINK:

- All cursors using the database link must be closed, and any transactions that reference the link (for UPDATE or SELECT purposes) must be ended (with COMMIT or ROLLBACK).

- The program does not assert a purity level with the RESTRICT_REFERENCES pragma.

Example. To close a database link named LOOPBACK, specify the following:

```
BEGIN
    DBMS_SESSION.CLOSE_DATABASE_LINK('LOOPBACK');
END;
```

Use of database links establishes a proxy session for the local user on the remote database, and this is a relatively expensive process. This is why Oracle keeps database links open rather than closing them immediately upon completion of the remote operation. Therefore, the CLOSE_DATABASE_LINK procedure probably should not be routinely called, especially for database links that are likely to be referenced again in the current session.

The DBMS_SESSION.FREE_UNUSED_USER_MEMORY procedure

The FREE_UNUSED_USER_MEMORY procedure is used to reclaim user session memory, especially when memory-intensive operations have been performed in the session. The header for this procedure follows:

```
PROCEDURE DBMS_SESSION.FREE_UNUSED_USER_MEMORY;
```

The FREE_UNUSED_USER_MEMORY procedure does not raise any exceptions and does not assert a purity level with the RESTRICT_REFERENCES pragma.

Oracle Corporation recommends that this procedure be used only when memory is at a premium and the session has allocated large (greater than 100 Kb) amounts. This caution indicates that calling the FREE_UNUSED_USER_MEMORY procedure is itself a relatively expensive operation and should be done only when really necessary. Calling the procedure forces Oracle to deallocate any session memory previously allocated but currently unused.

The following examples are the kinds of operations that can lead to large memory allocations:

- In-memory sorts where the SORT_AREA_SIZE initialization parameter is large
- Compilation of large PL/SQL packages, procedures, and functions
- Use of PL/SQL tables to store large amounts of data

In each of these cases, memory allocated for a specific purpose can only be re-used by Oracle for that same purpose. For example, memory allocated to the session for large PL/SQL compilations will not be reused later for anything but compilation of PL/SQL. If no more compilation is anticipated and memory is scarce, this is a good time to call FREE_UNUSED_USER_MEMORY.

In the case of PL/SQL tables, the scope of the table determines when memory allocated to the table is no longer in use and can be freed. Memory allocated for tables declared locally by procedures and functions becomes unused once the module completes execution. Other PL/SQL tables (local or global) can then make use of this memory. However, the memory remains allocated to the session. Global tables (i.e., tables declared at the package level) have persistent scope, and the memory associated with them can be made reusable only by assigning a NULL table to them. In either case, once the memory is made reusable, it is also eligible to be freed (deallocated from the session) using the FREE_UNUSED_ USER_MEMORY procedure.

Figure 11-1 illustrates the relationship between session memory and local versus global PL/SQL tables. In the figure, after package1.procedure1 executes and FREE_ UNUSED_USER_MEMORY is called, the memory for PL/SQL table2 is still allocated to the session. On the other hand, package2.procedure1 declares both tables locally, so that all the memory they use can be freed after the procedure completes.

Memory freed by calling this procedure is returned to either the operating system or the Oracle shared pool. This depends on the Oracle configuration and session connection as follows:

- Sessions connected through multithreaded servers return memory to the shared pool.
- Sessions with dedicated server connections return memory to the operating system.

Session memory can be monitored through the statistics for "session uga memory" and "session pga memory" found in the V$SESSTAT virtual table.

See the DBMS_SESSION package specification in the *dbmsutil.sql* file for more information on session memory and the effects of the FREE_UNUSED_USER_MEM-ORY procedure.

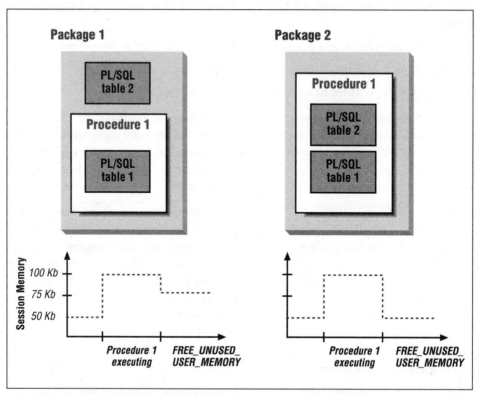

Figure 11-1. Package architecture and persistent session memory

The DBMS_SESSION.RESET_PACKAGE procedure

The RESET_PACKAGE procedure resets all package states for the session. The values of any persistent package variables will be lost after execution of this procedure. The header for this procedure follows:

```
PROCEDURE DBMS_SESSION.RESET_PACKAGE;
```

The RESET_PACKAGE procedure does not raise any exceptions.

Restrictions. Note the following restrictions on calling RESET_PACKAGE:

- Use the RESET_PACKAGE procedure with great caution, as it will cause the loss of package state in all packages for the current session. Applications making use of persistent package variables may be compromised and fail to work properly after calls to RESET_PACKAGE. Therefore, in general, don't embed calls to this procedure in application programs.

- The program does not assert a purity level with the RESTRICT_REFERENCES pragma.

Example. The output buffer used by DBMS_OUTPUT is actually a global package data structure that is initialized when either DBMS_OUTPUT.ENABLE or SET SERV-EROUTPUT ON is called in PL/SQL or SQL*Plus, respectively.

The following PL/SQL block will not display the message, because the call to RESET_PACKAGE clears out the DBMS_OUTPUT buffer:

```
BEGIN
   DBMS_SESSION.RESET_PACKAGE;
   DBMS_OUTPUT.PUT_LINE('This is an invisible message');
END;
```

Although calling RESET_PACKAGE will clear all persistent package variables, including PL/SQL tables and records, it will not automatically release the session memory used by these structures. To release session memory back to the operating system (or Oracle shared pool), use the FREE_UNUSED_USER_MEMORY procedure.

Note that package states cannot be reinstantiated until the outermost PL/SQL calling scope within which RESET_PACKAGE was called completes. This variation on the previous example illustrates the effect of RESET_PACKAGE within its calling scope:

```
/* Filename on companion disk: sess1.sql */
set serveroutput on size 1000000
BEGIN
   DBMS_SESSION.RESET_PACKAGE;
   DBMS_OUTPUT.PUT_LINE('You will not see this');
   DBMS_OUTPUT.ENABLE;
   DBMS_OUTPUT.PUT_LINE('Also invisible, since in same scope '||
                        'as RESET_PACKAGE call');
END;
/
set serveroutput on size 1000000
BEGIN
   DBMS_OUTPUT.PUT_LINE('New package states instantiated '||
                        'messages visible again!');
END;
/
```

Output from running this script follows:

```
SQL> @c:\opbip\examples\sess1.sql

PL/SQL procedure successfully completed.

New package states instantiated messages visible again!

PL/SQL procedure successfully completed.
```

As you can see, only the final call to DBMS_OUTPUT.PUT_LINE displays its message. The second call to DBMS_OUTPUT.PUT_LINE in the first block fails to produce output because the buffer used by DBMS_OUTPUT cannot be reinitialized within the same calling scope as RESET_PACKAGE.

The DBMS_SESSION.SET_CLOSE_CACHED_OPEN_CURSORS procedure

The SET_CLOSE_CACHED_OPEN_CURSORS procedure is used to set the close_cached_open_cursors property at the session level, overriding the database-wide setting established by the CLOSE_CACHED_OPEN_CURSORS initialization parameter. The header for this procedure looks like this:

```
PROCEDURE DBMS_SESSION.SET_CLOSE_CACHED_OPEN_CURSORS
   (close_cursors IN BOOLEAN);
```

The close_cursors parameter causes cached PL/SQL cursors to be automatically closed with a value of TRUE or kept open with a value of FALSE.

The SET_CLOSE_CACHED_OPEN_CURSORS procedure does not raise any declared exceptions and does not assert a purity level with the RESTRICT_REFERENCES pragma.

Example. To set CLOSE_CACHED_OPEN_CURSORS to on for the current session, specify the following:

```
BEGIN
   DBMS_SESSION.SET_CLOSE_CACHED_OPEN_CURSORS(TRUE);
END;
```

Most applications will probably have no need to use this procedure. When set to TRUE, the Oracle database will automatically close any cached PL/SQL cursors after a COMMIT or ROLLBACK, which releases the memory used by these cursors. When set to FALSE, cursors are held open in the cache across transactions, making subsequent executions somewhat faster. Applications that tend to use large cursors in a one-time or infrequent fashion (e.g., ad hoc query systems against a data warehouse) may benefit from setting this value to TRUE.

See the *Oracle7 Server Reference Manual* for more information on the CLOSE_CACHED_OPEN_CURSORS initialization parameter.

The DBMS_SESSION.SET_SQL_TRACE procedure

The SET_SQL_TRACE procedure is equivalent to the ALTER SESSION SET SQL_TRACE command. It is used to turn the Oracle SQL trace facility on or off for the session, primarily while debugging application problems. The SET_SQL_TRACE header looks like this:

```
PROCEDURE DBMS_SESSION.SET_SQL_TRACE
   (sql_trace IN BOOLEAN);
```

The sql_trace parameter sets the trace on if TRUE, off if FALSE.

The SET_SQL_TRACE procedure does not raise any exceptions.

Restrictions. Note the following restrictions on calling SET_SQL_TRACE:

- In general, use the SET_SQL_TRACE procedure only when debugging application problems. Tracing session SQL calls adds overhead to the database and can generate numerous and sizable trace files on the host server.

- The SET_SQL_TRACE procedure does not assert a purity level with the RESTRICT_REFERENCES pragma.

Example. Generate a trace file for the execution of a specific PL/SQL procedure call like this:

```
BEGIN
   DBMS_SESSION.SET_SQL_TRACE(TRUE);
   plsql_procedure_call;
   DBMS_SESSION.SET_SQL_TRACE(FALSE);
END;
```

The trace files generated when SQL tracing is turned on are created in the directory specified by the USER_DUMP_DEST initialization parameter for the Oracle database to which the session is connected.

Trace file naming conventions often make it difficult to identify the correct trace file when there are many in the directory specified by USER_DUMP_DEST. Executing a "tag" SQL statement after turning tracing on can facilitate trace file identification.

The trace files generated when SQL tracing is turned on are not directly readable. The Oracle utility program TKPROF can be used to generate a formatted summary of the trace file contents. The TKPROF output contains statistics on CPU time, elapsed time, and disk reads for the parse, execute, and fetch steps of each SQL statement in the trace file. This information can be invaluable when tracking down performance problems in complex applications. See the *Oracle7 Server Tuning* manual for instructions on using TKPROF.

DBMS_SESSION Examples

The DBMS_SESSION package is a kind of grab bag of ways to alter the user's current session characteristics in an Oracle database. Oracle provides a great deal of flexibility with respect to language settings and security. DBMS_SESSION includes several programs that are equivalent to the SQL commands SET ROLE and ALTER

SESSION normally used to establish these settings. The following programs in DBMS_SESSION fall into this category:

```
SET_LABEL
SET_MLS_LABEL_FORMAT
SET_NLS
SET_ROLE
```

These programs are "high-level," in that they would normally be called directly from an application program and not be buried deep inside layers of PL/SQL code. In fact, the SET_ROLE procedure can only be called from anonymous PL/SQL blocks and not from within stored program (procedures and functions) code. So in practice, an application would begin by prompting the user for preferences, issue the appropriate DBMS_SESSION.SET procedure calls, and then move on to the real work.

Other programs in DBMS_SESSION are geared toward manipulating session-level resource utilization, particularly memory. In this category are the following DBMS_SESSION programs:

```
SET_CLOSE_CACHED_OPEN_CURSORS
CLOSE_DATABASE_LINK
FREE_UNUSED_USER_MEMORY
RESET_PACKAGE
```

These are also quite "high-level" routines, but more likely to find their way into application code under the right circumstances.

One thing that DBMS_SESSION does not have (and that it should) is a function to return the current session id. This is frequently asked for by developers and DBAs and is relatively easy to provide.

NOTE   The source code for all of the examples is in a file called *mysess.sql,*
            which creates the package called my_session shown in this section
            that includes these examples.

Adding value to DBMS_SESSION

Let's take a look at how we can use DBMS_SESSION and add a little value along the way. I've created a package called my_session to do just that. Here is the package specification:

```
/* Filename on companion disk: mysess.sql */
CREATE OR REPLACE PACKAGE my_session
    /*
```

```
|| Extends some of the functionality of DBMS_SESSION
|| and provides access to additional session-level
|| information.
||
|| Author:  John Beresniewicz, Savant Corp
||
|| 12/22/97: exposed load_unique_id as/per Phil Pitha
|| 09/07/97: modified function SID to assert WNPS
||           and not call load_my_session_rec
|| 07/27/97: created
||
|| Compilation Requirements:
||
|| SELECT on sys.v_$session
|| SELECT on sys.v_$sesstat
|| SELECT on sys.v_$statname
||
|| Execution Requirements:
||
|| ALTER SESSION
*/
AS
   /* same as DBMS_SESSION.UNIQUE_SESSION_ID but callable in SQL */
   FUNCTION unique_id RETURN VARCHAR2;
   PRAGMA RESTRICT_REFERENCES(unique_id, WNDS,WNPS);

   /*
   || loads unique_session_id into global variable, must be called
   || prior to using function unique_id
   */
   PROCEDURE load_unique_id;

   /* returns session id of current session, callable in SQL */
   FUNCTION sid RETURN NUMBER;
   PRAGMA RESTRICT_REFERENCES(sid,WNDS,WNPS);

   /* closes any open database links not in use */
   PROCEDURE close_links
      (force_with_commit_TF IN BOOLEAN DEFAULT FALSE);

   /* loads session data, should be private but needs to assert purity */
   PROCEDURE load_my_session_rec;
   PRAGMA RESTRICT_REFERENCES(load_my_session_rec,WNDS);

   /* resets package states and frees memory */
   PROCEDURE reset;

   /* returns current stat value from V$SESSTAT for this session */
   FUNCTION statval(statname_IN IN VARCHAR2) RETURN NUMBER;

   /* displays session uga and pga using DBMS_OUTPUT */
   PROCEDURE memory;

   /* turns SQL tracing on/off with tag for file identification */
```

```
PROCEDURE set_sql_trace
   (trace_TF IN  BOOLEAN
   ,tag_IN  IN  VARCHAR2 DEFAULT USER);


END my_session;
```

You will notice that several of the programs seem very similar to programs in DBMS_SESSION. Well, they are, but with some important differences.

The unique_id function

Prior to Oracle 7.3.3, the DBMS.SESSION.UNIQUE_SESSION_ID function did not assert any purity level using the RESTRICT_REFERENCES pragma and thus could not be called directly from SQL statements. This is unfortunate, because one nice potential use of the function is as an identifier for applications making use of shared temporary tables. In other words, some applications will find it useful to do things like the following:

```
INSERT INTO temp_table (session_id, other_columns...)
VALUES (DBMS_SESSION.UNIQUE_SESSION_ID, other_columns...);

DELETE FROM temp_table
 WHERE session_id = DBMS_SESSION.UNIQUE_SESSION_ID;
```

Thankfully, Oracle Corporation has corrected this shortcoming in the latest releases of DBMS_SESSION. For those not fortunate enough to be using 7.3.3 or 8.0, the my_session.unique_id function can be used as a workaround. This function returns the same string as DBMS_SESSION.UNIQUE_SESSION_ID, yet it asserts a purity level of WNDS and can thus be called from SQL.

Here is the source to unique_id and its companion procedure load_unique_id:

```
/* Filename on companion disk: mysess.sql */
/* private global to hold DBMS_SESSION.UNIQUE_SESSION_ID */
   unique_id_  VARCHAR2(40);

   /*
   || loads unique_session_id into global variable, must be called
   || prior to using function unique_id
   */
   PROCEDURE load_unique_id
   IS
   BEGIN
    unique_id_ := DBMS_SESSION.UNIQUE_SESSION_ID;
   END load_unique_id;


   /*
   || returns unique_id_ loaded by call to load_unique_id
   */
   FUNCTION unique_id RETURN VARCHAR2
   IS
```

```
BEGIN
   RETURN unique_id_;
END unique_id;
```

As you can see, unique_id simply returns the value of a private package global variable that is set by the load_unique_id procedure to the value returned by DBMS_SESSION.UNIQUE_SESSION_ID. The only caveat is that load_unique_id must be called in the session prior to calling unique_id (or a NULL value will be returned). Note that using a private global and function is safer than using a public global, since the public global cannot be protected from inadvertent modification.

The load_my_session_rec procedure

Each session has a unique row in the V$SESSION virtual table with various columns containing identification and activity information about the session. The load_my_session_rec procedure selects the row in V$SESSION corresponding to the current session and loads it into a package global record called my_session_rec.

```
/* Filename on companion disk: mysess.sql */
/*
|| my_session_cur and my_session_rec are both declared
|| to always hold all columns of V$SESSION
*/
CURSOR my_session_cur
IS
SELECT  *
    FROM  sys.v_$session
    WHERE  audsid = USERENV('SESSIONID');

my_session_rec  sys.v_$session%ROWTYPE;

/*
|| loads V$SESSION data into global record for current session
*/
PROCEDURE load_my_session_rec
IS
BEGIN
    OPEN my_session_cur;
    FETCH my_session_cur INTO my_session_rec;
    CLOSE my_session_cur;
END load_my_session_rec;
```

Notice that load_my_session_rec is written in a way that ensures it always gets all columns of V$SESSION. This is accomplished by anchoring the package global my_session_rec to V$SESSION using %ROWTYPE in the declaration. Similarly, the cursor my_session_cur used to fetch into my_session_rec is anchored to V$SESSION by using the SELECT * syntax. This is a nice technique. Since V$SESSION can change with Oracle versions, writing the procedure in this way allows it to adjust itself to the particular version of Oracle under which it is executing.

The sid function

Several of the Oracle dynamic performance (V$) views are keyed by session id because they contain session-level performance data. Many developers and DBAs have had to answer the question "What is my current sid?" when delving into these performance tables. I don't know why DBMS_SESSION does not come with a sid function, but my_session sure does. Here is the relevant source code:

```
/* Filename on companion disk: mysess.sql */
/*
   || returns the session id of current session
*/
FUNCTION sid RETURN NUMBER
   temp_session_rec sys.v_$session%ROWTYPE;
BEGIN
   IF my_session_rec.sid IS NULL
   THEN
       OPEN my_session_cur;
       FETCH my_session_cur INTO temp_session_rec;
       CLOSE my_session_cur;
   ELSE
       temp_session_rec := my_session_rec;
       END IF;
       RETURN temp_session_rec.sid;
   END sid;
```

The sid function itself is quite simple, yet it has a subtle but important performance optimization. Since the session id will never change for the duration of the session, it is necessary to load it only once, and this can be done using the load_my_session_rec procedure. The IF statement checks to see if we've already loaded the my_session_rec.sid and bypasses opening my_session_cur in that case. Remember that we intend to use the function in SQL statements, and it will be executed for every row returned in which the function is referenced. That simple IF statement could save hundreds (or even thousands) of scans on the V$SESSION view per SQL statement. Be sure to execute load_my_session_rec before using the sid function to avoid the unnecessary performance penalty.

We can use the my_session.sid function to view our current performance statistics from V$SESSTAT as follows:

```
SELECT n.name,s.value
  FROM v$statname n, v$sesstat s
 WHERE n.statistic# = s.statistic#
   AND s.sid = my_session.sid;
```

NOTE   Astute readers may ask: Why not just call load_my_session_rec from the sid function if my_session_rec.sid has not been initialized? Well, originally this is exactly the way sid was written. However, since load_my_session_rec modifies package state, this meant that WNPS (Writes No Package State) purity could not be asserted for the sid function. In order to use a PL/SQL function in the WHERE clause of a SQL statement, the function must assert WNPS, so sid had to be modified to not call load_my_session_rec.

The close_links procedure

The Oracle initialization parameter OPEN_LINKS controls the maximum number of concurrent open connections to remote databases per user session. When a session exceeds this number, the following Oracle error is raised:

ORA-02020
    Too many database links in use.

Generally, the database administrator should set the OPEN_LINKS parameter to a value that will accommodate the needs of distributed applications accessing the database. However, in highly distributed environments with multiple applications, it's possible that users could receive the ORA-02020 error. Presumably, this is the purpose of the CLOSE_DATABASE_LINK procedure; however, there is a serious problem. Quite simply, users should not have to know anything about database links nor, for that matter, should applications. Database links are an implementation detail that should be kept transparent to users and applications. The real question is: When an ORA-02020 is incurred, how is a user or application supposed to know which links are open and can be closed?

Well, it's my opinion that users should not have to know about specific database links and yet should be able to do something in case of an ORA-02020 error. That is precisely the purpose of my_session.close_links. That procedure will close any open links that are not in use and can be closed. A link is considered in use if it has been referenced within the current transaction (i.e., since the last COMMIT or ROLLBACK). Alternatively, close_links will close all open links by issuing a COMMIT to terminate the current transaction and free all links for closure.

```
/* Filename on companion disk: mysess.sql */
/*
|| closes all open database links not in use by session,
|| or all if forced_with_commit_TF is TRUE
*/
PROCEDURE close_links
    (force_with_commit_TF IN BOOLEAN DEFAULT FALSE)
```

```
    IS

        /* declare exceptions for ORA errors */
        dblink_in_use EXCEPTION;
        PRAGMA EXCEPTION_INIT(dblink_in_use,-2080);

        dblink_not_open EXCEPTION;
        PRAGMA EXCEPTION_INIT(dblink_not_open,-2081);

        /* cursor of all db links available to user */
        CURSOR all_links_cur
        IS
        SELECT db_link
          FROM all_db_links;

    BEGIN
        /* try all links and close the ones you can */
        FOR dblink_rec IN all_links_cur
        LOOP
            BEGIN
                DBMS_SESSION.CLOSE_DATABASE_LINK(dblink_rec.db_link);
            EXCEPTION
                WHEN dblink_not_open
                    THEN null;
                WHEN dblink_in_use
                    THEN
                        IF force_with_commit_TF
                        THEN
                            COMMIT;
                            DBMS_SESSION.CLOSE_DATABASE_LINK(dblink_rec.db_link);
                        END IF;
                WHEN OTHERS
                    THEN null;
            END;
        END LOOP;
    END close_links;
```

There are a few things to note in this procedure. First, exceptions are declared and assigned to the two Oracle errors that can be raised by the DBMS_SES-SION.CLOSE_DATABASE_LINK procedure. This is done using PRAGMA EXCEPTION_INIT compiler directives. Next comes a loop through all database links available to the user. For each link in the loop, we execute DBMS_SES-SION.CLOSE_DATABASE_LINK in a BEGIN...END block and trap the exceptions raised by links that were not open or in use. Trapping the exceptions allows the loop to continue until all links have been processed.

Originally, the procedure would close only links that were not in use. I decided to enhance it to accept a BOOLEAN parameter called force_with_commit_TF. When this parameter is TRUE, the dblink_in_use exception handler issues a COM-MIT. This terminates the current transaction and frees all database links to be closed, including the one that raised the exception that is closed in the exception handler. This enhancement allows the procedure to close all database links for the session.

The set_sql_trace procedure

The SQL trace facility is an invaluable tool for debugging application performance problems. However, one problem that developers and DBAs often run into when using SQL trace is identifying the correct trace file from among the possibly hundreds of trace files that tend to collect and hang around in the directory specified by the USER_DUMP_DEST parameter. One technique is to put a literal tag in trace files by executing a SQL command such as the following:

```
SELECT 'JOHN B: TRACE 1' FROM DUAL;
```

When issued immediately after setting SQL_TRACE to TRUE, the statement will appear in the trace file, and a utility like *grep* or *awk* can be used to scan the directory for the file with the correct literal tag. In my_session.set_sql_trace, I've enhanced DBMS_SESSION.SET_SQL_TRACE to accept a string tag and place it into the trace file when turning trace on. The DBMS_SQL package is used to build and parse a SQL statement dynamically with the tag literal in it.

```
/* Filename on companion disk: mysess.sql */
/*
|| turns SQL tracing on/off with tag for file identification
*/
PROCEDURE set_sql_trace
    (trace_TF IN   BOOLEAN
    ,tag_IN   IN   VARCHAR2 DEFAULT USER)
IS
    cursor_id  INTEGER;
BEGIN
    DBMS_SESSION.SET_SQL_TRACE(trace_TF);

    IF trace_TF
    THEN
        cursor_id := DBMS_SQL.OPEN_CURSOR;

        /* parse a SQL stmt with the tag in it */
        DBMS_SQL.PARSE
            (cursor_id
            ,'SELECT '''||tag_IN||''' FROM DUAL'
            ,DBMS_SQL.native);

    DBMS_SQL.CLOSE_CURSOR(cursor_id);
```

```
      END IF;
   END set_sql_trace;
```

Note that it is not necessary to execute the tag SQL statement; the parse will get it into the trace file. After all, there is no need to do more work than absolutely required.

The reset procedure

The DBMS_SESSION.RESET_PACKAGE procedure invalidates all package states, including all global variables and PL/SQL tables. However, it does not free the memory associated with these now empty structures; that is the job of DBMS_SES-SION.FREE_UNUSED_USER_MEMORY. The my_session.reset procedure combines these into a single call.

```
/* Filename on companion disk: mysess.sql */
/*
|| resets all package states and frees memory
*/
PROCEDURE reset
IS
BEGIN
    DBMS_SESSION.RESET_PACKAGE;
    DBMS_SESSION.FREE_UNUSED_USER_MEMORY;
END reset;
```

Originally, I designed the reset procedure to call load_unique_id and load_my_ session_rec immediately after initializing the package and freeing memory. The idea was that some package states should always be available, so why not reinitialize them immediately? However, I had stepped into the DBMS_SES-SION.RESET_PACKAGE trap, which prevents any package state from being established within the same calling scope as the call to RESET_PACKAGE.

It is good practice for programs that rely on package state to check expected package variables and initialize them if necessary.

The memory procedure

The my_session.memory procedure was developed to provide experimental results from using DBMS_SESSION.RESET and DBMS_SESSION.FREE_UNUSED_ USER_MEMORY. It uses DBMS_OUTPUT to display the current session memory's UGA and PGA sizes. If you ever wondered how much memory that big package really uses, check it out with my_session.memory.

```
/* Filename on companion disk: mysess.sql */
/*
|| displays session uga and pga using DBMS_OUTPUT
*/
PROCEDURE memory
IS
```

```
BEGIN
    DBMS_OUTPUT.ENABLE;
    DBMS_OUTPUT.PUT_LINE('session UGA: '||
        TO_CHAR(my_session.statval('session uga memory') ) );
    DBMS_OUTPUT.PUT_LINE('session PGA: '||
        TO_CHAR(my_session.statval('session pga memory') ) );
END memory;
```

The memory procedure uses a function called statval, which returns the value of a V$SESSTAT statistic for the current session by name. It's a handy little function.

```
/* Filename on companion disk: mysess.sql */
/*
|| returns current value of a statistic from
|| V$SESSTAT for this session
*/
FUNCTION statval(statname_IN IN VARCHAR2) RETURN NUMBER
IS
    CURSOR sesstat_cur (statname VARCHAR2)
    IS
        SELECT  s.value
            FROM  sys.v_$sesstat s
                ,sys.v_$statname n
        WHERE  s.statistic# = n.statistic#
            AND  s.sid  = my_session.sid
            AND  n.name = statname;
    return_temp  NUMBER;
BEGIN
    OPEN sesstat_cur(statname_IN);
    FETCH sesstat_cur INTO return_temp;
    CLOSE sesstat_cur;
    RETURN return_temp;
EXCEPTION
    WHEN OTHERS THEN
        IF sesstat_cur%ISOPEN
        THEN
            CLOSE sesstat_cur;
        END IF;
        RETURN NULL;
END statval;
```

Notice that statval uses the my_session.sid funtion in the cursor sesstat_cur.

The following script demonstrates the inefficiency of PL/SQL tables of VARCHAR2 under Oracle 7.3 using my_session.memory:

```
/* Filename on companion disk: sess2.sql */
set serveroutput on size 100000

DECLARE
    TYPE my_tabtype IS TABLE OF VARCHAR2(2000)
        INDEX BY BINARY_INTEGER;

    my_tab my_tabtype;
BEGIN
```

```
    my_session.memory;
    FOR i IN 1..1000
    LOOP
        my_tab(i) := TO_CHAR(i);
    END LOOP;
    my_session.memory;
END;
/
```

Here is sample output from executing this script:

```
session UGA: 36048
session PGA: 103328
session UGA: 36048
session PGA: 2248352

PL/SQL procedure successfully completed.
```

Even though each entry in the PL/SQL table my_tab has at most three characters, session PGA memory grew by more than two megabytes! Luckily, this problem is fixed in PL/SQL8.

DBMS_SYSTEM: Setting Events for Debugging

The DBMS_SYSTEM package contains procedures for setting special internal trace events that can help the DBA or Oracle Technical Support personnel diagnose and debug serious database problems.

The procedures in DBMS_SYSTEM are used by DBAs under special circumstances and should not be used by end users or coded into applications. Most of the procedures should be used only under specific instructions from Oracle Technical Support, as improper usage can actually crash or damage the database. The extremely useful SET_SQL_TRACE_IN_SESSION procedure, however, has less serious implications. Both DBAs and developers should be aware of and know how to use it.

Getting Started with DBMS_SYSTEM

The DBMS_SYSTEM package is created when the Oracle database is installed. The *dbmsutil.sql* script (found in the built-in packages source code directory, as described in Chapter 1) contains the source code for this package's specification. This script is called by *catproc.sql*, which is normally run immediately after database creation.

Unlike the other packages created by the *dbmsutil.sql* script, no public synonym for DBMS_SYSTEM is created, and no privileges on the package are granted.

Thus, only the SYS user can normally reference and make use of this package. Other users (or roles) can be granted access to DBMS_SYSTEM by having the SYS user issue the following SQL command:

```
GRANT EXECUTE ON DBMS_SYSTEM TO username;
```

In practice, it is probably better and safer to create a cover package around DBMS_SYSTEM and grant EXECUTE privilege on the cover package to specific users or roles, as indiscriminate use of the DBMS_SYSTEM procedures can cause serious problems.

NOTE   In Oracle 8.0, the DBMS_SYSTEM package specification was moved from the *dbmsutil.sql* script into *prvtutil.plb* (the "wrapped" file), protecting it further from inadvertent access.

Table 11-2 lists the programs provided by this package.

Table 11-2. DBMS_SYSTEM Programs

Name	Description	Use in SQL?
READ_EV	Reads trace event level for current session	No
SET_EV	Sets trace event levels in user session	No
SET_SQL_TRACE_IN_SESSION	Sets SQL tracing on or off in user session	No

DBMS_SYSTEM does not declare any exceptions or any non-program elements.

DBMS_SYSTEM Interface

This section describes the programs defined in the DBMS_SYSTEM package.

The DBMS_SYSTEM.READ_EV procedure

The READ_EV procedure is used to read trace event level settings for the current session. Here's the header for this program:

```
PROCEDURE DBMS_SYSTEM.READ_EV
    (iev BINARY_INTEGER
    ,oev OUT BINARY_INTEGER);
```

Parameters are summarized in the following table.

Parameter	Value
iev	Event number
oev	Event level

The program does not raise any exceptions.

Restrictions. Note the following restrictions on calling READ_EV:

* The READ_EV procedure should not be invoked by end users or called by PL/ SQL programs. Its usage is limited to Oracle internal purposes or under instruction of Oracle Technical Support. Improper use of the procedure by end users can have adverse effects on database performance.

* The program does not assert a purity level with the RESTRICT_REFERENCES pragma.

Example. The following example[*] will display event-level settings for the current session:

```
/* Filename on companion disk: readev.sql */
DECLARE
    event_level number;
BEGIN
    FOR i IN 10000..10999 LOOP
        DBMS_SYSTEM.READ_EV(i,event_level);
        IF (event_level > 0)
        THEN
            DBMS_OUTPUT.PUT_LINE('Event '||TO_CHAR(i)||' set at level '||
                TO_CHAR(event_level) );
        END IF;
    END LOOP;
END;
/
```

The DBMS_SYSTEM.SET_EV procedure

The SET_EV procedure is used to set trace event levels in another user session. It is equivalent to having that session issue the ALTER SESSION SET EVENTS event syntax command. Since the other session may be engaged in an application, set-ting an event may not be possible. Here's the header for this program:

```
PROCEDURE DBMS_SYSTEM.SET_EV
    (si BINARY_INTEGER
    ,se BINARY_INTEGER
    ,ev BINARY_INTEGER
    ,le BINARY_INTEGER
    ,nm IN VARCHAR2);
```

---

[*] Supplied by Ken Robinson of Oracle Technical Support.

Parameters are summarized in the following table.

Parameter	Description
si	User session id
se	User session serial number
ev	Trace event number
le	Trace event level
nm	Trace event name

The program does not raise any exceptions.

Restrictions. Note the following restrictions on calling SET_EV:

- The SET_EV procedure should not be invoked by end users or called by PL/SQL programs. Its usage is limited to Oracle internal purposes or under instruction of Oracle Technical Support. Improper use of the procedure by end users can have adverse effects on database performance or cause database crashes.

- The program does not assert a purity level with the RESTRICT_REFERENCES pragma.

To learn more about Oracle trace events and their usage in diagnosing and debugging serious database problems, see the *Oracle Backup & Recovery Handbook*, by Rama Velpuri (Oracle Press, 1995).

The DBMS_SYSTEM.SET_SQL_TRACE_IN_SESSION procedure

The SET_SQL_TRACE_IN_SESSION procedure enables or disables SQL tracing in another user's session. It is especially useful for analyzing and debugging runtime performance issues in applications. Here's the header for this program:

```
PROCEDURE DBMS_SYSTEM.SET_SQL_TRACE_IN_SESSION
   (sid IN NUMBER
   ,serial# IN NUMBER
   ,sql_trace IN BOOLEAN);
```

Parameters are summarized in the following table.

Parameter	Value
sid	Session id
serial#	Session serial number
sql_trace	TRUE turns trace on, FALSE turns trace off

The program does not raise any exceptions, nor does it assert a purity level with the RESTRICT_REFERENCES pragma.

Example. Set SQL tracing on in a session identified by sid = 15 and serial number
= 4567 like this:

```
BEGIN
    SYS.DBMS_SYSTEM.SET_SQL_TRACE_IN_SESSION(15,4567,TRUE);
END;
```

The sid, serial number, and username for all sessions currently connected to the
database can be obtained using the following query:

```
SELECT sid, serial#, username
  FROM v$session;
```

Trace files generated when SQL tracing is turned on are created in the directory
specified by the USER_DUMP_DEST initialization parameter for the Oracle database to which the session is connected. SQL trace files can be formatted for readability using the TKPROF utility. See the *Oracle7 Server Tuning* manual for instructions on using TKPROF.

DBMS_SYSTEM Examples

DBMS_SYSTEM has some mysterious and apparently dangerous procedures in it.
Obtaining any information about SET_EV and READ_EV was very difficult and
promises to be more difficult in the future since the package header is no longer
exposed in Oracle 8.0.

In spite of Oracle's desire to keep DBMS_SYSTEM "under wraps," I feel strongly
that the SET_SQL_TRACE_IN_SESSION procedure is far too valuable to be hidden
away in obscurity. DBAs and developers need to find out exactly what is happening at runtime when a user is experiencing unusual performance problems, and
the SQL trace facility is one of the best tools available for discovering what the
database is doing during a user's session. This is especially useful when investigating problems with software packages where source code (including SQL) is generally unavailable.

So how can we get access to the one program in DBMS_SYSTEM we want without exposing those other dangerous elements to the public? The answer, of
course, is to build a package of our own to encapsulate DBMS_SYSTEM and
expose only what is safe. In the process, we can make DBMS_SYSTEM easier to
use as well. Those of us who are "keyboard-challenged" (or just plain lazy) would
certainly appreciate not having to type a procedure name with 36 characters.

I've created a package called trace to cover DBMS_SYSTEM and provide friendlier
ways to set SQL tracing on or off in other user's sessions. Here is the package
specification:

```
*/ Filename on companion disk: trace.sql */
CREATE OR REPLACE PACKAGE trace
IS
```

```
/*
|| Exposes DBMS_SYSTEM.SET_SQL_TRACE_IN_SESSION
|| with easier to call programs
||
|| Author:  John Beresniewicz, Savant Corp
|| Created: 07/30/97
||
|| Compilation Requirements:
|| SELECT on SYS.V_$SESSION
|| EXECUTE on SYS.DBMS_SYSTEM (or create as SYS)
||
|| Execution Requirements:
||
*/

/* turn SQL trace on by session id */
PROCEDURE Xon(sid_IN IN NUMBER);

/* turn SQL trace off by session id */
PROCEDURE off(sid_IN IN NUMBER);

/* turn SQL trace on by username */
PROCEDURE Xon(user_IN IN VARCHAR2);

/* turn SQL trace off by username */
PROCEDURE off(user_IN IN VARCHAR2);

END trace;
```

The trace package provides ways to turn SQL tracing on or off by session id or username. One thing that annoys me about DBMS_SYSTEM.SET_SQL_TRACE_IN_SESSION is having to figure out and pass a session serial number into the procedure. There should always be only one session per sid at any time connected to the database, so trace takes care of figuring out the appropriate serial number behind the scenes.

Another improvement (in my mind) is replacing the potentially confusing BOOLEAN parameter sql_trace with two distinct procedures whose names indicate what is being done. Compare the following commands, either of which might be used to turn SQL tracing off in session 15 using SQL*Plus:

```
SQL> execute trace.off(sid_IN=>15);

SQL> execute SYS.DBMS_SYSTEM.SET_SQL_TRACE_IN_SESSION(15,4567,FALSE);
```

The first method is both more terse and easier to understand.

The xon and off procedures are both overloaded on the single IN parameter, with versions accepting either the numeric session id or a character string for the session username. Allowing session selection by username may be easier than by sids. Why? Because sids are transient and must be looked up at runtime, whereas username is usually permanently associated with an individual. Beware, though, that multiple sessions may be concurrently connected under the same username, and invoking trace.xon by username will turn tracing on in all of them.

Let's take a look at the trace package body:

```
/* Filename on companion disk: trace.sql */
CREATE OR REPLACE PACKAGE BODY trace
IS

   /*
   || Use DBMS_SYSTEM.SET_SQL_TRACE_IN_SESSION to turn tracing on
   || or off by either session id or username.  Affects all sessions
   || that match non-NULL values of the user and sid parameters.
   */
   PROCEDURE set_trace
      (sqltrace_TF BOOLEAN
      ,user IN VARCHAR2 DEFAULT NULL
      ,sid IN NUMBER DEFAULT NULL)
   IS
   BEGIN
      /*
      || Loop through all sessions that match the sid and user
      || parameters and set trace on in those sessions.  The NVL
      || function in the cursor WHERE clause allows the single
      || SELECT statement to filter by either sid OR user.
      */
      FOR sid_rec IN
         (SELECT sid,serial#
            FROM sys.v_$session    S
           WHERE S.type='USER'
             AND S.username = NVL(UPPER(user),S.username)
             AND S.sid      = NVL(sid,S.sid) )
      LOOP
         SYS.DBMS_SYSTEM.SET_SQL_TRACE_IN_SESSION
            (sid_rec.sid, sid_rec.serial#, sqltrace_TF);
      END LOOP;
   END set_trace;

   /*
   || The programs exposed by the package all simply
   || call set_trace with different parameter combinations.
   */
   PROCEDURE Xon(sid_IN IN NUMBER)
   IS
   BEGIN
      set_trace(sqltrace_TF => TRUE, sid => sid_IN);
   END Xon;

   PROCEDURE off(sid_IN IN NUMBER)
   IS
   BEGIN
      set_trace(sqltrace_TF => FALSE, sid => sid_IN);
   END off;
```

```
PROCEDURE Xon(user_IN IN VARCHAR2)
IS
BEGIN
   set_trace(sqltrace_TF => TRUE, user => user_IN);
END Xon;

PROCEDURE off(user_IN IN VARCHAR2)
IS
BEGIN
   set_trace(sqltrace_TF => FALSE, user => user_IN);
END off;

END trace;
```

All of the real work done in the trace package is contained in a single private procedure called set_trace. The public procedures merely call set_trace with different parameter combinations. This is a structure that many packages exhibit: private programs with complex functionality exposed through public programs with simpler interfaces.

One interesting aspect of set_trace is the cursor used to get session identification data from V_$SESSION. I wanted to identify sessions for tracing by either session id or username. I could have just defined two cursors on V_$SESSION with some conditional logic deciding which cursor to use, but that just did not seem clean enough. After all, less code means fewer bugs. The solution I arrived at: make use of the NVL function to have a single cursor effectively ignore either the sid or the user parameter when either is passed in as NULL. Since set_trace is always called with either sid or user, but not both, the NVLs act as a kind of toggle on the cursor. I also supplied both the sid and user parameters to set_trace with the default value of NULL so that only the parameter being used for selection needs be passed in the call.

Once set_trace was in place, the publicly visible procedures were trivial.

A final note about the procedure name "xon": I wanted to use the procedure name "on," but ran afoul of the PL/SQL compiler since ON is a reserved word in SQL and PL/SQL.

12

Managing Server Resources

Through built-in packages, Oracle is now exposing more information about database internals—information that is not directly visible in the catalog. This chapter describes two packages that expose useful information.

DBMS_SPACE

> Gives DBAs an analysis of the amount of space both used and free within a table, index, or cluster segment. It also provides information about segment free list sizes—information of special interest to Oracle Parallel Server administrators.

DBMS_SHARED_POOL

> On the memory side, gives DBAs some measure of control over the Oracle System Global Area's (SGA's) shared pool. By pinning large packages into the shared pool, expensive runtime memory management (and even errors) can be avoided.

DBMS_SPACE: Obtaining Space Information

The DBMS_SPACE package provides procedures for obtaining space utilization information about table, index, and cluster segments. This information is not directly available through the Oracle data dictionary views. It can be used to report on and track segment space consumption in an Oracle database more accurately than by monitoring extent allocation alone. By measuring segment growth rates over time, DBAs can better predict the need for additional space in the database.

Getting Started with DBMS_SPACE

The DBMS_SPACE package is created when the Oracle database is installed. The *dbmsutil.sql* script (found in the built-in packages source code directory, as described in Chapter 1, *Introduction*) contains the source code for this package's specification. This script is called by *catproc.sql*, which is normally run immediately after database creation. The script creates the public synonym DBMS_SPACE for the package and grants EXECUTE privilege on the package to public. All Oracle users can reference and make use of this package.

Table 12-1 lists the programs in the DBMS_SPACE package.

Table 12-1. DBMS_SPACE Programs

Name	Description	Use in SQL?
FREE_BLOCKS	Returns information on free blocks for a segment	No
UNUSED_SPACE	Returns unused space information for a segment	No

The DBMS_SPACE package does not declare any exceptions or nonprogram elements.

The DBMS_SPACE Interface

This section describes the programs defined in DBMS_SPACE.

The DBMS_SPACE.FREE_BLOCKS procedure

The FREE_BLOCKS procedure returns information about the number of blocks on Oracle's freelist groups for a table, index, or cluster segment. Specifications for Oracle7 and Oracle8 vary as follows.

Here is the Oracle 7.x specification:

```
PROCEDURE DBMS_SPACE.FREE_BLOCKS
    (segment_owner IN VARCHAR2
    ,segment_name IN VARCHAR2
    ,segment_type IN VARCHAR2
    ,freelist_group_id IN NUMBER
    ,free_blks OUT NUMBER
    ,scan_limit IN NUMBER DEFAULT NULL);
```

Here is the Oracle 8.0 specification:

```
PROCEDURE DBMS_SPACE.FREE_BLOCKS
    (segment_owner IN VARCHAR2
    ,segment_name IN VARCHAR2
    ,segment_type IN VARCHAR2
    ,freelist_group_id IN NUMBER
    ,free_blks OUT NUMBER
```

```
,scan_limit IN NUMBER DEFAULT NULL
,partition_name IN VARCHAR2 DEFAULT NULL);
```

Parameters are summarized in the following table.

Parameter	Description
segment_owner	Schema of segment
segment_name	Name of segment
segment_type	Type of segment
freelist_group_id	Freelist group to compute
free_blks	Number of blocks on freelist
scan_limit	Maximum blocks to read
partition_name	Name of partition (8.0 only)

Exceptions. The FREE_BLOCKS procedure does not raise any package exceptions. FREE_BLOCKS will raise the following Oracle exception if invalid segment data is passed in or if the executing user does not have privileges to use the procedure on the segment:

ORA-00942

Table or view does not exist.

Restrictions. Note the following restrictions on using FREE_BLOCKS:

- The user must have the ANALYZE ANY system privilege to use DBMS_SPACE.FREE_BLOCKS on segments from schemas other than the current session schema.

- The program does not assert a purity level with the RESTRICT_REFERENCES pragma.

Example. The following code block is a simple SQL*Plus report on the size of freelist number 0 for all tables in the current session schema:

```
/* Filename on companion disk: spcex1.sql */
DECLARE
    free_blocks    NUMBER;
BEGIN
    DBMS_OUTPUT.PUT_LINE(RPAD('TABLE NAME',30)||' FREELIST BLOCKS');

    FOR user_tables_rec IN
        (SELECT table_name
            FROM user_tables)
    LOOP
        DBMS_SPACE.FREE_BLOCKS
            (segment_owner => USER
            ,segment_name  => user_tables_rec.table_name
            ,segment_type  => 'TABLE'
```

```
                    ,freelist_group_id => 0
                    ,free_blks => free_blocks
                    ,scan_limit => NULL);

               DBMS_OUTPUT.PUT_LINE(RPAD(user_tables_rec.table_name,30)||' '||
                         TO_CHAR(free_blocks));
          END LOOP;
     END;
     /
```

This is a sample of the report output:

```
     TABLE NAME                     FREELIST BLOCKS
     Q$BGP_CONFIG                   1
     Q$BGP_DEBUG                    1
     Q$DICACHE_DETL                 2
     Q$INSTAT_DETL                  1
     Q$INSTAT_LOG                   159
     Q$IOWAITS_DETL                 1
     Q$LATCHSTAT_DETL               2
     Q$LIBCACHE_DETL                1
     Q$MTSDISP_DETL                 1
     Q$MTSSERV_DETL                 1
     Q$PLAN_TABLE                   1
     Q$SEG                          3
     Q$SEGFAIL_DETL                 1
     Q$SEGWATCH                     1
     Q$SESSIONWAIT_DETL             1
```

Blocks are added to free lists when the percentage of free space in the block is less that the PCTUSE setting for the segment. These blocks are below the segment highwater mark, and thus are not included in the unused blocks reported by DBMS_SPACE.UNUSED_SPACE.

Freelist groups are used to reduce contention in Oracle Parallel Server installations by helping to partition data among the instances. Most DBAs will thus have less use for the FREE_BLOCKS procedure than for the UNUSED_SPACE procedure.

For more information about freelists and how they can be used to minimize contention, see the *Oracle7 Parallel Server Concepts and Administration* manual.

The DBMS_SPACE.UNUSED_SPACE procedure

The UNUSED_SPACE procedure returns information about the unused space and the position of the highwater mark in a table, index, or cluster segment. Specifications for Oracle7 and Oracle8 differ as follows.

Here is the Oracle 7.x specification:

```
     PROCEDURE DBMS_SPACE.UNUSED_SPACE
          (segment_owner IN VARCHAR2
          ,segment_name IN VARCHAR2
          ,segment_type IN VARCHAR2
```

```
          ,total_blocks OUT NUMBER
          ,total_bytes OUT NUMBER
          ,unused_blocks OUT NUMBER
          ,unused_bytes OUT NUMBER
          ,last_used_extent_file_id OUT NUMBER
          ,last_used_extent_block_id OUT NUMBER
          ,last_used_block OUT NUMBER);
```

Here is the Oracle 8.0 specification:

```
PROCEDURE DBMS_SPACE.UNUSED_SPACE
          (segment_owner IN VARCHAR2
          ,segment_name IN VARCHAR2
          ,segment_type IN VARCHAR2
          ,total_blocks OUT NUMBER
          ,total_bytes OUT NUMBER
          ,unused_blocks OUT NUMBER
          ,unused_bytes OUT NUMBER
          ,last_used_extent_file_id OUT NUMBER
          ,last_used_extent_block_id OUT NUMBER
          ,last_used_block OUT NUMBER
          ,partition_name IN VARCHAR2 DEFAULT NULL);
```

Parameters are summarized in the following table.

Name	Description
segment_owner	Schema of segment
segment_name	Name of segment
segment_type	Type of segment
total_blocks	Total data blocks in segment
total_bytes	Total bytes in segment
unused_blocks	Total unused blocks in segment
unused_bytes	Total unused bytes in segment
last_used_extent_file_id	File id of last used extent
last_used_extent_block_id	Block id of last used extent
last_used_block	Last used block in extent
partition_name	Name of partition (8.0 only)

Exceptions. The UNUSED_SPACE procedure does not raise any package exceptions. UNUSED_SPACE will raise the following Oracle exception if invalid segment data is passed in or if the executing user does not have privileges to use the procedure on the segment:

ORA-00942

Table or view does not exist.

Restrictions. Note the following restrictions on calling the UNUSED_SPACE procedure:

- The user must have the ANALYZE ANY system privilege to use UNUSED_ SPACE on segments from schemas other than the current session schema.

- The program does not assert a purity level with the RESTRICT_REFERENCES pragma.

Example. The following is a simple SQL*Plus report on space utilization by tables in the current session schema. It displays total space allocated, total unused space, and the percentage of allocated space that is unused.

```
//* Filename on companion disk: spcex1.sql */
DECLARE
    total_blocks  NUMBER;
    total_bytes   NUMBER;
    unused_blocks NUMBER;
    unused_bytes  NUMBER;
    last_extent_file  NUMBER;
    last_extent_block NUMBER;
    last_block    NUMBER;
    grand_total_blocks NUMBER := 0;
    grand_total_unused NUMBER := 0;

BEGIN
    FOR user_tables_rec IN
        (SELECT table_name
           FROM user_tables)
    LOOP
        DBMS_SPACE.UNUSED_SPACE
            (segment_owner => USER
            ,segment_name  => user_tables_rec.table_name
            ,segment_type  => 'TABLE'
            ,total_blocks  => total_blocks
            ,total_bytes   => total_bytes
            ,unused_blocks => unused_blocks
            ,unused_bytes  => unused_bytes
            ,last_used_extent_file_id => last_extent_file
            ,last_used_extent_block_id => last_extent_block
            ,last_used_block => last_block
            );

        grand_total_blocks := grand_total_blocks + total_blocks;
        grand_total_unused := grand_total_unused + unused_blocks;
    END LOOP;

    DBMS_OUTPUT.PUT_LINE('Space utilization (TABLES) ');
    DBMS_OUTPUT.PUT_LINE('total blocks: '||
                            TO_CHAR(grand_total_blocks) );
    DBMS_OUTPUT.PUT_LINE('unused blocks: '||
                            TO_CHAR(grand_total_unused) );
    DBMS_OUTPUT.PUT_LINE('pct unused: '||
        TO_CHAR(ROUND((grand_total_unused/grand_total_blocks)*100) ) );
```

```
END;
/
```

This is a sample of the report output:

```
Space utilization (TABLES)
total blocks: 1237
unused blocks: 613
pct unused: 50
```

In Oracle 8.0, the partition_name parameter was added to support space analysis for partitioned segments. Since the new parameter has a default value, calls to UNUSED_SPACE written to the version 7.x specification will continue to work under 8.0.

WARNING   Under Oracle 8.0, calling DBMS_SPACE.UNUSED_SPACE for a segment results in a DDL lock being held on the segment until the PL/
SQL scope within which the call is made completes. This prevents
any other DDL from being executed on the segment, so long-running programs that use the UNUSED_SPACE procedure could cause
unexpected interference with other DDL operations in the database.

Unused space can be deallocated from segments and returned to the free space for the segment's tablespace using the following SQL command:

```
ALTER [ TABLE | INDEX | CLUSTER ] segment_name DEALLOCATE UNUSED;
```

For information on how Oracle allocates and manages segment space, see the *Oracle7 Server Concepts* manual. For information on the DEALLOCATE UNUSED clause of the ALTER TABLE statement, see the *Oracle7 Server SQL Reference*.

DBMS_SPACE Examples

The DBMS_SPACE package is a good example of how Oracle Corporation is using the built-in packages to expose, in a controlled way, information about database internals not found in the data dictionary.

DBAs managing large transaction-oriented databases must pay attention to space utilization within segments. The UNUSED_SPACE procedure provides an additional level of detail that can help the DBAs make better use of space. For instance, wasted space that can be freed back to the tablespace for use by other segments can be detected and measured. Also, segment growth rates can be measured more accurately than by monitoring extent allocation, providing better information on the need to expand tablespaces.

DBAs, especially those with Oracle parallel server installations, will be interested additionally in monitoring the segment freelist information exposed by the FREE_BLOCKS procedure.

Figure 12-1 illustrates how the blocks of a segment fall into one of three categories: used, unused (above the highwater mark), and on the free list. The latter two categories are the subject of the UNUSED_SPACE and FREE_BLOCKS procedures, respectively.

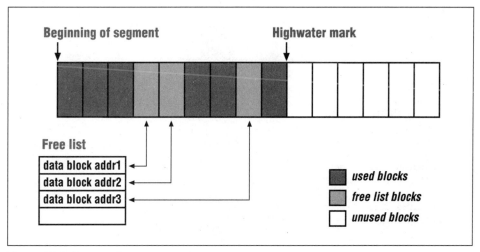

Figure 12-1. Space utilization in a segment

I really like the information available in the DBMS_SPACE programs. However, I find that the programs are very unwieldy to use, due to their long, cumbersome parameter lists. The UNUSED_SPACE procedure has at least three IN parameters and seven OUT parameters! Even the earlier simple illustrative example is many lines long. What if you're interested in only one of the OUT parameters—say, unused_blocks? You still have to allocate variables to hold all the other OUT parameters just to make the procedure call. Wouldn't it be nice to simply call a function that returns the unused blocks number for a given segment?

The segspace package

As usual, the solution to such usability issues lies in creating a package to encapsulate those unwieldy program calls with an easier-to-use layer of programs. Here is the specification for my own package called segspace:

```
//* Filename on companion disk: segspace.sql */
CREATE OR REPLACE PACKAGE segspace
   /*
   || Extends the DBMS_SPACE package by creating function
   || calls to return individual parameter values
   ||
   || Author:  John Beresniewicz, Savant Corp
   || Created: 07/29/97
   ||
```

```
|| Compilation Requirements:
||
|| Execution Requirements:
||
|| ANALYZE ANY system privilege
||
*/
AS

   /*
   || sets the specified segment as current context
   */
   PROCEDURE set_segment
      (name_IN IN VARCHAR2
      ,type_IN IN VARCHAR2
      ,schema_IN IN VARCHAR2
      ,partition_IN IN VARCHAR2 DEFAULT NULL);

   /* returns current segment name */
   FUNCTION current_name RETURN VARCHAR2;

   /* returns current segment type */
   FUNCTION current_type RETURN VARCHAR2;

   /* returns current segment schema */
   FUNCTION current_schema RETURN VARCHAR2;

   /*
   || returns total_blocks from DBMS_SPACE.UNUSED_SPACE
   || for the segment specified
   */
   FUNCTION total_blocks
      (name_IN IN VARCHAR2 DEFAULT current_name
      ,type_IN IN VARCHAR2 DEFAULT current_type
      ,schema_IN IN VARCHAR2 DEFAULT current_schema)
   RETURN NUMBER;


   /*
   || returns unused_blocks from DBMS_SPACE.UNUSED_SPACE
   || for the segment specified
   */
   FUNCTION unused_blocks
      (name_IN IN VARCHAR2 DEFAULT current_name
      ,type_IN IN VARCHAR2 DEFAULT current_type
      ,schema_IN IN VARCHAR2 DEFAULT current_schema)
   RETURN NUMBER;


   /*
   || returns number of blocks on segment freelist using
   || DBMS_SPACE.FREE_BLOCKS
   */
   FUNCTION freelist_blocks
```

```
      (name_IN IN VARCHAR2 DEFAULT current_name
      ,type_IN IN VARCHAR2 DEFAULT current_type
      ,schema_IN IN VARCHAR2 DEFAULT current_schema
      ,freelist_group_IN IN NUMBER DEFAULT 0
      ,partition_IN IN VARCHAR2 DEFAULT NULL)
   RETURN NUMBER;

END segspace;
```

The segspace package has functions called total_blocks and unused_blocks. These functions both accept segment identification information as IN parameters and return the value of their corresponding OUT parameters from DBMS_SPACE.UNUSED_SPACE. So in SQL*Plus, you can use these functions as follows:

```
SQL> var tot_blks NUMBER
SQL> execute :tot_blks := segspace.total_blocks('TENK','TABLE','LOAD1');

PL/SQL procedure successfully completed.

SQL> print tot_blks

   TOT_BLKS
 ---------
        455
```

Well, this sure is a lot easier than calling the UNUSED_SPACE procedure directly! Notice, however, that the IN parameters to these functions also all have default values, which means that they can be suppressed when making the function call (as long as the default is the desired value). The default values used are the segment identifiers (name, type, and schema) most recently specified. Thus we can find out the unused blocks for the LOAD1.TENK table by immediately following the preceding call with this:

```
SQL> var unused_blks number
SQL> execute :unused_blks := segspace.unused_blocks;

PL/SQL procedure successfully completed.

SQL> print unused_blks

UNUSED_BLKS
 -----------
         10
```

By retaining the current segment context set by the previous call and using default values, a complex procedure call (UNUSED_SPACE) with ten parameters is transformed into a simple function call requiring only a target variable for its result.

Now, this is something I might be able (and want) to actually use.

The set_segment procedure is used to set the current segment context, which amounts to establishing the default IN parameters for all the functions.

Astute readers will suspect that private package globals play a part in this trickery, and they are correct. They may also raise questions about the performance implications of splitting the OUT parameters of UNUSED_SPACE into individual function calls, as this is a relatively "expensive" procedure call to make and should not be redundantly or needlessly invoked. Well, segspace is designed to be both useful and efficient.

Here is the package body for segspace (an explanation follows the code):

```
//* Filename on companion disk: segspace.sql */
CREATE OR REPLACE PACKAGE BODY segspace
AS

    /* record type to hold data on segment */
    TYPE segdata_rectype IS RECORD
        (name      VARCHAR2(30)
        ,schema    VARCHAR2(30) DEFAULT USER
        ,type      VARCHAR2(30) DEFAULT 'TABLE'
        ,partition VARCHAR2(30) DEFAULT NULL
        ,total_blocks  NUMBER
        ,total_bytes   NUMBER
        ,unused_blocks NUMBER
        ,unused_bytes  NUMBER
        ,last_extent_file  NUMBER
        ,last_extent_block NUMBER
        ,last_block    NUMBER
        ,last_segload  DATE := SYSDATE - 1
        );

    /* global rec for current segment data */
    segdata_rec   segdata_rectype;

    /* reload timeout in seconds */
    segload_timeout   INTEGER := 60;

    /* flag for new segment */
    newseg_TF   BOOLEAN := TRUE;

    /*
    || returns the segment name from segdata_rec
    */
    FUNCTION current_name RETURN VARCHAR2
    IS
    BEGIN
       RETURN segdata_rec.name;
    END current_name;

    /*
    || returns the segment type from segdata_rec
    */
    FUNCTION current_type RETURN VARCHAR2
    IS
    BEGIN
```

```
      RETURN segdata_rec.type;
   END current_type;


   /*
   || returns the segment schema from segdata_rec
   */
   FUNCTION current_schema RETURN VARCHAR2
   IS
   BEGIN
      RETURN segdata_rec.schema;
   END current_schema;


   /*
   || sets specific segment as context
   */
   PROCEDURE set_segment
      (name_IN IN VARCHAR2
      ,type_IN IN VARCHAR2
      ,schema_IN IN VARCHAR2
      ,partition_IN IN VARCHAR2 DEFAULT NULL)
   IS
   BEGIN
      /* check if new segment and set flag */
      IF ( segdata_rec.schema != schema_IN
        OR segdata_rec.name    != name_IN
        OR segdata_rec.type    != type_IN
        OR segdata_rec.partition != partition_IN
          )
      THEN
         newseg_TF := TRUE;
      ELSE
         newseg_TF := FALSE;
      END IF;

      /* set segment globals */
      segdata_rec.schema := schema_IN;
      segdata_rec.name    := name_IN;
      segdata_rec.type    := type_IN;
      segdata_rec.partition := partition_IN;
   END set_segment;



   FUNCTION reload_TF RETURN BOOLEAN
   IS
   /*
   || returns TRUE if timed out or new segment since last load
   */
   BEGIN
      RETURN ( SYSDATE > segdata_rec.last_segload +
                         segload_timeout/(24*60*60)
             )
          OR newseg_TF;
   END reload_TF;



   PROCEDURE load_unused
```

```
IS
/*
|| loads segment unused space data for current segment using
|| DBMS_SPACE.UNUSED_SPACE if the segment is new or timeout limit
|| reached since last load
*/
BEGIN
   IF reload_TF
   THEN
      DBMS_SPACE.UNUSED_SPACE
         (segment_owner => segdata_rec.schema
         ,segment_name  => segdata_rec.name
         ,segment_type  => segdata_rec.type
         ,total_blocks  => segdata_rec.total_blocks
         ,total_bytes   => segdata_rec.total_bytes
         ,unused_blocks => segdata_rec.unused_blocks
         ,unused_bytes  => segdata_rec.unused_bytes
         ,last_used_extent_file_id => segdata_rec.last_extent_file
         ,last_used_extent_block_id => segdata_rec.last_extent_block
         ,last_used_block => segdata_rec.last_block
      /* ------------------------------------------ */
      /* NOTE: uncomment following line for Oracle 8 */
      /* ------------------------------------------ */
      /* ,partition_name  => segdata_rec.partition    */
         );

         segdata_rec.last_segload := SYSDATE;
      END IF;
END load_unused;


FUNCTION total_blocks
   (name_IN IN VARCHAR2
   ,type_IN IN VARCHAR2
   ,schema_IN IN VARCHAR2)
RETURN NUMBER
IS
/*
|| sets current segment and calls load_unused
*/
BEGIN
   set_segment(name_IN, type_IN, schema_IN);
   load_unused;
   RETURN segdata_rec.total_blocks;
END total_blocks;


FUNCTION unused_blocks
   (name_IN IN VARCHAR2
   ,type_IN IN VARCHAR2
   ,schema_IN IN VARCHAR2)
RETURN NUMBER
IS
/*
```

```
     || sets current segment and calls load_unused
     */
     BEGIN
        set_segment(name_IN, type_IN, schema_IN);
        load_unused;
        RETURN segdata_rec.unused_blocks;
     END unused_blocks;


     /*
     || returns number of blocks on segment freelist using
     || DBMS_SPACE.FREE_BLOCKS
     */
     FUNCTION freelist_blocks
        (name_IN IN VARCHAR2 DEFAULT current_name
        ,type_IN IN VARCHAR2 DEFAULT current_type
        ,schema_IN IN VARCHAR2 DEFAULT current_schema
        ,freelist_group_IN IN NUMBER DEFAULT 0
        ,partition_IN IN VARCHAR2 DEFAULT NULL)
     RETURN NUMBER
     IS
        /* variable to hold output from call to FREE_BLOCKS */
        temp_freelist_blocks NUMBER;

        /*
        || loads segment freelist size using DBMS_SPACE.FREE_BLOCKS
        || scan limit NULL means no limit
        */
        BEGIN
           DBMS_SPACE.FREE_BLOCKS
              (segment_owner => schema_IN
              ,segment_name  => name_IN
              ,segment_type  => type_IN
              ,freelist_group_id => freelist_group_IN
              ,free_blks => temp_freelist_blocks
              ,scan_limit => NULL
           /* ------------------------------------------- */
           /* NOTE: uncomment following line for Oracle 8  */
           /* ------------------------------------------- */
           /* ,partition_name  => partition_IN            */
              );

        RETURN temp_freelist_blocks;
     END freelist_blocks;

  END segspace;
```

The segspace package body declares a record type called segdata_rectype and a private global of that type called segdata_rec. This record is designed to hold a copy of all parameters (both IN and OUT) used by the UNUSED_SPACE procedure. The name, schema, type, and partition fields in segdata_rec correspond to the IN parameters of UNUSED_SPACE. These are set using the set_segment procedure. Think of this as the current segment context—the segment currently being analyzed. The functions current_name, current_schema, and current_type simply return the corresponding elements of the current segment context.

The load_unused procedure is the one that actually calls UNUSED_SPACE. It takes as IN parameters the appropriate field values from segdata_rec, and assigns its OUT values to the corresponding fields in segdata_rec. Now the individual OUT parameters from UNUSED_SPACE can be exposed through individual function calls that return fields from segdata_rec.

So the basic logic is quite simple:

1. The set_segment procedure establishes a segment context in segdata_rec.

2. The load_unused procedure loads UNUSED_SPACE information for the current segment into segdata_rec.

3. Individual field values from segdata_rec are returned through functions such as total_blocks and unused_block.

Now, a three-step process to retrieve the data items individually does not really represent an increase in usability, so what really happens is that the functions total_blocks and unused_blocks each do all three steps.

```
FUNCTION unused_blocks
    (name_IN IN VARCHAR2
    ,type_IN IN VARCHAR2
    ,schema_IN IN VARCHAR2)
RETURN NUMBER
IS
/*
|| sets current segment and calls load_unused
*/
BEGIN
    set_segment(name_IN, type_IN, schema_IN);
    load_unused;
    RETURN segdata_rec.unused_blocks;
END unused_blocks;
```

Remember that calling DBMS_SPACE.UNUSED_SPACE is relatively expensive, and we want to avoid calling it more often than necessary. It would be nice to be able to do the following without calling UNUSED_SPACE twice:

```
BEGIN
    pct_free := 100*
                (segspace.unused_blocks('TABLENAME','TABLE','SCHEMA') /
                segspace.total_blocks('TABLENAME','TABLE','SCHEMA')
                );
END;
```

The load_unused procedure avoids calling UNUSED_SPACE too often by checking a function called reload_TF, which returns a BOOLEAN indicating whether to reload segment data. The reload_TF function will return TRUE (reload) if either of the following is TRUE:

- It has been longer than segload_timeout seconds since the last call to DBMS_SPACE.LOAD_UNUSED.

- The current segment context is different than the context for the last call to DBMS_SPACE.LOAD_UNUSED.

Thus the previous PL/SQL block will call UNUSED_SPACE at most once (and perhaps not at all, if it was recently called for the same segment). The private global newseg_TF is a BOOLEAN flag indicating a new context. This is maintained by the set_segment procedure: whenever a context is established, the flag is set to TRUE, if it is a new context.

Additional usability in the total_blocks and unused_blocks functions is achieved by using default values for the IN parameters and careful ordering of the parameters. The default values for name_IN, type_IN, and schema_IN are assigned by the functions current_name, current_type, and current_schema. The parameters are ordered such that the most likely to change (name) is first, followed by type, and then schema. This is based on the reasonable assumption that when doing space analysis, the user will probably do all tables by schema or all indexes by schema. Additionally, the initial default prior to setting a context at all is the current user schema and segment type TABLE.

Q: Why did I use functions for the default values instead of direct reference to segdata_rec?

A: In order to directly reference the segdata_rec components for parameter defaults in the package specification, I would have also had to declare segdata_rec in the specification. This would expose segdata_rec such that it could be inadvertently modified by other programs. By using functions for the default values, segdata_rec can be declared privately (and thus protected) in the package body.

The function freelist_blocks simply calls DBMS_SPACE.FREE_BLOCKS and returns its single OUT parameter free_blks. Because FREE_BLOCKS has only a single OUT parameter, it was not really necessary to implement the optimizations discussed previously to avoid redundant calls. The function does improve usability by supplying defaults for the IN parameters to FREE_BLOCKS, reducing the calling profile where the defaults are correct. Be careful, though, because freelist_blocks does not do a set_segment to establish a context. If it is used alone (i.e., not in conjunction with total_blocks or unused_blocks), it is best to specify a full segment context in the call.

Q: Why did I choose to not have freelist_blocks call set_segment to establish a segment context?

A: The unused_blocks function relies on segdata_rec to provide information about the current segment context loaded by the load_unused procedure. If the freelist_ blocks function were to call set_segment to establish a context, it would also have to call load_unused to keep segdata_rec in synch with the context. This would introduce significant and unnecessary overhead, when only freelist information is desired.

Here is an example of using the segspace package in a SQL*Plus script to report on unused space in segments for a specific tablespace:

```
/* Filename on companion disk: spcex2.sql */
undefine tablespace_name
set serveroutput on size 100000
set verify off

DECLARE
   total_blocks NUMBER :=0;
   unused_blocks NUMBER :=0;
BEGIN
   DBMS_OUTPUT.PUT_LINE('TABLESPACE: '||UPPER('&&tablespace_name'));
   FOR seg_rec IN
      (SELECT segment_name, segment_type, owner
         FROM dba_segments
        WHERE tablespace_name = UPPER('&&tablespace_name') )
   LOOP
      total_blocks := total_blocks +
                         segspace.total_blocks
                            (seg_rec.segment_name
                            ,seg_rec.segment_type
                            ,seg_rec.owner);

      unused_blocks := unused_blocks + segspace.unused_blocks;
   END LOOP;
   DBMS_OUTPUT.PUT_LINE('Total Blocks: '||TO_CHAR(total_blocks));
   DBMS_OUTPUT.PUT_LINE('Unused Blocks: '||TO_CHAR(unused_blocks));
   DBMS_OUTPUT.PUT_LINE('Pct Unused: '||
           TO_CHAR(ROUND(unused_blocks/total_blocks*100)) );
END;
/
```

This is sample output from executing the script:

```
Enter value for tablespace_name: LOAD_DATA
TABLESPACE: LOAD_DATA
Total Blocks: 9195
Unused Blocks: 1300
Pct Unused: 14

PL/SQL procedure successfully completed.
```

I like using segspace to probe space utilization within segments. With segspace, I can obtain useful reports like the previous one with a few quick lines. Direct use of DBMS_SPACE would require much more time and effort.

DBMS_SHARED_POOL: Pinning Objects

The DBMS_SHARED_POOL package provides procedures that allow PL/SQL objects and SQL cursors to be pinned (kept) in the Oracle shared pool. Once pinned, objects are not subject to the normal aging-out processes of the shared pool.

DBMS_SHARED_POOL is used primarily by DBAs to help solve memory management and performance issues that can arise when applications make use of large PL/SQL objects or SQL cursors. Two problems can arise when large objects need to be loaded into the shared pool:

- ORA-04031 errors where insufficient memory is available and the user call fails to execute.

- Degraded performance due to the memory management overhead involved in finding and making room to load large objects.

Pinning large objects into the shared pool when the Oracle instance is first started can reduce or eliminate these problems. Some DBAs use DBMS_SHARED_POOL in their database startup scripts to help ensure that shared pool memory is used efficiently.

Getting Started with DBMS_SHARED_POOL

The DBMS_SHARED_POOL package is created when the Oracle database is installed. The *dbmspool.sql* script (found in the built-in packages source code directory, as described in Chapter 1) contains the source code for this package's specification. Unlike many of the other built-in package scripts, this script is not called by *catproc.sql*. Thus, the DBA must manually build this package. This is accomplished by executing the *dbmspool.sql* and *prvtpool.plb* scripts (in order) from SQLDBA or Server Manager when connected as the INTERNAL user.

Access to the DBMS_SHARED_POOL package is not automatically granted to any users, nor is a public synonym referencing the package created. The package is intended for use strictly by the Oracle DBA, usually when connected as the SYS user. Under Oracle8, the EXECUTE_CATALOG_ROLE role is granted EXECUTE privilege on DBMS_SHARED_POOL, so any users with this role can use the package.

Table 12-2 lists the programs available in this package.

Table 12-2. DBMS_SHARED_POOL Programs

Name	Description	Use in SQL?
ABORTED_REQUEST_ THRESHOLD	Sets size threshold for aborting object loads if memory is low	No
KEEP	Pins object into shared pool	No
SIZES	Displays shared pool objects larger than given size	No
UNKEEP	Unpins object from shared pool	No

DBMS_SHARED_POOL does not declare any exceptions or nonprogram elements.

Pinning and Unpinning Objects

The KEEP and UNKEEP procedures are used to pin and unpin objects in the Oracle shared pool.

The DBMS_SHARED_POOL.KEEP procedure

The KEEP procedure allows DBAs to pin PL/SQL or cursor objects into the Oracle shared pool. Pinning objects into the shared pool eliminates the need for Oracle to do dynamic memory management when users reference the object. The program header follows:

```
PROCEDURE DBMS_SHARED_POOL.KEEP
    (name IN VARCHAR2
    ,flag IN CHAR DEFAULT 'P');
```

Parameters are summarized in the following table.

Parameter	Description
name	Name of the object to pin
flag	Notifies the KEEP procedure of the kind of object specified in the name parameter

The flag parameter can take the following values:

flag Value	Object Type
P or p	Package, procedure, or function name
Q or q (v8 only)	Sequence name
R or r	Trigger name
Any other character	Cursor specified by address and hash value

Exceptions. The KEEP procedure does not raise any package exceptions. It can raise the following Oracle exceptions if the name parameter does not resolve to a real object or an object of the proper type:

ORA-06564

Object <object name> does not exist.

ORA-06502

PL/SQL: numeric or value error.

Restrictions. Note the following restrictions on calling KEEP:

- TABLE and VIEW objects cannot be pinned using KEEP. Pinning sequences are supported in the Oracle8 version only.

- Oracle warns that the KEEP procedure may not be supported in future releases.

- The program does not assert a purity level with the RESTRICT_REFERENCES pragma.

Example. This example illustrates using SQL*Plus to pin the package SYS.STANDARD into the shared pool:

```
SQL> BEGIN
  2      SYS.DBMS_SHARED_POOL.KEEP('SYS.STANDARD','P');
  3   END;
  4   /

PL/SQL procedure successfully completed.
```

In the example for DBMS_SHARED_POOL.SIZES, we see that the SYS.STANDARD package is 119 kilobytes in size. This is a good candidate for routinely pinning into the shared pool. Other Oracle packages that are probably good to keep in the shared pool are SYS.DBMS_STANDARD, SYS.DIUTIL, and SYS.DBMS_SYS_SQL.

It is best to pin any objects that are relatively large (larger than 10–20 kilobytes), especially if they are used intermittently. Doing so minimizes the likelihood that dynamic object loading will flush items out of the shared pool to make room for the object.

For an example of pinning a cursor into the shared pool, see the "DBMS_SHARED_POOL Examples" section.

The DBMS_SHARED_POOL.UNKEEP procedure

The UNKEEP procedure allows the DBA to release from the Oracle shared pool a pinned object that has previously been pinned using the KEEP procedure. Once unpinned, the object is subject to the normal shared pool memory management aging and flushing routines. Here's the header for this program:

```
PROCEDURE DBMS_SHARED_POOL.UNKEEP
    (name IN VARCHAR2
    ,flag IN CHAR DEFAULT 'P');
```

Parameters are summarized in the following table.

Parameter	Description
name	Name of the object to unpin
flag	Notifies the UNKEEP procedure of the kind of object specified in the name parameter

The flag parameter can take the following values:

flag Value	Object Type
P or p	Package, procedure, or function name
Q or q (v8 only)	Sequence name
R or r	Trigger name
Any other character	Cursor specified by address and hash value

Exceptions. The UNKEEP procedure does not raise any package exceptions. It can raise the following Oracle exceptions if the name parameter does not resolve to a real object or an object of the proper type:

ORA-06564

> Object <object name> does not exist.

ORA-06502

> PL/SQL: numeric or value error.

Restrictions. Note the following restrictions on calling UNKEEP:

- Oracle warns that the UNKEEP procedure may not be supported in future releases.

- The program does not assert a purity level with the RESTRICT_REFERENCES pragma.

Example. This example releases the object pinned by the KEEP procedure (see the example for KEEP earlier):

```
SQL> BEGIN
  2      SYS.DBMS_SHARED_POOL.UNKEEP('SYS.STANDARD','P');
  3  END;
  4  /

PL/SQL procedure successfully completed.
```

Usually an object is pinned into the shared pool for a reason, so it is not likely that you would need to call UNKEEP regularly. However, if large objects that have been pinned into the shared pool are definitely no longer needed, then memory can be made available to the shared pool by executing UNKEEP on these objects.

Monitoring and Modifying Shared Pool Behavior

You can monitor the behavior of objects in the shared pool with the SIZES procedure. You can modify that behavior with the ABORTED_REQUEST_THRESHOLD procedure.

The DBMS_SHARED_POOL.SIZES procedure

The SIZES procedure displays objects (including cursors and anonymous PL/SQL blocks) that are currently in the shared pool and that exceed the size (in kilobytes) specified by the minsize parameter. The program header follows:

```
PROCEDURE DBMS_SHARED_POOL.SIZES
    (minsize IN NUMBER);
```

The minsize parameter specifies the minimum size in kilobytes of shared pool objects that are displayed.

The program does not raise any package exceptions, nor does it assert a purity level with the RESTRICT_REFERENCES pragma.

Example. The following example demonstrates using the SIZES procedure in a SQL*Plus session to find all objects currently in the Oracle shared pool using more than 70 kilobytes of memory:

```
SQL> set serveroutput on size 100000
SQL> execute SYS.DBMS_SHARED_POOL.SIZES(70);

SIZE(K) KEPT                                                    NAME
------  --------------------------------------------------      ----------
119     SYS.STANDARD                                            (PACKAGE)
87      YES    QDBA.Q$INSTAT                                    (PACKAGE BODY)
80      YES    QDBA.Q$BGPROC                                    (PACKAGE BODY)
77      YES    QDBA.Q$CVAR                                      (PACKAGE)
72      begin :r:="LOADX"."RAND1";end;    (0D953BE8,3990841093) (CURSOR)

PL/SQL procedure successfully completed.
```

Notice that a cursor object's name is composed of the address and hash value for the cursor. These are the values to use in calls to DBMS_SHARED_POOL.KEEP for pinning cursor objects. See the "DBMS_SHARED_POOL Examples" section for an example of pinning a cursor.

The SIZES procedure is normally used from the SQL*Plus, SQLDBA, or Sever Manager utilities. In order to display the results, issue the SET SERVEROUTPUT ON SIZE NNNNNN command prior to calling this program, as shown in the example.

The DBMS_SHARED_POOL.ABORTED_REQUEST_THRESHOLD procedure

The ABORTED_REQUEST_THRESHOLD procedure allows the DBA to set a size threshold for restricting Oracle from dynamically flushing unpinned shared pool objects in order to make room for a large object greater than this size. When the threshold is set, any objects larger than the threshold for which sufficient free memory does not exist in the shared pool will fail to load with an ORA-4031 error (rather than flush other objects to make room). The program header follows:

```
PROCEDURE DBMS_SHARED_POOL.ABORTED_REQUEST_THRESHOLD
     (threshold_size IN NUMBER);
```

The threshold_size is a NUMBER, in bytes, that specifies the maximum size of objects that can be loaded if shared pool space is not available.

Exceptions. The ABORTED_THRESHOLD_REQUEST procedure does not raise any package exceptions. It can raise the following Oracle exceptions if the threshold_size parameter is out of range:

ORA-20000
   threshold_size not in valid range: (5000 – 2147483647).

Restrictions. Note the following restrictions on calling ABORTED_THRESHOLD_REQUEST:

- The range of valid values for the threshold_size is 5000 to 2147483647, inclusive.

- The program does not assert a purity level with the RESTRICT_REFERENCES pragma.

Example. The following shows how to keep objects larger than 50,000 bytes in size from flushing the shared pool when there is insufficient memory to load them:

```
SQL> BEGIN
  2      SYS.DBMS_SHARED_POOL.ABORTED_REQUEST_THRESHOLD(50000);
  3   END;
  4   /

PL/SQL procedure successfully completed.
```

ABORTED_REQUEST_THRESHOLD allows the DBA to control the negative impact of dynamically loading large objects into a fragmented or very active Oracle shared pool. Normally, these objects should be pinned into the shared pool using the KEEP procedure.

By setting the aborted request threshold, the DBA can avoid performance degradation for all users in cases of extreme pressure on shared pool resources. However, this may result in some users receiving the ORA-4031 error. In these cases, the DBA should determine the source of the ORA-4031 errors and pin the appropriate objects into the shared pool using KEEP.

DBMS_SHARED_POOL Examples

The DBMS_SHARED_POOL package is quite specialized and is intended for use by Oracle DBAs to help manage shared pool memory allocation problems. It would be unusual to see it used in applications, although a package-based application may try to pin itself into the shared pool using the KEEP procedure.

One problem with the SIZES procedure is that it uses DBMS_OUTPUT to display its results. It is used primarily interactively from the SQL*Plus, SQLDBA, or Server Manager utilities. This is unfortunate, because the natural way to use these results programmatically would be as input to the KEEP procedure. Ambitious DBAs might explore using the UTL_FILE package to pass results from SIZES to KEEP.

Pinning packages automatically

The best time to pin packages into the shared pool is immediately after the Oracle instance is first started and the database mounted. This is when shared pool memory is largely unallocated and has not become fragmented. It is a good DBA practice to call KEEP for any large packages as part of the database startup routine. Under UNIX, the Oracle-supplied script *dbstart* is often used to start databases. The DBA can customize this script to call KEEP and be sure the objects are pinned.

One thing about database startup and shutdown scripts is that once they are working, you really do not want to modify them unless absolutely necessary. However, the need to pin new packages into the shared pool can come up at any time, and different databases may need to pin different sets of objects. In order to minimize maintenance of database startup scripts, I decided to write a simple procedure called object_keeper, which uses a table of object names and pins all objects in the table when called. Each database's startup script can call object_keeper once to pin all objects, eliminating script maintenance to add or delete objects from the list. The table also allows each database to maintain a separate list of objects to pin.

The table that object_keeper uses is called keep_objects and is created as follows:

```
//* Filename on companion disk: keeper.sql */
CREATE TABLE keep_objects
    (
    obj_schema    VARCHAR2(30)  NOT NULL
```

```
     ,obj_name        VARCHAR2(30)   NOT NULL
     ,CONSTRAINT ko_PK PRIMARY KEY
                       (obj_schema, obj_name)
     )
TABLESPACE USER_DATA
STORAGE (INITIAL 2
        NEXT    2
        PCTINCREASE 0);
```

The object_keeper procedure opens a cursor that joins keep_objects to DBA_
OBJECTS and attempts to pin each of the objects in the cursor. Objects in keep_
objects not found in DBA_OBJECTS will not be in the cursor, and thus will not
attempt to be pinned. The call to DBMS_SHARED_POOL is contained in a
BEGIN...END sub-block to allow exception trapping and continuation to the next
object in the cursor.

```
//* Filename on companion disk: keeper.sql */
CREATE OR REPLACE PROCEDURE object_keeper
   /*
   || Procedure to pin objects into the shared pool
   || using DBMS_SHARED_POOL.KEEP procedure.  All
   || objects found in the keep_objects table will
   || be KEEPed.
   ||
   || For best results, procedure should be created
   || in the SYS schema.
   ||
   || Author:  John Beresniewicz, Savant Corp
   || Created: 09/18/97
   ||
   || Compilation Requirements:
   ||
   || SELECT on SYS.DBA_OBJECTS
   || EXECUTE on SYS.DBMS_SHARED_POOL
   ||
   || Execution Requirements:
   ||
   || Some SYS objects may get ORA-1031 unless
   || the procedure is run by SYS
   ||
   */
IS
   CURSOR keep_objects_cur
   IS
   SELECT  DO.owner||'.'||DO.object_name    object
          ,DECODE(DO.object_type
                  ,'PACKAGE','P'
                  ,'PROCEDURE','P'
                  ,'FUNCTION','P'
                  ,'TRIGGER','R'
                  ,null
                  )                         type
      FROM   keep_objects  KO
```

```
                     ,dba_objects    DO
          WHERE UPPER(KO.obj_schema) = DO.owner
            AND UPPER(KO.obj_name)   = DO.object_name
            AND DO.object_type IN
                    ('PACKAGE','PROCEDURE','FUNCTION','TRIGGER');
BEGIN
     FOR ko_rec IN keep_objects_cur
     LOOP
         BEGIN
             SYS.DBMS_SHARED_POOL.KEEP
                  (ko_rec.object, ko_rec.type);
             DBMS_OUTPUT.PUT_LINE
                  ('KEPT:  '||ko_rec.object);

         EXCEPTION
             WHEN OTHERS THEN
                 DBMS_OUTPUT.PUT_LINE(SQLERRM);
                 DBMS_OUTPUT.PUT_LINE
                     ('KEEP FAIL: '||ko_rec.object||' '||ko_rec.type);
         END;
     END LOOP;
END object_keeper;
```

The object_keeper procedure uses DBMS_OUTPUT to display the results of the
calls to KEEP. This is primarily for testing to make sure that all objects actually do
get pinned. Use the SET SERVEROUTPUT ON SIZE nnnnnn command to enable
the output display.

The following shows the results in SQL*Plus of inserting several rows into
keep_objects and executing the object_keeper procedure. This script is available on the disk in the *keeptst.sql* file.

```
SQL> INSERT INTO keep_objects
  2  VALUES ('SYS','STANDARD');

1 row created.

SQL> INSERT INTO keep_objects
  2  VALUES ('SYS','DBMS_STANDARD');

1 row created.

SQL> INSERT INTO keep_objects
  2  VALUES ('BOGUS','PACKAGE');

1 row created.

SQL> INSERT INTO keep_objects
  2  VALUES ('SYS','DIUTIL');

1 row created.

SQL> INSERT INTO keep_objects
```

```
  2  VALUES ('SYS','DBMS_SQL');

1 row created.

SQL> set serveroutput on size 100000
SQL> execute object_keeper;
KEEPED: SYS.DBMS_SQL
KEEPED: SYS.DBMS_STANDARD
KEEPED: SYS.DIUTIL
KEEPED: SYS.STANDARD

PL/SQL procedure successfully completed.
```

Pinning cursors into the shared pool

The DBMS_SHARED_POOL.KEEP procedure can be used to pin large cursors into the shared pool, as well as packages, procedures, and functions. In practice, it would be very unusual to need to do this. One reason might be in the case of a very large and complex view definition. Pinning the cursor associated with the view's SELECT statement into the shared pool may avoid memory management issues when users access the view.

In order to pin a cursor, the DBMS_SHARED_POOL.SIZES procedure is used to identify the cursor's address and hash value. These values are then passed as the name parameter in the call to DBMS_SHARED_POOL.KEEP. Note that because the cursor address is not identifiable until after the cursor is already in the shared pool, it is impossible to pre-pin a cursor object prior to its first reference by a user.

The following is output from a SQL*Plus session in which a cursor is identified using the SIZES procedure and is then pinned into the shared pool using KEEP:

```
SQL> execute dbms_shared_pool.sizes(50);

SIZE(K)     KEPT                                            NAME
------      -------------------------------------------     --------------
180         SYS.STANDARD                                    (PACKAGE)
78   YES    QDBA.Q$CVAR                                     (PACKAGE)
74   SELECT JOB   FROM SYS.DBA_JOBS_RUNNING  WHERE JOB = :b1
            (0F884588,518752523)                           (CURSOR)
71   YES    QDBA.Q$INSTAT                                   (PACKAGE BODY)
62   YES    QDBA.Q$BGPROC                                   (PACKAGE BODY)

PL/SQL procedure successfully completed.

SQL> execute dbms_shared_pool.keep('0F884588,518752523','C');

PL/SQL procedure successfully completed.

SQL> execute dbms_shared_pool.sizes(50);

SIZE(K) KEPT  NAME
```

```
SIZE(K)    KEPT                                                         NAME
------     ----------------------------------------                    --------------
180        SYS.STANDARD                                                 (PACKAGE)
78   YES   QDBA.Q$CVAR                                                  (PACKAGE)
74   YES(1) SELECT JOB FROM SYS.DBA_JOBS_RUNNING WHERE JOB = :b1
           (0F884588,518752523)                                        (CURSOR)
71   YES    QDBA.Q$INSTAT                                              (PACKAGEBODY)
62   YES   QDBA.Q$BGPROC                                               (PACKAGE BODY)
PL/SQL procedure successfully completed.
```

After the cursor is pinned, the second call to the SIZES procedure indicates this by showing "YES" in the KEPT output column. It is interesting (and somewhat confusing) that such a simple SELECT statement results in a cursor that uses 74K of shared pool memory.

The DBA_KEEPSIZES view

DBA_KEEPSIZES is a view that makes available the size PL/SQL objects will occupy in the shared pool when kept using the DBMS_SHARED_POOL.KEEP procedure. This view can be used by the DBA to plan for shared pool memory requirements of large PL/SQL objects. The actual view definition, contained in the *dbmspool.plb* file, follows:

```
CREATE OR REPLACE VIEW DBA_KEEPSIZES
    (totsize, owner, name)
AS
SELECT  TRUNC((SUM(parsed_size)+SUM(code_size))/1000)
        ,owner
        ,name
  FROM dba_object_size
 WHERE TYPE IN
        ('PACKAGE','PROCEDURE','FUNCTION','PACKAGE BODY','TRIGGER')
 GROUP BY owner, name;
```

The columns for DBA_KEEPSIZES are defined in the following table.

Column	Datatype	Description
TOTSIZE	NUMBER	Size in shared pool if object kept (via KEEP)
OWNER	VARCHAR2(30)	Schema of the stored PL/SQL object
NAME	VARCHAR2(30)	Name of the stored PL/SQL object

You can query DBA_KEEPSIZES to get an idea of which packages, procedures, and functions are relatively large, and thus may be good candidates for pinning into the shared pool.

13

In this chapter:
• Getting Started with
  DBMS_JOB
• Job Queue
  Architecture
• Tips on Using DBMS_
  JOB
• DBMS_JOB Examples

Job Scheduling in the Database

The DBMS_JOB package is actually an API into an Oracle subsystem known as the *job queue*. The Oracle job queue allows for the scheduling and execution of PL/SQL routines (jobs) at predefined times and/or repeated job execution at regular intervals. The DBMS_JOB package provides programs for submitting and executing jobs, changing job execution parameters, and removing or temporarily suspending job execution. This package is the only interface with the Oracle job queue.

DBMS_JOB is used to schedule many different types of tasks that can be performed in PL/SQL and that require regular execution. The job queue is used extensively by Oracle replication facilities, and was originally developed for the purpose of refreshing Oracle snapshots. DBMS_JOB is often used by DBAs to schedule regular maintenance activities on databases, typically during periods of low usage by end users. It can similarly be used by applications to schedule large batch operations during off hours. The job queue can also be used to start up service programs that listen on database pipes and respond to service requests by user sessions.

Getting Started with DBMS_JOB

The DBMS_JOB package is created when the Oracle database is installed. The *dbmsjob.sql* script (found in the built-in packages source code directory, as described in Chapter 1, *Introduction*) contains the source code for this package's specification. This script is called by *catproc.sql*, which is normally run immediately after database creation. The script creates the public synonym DBMS_JOB for the package and grants EXECUTE privilege on the package to public. All Oracle users can reference and make use of this package.

There are several data dictionary views that display information about the Oracle job queue. These are called DBA_JOBS, USER_JOBS, and DBA_JOBS_RUNNING, and are created by the script *catjobq.sql*. This script is also located in the built-in packages source code directory and is automatically run by *catproc.sql*.

Finally, the job queue must have its dedicated background processes started in order to operate properly. This is accomplished by setting an initialization parameter in the *INIT.ORA* file for the database. The parameter is,

```
JOB_QUEUE_PROCESSES = n
```

where n is a number between 1 and 36. Other INIT.ORA parameters that affect job queue behavior are discussed in the "Job Queue Architecture" section.

DBMS_JOB Programs

Table 13-1 lists the programs defined for the DBMS_JOB packages.

Table 13-1. DBMS_JOB Programs

Name	Description	Use in SQL?
BROKEN	Marks the job as broken; do not re-execute	No
CHANGE	Changes job parameters that can be set by user	No
CHECK_PRIVS	Unknown	No
INTERVAL	Changes execution interval for job	No
ISUBMIT	Submits a new job specifying job number	No
NEXT_DATE	Changes next execution date for job	No
REMOVE	Removes existing job from the queue	No
RUN	Runs the job immediately in current session	No
SUBMIT	Submits a new job obtaining new job number	No
USER_EXPORT	Creates text of call to recreate a job	No
WHAT	Changes PL/SQL executed for job	No

The DBMS_JOB package does not declare any package exceptions or nonprogram elements. In addition, none of the programs in this package asserts a purity level with the RESTRICT_REFERENCES pragma.

Job Definition Parameters

The programs in DBMS_JOB share a set of parameters that define jobs, their execution times, and frequency of execution. All of the DBMS_JOB procedures manipulate one or more of these parameters:

Parameter	Description
job	Unique identifier of the job
what	PL/SQL code to execute as a job
next_date	Next execution date of the job
interval	Date function to compute next execution date of job
broken	Flags job as broken and not to be executed

The following sections describe the characteristics of these parameters that apply to all of the procedures that contain them as formal parameters.

The job parameter

The job parameter is an integer that uniquely identifies the job. It can be either selected by the user or automatically assigned by the system, depending on which of the two job submission procedures is used to enter the job into the job queue. The DBMS_JOB.SUBMIT procedure automatically assigns the job number by obtaining the next value from the sequence SYS.JOBSEQ. It is returned as an OUT parameter so the caller can subsequently identify the job submitted. DBMS_JOB.ISUBMIT allows the user to assign a specific integer identifier to the job, and it is up to the caller to ensure that this number is unique.

Job numbers cannot be changed other than by removing and resubmitting the job. The job number is retained even when the database is exported and imported. Be aware of the potential for job number conflicts when performing export/import between databases that contain jobs.

The what parameter

The what parameter is a character string that evaluates to a valid PL/SQL call to be executed automatically by the job queue. You must enclose the what parameter in single quotes if you are using a string literal. Alternatively, you can use a VARCHAR2 variable containing the desired string value. The actual PL/SQL call must be terminated with a semicolon. To embed literal strings in the PL/SQL call, include two single quotes around the literal.

The length of the what parameter is limited to 2000 bytes under Oracle 7.3 and 4000 bytes under Oracle 8.0. These limits should be more than sufficient for all practical purposes. The value of the parameter is normally a call to a stored PL/SQL program. It is best to avoid using large anonymous PL/SQL blocks, although these are legal values. Another good tip is to always wrap stored procedure invocations in an anonymous block, as some subtle difficulties are possible otherwise. Thus, instead of,

```
what => 'my_proc(parm1);'
```

it is safer to use:

```
what => 'begin my_proc(parm1); end;'
```

Whenever the what parameter is modified to change the job to execute, the user's current session settings are recorded and become part of the job's execution environment. This could alter the expected execution behavior of the job if the session settings were different from those in place when the job was originally submitted. It is important to be aware of this potential side effect and be sure that session settings are correct whenever the what parameter is used in a DBMS_JOB procedure call. See the "Job Queue Architecture" section for more discussion of the job execution environment.

Jobs that reference database links will fail if the database link is not fully qualified with the username and password. This is another subtle consequence of the execution environment of jobs.

The job definition specified by the what parameter can also reference the following "special" job parameter values:

Parameter	Mode
job	IN
next_date	IN/OUT
broken	IN/OUT

When the job definition references these job parameters in its own parameter list, their values are assigned to the parameters in the job definition when the job executes. For example, suppose that a procedure called proc1 has the following specification:

```
PROCEDURE proc1 (my_job_number IN INTEGER);
```

Suppose also that we submit proc1 to be executed by the job queue as follows:

```
DECLARE
    jobno   INTEGER;
BEGIN
    DBMS_JOB.SUBMIT(jobno, 'proc1(my_job_number=>job);');
END;
/
```

When proc1 is executed by the queue, the my_job_number parameter is assigned the job's job number, and thus proc1 will "know" what job number it is.

The ability to reference and modify job parameters from within the job itself enables the creation of self-modifying and self-aware jobs. See the "DBMS_JOB Examples" section for an example of a job that demonstrates these powerful characteristics.

The next_date parameter

The next_date parameter tells the job queue when a job should be executed next. This parameter defaults to SYSDATE in both the DBMS_JOB.SUBMIT and BROKEN procedures, indicating that the job should be run immediately.

Whenever a NULL value is passed for the next_date parameter, the next execution date for the job is set to January 1, 4000. This effectively keeps the job from being executed without removing it from the job queue.

The next_date parameter can be set to a time in the past. Jobs are chosen for execution in order of their next execution dates, so setting a job's next_date back can effectively move the job ahead in the queue. This can be useful in systems where the job queue processes are not keeping up with jobs to be executed, and a specific job needs to be executed as soon as possible.

The interval parameter

The interval parameter is a character string representing a valid Oracle date expression. This date expression is evaluated each time the job begins execution. When a job completes successfully, this date becomes the next execution date for the job. It is important to remember that interval evaluation and updating the job's next execution date happen at different times. For instance, a job that takes one hour to complete and has interval set to SYSDATE+1/48 (every 30 minutes) will constantly execute, because each time it completes, it will already be 30 minutes late to execute again.

The interval expression must evaluate to either a NULL value or a time in the future. When interval evaluates to a NULL value, the job will not be re-executed after the next execution and will be automatically removed from the job queue. Thus, to execute a job one time only, pass a NULL value for the interval parameter.

Jobs may have complex execution schedules, requiring complex date arithmetic expressions for the interval parameter. The interval parameter can contain a call to a PL/SQL function with a return datatype of DATE, suggesting a nice way to encapsulate complex execution schedules within simple interval parameter values. However, experimentation with using function calls for interval resulted in erratic job execution behavior. Thus, unfortunately, a useful alternative to embedding complex date arithmetic into the interval parameter does not appear to be currently available.

The broken parameter

The broken parameter is a BOOLEAN flag used to indicate that the job is to be marked as broken (TRUE) or unbroken (FALSE). The job queue processes will not attempt to execute jobs marked as broken.

Job Queue Architecture

The job queue is really a subsystem within an Oracle database, which uses dedicated background processes and catalog tables to execute user PL/SQL procedures automatically without user intervention. It is useful to get a good conceptual understanding of the job queue, because some of the behavior of this queue is not obvious. Figure 13-1 shows a schematic of the job queue architecture.

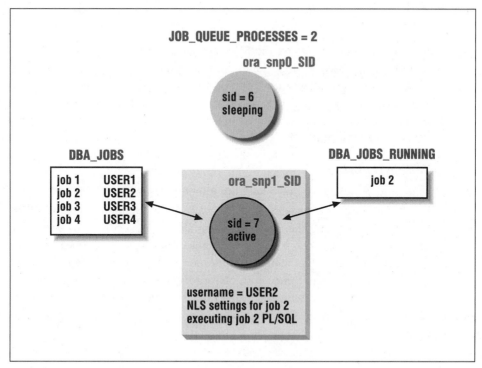

Figure 13-1. Schematic of job queue architecture

INIT.ORA Parameters and Background Processes

These three *INIT.ORA* parameters are instrumental in controlling the job queue:

    JOB_QUEUE_PROCESSES
    JOB_QUEUE_INTERVAL
    JOB_QUEUE_KEEP_CONNECTIONS

JOB_QUEUE_PROCESSES

The job queue (or SNP*) background processes are started when the Oracle instance is started. There are as many SNP processes started as specified in the *INIT.ORA* parameter JOB_QUEUE_PROCESSES. The range of valid values is from 0 to 36, so there can be a maximum of 36 SNP processes per Oracle instance. Under most operating systems, the characters SNP will appear as part of the process name. For example, under UNIX, an Oracle instance called DEV with three job queue processes would show the following process names:

    ora_DEV_snp0
    ora_DEV_snp1
    ora_DEV_snp2

One significant difference between the SNP background processes and other Oracle background processes is that killing an SNP process will not crash the instance. While you're not likely to want to do this very often, this behavior is useful to know in case a job queue process "runs away" and consumes excessive resources. When an SNP process is killed or fails on its own, Oracle automatically starts a new one to replace it.

JOB_QUEUE_INTERVAL

The job queue processes "wake up" periodically and check the job queue catalog to see if any jobs are due to execute. The *INIT.ORA* parameter JOB_QUEUE_INTERVAL controls how long the SNP processes "sleep" (in seconds) between catalog checks. Setting the interval too low can cause unnecessary overhead as SNP processes constantly check the catalog. Setting the interval too high can keep jobs from executing at the expected time if an SNP process does not awaken promptly enough. The proper balance will depend on the specific mix of jobs in a given environment. For most purposes, the default setting of 60 seconds is adequate.

---

* The SNP acronym results from the fact that these special background processes were originally developed to refresh Oracle snapshots.

JOB_QUEUE_KEEP_CONNECTIONS

The third *INIT.ORA* parameter that affects the behavior of the SNP processes is JOB_QUEUE_KEEP_CONNECTIONS. When this parameter is TRUE, the SNP processes will retain open connections to Oracle between job executions during their sleep periods. When FALSE, the SNP processes will disconnect from the database and reconnect when it is time to awaken and check the queue. The primary tradeoff is between job queue efficiency and database shutdown methods. Keeping connections open is more efficient, but can interfere with doing a normal shutdown of the database. This is because the job queue processes appear as user processes to Server Manager and a normal shutdown requires all users to be disconnected. Disconnecting and reconnecting the SNP processes involves significant overhead, yet you should periodically leave the database with no connected SNP processes, permitting a normal shutdown to proceed.

Environments with many jobs or relatively short execution intervals (one hour or less) will probably want to set JOB_QUEUE_KEEP_CONNECTIONS to TRUE and modify the shutdown script to do an immediate shutdown. Environments with strict requirements to do a normal shutdown and relatively few jobs with long intervals can set the value to FALSE. Of course, if immediate shutdowns are already being done, the value should be set to TRUE. Also keep in mind that the SNP processes will only disconnect when not executing a job, so long-running jobs will keep open connections for their duration and may delay normal shutdowns.

Job Execution and the Job Execution Environment

When an SNP process wakes up, it looks in the catalog to see if the current date exceeds the next execution date for any jobs in the queue. If a job is due to execute, the SNP process will dynamically do the following:

- Become a database session with the username of the job's owner
- Alter session NLS (National Language Support) settings to match those in place when the job was submitted or last modified
- Calculate the next execution date by applying the interval date expression to SYSDATE
- Execute the PL/SQL job definition
- If execution succeeds, upate next_date for the job with the previously calculated next execution date; otherwise, increment the number of failures
- Repeat if another job is due to run or sleep for JOB_QUEUE_INTERVAL seconds

In the first two steps, the SNP process creates a job execution environment that mimics that of a real user session that is executing the job definition's PL/SQL. This includes setting the following NLS settings:

NLS_LANGUAGE
NLS_TERRITORY
NLS_CURRENCY
NLS_ISO_CURRENCY
NLS_NUMERIC_CHARACTERS
NLS_DATE_FORMAT
NLS_DATE_LANGUAGE
NLS_SORT

In Trusted Oracle databases, the session also sets the session label and high/low clearances.

The execution environment does not exactly mimic a user session, and this has some consequences worth noting. First, any nondefault roles that were enabled when the job was submitted will not be enabled in the job execution environment. Therefore, jobs that rely on privileges obtained through nondefault roles should not be submitted, and modification of user default roles can compromise the future execution of existing jobs. Also, any database links used in the job definition itself, or the procedures executed by it, must be fully qualified with a remote username and password. The SNP process is not able to initiate a remote session without an explicit password. Apparently, it does not assume the local user's password as part of the execution environment session settings.

When job execution fails, the SNP processes attempts to rerun the job one minute later. If this run fails, another attempt is made in two minutes and another in four minutes. The job queue doubles the retry interval until it exceeds the normal execution interval, which is then used. After 16 consecutive failures, the job is flagged as broken and will not be re-executed by the job queue without user intervention.

Miscellaneous Notes

The Oracle export and import utilities preserve job numbers. Therefore, when you are importing into a database with jobs in the job queue, job number conflicts are possible. The same consideration applies when using DBMS_JOB.USER_EXPORT to transfer jobs from one database to another.

The job queue is not designed to function well under Oracle Parallel Server configurations. In particular, here are two significant limitations:

- Jobs cannot be specified to run in a specific Oracle instance.

- The SYS.JOB$ catalog table is not partitioned by instance and will be subject to "pinging" by job queue processes from different instances.

The workaround to these problems is to only run the job queue in a single instance of an OPS environment. This is done by setting JOB_QUEUE_PROCESSES to zero in all but one of the Oracle instances.

DBMS_JOB Interface

This section describes the programs available in the DBMS_JOB package.

Submitting Jobs to the Job Queue

Use the SUBMIT and ISUBMIT procedures to submit jobs to the job queue.

The DBMS_JOB.SUBMIT procedure

The SUBMIT procedure submits a new job to the job queue. The job number is obtained from the sequence SYS.JOBSEQ and returned as an OUT parameter. Here's the header for this program:

```
PROCEDURE DBMS_JOB.SUBMIT
    (job OUT BINARY_INTEGER
    ,what IN VARCHAR2
    ,next_date IN DATE DEFAULT SYSDATE
    ,interval IN VARCHAR2 DEFAULT 'null'
    ,no_parse IN BOOLEAN DEFAULT FALSE);
```

Parameters are summarized in the following table.

Parameter	Description
job	Unique identifier of the job
what	PL/SQL code to execute as a job
next_date	Next execution date of the job
interval	Date expression to compute next execution date of job
no_parse	Flag indicating whether to parse job PL/SQL at time of submission (FALSE) or execution (TRUE)

Exceptions. The program does not raise any package exceptions. The interval date expression must evaluate to a future date or the following Oracle exception will be raised:

ORA-23420
   Interval must evaluate to a time in the future.

Example. This SQL*Plus script submits a job that uses DBMS_DDL.ANALYZE_OBJECT to analyze a particular table every day at midnight:

```
var jobno NUMBER

BEGIN
   DBMS_JOB.SUBMIT
      (job => :jobno
      ,what => 'DBMS_DDL.ANALYZE_OBJECT(''TABLE'',''LOAD1'',''TENK'',
                  ''ESTIMATE'',null,estimate_percent=>50);'
      ,next_date => TRUNC(SYSDATE+1)
      ,interval => 'TRUNC(SYSDATE+1)'
      );
END;
/
print jobno
```

The what parameter must be enclosed in single quotes and the PL/SQL call terminated with a semicolon. To embed literal strings in the PL/SQL call, use two single quotes around the literal.

The no_parse parameter controls when the job's PL/SQL definition is actually parsed. The default value of FALSE specifies that the PL/SQL is parsed immediately when the job is submitted. Alternatively, if you specify TRUE, parsing can be deferred until the first execution of the job. This allows jobs to be submitted into the queue for future execution where objects necessary for execution (tables, packages, etc.) are not in place at the time of submission.

TIP   On some platforms and versions of Oracle, a COMMIT is required
               for the job to be picked up by the job queue for execution. If sub-
               mitted jobs do not seem to be executing at all, this may be the
               cause. The workaround for this problem is to always COMMIT
               immediately after calling SUBMIT.

               To execute a job one time only, pass a NULL value for the interval
               parameter.

The DBMS_JOB.ISUBMIT procedure

The ISUBMIT procedure submits a new job to the job queue with the specified job number. Here's the header for this program:

```
PROCEDURE DBMS_JOB.ISUBMIT
   (job IN BINARY_INTEGER
   ,what IN VARCHAR2
   ,next_date IN VARCHAR2
   ,interval IN VARCHAR2 DEFAULT 'null'
   ,no_parse IN BOOLEAN DEFAULT FALSE);
```

Parameters are summarized in the following table.

Parameter	Description
job	Unique identifier of the job
what	PL/SQL code to execute as a job
next_date	Next execution date of the job
interval	Date expression to compute next execution date of job
no_parse	Flag indicating whether to parse job PL/SQL at time of submission (FALSE) or execution (TRUE)

Exceptions. The program does not raise any packaged exceptions. The interval date expression must evaluate to a future date or the following Oracle exception will be raised:

ORA-23420

Interval must evaluate to a time in the future.

The catalog table that records job queue entries is protected by a unique constraint on the job number. Therefore, using the ISUBMIT procedure to submit a job number that already exists results in the following error:

ORA-00001

Unique constraint (SYS.I_JOB_JOB) violated.

Example. The following example submits three jobs to the job queue, numbered 1, 2, and 3. Job 1 passes a string and number into procedure my_job1, runs it in one hour, and executes it every day thereafter. Job 2 passes a date into procedure my_job2, executes for the first time tomorrow, and execute it every 10 minutes thereafter. Job 3 is a PL/SQL block that does nothing, executes immediately, and will be removed from the queue automatically.

```
BEGIN
    DBMS_JOB.ISUBMIT
        (job  => 1
        ,what => 'my_job1(''string_parm_value'',120);'
        ,next_date => SYSDATE + 1/24
        ,interval => 'SYSDATE +1');

    DBMS_JOB.ISUBMIT
        (2, 'my_job2(date_IN=>SYSDATE);'
          ,SYSDATE+1,'SYSDATE+10/1440');

    DBMS_JOB.ISUBMIT(3,'BEGIN null; END;',SYSDATE,null);
END;
```

The ISUBMIT procedure allows the calling user or application to decide the job identification number. Collisions in job numbers will result in the unique constraint violation noted earlier. Therefore, it is probably better not to embed fixed job numbers into applications (as this will increase the chances for collisions) and to use SUBMIT instead of ISUBMIT. If specific job numbering is required, then you can minimize job number collisions by pushing the SYS.JOBSEQ sequence out to a number greater than those used in calls to ISUBMIT. This can be accomplished by consuming sequence numbers as follows:

```
SELECT SYS.JOBSEQ.NEXTVAL
   FROM dictionary
   WHERE rownum < 101;
```

After issuing the previous command, DBMS_JOB.SUBMIT will always return job numbers higher than 100. Note that in this command, the dictionary view is not special, but is used because it is publicly accessible and contains more than 100 rows. You can substitute any table or view accessible to the user.

WARNING   A potential problem with the ISUBMIT procedure arises from the fact that the next_date parameter has datatype VARCHAR2 instead of DATE (which SUBMIT has). At least one user has reported problems with unexpected job execution dates that seemed related to this; however, I have not been able to duplicate the problem. It is curious, and somewhat suspect, that next_date would have different datatypes between the SUBMIT and ISUBMIT procedures.

Modifying Job Characteristics

This section describes the procedures you use to modify job characteristics: CHANGE, INTERVAL, NEXT_DATE, and WHAT.

The DBMS_JOB.CHANGE procedure

The CHANGE procedure alters one or more of the user-definable parameters of a job. When a null value is passed for any of these parameters (what, next_date, or interval) the current setting is not modified. Here's the header for this program:

```
PROCEDURE DBMS_JOB.CHANGE
      (job IN BINARY_INTEGER
      ,what IN VARCHAR2
      ,next_date IN DATE
      ,interval IN VARCHAR2);
```

Parameters are summarized in the following table.

Parameter	Description
job	Unique identifier of the job
what	PL/SQL code to execute as a job
next_date	Next execution date of the job
interval	Date expression to compute next execution date of job

Exceptions. The program does not raise any packaged exceptions. The interval date function must evaluate to a future date or the following Oracle exception will be raised:

ORA-23420

   Interval must evaluate to a time in the future.

Restrictions. The CHANGE procedure can be executed only for jobs owned by the username to which the session is connected. These jobs are visible in the dictionary view USER_JOBS. The USER_JOBS dictionary view is discussed in the "Tips on Using DBMS_JOB" section.

Example. The execution schedule of job 100 can be changed to next execute tomorrow at 6:00 a.m. and every two hours after that, as follows:

```
BEGIN
   DBMS_JOB.CHANGE(100,null,TRUNC(SYSDATE+1)+6/24,'SYSDATE+2/24');
END;
/
```

When the what parameter is changed to modify the actual job to execute, the user's current session NLS settings are also recorded and become part of the job's execution environment.

The DBMS_JOB.INTERVAL procedure

The INTERVAL procedure changes the date expression, which is used to determine the next execution date of a job. Here's the header for this program:

```
PROCEDURE DBMS_JOB.INTERVAL
   (job IN BINARY_INTEGER
   ,interval IN VARCHAR2);
```

Parameters are summarized in the following table.

Parameter	Description
job	Unique identifier of the job
interval	Date expression to compute next execution date of job

Exceptions. The program does not raise any package exceptions. The interval date expression must evaluate to a future date or the following Oracle exception will be raised:

ORA-23420

   Interval must evaluate to a time in the future.

Restrictions. The INTERVAL procedure can be executed only for jobs owned by
the username to which the session is connected. These jobs are visible in the dictionary view USER_JOBS. The USER_JOBS dictionary view is discussed in the
"Tips on Using DBMS_JOB" section.

Example. The following SQL*Plus command will modify job 100 to execute every
day at 6:00 a.m.:

```
SQL> execute DBMS_JOB.INTERVAL(100, 'TRUNC(SYSDATE+1)+6/24');
```

The date expression must be specified as a string literal or a VARCHAR2 variable
containing a string literal. Literals that evaluate to PL/SQL functions are accepted
by DBMS_JOB, but have been observed to cause erratic job execution behavior.

A job can be removed automatically from the job queue after its next execution
by passing NULL for the interval parameter.

The DBMS_JOB.NEXT_DATE procedure

The NEXT_DATE procedure changes the job's next scheduled date of execution.
Here's the header for this program:

```
PROCEDURE DBMS_JOB.NEXT_DATE
    (job IN BINARY_INTEGER
    ,next_date IN DATE);
```

Parameters are summarized in the following table.

Parameter	Description
job	Unique identifier of the job
next_date	Next execution date of the job

The program does not raise any named exceptions.

Restrictions. The NEXT_DATE procedure can be executed only for jobs owned by
the username to which the session is connected. These jobs are visible in the dictionary view USER_JOBS. The USER_JOBS dictionary view is discussed in the
"Tips on Using DBMS_JOB" section.

Example. This example shows a SQL*Plus example of how to schedule the next
execution of job 100 for next Monday:

```
SQL> execute DBMS_JOB.NEXT_DATE(100, NEXT_DAY(SYSDATE,'MONDAY'));
```

When a NULL value is passed for the next_date parameter, the next execution
date for the job is set to January 1, 4000. This effectively keeps the job from being
executed without removing it from the job queue.

The DBMS_JOB.WHAT procedure

The WHAT procedure changes the PL/SQL call that comprises the job's PL/SQL definition. Here's the header for this program:

```
PROCEDURE DBMS_JOB.WHAT
    (job IN BINARY_INTEGER
    ,what IN VARCHAR2);
```

Parameters are summarized in the following table.

Parameter	Description
job	Unique identifier of the job
what	PL/SQL code to execute as a job

Restrictions. The WHAT procedure can be executed only for jobs owned by the username to which the session is connected. These jobs are visible in the dictionary view USER_JOBS. The USER_JOBS dictionary view is discussed in the "Tips on Using DBMS_JOB" section.

Example. In this example, job 100 is modified to execute a procedure called my_package.proc1. When the job is run by the job queue, it will run in a session that has NLS_DATE_FORMAT set as in the ALTER SESSION command.

```
SQL> ALTER SESSION SET NLS_DATE_FORMAT='YYYY:MM:DD:HH24:MI:SS';

SQL> execute dbms_job.what(100,'my_package.proc1;');
```

When the what parameter is changed to modify the actual job to execute, the user's current session NLS settings are also recorded and become part of the job's execution environment.

The what parameter must be enclosed in single quotes and the PL/SQL call must be terminated with a semicolon. To embed literal strings in the PL/SQL call, use two single quotes around the literal.

Removing Jobs and Changing Job Execution Status

The REMOVE, BROKEN, and RUN procedures let you remove jobs from the job queue and change the execution status of jobs.

The DBMS_JOB.REMOVE procedure

The REMOVE procedure removes an existing job from the job queue. If the job is currently executing, it will run to normal completion, but will not be rescheduled. The header for this procedure is,

```
PROCEDURE DBMS_JOB.REMOVE
    (job IN BINARY_INTEGER);
```

where job is the unique identifier of the job. This program does not raise any package exceptions.

Restrictions. The REMOVE procedure can be executed only for jobs owned by the username to which the session is connected. These jobs are visible in the dictionary view USER_JOBS. The USER_JOBS dictionary view is discussed in the "Tips on Using DBMS_JOB" section.

Example. To remove job number 100 from the job queue in SQL*Plus, specify the following:

```
SQL> execute DBMS_JOB.REMOVE(100);
```

When REMOVE is executed for a job that is currently executing, the job is removed from the job queue, but the current execution is allowed to complete. Terminating a running job and removing it from the job queue is described in the "Tips on Using DBMS_JOB" section later in this chapter.

The DBMS_JOB.BROKEN procedure

The BROKEN procedure is used to set or unset the broken flag for a job. Jobs flagged as broken are not automatically re-executed. Here's the header for this program:

```
PROCEDURE DBMS_JOB.BROKEN
    (job IN BINARY_INTEGER
    ,broken IN BOOLEAN
    ,next_date IN DATE DEFAULT SYSDATE);
```

Parameters are summarized in the following table.

Parameter	Description
job	Unique identifier of the job
broken	Flag indicating job is broken (TRUE) or not broken (FALSE)
next_date	Next execution date of the job

The program does not raise any package exceptions.

Restrictions. The BROKEN procedure can be executed only for jobs owned by the username to which the session is connected. These jobs are visible in the dictionary view USER_JOBS. The USER_JOBS dictionary view is discussed in the "Tips on Using DBMS_JOB" section.

Example. All jobs owned by the current user are set to broken by this PL/SQL block:

```
BEGIN
    FOR job_rec IN (SELECT job FROM user_jobs)
```

```
      LOOP
         DBMS_JOB.BROKEN(job_rec.job,TRUE);
      END LOOP;
   END;
   /
```

Jobs are marked as broken by passing TRUE for the broken parameter. In this case, the next execution for the job date is automatically set to January 1, 4000, regardless of the value of the next_date parameter passed. Although it looks strange, this is not a problem and is merely another safeguard preventing the job queue processes from executing broken jobs.

When marking jobs as not broken by passing the value FALSE for the broken parameter, the value of next_date becomes the next execution date for the job. Since next_date has a default value of SYSDATE, marking a job as unbroken without specifying next_date explicitly indicates that the job should execute immediately. Be careful to pass an explicit value for next_date if immediate execution is not the desired behavior. Note also that DBMS_JOB.BROKEN (job,FALSE) will always modify the next execution date of the job, regardless of whether it was marked broken.

The DBMS_JOB.RUN procedure

The RUN procedure immediately executes the job in the current session. The header for this program follows:

```
PROCEDURE DBMS_JOB.RUN
   (job IN BINARY_INTEGER);
```

The job parameter is the unique identifier for the job. The program does not raise any package exceptions.

Restrictions. The RUN procedure can be executed only for jobs owned by the username to which the session is connected. These jobs are visible in the dictionary view USER_JOBS. The USER_JOBS dictionary view is discussed in the "Tips on Using DBMS_JOB" section.

Example. To run job number 100 immediately in the current session, specify the following:

```
SQL> execute DBMS_JOB.RUN(100);
```

The RUN procedure performs an implicit COMMIT in the current session. It runs the job with the current session's settings and privileges as the execution environment. Be aware that these could be different from the execution environment settings specified for the job and used by the job queue when it runs the job. This could cause unexpected results, so it is best to execute RUN from a session with the same environment as the job.

Also, issuing the RUN procedure computes the next execution date for the job using the current SYSDATE as the seed value. This could throw off the execution schedule of some jobs, depending on how the interval is defined. See "Tips on Using DBMS_JOB" for a discussion of job intervals and date arithmetic.

Transferring Jobs

The USER_EXPORT procedure lets you export jobs in the job queue to a file for re-creation or transfer to another database.

The DBMS_JOB.USER_EXPORT procedure

The USER_EXPORT procedure produces a character string that can be used to re-create an existing job in the job queue. The string contains a call to the ISUBMIT procedure for the job, which specifies the current values for the job definition parameters. Here's the header for the program:

```
PROCEDURE DBMS_JOB.USER_EXPORT
    (job IN BINARY_INTEGER
    ,mycall IN OUT VARCHAR2);
```

Parameters are summarized in the following table.

Parameter	Description
job	Unique identifier of the job
mycall	String containing call to the ISUBMIT procedure to re-create job

The program does not raise any package exceptions.

Example. This SQL*Plus script shows that current settings for the job definition parameters are placed into the mycall parameter of USER_EXPORT:

```
/* Filename on companion disk: job1.sql */
set array 1
var job number
var jobstring VARCHAR2(2000)
col jobstring format a50 word_wrap
col what format a25 word_wrap
col interval format a20

ALTER SESSION SET NLS_DATE_FORMAT='YYYY:MM:DD:HH24:MI:SS';

BEGIN
    /* submit no-op job to execute every 30 seconds */
    DBMS_JOB.SUBMIT(:job,'begin null;end;',SYSDATE,'SYSDATE+1/2880');

    /* commit to make sure the submit "takes" */
    COMMIT;
    /* sleep for two minutes to let job execute a few times */
```

```
        DBMS_LOCK.SLEEP(120);
END;
/

SELECT job,what,next_date,interval
  FROM dba_jobs
 WHERE job = :job;

BEGIN
   /* export the job */
   DBMS_JOB.USER_EXPORT(:job,:jobstring);
END;
/

print jobstring
```

The following output was generated by the script. Notice that the current value of NEXT_DATE (as shown by querying DBA_JOBS) is extracted and placed into the string value returned in the mycall parameter as the value for next_date in the call to ISUBMIT.

```
Session altered.


PL/SQL procedure successfully completed.


   JOB WHAT                         NEXT_DATE           INTERVAL
------ ---------------------------- ------------------- --------------
   175 begin null;end;              1997:11:16:16:22:59 SYSDATE+1/2880


PL/SQL procedure successfully completed.


JOBSTRING
--------------------------------------------------
dbms_job.isubmit(job=>175,what=>'begin
null;end;',next_date=>to_date('1997-11-16:16:22:59
','YYYY-MM-DD:HH24:MI:SS'),interval=>'SYSDATE+1/28
80',no_parse=>TRUE);
```

Tips on Using DBMS_JOB

This section discusses several useful tips for using DBMS_JOB.

Job Intervals and Date Arithmetic

Job execution intervals are determined by the date expression set by the interval parameter. Getting jobs to run at the desired times can be one of the more confusing aspects of using DBMS_JOB and the job queue. One key to setting the interval correctly is determining which of the following applies to the job:

- Each execution of the job should follow the last by a specific time interval.

- The job should execute on specific dates and times.

Jobs of type 1 usually have relatively simple date arithmetic expressions of the type SYSDATE+N, where N represents the time interval expressed in days. The following table provides examples of these types of intervals.

Action	Interval Value
Execute daily	'SYSDATE + 1'
Execute hourly	'SYSDATE + 1/24'
Execute every 10 minutes	'SYSDATE + 10/1440'
Execute every 30 seconds	'SYSDATE + 30/86400'
Execute every 7 days	'SYSDATE + 7'
Do not re-execute and remove job	NULL

Remember that job intervals expressed as shown in the previous table do not guarantee that the next execution will happen at a specific day or time, only that the spacing between executions will be at least that specified. For instance, if a job is first executed at 12:00 p.m. with an interval of SYSDATE + 1, it will be scheduled to execute the next day at 12:00 p.m. However, if a user executes the job manually at 4:00 p.m. using DBMS_JOB.RUN, then it will be rescheduled for execution at 4:00 p.m. the next day. Another possibility is that the database is down or the job queue so busy that the job cannot be executed exactly at the time scheduled. In this case, the job will run as soon as it can, but the execution time will have migrated away from the original submission time due to the later execution. This "drift" in next execution times is characteristic of jobs with simple interval expressions.

Jobs with type 2 execution requirements involve more complex interval date expressions, as seen in the following table.

Action	Interval Value
Every day at 12:00 midnight	TRUNC(SYSDATE + 1)
Every day at 8:00 p.m.	TRUNC(SYSDATE + 1) + 8/24
Every Tuesday at 12:00 noon	NEXT_DAY(TRUNC(SYSDATE), "TUESDAY") + 12/24

Action	Interval Value
First day of the month at midnight	TRUNC(LAST_DAY(SYSDATE) + 1)
Last day of the quarter at 11:00 p.m.	TRUNC(ADD_MONTHS(SYSDATE + 2/24, 3), 'Q') - 1/24
Every Monday, Wednesday, and Friday at 9:00 a.m.	TRUNC(LEAST(NEXT_DAY(SYSDATE, "MONDAY"), NEXT_DAY(SYSDATE, "WEDNESDAY"), NEXT_DAY(SYSDATE, "FRIDAY"))) + 9/24

Specifying intervals like these can get tricky, so be sure that your date arithmetic expression is correct.

I had hoped that another option for evaluating complex job execution intervals would be to write PL/SQL functions with DATE return values that perform the interval calculations. However, my experiments in this area showed that job intervals that call date functions can be successfully submitted to the job queue but may not be properly executed. The SNP processes appeared to have difficulty properly updating the catalog, and jobs became locked in an endless cycle of execution. Perhaps this limitation will be corrected in future releases.

Viewing Job Information in the Data Dictionary

Information about jobs in the job queue is available through several data dictionary views (see Table 13-2) created by the *catproc.sql* script.

Table 13-2. Data Dictionary Views for DBMS_JOB

View Name	Description
DBA_JOBS	All jobs defined to the job queue in this database
DBA_JOBS_RUNNING	All jobs in the database which are currently executing
USER_JOBS	Jobs in the database owned by the current user

Table 13-3 summarizes the various columns in the DBA_JOBS and USER_JOBS views.

Table 13-3. Columns in DBA_JOBS and USER_JOBS Views

Column	Datatype	Description
JOB	NUMBER	Unique identifier of the job
LOG_USER	VARCHAR2(30)	User who submitted the job
PRIV_USER	VARCHAR2(30)	User whose privileges apply to the job
SCHEMA_USER	VARCHAR2(30)	User schema to parse the job under
LAST_DATE	DATE	Last successful execution date

Table 13-3. Columns in DBA_JOBS and USER_JOBS Views (continued)

Column	Datatype	Description
LAST_SEC	VARCHAR2(8)	Hour, minute, and second portion of last_date formatted as HH24:MI:SS
THIS_DATE	DATE	Date current execution began, or NULL if not executing
THIS_SEC	VARCHAR2(8)	Hour, minute, and second portion of this_date formatted as HH24:MI:SS
NEXT_DATE	DATE	Date of next scheduled execution
NEXT_SEC	VARCHAR2(8)	Hour, minute, and second portion of next_date formatted as HH24:MI:SS
TOTAL_TIME	NUMBER	Total elapsed time in seconds for all executions of this job
BROKEN	VARCHAR2(1)	Flag value Y indicates job broken, will not run
INTERVAL	VARCHAR2(200)	Date function used to compute next_date
FAILURES	NUMBER	Number of consecutive unsuccessful executions
WHAT	VARCHAR2(2000)	PL/SQL block executed as the job
CURRENT_SESSION_LABEL	RAW MLSLABEL	Trusted Oracle session label for the job
CLEARANCE_HI	RAW MLSLABEL	Trusted Oracle high clearance for the job
CLEARANCE_LO	RAW MLSLABEL	Trusted Oracle low clearance for the job
NLS_ENV	VARCHAR2(2000)	NLS session settings for job execution
MISC_ENV	RAW(32)	Other session parameters for job execution

Table 13-4 shows the columns in the DBA_JOBS_RUNNING view.

Table 13-4. Columns in DBA_JOBS_RUNNING View

Column	Datatype	Description
SID	NUMBER	Session ID currently executing the job
JOB	NUMBER	Unique identifier of the job
FAILURES	NUMBER	Number of consecutive unsuccessful executions
LAST_DATE	DATE	Last successful execution date
LAST_SEC	VARCHAR2(8)	Hour, minute, and second portion of last_date formatted as HH24:MI:SS

Table 13-4. Columns in DBA_JOBS_RUNNING View (continued)

Column	Datatype	Description
THIS_DATE	DATE	Date current execution began
THIS_SEC	VARCHAR2(8)	Hour, minute, and second portion of this_date formatted as HH24:MI:SS

The number and size of the columns in DBA_JOBS and USER_JOBS can make them awkward to query interactively. Several examples of useful scripts to run against the job queue dictionary views follow. One thing I usually do is to set my session NLS_DATE_FORMAT to display the full date and time; in this way, I avoid selecting the date and time portions separately. Note that the date columns in these views contain full date values down to the second; the formatted timestamp columns (LAST_SEC, THIS_SEC, NEXT_SEC) are actually derived from them in the views.

This script shows which jobs are currently executing, who owns them, and when they began:

```
/* Filename on companion disk: job2.sql */
col job_definition format a30 word_wrap
col username format a15

ALTER SESSION SET NLS_DATE_FORMAT='YYYY:MM:DD:HH24:MI:SS';

SELECT  jr.job        job_id
        ,username      username
        ,jr.this_date  start_date
        ,what          job_definition
  FROM
        dba_jobs_running  jr
        ,dba_jobs         j
        ,v$session        s
  WHERE
        s.sid = jr.sid
  AND   jr.job = j.job
ORDER BY jr.this_date;
```

The following script shows failing or broken jobs (i.e., jobs that may need attention):

```
/* Filename on companion disk: job2.sql */
col job_owner format a15
col job_definition format a30 word_wrap

SELECT  job
        ,log_user      job_owner
        ,failures
        ,broken
        ,what          job_definition
  FROM
```

```
        dba_jobs
WHERE
        broken = 'Y' OR NVL(failures,0) > 0 ;
```

The next script shows jobs queued up to be executed in order of next execution date. Jobs with negative values in the mins_to_exec column indicate that the job queue is not keeping up with its workload and may need extra job queue processes initiated. The script excludes currently executing jobs because next_date will not be updated until the current execution completes.

```
/* Filename on companion disk: job2.sql */
col job_definition format a30 word_wrap
col username format a15

ALTER SESSION SET NLS_DATE_FORMAT='YYYY:MM:DD:HH24:MI:SS';

SELECT   job
        ,username
        ,next_date
        ,ROUND((next_date - SYSDATE)*24*60)  mins_to_exec
        ,what                      job_definition
   FROM
        dba_jobs
WHERE
        broken != 'Y'
  AND job NOT IN
         (SELECT job
            FROM dba_jobs_running)
  ORDER BY next_date ASC;
```

Here is sample output from the preceding script on a system that has a very busy job queue. Job number 10 will be run next but is already 21 minutes late for execution.

```
  JOB NEXT_DATE           MINS_TO_EXEC JOB_DEFINITION
----- ------------------- ------------ ----------------------------
   10 1997:11:25:17:04:10          -21 load3.loadx.loop_and_execute(5
                                        ,30,'begin
                                        loadx.table_scanner(5,5);end;'
                                        );

    5 1997:11:25:17:25:21            0 load3.loadx.loop_and_execute(1
                                        0,90,'begin
                                        loadx.cpu_hog(20,20,20);end;')
                                        ;

   12 1997:11:25:17:29:08            4 load2.loadx.loop_and_execute(2
                                        0,60,'begin
                                        loadx.grow_table(''LOAD2'',''T
                                        ABLE2'',500,500);end;');
```

DBMS_IJOB: Managing Other Users' Jobs

One of the most frustrating aspects of the DBMS_JOB package for DBAs is that its procedures can be executed only against jobs owned by the current user. Even the SYS user cannot remove or set the broken flag for other user's jobs. Thus, job queue environments with multiple job owners can become problematic to administer using the DBMS_JOB package. On the other hand, requiring all jobs to be submitted under a single schema can introduce significant administrative overhead and complexity.

Fortunately, there is a way out of this dilemma. While it is not widely documented (until now), there is a hidden package interface into the job queue, which allows administrators to manipulate jobs that are not their own. This package is called DBMS_IJOB and it is created entirely in the *prvtjob.plb* script. DBMS_IJOB allows properly authorized users to manipulate any job in the job queue.

The following procedure uses DBMS_IJOB.BROKEN to set or unset the broken flag for all jobs in the job queue:

```
/* Filename on companion disk: job3.sql */
PROCEDURE break_all_jobs (set_broken_IN IN BOOLEAN)
   IS
      /*
      || Sets the broken flag to TRUE or FALSE for all
      || jobs in the job queue
      ||
      || Requirements:
      ||
      || SELECT on DBA_JOBS
      || EXECUTE on DBMS_IJOB
      */
   BEGIN
      FOR job_rec IN
            (SELECT job
                FROM dba_jobs)
      LOOP
         SYS.DBMS_IJOB.BROKEN(job_rec.job, set_broken_IN);
      END LOOP;
   END break_all_jobs;
```

Another useful administrative feature of DBMS_IJOB is the ability to remove other users' jobs from the queue. Again, such activities should typically be done by DBAs and only when necessary. Here is a handy procedure similar to the previous one that will remove all jobs by user, or all jobs if NULL is explicitly passed in for the owner_IN parameter. If no job owner is specified, the procedure removes all jobs owned by the caller.

```
/* Filename on companion disk: job3.sql */
PROCEDURE remove_all_jobs
   (owner_IN IN VARCHAR2 := USER )
```

```
IS
    /*
    || Removes all jobs from the job queue owned by
    || a specific user, defaults to current user
    ||
    || Requirements:
    ||
    || SELECT on DBA_JOBS
    || EXECUTE on DBMS_IJOB
    */
BEGIN
    FOR job_rec IN
            (SELECT job
                FROM dba_jobs
               WHERE priv_user = NVL(owner_IN,priv_user) )
    LOOP
        SYS.DBMS_IJOB.REMOVE(job_rec.job);
    END LOOP;
END remove_all_jobs;
```

These two procedures may come in handy when manipulation of large numbers
of jobs is necessary (e.g., when trying to quiesce an environment with many busy
job queue processes).

DBMS_JOB Examples

The DBMS_JOB package has all kinds of useful applications waiting to be discovered. DBAs can schedule jobs that look for problem conditions in the database or
track and record resource utilization. Developers can schedule large batch operations at off hours without requiring operator intervention.

Tracking Space in Tablespaces

I decided to implement a very simple tracking system that can be used to track
the growth of data in tablespaces. Such a system could be used for capacity plan-
ning or to trigger an alert of impending space problems.

The system consists of a table called db_space, a view called tbs_space, and a procedure called space_logger. Here is the source code for the system:

```
/* Filename on companion disk: job6.sql */
CREATE TABLE db_space
    (tablespace_name   VARCHAR(30)   NOT NULL
    ,calc_date         DATE       NOT NULL
    ,total_bytes       NUMBER     NOT NULL
    ,free_bytes        NUMBER     NOT NULL);

CREATE OR REPLACE VIEW tbs_space
    (tablespace_name
    ,total_bytes
```

```
            ,free_bytes)
AS
    SELECT  DF.tbsname          tablespace_name
            ,DF.totbytes         total_bytes
            ,FS.freebytes        free_bytes
      FROM
            (SELECT  tablespace_name    tbsname
                    ,SUM(bytes)          totbytes
               FROM  dba_data_files
             GROUP BY tablespace_name
            ) DF
            ,(SELECT  tablespace_name    tbsname
                    ,SUM(bytes)          freebytes
               FROM   dba_free_space
             GROUP BY tablespace_name
            ) FS
    WHERE
            DF.tbsname = FS.tbsname;


CREATE OR REPLACE PROCEDURE space_logger
AS
    /*
    || records total size and free space for all
    || tablespaces in table db_space
    ||
    || Author:  John Beresniewicz, Savant Corp
    ||
    || 01/26/98: created
    ||
    || Compilation requirements:
    ||
    || SELECT on TBS_SPACE view
    || INSERT on DB_SPACE table
    */
    CURSOR tbs_space_cur
    IS
    SELECT tablespace_name, total_bytes, free_bytes
      FROM tbs_space;

BEGIN
    FOR tbs_space_rec IN tbs_space_cur
    LOOP
        INSERT INTO db_space VALUES
            (tbs_space_rec.tablespace_name
            ,SYSDATE
            ,tbs_space_rec.total_bytes
            ,tbs_space_rec.free_bytes);
    END LOOP;
    COMMIT;
END space_logger;
```

To set the system in motion, the space_logger procedure can be submitted to the job queue for regular execution as follows:

```
DECLARE
    jobno   NUMBER;
BEGIN
    DBMS_JOB.SUBMIT
        (job  => jobno
        ,what => 'begin space_logger; end;'
        ,next_date => SYSDATE
        ,interval  => 'SYSDATE+1/24');
    COMMIT;
END;
/
```

Each time space_logger executes, it records total space, free space, tablespace name, and a timestamp for each tablespace in the database. Adjusting the interval parameter for the job adjusts the frequency of data collection.

Fixing Broken Jobs Automatically

Charles Dye recommended the next example, probably based on his experiences with replication. When jobs have relatively complex execution requirements in terms of the database objects on which they depend, they can easily become broken by incurring multiple execution failures. Perhaps the DBA has modified some database links or recreated tables or views, and the job's definition has been temporarily compromised. Well, it's a pain to manually reset the broken flag for these "not really broken" jobs, so why not have a job that regularly tries to unbreak jobs? Sounds good to me; here is a procedure called job_fixer to do just that:

```
/* Filename on companion disk: job5.sql */
CREATE OR REPLACE PROCEDURE job_fixer
    AS
        /*
        || calls DBMS_JOB.BROKEN to try and set
        || any broken jobs to unbroken
        */

        /* cursor selects user's broken jobs */
        CURSOR broken_jobs_cur
        IS
        SELECT job
          FROM user_jobs
         WHERE broken = 'Y';

BEGIN
    FOR job_rec IN broken_jobs_cur
    LOOP
        DBMS_JOB.BROKEN(job_rec.job,FALSE);
    END LOOP;
END job_fixer;
```

The job_fixer procedure works only on a user's own jobs, so each user submitting jobs to the queue will need a separate job_fixer in the queue.

Self-Modifying and Self-Aware Jobs

The ability to reference the job, next_date, and broken parameters in the job definition allows the procedure executed to alter its own job characteristics. Thus, a job could remove itself from the job queue, or assign its own next execution date based on some criteria decided at runtime by the procedure itself. I've written a small skeleton procedure that demonstrates this capability. It is called smart_job, and makes use of all three of the referenceable parameters when submitted as a job.

When submitted to the job queue, smart_job uses the job definition parameters to modify itself in the following ways:

- Reschedules itself to parm1_IN minutes after finishing if parm2_IN = "RESTART"

- Sets next_date NULL causing automatic removal from queue if parm2_IN != "RESTART"

- Flags itself as broken if any exceptions are encountered

- Uses the job number to raise an exception

Pay close attention to how the smart_job procedure modifies itself. It uses the fact that the next_date and broken parameters support both IN and OUT modes when referenced by the job definition. Thus, when the broken_out parameter of smart_job has the broken parameter assigned to it in the call to DBMS_JOB.SUBMIT, the value set for broken_out by the procedure gets set for the job by the job queue when the job completes. In this way, smart_job changes its job characteristics without calling any DBMS_JOB procedures.

Here is the source code for smart_job:

```
/* Filename on companion disk: job4.sql */
PROCEDURE smart_job
    (parm1_IN IN INTEGER
    ,parm2_IN IN VARCHAR2
    ,next_date_OUT IN OUT DATE
    ,broken_OUT IN OUT BOOLEAN
    ,job_IN IN INTEGER := -1)
IS
    /* declare an exception for testing */
    JOB_LESSTHAN_100  EXCEPTION;

BEGIN
    /*
    || Do the procedure main line functions
```

```
    */
    null;

    /*
    || use job_IN to branch to exception handler
    || for testing self-breaking
    */
    IF job_IN < 100
    THEN
        RAISE JOB_LESSTHAN_100;
    END IF;

    /*
    || After main processing is finished, job decides
    || if it should re-execute and determines its own
    || next execution date by adding parm1_IN minutes to
    || the current time
    */
    IF parm2_IN = 'RESTART'
    THEN
        next_date_OUT := SYSDATE + parm1_IN/1440;
    ELSE
        /*
        || NULL next_date will cause automatic removal of
        || job from queue
        */
        next_date_OUT := NULL;
    END IF;

EXCEPTION
    /*
    || job "breaks" itself if unexpected error occurs
    */
    WHEN OTHERS
    THEN
        broken_OUT := TRUE;

END smart_job;
```

The following test script exercises smart_job:

```
/* Filename on companion disk: job4.sql */
var jobno NUMBER
BEGIN
    /*
    || Test the ability to modify next_date.
    */
    DBMS_JOB.SUBMIT
        (:jobno
        ,'smart_job(180,''RESTART'',next_date,broken,job);'
        ,SYSDATE + 1/1440
        ,'SYSDATE + 1');

    COMMIT WORK;
END;
```

```
/
print jobno

BEGIN
    /*
    || Test the ability to autoremove
    */
    DBMS_JOB.SUBMIT
        (:jobno
        ,'smart_job(180,''NO_RESTART'',next_date,broken,job);'
        ,SYSDATE + 1/1440
        ,'SYSDATE + 1');

    COMMIT WORK;
END;
/
print jobno

BEGIN
    /*
    || Test the ability to break itself.
    */
    DBMS_JOB.ISUBMIT
        (99
        ,'smart_job(180,''RESTART'',next_date,broken,job);'
        ,SYSDATE + 1/1440
        ,'SYSDATE + 1');

    COMMIT WORK;
END;
/
```

After executing the test script in SQL*Plus, the following jobs are in the queue:

```
SQL> SELECT job,last_date,next_date,broken FROM user_jobs;


JOB        LAST_DATE           NEXT_DATE           B
--------- ------------------- ------------------- -
      307                     1997:11:25:11:50:39 N
      308                     1997:11:25:11:50:39 N
       99                     1997:11:25:11:50:40 N
```

A few minutes later, the job queue looks like this:

```
SQL> SELECT job,last_date,next_date,broken FROM user_jobs;

JOB        LAST_DATE           NEXT_DATE           B
--------- ------------------- ------------------- -
      307 1997:11:25:11:50:42 1997:11:25:14:50:42 N
       99 1997:11:25:11:50:42 1997:11:26:11:50:42 Y
```

The tests worked! Job 308 ran once and was removed from the queue for having a NULL next_date. Job 307 ran and rescheduled itself three hours later, which is different from the interval specified in the call to DBMS_JOB.SUBMIT. Finally, job 99 set itself to broken status because its job number was less than 100.

Distributed Database Packages

This part of the book describes the built-in distributed database packages:

- Chapter 14, *Snapshots*, explores the packages, DBMS_SNAPSHOT, DBMS_REFRESH, and DBMS_OFFLINE_SNAPSHOT, and some programs in DBMS_REPCAT that show how to maintain snapshots, snapshot groups, and snapshot logs.

- Chapter 15, *Advanced Replication*, explains how to use DBMS_REPCAT, DBMS_REPUTIL, DBMS_OFFLINE_OG, DBMS_REPCAT_ADMIN, DBMS_REPCAT_AUTH, and DBMS_RECTIFIER_DIFF to create and to administer your replicated databases.

- Chapter 16, *Conflict Resolution*, shows you how to configure Oracle to automatically detect, correct, and report many forseeable conflicts by using procedures in DBMS_REPCAT to create and maintain custom resolution methods.

- Chapter 17, *Deferred Transactions and Remote Procedure Calls*, introduces the DBMS_DEFER package and shows you how to queue deferred remote procedure calls (RPCs) and use DBMS_DEFER_QUERY and DBMS_DEFER_SYS to perform administrative and diagnostic activities.

14

Snapshots

Oracle provides a number of packages that let you perform various types of administrative operations on snapshots and snapshot logs. Most of these administrative operations are relevant only if you are using snapshot groups or the Oracle advanced replication option. This chapter describes the following packages:

DBMS_SNAPSHOT

Lets you maintain snapshots and snapshot logs.

DBMS_OFFLINE_SNAPSHOT

Allows you to instantiate snapshots without having to run the CREATE SNAPSHOT command over the network. This package is particularly useful if you need to instantiate extremely large snapshots.

DBMS_REFRESH

Administers snapshot groups at a snapshot site.

DBMS_REPCAT

Performs a number of advanced replication operations. This chapter describes only the DBMS_REPCAT programs that deal with snapshots; all other programs are described in Chapter 15, *Advanced Replication*.

Even if you are using PL/SQL's built-in snapshot packages, you will continue to use the CREATE SNAPSHOT command to create your snapshots.

DBMS_SNAPSHOT: Managing Snapshots

The DBMS_SNAPSHOT package contains programs that allow you to maintain snapshots and snapshot logs, and to set and query package state variables associated with the advanced replication option.

Getting Started with DBMS_SNAPSHOT

The DBMS_SNAPSHOT package is created when the Oracle database is installed. The *dbmssnap.sql* script (found in the built-in packages source directory, as described in Chapter 1, *Introduction*) contains the source code for this package's specification. This script is called by *catproc.sql*, which is normally run immediately after database creation. The script creates the public synonym DBMS_SNAPSHOT for the package and grants EXECUTE privilege on the package to public. All Oracle users can reference and make use of this package.

Table 14-1 lists the programs contained in the DBMS_SNAPSHOT package.

Table 14-1. DBMS_SNAPSHOT Packages

Name	Description	Use in SQL?
BEGIN_TABLE_REORGANIZA-TION (Oracle8 only)	Called prior to reorganizing a master table (e.g., through export/import); saves data required to refresh snapshots	No
END_TABLE_REORGANIZA-TION (Oracle8 only)	Called after reorganizing a master table (e.g., through export/import); validates data required to refresh snapshots	No
I_AM_A_REFRESH	Returns value of REP$WHAT_AM_I.I_AM_A_SNAPSHOT	No
PURGE_LOG	Purges snapshot log	No
REFRESH	Refreshes a snapshot	No
REGISTER_SNAPSHOT (Oracle8 only)	Records information about snapshots at the master site in the DBA_REGISTERED_SNAPSHOTS data dictionary view	No
SET_I_AM_A_REFRESH	Sets REP$WHAT_AM_I.I_AM_A_SNAPSHOT to specified value	No
UNREGISTER_SNAPSHOT (Oracle8 only)	Removes information about snapshots at the master site from the DBA_REGISTERED_SNAPSHOTS data dictionary view	No

DBMS_SNAPSHOT does not define any exceptions.

NOTE All of the programs in DBMS_SNAPSHOT are available regardless of whether you are using snapshot groups or the advanced replication option.

Using the I_AM_A_REFRESH Package State Variable

The I_AM_A_REFRESH and SET_I_AM_A_REFRESH programs query and set Oracle's REP$I_AM_A_REFRESH package variable. Oracle uses this variable in replication triggers and elsewhere internally to determine whether a given DML statement should be replicated to other master sites.

The DBMS_SNAPSHOT.I_AM_A_REFRESH function

The I_AM_A_REFRESH function queries the REP$I_AM_A_REFRESH package variable. If this variable equals "Y," then the session is refreshing a snapshot or applying propagated DML to a replicated table. The header for the function follows:

```
FUNCTION DBMS_SNAPSHOT.I_AM_A_REFRESH RETURN BOOLEAN;
```

The function does not raise any exceptions.

Examples. Let's look at several examples of querying the I_AM_A_REFRESH package variable.

Generating replication support. Suppose now that you are replicating a table named COUNTRIES in the SPROCKET schema:

```
SQL> DESC sprocket.countries
Name                     Null?          Type
----------------         --------       --------------
COUNTRY_ID               NOT NULL       NUMBER(6)
ISO3166_NUMBER           NOT NULL       NUMBER(3)
ISO3166_NAME             NOT NULL       VARCHAR2(50)
ISO2_CODE                NOT NULL       VARCHAR2(2)
ISO3_CODE                NOT NULL       VARCHAR2(3)
AUDIT_DATE               NOT NULL       DATE
AUDIT_USER               NOT NULL       VARCHAR2(30)
GLOBAL_NAME              NOT NULL       VARCHAR2(20)
```

When you generate replication support for this table with DBMS_REPCAT.GENERATE_REPLICATION_SUPPORT (described in Chapter 15), Oracle creates an AFTER ROW trigger named COUNTRIES$RT, which queues DML to other master sites. The text of the trigger follows:

```
   after delete or insert or update on "SPROCKET"."COUNTRIES"
   for each row
declare
   flag char;
begin
   if "COUNTRIES$TP".active then
      if inserting then
         flag := 'I';
      elsif updating then
         flag := 'U';
      elsif deleting then
         flag := 'D';
      end if;
      "COUNTRIES$TP".replicate(
         :old."AUDIT_DATE",:new."AUDIT_DATE",
         :old."AUDIT_USER",:new."AUDIT_USER",
```

```
            :old."COUNTRY_ID",:new."COUNTRY_ID",
            :old."GLOBAL_NAME",:new."GLOBAL_NAME",
            :old."ISO2_CODE",:new."ISO2_CODE",
            :old."ISO3166_NAME",:new."ISO3166_NAME",
            :old."ISO3166_NUMBER",:new."ISO3166_NUMBER",
            :old."ISO3_CODE",:new."ISO3_CODE",
            flag);
      end if;
    end;
```

As you can see, this trigger replicates DML only if the function COUN-TRIES$TP.active is TRUE. This ACTIVE function uses DBMS_SNAPSHOT.I_AM_A_REFRESH as follows:

```
function active return boolean
is
begin
return (not((is_snapshot and dbms_snapshot.I_am_a_refresh) or
not dbms_reputil.replication_is_on));
end active;
```

Oracle uses the active function, which calls DBMS_SNAPSHOT.I_AM_A_REFRESH, to distinguish between your application's DML operations and the DML that is being propagated from another master site.

The base table of an updateable snapshot has a trigger that also uses the I_AM_A_REFRESH function.

Auditing triggers. Under some circumstances, you may need to determine the source of DML statements. For example, you will notice that the countries table has a number of fields used for auditing: audit_date, audit_user, and global_name. We have a BEFORE ROW trigger that populates these fields.

```
CREATE OR REPLACE TRIGGER countries_audit
BEFORE INSERT OR UPDATE ON countries
FOR EACH ROW

DECLARE
        vGlobalName      VARCHAR2(30) := DBMS_REPUTIL.GLOBAL_NAME;
BEGIN
        IF NOT (DBMS_SNAPSHOT.I_AM_A_REFRESH) THEN
        BEGIN
                :new.audit_date       := SYSDATE;
                :new.audit_user       := USER;
                :new.global_name      := vGlobalName;
        END IF;
END;
```

This trigger fires when an application performs an INSERT or UPDATE, but not when the DML is propagated from other sites.

TIP	All row-level replication triggers are AFTER ROW triggers. Although a table can have multiple triggers of the same type, you cannot control the order in which they are fired. Therefore, it is safest to use BEFORE ROW triggers to perform auditing on replicated tables; in this way, you are guaranteed that BEFORE ROW triggers fire before AFTER ROW triggers.

The DBMS_SNAPSHOT.SET_I_AM_A_REFRESH procedure

The SET_I_AM_A_REFRESH procedure sets the I_AM_A_REFRESH package variable. The header for the procedure is;

```
PROCEDURE DBMS_SNAPSHOT.SET_I_AM_A_REFRESH  (value IN  BOOLEAN);
```

where value is the value (Y or N) being set. This procedure does not raise any exceptions.

Example. If you need to enable and disable replication triggers at the session level, you can do so with the SET_I_AM_A_REFRESH procedure. To enable the triggers, specify the following:

```
DBMS_SNAPSHOT.SET_I_AM_A_REFRESH( value => FALSE )
```

To disable them, specify the following:

```
DBMS_SNAPSHOT.SET_I_AM_A_REFRESH( value => TRUE )
```

Use this package carefully, because disabling replication triggers effectively disables any conflict resolution mechanisms you may have defined. (See Chapter 17, *Deferred Transactions and Remote Procedure Calls*, for a discussion of these mechanisms.)

Refreshing Snapshots

Calling the REFRESH procedure from a snapshot site forces the refresh of the specified snapshot(s). Typically, this procedure is used to refresh an individual snapshot, or a group of snapshots that are not in the same snapshot refresh group.

The DBMS_SNAPSHOT.REFRESH procedure

Call the REFRESH procedure to force a snapshot refresh. The specifications for the Oracle7 and Oracle8 versions of the REFRESH procedure differ. Note that the Version 8.0 implementation adds parameters that support parallelism, and drops the execute_as_user parameter. Both versions are overloaded, allowing you to specify the list of snapshots as a comma-delimited string in the list parameter, or as a PL/SQL table in the tab parameter. The other parameters are identical for the two versions.

Here is the Oracle7 specification:

```
PROCEDURE DBMS_SNAPSHOT.REFRESH
   (list IN VARCHAR2,
    method IN VARCHAR2 DEFAULT NULL,
    rollback_seg IN VARCHAR2 DEFAULT NULL,
    push_deferred_rpc IN BOOLEAN DEFAULT TRUE,
    refresh_after_errors IN BOOLEAN DEFAULT FALSE,
    execute_as_user IN BOOLEAN DEFAULT FALSE );

PROCEDURE DBMS_SNAPSHOT.REFRESH
   (ab IN OUT dbms_utility.uncl_array,
    method  IN VARCHAR2 DEFAULT NULL,
    rollback_seg IN VARCHAR2 DEFAULT NULL,
    push_deferred_rpc IN BOOLEAN DEFAULT TRUE,
    refresh_after_errors IN BOOLEAN DEFAULT FALSE,
    execute_as_user IN BOOLEAN DEFAULT FALSE );
```

Here is the Oracle8 specification:

```
PROCEDURE DBMS_SNAPSHOT.REFRESH
   (list IN VARCHAR2,
    method  IN VARCHAR2 := NULL,
    rollback_seg IN VARCHAR2 := NULL,
    push_deferred_rpc IN BOOLEAN := TRUE,
    refresh_after_errors IN BOOLEAN := FALSE,
    purge_option IN BINARY_INTEGER := 1,
    parallelism IN BINARY_INTEGER := 0,
    heap_size IN BINARY_INTEGER := 0);

PROCEDURE DBMS_SNAPSHOT.REFRESH
   (tab IN OUT dbms_utility.uncl_array,
    method IN VARCHAR2 := NULL,
    rollback_seg IN VARCHAR2 := NULL,
    push_deferred_rpc IN BOOLEAN := TRUE,
    refresh_after_errors IN BOOLEAN := FALSE,
    purge_option IN BINARY_INTEGER := 1,
    parallelism IN BINARY_INTEGER := 0,
    heap_size  IN BINARY_INTEGER := 0);
```

Parameters are summarized in the following table.

Name	Description
list	Comma-separated list of snapshots to be refreshed. Use list or tab.
tab	PL.SQL table of snapshots to be refreshed. Use list or tab.

Name	Description
method	Refresh method: '?' uses the default refresh method. If you specified a refresh method when you created the snapshot, that is the default method. Otherwise, Oracle uses a fast refresh if possible, and a complete refresh if not. 'F' or 'f' uses fast refresh if possible, and returns ORA-12004 if not. 'C' or 'c' uses a COMPLETE refresh. This parameter should include a single character for each snapshot specified in list or tab, in the same order as the snapshot names appear. If list or tab contains more snapshots than the method list, the additional snapshots are refreshed with their default method.
rollback_seg	Optional; specifies the rollback segment to use for the refresh.
push_deferred_rpc	Optional; for updateable snapshots only. If TRUE (the default), then local updates are sent back to the master site before the snapshot is refreshed (otherwise, local updates will be temporarily overwritten).
refresh_after_errors	Optional; for updateable snapshots only. If TRUE, proceed with the refresh even if outstanding errors (conflicts) are logged in the DEFERROR data dictionary view at the master site. Default is FALSE.
execute_as_user (Version 7 only)	If FALSE (the default) then the call to the remote system is performed under the privilege domain of the user that created the snapshot. If TRUE, the call is performed as the user calling the refresh procedure.
purge_option (Oracle8 only)	If push_deferred_rpc is TRUE, this designates the purge method; default is 1. • 0 No purge • 1 Lazy purge (optimized for time) • 2 Aggressive purge (complete)
parallelism (Oracle8 only)	If push_defered_rpc is TRUE, this determines the maximum degree of parallelism; default is 1. • 0 Serial • 1 Parallel with one slave • N Parallel with N slaves (N > 1)
heap_size (Oracle8 only)	Used only if parallelism > 0. Sets the maximum number of transactions to be examined simultaneously for determining parallel scheduling. Oracle determines this value internally; you are advised not to use it.

The REFRESH procedure does not raise any exceptions.

All of the snapshots passed to list or tab are refreshed as a single transaction; all or none are refreshed. In addition, the refreshed snapshots will respect all integrity constraints that exist among the master tables.

You might want to force a manual refresh of a snapshot if the next scheduled refresh is too far in the future, or if you have repaired a problem that caused the scheduled refresh job to break. Forcing a manual refresh of a snapshot does not alter its refresh schedule.

A FAST refresh requires a snapshot log on the master table, and is possible only for simple snapshots in Oracle7; Oracle8 supports fast refreshes subquery snapshots meeting certain conditions. Fast refreshes read the snapshot log to determine which rows have changed since the last refresh, and only those rows are updated.

If you are concerned about the amount of rollback the refresh will require, you can use the rollback_seg parameter to designate a rollback segment that is suitably sized for the transaction. However, you are not guaranteed that no other transactions will use this rollback segment. In general, you should consider making relatively large rollback segments if you anticipate frequent refreshes of large snapshots.

Restrictions. You can call REFRESH only from a snapshot site.

Examples. Once you are familiar with the various parameters to the REFRESH procedure, it becomes simple to use, as the following examples illustrate.

Read-only snapshot. This example shows a refresh as a read-only snapshot named PRICE_LIST:

```
BEGIN
    DBMS_SNAPSHOT.REFRESH (list => 'PRICES');
END;
```

This is the simplest possible refresh method. Note that since we have not provided a schema name, this would have to be executed from the snapshot owner's account.

Related read-only snapshots. In the next example, we refresh a set of related read-only snapshots.

```
DECLARE
vSnapshotList dbms_utility.uncl_array
BEGIN
    vSnapshotList(1) = 'COUNTRIES'
    vSnapshotList(2) = 'STATES'
    vSnapshotList(3) = 'POSTAL_CODES'
    vSnapshotList(4) = 'CUSTOMER_ADDRESSES'

    DBMS_SNAPSHOT.REFRESH(   tab => vSnapShotList,
                             method => 'CCF?',
                             rollback_segment => 'RB1'
                             execute_as_user => FALSE);
END;
```

This example illustrates several points:

1. You can provide the list of snapshots as a PL/SQL table. Oracle will refresh all of the snapshots in one atomic transaction; either all or none of the snapshots are refreshed. All referential consistencies among the master tables will be preserved in the snapshot tables.

2. You can specify different refresh methods for each snapshot. This example performs a complete refresh on COUNTRIES and STATES, a full refresh on POSTAL_CODES, and a fast refresh (if possible) on CUSTOMER_ADDRESSES. If Oracle cannot use a fast refresh on the CUSTOMER_ADDRESS table, it will perform a complete refresh instead.

3. You can designate a specific, suitably sized rollback segment for the refresh.

4. You can set the parameter, execute_as_user, to FALSE to force Oracle to refresh the snapshot under the privilege domain of the snapshot owner.

Updateable snapshot. In the next example, we refresh the updateable snapshot DAILY_STORE_SALES.

```
DECLARE
vSnapshotList dbms_utility.uncl_array
BEGIN
    vSnapshotList(1) = 'DAILY_STORE_SALES'

    DBMS_SNAPSHOT.REFRESH(   tab => vSnapShotList,
                             method => '?'
                             push_deferred_rpc => FALSE);
END;
```

Since we set push_deferred_rpc to FALSE (the default is TRUE), the refresh will overwrite any local changes. The local changes will be visible again after the remote procedure call (RPC) pushes them to the master site and snapshot is refreshed again.

Parallel refreshes. In this example, the parallelism feature of Oracle8 allows us to use four processes to refresh the updateable snapshot DAILY_STORE_SALES:

```
DECLARE
vSnapshotList dbms_utility.uncl_array
BEGIN
    vSnapshotList(1) = 'DAILY_STORE_SALES'

    DBMS_SNAPSHOT.REFRESH(   tab => vSnapShotList,
                             method => '?'
                             parallelism => 4,
                             purge_option = 2);
END;
```

The purge_option parameter controls how Oracle purges the snapshot site's deferred transaction queue; Oracle8 does not purge the queue automatically when the transactions propagate, so you must use DBMS_DEFER_SYS.SCHEDULE_ PURGE (described in Chapter 17) to schedule a job to purge the queue, lest it become large and unmanageable. The purge_option parameter in REFRESH provides an opportunity to purge the queue of transactions associated with the updateable snapshot(s) you are refreshing.

NOTE   Purging the deferred transaction queue is not the same thing as purging a snapshot log!

Purging the Snapshot Log

The PURGE_LOG procedure deletes records from the snapshot log on a master table. You may wish to do this if the snapshot log becomes very large, or if you drop a subset of the snapshots for which the table is a master.

The DBMS_SNAPSHOT.PURGE.LOG procedure

Call the PURGE_LOG procedure to delete snapshot log records. The specification for the PURGE_LOG procedure follows:

```
PROCEDURE DBMS_SNAPSHOT.PURGE_LOG
    (master VARCHAR2
    ,num BINARY_INTEGER DEFAULT 1
    ,flag VARCHAR2 DEFAULT 'NOP' );
```

Parameters are summarized in the following table.

Name	Description
master	Name of the master table
num	Delete records required to refresh the oldest number of unrefreshed snapshot; default is 1
flag	Set to DELETE to guarantee that records are deleted for at least one snapshot regardless of the setting of num

The PURGE_LOG procedure does not raise any exceptions.

Examples. The following examples illustrate the use of the PURGE_LOG procedure. The first example shows the simplest form of the procedure; the only parameter is master:

```
BEGIN
    DBMS_REFRESH.PURGE_LOG( master => 'COUNTRIES' );
END;
```

Since the call uses the default value for num, 1, it will purge the snapshot log records required for a fast refresh of the least recently refreshed snapshot—that is, the most stale snapshot.

This example shows the use of several parameters:

```
BEGIN
    DBMS_REFRESH.PURGE_LOG
    ( master => 'COUNTRIES', num => 5, flag => 'DELETE' );
END;
```

In this example, the procedure deletes snapshot log records required for a fast refresh of the five most stale snapshots. However, since we have set the flag parameter to DELETE, the call is guaranteed to delete the records for at least one snapshot, even if the table masters fewer than five snapshots.

TIP   To delete all records from a snapshot log, set the num parameter to a high value (greater than the number of snapshots mastered to the master table, specified in the master parameter).

Reorganizing Tables

Occasionally a DBA must reorganize a table—in other words, coalesce its extents and reduce row chaining. Two new programs in Oracle8 allow you to reorganize a master table without invalidating its snapshot log: BEGIN_TABLE_REORGANIZATION and END_TABLE_REORGANIZATION. Therefore, you do not have to perform complete refreshes of the table's snapshots after it is reorganized. To take advantage of this new feature, you must be using primary key snapshots.

The DBMS_SNAPSHOT.BEGIN_TABLE_REORGANIZATION procedure (Oracle8 only)

If you are reorganizing a table, call the BEGIN_TABLE_REORGANIZATION procedure before reorganizing the table, and the END_TABLE_REORGANIZATION procedure when you are finished. The specification for BEGIN_TABLE_REORGANIZATION follows:

```
PROCEDURE DBMS_SNAPSHOT.BEGIN_TABLE_REORGANIZATION
    (tabowner IN VARCHAR2
    ,tabname  IN VARCHAR2);
```

Parameters are summarized in the following table.

Name	Description
tabowner	Owner of the master table
tabname	Name of the master table being reorganized

This procedure does not raise any exceptions.

The DBMS_SNAPSHOT.END_TABLE_REORGANIZATION procedure (Oracle8 only)

Call the END_TABLE_REORGANIZATION procedure when you are finished reorganizing a table. The specification for END_TABLE_REORGANIZATION follows:

```
PROCEDURE DBMS_SNAPSHOT.END_TABLE_REORGANIZATION
    (tabowner IN VARCHAR2
```

Parameters are the same as those for BEGIN_TABLE_REORGANIZATION. This procedure does not raise any exceptions.

Examples. The following examples illustrate how to use these procedures as part of a table reorganization. The first example shows the steps for reorganizing a master table using truncation.

1. Call DBMS_SNAPSHOT.BEGIN_TABLE_REORGANIZATION:

   ```
   BEGIN
       EXECUTE DBMS_SNAPSHOT.BEGIN_TABLE_REORGANIZATION (
           tabowner => 'SPROCKET', tabname => 'COUNTRIES');
   END;
   ```

2. Back up the table by exporting it, or spooling it to a flat file.

3. Truncate the master table, preserving the snapshot log:

   ```
   TRUNCATE TABLE countries PRESERVE SNAPSHOT LOG;
   ```

4. Restore the table from the export file or flat file.

5. Call DBMS_SNAPSHOT.END_TABLE_REORGANIZATION:

   ```
   BEGIN
       EXECUTE DBMS_SNAPSHOT.END_TABLE_REORGANIZATION (
           tabowner => 'SPROCKET', tabname => 'COUNTRIES');
   END;
   ```

The next example shows the steps for reorganizing a master table using RENAME TABLE.

1. Call DBMS_SNAPSHOT.BEGIN_TABLE_REORGANIZATION:

   ```
   BEGIN
       EXECUTE DBMS_SNAPSHOT.BEGIN_TABLE_REORGANIZATION (
           tabowner => 'SPROCKET', tabname => 'COUNTRIES');
   END;
   ```

2. Rename the table:

```
        RENAME TABLE countries TO countries_pre_reorg;
```

3. Create a new version of the table:

```
        CREATE TABLE countries AS SELECT * FROM countrie_pre_reorg;
```

4. Call DBMS_SNAPSHOT.END_TABLE_REORGANIZATION:

```
    BEGIN
        EXECUTE DBMS_SNAPSHOT.END_TABLE_REORGANIZATION (
            tabowner => 'SPROCKET', tabname => 'COUNTRIES');
    END;
```

5. Recreate any triggers that were defined on the table.

In both of these examples, snapshots will be able to use the snapshot log for fast refreshes after the table reorganization is complete.

Registering Snapshots

One of the most significant improvements in Oracle8 is the automatic registration of snapshots at the master site. In Oracle7, there was no easy way to determine the location—or even the existence—of snapshots with master table(s) in your instance. But when you create a snapshot in Oracle8, Oracle puts a record in the DBA_REGISTERED_SNAPSHOTS data dictionary view. Similarly, when you drop a snapshot, Oracle deletes the record from DBA_REGISTERED_SNAPSHOTS.

The REGISTER and UNREGISTER procedures let you manually maintain this data dictionary view, shown in Table 14-2.

Table 14-2. DBA_REGISTERED_SNAPSHOTS Data Dictionary View

Column Name	Description
OWNER	Snapshot owner.
NAME	Snapshot name.
SNAPSHOT_SITE	Global name of database where snapshot resides.
CAN_USE_LOG	If YES, then snapshot refreshes can use snapshot log.
UPDATABLE	If YES, then snapshot is an updateable snapshot.
REFRESH_METHOD	Refresh method; either ROWID or PRIMARY KEY.
SNAPSHOT_ID	Unique ID of snapshot used for fast refreshes.
VERSION	Version of the snapshot. Possible values are REG_UNKNOWN, REG_V7_GROUP, REG_V8_GROUP, and REG_REPAPI_GROUP.
QUERY_TXT	Text of the snapshot's query.

The DBMS_SNAPSHOT.REGISTER_SNAPSHOT procedure (Oracle 8 only)

Generally, the registration and unregistration of snapshots is automatic if both the master and snapshot databases are Oracle8. However, in case the snapshot site is running Oracle7, or if the automatic registration fails, you can use the Oracle8 procedure, REGISTER_SNAPSHOT, to register the snapshot manually.

NOTE   The registration of snapshots is not mandatory; it records data in DBA_REGISTERED_SNAPSHOTS that is for informational use only. You should not rely on the contents of this data dictionary view.

The specification for the REGISTER_SNAPSHOT procedure is as follows:

```
PROCEDURE DBMS_SNAPSHOT.REGISTER_SNAPSHOT
    (snapowner     IN VARCHAR2,
     snapname      IN VARCHAR2,
     snapsite      IN VARCHAR2,
     snapshot_id IN DATE | BINARY_INTEGER,
     flag          IN BINARY_INTEGER,
     qry_txt       IN VARCHAR2,
     rep_type      IN BINARY_INTEGER := dbms_snapshot.reg_unknown);
```

The REGISTER_SNAPSHOT procedure is overloaded; snapshot_id is a DATE type if the snapshot site is an Oracle7 database, and BINARY_INTEGER if it is an Oracle8 database. Parameters are summarized in the following table.

Name	Description
snapowner	Owner of the snapshot.
snapname	Name of the snapshot.
snapsite	Global name of snapshot site database instance.
snapshot_id	ID of the snapshot. Use DATE datatype for Oracle7 snapshot sites, BINARY_INTEGER for Oracle8 snapshot sites. The snapshot_id and flag parameters are mutually exclusive.
flag	PL/SQL variable dictating whether future moves and creates are registered in the qry_text parameter; this flag does not appear to be used.
qry_text	Up to 32000 characters of the text of the snapshot query.
rep_type	Binary integer indicating the version of the snapshot. Possible values are: • reg_unknown = 0 (the default) • reg_v7_group = 1 • reg_v8_group = 2 • reg_repapi_group = 3

REGISTER_SNAPSHOT does not raise any exceptions.

Example. Registration of Oracle7 snapshots is never automatic; you must call REGISTER_SNAPSHOT if you want to see Oracle7 snapshots in the DBA_REGISTERED_SNAPSHOTS data dictionary view. You must provide all of the information you want to see. In the following example, you register a snapshot from an Oracle7 snapshot site to an Oracle8 master:

```
BEGIN
    DBMS_SNAPSHOT.REGISTER_SNAPSHOT(
                snapowner    => 'SPROCKET',
                snapname     => 'COUNTRIES',
                snapsite     => 'D7CA.BIGWHEEL.COM',
                snapshot_id  => sysdate,
                flag         => 0,
                qry_text     => 'SELECT * FROM countries@D8CA.BIGWHEEL.COM',
                rep_type     => reg_v7_group);
END;
```

The DBMS_SNAPSHOT.UNREGISTER_SNAPSHOT procedures (Oracle8 only)

The UNREGISTER_SNAPSHOT procedure is the flip side of the REGISTER_SNAP-
SHOT procedure. You use UNREGISTER_SNAPSHOT when you need to manually
unregister a snapshot. This procedure unregisters snapshots at the master site,
regardless of whether they were registered manually or automatically.

The specification is as follows:

```
PROCEDURE DBMS_SNAPSHOT.UNREGISTER_SNAPSHOT
    (snapowner IN VARCHAR,
     snapname IN VARCHAR2,
     snapsite IN VARCHAR2)
```

See the description of parameters under the REGISTER procedure.

UNREGISTER_SNAPSHOT does not raise any exceptions.

NOTE   Unregistering a snapshot has no effect on the snapshot itself.

Example. In this example, we unregister the snapshot that we created in the previous section:

```
BEGIN
    DBMS_SNAPSHOT.UNREGISTER_SNAPSHOT(
                snapowner    => 'SPROCKET',
                snapname     => 'COUNTRIES',
                snapsite     => 'D7CA.BIGWHEEL.COM');
END
```

For a detailed example, see the *mastsnap.sql* file on the companion disk.
This script lists registered snapshots at a master site, including their last
refresh time. It requires Oracle8.

DBMS_REFRESH: Managing Snapshot Groups

The DBMS_REFRESH package contains procedures for administrating snapshot groups. A snapshot group is a collection of one or more snapshots that Oracle refreshes in an atomic transaction, guaranteeing that relationships among the master tables are preserved in the snapshot tables. The DBMS_REFRESH package includes packages that perform the following functions:

- Create and destroy snapshot groups

- Add and subtract snapshots from snapshot groups

- Manually refresh snapshot groups

- Change properties of the snapshot group, such as the refresh interval

Figure 14-1 shows how DBMS_REFRESH works and Figure 14-2 illustrates snapshot groups.

Getting Started with DBMS_REFRESH

The DBMS_REFRESH package is created when the Oracle database is installed. The *dbmssnap.sql* script (found in the built-in packages source directory, as described in Chapter 1) contains the source code for this package's specification. This script is called by *catproc.sql*, which is normally run immediately after database creation. The script creates the public synonym DBMS_REFRESH for the package and grants EXECUTE privilege on the package to public. All Oracle users can reference and make use of this package.

Table 14-3 lists the programs available in the DBMS_REFRESH package.

Table 14-3. DBMS_REFRESH Programs

Name	Description	Use in SQL?
ADD	Adds one or more snapshots to an existing refresh group	No
CHANGE	Changes parameters associated with a refresh group	No
DESTROY	Removes a refresh group	No
MAKE	Creates a refresh group	No
REFRESH	Forces a refresh of a refresh group	No
SUBTRACT	Removes one or more snapshots from a refresh group	No

DBMS_REFRESH does not define any exceptions.

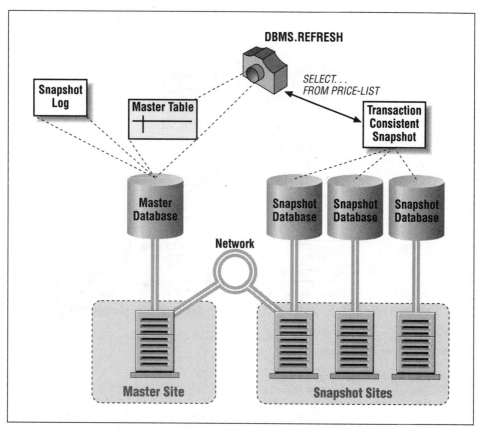

Figure 14-1. DBMS_REFRESH components

Creating and Destroying Snapshot Groups

The MAKE and DESTROY procedures create and destroy snapshot groups, respectively. You call these procedures from the snapshot site.

The DBMS_REFRESH.MAKE procedure

Call the MAKE procedure to create a snapshot group. Note that you must select either the list or tab parameter, but not both. The specifications for Oracle7 and Oracle8 versions differ as follows.

Here is the Oracle7 specification:

```
PROCEDURE DBMS_REFRESH.MAKE
    (name IN VARCHAR2,
    {list IN VARCHAR2,| tab IN dbms_utility.uncl_array,}
    next_date IN DATE,
    interval IN VARCHAR2,
    implicit_destroy IN BOOLEAN DEFAULT FALSE,
```

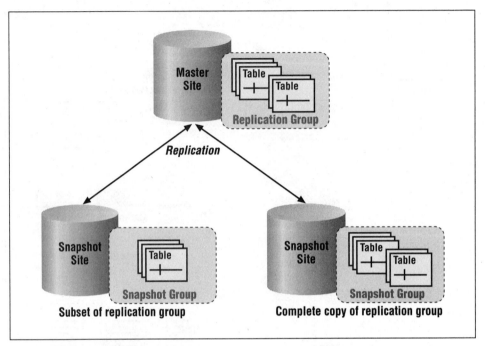

Figure 14-2. A snapshot group

```
lax IN BOOLEAN DEFAULT FALSE,
job IN BINARY_INTEGER DEFAULT 0,
rollback_seg IN VARCHAR2 DEFAULT NULL,
push_deferred_rpc IN BOOLEAN DEFAULT TRUE,
refresh_after_errors IN BOOLEAN DEFAULT FALSE );
```

Here is the Oracle8 specification:

```
PROCEDURE DBMS_REFRESH.MAKE
    (name IN VARCHAR2,
    {list IN VARCHAR2,| tab IN dmbs_utility.uncl_array,}
    next_date IN DATE,
    interval IN VARCHAR2,
    implicit_destroy IN BOOLEAN := FALSE,
    lax IN BOOLEAN := FALSE,
    job IN BINARY_INTEGER := 0,
    rollback_seg IN VARCHAR2 := NULL,
    push_deferred_rpc IN BOOLEAN := TRUE,
    refresh_after_errors IN BOOLEAN := FALSE,
    purge_option  IN BINARY_INTEGER := 1,
    parallelism IN BINARY_INTEGER := 0,
    heap_size IN BINARY_INTEGER := 0);
```

In both Oracle7 and Oracle8, the MAKE procedure is overloaded; you can supply
the list of snapshots either as a comma-separated string with the list parameter, or
as a PL/SQL table with the tab parameter.

Parameters are summarized in the following table.

Name	Description
name	Name of the refresh group to create.
list	A comma-delimited string of snapshots to include in the new refresh group. Use either list or tab to specify the snapshot(s) you want to add.
tab	A PL/SQL table of snapshots to include in the new refresh group. Use either list or tab to specify the snapshot(s) you want to add.
next_date	The time of the next refresh.
interval	A DATE expression indicating the snapshot group's refresh interval.
implicit_destroy	If set to TRUE, the snapshot group is destroyed if all snapshots are removed from it.
lax	If set to TRUE and the snapshot(s) already exist in a refresh group other than name, the snapshot(s) are first removed from the other group.
job	Used by import utility. Always use default value of 0.
rollback_seg	Specifies the rollback segment to use during snapshot refreshes. If set to NULL, the default rollback segment is used.
push_deferred_rpc	For updateable snapshots only. Setting this parameter to TRUE indicates that local updates will be pushed back to the master site (otherwise, local updates will not be visible during the refresh).
refresh_after_errors	For updateable snapshots only. Setting this parameter to TRUE indicates that refreshes should occur even if errors exist in the DEFERROR data dictionary view.
purge_option (Oracle8 only)	If *push*_deferred_rpc is TRUE, this designates the purge method; default is 1. • 0 No purge • 1 Lazy purge (optimized for time) • 2 Aggressive purge (complete)
parallelism (Oracle8 only)	• If push_defered_rpc is TRUE, this determines the maximum degree of parallelism; default is 1. • 0 Serial • 1 Parallel with 1 slave • N Parallel with N slaves (N > 1)
heap_size (Oracle8 only)	Used only if parallelism > 0. Sets the maximum number of transactions to be examined simultaneously for determining parallel scheduling. Oracle determines this value internally; you are advised not to use it.

The MAKE procedure does not raise any exceptions.

Examples. The following examples illustrate how the MAKE procedure may be used.

Read-only snapshot. group. In this example, we create a snapshot refresh group of read-only snapshots:

```
DECLARE
vSnapshotList dbms_utility.uncl_array
BEGIN
    vSnapshotList(1) = 'COUNTRIES'
    vSnapshotList(2) = 'STATES'
    vSnapshotList(3) = 'POSTAL_CODES'
    vSnapshotList(4) = 'CUSTOMER_ADDRESSES'

    DBMS_REFRESH.MAKE(name => 'SG_ADDR_TABS',
                      tab => vSnapShotList,
                      next_date => TRUNC(sysdate) + 1,
                      interval => 'SYSDATE + 1');
END;
```

This example shows the simplest invocation of DBMS_REFRESH.MAKE; defaults are used for all possible parameters. This call creates a snapshot group on four related tables, and schedules them to be refreshed at every day at midnight.

Read-only snapshot group with specialized parameters. In the following example, we create a snapshot refresh group of read-only snapshots with specialized parameters:

```
DECLARE
vSnapshotList dbms_utility.uncl_array
BEGIN
    vSnapshotList(1) = 'COUNTRIES'
    vSnapshotList(2) = 'STATES'
    vSnapshotList(3) = 'POSTAL_CODES'
    vSnapshotList(4) = 'CUSTOMER_ADDRESSES'

    DBMS_REFRESH.MAKE(name => 'SG_ADDR_TABS',
                      tab => vSnapShotList,
                      next_date => TRUNC(sysdate) + 1,
                      interval => 'SYSDATE + 1',
                      implicit_destroy => TRUE,
                      lax => TRUE,
                      rollback_segment 'RB1');
END;
```

This example creates the same snapshot group as in the previous example, but with some additional properties:

implicit_destroy = TRUE

This setting causes the snapshot group SG_ADDR_TABS to be destroyed if all of the snapshots in the group are dropped. The default behavior is to preserve the snapshot group, even if it has no members.

lax = TRUE

> If any of the snapshots being added to SG_ADDR_TABS exist in another snap-
> shot group, this setting instructs Oracle to remove them from the other group
> before adding them to the new group. A snapshot cannot be a member of
> more than one snapshot group.

rollback_segment = 'RB1'

> This setting causes Oracle to use rollback segment RB1 whenever it refreshes
> snapshot group SG_ADDR_TABS. You should consider specifying rollback
> segments if your snapshot refreshes result in long transactions requiring a
> large rollback segment.

Parallel propagation. In the next example, we create a snapshot refresh group
that uses parallel propagation (Oracle8 only):

```
DECLARE
vSnapshotList dbms_utility.uncl_array
BEGIN
    vSnapshotList(1) = 'COUNTRIES'
    vSnapshotList(2) = 'STATES'
    vSnapshotList(3) = 'POSTAL_CODES'
    vSnapshotList(4) = 'CUSTOMER_ADDRESSES'

    DBMS_REFRESH.MAKE(name => 'SG_ADDR_TABS',
                      tab => vSnapShotList,
                      next_date => TRUNC(sysdate) + 1,
                      interval => 'SYSDATE + 1',
                      parallelism => 4,);
END;
```

This example sets parallelism to 4, so that Oracle uses four processes to perform
the refresh.

The DBMS_REFRESH.DESTROY procedure

Call the DESTROY procedure to destroy a snapshot group. For both Oracle7 and
Oracle8, you call DESTROY as follows,

```
PROCEDURE DBMS_REFRESH.DESTROY (name IN VARCHAR2);
```

where name is the name of the snapshot group to be destroyed.

The DESTROY procedure raises the following exception:

Name	Number	Description
ORA-23404	–23404	Refresh group name does not exist

Example. This example destroys the snapshot group SG_ADDR_TABS:

```
BEGIN
    DBMS_REFRESH.DESTROY( name => 'SG_ADDR_TABS' );
END;
```

This example does not drop the member snapshots themselves; however, they will not be refreshed again unless you either add them to another snapshot group, or refresh them manually with the DBMS_SNAPSHOT.REFRESH procedure.

Adding and Subtracting Snapshots from Snapshot Groups

With the ADD and SUBTRACT procedures, you can add and subtract the snapshots in a snapshot group after you have created the group. As with the other DBMS_REFRESH procedures, you must call these procedures from the snapshot site.

NOTE   A snapshot group cannot have more than 100 members.

The DBMS_REFRESH.ADD procedure

Call the ADD procedure to add a snapshot group. The specification follows:

```
PROCEDURE DBMS_REFRESH.ADD
    (name IN VARCHAR2,
    {list IN VARCHAR2,| tab IN dbms_utility.uncl_array,}
     lax IN BOOLEAN  DEFAULT FALSE );
```

The parameters for the ADD procedure have the same meaning as in the MAKE procedure; refer to the parameter table in that section. Note that you must select the list or tab parameter, but not both.

The ADD procedure does not raise any exceptions.

Example. This example uses the ADD procedure to add the snapshots PROVINCES and CONTINENTS to the existing snapshot group SG_ARR_TABS:

```
BEGIN
    DBMS_REFRESH.ADD
            (name => 'SG_ADDR_TABS', list => 'PROVINCES', CONTINENTS');
END;
```

The DBMS_REFRESH.SUBTRACT procedure

Call the SUBTRACT procedure to subtract a snapshot group. The specification follows:

```
PROCEDURE DBMS_REFRESH.SUBTRACT
    (name IN VARCHAR2,
    {list IN VARCHAR2,| tab IN dbms_utility.uncl_array,}
     lax IN BOOLEAN  DEFAULT FALSE );
```

The parameters for the SUBTRACT procedure have the same meaning as in the MAKE procedure; refer to the parameter table in that section. Note that you must select the list or tab parameter, but not both.

The SUBTRACT procedure does not raise any exceptions.

Example. The following example removes the snapshots STATES and COUNTRIES from the existing snapshot group SG_ADDR_TABS. Since we also specified lax = TRUE, the call also drops the snapshot group if there are no other member snapshots remaining.

```
BEGIN
    DBMS_REFRESH.SUBTRACT( name => 'SG_ADDR_TABS',
                           list => 'STATES', COUNTRIES',
                           lax => TRUE);
END;
```

Altering Properties of a Snapshot Group

The CHANGE procedure allows you to modify settings associated with a snapshot group. You can change any of the parameters that are available in DBMS_REFRESH.MAKE:

interval
implicit_destroy
rollback_segment
push_deferred_rpc
refresh_after_errors
purge_option (Oracle8 only)
parallelism (Oracle8 only)
heap_size (Oracle8 only)

Refer to the MAKE section for an explanation of these parameters.

The DBMS_REFRESH.CHANGE procedure

Call the CHANGE procedure to modify a snapshot group's setting. The specifications for CHANGE differ for Oracle7 and Oracle8 as follows.

Here is the Oracle7 specification:

```
PROCEDURE DBMS_REFRESH.CHANGE
    (name IN VARCHAR2,
     next_date IN DATE DEFAULT NULL,
     interval IN VARCHAR2 DEFAULT NULL,
     implicit_destroy IN BOOLEAN DEFAULT NULL,
     rollback_seg IN VARCHAR2 DEFAULT NULL,
     push_deferred_rpc IN BOOLEAN DEFAULT NULL,
     refresh_after_errors IN BOOLEAN DEFAULT NULL);
```

Here is the Oracle8 specification:

```
PROCEDURE DBMS_REFRESH.CHANGE
    (name IN VARCHAR2,
     next_date IN DATE := NULL,
     interval IN VARCHAR2 := NULL,
     implicit_destroy IN BOOLEAN := NULL,
     rollback_seg IN VARCHAR2 := NULL,
     push_deferred_rpc IN BOOLEAN := NULL,
     refresh_after_errors IN BOOLEAN := NULL,
     purge_option IN BINARY_INTEGER := NULL,
     parallelism IN BINARY_INTEGER := NULL,
     heap_size IN BINARY_INTEGER := NULL);
```

As with the MAKE procedure, the difference between the Oracle7 and Oracle8 CHANGE specifications is the inclusion of support for parallel propagation and purging in the Oracle8 version.

The CHANGE procedure does not raise any exceptions

Manually Refreshing Snapshot Groups

The REFRESH procedure refreshes a snapshot group.

The DBMS_REFRESH.REFRESH procedure

Call REFRESH to refresh a snapshot group. A call to REFRESH causes all members of snapshot group name to be refreshed with the settings that you have designated in DBMS_REFRESH.MAKE and/or DBMS_REFRESH.CHANGE. The specification is,

```
PROCEDURE DBMS_REFRESH.REFRESH (name IN VARCHAR2);
```

where name identifies the snapshot group.

The REFRESH procedure does not raise any exceptions.

DBMS_OFFLINE_SNAPSHOT: Performing Offline Snapshot Instantiation

The DBMS_OFFLINE_SNAPSHOT package allows you to instantiate snapshots without having to run the CREATE SNAPSHOT command or the DBMS_REPEAT.SNAPSHOT_REPOBJECT procedure over the network (those methods are described under DBMS_REPCAT, later in this chapter). Doing offline instantiation in this way is particularly useful in cases where you wish to instantiate a snapshot site with a large amount of data in an advanced replication environment. Offline instantiation refers to the population of snapshots with the import and export utilities, as opposed to using the DBMS_SNAPSHOT.REFRESH procedure. This technique is less time-consuming and less taxing on your network, and it minimizes the time your environment must be quiesced.

You will typically use DBMS_OFFLINE_SNAPSHOT's BEGIN_LOAD and END_LOAD procedures in conjunction with the DBMS_REPCAT package's CREATE_SNAPSHOT_REPGROUP procedure; this procedure creates a new replicated snapshot group. The following sections summarize the syntax of the calls to BEGIN_LOAD and END_LOAD. See the later section "DBMS_REPCAT: Managing Snapshot Replication Groups" for a discussion of the DBMS_REPCAT procedure and how these procedures work together to instantiate snapshots in an advanced replication environment.

Getting Started with DBMS_OFFLINE_SNAPSHOT

The DBMS_OFFLINE_SNAPSHOT package is created when the Oracle database is installed. The *dbmsofln.sql* script (found in the built-in packages source directory, as described in Chapter 1) contains the source code for this package's specification. This script is called by *catrep.sql*, which must be run to install the advanced replication packages. The wrapped sql script *prvtofln.plb* creates the public synonym DBMS_OFFLINE_SNAPSHOT. No EXECUTE privileges are granted on DBMS_OFFLINE_SNAPSHOT; only the owner (SYS) and those with the EXECUTE ANY PROCEDURE system privilege may execute the package.

DBMS_OFFLINE_SNAPSHOT programs

Table 14-4 summarizes the programs available through DBMS_OFFLINE_SNAPSHOT.

Table 14-4. DBMS_OFFLINE_SNAPSHOT Programs

Name	Description	Use in SQL?
BEGIN_LOAD	Call before beginning to load data from an export file	No
END_LOAD	Call after the load is complete	No

DBMS_OFFLINE_SNAPSHOT exceptions

The DBMS_OFFLINE_SNAPSHOT package raises the following exceptions:

Name	Number	Description
badargument	−23430	The gname, sname, master_site, or snapshot_oname parameter is NULL or".
missingremotesnap	−23361	The snapshot_oname parameter does not exist at the remote master site (master_site parameter).
snaptabmismatch	−23363	The base table name of the snapshot at master site and snapshot site do not match.

DBMS_OFFLINE_SNAPSHOT Interface

This section describes the programs available through the DBMS_OFFLINE_SNAP-SHOT package.

The DBMS_OFFLINE_SNAPSHOT.BEGIN_LOAD procedure

Call the BEGIN_LOAD procedure before beginning to load data from an export file. The specifications for the Oracle7 and Oracle8 versions differ as follows.

Here is the Oracle7 specification:

```
PROCEDURE DBMS_OFFLINE_SNAPSHOT.BEGIN_LOAD
   (gname IN VARCHAR2,
    sname IN VARCHAR2,
    master_site IN VARCHAR2,
    snapshot_oname IN VARCHAR2,
    storage_c IN VARCHAR2 := '',
    comment IN VARCHAR2 := '');
```

Here is the Oracle8 specification:

```
PROCEDURE DBMS_OFFLINE_SNAPSHOT.BEGIN_LOAD
   (gname IN VARCHAR2,
    sname IN VARCHAR2,
    master_site IN VARCHAR2,
    snapshot_oname IN VARCHAR2,
    storage_c IN VARCHAR2 := '',
    comment IN VARCHAR2 := '',
    min_communicatio IN BOOLEAN := TRUE );
```

Parameters are summarized in the following table.

Name	Description
gname	The replication group to which the new snapshot belongs.
sname	The schema that owns the new snapshot.
master_site	The global name of the snapshot master site.
snapshot_oname	The name of the temporary snapshot created at the master site.
storage_c	Optional storage clause for the new snapshot.
comment	Optional comment for the snapshot; stored with entry in DBA_SNAPSHOTS if supplied.
min_communication (Oracle8 only)	The min_communication parameter controls how the update trigger on updateable snapshots queues changes back to the master site. If this parameter is set to TRUE (the default), then old column values are sent only if the update changes their value. New column values are sent only if the column is part of primary key, or if the column is in a column group that has been modified.

The BEGIN_LOAD procedure does not raise any exceptions.

The DBMS_OFFLINE_SNAPSHOT.END_LOAD procedure

Call the END_LOAD procedure after the data import (initiated by the BEGIN_ LOAD procedure) is complete. The specification is the same for Oracle7 and Oracle8:

```
PROCEDURE DBMS_OFFLINE_SNAPSHOT.END_LOAD
    (gname IN VARCHAR2,
     sname IN VARCHAR2,
     snapshot_oname IN VARCHAR2);
```

Parameters have the same meanings as for the BEGIN_LOAD procedure (see the previous section). The END_LOAD procedure does not raise any exceptions.

DBMS_REPCAT: Managing Snapshot Replication Groups

Although most of the procedures in the DBMS_REPCAT package are used to create and maintain the advanced replication environment, some of the procedures let you manipulate snapshot replication groups. This section describes only the snapshot-related programs. The bulk of the DBMS_REPCAT programs are described in Chapters 15 and 16.

The procedures in DBMS_REPCAT used for manipulating snapshot replication groups are in large measure analogous to the procedures DBMS_REFRESH provides for manipulating simple snapshot groups.

Getting Started with DBMS_REPCAT

The DBMS_REPCAT package is created when the Oracle database is installed. The *dbmsrepc.sql* script (found in the built-in packages source directory, as described in Chapter 1) contains the source code for this package's specification. This script is called by *catrep.sql*, which must be run to install the advanced replication packages. The script creates the public synonym DBMS_REPCAT. The package procedure DBMS_REPCAT_AUTH.GRANT_SURROGATE_REPCAT grants EXECUTE privileges on the package to the specified grantee. In addition, the package owner (SYS) and users with the EXECUTE ANY PROCEDURE system privilege may execute it.

DBMS_REPCAT programs

Table 14-5 lists only the DBMS_REPCAT snapshot-related programs; see Tables 15-3 and 16-10 for the remaining DBMS_REPCAT programs.

Table 14-5. DBMS_REPCAT Programs (Snapshots Only)

Name	Description	Use in SQL
ALTER_SNAPSHOT_PROPAGATION	Changes a snapshot replication group's propagation mode	No
CREATE_SNAPSHOT_REPGROUP	Creates a snapshot replication group	No
CREATE_SNAPSHOT_REPOBJECT	Adds an object to a snapshot replication group	No
DROP_SNAPSHOT_REPGROUP	Drops a snapshot replication group	No
DROP_SNAPSHOT_REPOBJECT	Drops an object from a snapshot replication group	No
REFRESH_SNAPSHOT_REPGROUP	Refreshes a snapshot replication group	No
SWITCH_SNAPSHOT_MASTER	Remasters a snapshot site to another master site	No

DBMS_REPCAT exceptions

DBMS_REPCAT defines the following exceptions for the programs listed in Table 14-6.

Table 14-6. DBMS_REPCAT Exceptions

Name	Number	Description
commfailure	−23317	Unable to communicate with master
dbnotcompatible	−23375	Attempt to use SYNCHRONOUS propagation in Pre-7.3 database
ddlfailure	−23318	Unable to perform DDL
duplicateobject	−23309	Object oname already exists
duplicaterepgroup	−23374	Replication group gname already exists
missingobject	−23308	Object oname does not exist in master's replication group gname
missingremoteobject	−23381	Master site has not generated replication support for oname
missingrepgroup	−23373	Replication group gname does not exist
missingschema	−23306	Schema sname does not exist
misssnapobject	−23355	Object oname does not exist at master
nonmaster	−23312	Master site associated with snapshot group is no longer a master site
nonsnapshot	−23314	Calling site is not a snapshot site

Table 14-6. DBMS_REPCAT Exceptions (continued)

Name	Number	Description
norepoption	–23364	Replication option not installed
typefailure	–23319	propagation_mode not specified correctly

Creating and Dropping Snapshot Replication Groups

The CREATE_SNAPSHOT_REPGROUP and DROP_SNAPSHOT_REPGROUP procedures allow you to create and destroy snapshot replication groups.

The DBMS_REPCAT.CREATE_SNAPSHOT_REPGROUP procedure

This procedure creates a new, empty snapshot replication group. You must invoke it from the snapshot site. The program specification follows:

```
PROCEDURE DBMS_REPCAT.CREATE_SNAPSHOT_REPGROUP
    (gname IN VARCHAR2,
     master IN VARCHAR2,
     comment IN VARCHAR2 := '',
     propagation_mode IN VARCHAR2  := 'ASYNCHRONOUS');
```

Parameters are summarized in the following table.

Name	Description
gname	Name of the new snapshot group
master	Global name of master site
comment	Comment for the snapshot group; visible in DBA_REPSITES data dictionary view
propagation_mode	Snapshot propagation mode (SYNCHRONOUS, or ASYNCHRONOUS)

Exceptions. The CREATE_SNAPSHOT_REPGROUP procedure raises the following exceptions:

Name	Number	Description
commfailure	–23317	Unable to communicate with master
dbnotcompatible	–23375	Attempt to use SYNCHRONOUS propagation in pre-7.3 database
duplicaterepgroup	–23374	Replication group gname already exists
nonmaster	–23312	The master parameter is not a master site
norepoption	–23364	Replication option not installed
typefailure	–23319	propagation_mode not specified correctly

Restrictions. Note the following restrictions on calling CREATE_SNAPSHOT_REP-
GROUP:

- You must be connected to the replication administrator account (typically REPADMIN) to call the CREATE_SNAPSHOT_REPGROUP procedure.

- The snapshot group name must match the name of the master replication group.

The offline snapshot instantiation procedure

The procedure for performing offline instantiation of snapshots in an advanced replication environment (using the CREATE SNAPSHOT command and the DBMS_ OFFLINE_SNAPSHOT and DBMS_REPCAT packages) follows:

1. Create a snapshot log for each master table if one does not already exist.

2. Create a snapshot of each master table *in the master database*, and *in the same schema as the master table*. Of course, the name of the snapshot will have to be different from the name of the master table. The CREATE SNAP-SHOT statement must also include a loopback database link qualifier.

   ```
   CREATE SNAPSHOT snp_countries
   AS SELECT * FROM countries@D7CA.BIGWHEEL.COM@TCPIP
   ```

3. Perform user exports of all schema that own master tables. You should be logged on to the schema owner account for these exports. The only tables that you need to export are the snapshot base tables—that is, those whose names begin with "SNAP$_".

4. Copy the export dump file(s) to the new snapshot site(s).

5. Use CREATE_SNAPSHOT_REPGROUP at the snapshot sites to create a new snapshot replication object group. The name of this object group should be the same as the name of the replication group of which the master tables are members.

   ```
   BEGIN
       DBMS_REPCAT.CREATE_SNAPSHOT_REPGROUP(
           gname            => 'SPROCKET',
           master           => 'D7CA.BIGWHEEL.COM',
           comment          => 'Group created on '||sysdate|| ' by '||user,
           propagation_mode => 'ASYNCHRONOUS');
   END;
   ```

6. Call DBMS_OFFLINE_SNAPSHOT.BEGIN_LOAD to begin loading the data from the export file(s). You must call the procedure for every snapshot you plan to import.

   ```
   BEGIN
       DBMS_OFFLINE_SNAPSHOT.BEGIN_LOAD(
           gname       =>   'SPROCKET',
           sname       =>   'SPROCKET',
   ```

```
         master_site  =>   'D7CA.BIGWHEEL.COM'
         snapshot_oname=> 'SNP_COUNTRIES'
         storage_c    =>   'TABLESPACE sprocket_data STORAGE (INITIAL 64K)'
         comment      =>   'Load of COUNTRIES snapshot begun at '||sysdate);
    END;
```

7. Import the snapshot base table(s) from the export file(s) created in step 4.

8. Call DBMS_OFFLINE_SNAPSHOT.END_LOAD for each snapshot when the load is complete.

```
    BEGIN
        DBMS_OFFLINE_SNAPSHOT.END_LOAD(
            gname        => 'SPROCKET'
            sname        => 'SPROCKET'
            snapshot_oname=> 'SNP_COUNTRIES');
    END;
```

The DBMS_REPCAT.DROP_SNAPSHOT_REPGROUP procedure

The DBMS_REPCAT package's DROP_SNAPSHOT_REPGROUP procedure is the counterpart to the CREATE_SNAPSHOT_REPGROUP procedure. As you would suspect, this procedure drops an existing snapshot replication group, and optionally, all member snapshots. Here's the specification:

```
    PROCEDURE DBMS_REPCAT>DROP_SNAPSHOT_REPGROUP
        (gname IN VARCHAR2,
         drop_contents IN BOOLEAN := FALSE);
```

Parameters are summarized in the following table.

Name	Description
gname	Name of the snapshot group.
drop_contents	If TRUE, objects in gname are dropped. If FALSE (the default) they are simply no longer replicated.

Exceptions. The DROP_SNAPSHOT_REPGROUP procedure raises the following exceptions:

Name	Number	Description
missingrepgroup	−23373	Replication group gname does not exist
nonmaster	−23313	Calling site is not a snapshot site

Restrictions. If drop_contents is set to FALSE, the triggers created to support snapshot modifications remain.

Example. The following example illustrates the dropping of a snapshot replication group with the DROP_SNAPSHOT_REPGROUP procedure:

```
    BEGIN
        DBMS_REPCAT.DROP_SNAPSHOT_REPGROUP(
```

```
        gname        => 'SPROCKET',
        drop_objects=> TRUE);
END;
```

Here, we drop the snapshot replication group SPROCKET and drop the member
snapshots as well.

Adding and Removing Snapshot Replication Group Objects

The CREATE_SNAPSHOT_REPOBJECT and DROP_SNAPSHOT_REPOBJECT procedures add and remove objects, respectively, from a snapshot replication group.
These objects may be snapshots, packages, package bodies, procedures, synonyms, or views.

The DBMS_REPCAT.CREATE_SNAPSHOT_REPOBJECT procedure

The CREATE_SNAPSHOT_REPOBJECT procedure adds an object to a snapshot
replication group. For new snapshot objects, this procedure generates row-level
replication triggers for snapshots if the master table uses row-level replication.
The specifications differ for Oracle7 and Oracle8 as follows.

Here is the Oracle7 specification:

```
PROCEDURE DBMS_REPCAT. CREATE_SNAPSHOT_REPOBJECT
    (sname IN VARCHAR2,
     oname IN VARCHAR2,
     type IN VARCHAR2,
     ddl_text IN VARCHAR2 := '',
     comment IN VARCHAR2 := '',
     gname IN VARCHAR2 := '',
     gen_objs_owner IN VARCHAR2 := '');
```

Here is the Oracle8 specification:

```
PROCEDURE DBMS_REPCAT.CREATE_SNAPSHOT_REPOBJECT
    (sname IN VARCHAR2,
     oname IN VARCHAR2,
     type IN VARCHAR2,
     ddl_text IN VARCHAR2 := '',
     comment IN VARCHAR2 := '',
     gname IN VARCHAR2 := '',
     gen_objs_owner IN VARCHAR2 := '',
     min_communication IN BOOLEAN  := TRUE);
```

NOTE   The only difference between the Orace7 and Oracle8 implementa-
          tions is the addition of the min_communication parameter in
          Oracle8.

Parameters are summarized in the following table.

Name	Description
sname	Name of schema to which oname belongs.
oname	Name of object to be added.
type	Object type. Supported types are PACKAGE, PACKAGE BODY, PROCEDURE, SNAPSHOT, SYNONYM, and VIEW.
ddl_text	DDL used to create object (for type SNAPSHOT only).
comment	Comment on object, visible in DBA_REPOBJECT data dictionary view.
gname	Name of snapshot group to which object is being added. Defaults to sname if not specified.
gen_objs_owner	Name of the schema in which to create the generated trigger and trigger package or procedure wrapper for the object. Defaults to sname.
drop_objects	If set to TRUE, object is dropped too. If FALSE (the default), object is only removed from the snapshot group.
min_communication (Oracle8 only)	Must be FALSE if any master site is running Oracle7. TRUE, the default setting, uses the minimum communication algorithm.

Exceptions. CREATE_SNAPSHOT_REPGROUP raises the following exceptions:

Name	Number	Description
commfailure	−23317	Unable to communicate with master site
ddlfailure	−23318	Unable to perform DDL
duplicateobject	−23309	Object oname already exists
missingobject	−23308	Object oname does not exist in master's replication group gname
missingremoteobject	−23381	Master site has not generated replication support for oname
missingschema	−23306	Schema sname does not exist
misssnapobject	−23355	Object oname does not exist at master
nonmaster	−23312	Master site associated with snapshot group is no longer a master site
nonsnapshot	−23314	Calling site is not a snapshot site
typefailure	−23319	Invalid value for type

TIP CREATE_SNAPSHOT_REPOBJECT is called from the replication administrator (typically REPADMIN) account. If you are creating an snapshot with ddl_text, be sure to specify the schema in which it should be created (if other than the replication administrator account).

Example. The following example illustrates how to add an object to an existing snapshot replication group:

```
BEGIN
    DBMS_REPCAT.CREATE_SNAPSHOT_REPOBJECT(
        sname     => 'SPROCKET',
        oname     => 'PRICE_LIST',
        type      => 'SNAPSHOT' ,
        ddl_text=>
'CREATE SNAPSHOT  SPROCKET.PRICES AS SELECT * FROM
    PRICES@D7CA.BIGWHEEL.COM' ,
        gnam      => 'SPROCKET',
        gen_objs_owner => 'SPROCKET')
END;
BEGIN
```

The DBMS_REPCAT.DROP_SNAPSHOT_REPOBJECT procedure

The DROP_SNAPSHOT_REPOBJECT procedure drops an object from a snapshot replication group.

```
PROCEDURE DBMS_REPCAT.DROP_SNAPSHOT_REPOBJECT
    (sname IN VARCHAR2,
     oname IN VARCHAR2,
     type IN VARCHAR2,
     drop_objects IN BOOLEAN := FALSE);.
```

For parameter descriptions, see the table in the "The DBMS_REPCAT.CREATE_SNAPSHOT_REPOBJECT procedure" section.

Exceptions. DROP_SNAPSHOT_REPOBJECT raises the following exceptions:

Name	Number	Description
missingobject	−23308	Object oname does not exist in master's replication group gname
nonsnapshot	−23314	Calling site is not a snapshot site
typefailure	−23319	Invalid value for type

Restrictions. If the type parameter in DROP_REPOBJECT is SNAPSHOT and you do not set the drop_objects parameter to TRUE, replication triggers and associated packages remain in the schema, and deferred transactions (if any) remain in the DEFTRANS queue.

Example. The following example drops an object from a snapshot replication group:

```
DBMS_REPCAT.FTOP_SNAPSHOT_REPOBJECT(
    sname     => 'SPROCKET',
    oname     => 'PRICE_LIST',
    type      => 'SNAPSHOT',
```

```
            drop_objects=> TRUE);
    END;
```

Altering a Snapshot Replication Group's Propagation Mode

The ALTER_SNAPSHOT_PROPAGATION procedure changes a snapshot replication group's propagation mode. The propagation mode can be either SYNCHRONOUS or ASYNCHRONOUS. When you call this procedure, Oracle does the following:

- Pushes any transactions that exist in the deferred RPC queue for the group
- Locks the snapshot base tables (SNAP$_<tablename>)
- Regenerates replication triggers and packages for the objects in the group

The DBMS_REPCAT.ALTER_SNAPSHOT_PROPAGATION procedure

Call the ALTER_SNAPSHOT_PROPAGATION procedure to change the propagation mode of a particular snapshot. Specifications for Oracle7 and Oracle8 differ as follows.

Here is the Oracle7 specification:

```
PROCEDURE DBMS_REPCAT.ALTER_SNAPSHOT_PROPAGATION
    (alter_snapshot_propagation(
    gname IN VARCHAR2,
    propagation_mode IN VARCHAR2,
    comment IN VARCHAR2 := '',
    execute_as_user  IN BOOLEAN  := FALSE);
```

Here is the Oracle8 specification:

```
PROCEDURE DBMS_REPCAT.ALTER_SNAPSHOT_PROPAGATION
    (gname IN VARCHAR2,
    propagation_mode IN VARCHAR2,
    comment IN VARCHAR2 := '' );
```

Parameters are summarized in the following table.

Name	Description
gname	Name of the replication group to be altered
propagation_mode	The new propagation mode to use (SYNCHRONOUS or ASYNCHRONOUS)
comment	Comment visible in DBA_REPPROP data dictionary view
execute_as_user (Oracle7 only)	FALSE (default) indicates that remote system will authenticate calls using authentication context user who originally queued the RPC; TRUE indicates that remote system will use authentication context of the session user

Exceptions. ALTER_SNAPSHOT_PROPAGATION raises the following exceptions:

Name	Number	Description
dbnotcompatible	−23375	Database version is not 7.3 or later
missingrepgroup	−23373	Replication group gname does not exist
typefailure	−23319	Invalid propagation_mode

Restrictions. ALTER_SNAPSHOT_PROPAGATION must be called from a snapshot site.

Example. The following example shows how to switch from asynchronous to synchronous propagation for a given snapshot replication group:

```
BEGIN
    DBMS_REPCAT.ALTER_SNAPSHOT_PROPAGATION(
    gname                =>  'SPROCKET',
    propagation_mode     =>  'ASYNCHRONOUS',
    comment              =>  'Mode set to asynchronous on ' ||sysdate||
                             'by '||user);
END;
```

Manually Refreshing a Snapshot Replication Group

You can use the REFRESH_SNAPSHOT_REPGROUP to refresh manually a snapshot replication group. The procedure can optionally drop objects that are no longer in the group, and/or refresh the snapshots and other objects.

NOTE   The REFRESH_SNAPSHOT_REPGROUP procedure replaces the REFRESH_SNAPSHOT_REPSCHEMA procedure. Although REFRESH_SNAPSHOT_REPSCHEMA still exists (as of Oracle 7.3.3), do not use it; it does not exist in Oracle 8.0.3.

The DBMS_REPCAT.REFRESH_SNAPSHOT_REPGROUP procedure

Call the DBMS_REPCAT.REFRESH_SNAPSHOT_REPGROUP procedure to refresh a snapshot replication group manually. Specifications differ for Oracle7 and Oracle8 as follows.

Here is the Oracle7 specification:

```
PROCEDURE DBMS_REPCAT.REFRESH_SNAPSHOT_REPGROUP
    (gname IN VARCHAR2,
     drop_missing_contents IN BOOLEAN := FALSE,
     refresh_snapshots IN BOOLEAN := FALSE,
     refresh_other_objects IN BOOLEAN := FALSE,
     execute_as_user IN BOOLEAN:= FALSE);
```

Here is the Oracle8 specification:

```
PROCEDURE DBMS_REPCAT.REFRESH_SNAPSHOT_REPGROUP
    (gname IN VARCHAR2,
     drop_missing_contents IN BOOLEAN := FALSE,
     refresh_other_objects IN BOOLEAN := FALSE )
```

Parameters are summarized in the following table.

Name	Description
gname	Name of the replication group.
drop_missing_contents	If TRUE, drop schema objects that are no longer in the snapshot group. If FALSE (the default), objects are simply no longer replicated.
refresh_snapshots	If TRUE, force a refresh of snapshots in gname. Default is FALSE.
refresh_other_objects	If TRUE, refresh non-snapshot objects in gname, such as views and procedures. Non-snapshot objects are refreshed by dropping and recreating them. Default is FALSE.
execute_as_user (Oracle7 only)	FALSE (default) indicates that the remote system will authenticate calls using the authentication context user who originally queued the RPC; TRUE indicates that remote system will use authentication context of the session user.

Exceptions. REFRESH_SNAPSHOT_REPGROUP raises the following exceptions:

Name	Number	Description
commfailure	−23317	Unable to communicate with the master site
nonmaster	−23313	Master is no longer a master database
nonsnapshot	−23314	Calling site is not a snapshot site

Restrictions. REFRESH_SNAPSHOT_REPGROUP must be called from a snapshot site.

Example. The following example illustrates how REFRESH_SNAPSHOT_REP-GROUP is commonly used:

```
BEGIN
    DBMS_REPCAT.REFRESH_SNAPSHOT_REPGROUP(
        gname => 'SPROCKET',
        drop_missing_contents=> TRUE,
        refresh_snapshots=> TRUE,
        refresh_other_objects=> TRUE)
END;
```

This example refreshes all snapshots in group SPROCKET, drops schema objects that are no longer in the group, and recreates any views, procedures, or synonyms that have been created or altered at the master site.

Switching the Master of a Snapshot Replication Group

Should it ever become necessary to point a snapshot replication group to a different master site, you can do it with the SWITCH_SNAPSHOT_MASTER procedure.

The DBMS_REPCAT.SWITCH_SNAPSHOT_MASTER procedure

The SWITCH_SNAPSHOT_MASTER procedure lets you switch a snapshot replication group to a different master site. This procedure changes the master site for the specified snapshot group. The new master site must contain a replica of the replication group gname. The next time the snapshot group refreshes, Oracle performs a full refresh. The specifications for SWITCH_SNAPSHOT_MASTER differ for Oracle7 and Oracle8 as follows.

Here is the Oracle7 specification:

```
PROCEDUREDBMS_REPCAT.SWITCH_SNAPSHOT_MASTER
    (gname IN VARCHAR2 := '',
    master IN VARCHAR2,
    execute_as_user IN BOOLEAN  = FALSE,
    sname IN VARCHAR2 := '');
```

Here is the Oracle8 specification:

```
PROCEDURE DBMS_REPCAT.SWITCH_SNAPSHOT_MASTER
    (gname IN VARCHAR2 := '',
    master IN VARCHAR2)
```

Parameters are summarized in the following table.

Name	Description
gname	Name of the snapshot group
master	Name of the new master site
execute_as_user (Oracle7 only)	FALSE (default) indicates that the remote system will authenticate calls using the authentication context user who originally queued the RPC; TRUE indicates that remote system will use authentication context of the session user
sname (Oracle7 only)	Not used

Exceptions. The SWITCH_SNAPSHOT_MASTER procedure may raise the following exceptions:

Name	Number	Description
commfailure	–23317	Unable to communicate with master site

Name	Number	Description
nonmaster	−23312	The master parameter is not a master site
nonsnapshot	−23314	Calling site is not a snapshot site

Restrictions. Note the following restrictions on calling SWITCH_SNAPSHOT_MAS-
TER:

- The new master site must contain a replica of the replication group gname.

- Snapshots whose query is greater than 32K cannot be remastered.

Example. The following call remasters snapshot group SPROCKET to D7NY.BIG-
WHEEL.COM:

```
BEGIN
    DBMS_REPCAT.SWITCH_SNAPSHOT_MASTER(
        gname   => 'SPROCKET',
        master  => 'D7NY.BIGWHEEL.COM')
END
```

TIP   Put snapshot logs on the master tables at the new master site so that
                 you can use fast refreshes.

Figure 14-3 graphically illustrates this example.

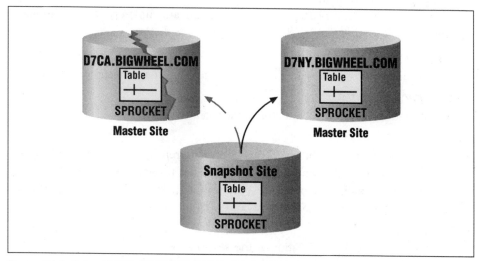

Figure 14-3. Using DBMS_REPCAT.SWITCH_SNAPSHOT_MASTER

15

Advanced Replication

If you are using the advanced replication option, you will use Oracle built-in packages to create and maintain a replicated environment. This chapter describes packages and the roles they play in the configuration and upkeep of a multi-master environment.

DBMS_REPCAT_AUTH

> Grants and revokes "surrogate SYS" privileges for an administrator account.

DBMS_REPCAT_ADMIN

> Creates administrator accounts for replication.

DBMS_REPCAT

> An enormous package that performs many different types of advanced replication operations. This chapter describes only the programs that deal with replication environment maintenance; the other DBMS_REPCAT programs are described in Chapter 14, *Snapshots*, and Chapter 16, *Conflict Resolution*.

DBMS_REPUTIL

> Enables and disables replication at the session level.

DBMS_OFFLINE_OG

> Instantiates sites—that is, lets you export data from an existing master site and import it into the new master site.

DBMS_RECTIFIER_DIFF

   Compares the replicated tables at two master sites and allows you to synchronize them if they are different.

In this chapter, the presentation is more or less chronological—the packages and
their programs are presented in roughly the order in which you would run them
in a real advanced replication situation.

DBMS_REPCAT_AUTH: Setting Up Administrative Accounts

The first step in creating an advanced replication environment is to create administrative and end user accounts. The DBMS_REPCAT_AUTH and DBMS_REPCAT_
ADMIN packages contain programs that grant and revoke the privileges required
in such an environment. This section describes the DBMS_REPCAT_AUTH operations; the next section describes DBMS_REPCAT_ADMIN.

Getting Started with DBMS_REPCAT_AUTH

The DBMS_REPCAT_AUTH package is created when the Oracle database is
installed. The *dbmsrepc.sql* script (found in the built-in packages source directory,
as described in Chapter 1, *Introduction*) contains the source code for this package's specification. This script is called by *catrep.sql*, which must be run to install
the advanced replication packages. The wrapped sql script *prvtrepc.sql* creates the
public synonym DBMS_REPCAT_AUTH. No EXECUTE privileges are granted on
DBMS_REPCAT_AUTH; only the owner (SYS) and those with the EXECUTE ANY
PROCEDURE system privilege may execute the package.

DBMS_REPCAT_AUTH programs

The DBMS_REPCAT_AUTH programs are listed in Table 15-1.

Table 15-1. DBMS_REPCAT_AUTH Programs

Name	Description	Use in SQL?
GRANT_SURROGATE_REPCAT	Grants required privileges to a specified user	No
REVOKE_SURROGATE_REPCAT	Revokes required privileges from a specified user	No

DBMS_REPCAT_AUTH exceptions

The DBMS_REPCAT_AUTH package may raise exception ORA-01917 if the specified user does not exist.

Granting and Revoking Surrogate SYS Accounts

The DBMS_REPCAT_AUTH package contains programs that let you grant and revoke "surrogate SYS" privileges to a user. Private database links owned by SYS connect to the surrogate SYS account at remote sites, thereby avoiding the need for any database links that connect to SYS.

The DBMS_REPCAT_AUTH.GRANT_SURROGATE_REPCAT procedure

The GRANT_SURROGATE_REPCAT procedure grants surrogate SYS privileges to a particular user. The specification is,

```
PROCEDURE DBMS_REPCAT_AUTH.GRANT_SURROGATE_REPCAT
    (userid IN VARCHAR2);
```

where userid is the Oracle userid for whom you are granting privileges.

Exceptions. The GRANT_SURROGATE_REPCAT procedure may raise the exception ORA-1917 if the specified user does not exist.

Example. The following example illustrates how you might use GRANT_SURROGATE_REPCAT:

```
BEGIN
    DBMS_REPCAT_AUTH.GRANT_SURROGATE_REPCAT('REPSYS');
END;
```

This call configures the REPSYS account to perform tasks required to replicate remote DML and DDL at this site. The SYS account from remote sites should have private database links connecting to this account. The privileges granted include EXECUTE privileges on replication packages. DML privileges are data dictionary tables associated with replication.

The DBMS_REPCAT_AUTH.REVOKE_SURROGATE_REPCAT procedure

The REVOKE_SURROGATE_REPCAT procedure revokes the surrogate SYS privileges that have previously been granted to an end user. The specification is,

```
PROCEDURE DBMS_REPCAT_AUTH.REVOKE_SURROGATE_REPCAT
    (userid IN VARCHAR2);
```

where userid is the Oracle userid for whom you are revoking privileges.

Exceptions. The REVOKE_SURROGATE_REPCAT procedure may raise the exception ORA-1917 if the specified user does not exist.

Example. The following example shows how to use REVOKE_SURROGATE_REP-CAT:

```
BEGIN
    DBMS_REPCAT_AUTH.REVOKE_SURROGATE_REPCAT('REPSYS');
END;
```

You must have only one surrogate SYS account at each site in a multimaster environment, and it is most convenient if the userid is the same at every site. Generally, the only usage of the surrogate SYS account is via a database link.

Granting and Revoking Propagator Accounts (Oracle8)

Oracle8 and Oracle7 use different mechanisms to propagate changes between sites. Oracle8 does not require a surrogate SYS account, as Oracle7 does. Instead, with Oracle8 you designate a propagator account that delivers queued transactions to remote databases and applies transactions locally on behalf of remote sites.

The programs to create and to drop propagator accounts, REGISTER_PROPAGA-TOR and UNREGISTER_PROPAGATOR, are contained in the DBMS_DEFER_SYS (described in Chapter 17, *Deferred Transactions and Remote Procedure Calls*).

NOTE   We recommend using the same username as the propagator at all database sites. Also, make the account the same as the replication administrator (REPADMIN) account.

DBMS_REPCAT_ADMIN: Setting Up More Administrator Accounts

Along with DBMS_REPCAT_AUTH, use the DBMS_REPCAT_ADMIN package to create administrator accounts for replication. This section explains how to do so.

Getting Started with DBMS_REPCAT_ADMIN

The DBMS_REPCAT_ADMIN package is created when the Oracle database is installed. The *dbmsrepc.sql* script (found in the built-in packages source directory, as described in Chapter 1) contains the source code for this package's specification. This script is called by *catrep.sql*, which must be run to install the advanced replication packages. The wrapped sql script *prvtrepc.sql* creates the public synonym DBMS_REPCAT_ADMIN. No EXECUTE privileges are granted on DBMS_REPCAT_ADMIN; only the owner (SYS) and those with the EXECUTE ANY PROCEDURE system privilege may execute the package.

DBMS_REPCAT_ADMIN programs

Table 15-2 lists the programs in DBMS_REPCAT_ADMIN.T

Table 15-2. DBMS_REPCAT_ADMIN Program

Name	Description	Use in SQL?
GRANT_ADMIN_ANY_REPGROUP	Grants privileges required to administer any replication group at the current site	No
GRANT_ADMIN_ANY_REPSCHEMA (Oracle8)	Grants privileges required to administer any replication schema at the current site	No
GRANT_ADMIN_REPGROUP	Grants privileges required to administer the replication group for which the user is the schema owner	No
GRANT_ADMIN_REPSCHEMA (Oracle8)	Grants privileges required to administer the replication schema for which the user is the schema owner	No
REVOKE_ADMIN_ANY_REPGROUP	Revokes privileges required to administer all replication groups	No
REVOKE_ADMIN_ANY_REPSCHEMA (Oracle8)	Revokes privileges required to administer all replication schemas	No
REVOKE_ADMIN_REPGROUP	Revokes privileges required to administer the replication group for which the user is the schema owner	No
REVOKE_ADMIN_REPSCHEMA (Oracle8)	Revokes privileges required to administer the replication schema for which the user is the schema owner.	No

DBMS_REPCAT_ADMIN exceptions

The DBMS_REPCAT_AUTH package may raise exception ORA-1917 if the specified user does not exist.

NOTE   Oracle8 documents only the REPGROUP procedures, although the REPSCHEMA procedures also exist. The functionality is identical.

Creating and Dropping Replication Administrator Accounts

Advanced replication also requires an account to maintain the environment. The replication administrator account (usually REPADMIN) performs tasks such as quiescing the environment, adding and removing master sites, and creating replication groups. For example, you'll use DBMS_REPCAT's ADMIN.GRANT_ADMIN_ ANY_REPGROUP procedure to set up the replication administrator account to maintain *all* replication groups in your environment. You can also configure an account to control exactly one schema in a replication group with the GRANT_ ADMIN_REPGROUP procedure. The recipient of this grant will be able to perform administrative tasks on objects it owns within a replication group; the account will not be able to administer objects it does not own. Because of this restriction, it usually makes sense to create administrative accounts for a specific group only if it is a single schema replication group and the administrative account is the schema account.

In most cases, the DBA opts for using a single replication administrator account over creating administrative accounts for every replication group.

The DBMS_REPCAT_ADMIN.GRANT_ADMIN_REPGROUP procedure

The GRANT_ADMIN_REPGROUP procedure grants the privileges required to administer a replication group for which the user is the schema owner. The specification is,

```
PROCEDURE DBMS_REPCAT_ADMIN.GRANT_ADMIN_REPGROUP
    (userid IN VARCHAR2);
```

where userid is the Oracle userid for whom you are granting privileges.

Exceptions. DBMS_REPCAT_ADMIN.GRANT_ADMIN.REPGROUP may raise exception ORA-1917 if the specified user does not exist.

Example. This call configures the SPROCKET account to administer its objects in a replication group:

```
BEGIN
    DBMS_REPCAT_ADMIN.GRANT_ADMIN_REPGROUP('SPROCKET');
END;
```

This approach is most viable when the name of the replication group is the same as the name of the schema, and when all objects in the replication group belong to that schema.

The DBMS_REPCAT_ADMIN.REVOKE_ADMIN_REPGROUP procedure

The REVOKE_ADMIN_REPGROUP procedure revokes the privileges required to administer the replication group for which the user is the schema owner. The specification is,

```
PROCEDURE DBMS_REPCAT_ADMIN.REVOKE_ADMIN_REPGROUP
    (userid IN VARCHAR2);
```

where userid is the Oracle userid for whom you are revoking privileges.

Exceptions. DBMS_REPCAT_ADMIN.REVOKE_ADMIN_REPGROUP   may   raise exception ORA-1917 if the specified user does not exist.

The DBMS_REPCAT_ADMIN.GRANT_ADMIN_ANY_REPGROUP procedure

The GRANT_ADMIN_ANY_REPGROUP procedure grants the privileges required to administer *any* replication group at the current site. The specification is,

```
PROCEDURE DBMS_REPCAT_ADMIN.GRANT_ADMIN_ANY_REPGROUP
    (userid IN VARCHAR2);
```

where userid is the Oracle userid for whom you are granting privileges.

Exceptions. DBMS_REPCAT_ADMIN.GRANT_ADMIN_ANY_REPGROUP may raise exception ORA-1917 if the specified user does not exist.

Example. The following call supplies the REPADMIN account with privileges to perform maintenance operations on all replication groups at the site:

```
BEGIN
    DBMS_REPCAT_ADMIN.GRANT_ADMIN_ANY_REPGROUP('REPADMIN');
END;
```

NOTE   Be sure to set up a replication administrator account at every master site of a multimaster replication environment. In addition, administration will be easiest if you use the same account name in all locations.

The DBMS_REPCAT_ADMIN.REVOKE_ADMIN_ANY_REPGROUP procedure

The REVOKE_ADMIN_ANY_REPGROUP procedure revokes the privileges required to administer *any* replication group at the current site. The specification is,

```
PROCEDURE DBMS_REPCAT_ADMIN.REVOKE_ADMIN_ANY_REPGROUP
    (userid IN VARCHAR2);
```

where userid is the Oracle userid for whom you are revoking privileges.

Exceptions. DBMS_REPCAT_ADMIN.REVOKE_ANY_REPGROUP may raise exception ORA-1917 if the specified user does not exist.

Example. This call revokes replication administrator privileges from the REPADMIN account:

```
BEGIN
    DBMS_REPCAT_ADMIN.REVOKE_ADMIN_ANY_REPGROUP('REPADMIN');
END;
```

DBMS_REPCAT: Replication Environment Administration

The DBMS_REPCAT package performs many advanced replication operations, including some described in other chapters. This section describes only the DBMS_REPCAT programs that you'll use to administer the advanced replication environment.

Getting Started with DBMS_REPCAT

The DBMS_REPCAT package is created when the Oracle database is installed. The *dbmsrepc.sql* script (found in the built-in packages source directory, as described in Chapter 1) contains the source code for this package's specification. This script is called by *catrep.sql*, which must be run to install the advanced replication packages. The script creates the public synonym DBMS_REPCAT. The package procedure DBMS_REPCAT_AUTH.GRANT_SURROGATE_REPCAT grants EXECUTE privileges on the package to the specified grantee. In addition, the package owner (SYS) and users with the EXECUTE ANY PROCEDURE system privilege may execute it.

DBMS_REPCAT programs

Table 15-3 lists in alphabetical order the DBMS_REPCAT procedures used to maintain an advanced replication environment. In the sections that follow, we divide these programs by category (replication groups, replication objects, replication support, master sites, the "repcatlog" queue, and quiescence); each section includes a table showing the programs available in that category. For example, the section "Replication Groups with DBMS_REPCAT" describes only the replication group programs.

Table 15-3. DBMS_REPCAT Programs (Replication Administration Only)

Name	Description	Use in SQL?
ADD_MASTER_DATABASE	Adds master database to replication group	No
ALTER_MASTER_PROPAGATION	Alters propagation method for a replication group at a given site (options are SYNCHRONOUS or ASYNCHRONOUS)	No
ALTER_MASTER_REPOBJECT	Performs DDL on a replicated object	No
COMMENT_ON_REPGROUP	Creates or updates a comment on a replication group; visible in DBA_REPGROUP data dictionary view	No
COMMENT_ON_REPSITES	Creates or updates a comment on a replication site; visible in DBA_REPSITES data dictionary view	No
COMMENT_ON_REPOBJECT	Creates or updates a comment on a replicated object; visible in DBA_REPOBJECT data dictionary view	No
CREATE_MASTER_REPGROUP	Creates a master replication group	No
CREATE_MASTER_REPOBJECT	Adds an object to a replication group	No
DO_DEFERRED_REPCAT_ADMIN	Performs outstanding administrative tasks at local master site	No
DROP_MASTER_REPGROUP	Drops a replication group	No
DROP_MASTER_REPOBJECT	Drops an object from a replication group	No
EXECUTE_DDL	Specifies DDL to execute at master sites	No
GENERATE_REPLICATION_PACKAGE	Generates packages required to replicate a given table	No
GENERATE_REPLICATION_SUPPORT	Generates triggers, packages, and procedures required to replicate a given table	No
GENERATE_REPLICATION_TRIGGER	Generates triggers and packages required to replicate a given table	No
PURGE_MASTER_LOG	Deletes entries from the local RepCatLog (DBA_REPCATLOG)	No
RELOCATE_MASTERDEF	Changes the master definition site for a replication group	No
REMOVE_MASTER_DATABASES	Drops one or more master databases from a replication group	No
REPCAT_IMPORT_CHECK	Confirms a replicated object's validity after an import	No
RESUME_MASTER_ACTIVITY	Enables propagation of a replication group that had been quiesced	No
SEND_AND_COMPARE_OLD_VALUES	Reduces propagation overhead by not sending unchanged columns to a master site.	No

Table 15-3. DBMS_REPCAT Programs (Replication Administration Only) (continued)

Name	Description	Use in SQL?
SET_COLUMNS	Designates alternative column(s) to use instead of a primary to uniquely identify rows of a replicated table	No
SUSPEND_MASTER_ACTIVITY	Quiesces a replication group	No
WAIT_MASTER_LOG	Determines whether asynchronous DML has been applied at a master site	No

Exceptions

Table 15-4 describes exceptions raised by the DBMS_REPCAT programs described in this chapter.

Table 15-4. DBMS_REPCAT Exceptions

Name	Number	Description
commfailure	−23317	Unable to communicate with remote site
dbnotcompatible	−23375	Operation not available for current version of RDBMS
ddlfailure	−23318	DDL failed during object creation or maintenance activity
duplicateobject	−23309	Replicated object already exists
duplicateschema	−23307	Attempt to create duplicate replication group
fullqueue	−23353	Attempt to drop replication group or schema for which RPC entries are queued
invalidpropmode	−23380	Invalid propagation mode (used internally)
missingcolumn	−23334	Reference to nonexistent column
missinggroup	−23331	Replication group does not exist
missingobject	−23308	Object does not exist
missingrepgroup	−23373	Replication group does not exist
missingschema	−23306	Schema does not exist
missingvalue	−23337	Missing value (used internally)
nonmaster	−23313	Site is not a master site
nonmasterdef	−23312	Site is not a master definition site
nonsnapshot	−23314	Site is not a snapshot site
norepoption	−23364	Replication option not installed
notnormal	−23311	Replication group is not in normal propagation mode
notquiesced	−23310	Replication group is not quiesced
paramtype	−23325	Invalid parameter type (used internally)
reconfigerror	−23316	Attempt to drop master definition site with REMOVE_MASTER_DATABASES
repnotcompatible	−23376	Replication versions not compatible (used internally)

Table 15-4. DBMS_REPCAT Exceptions (continued)

Name	Number	Description
typefailure	−23319	Attempt to replicate nonsupported datatype
version	−23315	Replication versions not compatible (used internally)

Replication Groups with DBMS_REPCAT

Once you have created administrative accounts for your advanced replication environment and established the appropriate database links among your various sites, you are ready for the next step, which is to create a replication group. Here are the procedures you will use:

    DBMS_REPCAT.CREATE_MASTER_REPGROUP
    DBMS_REPCAT.DROP_MASTER_REPGROUP
    DBMS_REPCAT.COMMENT_ON_REPGROUP

The following sections describe these programs in detail.

Replication Groups versus Replication Schema

Prior to Oracle 7.3, the concept of a *replication group* does not exist. Instead, you have to replicate *replication schema groups*. As you would suspect, schema groups can contain only objects from a single schema. In addition, the name of the group has to be the same as the name of the schema.

In Version 7.3, Oracle introduced replication groups, which can contain objects from one or more schema. Replication groups do not have to have the same name as any of the schema they contain. In Oracle 8.0, Oracle improved the manageability of replication groups by allowing you to quiesce a single replication group at a time. (The *syntax* for quiescing a single group exists in 7.3, but it does not work!)

As you configure and manage a replicated environment, you may notice that for each program that operates on a replication group, such as DBMS_REPCAT.GRANT_ADMIN_ANY_REPGROUP, there is a corresponding procedure that operates on a replication schema, such as DBMS_REPCAT.GRANT_ADMIN_ANY_REPSCHEMA. You may also notice that many of the Oracle 7.3 procedure calls contain an undocumented sname parameter.

Oracle provided these procedures and parameters for backward compatibility only. Although the REPSCHEMA procedures exist in Versions 7.3 and 8.0, you are strongly encouraged *not* to use them, as their support will not continue indefinitely. The sname parameters are already gone from many programs in the first Oracle8 release.

Figure 15-1 shows how replication groups work.

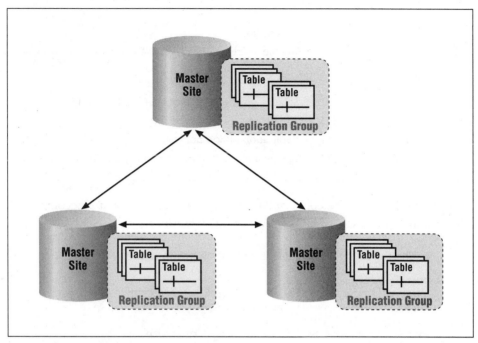

Figure 15-1. Replication groups

The DBMS_REPCAT.CREATE_MASTER_REPGROUP procedure

The CREATE_MASTER_REPGROUP procedure creates a replication group at the master definition site. Here's the specification:

```
PROCEDURE DBMS_REPCAT.CREATE_MASTER_REPGROUP
   (gname IN VARCHAR2,
    group_comment  IN VARCHAR2 := '',
    master_comment IN VARCHAR2 := '',
    qualifier      IN VARCHAR2 := '');
```

Parameters are summarized in the following table.

Name	Description
gname	Name of the new replication group
group_comment	Comment for new replication group visible in DBA_REPGROUP data dictionary view
master_comment	Comment for the calling site, visible in DBA_REPSITES data dictionary view
qualifier	For internal use

Exceptions. The CREATE_MASTER_REPGROUP procedure may raise the following exceptions:

Name	Number	Description
ddlfailure	−23318	Unable to create REP$WHAT_AM_I package or package body
duplicaterepgroup	−23374	Replication group gname already exists
duplicateschema	−23307	Schema gname is already a replication group
missingrepgroup	−23373	The gname was not specified correctly
norepoption	−23364	Replication option not installed
dbnotcompatible	−23375	The gname is not a schema name, and RDBMS is a pre-7.3 release

Restrictions. You must be connected to the replication administrator account (typically REPADMIN) to call CREATE_MASTER_REPGROUP.

Example. The following call creates a replication group named SPROCKET:

```
BEGIN
    DBMS_REPCAT.CREATE_MASTER_REPGROUP(gname=> 'SPROCKET', -
    group_comment => 'Replication group SPROCKET created on
        '||sysdate|| ' by ' ||user, -
    master_comment => 'Master  Definition Site created on
        '||sysdate|| ' by ' ||user);
END;
```

This call creates a replication group with no objects. The site from which you make the call is the master definition site for the group.

For an additional example, see the *repgroup.sql* file on the companion disk. That example queries the DBA_REPGROUP data dictionary view and lists all replication groups in the database.

The DBMS_REPCAT.DROP_MASTER_REPGROUP procedure

The DROP_MASTER_REPGROUP procedure drops one or more replication groups at the master definition site. Here's the specification:

```
PROCEDURE DBMS_REPCAT.DROP_MASTER_REPGROUP
    (gname IN VARCHAR2,
     drop_contents IN BOOLEAN := FALSE,
     all_sites IN BOOLEAN := FALSE);
```

Parameters are summarized in the following table.

Name	Description
all_sites	If TRUE and call is the master definition site, then drop the replication group from all sites in the environment
drop_contents	If TRUE, drop the objects in the replication group as well as the group itself
gname	Name of the new replication group

Exceptions. The DROP_MASTER_REPGROUP procedure raises the following exceptions:

Name	Number	Description
commfailure	−23317	Unable to communicate with all masters, and all_sites is TRUE
fullqueue	−23353	Outstanding transactions queued for replication group gname
missingrepgroup	−23373	gname is not specified correctly
nonmaster	−23313	Calling site is not a master site
nonmasterdef	−23312	Calling site is not a master definition site, and all_sites is TRUE

Restrictions. Note the following restrictions on calling DROP_MASTER_REP-GROUP:

- You must be connected to the replication administrator account (typically REPADMIN) to call DROP_MASTER_REPGROUP.

- DROP_MASTER_REPGROUP does not drop all snapshots if the gname parameter is the master of any snapshot groups. Dropping a master site does not necessarily remove it from the DBA_REPSITES at other masters.

TIP   Before calling DROP_MASTER_REPGROUP, call DBMS_REPCAT.REMOVE_MASTER_DATABASES from the master definition site to remove all masters for which you plan to drop the group and that do not contain any other replication groups. In addition, you can avoid the full queue error by quiescing the replication group before attempting to drop the replication group.

Example. This call, from the master definition site, drops a replication group from all sites where it exists:

```
BEGIN
    DBMS_REPCAT.DROP_MASTER_REPGROUP(
        gname => 'SPROCKET',
```

```
            all_sites => TRUE );
    END;
```

The next call drops a replication group and all of its objects from the calling site, assumed to be a master site (not a master definition site):

```
    BEGIN
        DBMS_REPCAT.DROP_MASTER_REPGROUP(
            gname => 'SPROCKET',
            drop_contents => TRUE );
    END;
```

If you want to drop a replication group from all master sites, along with the replicated objects, you can do the following:

```
    BEGIN
        DBMS_REPCAT.DROP_MASTER_REPGROUP(
            gname => 'SPROCKET',
            all_sites => TRUE
            drop_contents => TRUE );
    END;
```

The DBMS_REPCAT.COMMENT_ON_REPGROUP procedure

This procedure adds a new schema comment field to the DBA_REPCAT data dictionary view, or changes an existing one. The specifications differ for Oracle7 and Oracle8 as follows.

Here is the Oracle7 specification:

```
    PROCEDURE DMBS_REPCAT.COMMENT_ON_REPGROUP
        (gname IN VARCHAR2 := '',
         comment IN VARCHAR2,
         sname IN VARCHAR2 := '');
```

Here is the Oracle8 specification:

```
    PROCEDURE DMBS_REPCAT.COMMENT_ON_REPGROUP
        (gname IN VARCHAR2,
         comment IN VARCHAR2);
```

Parameters are summarized in the following table.

Name	Description
gname	Replication group to which comment is added
comment	Comment
sname	Not used

NOTE   As noted in the earlier sidebar entitled "Replication Groups versus Replication Schema," you can see that Oracle has dispensed with the sname parameter in Oracle8.

Exceptions. The COMMENT_ON_REPROUP procedure may raise the following exceptions:

Name	Number	Description
commfailure	−23317	Unable to communicate with one or more master sites
missinggroup	−23331	Replication group gname does not exist
nonmasterdef	−23312	Calling site is not master definition site

Restrictions. The COMMENT_ON_REPGROUP procedure must be called from the master definition site.

Example. This call adds or replaces the comment in DBA_REPGROUP for the SPROCKET replication group:

```
BEGIN
    DBMS_REPCAT.COMMENT_ON_REPGROUP(
        gname 'SPROCKET',
        comment => 'Comment added on '||sysdate|| ' by '||user);
END;
```

COMMENT_ON_REPGROUP queues an RPC to update the field at all other master sites.

Replicated Objects with DBMS_REPCAT

After you have created your replication group(s) (with or without comments), you are ready to add, alter, and remove member objects. Here are the procedures you need:

```
DBMS_REPCAT.CREATE_MASTER_REPOBJECT
DBMS_REPCAT.SET_COLUMNS
DBMS_REPCAT.DROP_MASTER_REPOBJECT
DBMS_REPCAT.COMMENT_ON_REPOBJECT
DBMS_REPCAT.ALTER_MASTER_REPOBJECT
DBMS_REPCAT.EXECUTE_DDL
```

The following sections describe these programs in detail.

The DBMS_REPCAT.CREATE_MASTER_REPOBJECT procedure

The CREATE_MASTER_REPOBJECT procedure creates a replicated object. Its specification follows:

```
PROCEDURE DBMS_REPCAT.CREATE_MASTER_REPOBJECT(
    sname IN VARCHAR2,
    oname IN VARCHAR2,
    type IN VARCHAR2,
    use_existing_object IN BOOLEAN := TRUE,
    ddl_text IN VARCHAR2 := NULL,
```

```
comment IN VARCHAR2 := '',
retry IN BOOLEAN := FALSE,
copy_rows IN BOOLEAN := TRUE,
gname IN VARCHAR2 := '');
```

Parameters are summarized in the following table.

Name	Description
sname	Name of the schema to which oname belongs.
oname	Name of the object to be added.
type	Object type. Valid types: TABLE, INDEX, SYNONYM, TRIGGER, VIEW, PROCEDURE, FUNCTION, PACKAGE, and PACKAGE BODY.
use_existing_object	Set to TRUE to reuse existing objects with the same name and structure at master sites.
ddl_text	Text of DDL statement to create object oname (use this parameter if and only if object does not already exist).
comment	Comment on replicated object, visible in DBA_REPOBJECT data dictionary view.
retry	Flag indicating that this call is a reattempt of an earlier call. An attempt is made to create object only at master sites where it does not exist with a status of valid.
copy_rows	Populate tables and other master sites with data from master definition site.
gname	Name of the replication group to which oname should be added.

Exceptions. The CREATE_MASTER_REPOBJECT procedure may raise the following exceptions:

Name	Number	Description
commfailure	−23317	Not all master sites are reachable
ddlfailure	−23309	Object oname already exists in replication group gname, and retry is not set to TRUE
duplicateobject	−23374	Replication group gname already exists
missingobject	−23308	Object oname does not exist
nonmasterdef	−23373	Calling site is not the master definition site for replication group gname
notquiesced	−23310	Replication group gname is not quiesced
typefailure	−23319	The type is not supported

Restrictions. Note the following restrictions on calling CREATE_MASTER_REPOBJECT:

- This procedure must be called from the master definition site.
- The replication group must already exist and be quiesced.

Example. This section contains a series of examples showing how to create replication objects.

Adding an existing table to a replication group. This call adds table SPROCKET. PRODUCTS to the replication group SPROCKET:

```
BEGIN
    DBMS_REPCAT.CREATE_MASTER_REPOBJECT(sname    =>    'SPROCKET',
                                        oname    =>    'PRODUCTS',
                                        type     =>    'TABLE',
                                        gname    =>    'SPROCKET');
END;
```

Since we have not specified ddl_text in this example, the table must already exist.

Creating an object at the master definition site. In this next example, we use CREATE_MASTER_REPOBJECT to create an object at the master definition site and add it to the replication group:

```
BEGIN
    DBMS_REPCAT.CREATE_MASTER_REPOBJECT(
        sname    =>   'SPROCKET',
        oname    =>   'STATES',
        type     =>   'TABLE'
        ddl_text =>   'CREATE TABLE sprocket.states(state_id VARCHAR2(2),
                       state_name VARCHAR2(20))',
        gname    =>   'SPROCKET');
END;
```

Notice that the CREATE TABLE statement in this example specifies the owner of the table. Typically, the replication administrator account uses DBMS_REPCAT, not the owner of the replicated schema. When this is the case, you must be sure to specify the schema in which to create objects. One of the privileges granted through DBMS_REPCAT_ADMIN.GRANT_ADMIN_ANY_REPGROUP is CREATE ANY TABLE.

In all likelihood, you will not create objects with the CREATE_MASTER_REPOBJECT procedure very often, because doing so is rather clumsy for all but the most simple objects. But it's there if you want it.

Setting the retry and use_existing_object parameters to TRUE in this third example creates the table PRODUCTS at all master sites where it does not already exist; setting copy_rows to TRUE copies the data from the master definition site to the master sites.

```
BEGIN
    DBMS_REPCAT.CREATE_MASTER_REPOBJECT(
        sname         =>   'SPROCKET',
        oname         =>   'PRODUCTS',
        type          =>   'TABLE',
```

```
                use_existing_object =>TRUE,
                retry          =>    TRUE,
                copy_rows      =>    TRUE,
                gname          =>    'SPROCKET');
        END;
```

If tables exist at master sites, but do not have the same definition as at the master definition site, Oracle returns an error.

TIP   If you are incorporating an existing database into a replication group, you should consider precreating all of the objects at the new site manually, especially if the objects have interdependencies. At my sites, we always run a "catalog" script to create all schema objects, including triggers, primary and foreign key definitions, check constraints, etc. We then let Oracle generate the replication support objects. This methodology gives us complete control over how the schema is created, and we can easily reproduce the objects in other environments.

Replicating a package. In this final example, we replicate a package. To replicate a package, you must make two calls to CREATE_MASTER_REPOBJECT, one for the package, and one for the package body.

```
    BEGIN
        DBMS_REPCAT.CREATE_MASTER_REPOBJECT
            sname                => 'SPROCKET',
            oname                => 'PRODUCTMAINT',
            type                 => 'PACKAGE',
            use_existing_object  => TRUE,
            comment              => 'Added on '||sysdate,
            retry                => FALSE,
            gname                => 'SPROCKET');

        DBMS_REPCAT.CREATE_MASTER_REPOBJECT
            sname                => 'SPROCKET',
            oname                => 'PRODUCTMAINT',
            type                 => 'PACKAGE BODY',
            use_existing_object  => TRUE,
            comment              => 'Added on '||sysdate,
            retry                => FALSE,
            gname                => 'SPROCKET');
    END;
```

For an additional example, see the *repobjs.sql* file on the companion disk. The example queries the DBA_REPOBJECT data dictionary view and lists all replicated objects in the database.

The DBMS_REPCAT.SET_COLUMNS procedure

When you replicate a table, Oracle must be able to uniquely identify each record in the table so that it can propagate changes to the correct row or rows. By default, the advanced replication facility uses the primary key to identify rows. However, if your table does not have a primary key, or if you wish to use a different criteria to uniquely identify records, you can use SET_COLUMNS to designate a pseudo-primary key.

Here's the specification for the package:

```
PROCEDURE DBMS_REPCAT.SET_COLUMNS
   (sname IN VARCHAR2,
    oname IN VARCHAR2,
    column_list IN VARCHAR2 | column_table IN
    dbms_utility.name_array);
```

Parameters are summarized in the following table.

Name	Description
sname	Name of the schema that owns the replicated table.
oname	Name of the table with the column_group.
column_list	A comma-delimited list of column names to use as the pseudo-primary key. Use either column_list or column_table.
column_table	A PL/SQL table of column names. Use either column_list or column_table.

Exceptions. DBMS_REPCAT.SET_COLUMNS may raise the following exceptions:

Name	Number	Description
nonmasterdef	–23312	Invoking site is not master definition site
missingobject	–23308	Table oname does not exist
missingcolumn	–23334	Column(s) specified do not exist in table *oname*

Restrictions. Note the following restrictions on calling DBMS_REPCAT.SET_COLUMNS.

- DBMS_REPCAT.SET_COLUMNS must be run from the master definition site.

- The changes do not take effect until the next call to DBMS_REPCAT.GENERATE_REPLICATION_SUPPORT.

Example. The following call designates columns COLOR, MODEL, and YEAR as the pseudo-primary key columns in table SPROCKET.PRODUCTS:

```
BEGIN
    DBMS_REPCAT.SET_COLUMNS(sname    => 'SPROCKET',
```

```
                                    oname   => 'PRODUCTS',
                                    column_list=> 'COLOR,MODEL,YEAR');
        END;
```

The DBMS_REPCAT.DROP_MASTER_REPOBJECT procedure

The DROP_MASTER_REPOBJECT procedure drops a replicated object at the master site. The specification follows:

```
PROCEDURE DBMS_REPOBJECT.DROP_MASTER_REPOBJECT
   (sname IN VARCHAR2,
    oname IN VARCHAR2,
    type IN VARCHAR2,
    drop_objects IN BOOLEAN := FALSE);
```

Parameters are summarized in the following table.

Name	Description
sname	Name of the schema to which oname belongs.
oname	Name of the object to be added.
type	Object type. Valid types: TABLE, INDEX, SYNONYM, TRIGGER, VIEW, PROCEDURE, FUNCTION, PACKAGE, and PACKAGE BODY.
drop_objects	If TRUE, drop the object at all master sites; default is FALSE.

Exceptions. The DROP_MASTER_REPOBJECT procedure may raise the following exceptions:

Name	Number	Description
commfailure	−23317	Not all master sites are reachable
missingobject	−23308	Object oname does not exist
nonmasterdef	−23373	Calling site is not the master definition site for replication group gname
typefailure	−23319	The type is not supported

Restrictions. Note the following restrictions on calling DROP_MASTER_REPOBJECT:

*   This procedure must be called from the master definition site.
*   The replication group must already exist and be quiesced.

Examples. The following call removes table SPROCKET.PRODUCTS from the SPROCKET replication group, but preserves the table:

```
    BEGIN
        DBMS_REPCAT.DROP_MASTER_REPOBJECT(
                           sname   => 'SPROCKET',
                           oname   => 'PRODUCTS',
```

```
                                type    => 'TABLE');
    END;
```

Dropping a table from a replication group automatically drops all replication triggers associated with the table and removes it from the replication data dictionary views.

The DROP_MASTER_REPOBJECT procedure can remove the object from the replication group, and also drop the object from the schema by setting the drop_objects parameter to TRUE, as shown in this example:

```
    BEGIN
        DBMS_REPCAT.DROP_MASTER_REPOBJECT(
                            sname       => 'SPROCKET',
                            oname       => 'PRODUCTS',
                            type        => 'TABLE',
                            drop_objects=>  TRUE);
    END;
```

The DBMS_REPCAT.EXECUTE_DDL procedure

DBMS_REPCAT.CREATE_MASTER_REPOBJECT and DBMS_REPCAT.DROP_MASTER_REPOBJECT do not support every type of object. For example, you cannot use these procedures to drop and create constraints. Enter DBMS_REPCAT's EXECUTE_DDL procedure.

The EXECUTE_DDL procedure allows you to perform DDL at multiple sites. The specification follows:

```
    PROCEDURE DBMS_REPCAT.EXECUTE_DDL
        (gname          IN VARCHAR2 := '',
        {master_list IN VARCHAR2 := NULL, |
        master_table IN dbms_utility.dblink_array,}
        ddl_text       IN VARCHAR2,
        sname          IN VARCHAR2 := '');
```

Parameters are summarized in the following table.

Name	Description
gname	Name of the replicated object group.
master_list	Comma-separated string of master site global names at which DDL is to be performed. If NULL (the default), DDL is applied at all master sites in the replication group. Use either parameter master_list or master_table.
master_table	PL/SQL table of master site global names at which DDL is to be performed. Use either parameter master_list or master_table.
ddl_text	DDL statement to apply.
sname	Not used.

Exceptions. The EXECUTE_DDL procedure may raise the following exceptions:

Name	Number	Description
commfailure	−23317	Unable to communicate with master site
ddlfailure	−23318	Unable to perform DDL
nonmaster	−23312	At least one site in master_list or master_table is not a master site
nonmasterdef	−23312	Calling site is not a master definition site

Restrictions. Note the following restrictions on calling EXECUTE_DDL:

- This procedure must be called from the master definition site.

- The replication group must already exist.

NOTE   The environment does not have to be quiesced.

Example. This example creates an index on the SPROCKET.STATES table at sites D7CA.BIGWHEEL.COM and D7NY.BIGWHEEL.COM. Note that as in the example of CREATE_MASTER_REPOBJECT, we must specify the schema in which to create the index.

```
DECLARE vMasters VARCHAR2(30);
BEGIN
    vMasters := 'D7CA.BIGWHEEL.COM,D7NY.BIGWHEEL.COM';
    DBMS_REPCAT.EXECUTE_DDL(
        gname       => 'SPROCKET',
        master_list => vMasters,
        ddl_text    =>'CREATE INDEX sprocket.i_state_id ON
           sprocket.tstates(state_id)',
        sname       =>'SPROCKET');
END;
```

The DBMS_REPCAT.ALTER_MASTER_REPOBJECT procedure

Just as you can propagate DDL to create objects with the EXECUTE_DDL procedure, you can also propagate DDL to alter objects with DBMS_REPCAT.ALTER_MASTER_REPOBJECT. Unlike EXECUTE_DDL, ALTER_MASTER_REPOBJECT does not allow you to specify a list of master sites; the call affects all masters. In other words, Oracle does not support site-specific customizations of replicated objects. The specification follows:

```
PROCEDURE DBMS_REPCAT.ALTER_MASTER_REPOBJECT
    (sname IN VARCHAR2,
     oname IN VARCHAR2,
     type IN VARCHAR2,
```

```
ddl_text IN VARCHAR2,
comment IN VARCHAR2 := '',
retry IN BOOLEAN := FALSE);
```

Parameters are summarized in the following table.

Name	Description
sname	Name of the schema to which object oname belongs.
oname	Name of the object to alter.
type	The oname object type. Supported types: FUNCTION, INDEX, PACKAGE, PACKAGE BODY, SYNONYM, TABLE, TRIGGER, and VIEW.
ddl_text	Text of DDL statement to apply.
comment	Comment visible in DBA_REPOBJECT data dictionary view.
retry	If set to TRUE, procedure alters only objects whose status is not VALID at master sites.

Exceptions. The ALTER_MASTER_REPOBJECT procedure may raise the following exceptions:

Name	Number	Description
commfailure	−23317	Unable to communicate with one or more master site(s)
ddlfailure	−23318	DDL at master definition site failed
missingobject	−23308	Object oname does not exist
nonmasterdef	−23312	Calling site is not the master definition site
notquiesced	−23310	Replication group gname is not quiesced
typefailure	−23319	DDL on objects of type type is not supported

Restrictions. Note the following restrictions on calling ALTER_MASTER_REPOB-JECT:

- This procedure must be run from the master definition site.

- The replication group must be quiesced.

- You must call DBMS_REPCAT.GENERATE_REPLICATION_SUPPORT for the altered object before resuming replication.

Example. If you set the retry parameter to TRUE, ALTER_MASTER_REPOBJECT applies the DDL only at sites where the object has a status of INVALID in the DBA_OBJECTS data dictionary view.

```
BEGIN
DBMS_REPCAT.ALTER_MASTER_REPOBJECT(
        sname    => 'SPROCKET',
        oname    => 'PRODUCTMAINT',
        type     => 'PACKAGE BODY'
```

```
               ddl_text => 'ALTER PACKAGE SPROCKET.PRODUCTMAINT COMPILE BODY',
               comment => 'Recompiled on '||sysdate|| ' by '||user,
               retry    => TRUE );
       END;
```

Notice that we specify the schema for the object that we are altering. As with DBMS_REPCAT.EXECUTE_DDL, the ALTER_MASTER_REPOBJECT procedure operates on objects in the caller's schema by default, and the caller is generally the replication administrator account, not the schema account.

This example alters the width of the state_id column in table SPROCKET.STATES at *all* sites:

```
BEGIN
DBMS_REPCAT.ALTER_MASTER_REPOBJECT(
        sname    => 'SPROCKET',
        oname    => 'PRODUCTMAINT',
        type     => 'PACKAGE BODY'
        ddl_text => 'ALTER TABLE SPROCKET.STATES MODIFY
           (STATE_ID NUMBER(10))' ,
        comment => 'state_id widened on '||sysdate|| ' by '||user);
    END;
```

The DBMS_REPCAT.COMMENT_ON_REPOBJECT procedure

As you have seen in the previous examples, you can associate comments with a replicated object when you create or alter it by passing a VARCHAR2 string to the comment parameter. You can see these comments in the object_comment field of DBA_REPOBJECTS.

You can also create comments without creating or altering the object with DBMS_REPCAT's COMMENT_ON_REPOBJECT procedure. The specification follows:

```
PROCEDURE DBMS_REPCAT.COMMENT_ON_REPOBJECT
       (sname IN VARCHAR2,
        oname IN VARCHAR2,
        type IN VARCHAR2,
        comment IN VARCHAR2);
```

Parameters are summarized in the following table.

Name	Description
sname	Name of schema to which object belongs
oname	Name of the object
type	Object type
comment	Comment

Exceptions. The COMMENT_ON_REPOBJECT procedure may raise the following exceptions:

Name	Number	Description
commfailure	−23317	Unable to communicate with one or more master sites
missingobject	−23308	Object oname does not exist
nonmasterdef	−23312	Calling site is not master definition site
typefailure	−23319	Object type is not supported

Restrictions. The COMMENT_ON_REPOBJECT procedure must be called from the master definition site.

Example. The following call updates the comment for replicated table SPROCKET.PRICES:

```
BEGIN
    DBMS_REPCAT.COMMENT_ON_REPOBJECT(
            sname   =>  'SPROCKET', -
            oname   =>  'PRICES', -
            type    =>  'TABLE', -
            comment =>  'Headquarters updates this table once a month.');
END;
```

Replication Support with DBMS_REPCAT

The next step in the creation of a replicated environment is to generate replication support for your replicated tables, packages, and package bodies. In the case of replicated tables, this step creates a BEFORE ROW trigger, called tablename$RT, and three packages:

> tablename$RP
> tablename$RR
> tablename$TP

This code propagates DML to remote sites, and applies DML on behalf of remote sites. We'll examine this code in the examples of these procedures:

> DBMS_REPCAT.GENERATE_REPLICATION_SUPPORT
> DBMS_REPCAT.GENERATE_REPLICATION_PACKAGE
> DBMS_REPCAT.GENERATE_REPLICATION_TRIGGER

The DBMS_REPCAT.GENERATE_REPLICATION_SUPPORT procedure

The GENERATE_REPLICATION_SUPPORT procedure generates support for replicated tables, packages, and package bodies. The specifications differ for Oracle7 and Oracle8 as follows.

Here is the Oracle7 specification:

```
PROCEDURE DBMS_REPCAT.GENERATE_REPLICATION_SUPPORT
     (sname            IN VARCHAR2,
      oname            IN VARCHAR2,
      type             IN VARCHAR2,
      package_prefix   IN VARCHAR2 := NULL,
      procedure_prefix IN VARCHAR2 := NULL,
      distributed      IN BOOLEAN  := TRUE,
      gen_objs_owner   IN VARCHAR2 := NULL,
      gen_rep2_trigger IN BOOLEAN  := FALSE);
```

Here is the Oracle8 specification:

```
PROCEDURE DBMS_REPCAT.GENERATE_REPLICATION_SUPPORT
     (sname             IN VARCHAR2,
      oname             IN VARCHAR2,
      type              IN VARCHAR2,
      package_prefix    IN VARCHAR2 := NULL,
      procedure_prefix  IN VARCHAR2 := NULL,
      distributed       IN BOOLEAN  := TRUE,
      gen_objs_owner    IN VARCHAR2 := NULL,
      min_communication IN BOOLEAN  := TRUE);
```

Parameters are summarized in the following table.

Name	Description
sname	Name of the schema to which table oname belongs.
oname	Name of table for which package is being generated.
type	Object type. Supported types: TABLE, PROCEDURE, PACKAGE, and PACKAGE BODY.
package_prefix	Prefix used to name generated wrapper package for packages and package bodies.
procedure_prefix	Prefix used to name generated wrapper package for procedures.
distributed	If TRUE (the default), generate replication support for the object at each master; if FALSE, copy the reapplication support objects generated at the master definition site.
gen_objs_owner	Specifies schema in which to generate replication support objects; if NULL (the default), objects are generated under schema sname.
gen_rep2_trigger (Oracle7 only)	Provided for backward compatibility; if any masters are pre-7.3 releases, this must be set to TRUE. The default is FALSE.
min_communication (Oracle8 only)	If TRUE (the default), Oracle propagates changes with the minimum communication parameter, which avoids sending the old and new column values of unmodified fields.

Exceptions. The GENERATE_REPLICATION_SUPPORT procedure may raise the following exceptions:

Name	Number	Description
commfailure	–23317	Unable to communicate with all masters
dbnotcompatible	–23375	One or more masters is a pre-7.3 release
missingobject	–23308	Table oname does not exist in schema sname
missingschema	–23306	Schema sname does not exist
nonmasterdef	–23312	Calling site is not a master definition site
notquiesced	–23310	Replication group to which object belongs is not quiesced
typefailure	–23319	Specified type is not a supported type

Restrictions. Note the following restrictions on calling GENERATE_REPLICATION_ SUPPORT:

- You must call this procedure from the master definition site for each object in the replication group.

- The replication group must be quiesced.

- If the object is not owned by the replication administrator account, the owner must have explicit EXECUTE privileges on the DBMS_DEFER package (described in Chapter 17).

- If the *INIT.ORA* parameter COMPATIBLE is 7.3 or higher, the distributed parameter must be set to TRUE.

- If the *INIT.ORA* parameter COMPATIBLE is less than 7.3 in any snapshot sites, the gen_rep2_trigger parameter must be set to TRUE, and the COMPATIBLE parameter at the master definition site must be set to 7.3.0.0 or greater.

Example. Suppose that we have a table SPROCKET.REON defined as follows:

Field Name	Nullable?	Datatype
region_id	NOT NULL	NUMBER(6)
region_name	NOT NULL	VARCHAR2(15)

Assuming that we have already added this table to the SPROCKET replication group, here is how we would generate replication support for it:

```
BEGIN
EXECUTE dbms_repcat.generate_replication_support( -
        sname => 'SPROCKET',-
        oname => 'REGION',-
        type => 'TABLE', -
        distributed => TRUE,-
        gen_objs_owner=> 'SPROCKET',-
```

```
            gen_rep2_trigger=> FALSE);
END;
```

This call creates a trigger and three packages, as described in the following table. Oracle immediately creates these objects at the master definition site, as well as the participating master sites.

Object Name	Object Type	Description
REGION$RT	BEFORE ROW Trigger	Invokes procedure REGION$TP.REPLICATE.
REGION$RR	Package + Body	Invokes conflict resolution handler. REGIONS$RP invokes this procedure only in the event of a conflict.
REGION$RP	Package + Body	Applies DML that originated at a remote site.
REGION$TP	Package + Body	Determines whether DML originates locally, and if so, queues as an RPC call the REGION$RP procedure corresponding to the type of DML (insert, update, or delete). Oracle propagates this RPC call to all master sites.

In the next sections, we examine what Oracle creates for us when we generate replication support for this table.

The replication support trigger. The following example shows the text of the REGION$RT trigger that the GENERATE_REPLICATION_SUPPORT call generates:

```
declare
  flag char;
begin
  if "REGION$TP".active then
    if inserting then
      flag := 'I';
    elsif updating then
      flag := 'U';
    elsif deleting then
      flag := 'D';
    end if;
    "REGION$TP".replicate(
      :old."REGION_ID",:new."REGION_ID",
      :old."REGION_NAME",:new."REGION_NAME",
      flag);
  end if;
end;
```

As you can see, this BEFORE ROW trigger simply sets a flag to indicate the type of DML being performed: "I" for inserts, "U" for updates, and "D" for deletes. It then passes this flag, along with the new and old values of each field, to the REGIONS$TP.REPLICATE procedure.

The replication support packages. The replication package REGION$TP invokes DBMS_SNAPSHOT.I_AM_A_REFRESH (see the description of this procedure in Chapter 14) to determine if the DML that fired the REGION$RT trigger originated locally, or if it is DML that another site has propagated. If the DML originated locally, then the REGION$TP builds a deferred call—one of the REGION$RP procedures (REP_UPDATE, REP_INSERT, or REP_DELETE), as appropriate. Oracle queues this deferred call to all master sites. Here is the Oracle-generated code:

```
package body"REGION$TP" as
  I_am_a_snapshot CHAR;
  is_snapshot BOOLEAN;
  function active return boolean
  is
  begin
    return (not((is_snapshot and dbms_snapshot.I_am_a_refresh) or
        not dbms_reputil.replication_is_on));
  end active;
  procedure replicate(
    "REGION_ID1_o" IN NUMBER,
    "REGION_ID1_n" IN NUMBER,
    "REGION_NAME2_o" IN VARCHAR2,
    "REGION_NAME2_n" IN VARCHAR2,
    flag IN CHAR)
  is
  begin
    if flag = 'U' then
      dbms_defer.call('SPROCKET','REGION$RP','REP_UPDATE',6,'SPROCKET');
      dbms_defer.number_arg("REGION_ID1_o");
      dbms_defer.number_arg("REGION_ID1_n");
      dbms_defer.varchar2_arg("REGION_NAME2_o");
      dbms_defer.varchar2_arg("REGION_NAME2_n");
    elsif flag = 'I' then
      dbms_defer.call('SPROCKET','REGION$RP','REP_INSERT',4,'SPROCKET');
      dbms_defer.number_arg("REGION_ID1_n");
      dbms_defer.varchar2_arg("REGION_NAME2_n");
    elsif flag = 'D' then
      dbms_defer.call('SPROCKET','REGION$RP','REP_DELETE',4,'SPROCKET');
      dbms_defer.number_arg("REGION_ID1_o");
      dbms_defer.varchar2_arg("REGION_NAME2_o");
    end if;
    dbms_defer.varchar2_arg(dbms_reputil.global_name);
    dbms_defer.char_arg(I_am_a_snapshot);
  end replicate;
begin
  select decode(master, 'N', 'Y', 'N')
    into I_am_a_snapshot
    from all_repcat where gname = 'SPROCKET';
  is_snapshot := (I_am_a_snapshot = 'Y');
end "REGION$TP";
```

Notice that Oracle passes the old and new values of each column in the table to the REGION$RP procedure. Oracle uses these values to confirm that the version of the row at the originating site is the same as the version of the row at the destination sites. If the old column values at the originating site do not match the current column values at the destination site, then Oracle detects a conflict and invokes the appropriate conflict resolution method.

You can see this logic in the package body of REGION$RP:

```
package body"REGION$RP" as
  procedure rep_delete(
    "REGION_ID1_o" IN NUMBER,
    "REGION_NAME2_o" IN VARCHAR2,
    site_name IN VARCHAR2,
    propagation_flag IN CHAR) is
  begin
    if propagation_flag = 'N' then
      dbms_reputil.replication_off;
    end if;
    dbms_reputil.rep_begin;
    dbms_reputil.global_name := site_name;
    delete from "REGION"
    where ("REGION_ID1_o" = "REGION_ID"
    and    "REGION_NAME2_o" = "REGION_NAME");
    if sql%rowcount = 0 then
      raise no_data_found;
    elsif sql%rowcount > 1 then
      raise too_many_rows;
    end if;
    dbms_reputil.rep_end;
  exception
    when no_data_found then
      begin
    if not "REGION$RR".delete_conflict_handler(
      "REGION_ID1_o",
      "REGION_NAME2_o",
      site_name,
      propagation_flag) then
      dbms_reputil.rep_end;
      raise;
    end if;
    dbms_reputil.rep_end;
      exception
    when others then
      dbms_reputil.rep_end;
      raise;
      end;
    when others then
      dbms_reputil.rep_end;
      raise;
  end rep_delete;
  procedure rep_insert(
    "REGION_ID1_n" IN NUMBER,
    "REGION_NAME2_n" IN VARCHAR2,
    site_name IN VARCHAR2,
```

```
      propagation_flag IN CHAR) is
begin
   if propagation_flag = 'N' then
      dbms_reputil.replication_off;
   end if;
   dbms_reputil.rep_begin;
   dbms_reputil.global_name := site_name;
   insert into "REGION" (
      "REGION_ID",
      "REGION_NAME")
   values (
      "REGION_ID1_n",
      "REGION_NAME2_n");
   dbms_reputil.rep_end;
exception
   when dup_val_on_index then
      begin
   if not "REGION$RR".unique_conflict_insert_handler(
      "REGION_ID1_n",
      "REGION_NAME2_n",
      site_name,
      propagation_flag,
      SQLERRM) then
      dbms_reputil.rep_end;
      raise;
   end if;
   dbms_reputil.rep_end;
      exception
   when others then
      dbms_reputil.rep_end;
      raise;
      end;
   when others then
      dbms_reputil.rep_end;
      raise;
end rep_insert;
procedure rep_update(
   "REGION_ID1_o" IN NUMBER,
   "REGION_ID1_n" IN NUMBER,
   "REGION_NAME2_o" IN VARCHAR2,
   "REGION_NAME2_n" IN VARCHAR2,
   site_name IN VARCHAR2,
   propagation_flag IN CHAR) is
begin
   if propagation_flag = 'N' then
      dbms_reputil.replication_off;
   end if;
   dbms_reputil.rep_begin;
   dbms_reputil.global_name := site_name;
   update "REGION" set
      "REGION_ID" = "REGION_ID1_n",
      "REGION_NAME" =
   decode("REGION_NAME2_o",
            "REGION_NAME2_n", "REGION_NAME",
```

```
           "REGION_NAME2_n")
      where (((1 = 1 and
         "REGION_NAME2_o" = "REGION_NAME2_n")) or
        (1 = 1 and
         "REGION_NAME2_o" = "REGION_NAME"))
       and "REGION_ID1_o" = "REGION_ID";
    if sql%rowcount = 0 then
      raise no_data_found;
    elsif sql%rowcount > 1 then
      raise too_many_rows;
    end if;
    dbms_reputil.rep_end;
  exception
    when no_data_found then
      begin
      if not "REGION$RR".update_conflict_handler(
        "REGION_ID1_o",
        "REGION_ID1_n",
        "REGION_NAME2_o",
        "REGION_NAME2_n",
        site_name,
        propagation_flag) then
        dbms_reputil.rep_end;
        raise;
      end if;
      dbms_reputil.rep_end;
        exception
      when others then
        dbms_reputil.rep_end;
        raise;
        end;
    when dup_val_on_index then
      begin
      if not "REGION$RR".unique_conflict_update_handler(
        "REGION_ID1_o",
        "REGION_ID1_n",
        "REGION_NAME2_o",
        "REGION_NAME2_n",
        site_name,
        propagation_flag,
        SQLERRM) then
        dbms_reputil.rep_end;
        raise;
      end if;
      dbms_reputil.rep_end;
        exception
      when others then
        dbms_reputil.rep_end;
        raise;
        end;
    when others then
      dbms_reputil.rep_end;
      raise;
  end rep_update;
end "REGION$RP";
```

As you can see, Oracle invokes REGION$RR, the conflict resolution package:

```
package body"REGION$RR" as
  function unique_conflict_insert_handler(
    "REGION_ID1_n" IN NUMBER,
    "REGION_NAME2_n" IN VARCHAR2,
    site_name IN VARCHAR2,
    propagation_flag IN CHAR,
    errmsg IN VARCHAR2) return boolean is
  begin
    return FALSE;
  end unique_conflict_insert_handler;

  function delete_conflict_handler(
    "REGION_ID1_o" IN NUMBER,
    "REGION_NAME2_o" IN VARCHAR2,
    site_name IN VARCHAR2,
    propagation_flag IN CHAR) return boolean is
  begin
    return FALSE;
  end delete_conflict_handler;

  function update_conflict_handler(
    "REGION_ID1_o" IN NUMBER,
    "REGION_ID1_n" IN NUMBER,
    "REGION_NAME2_o" IN VARCHAR2,
    "REGION_NAME2_n" IN VARCHAR2,
    site_name IN VARCHAR2,
    propagation_flag IN CHAR) return boolean is
  begin
    return FALSE;
  end update_conflict_handler;

  function unique_conflict_update_handler(
    "REGION_ID1_o" IN NUMBER,
    "REGION_ID1_n" IN NUMBER,
    "REGION_NAME2_o" IN VARCHAR2,
    "REGION_NAME2_n" IN VARCHAR2,
    site_name IN VARCHAR2,
    propagation_flag IN CHAR,
    errmsg IN VARCHAR2) return boolean is
  begin
    return FALSE;
  end unique_conflict_update_handler;
end "REGION$RR";
```

This is the default conflict handling package that GENERATE_REPLICATION_SUPPORT creates. Since no conflict resolution methods are defined for REGION, the unique_conflict_insert_handler, delete_conflict_handler, update_conflict_handler, and unique_conflict_update_handler programs all return FALSE, indicating that they cannot resolve the conflict. Chapter 17 contains details about how to define conflict resolution handlers.

Generating replication support for packages and procedures. As well as tables, you can also replicate procedures and packages. When you call a replicated procedure, Oracle builds a deferred RPC that it propagates to all master sites. This deferred RPC invokes the same procedure with the same arguments as the originating call. Oracle recommends procedural replication for situations that call for massive updates to tables (i.e., updates affecting tens of thousands of rows). Procedural replication duplicates the procedure call only, which is more efficient and network-friendly than row-level replication. (Row-level replication sends the old and new column values for every field of every row.)

Just as we made two calls to CREATE_MASTER_REPOBJECT to create a replicated package, we must also make two calls to GENERATE_REPLICATION_SUPPORT:

```
BEGIN
    DBMS_REPCAT.GENERATE_REPLICATION_SUPPORT(
            sname            => 'SPROCKET',
            oname            => 'PRODUCTMAINT',
            type             => 'PACKAGE',
            distributed      => TRUE,
            gen_objs_owner   => 'SPROCKET',
            gen_rep2_trigger => FALSE);

    DBMS_REPCAT.GENERATE_REPLICATION_SUPPORT(
            sname            => 'SPROCKET',
            oname            => 'PRODUCTMAINT',
            type             => 'PACKAGE BODY',
            distributed      => TRUE,
            gen_objs_owner   => 'SPROCKET',
            gen_rep2_trigger => FALSE);
END;
```

These two calls create a "wrapper" package and package body, named DEFER_ PRODUCTMAINT. This package uses DBMS_DEFER.CALL (described in Chapter 17) to build RPCs to PRODUCTMAINT. To replicate a call to procedure ADDPRODUCT, we would call DEFER_PRODUCTMAINT.ADDPRODUCT.

```
package "DEFER_PRODUCTMAINT" as
  I_am_a_snapshot CHAR;
  procedure "ADDPRODUCT"(
    "PRODUCT_TYPE_IN" IN number,
    "CATALOG_ID_IN" IN varchar2,
    "DESCRIPTION_IN" IN varchar2,
    "REV_LEVEL_IN" IN varchar2,
    "PRODUCTION_DATE_IN" IN date,
    "PRODUCT_STATUS_IN" IN varchar2,
    call_local IN char := 'N',
    call_remote IN char := 'Y');
end "DEFER_PRODUCTMAINT";

package body "DEFER_PRODUCTMAINT" as
  procedure "ADDPRODUCT"(
```

```
          "PRODUCT_TYPE_IN" IN NUMBER,
          "CATALOG_ID_IN" IN VARCHAR2,
          "DESCRIPTION_IN" IN VARCHAR2,
          "REV_LEVEL_IN" IN VARCHAR2,
          "PRODUCTION_DATE_IN" IN DATE,
          "PRODUCT_STATUS_IN" IN VARCHAR2,
          call_local IN char := 'N',
          call_remote IN char := 'Y') is
       begin
          select decode(master, 'N', 'Y', 'N')
            into I_am_a_snapshot
            from all_repcat where gname = 'SPROCKET';
          if call_local = 'Y' then
            "SPROCKET"."PRODUCTMAINT"."ADDPRODUCT"(
          "PRODUCT_TYPE_IN",
          "CATALOG_ID_IN",
          "DESCRIPTION_IN",
          "REV_LEVEL_IN",
          "PRODUCTION_DATE_IN",
          "PRODUCT_STATUS_IN");
          end if;
          if call_remote = 'Y' then
          dbms_defer.call('SPROCKET', 'DEFER_PRODUCTMAINT', 'ADDPRODUCT',
          8, 'SPROCKET');
            dbms_defer.number_arg("PRODUCT_TYPE_IN");
            dbms_defer.varchar2_arg("CATALOG_ID_IN");
            dbms_defer.varchar2_arg("DESCRIPTION_IN");
            dbms_defer.varchar2_arg("REV_LEVEL_IN");
            dbms_defer.date_arg("PRODUCTION_DATE_IN");
            dbms_defer.varchar2_arg("PRODUCT_STATUS_IN");
            dbms_defer.char_arg('Y');
            dbms_defer.char_arg(I_am_a_snapshot);
          end if;
        end "ADDPRODUCT";
     begin
        select decode(master, 'N', 'Y', 'N')
          into I_am_a_snapshot
          from all_repcat where gname = 'SPROCKET';
     end "DEFER_PRODUCTMAINT";
```

The DBMS_REPCAT.GENERATE_REPLICATION_PACKAGE procedure

In some situations, you may wish to generate only replication support triggers or replication support packages. For example, if you use DBMS_REPCAT's ALTER_MASTER_PROPAGATION procedure to change from synchronous to asynchronous replication, you will have to recreate replication triggers. The GENERATE_REPLICATION_PACKAGE and GENERATE_REPLICATION_TRIGGERS procedures provide this functionality.

The GENERATE_REPLICATION_PACKAGE procedure allows you to generate replication support packages. The specification follows:

```
PROCEDURE DBMS_REPCAT.GENERATE_REPLICATION_PACKAGE
```

```
(sname IN VARCHAR2,
 oname IN VARCHAR2);
```

Parameters are summarized in the following table.

Name	Description
sname	Name of the schema to which table oname belongs
oname	Name of table for which package is being generated

Exceptions. The GENERATE_REPLICATON_PACKAGE procedure may raise the following exceptions:

Name	Number	Description
commfailure	−23317	Unable to communicate with all masters
dbnotcompatible	−23375	One or more masters is a pre-7.3 release
missingobject	−23308	Table oname does not exist in schema sname
nonmasterdef	−23312	Calling site is not a master definition site
notquiesced	−23310	Replication group to which object belongs is not quiesced

Restrictions. Note the following restrictions on calling GENERATE_REPLICATION_PACKAGE:

- You must call this procedure from the master definition site.
- The replication group must be quiesced.
- The Oracle version must be 7.3 or later.

Example. The following call generates the replication support packages for table SPROCKET.PRODUCTS in all master sites:

```
BEGIN
    DBMS_REPCAT.GENERATE_REPLICATION_PACKAGE(
            sname    => 'SPROCKET',
            oname    => 'PRODUCTS');
END;
```

The DBMS_REPCAT.GENERATE_REPLICATION_TRIGGER procedure

The GENERATE_REPLICATION_TRIGGER procedure allows you to generate replication support triggers. The specifications differ for Oracle7 and Oracle8 as follows.

Here is the Oracle7 specification:

```
PROCEDURE DBMS_REPCAT.GENERATE_REPLICATION_TRIGGER
    (sname IN VARCHAR2,
```

```
      oname IN VARCHAR2,
      gen_objs_owner IN VARCHAR2 := NULL,
      gen_rep2_trigger IN BOOLEAN := FALSE);

   PROCEDURE DBMS_REPCAT.GENERATE_REPLICATION_TRIGGER
      (gname IN VARCHAR2,
      {master_list IN VARCHAR2 := NULL
      | master_table IN dbms_utility.dblink_array},
      gen_objs_owner IN VARCHAR2 := NULL);
```

Here is the Oracle8 specification:

```
   PROCEDURE DBMS_REPCAT.GENERATE_REPLICATION_TRIGGER
      (sname IN VARCHAR2,
      oname IN VARCHAR2,
      gen_objs_owner IN VARCHAR2 := NULL,
      min_communication IN BOOLEAN  := TRUE);

   PROCEDURE DBMS_REPCAT.GENERATE_REPLICATION_TRIGGER
      (gname IN VARCHAR2,
      gen_objs_owner IN VARCHAR2 := NULL,
      min_communication IN BOOLEAN := NULL);
```

Parameters are summarized in the following table.

Name	Description
sname	Name of the schema to which table oname belongs.
oname	Name of object for which support objects are being generated.
gen_rep2_trigger (Oracle7 only)	Provided for backward compatibility; if any master sites are pre-7.3 releases, this parameter must be set to TRUE (default is FALSE).
gname	The replication group to which oname belongs.
master_list	Comma-delimited string of global names for masters in which support objects are to be generated.
master_table	PL/SQL table of global names for masters in which support objects are to be generated.
gen_objs_owner	Specifies schema in which to generate replication support objects; if NULL (the default), objects are generated under schema in which they currently reside.
min_communication (Oracle8 only)	If TRUE (the default) the generated trigger sends the new value of a column only if the value has changed. Old field values are sent only if the field is part of the primary key, or part of a column group for which member columns have changed.

Exceptions. The GENERATE_REPLICATION_TRIGGER procedure may raise the following exceptions:

Name	Number	Description
commfailure	−23317	Unable to communicate with all masters
dbnotcompatible	−23375	One or more masters is a pre-7.3 release and gen_rep2_ trigger is not set to TRUE
missingobject	−23308	Table oname does not exist in schema sname
missingschema	−23306	Schema sname does not exist
nonmasterdef	−23312	Calling site is not a master definition site
notquiesced	−23310	Replication group to which object belongs is not quiesced

Restrictions. Note the following restrictions on calling GENERATE_REPLICATION_TRIGGER:

- You must call this procedure from the master definition site.

- The replication group must be quiesced.

- The GENERATE_REPLICATION_SUPPORT or GENERATE_PACKAGE_SUPPORT must previously have been called for the object specified in the oname parameter.

Examples. The simplest invocation of the GENERATE_REPLICATION_TRIGGER procedure does the most work; this call generates replication triggers for all replicated tables at all master sites:

```
BEGIN
    DBMS_REPCAT.GENERATE_REPLICATION_TRIGGER(gname=> 'SPROCKET' );
END;
```

This next example generates replication triggers for the replicated table SPROCKET.PRODUCTS at all master sites:

```
BEGIN
    DBMS_REPCAT.GENERATE_REPLICATION_TRIGGER(
        gname   => 'SPROCKET',
        oname   => 'PRODUCTS' );
END;
```

The following call generates replication triggers for all replicated tables in the SPROCKET replication group at the master sites D7HI.BIGWHEEL.COM and D7WA.BIGWHEEL.COM:

```
BEGIN
    DBMS_REPCAT.GENERATE_REPLICATION_TRIGGER(
        gname      => 'SPROCKET',
        master_list=> 'D7HI.BIGWHEEL.COM, D7WA.BIGWHEEL.COM' );
END;
```

The following call regenerates the replication support for all objects in replication group SPROCKET at all master sites:

```
EXECUTE DBMS_REPCAT.GENERATE_REPLICATION_TRIGGER(gname=> 'SPROCKET' )
```

For an additional example, see the *invalids.sql* file on the companion disk. The example lists all objects in the database with a status of INVALID and generates the appropriate SQL statements to attempt to validate them.

Adding and Removing Master Sites with DBMS_REPCAT

Now you have generated replication support for those objects you intend to replicate, and you are ready to add master sites to your environment. In advanced replication parlance, a *master site* is a database instance where replicated objects and their replication support triggers and packages exist. Master sites are sometimes called *peers*, because every master site has the same objects and identical (or nearly identical) data. Any master site can perform DML on a replicated table, and Oracle propagates the DML to all other master sites. There is no single authoritative site, not even the master definition site. The distinction between the master definition site and the other masters is that the master definition site is the only site that can perform DDL on replicated objects, and the only one that can suspend or resume replication activity.

Here are the DBMS_REPCAT programs associated with creating and maintaining master sites in your replicated environment:

> DBMS_REPCAT.ADD_MASTER_DATABASE
> DBMS_REPCAT.REMOVE_MASTER_DATABASES
> DBMS_REPCAT.COMMENT_ON_REPSITES
> DBMS_REPCAT.RELOCATE_MASTERDEF

We describe these programs in the following sections.

The DBMS_REPCAT.ADD_MASTER_DATABASE procedure

The ADD_MASTER_DATABASE procedure adds a master site. The specifications differ for Oracle7 and Oracle8 as follows. (Note that the sname parameter no longer exists in Oracle8.)

Here is the Oracle7 specification:

```
PROCEDURE DBMS_REPCAT.ADD_MASTER_DATABASE
    (gname      IN VARCHAR2 := '',
     master     IN VARCHAR2,
     use_existing_objects IN BOOLEAN := TRUE,
     copy_rows IN BOOLEAN := TRUE,
```

```
        comment   IN VARCHAR2 := '',
        propagation_mode IN VARCHAR2 := 'ASYNCHRONOUS',
        sname N VARCHAR2 := '');
```

Here is the Oracle8 specification:

```
PROCEDURE DBMS_REPCAT.ADD_MASTER_DATABASE
     (gname     IN VARCHAR2 := '',
      master    IN VARCHAR2,
      use_existing_objects IN BOOLEAN := TRUE,
      copy_rows IN BOOLEAN := TRUE,
      comment   IN VARCHAR2 := '',
      propagation_mode IN VARCHAR2 := 'ASYNCHRONOUS');
```

Parameters are summarized in the following table.

Name	Description
gname	Name of the replication group to which master site is being added
master	Global name of the new master site
use_existing_objects	Reuse existing objects at the new site
copy_rows	Copy rows from the invoking site to the new master site
comment	Comment on new master site, visible in DBA_REPSITES data dictionary view
propagation_mode	Propagation mode (SYNCHRONOUS or ASYNCHRONOUS)
sname (Oracle7 only)	Schema name (not used)

Exceptions. The ADD_MASTER_DATABASE procedure may raise the following exceptions:

Name	Number	Description
commfailure	−23317	Site master is not reachable
duplicateschema	−23307	Replication group gname already exists at site master
invalidpropmode	−23380	Propagation_mode is not SYNCHRONOUS or ASYNCHRONOUS
missingrepgroup	−23373	Replication group gname does not exist at the calling site
nonmasterdef	−23312	Calling site is not the master definition site
notquiesced	−23310	Replication group gname is not quiesced
repnotcompatible	−23376	Replication group gname does not exist at master, and master is a pre-7.3 release

Restrictions. Note the following restrictions on calling ADD_MASTER_DATABASE:

- This procedure must be run from the master definition site.
- The replication group must be quiesced.

Example. The ADD_MASTER_DATABASE procedure is relatively simple to use. For example, this call adds site D7NY.BIGWHEEL.COM to the SPROCKET replication group and instantiates all objects there:

```
BEGIN
    DBMS_REPCAT.ADD_MASTER_DATABASE(
        gname               => 'SPROCKET',
        master              => 'D7NY.BIGWHEEL.COM',
        use_existing_objects=> 'FALSE',
        copy_rows           => 'TRUE',
        propagation_mode => 'ASYNCHRONOUS');
END;
```

For additional examples, see the *repsites.sql* and *links.sql* files on the companion disk. The *repsites.sql* example queries all replication sites, sorted by replication group, and queries the DBA_REPSITES data dictionary view. The *links.sql* example lists all database links in the database (but not the passwords for those that were created using a CONNECT clause).

TIP   It is generally easier to instantiate all objects at the new master site first. That way, the call to ADD_MASTER_DATABASE does not have to perform DDL to create the schema or send all of the data across a network link. If you instantiate the objects first, the call to ADD_MASTER_DATABASE has to generate replication support only for the objects at the new site and update other master sites with the new master's existence.

The DBMS_REPCAT.REMOVE_MASTER_DATABASES procedure

The REMOVE_MASTER_DATABASES procedure complements the ADD_MASTER_DATABASE procedure by removing master sites. The master sites being removed do not need to be accessible, but all other masters do. As with the ADD_MASTER_DATABASE procedure, the Oracle7 and Oracle8 specifications differ; Oracle8 does not have the sname parameter.

Here is the Oracle7 specification:

```
PROCEDURE DBMS_REPCAT.REMOVE_MASTER_DATABASES
    (gname IN VARCHAR2 := '',
     master_list IN VARCHAR2,
     sname IN VARCHAR2 := '');
```

Here is the Oracle8 specification:

```
PROCEDURE DBMS_REPCAT.REMOVE_MASTER_DATABASES
    (gname IN VARCHAR2 := '',
     master_list IN VARCHAR2);;
```

Parameters are summarized in the following table.

Name	Description
gname	Name of the replication group from which master site(s) will be removed
master_list	A comma-delimited list of global_names of master sites to be removed; use either master_list or master_table
sname (Oracle7 only)	Schema name (not used)

Exceptions. The REMOVE_MASTER_DATABASES procedure may raise the following exceptions:

Name	Number	Description
commfailure	−23317	One or more remaining master sites is not reachable
nonmaster	−23313	One or more of the specified masters is not a master database
nonmasterdef	−23312	Calling site is not the master definition site
reconfigerror	−23316	One of the specified masters in the master definition site

Restrictions. The REMOVE_MASTER_DATABASES procedure must be run from the master definition site.

Example. To remove site D7NY.BIGWHEEL.COM from the SPROCKET replication group and inform all other master sites, specify the following:

```
BEGIN
    DBMS_REPCAT.REMOVE_MASTER_DATABASES(
        name       => 'SPROCKET',
        master_list => 'D7NY.BIGWHEEL.COM');
END;
```

TIP   After removing master sites with REMOVE_MASTER_DATABASES, you should call DBMS_REPCAT.DROP_MASTER_REPGROUP at each of the master sites you removed. Although you do not need to quiesce the replication group to remove one or more master database(s), you are strongly encouraged to do so. Otherwise, you will have to manually clear the RPC queue and resolve any inconsistencies.

The DBMS_REPCAT.COMMENT_ON_REPSITES procedure

The COMMENT_ON_REPSITES procedure allows you to add or change a comment associated with a master site specified in the DBA_REPSITES data dictionary view. Here's the specification:

```
PROCEDURE DBMS_REPCAT.COMMENT_ON_REPSITES
    (gname IN VARCHAR2,
```

```
master IN VARCHAR,
comment IN VARCHAR2);
```

Parameters are summarized in the following table.

Name	Description
gname	Name of the replication group to which master belongs
master	Global name of master site
comment	Comment

Exceptions. The COMMENT_ON_REPSITES procedure may raise the following exceptions:

Name	Number	Description
commfailure	−23317	Unable to communicate with one or more master sites
nonmaster	−23313	The master is not a master site
nonmasterdef	−23312	Calling site is not master definition site

Restrictions. You must call the COMMENT_ON_REPSITES procedure from the master definition site.

Example. The following call updates the comment for master site D7NY. BIG-WHEEL.COM:

```
BEGIN
    DBMS_REPCAT.COMMENT_ON_REPSITES(
        gname   => 'SPROCKET',
        master  => 'D7NY.BIGWHEEL.COM',
        comment => 'Comment added on '||sysdate|| ' by ' ||user)
END;
```

The DBMS_REPCAT.RELOCATE_MASTERDEF procedure

If your master definition site becomes unusable, or if you simply want another site to serve that role, you can configure a different master site as the master definition site with the RELOCATE_MASTERDEF procedure described in this section. Follow these guidelines:

- If your relocation is planned (i.e., all sites are up and reachable), set the notify_masters and include_old_masterdef parameters to TRUE.

- If the current master definition site is not available, set the notify_masters parameter to TRUE and set include_old_masterdef to FALSE.

- If the master definition site as well as some master sites are unavailable, invoke the RELOCATE_MASTERDEF procedure from each functioning master site with both the notify_masters and the include_old_masterdef parameters set to FALSE.

The specifications differ for Oracle7 and Oracle8 as follows.

Here is the Oracle7 specification:

```
PROCEDURE DBMS_REPCAT.RELOCATE_MASTERDEF
    (gname IN VARCHAR2 := '',
     old_masterdef IN VARCHAR2,
     new_masterdef IN VARCHAR2,
     notify_masters IN BOOLEAN := TRUE,
     include_old_masterdef IN BOOLEAN := TRUE,
     sname IN VARCHAR2 := '')
```

Here is the Oracle8 specification:

```
PROCEDURE DBMS_REPCAT.RELOCATE_MASTERDEF
    (gname IN VARCHAR2,
     old_masterdef IN VARCHAR2,
     new_masterdef IN VARCHAR2,
     notify_masters IN BOOLEAN := TRUE,
     include_old_masterdef IN BOOLEAN := TRUE);
```

Parameters are summarized in the following table.

Name	Description
gname	Name of the replication group.
old_masterdef	Global name of the current master definition site.
new_masterdef	Global name of the new master definition site.
notify_masters	If TRUE (the default), synchronously multicast information about the change to all masters; if FALSE, do not inform masters.
include_old_masterdef	If TRUE (the default), notify current master definition site of the change.
sname (Oracle7 only)	Not used.

Exceptions. The RELOCATE_MASTERDEF procedure may raise the following exceptions:

Name	Number	Description
commfailure	−23317	Unable to communicate with master site(s) and notify_masters is TRUE
nonmaster	−23313	The new_masterdef is not a master site
nonmasterdef	−23312	The old_masterdef is not the master definition site

Restrictions. You must call RELOCATE_MASTERDEF from a master or master definition site.

Example. The following call relocates the master definition site for replication group SPROCKET from D7CA.BIGWHEEL.COM to D7NY.BIGWHEEL.COM, and informs all masters, as well as the master definition site, of the change:

```
BEGIN
    DBMS_REPCAT.RELOCATE_MASTERDEF(
            gname             => 'SPROCKET',
            old_master_def    => 'D7CA.BIGWHEEL.COM',
            new_master_def    => 'D7NY.BIGWHEEL.COM',
            notify_masters    => TRUE,
            include_old_masterdef=> TRUE);
END;
```

Suppose that the master definition site D7CA.BIGWHEEL.COM becomes permanently unavailable. We can convert another site, such as D7NY.BIGWHEEL.COM, into the master definition site without having to communicate with D7CA.BIGWHEEL.COM. We set the include_old_masterdef parameter to FALSE.

```
BEGIN
    DBMS_REPCAT.RELOCATE_MASTERDEF(
            gname             => 'SPROCKET',
            old_master_def    => 'D7CA.BIGWHEEL.COM',
            new_master_def    => 'D7NY.BIGWHEEL.COM',
            notify_masters    => TRUE,
            include_old_masterdef=> FALSE);
END;
```

Maintaining the Repcatlog Queue with DBMS_REPCAT

The programs in this category maintain the "repcatlog" queue. You'll use these procedures:

> DBMS_REPCAT.DO_DEFERRED_REPCAT_ADMIN
> DBMS_REPCAT.WAIT_MASTER_LOG
> DBMS_REPCAT.PURGE_MASTER_LOG

The following sections describe these programs.

The DBMS_REPCAT.DO_DEFERRED_REPCAT_ADMIN procedure

Whenever you create or alter replicated objects—for example, with the GENERATE_REPLICATION_SUPPORT or ALTER_MASTER_REPOBJECT procedure—Oracle queues the changes in the "repcatlog" queue; the entries in this queue correspond to entries in the DBA_REPCATLOG data dictionary view. All DDL changes must originate at the master definition site, but the repcatlog queue exists at every master site.

The DO_DEFERRED_REPCAT_ADMIN procedure processes entries in the repcatlog queue at all master sites. You may have noticed this job in the job queue, scheduled to run once every ten minutes. Oracle creates this scheduled job the first time you execute one of the packages that performs DDL.

The specifications differ for Oracle7 and Oracle8 as follows.

Here is the Oracle7 specification:

```
PROCEDURE DBMS_REPCAT.DO_DEFERRED_REPCAT_ADMIN
    (gname IN VARCHAR2 := '',
     all_sites IN BOOLEAN := FALSE,
     sname IN VARCHAR2 := '');
```

Here is the Oracle8 specification:

```
PROCEDURE DBMS_REPCAT.DO_DEFERRED_REPCAT_ADMIN
    (gname IN VARCHAR2,
     all_sites IN BOOLEAN := FALSE);
```

As with all of the other DBMS_REPCAT procedures, the Oracle8 version does not have the sname parameter.

Parameters are summarized in the following table.

Name	Description
gname	Name of the replication group for which to push the repcatlog queue
all_sites	If TRUE, execute queued procedures at every master site
sname (Oracle7 only)	Not used

Exceptions. The DO_DEFERRED_REPCAT_ADMIN procedure may raise the following exceptions:

Name	Number	Description
commfailure	−23317	Unable to communicate with master site
nonmaster	−23312	Master site associated with snapshot group is no longer a master site

Restrictions. The DO_DEFERRED_REPCAT_ADMIN procedure performs only the procedures that have been queued by the invoking user. Note that the job queue is used to perform the queued procedures automatically.

Example. If you want to run DO_DEFERRED_REPCAT_ADMIN manually, either because you do not have DBMS_JOB background processes running, or because you want to push the repcatlog queue immediately, you can do so. Here is an example:

```
BEGIN
    DBMS_REPCAT.DO_DEFFERED_REPCAT_ADMIN
    ( gname => 'SPROCKET',  all_sites => TRUE);
```

```
END;
```

For an additional example, see the *catlog.sql* file on the companion disk. The example lists entries in the repcatlog (DBA_REPCATLOG) with the time of submission in hours, minutes, and seconds.

The DBMS_REPCAT.WAIT_MASTER_LOG procedure

You can use the WAIT_MASTER_LOG procedure to ascertain whether the changes in the repcatlog queue have reached the master sites. This procedure has an OUT parameter, true_count, which the procedure populates with the number of outstanding tasks. The specifications differ for Oracle7 and Oracle8 as follows.

Here is the Oracle7 specification:

```
PROCEDURE DBMS_REPCAT.WAIT_MASTER_LOG
    (gname IN VARCHAR2 := '',
    record_count IN NATURAL,
    timeout IN NATURAL,
    true_count OUT NATURAL,
    sname IN VARCHAR2 := '');
```

Here is the Oracle8 specification:

```
PROCEDURE DBMS_REPCAT.WAIT_MASTER_LOG
    (gname IN VARCHAR2,
    record_count IN NATURAL,
    timeout IN NATURAL,
    true_count OUT NATURAL);
```

Parameters are summarized in the following table.

Name	Description
gname	Name of the replication group
record_count	Number of records to allow to be entered in the DBA_REPCATLOG data dictionary view before returning
timeout	Number of seconds to wait before returning
true_count	Output variable containing the actual number of incomplete activities queued in the DBA_REPCATLOG data dictionary view
sname	Not used

There are no restrictions on calling WAIT_MASTER_LOG.

Exceptions. The WAIT_MASTER_LOG procedure may raise the following exception:

Name	Number	Description
nonmaster	−23312	Calling site is not a master site

Example. The following call returns after 60 seconds, or after five entries have
been entered into the DBA_REPCATLOG data dictionary view at the current master for replication group SPROCKET. The number of records (corresponding to
incomplete tasks) is stored in the variable vRecCount.

```
VARIABLE vRecCount NATURAL
BEGIN
    DBMS_REPCAT.WAIT_MASTER_LOG(gname=> 'SPROCKET',
                                record_count => 5,
                                timeout => 60,
                                true_count => vRecCount);
END;
```

TIP   You might find it more convenient to query the DBA_REPCATLOG
               data dictionary view directly.

The DBMS_REPCAT.PURGE_MASTER_LOG procedure

The DBA_REPCATLOG data dictionary view retains entries on DDL propagations
that have failed; these entries are not removed when you resolve the problem that
caused the failure. You may notice entries such as these:

```
  1  SELECTsource, status, request, to_char(timestamp, 'HH24:MI:SS') timestamp
  2  FROM dba_repcatlog
  3* ORDER BY id
system@d7ca SQL> /
```

Source	Status	Request	Time
D7CA.BIGWHEEL.COM	ERROR	CREATE_MASTER_REPOBJECT	23:13:07
D7CA.BIGWHEEL.COM	ERROR	CREATE_MASTER_REPOBJECT	23:13:07
D7CA.BIGWHEEL.COM	ERROR	CREATE_MASTER_REPOBJECT	23:25:20
D7CA.BIGWHEEL.COM	ERROR	CREATE_MASTER_REPOBJECT	23:25:20
D7CA.BIGWHEEL.COM	ERROR	CREATE_MASTER_REPOBJECT	23:26:53
D7CA.BIGWHEEL.COM	ERROR	CREATE_MASTER_REPOBJECT	23:26:53
D7CA.BIGWHEEL.COM	ERROR	DROP_MASTER_REPOBJECT	14:03:27
D7CA.BIGWHEEL.COM	ERROR	DROP_MASTER_REPOBJECT	14:03:27

```
8 rows selected.
```

You must use the PURGE_MASTER_LOG procedure to remove these entries from
DBA_REPCATLOG. You can specify records to delete by id, originating master,
replication group, and schema. If a parameter is NULL, it is treated as a wildcard.
Specifications differ for Oracle7 and Oracle8 as follows.

Here is the Oracle7 specification:

```
PROCEDURE DBMS_REPCAT.PURGE_MASTER_LOG
    (id IN NATURAL,
     source IN VARCHAR2,
     gname IN VARCHAR2 := '',
```

```
        sname IN VARCHAR2 := '');
```

Here is the Oracle8 specification:

```
PROCEDURE DBMS_REPCAT.PURGE_MASTER_LOG
    (id IN NATURAL,
     source IN VARCHAR2,
     gname IN VARCHAR2);
```

Parameters are summarized in the following table.

Name	Description
id	Identification of the request (i.e., the ID field in DBA_REPCAT-LOG data dictionary view)
source	Global name of originating master
gname	Name of the replication group for which request was made
sname (Oracle7 only)	Not used

Exceptions. The PURGE_MASTER_LOG procedure may raise the following exception:

Name	Number	Description
nonmaster	−23312	The gname is NULL and calling site is not a master site

Restrictions. The calling site must be a master site.

Example. The following call removes all entries associated with replication group SPROCKET from the DBA_REPCATLOG data dictionary view:

```
BEGIN
    DBMS_REPCAT.PURGE_MASTER_LOG(gname=> 'SPROCKET' );
END;
```

For an additional example, see the *caterr.sql* file on the companion disk. The example lists entries in the repcatlog (DBA_REPCATLOG) containing errors, and displays the error message associated with each error.

TIP   To clear all entries from the DBA_REPCATLOG data dictionary view, set all parameters to NULL.

Quiescence with DBMS_REPCAT

You may have noticed that many of the DBMS_REPCAT packages require you to quiesce the environment before using them. *Quiescence,* as it is called, accomplishes two things:

1. It applies all outstanding DML for the replication group at all master sites.

2. It prevents any additional DML on any of the replicated objects at all master sites.

In other words, quiescence ensures that all sites are up to date, and forces the replicated environment to stand still.

WARNING   Do not attempt to quiesce an environment that has unresolved errors or any other serious problems. If you cannot complete outstanding transactions, you will not be able to quiesce the environment.

You will use the following programs to quiesce your environment and start it up again:

    DBMS_REPCAT.SUSPEND_MASTER_ACTIVITY
    DBMS_REPCAT.RESUME_MASTER_ACTIVITY

The DBMS_REPCAT.SUSPEND_MASTER_ACTIVITY procedure

The SUSPEND_MASTER_ACTIVITY procedure quiesces an environment. The specifications differ for Oracle7 and Oracle8 as follows.

Here is the Oracle7 specification:

```
PROCEDURE DBS_REPCAT.SUSPEND_MASTER_ACTIVITY
    (gname IN VARCHAR2 := '',
     execute_as_user IN BOOLEAN   := FALSE,
     sname IN VARCHAR2 := '');
```

Here is the Oracle8 specification:

```
PROCEDURE DBMS_REPCAT.SUSPEND_MASTER_ACTIVITY
    (gname IN VARCHAR2,
     override IN BOOLEAN   := FALSE);
```

Parameters are summarized in the following table.

Name	Description
gname	Name of the replication group for which replication activity is to be suspended
execute_as_user	FALSE (default), indicates that remote system will authenticate calls using authentication context user who originally queued the RPC; TRUE indicates that remote system will use authentication context of the session user
sname (Oracle7 only)	Not used

Exceptions. The SUSPEND_MASTER_ACTIVITY procedure may raise the following exceptions:

Name	Number	Description
commfailure	–23317	Unable to communicate with one or more master site(s)
nonmasterdef	–23312	Calling site is not the master definition site
notnormal	–23311	Replication group gname is not in NORMAL state

Restrictions. Note the following restrictions on calling SUSPEND_MASTER_ACTIV-ITY:

* You must run this procedure from the master definition site.

* Prior to Oracle8, this procedure quiesces all replication groups at the master definition site, not just the group specified by the gname parameter.

Example. The following call suspends replication activity for the SPROCKET replication group:

```
BEGIN
    DBMS_REPCAT.SUSPEND_MASTER_ACTIVITY( gname => 'SPROCKET' );
END;
```

TIP   This call can take some time to complete if you have many master sites and/or many outstanding transactions. You can monitor the progress by querying the status field in the DBA_REPCATLOG data dictionary view.

The DBMS_REPCAT.RESUME_MASTER_ACTIVITY procedure

The RESUME_MASTER_ACTIVITY procedure starts up an environment that has been quiesced. The specifications differ for Oracle7 and Oracle8 as follows.

Here is the Oracle7 specification:

```
PROCEDURE DBMS_REPCAT.RESUME_MASTER_ACTIVITY
```

```
(gname IN VARCHAR2 := '',
 override IN BOOLEAN := FALSE,
 sname IN VARCHAR2 := '');
```

Here is the Oracle8 specification:

```
PROCEDURE DBMS_REPCAT.RESUME_MASTER_ACTIVITY
    (gname IN VARCHAR2,
     override IN BOOLEAN := FALSE);
```

Parameters are summarized in the following table.

Name	Description
gname	Name of the replication group for which replication activity is to be resumed.
override	If FALSE (the default), activity is resumed only after all deferred REPCAT activity is completed; if set to TRUE, activity is resumed as soon as possible
sname	Not used

Exceptions. The RESUME_MASTER_ACTIVITY procedure may raise the following exceptions:

Name	Number	Description
commfailure	−23317	Unable to communicate with one or more master site(s)
nonmasterdef	−23312	Calling site is not the master definition site
notquiesced	−23310	Replication group gname is not quiesced

Restrictions. Note the following restrictions on calling RESUME_MASTER_ACTIVITY:

- You must run this procedure from the master definition site.
- The replication group must be quiesced or quiescing.

Example. The following example resumes replication activity for a replication group:

```
BEGIN
    DBMS_REPCAT.RESUME_MASTER_ACTIVITY( gname => 'SPROCKET' );
END;
```

Miscellaneous DBMS_REPCAT Procedures

This section describes several DBMS_REPCAT programs that don't fall into any of the earlier categories.

NOTE	We describe the IMPORT_CHECK, ALTER_MASTER_PROPAGA-TION, and SEND_AND_COMPARE_OLD_VALUES procedures here because they are a part of the DBMS_REPCAT package. However, you will probably run these procedures after using the DBMS_OFFLINE_OG and/or DBMS_RECTIFIER_DIFF packages described in the next major section.

The DBMS_REPCAT.REPCAT_IMPORT_CHECK procedure

From time to time, you may need to rebuild a master site from an export dump file as either a recovery or maintenance procedure. Because object id numbers (as seen in SYS.OBJ$.OBJ# and DBA_OBJECTS.OBJECT_ID) change during these rebuilds, Oracle supplies a procedure (REPCAT_IMPORT_CHECK) that you must run immediately after an import of any master site to synchronize the new id numbers with the data stored in the table SYSTEM.REPCAT$_REPOBJECT.

You must run the REPCAT_IMPORT_CHECK procedure immediately after you import any master site. The specifications differ for Oracle7 and Oracle8 as follows.

Here is the Oracle7 specification:

```
PROCEDURE DBMS_REPCAT.REPCAT_IMPORT_CHECK
    (gname IN VARCHAR2 := '',
     master IN BOOLEAN,
     sname IN VRCHAR2 := '');
```

Here is the Oracle8 specification:

```
PROCEDURE DBMS_REPCAT.REPCAT_IMPORT_CHECK
    (gnamee in VARCHAR2 := '',
     master IN BOOLEAN);
```

Parameters are summarized in the following table.

Name	Description
gname	Name of the replication group being revalidated
master	Set to TRUE if site is a master, FALSE if it is a snapshot site
sname (Oracle7 only)	Not used

Exceptions. The REPCAT_IMPORT_CHECK procedure may raise the following exceptions:

Name	Number	Description
missingobject	−23308	Object with a status of VALID in REPCAT$_REPOBJECT does not exist
missingschema	−23306	Schema sname does not exist

Name	Number	Description
nonmaster	−23312	Master is set to TRUE, but the calling site is not a master, or not the expected database
nonsnapshot	−23314	Master is set to FALSE but the calling site is not a snapshot site

Example. The following call revalidates all replicated objects and supporting objects for the SPROCKET replication group. Issue this call after an import:

```
BEGIN
    DBMS_REPCAT.REPCAT_IMPORT_CHECJ(sname=> 'SPROCKET',  master => TRUE );
END;
```

TIP   Call REPCAT_IMPORT_CHECK with sname and master set to NULL
             (or with no parameters) to validate all replication groups at the site.

The DBMS_REPCAT.ALTER_MASTER_PROPAGATION procedure

The advanced replication option supports two modes of propagation: synchronous and asynchronous. The following table summarizes the pros and cons of each mode.

Mode	Advantages	Disadvantages
Synchronous	Data is always up to date at all sites. No possibility of conflicts.	Requires 100% availability of network connections. If a site is unreachable, transactions are blocked.
Asynchronous	Master sites can go offline temporarily with no adverse impact.	Must build conflict resolution into replicated applications and monitor unresolved conflicts.

As a practical matter, you should opt for synchronous replication only if your sites are tightly linked to each other in your network, both physically and logically. Examples of acceptably tight links include two machines sharing a hub, or two machines connected by a crossover cable.

Regardless of the propagation method you choose, Oracle lets you change a replication group's propagation mode later with the ALTER_MASTER_PROPAGATION procedure. Call this procedure to change the propagation mode of a replication group (from synchronous to asynchronous, or vice versa). Here's the specification:

```
PROCEDURE DBMS_REPCAT.ALTER_MASTER_PROPAGATION
    (gname IN VARCHAR2,
     master IN VARCHAR2,
     {dblink_table IN dbms_utility.dblink_array | dblink_list IN VARCHAR2},
     propagation_modee IN VARCHAR2 := 'ASYNCHRONOUS',
     comment IN VARCHAR2 := '');
```

Parameters are summarized in the following table.

Name	Description
gname	Name of the replication group whose propagation mode is being altered
master	Global name of the master site having its propagation mode altered
dblink_list	List of database links for which the master's propagation mode is being altered
propagation_mode	New propagation mode (SYNCHRONOUS or ASYNCHRONOUS)
comment	Comment visible in DBA_REPPROP data dictionary view

Exceptions. The ALTER_MASTER_PROPAGATION procedure may raise the following exceptions:

Name	Number	Description
nonmaster	−23312	One of the sites in dblink_list is not a master site
nonmasterdef	−23312	Calling site is not the master definition site
notquiesced	−23310	Replication group gname is not quiesced
typefailure	−23319	The propagation_mode is not SYNCHRONOUS or ASYNCHRONOUS

Restrictions. Note the following restrictions on calling ALTER_MASTER_PROPAGATION:

- You must run this procedure from the master definition site.

- The replication group must be quiesced.

Example. The following call changes the propagation mode between D7CA.BIGWHEEL.COM and D7NY.BIGWHEEL.COM to SYNCHRONOUS:

```
BEGIN
    DBMS_REPCAT.ALTER_MASTER_PROPAGATION(
        gname            => 'SPROCKET',
        master           => 'D7CA.BIGWHEEL.COM',
        dblink_list      => 'D7NY.BIGWHEEL.COM',
        use_existing_objects=> 'FALSE',
        propagation_mode => 'SYNCHRONOUS');
END;
```

TIP   If you change the propagation mode, you must also regenerate the
                 replication support triggers for all replicated tables; ALTER_MASTER_
                 PROPAGATION does not do this automatically. After altering the
                 propagation method, you must call DBMS_REPCAT.GENERATE_
                 REPLICATION_TRIGGERS for all replicated tables in the replication
                 group.

The DBMS_REPCAT.SEND_AND_COMPARE_OLD_VALUES procedure (Oracle8 only)

The default behavior of advanced replication is to send the old and new values of
every column to participating master sites whenever you update a row in a replicated table. At the destination sites, Oracle uses this information to ensure that the
version of the row that you updated matches the version of the row currently at
the destination. However, if you know that certain columns in a table will never
change, you can avoid sending the data in these columns when you propagate
updates to participating master sites. Using the SEND_AND_COMPARE_OLD_VAL-
UES procedure (available only in Oracle8) in this way, you'll reduce propagation
overhead. Here is the specification:

```
PROCEDURE DBMS_REPCAT.SEND_AND_COMPARE_OLD_VALUES
    (sname IN VARCHAR2
    oname IN VARCHAR2,
    {column_list IN VARCHAR2 | column_table IN dbms_repcat.varchar2s},
    operation IN VARCHAR2 := 'UPDATE',
    send IN BOOLEAN := TRUE);
```

Parameters are summarized in the following table.

Name	Description
sname	Name of the replication group whose propagation mode is being altered
oname	Table being altered
column_list	Comma-separated list of columns whose propagation mode is being altered; "*" indicates all nonkey columns
column_table	PL/SQL table of containing columns whose propagation is being altered
operation	Operation for which this change applies; this may be UPDATE, DELETE, or "*" (indicating both updates and deletes)
send	If TRUE (the default), then the old values for the columns are sent; if FALSE, then old values are not sent

---

NOTE   The configuration changes you specify with this procedure do not take effect unless the min_communication parameter is TRUE for the table in question. That is, you must have executed DBMS_REP-CAT.GENERATE_REPLICATION_SUPPORT for the table with min_communication = TRUE.

Exceptions. The SEND_AND_COMPARE_OLD_VALUES procedure may raise the following exceptions:

Name	Number	Description
missingobject	–23308	Object oname does not exist
missingcolumn	–23334	Column(s) specified do not exist in table oname
nonmasterdef	–23312	Calling site is not the master definition site
notquiesced	–23310	Replication group gname is not quiesced
typefailure	–23319	The oname is not a table

Restrictions. Note the following restrictions on calling SEND_AND_COMPARE_OLD_VALUES:

- You must call this procedure from the master definition site.
- The replication group sname must be quiesced.

DBMS_OFFLINE_OG: Performing Site Instantiation

When you add a new site to your replicated environment, you must not only create the replicated objects, but also populate snapshots and replicated tables with a copy of the current data. Although you can set the copy_rows parameter to TRUE in your call to the DBMS_REPCAT package's CREATE_MASTER_REPOBJECT or ADD_MASTER_DATABASE procedure, this option is not practical for schemas that are large or complex.

The DBMS_OFFLINE_OG package provides a more feasible method of site instantiation. The general idea is that you export data from an existing master site and import it into the new master site. While the import is taking place, the existing master sites queue data updates to the new site, but do not actually send the updates until the load is complete.

Getting Started with DBMS_OFFLINE_OG

The DBMS_OFFLINE_OG package is created when the Oracle database is installed. The *dbmsofln.sql* script (found in the built-in packages source directory, as described in Chapter 1) contains the source code for this package's specification. This script is called by *catrep.sql*, which must be run to install the advanced replication packages. The wrapped sql script *prvtofln.plb* creates the public synonym DBMS_OFFLINE_OG. No EXECUTE privileges are granted on DBMS_OFFLINE_OG; only the owner (SYS) and those with the EXECUTE ANY PROCEDURE system privilege may execute the package.

The programs in DBMS_OFFLINE_OG are listed in Table 15-5.

Table 15-5. DBMS_OFFLINE_OG: Programs

Name	Description	Use in SQL?
BEGIN_INSTANTIATION	Call from master definition site to flag beginning of offline instantiation	No
BEGIN_LOAD	Call from new master site prior to importing data	No
END_INSTANTIATION	Call from master definition site to flag end of offline instantiation	No
END_LOAD	Call from new master site after importing data	No
RESUME_SUBSET_OF_MASTERS	Call from master definition site to resume replication activity for existing sites while new site is instantiated	No

DBMS_OFFLINE_OG Interface

This section describes the programs available in the DBMS_OFFLINE_OG package.

The DBMS_OFFLINE_OG.BEGIN_INSTANTIATION procedure

The BEGIN_INSTANTIATION procedure is called from the master definition site to flag the beginning of offline instantiation. Here's the specification:

```
PROCEDURE DBMS_OFFLINE_OG.BEGIN_INSTANTIATION
    (gname IN VARCHAR2,
     new_site IN VARCHAR2);
```

Parameters are summarized in the following table.

Name	Description
gname	The replication group to which the site is being added
new_site	The global_name of the new_site

Exceptions. The BEGIN_INSTANTIATION procedure may raise the following exceptions:

Name	Number	Description
badargument	−23430	gname is NULL or ' '
missingrepgroup	−23373	Group gname does not exist
nonmasterdef	−23312	Routine is not being called from master definition site
sitealreadyexists	−23432	New_site already exists
wrongstate	−23431	Group gname is not in NORMAL state at master definition site

Restrictions. The procedures in DBMS_OFFLINE_OG must be called in the appropriate order from the appropriate sites. The following example illustrates the proper use of this package.

Example. The following table summarizes the steps you should follow when you use the procedures in the DBMS_OFFLINE_OG package.

Step	Where Performed	Activity
1	Master definition site	DBMS_REPCAT.ADD_MASTER_DATABASE
2	Master definition site	DBMS_REPCAT.SUSPEND_MASTER_ACTIVITY
3	Master definition site	DBMS_OFFLINE_OG.BEGIN_INSTANTIATION
4	Any master site	Export replicated schema
5	Master definition site	DBMS_OFFLINE_OG.RESUME_SUBSET_OF_MASTERS
6	New site	DBMS_OFFLINE_OG.BEGIN_LOAD
7	New site	Import data from step 4
8	New site	DBMS_OFFLINE_OG.END_LOAD
9	Master definition site	DBMS_OFFLINE_OG.END_INSTANTIATION

The following scenario shows how instantiate a new site. Here we add the site D7NY.BIGWHEEL.COM to the replication group SPROCKET using DBMS_OFFLINE_OG. Assume that the master definition site is D7CA.BIGWHEEL.COM.

1. From master definition site D7CA.BIGWHEEL.COM, we add the new master site, quiesce the replication group, and call DBMS_OFFLINE_OG.BEGIN_INSTANTIATION.

```
BEGIN
    DBMS_REPCAT.ADD_MASTER_DATABASE(
        gname   => 'SPROCKET',
        master  =>'D7NY.BIGWHEEL.COM');;
    DBMS_REPCAT.SUSPEND_MASTER_ACTIVITY(gname => 'SPROCKET');
    DBMS_OFFLINE_OG.BEGIN_INSTANTIATION(
        gname   =>   'SPROCKET',
```

```
                            new_site=> 'D7NY.BIGWHEEL.COM');
          END;
```

2. Perform export of schema SPROCKET from any existing master site.

3. Call RESUME_SUBSET_OF_MASTERS at master definition site.

4. Call BEGIN_LOAD from the new master site D7NY.BIGWHEEL.COM.

```
          BEGIN
              DBMS_OFFLINE_OG.BEGIN_LOAD(
                  gname    => 'SPROCKET',
                  new_site=> 'D7NY.BIGWHEEL.COM');
          END;
```

5. Import the SPROCKET schema into D7NY.BIGWHEEL.COM using the export file created in step 2.

6. Call END_LOAD from the new master site, D7NY.BIGWHEEL.COM.

```
          BEGIN
              DBMS_OFFLINE_OG.END_LOAD(
                  gname    => 'SPROCKET',
                  new_site=> 'D7NY.BIGWHEEL.COM');
          END;
```

7. Call END_INSTANTIATION from the master definition site.

```
          BEGIN
              DBMS_OFFLINE_OG.END_INSTANTIATION(
                  gname => 'SPROCKET',
                  new_site => 'D7NY.BIGWHEEL.COM');
          END;
```

The DBMS_OFFLINE_OG.BEGIN_LOAD procedure

Call the BEGIN_LOAD procedure from the new master site before you begin importing data. The specification follows:

```
    PROCEDURE DBMS_OFFLINE_OG.BEGIN_LOAD
        (gname IN VARCHAR2,
        new_site IN VARCHAR2);
```

These parameters are identical to those described for the BEGIN_INSTANTIA-TION procedure. See that section as well for an example of using the procedures in the DBMS_OFFLINE_OG procedure.

Exceptions. The BEGIN_LOAD procedure may raise the following exceptions:

Name	Number	Description
badargument	−23430	gname is NULL or ' '
missingrepgroup	−23373	Group gname does not exist

Name	Number	Description
wrongsite	−23433	Raised if BEGIN_LOAD or END_LOAD is executed at a site other than new_site
wrongstate	−23431	Group gname is not in NORMAL state at the master definition site

Restrictions. The procedures in DBMS_OFFLINE_OG must be called in the appropriate order from the appropriate sites. The example under BEGIN_INSTANTIATION illustrates the proper use of this package.

The DBMS_OFFLINE_OG.END_INSTANTIATION procedure

You call the END_INSTANTIATION procedure from the master definition site to flag the end of offline instantiation. The specification follows:

```
PROCEDURE DBMS_OFFLINE_OG.END_INSTANTIATION
    (gname IN VARCHAR2,
     new_site IN VARCHAR2);
```

These parameters are identical to those described for the BEGIN_INSTANTIATION procedure. See that section as well for an example of using the procedures in the DBMS_OFFLINE_OG package.

Exceptions. The END_INSTANTIATION procedure may raise the following exceptions:

Name	Number	Description
badargument	−23430	gname is NULL or ' '
missingrepgroup	−23373	Group gname does not exist
nonmasterdef	−23312	Routine is not being called from master definition site
sitealreadyexists	−23432	New_site already exists
wrongstate	−23431	Group gname is not in NORMAL state at the master definition site

Restrictions. The procedures in DBMS_OFFLINE_OG must be called in the appropriate order from the appropriate sites. The example under BEGIN_INSTANTIATION illustrates the proper use of this package.

The DBMS_OFFLINE_OG.END_LOAD procedure

Call the END_LOAD procedure from the new master site when you are finished importing data. The specification follows:

```
PROCEDURE DBMS_OFFLINE_OG.END_LOAD
    (gname IN VARCHAR2,
     new_site IN VARCHAR2);
```

These parameters are identical to those described for the BEGIN_INSTANTIA-TION procedure. See that section as well for an example of using the procedures in the DBMS_OFFLINE_OG package.

Exceptions. The END_LOAD procedure may raise the following exceptions:

Name	Number	Description
badargument	−23430	gname is NULL or ' '
missingrepgroup	−23373	Group gname does not exist
wrongsite	−23433	Raised if BEGIN_LOAD or END_LOAD is executed at a site other than new_site
wrongstate	−23431	Group gname is not in NORMAL state at master definition site

Restrictions. The procedures in DBMS_OFFLINE_OG must be called in the appropriate order from the appropriate sites. The example under BEGIN_INSTANTIA-TION illustrates the proper use of this package.

The DBMS_OFFLINE_OG.RESUME_SUBSET_OF_MASTERS procedure

Call this procedure from the master definition site to resume replication activity for existing sites while the new site is instantiated. The specification follows:

```
PROCEDURE DBMS_OFFLINE_OG.RESUME_SUBSET_OF_MASTERS
    (gname IN VARCHAR2,
     new_site IN VARCHAR2);
```

These parameters are identical to those described for the BEGIN_INSTANTIA-TION procedure. See that section as well for an example of using the procedures in the DBMS_OFFLINE_OG package.

Exceptions. The RESUME_SUBSET_OF_MASTERS procedure may raise the following exceptions:

Name	Number	Description
badargument	−23430	gname is NULL or ' '
missingrepgroup	−23373	Group gname does not exist
nonmasterdef	−23312	Routine is not being called from master definition site
sitealreadyexists	−23432	New_site already exists
wrongstate	−23431	Group gname is not in NORMAL state at master definition site

Restrictions. The procedures in DBMS_OFFLINE_OG must be called in the appropriate order from the appropriate sites. The example under BEGIN_INSTANTIA-TION illustrates the proper use of this package.

DBMS_RECTIFIER_DIFF: Comparing Replicated Tables

If you are not sure whether the data at two sites are identical, you can use the DBMS_RECTIFIER_DIFF package to find out. The DIFFERENCES procedure compares the data in a table at a master site with the same table at a reference site. After determining the differences, you can use DBMS_RECTIFIER_DIFF.RECTIFY to synchronize the tables.

Getting Started with DBMS_RECTIFIER_DIFF

The DBMS_RECTIFIER_DIFF package is created when the Oracle database is installed. The *dbmsrepc.sql* script (found in the built-in packages source directory, as described in Chapter 1) contains the source code for this package's specification. This script is called by *catrep.sql*, which must be run to install the advanced replication packages. The wrapped sql script *prvtrctf.sql* creates the public synonym DBMS_RECTIFIER_DIFF. No EXECUTE privileges are granted on DBMS_RECTIFIER_DIFF; only the owner (SYS) and those with the EXECUTE ANY PROCEDURE system privilege may execute the package.

Table 15-6 summarizes the DBMS_RECTIFIER_DIFF programs.

Table 15-6. DBMS_RECTIFIER_DIFF.DIFFERENCES Programs

Name	Description	Use in SQL?
DIFFERENCES	Determines differences between truth table and comparison table	No
RECTIFY	Synchronizes comparison table with truth table	No

DBMS_RECTIFIER_DIFF Interface

This section describes the programs available in the DBMS_RECTIFIER_DIFF package.

The DBMS_RECTIFIER.DIFFERENCES procedure

The DIFFERENCES procedure compares the data in a table at a master site with the same table at a reference site. The reference need not be the master definition site.

The procedure stores discrepancies between the reference table and comparison table in a "missing rows" table, which the user must create. It populates the table specified by the missing_rows_oname1 parameter with rows that exist in the reference table but not the comparison table, and rows that exist in the comparison table but not the reference table. The table identified by the missing_rows_oname2 parameter has one record for every record in missing_rows_oname1, which identifies which site has the record.

Here is the specification:

```
PROCEDURE DBMS_RECTIFIER_DIFF.DIFFERENCES
  (sname1 IN VARCHAR2,
   oname1 IN VARCHAR2,
   reference_site IN VARCHAR2 := '',
   sname2 IN VARCHAR2,
   oname2 IN VARCHAR2,
   comparison_site IN VARCHAR2 := '',
   where_clause IN VARCHAR2 := '',
   {column_list IN VARCHAR2 := '' |
   array_columns IN dbms_utility.name_array,},
   missing_rows_sname IN VARCHAR2,
   missing_rows_oname1 IN VARCHAR2,
   missing_rows_oname2 IN VARCHAR2,
   missing_rows_site IN VARCHAR2 := '',
   max_missing IN INTEGER,
   commit_rows IN INTEGER := 500);
```

Parameters are summarized in the following table.

Name	Description
sname1	Name of schema that owns oname1.
oname1	Table at reference_site (truth table).
reference_site	The global_name of site with truth table. If NULL or ' ' (default), truth table is assumed to be local.
sname2	Name of schema that owns oname2.
oname2	The comparison table.
comparison_site	The global_name of the site with comparison table. If NULL or ' ', table is assumed to be local.
where_clause	Optional predicate that can be used to limit set of rows compared (e.g.,'WHERE STATE = 'CA'').
column_list	Comma-separated list of one or more columns whose values are to be compared. If NULL or ' ' (default), then all columns are used. There should not be any whitespace after the commas.
array_columns	PL/SQL table of column names; either column_list or array_columns can be passed, not both.
missing_rows_sname	Name of schema that owns missing_rows_oname1.
missing_rows_oname1	Name of table containing records that do not exist in both truth table and comparison table.
missing_rows_oname2	Table that holds information telling which table owns each record in missing_rows_oname1.
missing_rows_site	The global_name of site where tables missing_rows_oname1 and missing_rows_oname2 exist; if NULL or ' ' (default), tables are assumed to be local.

Name	Description
max_missing	The maximum number or rows to insert into missing_rows_oname1 before exiting; can be any value > 1.
comming_rows	Commit rows inserted into missing_row_oname1 after this many records.

Exceptions. The DIFFERENCES procedure may raise the following exceptions:

Name	Number	Description
badmrname	−23377	The oname1 is the same as missing_rows_oname1
badname	−23368	The sname, oname, missing_rows_sname, or missing_rows_oname is NULL or ' '
badnumber	−23366	The max_missing is less than 1 or NULL
dbms_repcat.commfailure	−23302	Remote site is not accessible
dbms_repcat.missingobject	−23308	The tables oname1, oname2, missing_rows_oname1, or missing_rows_oname2 do not exist
nosuchsite	−23365	The reference_site, comparison_site, or missing_rows_site does not name a site

Restrictions. Note the following restrictions on calling the DIFFERENCES procedure:

- You must create tables missing_rows_sname.missing_rows_oname1 and missing_rows_sname.missing_rows_oname2 before running this procedure.

- The columns in table missing_rows_oname1 must match the columns passed to column_list or array_columns exactly.

- The replication group to which the tables belong must be quiesced.

Example. For an example of how to use the DIFFERENCES procedure, see the example under the RECTIFY procedure.

The DBMS_RECTIFIER_DIFF.RECTIFY procedure

The DIFFERENCES procedure paves the way for its companion procedure, REC-TIFY, which synchronizes the reference table. Before running the RECTIFY proce-dure, always make sure that the updates to the comparison table will not violate any integrity, check, or NOT NULL constraints. Note that this procedure does not modify the reference table. Here's the specification:

```
PROCEDURE DBMS_RECTIFIER_DIFF.RECTIFY
    (sname1 IN VARCHAR2,
    oname1 IN VARCHAR2,
    reference_site IN VARCHAR2 := '',
    sname2 IN VARCHAR2,
    oname2 IN VARCHAR2,
```

```
        comparison_site IN VARCHAR2 := '',
        {column_list IN VARCHAR2 := '' |
        array_columns IN dbms_utility.name_array},
        missing_rows_sname IN VARCHAR2,
        missing_rows_oname1 IN VARCHAR2,
        missing_rows_oname2 IN VARCHAR2,
        missing_rows_site IN VARCHAR2 := '',
        commit_rows IN INTEGER := 500);
```

Parameters are summarized in the following table.

Name	Description
sname1	Name of schema that owns oname1.
oname1	Table at reference_site (truth table).
reference_site	The global_name of site with truth table; if NULL or ' ' (default), truth table is assumed to be local.
sname2	Name of schema that owns oname2.
oname2	The comparison table.
comparison_site	The global_name of the site with comparison table. If NULL or ' ', table is assumed to be local.
column_list	A comma-separated list of one or more columns whose values are to be compared; if NULL or ' ' (default), then all columns are used. There should not be any white space after the commas.
array_columns	PL/SQL table of column names; either column_list or array_columns can be passed, not both.
missing_rows_sname	Name of schema that owns missing_rows_oname1.
missing_rows_oname1	The name of the table containing records that do not exist in both truth table and comparison table.
missing_rows_oname2	The table that holds information telling which table owns each record in missing_rows_oname1.
missing_rows_site	The global_name of the site where tables missing_rows_oname1 and missing_rows_oname2 exist; if NULL or ' ' (default), tables are assumed to be local.
comming_rows	Commit rows inserted into missing_row_oname1 after this many records.

Exceptions. The RECTIFY procedure may raise the following exceptions:

Name	Number	Description
badname	–23368	The sname, oname, missing_rows_sname, or missing_rows_oname is NULL or ' '
badnumber	–23366	The max_missing is less than 1 or NULL
dbms_repcat.commfailure	–23302	Remote site is not accessible
dbms_repcat.missingobject	–23308	The tables oname1, oname2, missing_rows_oname1, or missing_rows_oname2 do not exist

Name	Number	Description
dbms_repcat.norepoption	−2094	Replication option is not linked to kernel
nosuchsite	−23365	The reference_site, comparison_site, or missing_rows_site does not name a site

Restrictions. Note the following restrictions on calling RECTIFY:

- The DIFFERENCES procedure must have been run prior to running RECTIFY.

- The replication group to which the tables belong should still be quiesced.

- If duplicate rows exist in the reference table but not the comparison table they will be inserted into the comparison table.

- If duplicate rows exist in the comparison table but not the reference table they will be deleted from the comparison table.

Example. Assume that the table SPROCKET.DAILY_SALES is replicated between sites D7CA.BIGWHEEL.COM (the references site) and D7NY.BIGWHEEL.COM (the comparison site). The following table shows the description of the DAILY_SALES table.

Column Name	Data Type
sales_id	NUMBER(9)
distributor_id	NUMBER(6)
product_id	NUMBER(9)
units	NUMBER(9,2)

The following steps executed at D7CA.BIGWHEEL.COM would populate the tables missing_rows_daily_sales and missing_location_daily_sales and rectify these differences. These steps should be executed under the designated replication administrator account. Note that storage parameters are left out of the example for the sake of brevity and clarity, but they should be included whenever you run the DBMS_RECTIFIER_DIFF.DIFFERENCES procedure.

```
CREATE TABLE missing_rows_daily_sales (
sales_id      NUMBER(9),
distributor_idNUMBER(6),
product_id    NUMBER(9),
units         NUMBER(9,2)
);

CREATE TABLE missing_location_daily_sales (
present VARCHAR2(128),
absent  VARCHAR2(128),
r_id    ROWID
);

BEGIN
```

```
DBMS_REPCAT.SUSPEND_MASTER_ACTIVITY('SPROCKET');

DBMS_RECTIFIER_DIFF.DIFFERENCES( -
     sname1               => 'SPROCKET',
     oname1               => 'DAILY_SALES',
     reference_site       => 'D7CA.BIGWHEEL.COM',
     sname2               => 'SPROCKET',
     oname2               => 'SPROCKET',
     comparison_site      => 'D7NY.BIGWHEEL.COM',
     where_clause         => NULL,
     column_list          => 'SALES_ID,DISTRIBUTOR_ID,PRODUCT_
                              ID,UNITS',
     missing_rows_sname   => 'REPADMIN',
     missing_rows_oname1  => 'MISSING_ROWS_DAILY_SALES',
     missing_rows_oname2  => 'MISSING_LOCATIONS_DAILY_SALES ,
     missing_rows_site    => 'D7CA.BIGWHEEL.COM',
     max_missing          => 500,
     comit_rows           => 100);

DBMS_RECTIFIER_DIFF.RECTIFY( -
     sname1               => 'SPROCKET',
     oname1               => 'DAILY_SALES',
     reference_site       => 'D7CA.BIGWHEEL.COM',
     sname2               => 'SPROCKET',
     oname2               => 'SPROCKET',
     comparison_site      => 'D7NY.BIGWHEEL.COM',
     column_list          => 'SALES_ID,DISTRIBUTOR_ID,PRODUCT_
                              ID,UNITS',
     missing_rows_sname   => 'REPADMIN',
     missing_rows_oname1  => 'MISSING_ROWS_DAILY_SALES',
     missing_rows_oname2  => 'MISSING_LOCATIONS_DAILY_SALES -
     missing_rows_site    => 'D7CA.BIGWHEEL.COM',
     comit_rows           => 100);
END;
```

TIP   These procedures can take a long time to run. If the volume of data
               is significant, it will probably be easier for you to simply reinstanti-
               ate the comparison table by importing an export of the reference
               table.

DBMS_REPUTIL: Enabling and Disabling Replication

Situations will arise when you need to perform DML on a replicated table *without*
propagating the changes to other master sites. For example, if you have resolved
a conflict and wish to update a row manually, you would not want to propagate
your change. Or you might have a trigger on a replicated table that you want to

fire only for updates that originate locally. The DBMS_REPUTIL package allows you to control whether updates propagate for the current session.

Getting Started with DBMS_REPUTIL

The DBMS_REPUTIL package is created when the Oracle database is installed. The *dbmsgen.sql* script (found in the built-in packages source directory, as described in Chapter 1) contains the source code for this package's specification. This script is called by *catrep.sql*, which must be run to install the advanced replication packages. The script creates the public synonym DBMS_REPUTIL for the package and grants EXECUTE privilege on the package to public. All Oracle users can reference and make use of this package.

Table 15-7 lists the programs available in this package.

Table 15-7. DBMS_REPUTIL Programs

Name	Description	Use in SQL?
REPLICATION_OFF	Turns replication off for the current session	No
REPLICATION_ON	Turns replication on for the current session	No

DBMS_REPUTIL Interface

This section describes the programs available in the DBMS_REPUTIL package.

DBMS_REPUTIL.REPLICATION_OFF procedure

The REPLICATION_OFF procedure works by setting a package variable off. The replication triggers can subsequently query this variable. This procedure is as simple as it can be: no parameters and no exceptions.

```
PROCEDURE DBMS_REPUTIL.REPLICATION_OFF;
```

DBMS_REPUTIL.REPLICATION_ON procedure

The REPLICATION_ON procedure reverses the effect of the REPLICATION_OFF procedure. It sets the package variable on. The specification follows:

```
PROCEDURE DBMS_REPUTIL.REPLICATION_ON;
```

16

Conflict Resolution

Conflict resolution is perhaps the most difficult challenge for the administrator of a replicated environment that uses asynchronous replication. A conflict can arise when an insert, update, or delete to a replicated table occurs at two or more master sites. Oracle detects conflicts at the destination site when attempting to apply the changes. Three different types of conflicts can arise:

Insert conflicts

　　An inserted row has a primary key that already exists at the destination site.

Update conflicts

　　The pre-update data in a row at the originating site does not match the current data at the destination site.

Delete conflicts

　　A deleted row does not exist at the destination site.

Through the DBMS_REPCAT package, Oracle's advanced replication option gives you tools for identifying and resolving conflicts automatically. The goal is to ensure that data at all master sites converges—that is, all rows end up with identical data at all sites.

WARNING　　The procedures described in this chapter are no substitute for careful application and schema design, and they can't resolve *all* conflicts.

Getting Started with DBMS_REPCAT

Use the DBMS_REPCAT package to deal with conflict resolution. As we've seen in previous chapters, DBMS_REPCAT is an enormous package whose programs perform many different types of operations. Chapter 14, *Snapshots*, describes the snapshot-related programs; Chapter 15, *Advanced Replication*, describes the programs you call to create and maintain replicated environments. This chapter focuses on the programs you use in DBMS_REPCAT conflict resolution.

The DBMS_REPCAT package is created when the Oracle database is installed. The *dbmsrepc.sql* script (found in the built-in packages source directory, as described in Chapter 1, *Introduction*) contains the source code for this package's specification. This script is called by *catrep.sql*, which must be run to install the advanced replication packages. The script creates the public synonym DBMS_REPCAT. The package procedure DBMS_REPCAT_AUTH.GRANT_SURROGATE_REPCAT grants EXECUTE privileges on the package to the specified grantee. In addition, the package owner (SYS) and users with the EXECUTE ANY PROCEDURE system privilege may execute it.

DBMS_REPCAT Programs

Table 16-1 summarizes the DBMS_REPCAT procedures used in conflict resolution, and lists all of the programs in alphabetical order. In the sections that follow, we divide these programs by category (column groups, priority groups, site priorities, resolution method assignment, and conflict resolution monitoring). For example, the section "Column Groups" describes only the column group programs.

Table 16-1. DBMS_REPCAT Program (Conflict Resolution Only)

Name	Description	Use in SQL?
ADD_GROUPED_COLUMN	Adds table column(s) to an existing column group	No
ADD_PRIORITY_<datatype>	Adds a member to an existing priority group	No
ADD_SITE_PRIORITY_SITE	Adds a site to an existing site priority group	No
ADD_<conflicttype>_RESOLUTION	Adds custom conflict resolution handler for update, delete, or uniqueness conflicts	No
ALTER_PRIORITY	Changes priority level for a member of a priority group	No
ALTER_PRIORITY_<datatype>	Alters the value of a member of a priority group	No
ALTER_SITE_PRIORITY	Alters priority level of a site	No

Table 16-1. DBMS_REPCAT Program (Conflict Resolution Only) (continued)

Name	Description	Use in SQL?
ALTER_SITE_PRIORITY_SITE	Designates a site to a given priority level	No
CANCEL_STATISTICS	Cancels collection of statistics about conflict resolution for a table	No
COMMENT_ON_COLUMN_GROUP	Creates or updates a comment on a column group, visible in DBA_ REPCOLUMN_GROUP data dictionary view	No
COMMENT_ON_PRIORITY_GROUP	Creates or updates comment on a priority group, visible in DBA_ REPPRIORITY_GROUP	No
COMMENT_ON_SITE_PRIORITY	Creates or updates a comment on a site priority, visible in DBA_ REPRIORITY_GROUP data dictionary view	No
COMMENT_ON_<conflicttype>_ RESOLUTION	Creates a comment on a conflict resolution method, visible in DBA_ REPRESOLUTION data dictionary view	No
DEFINE_COLUMN_GROUP	Creates an empty column group for a replication group	No
DEFINE_PRIORITY_GROUP	Creates a priority group for a replication group	No
DEFINE_SITE_PRIORITY	Creates a site priority group for a replication group	No
DROP_COLUMN_GROUP	Drops a column group from a replication group	No
DROP_GROUPED_COLUMN	Drops a column from a column group	No
DROP_PRIORITY	Drops a member of a priority group, selected by priority level	No
DROP_PRIORITY_GROUP	Drops a priority group from a replication group	No
DROP_PRIORITY_<datatype>	Drops a member of a priority group, selected by value	No
DROP_SITE_PRIORITY	Drops a site priority group from a replication group	No
DROP_SITE_PRIORITY_SITE	Drops a site from a site priority group, selected by site name	No
DROP_<conflicttype>_RESOLUTION	Drops an update, delete, or uniqueness conflict resolution handling technique from a replication group	No

Table 16-1. DBMS_REPCAT Program (Conflict Resolution Only) (continued)

Name	Description	Use in SQL?
MAKE_COLUMN_GROUP	Creates a column group and adds one or more columns	No
PURGE_STATISTICS	Deletes entries from the DBA_ REPRESOLUTION_STATISTICS data dictionary view	No
REGISTER_STATISTICS	Starts collection of statistics for the resolution of update, delete, and uniqueness conflicts for a given table	No

DBMS-REPCAT Exceptions

Table 16-2 lists the exceptions that may be raised by programs in the DBMS_REP-CAT package that are specific to conflict resolution. Specific sections list the exceptions that may be raised by individual programs in DBMS_REPCAT.

Table 16-2. DBMS_REPCAT Exceptions (Conflict Resolution Only)

Name	Number	Description
duplicatecolumn	−23333	Attempt to add duplicate column to column group
duplicategroup	−23330	Attempt to add duplicate column group to a replicated table
duplicateprioritygroup	−23335	Attempt to create duplicate priority group
duplicaterepgroup	−23374	Attempt to create duplicate snapshot replication group
duplicateresolution	−23339	Attempt to create duplicate resolution method
duplicateschema	−23307	Attempt to create duplicate replication group
duplicatevalue	−23338	Attempt to create duplicate value in a priority group
invalidmethod	−23340	Attempt to use nonexistent conflict resolution method
invalidparameter	−23342	Invalid number of columns in call to ADD_ UNIQUE_RESOLUTION
missingcolumn	−23334	Reference to nonexistent column
missingconstraint	−23344	Missing constraint (used internally)
missingfunction	−23341	User function does not exist
missinggroup	−23331	Column group does not exist
missingobject	−23308	Object does not exist as a table
missingprioritygroup	−23336	Priority group does not exist
missingrepgroup	−23373	Replication group does not exists

Table 16-2. DBMS_REPCAT Exceptions (Conflict Resolution Only) (continued)

Name	Number	Description
missingresolution	−23343	Reference conflict resolution method does not exist
missingschema	−23306	Schema does not exist
missingvalue	−23337	Missing value (used internally)
nonmasterdef	−23312	Site is not a master definition site
nonsnapshot	−23314	Site is not a snapshot site
paramtype	−23325	Invalid parameter type (used internally)
referenced	−23332	Attempt to drop column group used for conflict resolution
statnotreg	−23345	Conflict resolution statistics not registered (used internally)
typefailure	−23319	Attempt to replicate nonsupported datatype

DBMS-REPCAT Nonprogram Elements

In addition to programs and exceptions, the DBMS_REPCAT package defines the following constant used for conflict resolution:

VARCHAR2S
   PL/SQL table of VARCHAR2(60) indexed by BINARY INTEGER.

Data Dictionary Views

Oracle provides a number of data dictionary views that are useful for analyzing the status and volume of conflicts, as listed in Table 16-3.

Table 16-3. Data Dictionary Views Associated with Conflict Resolution

View Name	Description
DBA_REPCOLUMN_ GROUP	Contains information about column groups.
DBA_REPCONFLICT	Contains information about all conflict resolution methods that have been defined.
DBA_REPGROUPED_ COLUMN	Contains information about all columns that are members of column groups.
DBA_REPPARAMETER_ COLUMN	Contains information about columns that are designated to resolve conflicts. These columns have been passed in the list_of_column_names parameter of DBMS_REPCAT.ADD_ <conflicttype>_RESOLUTION.
DBA_REPPRIORITY	Contains information about every value and priority that has been defined for all priority groups and site priority groups.
DBA_REPPRIORITY_ GROUP	Contains information about all priority groups and site priority groups.

Table 16-3. Data Dictionary Views Associated with Conflict Resolution (continued)

View Name	Description
DBA_REPRESOLUTION	Contains information about the conflict resolution technique that has been defined for all conflict types.
DBA_REPRESOL_STATS_CONTROL	Contains information about statistics that have been gathered for conflict resolution.
DBA_REPRESOLUTION_METHOD	Contains information about all available conflict resolution methods.
DBA_REPRESOLUTION_STATISTICS	If resolution statistics are being collected, contains information about the execution of conflict resolution handlers.

Tables 16-4 through 16-14 describe the contents of these views.

Table 16-4. Columns in DBA_REPCOLUMN_GROUP View

Column Name	Description
sname	Schema that owns table oname
oname	Name of the replicated table
group_name	Name of the column group
group_comment	Comment for the column group

Table 16-5. Columns in DBA_REPCONFLICT View

Column Name	Description
sname	Schema that owns table oname.
oname	Name of the replicated table.
conflict_type	Type of conflict the resolution method resolves.
reference_name	For DELETE conflicts, the table name. For UNIQUENESS conflicts, the unique constraint name. For UPDATE conflicts, the column group name.

Table 16-6. Columns in DBA_REPGROUPED_COLUMN View

Column Name	Description
sname	Schema that owns table oname
oname	Name of the replicated table
group_name	Name of the column group
group_comment	Comment for the column group

Table 16-7. Columns in DBA_REPPARAMETER_COLUMN View

Column Name	Description
sname	Schema that owns table oname.
oname	Name of the replicated table.
conflict_type	Type of conflict the method resolves.

Table 16-7. Columns in DBA_REPPARAMETER_COLUMN View (continued)

Column Name	Description
reference_name	For DELETE conflicts, the table name. For UNIQUE-NESS conflicts, the unique constraint name. For UPDATE conflicts, the column group name.
sequence_no	Order in which the method is attempted. 1 is first.
method_name	Name of the built-in resolution method, or 'USER FUNCTION' for user defined methods.
function_name	Name of the user defined function (if applicable).
priority_group	Name of the priority group (if applicable).
parameter_table_name	Name of the PL/SQL table containing columns that are passed to the resolution method.
parameter_column_name	Name of the column passed to parameter_column_name in ADD_<confllicttype>_RESOLUTION call.
parameter_sequence_no	Position of the column in the parameter_column_name parameter.

Table 16-8. Columns in DBA_REPPRIORITY View

Column Name	Description
sname	Name of the replicated schema. Obsolete with Version 7.3 onwards; replace by gname.
priority_group	Name of the priority group.
priority	Priority level (the higher the number, the higher the priority).
data_type	Datatype of the priority group.
fixed_data_length	Maximum length for CHAR datatypes.
char_value	For CHAR priority groups, the value associated with the priority.
varchar2_value	For VARCHAR2 priority groups, the value associated with the priority.
number_value	For NUMBER priority groups, the value associated with the priority.
date_value	For DATE priority groups, the value associated with the priority.
raw_value	For RAW priority groups, the value associated with the priority.
gname	Name of the replication group.
nchar_value (Oracle8 only)	For NCHAR priority groups, the value associated with the priority.
nvarchar2_value (Oracle8 only)	For NVARCHAR2 priority groups, the value associated with the priority.
large_char_value (Oracle8 only)	For LARGE_CHAR priority groups, the value associated with the priority.

Table 16-9. Columns in DBA_REPPRIORITY_GROUP View

Column Name	Description
sname	Name of the replicated schema. Obsolete with Version 7.3 onwards; replace by gname.
priority_group	Name of the priority group or site priority group.
data_type	Datatype of the priority group.
fixed_data_length	Maximum length for CHAR datatypes.
priority_comment	Comment for priority group.
gname	Replication group to which priority group belongs.

Table 16-10. Columns in DBA_REPRESOLUTION View

Column Name	Description
sname	Schema that owns table oname.
oname	Name of the replicated table.
conflict_type	Type of conflict the method resolves.
reference_name	For DELETE conflicts, the table name. For UNIQUENESS conflicts, the unique constraint name. For UPDATE conflicts, the column group name.
sequence_no	Order in which the method is attempted. 1 is first.
method_name	Name of the built-in resolution method, or USER FUNCTION for user-defined methods.
function_name	Name of the user-defined function (if applicable).
priority_group	Name of the priority group (if applicable).
resolution_comment	Comment on the resolution method.

Table 16-11. Columns in DBA_REPRESOL_STATS_CONTROL View

Column Name	Description
sname	Schema that owns table oname
oname	Name of the replicated table
created	Date statistics were first collected
status	Current status of statistics collection (ACTIVE or CANCELLED)
status_update_date	Date of last update to status
purged_date	Date of last purge of statistics
last_purge_start_date	Start Date passed to last call to PURGE_STATISTICS
last_purge_end_date	End Date passed to last call to PURGE_STATISTICS

Table 16-12. Columns in DBA_REPRESOLUTION_METHOD View

Column Name	Description
conflict_type	Type of conflict the method resolves (UPDATE, UNIQUENESS, or DELETE)
method_name	Name of the built in method, or name of user-supplied function

Table 16-13. Columns in DBA_REPRESOLUTION_STATISTICS View

Column Name	Description
sname	Schema that owns table oname.
oname	Name of the replicated table.
conflict_type	Type of conflict that Oracle resolved successfully (UPDATE, UNIQUENESS, or DELETE).
reference_name	For DELETE conflicts, the table name. For UNIQUENESS conflicts, the unique constraint name. For UPDATE conflicts, the column group name.
method_name	Name of the built-in resolution method, or 'USER FUNCTION' for user defined methods.
function_name	Name of the user defined function (if applicable).
priority_group	Name of the priority group (if applicable).
resolved_date	Date Oracle resolved the conflict.
primary_key_value	Value of the primary key for the resolved row.

Column Groups with DBMS_REPCAT

Column groups provide a mechanism for guaranteeing data consistency across one or more columns in a replicated table. Every replicated table has at least one column group, called the default column group, which Oracle creates automatically. You can also create your own column groups (and you probably should) in which you group logically related fields.

About Column Groups

Suppose that you have a customer table that contains address information, such as street address, city, state, and postal code, plus personal information such as last name, marital status, birth date, and phone number.

```
SQL> desc customer
Name                 Null?        Type
---------------      --------     ------
CUSTOMER_ID                       NUMBER(6)
NAME                              VARCHAR2(30)
MARITAL_STATUS                    VARCHAR2(1)
PHONE_NUMBER                      VARCHAR2(16)
STREET_ADDR                       VARCHAR2(30)
CITY                              VARCHAR2(30)
STATE                             VARCHAR2(30)
POSTAL_CODE                       VARCHAR2(12)
TIMESTAMP                         DATE
GLOBAL_NAME                       VARCHAR2(30)
```

In this table, the fields pertaining to the customer's address (i.e., STREET_ADDR, CITY, STATE, and POSTAL_CODE) are logically related. You would not want to allow an update at one site to set the CITY to "San Francisco" and an update at another site to set the STATE to "Mississippi" since (as of this writing) there is no such municipality as San Francisco, Mississippi.

Oracle's answer to this potential catastrophe is the column group. A column group is a logical grouping of columns whose collective values are treated as a unit. If we create a column group and add the address-related fields STREET_ADDR, CITY, STATE, and POSTAL_CODE, we can be sure that rows in this table will always contain consistent values for these columns. We can also make a second column group consisting of the fields NAME, MARITAL_STATUS, and PHONE_NUMBER. Note that a row in this table could contain address information that was entered at one site, and name information that was entered at another site.

As we shall see in the later section "Built-in Resolution Techniques," every column group needs to have a "governing" column that determines which data is to be considered correct. For example, if you want to use the Latest Timestamp resolution method for a given column group, then your table should include a DATE field, and your application should update this field with the current time whenever it performs inserts or updates on the table.

NOTE   Oracle automatically creates a default column group, called the *shadow column group*, when you generate replication support for a table. This column group contains every field that you do not explicitly place in a column group of your own.

The procedures you'll use to create and maintain column groups follow:

    DBMS_REPCAT.ADD_GROUPED_COLUMN
    DBMS_REPCAT.COMMENT_ON_COLUMN_GROUP
    DBMS_REPCAT.DEFINE_COLUMN_GROUP
    DBMS_REPCAT.DROP_COLUMN_GROUP
    DBMS_REPCAT.DROP_GROUPED_COLUMN
    DBMS_REPCAT.MAKE_COLUMN_GROUP

Creating and Dropping Column Groups

The DEFINE_COLUMN_GROUP, DROP_COLUMN_GROUP, and MAKE_COLUMN_GROUP procedures are used to create and drop column groups. The difference between DEFINE_COLUMN_GROUP and MAKE_COLUMN_GROUP is that the former creates a column group with no member columns, and the latter both creates the group and adds columns to it.

The DBMS_REPCAT.DEFINE_COLUMN_GROUP procedure

The DEFINE_COLUMN_GROUP procedure creates a column group with no member columns. Here's the specification:

```
PROCEDURE DBMS_REPCAT.DEFINE_COLUMN_GROUP
    (sname IN VARCHAR2,
     oname IN VARCHAR2,
     column_group IN VARCHAR2,
     comment IN VARCHAR@ := NULL);
```

Parameters are summarized in the following table.

Name	Description
sname	Name of the schema to which the replicated table belongs
oname	Name of the replicated table containing the column group
column_group	Name of the column group
comment	Comment

Exceptions. The DEFINE_COLUMN_GROUP procedure may raise the following exceptions:

Name	Number	Description
duplicategroup	−23330	Column_group already exists
missingobject	−23308	Object oname does not exist
nonmasterdef	−23312	Calling site is not master definition site

Restrictions. Note the following restrictions on calling the DEFINE_COLUMN_ GROUP:

- You must call this procedure from the quiesced master definition site.

- You must regenerate replication support for the table after defining the column group with the GENERATE_REPLICATION_SUPPORT procedure.

Example. The DEEFINE_COLUMN_GROUP creates an empty column group—that is, one with no members. After creating the column group, you can add columns to it with the DBMS_REPCAT.ADD_GROUPED_COLUMN procedure described later in this chapter. The following example creates an empty column group for table SPROCKET.PRODUCTS:

```
BEGIN
    DBMS_REPCAT.DEFINE_COLUMN_GROUP(sname=> 'SPROCKET',
            oname => 'PRODUCTS',
            column_group => 'CG_PRODUCTS_PRICE_COLS',
            comment => 'Comment added on '||sysdate|| ' by ' ||user);
END;
```

The DBMS_REPCAT.DROP_COLUMN_GROUP procedure

The DROP_COLUMN_GROUP procedure drops a column group that you've previously created. Here's the specification:

```
PROCEDURE DBMS_REPCAT.DROP_COLUMN_GROUP
    (sname IN VARCHAR2,
     oname IN VARCHAR2,
     column_group IN VARCHAR2);
```

Parameters are summarized in the following table.

Name	Description
sname	Name of the schema to which the replicated table belongs
oname	Name of the replicated table containing the column group
column_group	Name of the column group

Exceptions. The DROP_COLUMN_GROUP procedure may raise the following exceptions:

Name	Number	Description
missinggroup	−23331	The column_group does not exist
missingobject	−23308	The object oname does not exist
missingschema	−23306	The schema sname does not exist
nonmasterdef	−23312	Calling site is not master definition site
referenced	−23332	The column_group is used by existing conflict resolution methods

Restrictions. Note the following restrictions on calling DROP_COLUMN_GROUP:

- You must call this procedure from the quiesced master definition site.

- You must regenerate replication support for the table after defining the column group with the GENERATE_REPLICATION_SUPPORT procedure.

Example. This example drops the column group CG_PRODUCTS_PRICE_COLS that was created in the CREATE_COLUMN_GROUP example:

```
BEGIN
    DBMS_REPCAT.DROP_COLUMN_GROUP(sname > 'SPROCKET',
                                  oname => 'PRODUCTS',
                                  column_group => 'CG_PRODUCTS_PRICE_COLS');
END;
```

The DBMS_REPCAT.MAKE_COLUMN_GROUP procedure

The MAKE_COLUMN_GROUP procedure creates a column group and adds member columns to it. Here's the specification:

```
PROCEDURE DBMS_REPCAT.MAKE_COLUMN_GROUP
    (sname IN VARCHAR2,
     oname IN VARCHAR2,
     column_group IN VARCHAR2,
     {list_of_column_names IN VARCHAR2 |
     list_of_column_names IN dbms_repcat.varchar2s} );
```

Note that you must specify only one of the list_of_column_names parameters.

Parameters are summarized in the following table.

Name	Description
sname	Name of the schema to which the replicated table belongs.
oname	Name of the replicated table containing the column group.
column_group	Name of the column group.
list_of_column_names	A comma-delimited list of column names, or a PL/SQL table of column names. Use '*' to add all columns in the table.

Exceptions. The MAKE_COLUMN_GROUP procedure may raise the following exceptions:

Name	Number	Description
duplicatecolumn	−23333	Column(s) already a member of a different column group
duplicategroup	−23330	column_group already exists
missingcolumn	−23334	Column(s) specified do not exist in table oname
missingobject	−23308	Object oname does not exist
nonmasterdef	−23312	Calling site is not master definition site

Restrictions. Note the following restrictions on calling MAKE_COLUMN_GROUP:

- You must call this procedure from the quiesced master definition site.

- You must regenerate replication support for the table after defining the column group with the DBMS_REPCAT.GENERATE_REPLICATION_SUPPORT procedure.

Example. By passing "*" to the list_of_column_names parameter in MAKE_COLUMN_GROUP, you can create a column group consisting of all columns in the table.

```
BEGIN
    DBMS_REPCAT.MAKE_COLUMN_GROUP(sname=> 'SPROCKET',
                                  oname => 'PRODUCTS',
                                  column_group => 'CG_PRODUCTS_ALL_COLS',
                                  list_of_column_names => '*');
END;
```

You can also use MAKE_COLUMN_GROUP to create a column group containing whatever subset of columns you want.

```
BEGIN
    DBMS_REPCAT.MAKE_COLUMN_GROUP(
        sname              => 'SPROCKET',
        oname              => 'PRODUCTS',
        column_group       => 'CG_PRODUCTS_MFG_COLS',
        list_of_column_names=> 'REV_LEVEL, PRODUCTION_DATE,
            PRODUCTION_STATUS');
END;
```

Modifying Existing Column Groups

Once you have created a column group, you can add and remove member columns (with the ADD_GROUPED_COLUMN and DROP_GROUPED_COLUMN procedures), and you can add or change the comment associated with the group (with the COMMENT_ON_COLUMN_GROUP procedure).

The DBMS_REPCAT.ADD_GROUPED_COLUMN procedure

The ADD_GROUPED_COLUMN procedure adds a member column to a column group. You can call this procedure after you have created a new, empty column group with DBMS_REPCAT.DEFINE_COLUMN_GROUP, or if your schema or conflict resolution requirements change. Here's the specification:

```
PROCEDURE DBMS_REPCAT.ADD_GROUPED_COLUMN
    (sname IN VARCHAR2,
     oname IN VARCHAR2,
     column_group IN VARCHAR2,
     {list_of_column_names IN VARCHAR2 |
     list_of_column_names IN dbms_repcat.varchar2s});
```

Note that you must specify only one of the list_of_column_names parameters.

Parameters are summarized in the following table.

Name	Description
sname	Name of the schema that owns the replicated table.
oname	Name of the table with the column_group.
column_group	Name of the column_group to which column(s) will be added.
list_of_column_names	A comma-delimited list of column names, or a PL/SQL table of column names. Use "*" to add all columns in the table to the column group.

Exceptions. ADD_GROUPED_COLUMN may raise the following exceptions:

Name	Number	Description
nonmasterdef	−23312	Invoking site is not master definition site
missingobject	−23308	Table oname does not exist
missinggroup	−23331	Column group column_group does not exist
missingcolumn	−23334	Column(s) specified do not exist in table oname
duplicatecolumn	−23333	Column(s) specified already exist in column_group
missingschema	−23306	Schema sname does not exist

Restrictions. Note the following restrictions on calling ADD_GROUPED_COLUMN:

- You must call this procedure from the quiesced master definition site.

- You must regenerate replication support for the table after defining the column group with the GENERATE_REPLICATION_SUPPORT procedure.

Example. In this example, we add the columns CATALOG_ID and DESCRIPTION to the column group CG_PRODUCT_MFG_COLS that we created in the MAKE_COLUMN_GROUP example:

```
DECLARE cg_list DBMS_REPCAT.VARCHAR2(s);
BEGIN
    cg_list(1) := 'CATALOG_ID';
    cg_list(1) := 'DESCRIPTION';

    DBMS_REPCAT.ADD_GROUPED_COLUMN(sname=> 'SPROCKET',
                            oname => 'PRODUCTS',
                            column_group => 'CG_PRODUCT_MFG_COLS',
                            list_of_column_names => cg_list);
END;
```

The DBMS_REPCAT.DROP_GROUPED_COLUMN procedure

The DROP_GROUPED_COLUMN procedure allows you to drop a column from a column group. Dropping a column from a column group is quite similar to adding one. Make sure, however, that none of your conflict resolution methods reference the column(s) that you are dropping. And as with the other procedures with a "list_of_column_names" parameter, you can pass "*" to the parameter to indicate all fields in table oname. Here's the specification:

```
PROCEDURE DBMS_REPCAT.DROP_GROUPED_COLUMN
    (sname IN VARCHAR2,
     oname IN VARCHAR2,
     column_group IN VARCHAR2,
     {list_of_column_names IN VARCHAR2 |
      list_of_column_names IN dbms_repcat.varchar2s});
```

Note that you must specify only one of the list_of_column_names parameters.

Parameters are summarized in the following table.

Name	Description
sname	Name of the schema that owns the replicated table
oname	Name of the table with the column_group
column_group	Name of the column_group from which column(s) will be dropped
list_of_column_names	A comma-delimited list of column names, or a PL/SQL table of column names

Exceptions. The DROP_GROUPED_COLUMN procedure may raise the following exceptions:

Name	Number	Description
missinggroup	−23331	Column group column_group does not exist
missingobject	−23308	Table oname does not exist
missingschema	−23306	Schema sname does not exist
nonmasterdef	−23312	Invoking site is not the master definition site

Restrictions. Note the following restrictions on calling DROP_GROUPED_COLUMN:

- You must not call this procedure from the quiesced master definition site.
- You must regenerate replication support for the table after defining the column group with the GENERATE_REPLICATION_SUPPORT procedure.

Example. The following example shows how to drop a column from an existing column group:

```
BEGIN
    DBMS_REPCAT.DROP_GROUPED_COLUMN(
                    sname              => 'SPROCKET',
                    oname              => 'PRODUCTS',
                    column_group       => 'CG_PRODUCT_MFG_COLS',
```

```
              list_of_column_names    => 'CATALOG_ID, DESCRIPTION');
END;
```

The DBMS_REPCAT.COMMENT_ON_COLUMN_GROUP procedure

The COMMENT_ON_COLUMN_GROUP procedure adds or changes the comment associated with a column group. Here's the specification:

```
PROCEDURE DBMS_REPCAT.COMMENT_ON_COLUMN_GROUP
    (sname IN VARCHAR2,
     oname IN VARCHAR2,
     column_group IN VARCHAR2,
     comment IN VARCHAR2);
```

Parameters are summarized in the following table.

Name	Description
sname	Name of the schema to which the replicated table belongs
oname	Name of the replicated table containing the column group
column_group	Name of the column group
comment	Comment

Exceptions. The COMMENT_ON_COLUMN_GROUP procedure may raise the following exceptions:

Name	Number	Description
missinggroup	−23331	The column_group does not exist
nonmasterdef	−23312	Calling site is not the master definition site

Restrictions. The COMMENT_ON_COLUMN_GROUP procedure must be called from the master definition site.

Example. You can create or change the comment field in DBA_REPCOLUMN_GROUP with the COMMENT_ON_COLUMN_GROUP procedure, as the following example illustrates:

```
BEGIN
    DBMS_REPCAT.COMMENT_ON_COLUMN_GROUP(
            sname            => 'SPROCKET',
            oname            => 'PRODUCTS',
            column_group     => 'CG_PRODUCT_MFG_COLS',
            comment          => 'Added catalog_id + desc on '||sysdate);
```

Priority Groups with DBMS_REPCAT

Priority groups allow you to determine the validity of data based on its value. The priority group conflict resolution technique is most effective for data that has a finite range of possible values, and that goes through this range in a specific order.

About Priority Groups

Consider the products table:

```
SQL>desc products
Name                                  Null?        Type
------------------------------------- --------     ----
    PRODUCT_ID                        NOT NULL     NUMBER(9)
    PRODUCT_TYPE                      NOT NULL     NUMBER(6)
    CATALOG_ID                        NOT NULL     VARCHAR2(15)
    DESCRIPTION                       NOT NULL     VARCHAR2(30)
    REV_LEVEL                         NOT NULL     VARCHAR2(15)
    PRODUCTION_DATE                   NOT NULL     DATE
    PRODUCTION_STATUS                 NOT NULL     VARCHAR2(12)
    AUDIT_DATE                        NOT NULL     DATE
    AUDIT_USER                        NOT NULL     VARCHAR2(30)
    GLOBAL_NAME                       NOT NULL     VARCHAR2(20)
```

The PRODUCTION_STATUS field in this table can only take on certain values: CONCEPT, DEVELOPMENT, BETA, PRODUCTION, and DISCONTINUED. In addition, products must go through this range of values in the order given.

This concept of a sequential range of values is known as a *workflow*, and priority groups are designed to enforce the rules of a workflow in a replicated environment. Unlike column groups, which pertain to fields in a specific table, you can define a priority group for a specific column, which may appear in one or more tables. Once you define and configure a priority group, you can designate it to resolve update conflicts within a column group. The basic idea is that if a conflict arises, the row with the data corresponding to the higher priority in the workflow "wins."

Use the following programs to create and maintain priority groups:

DBMS_REPCAT.ADD_PRIORITY_<datatype>
DBMS_REPCAT.ALTER_PRIORITY
DBMS_REPCAT.ALTER_PRIORITY_<datatype>
DBMS_REPCAT.COMMENT_ON_PRIORITY_GROUPS
DBMS_REPCAT.DEFINE_PRIORITY_GROUPS
DBMS_REPCAT.DROP_PRIORITY
DBMS_REPCAT.DROP_PRIORITY_GROUP
DBMS_REPCAT.DROP_PRIORITY_<datatype>

Creating, Maintaining, and Dropping Priority Groups

DBMS_REPCAT's DEFINE_PRIORITY_GROUP and DROP_PRIORITY_GROUP procedures allow you to create and drop priority groups. You use the COMMENT_ON_PRIORITY_GROUP procedure to maintain the comment on the priority group.

The DBMS_REPCAT.DEFINE_PRIORITY_GROUP procedure

The DEFINE_PRIORITY_GROUP procedure creates a new priority group. The specifications differ for Oracle7 and Oracle8 as follows.

Here is the Oracle7 specification:

```
PROCEDURE DBMS_REPCAT.DEFINE_PRIORITY_GROUP
    (gname IN VARCHAR2 := '',
    pgroup IN VARCHAR2,
    datatype IN VARCHAR2,
    fixed_length IN INTEGER := NULL,
    comment IN VARCHAR2 := NULL,
    sname IN VARCHAR2 := '');
```

Here is the Oracle8 specification:

```
PROCEDURE DBMS_REPCAT.DEFINE_PRIORITY_GROUP
    (gname IN VARCHAR2 := '',
    pgroup IN VARCHAR2,
    datatype IN VARCHAR2,
    fixed_length IN INTEGER := NULL,
    comment IN VARCHAR2 := NULL);
```

Parameters are summarized in the following table.

Name	Description
gname	Name of the replication group containing the priority group.
pgroup	Name of the priority group.
datatype	Datatype for the value used in the priority group. Supported datatypes: • CHAR • NCHAR (Oracle8 only) • VARCHAR2 • NUMBER • DATE • RAW
fixed_length	Fixed length for values. Used only for datatype CHAR.
comment	Comment.
sname (Oracle7 only)	Not used.

Exceptions. The DEFINE_PRIORITY_GROUP procedure may raise the following exceptions:

Name	Number	Description
duplicateprioritygroup	−23335	Priority group pgroup already exists
missingschema	−23306	Schema does not exist
nonmasterdef	−23312	Calling site is not the master definition site
typefailure	−23319	Datatype not supported

Restrictions. Note the following restrictions on calling DEFINE_PRIORITY_GROUP:

- You must call the DEFINE_PRIORITY_GROUP procedure from the master definition site.

- You must call GENERATE_REPLICATION_SUPPORT for *any* object in the replication group for the new priority group to become active.

Example. Since priority groups are meant to work with a specific range of values, you must specify the datatype of these values when you create the group. Valid datatypes follow:

CHAR
NCHAR (Oracle8 only)
VARCHAR2
NUMBER
DATE
RAW

If the data type is CHAR, then you must also specify the length of the data with the fixed_length parameter. After you create a priority group, you must run DBMS_REPCAT.GENERATE_REPLICATION_SUPPORT for any object in the same replication group to propagate the new priority group to other master sites. (Since priority groups are not associated with a specific object, it does not matter what object you use in the call the GENERATE_REPLICATION_SUPPORT.)

Creating a priority group for datatype CHAR. This call creates a priority group for a CHAR datatype. For the sake of this example, assume that the range of values is GREEN, YELLOW, RED, and the longest string is six characters long.

```
BEGIN
    DBMS_REPCAT.DEFINE_PRIORITY_GROUP(
            gname           => 'SPROCKET',
            pgroup          => 'PG_SIGNAL_COLORS',
            datatype        => 'CHAR',
            fixed_length    => 6,
```

```
          comment          => 'PG_SIGNAL_COLORS created '||sysdate);
END;
```

Creating a priority group for datatype VARCHAR. For all other datatypes, the use of the fixed_length parameter does not apply. This statement creates a priority group for use with the PRODUCTION_STATUS field in the PRODUCTS table:

```
BEGIN
     DBMS_REPCAT.DEFINE_PRIORITY_GROUP(
          gname          => 'SPROCKET',
          pgroup         => 'PG_PRODUCTION_STATUS',
          datatype       => 'VARCHAR',
          comment        => 'PG_PRODUCTION_STATUS created '||sysdate);
END;
```

The DBMS_REPCAT.DROP_PRIORITY_GROUP procedure

The DROP_PRIORITY_GROUP procedure lets you drop a priority group that you have defined. The specifications differ for Oracle7 and Oracle8 as follows.

here is the Oracle7 specification:

```
PROCEDURE DBMS_REPCAT.DROP_PRIORITY_GROUP
     (gname IN VARCHAR2 := '',
      pgroup IN VARCHAR2,
      sname IN VARCHAR2 := '');
```

Here is the Oracle8 specification:

```
PROCEDURE DBMS_REPCAT.DROP_PRIORITY_GROUP
     (gname IN VARCHAR2 := '',
      pgroup IN VARCHAR2);
```

Parameters are summarized in the following table.

Name	Description
gname	Name of the replication group containing the priority group
pgroup	Name of the priority group to drop
sname (Oracle7 only)	Not used

WARNING   Do not drop a priority group that you have designated as an UPDATE conflict resolution method for a column group. You must first use DROP_UPDATE_RESOLUTION for the column group. Records in the data dictionary view DBA_REPRESOLUTION indicate if and where the priority group is used. Attempting to drop a priority group that is in use raises the *referenced* exception.

Exceptions. The DROP_PRIORITY_GROUP procedure may raise the following exceptions:

Name	Number	Description
missingrepgroup	–23373	Replication group gname does not exist
nonmasterdef	–23312	Calling site is not the master definition site
referenced	–23332	Priority group pgroup is used by existing conflict resolution methods

Restrictions. You must call DBMS_REPCAT.DROP_PRIORITY_GROUP from the master definition site.

Example. You can use DBMS_REPCAT.DROP_PRIORITY_GROUP as follows to remove a particular priority group from the replication group:

```
BEGIN
    DBMS_REPCAT.DROP_PRIORITY_GROUP(
        gname    =>'SPROCKET',
        pgroup   =>'PG_PRODUCTION_STATUS');
END;
```

The DBMS_REPCAT.COMMENT_ON_PRIORITY_GROUP procedure

The COMMENT_ON_PRIORITY_GROUP procedure allows you to create or replace the comment for a priority group (as seen in the DBA_REPPRIORITY_GROUP data dictionary view). The specifications for Oracle7 and Oracle8 differ as follows.

Here is the Oracle7 specification:

```
PROCEDURE DBMS_REPCAT.COMMENT_ON_PRIORITY_GROUP
    (gname IN VARCHAR2 := '',
    pgroup IN VARCHAR2,
    comment IN VARCHAR2,
    sname IN VARCHAR2 := '');
```

Here is the Oracle8 specification:

```
PROCEDURE DBMS_REPCAT.COMMENT_ON_PRIORITY_GROUP
    (gname IN VARCHAR2 := '',
    pgroup IN VARCHAR2,
    comment IN VARCHAR2);
```

Parameters are summarized in the following table.

Name	Description
gname	Name of the replication group containing the priority group
pgroup	Name of the priority group
comment	Comment
sname (Oracle7 only)	Not used

Exceptions. The COMMENT_ON_PRIORITY_GROUP procedure may raise the following exceptions:

Name	Number	Description
missingprioritygroup	−23336	Priority group pgroup does not exist
missingrepgroup	−23373	Replication group gname does not exist
nonmasterdef	−23312	Calling site is not the master definition site

Restrictions. You must call COMMENT_ON_PRIORITY_GROUP from the master definition site.

Example. The following illustrates how you can replace the comment for the PG_SIGNAL_COLORS priority group:

```
BEGIN
    DBMS_REPCAT.COMMENT_ON_PRIORITY_GROUP(
        gname   => 'SPROCKET',
        comment => 'Valid values are GREEN, YELLOW, and RED');
END;
```

Creating and Maintaining Priorities Within a Priority Group

The next step after creating a priority group is to add priorities to it. This task entails specifying every possible value for the data in the priority group, and assigning a priority to each value.

For example, recall the PRODUCTION_STATUS field we described earlier, which has this range of five possible values:

1. CONCEPT
2. DEVELOPMENT
3. BETA
4. PRODUCTION
5. DISCONTINUED

We want to resolve conflicts for this data by accepting the data that is furthest in the production cycle. If a conflict arises in which one update has PRODUCTION_STATUS set to "BETA," and another update has it set to "PRODUCTION," we would take the data from the latter update.

The examples in the following sections illustrate exactly how to implement this priority group. We will show the following packages:

```
DBMS_REPCAT.ADD_PRIORITY_<datatype>
DBMS_REPCAT.ALTER_PRIORITY
```

DBMS_REPCAT.ALTER_PRIORITY_<datatype>
DBMS_REPCAT.DROP_PRIORITY
DBMS_REPCAT.DROP_PRIORITY_<datatype>

NOTE	Each of the procedures containing the <datatype> suffix actually has five different versions in Oracle7, one for each of the datatypes CHAR, VARCHAR2, NUMBER, RAW, and DATE. Oracle8 adds support for two more datatypes: NCHAR and NVARCHAR2. The usage of each of these packages is identical. Most of the examples in the following sections will use the VARCHAR2 version of these packages.

The DBMS_REPCAT.ADD_PRIORITY_<datatype> procedure

The ADD_PRIORITY_<datatype> procedure adds a member (of the specified datatype) to an existing priority group. The specifications differ for Oracle7 and Oracle8 as follows.

Here is the Oracle7 specification:

```
PROCEDURE DBMS_REPCAT.ADD_PRIORITY_<datatype>
    (gname IN VARCHAR2 := '',
     pgroup IN VARCHAR2,
     value IN {CHAR|VARCHAR2|NUMBER|DATE|RAW,
     priority IN NUMBER,
     sname IN VARCHAR2 := '');
```

Here is the Oracle8 specification:

```
PROCEDURE DBMS_REPCAT.ADD_PRIORITY_<datatype>
    (gname IN VARCHAR2 := '',
     pgroup IN VARCHAR2,
     value IN {CHAR|NCHAR|VARCHAR2|NUMBER|DATE|RAW,
     priority IN NUMBER)
```

In these specifications, <datatype> can be any of the following, and value can be any of these types:

CHAR
VARCHAR2
NUMBER
DATE
RAW
NCHAR (Oracle8 only)
NVARCHAR2 (Oracle8 only)

Parameters are summarized in the following table.

Name	Description
gname	Name of the replication group to which priority group pgroup belongs
pgroup	Priority group to which new value and priority are being added
value	Literal value that is being assigned added to pgroup
priority	Priority designated to value
sname (Oracle7 only)	Not used

Exceptions. This procedure may raise the following exceptions:

Name	Number	Description
duplicatepriority	–23335	Another value is already designated with priority priority
duplicatevalue	–23338	Value is already in the priority group pgroup
missingprioritygroup	–23336	Priority group pgroup does not exist
missingrepgroup	–23373	Replication group gname does not exist
nonmasterdef	–23312	Calling site is not the master definition site
typefailure	–23319	Datatype of value is not the same as the datatype for priority group pgroup

Restrictions. Note the following restrictions on calling ADD_PRIORITY_ <datatype>:

- The new value must be unique within the priority group.

- The new priority must be unique within the priority group.

- ADD_PRIORITY_<datatype> must be called from the master definition site.

Example. To associate priorities with each of the five possible values of PRODUCTION_STATUS, we must make five calls to ADD_PRIORITY_VARCHAR2. After making these calls and a call to DBMS_REPCAT.GENERATE_REPLICATION_ SUPPORT, the column group is completely configured.

```
BEGIN
    DBMS_REPCAT.ADD_PRIORITY_VARCHAR2(
        gname       => 'SPROCKET',
        pgroup      => 'PG_PRODUCTION_STATUS',
        value       => 'CONCEPT',
        priority    => 10);
    DBMS_REPCAT.ADD_PRIORITY_VARCHAR2(
        gname       => 'SPROCKET',
        pgroup      => 'PG_PRODUCTION_STATUS',
        value       => 'DEVELOPMENT',
        priority    => 20);
    DBMS_REPCAT.ADD_PRIORITY_VARCHAR2(
```

```
                gname        => 'SPROCKET',
                pgroup       => 'PG_PRODUCTION_STATUS',
                value        => 'BETA',
                priority     => 30);
        DBMS_REPCAT.ADD_PRIORITY_VARCHAR2(
                gname        => 'SPROCKET',
                pgroup       => 'PG_PRODUCTION_STATUS',
                value        => 'PRODUCTION',
                priority     => 40);
        DBMS_REPCAT.ADD_PRIORITY_VARCHAR2(
                gname        => 'SPROCKET',
                pgroup       => 'PG_PRODUCTION_STATUS',
                value        => 'DISCONTINUED',
                priority     => 50);
    END;
```

TIP   It is a good idea to number priorities in multiples of 10 or more so that you can easily add new priority values later as requirements change.

The DBMS_REPCAT.ALTER_PRIORITY procedure

The ALTER_PRIORITY procedure lets you change the priority associated with a specific value in a priority group. The specifications differ for Oracle7 and Oracle8 as follows.

Here is the Oracle7 specification:

```
PROCEDURE DBMS_REPCAT.ALTER_PRIORITY
    (gname IN VARCHAR2 := '',
    pgroup IN VARCHAR2,
    old_priority IN NUMBER,
    new_priority IN NUMBER,
    sname IN VARCHAR2 := '');
```

Here is the Oracle8 specification:

```
PROCEDURE DBMS_REPCAT.ALTER_PRIORITY
    (gname IN VARCHAR2 := '',
    pgroup IN VARCHAR2,
    old_priority IN NUMBER,
    new_priority IN NUMBER)
```

Parameters are summarized in the following table.

Name	Description
gname	Name of the replication group to which priority group pgroup belongs
pgroup	Name of the priority group whose priority is being altered
old_priority	pgroup's previous priority value
new_priority	pgroup's new priority value
sname	Not used

Exceptions. The ALTER_PRIORITY procedure may raise the following exceptions:

Name	Number	Description
duplicatepriority	−23335	Priority new_priority already exists in priority group pgroup
missingprioritygroup	−23336	Priority group pgroup does not exist
missingvalue	−23337	Value was not registered (with a call to ADD_PRIORITY_<datatype>
nonmasterdef	−23312	Calling site is not the master definition site

Restrictions. Note the following restrictions on calling ALTER_PRIORITY:

- You must call the ALTER_PRIORITY procedure from the master definition site.
- The new priority must be unique within the priority group.

Examples. Suppose that our requirements change such that we want the PRODUCTION_STATUS value DEVELOPMENT to have higher priority than BETA. We can accomplish this by changing the priority associated with DEVELOPMENT from 30 to 45.

```
BEGIN
    DBMS_REPCAT.ALTER_PRIORITY(
        gname           => 'SPROCKET',
        pgroup          => 'PG_PRODUCTION_STATUS',
        old_priority    => 30,
        new_priority    => 45);
END;
```

As with the call to ADD_PRIORITY_<datatype>, this change takes effect after the next call to DBMS_REPCAT.GENERATE_REPLICATION_SUPPORT.

The DBMS_REPCAT.ALTER_PRIORITY_<datatype> procedure

The ALTER_PRIORITY_<datatype> procedures let you alter the data value associated with a specific priority for a priority group. The specifications differ for Oracle7 and Oracle8 as follows.

Here is the Oracle7 specification:

```
PROCEDURE DBMS_REPCAT.ALTER_PRIORITY_<datatype>
    (gname       IN VARCHAR2 := '',
     pgroup      IN VARCHAR2,
     old_value   IN {CHAR|VARCHAR2|NUMBER|DATE|RAW},
     new_value   IN {CHAR|VARCHAR2|NUMBER|DATE|RAW},
     sname       IN VARCHAR2 := '');
```

Here is the Oracle8 specification:

```
PROCEDURE DBMS_REPCAT.ALTER_PRIORITY_<datatype>
    (gname       IN VARCHAR2 := '',
```

```
pgroup     IN VARCHAR2,
old_value  IN {CHAR|NCHAR|VARCHAR2|NUMBER|DATE|RAW},
new_value  IN {CHAR|NCHAR|VARCHAR2|NUMBER|DATE|RAW});
```

<datatype> can be one of the following, and value and old_value can be any of these types:

CHAR

VARCHAR2

NUMBER

DATE

RAW

NCHAR (Oracle8 only)

NVARCHAR2 (Oracle8 only)

Parameters are summarized in the following table.

Name	Description
gname	Name of the replication group to which priority group pgroup belongs
pgroup	Name of the priority group whose priority is being altered
old_value	Current value of the priority group member
new_value	New value of the priority group member
sname (Oracle7 only)	Not used

Exceptions. The ALTER_PRIORITY_<datatype> procedure may raise the following exceptions:

Name	Number	Description
duplicatevalue	−23338	Value new_value is already designated a priority in priority group pgroup
missingprioritygroup	−23336	Priority group pgroup does not exist
missingvalue	−23337	Value was not registered (with a call to ADD_PRIORITY_<datatype>
nonmasterdef	−23312	Calling site is not the master definition site

Restrictions. Note the following restrictions on calling ALTER_PRIORITY_<datatype>:

• You must call the ALTER_PRIORITY_<datatype> procedure from the master definition site.

• The new priority must be unique within the priority group.

Example. Suppose that we want to change the data value associated with priority 50 from DISCONTINUED to OBSOLETE. We would make the following call:

```
BEGIN
    DBMS_REPCAT.ALTER_PRIORITY_VARCHAR2(
            gname       => 'SPROCKET',
            pgroup      => 'PG_PRODUCTION_STATUS',
            old_value   => 'DISCONTINUED',
            new_value   => 'OBSOLETE');
END;
```

This call would take effect after the next call to GENERATE_REPLICATION_SUP-PORT for an object in the SPROCKET replication group.

Dropping Priorities from a Priority Group

The DROP_PRIORITY and DROP_PRIORITY_<datatype> remove values from a priority group. You can specify the value to be removed by priority (with DROP_PRIORITY) or by data value (with DROP_PRIORITY_<datatype>).

The DBMS_REPCAT.DROP_PRIORITY procedure

The DROP_PRIORITY procedure removes a value from a priority group. In this version of the procedure, you must specify the value by priority. The specifications differ for Oracle7 and Oracle 8 as follows.

Here is the Oracle7 specification:

```
PROCEDURE DBMS_REPCAT.DROP_PRIORITY
    (gname IN VARCHAR2 := '',
     pgroup IN VARCHAR2,
     priority_num IN NUMBER,
     sname IN VARCHAR2 := '');
```

Here is the Oracle8 specification:

```
PROCEDURE DBMS_REPCAT.DROP_PRIORITY
    (gname IN VARCHAR2 := '',
     pgroup IN VARCHAR2,
     priority_num IN NUMBER);
```

Parameters are summarized in the following table.

Name	Description
gname	Name of the replication group to which priority group pgroup belongs
pgroup	Name of the priority group whose priority is being altered
priority_num	Priority for the value to be dropped
sname	Not used

Exceptions. The DROP_PRIORITY procedure may raise the following exceptions:

Name	Number	Description
missingprioritygroup	−23336	Priority group pgroup does not exist.
missingrepgroup	−23373	Replication group gname does not exist.
nonmasterdef	−23312	Calling site is not the master definition site.

Restrictions. You must call the DROP_PRIORITY procedure from the master definition site.

Example. In the following example, we drop the member of the PG_
PRODUCTION_STATUS priority group whose priority is 50:

```
BEGIN
    DBMS_REPCAT.DROP_PRIORITY(
        gname       => 'SPROCKET',
        pgroup      => 'PG_PRODUCTION_STATUS',
        priority    => 50);
END;
```

This change takes effect the next time we run DBMS_REPCAT.GENERATE_
REPLICATION_SUPPORT for an object in the SPROCKET replication group.

The DBMS_REPCAT.DROP_PRIORITY_<datatype> procedure

The DROP_PRIORITY_<datatype> procedure removes a value from a priority
group. In this version of the procedure, you can specify the value by data value.
The specifications differ for Oracle7 and Oracle 8 as follows.

Here is the Oracle7 specification:

```
PROCEDURE DBMS_REPCAT.DROP_PRIORITY_<datatype>
    (gname  IN VARCHAR2 := '',
     pgroup IN VARCHAR2,
     value  IN {CHAR|VARCHAR2|NUMBER|DATE|RAW},
     sname  IN VARCHAR2 := '');
```

Here is the Oracle8 specification:

```
PROCEDURE DBMS_REPCAT.DROP_PRIORITY_<datatype>
    (name   IN VARCHAR2 := '',
     pgroup IN VARCHAR2,
     value  IN {CHAR|NCHAR|VARCHAR2|NUMBER|DATE|RAW},
     sname  IN VARCHAR2 := '');
```

<datatype> can be any of the following, and value can be any of these types:

CHAR
VARCHAR2
NUMBER
DATE

RAW

NCHAR (Oracle8 only)

NVARCHAR2 (Oracle8 only)

Parameters are summarized in the following table.

Name	Description
gname	Name of the replication group to which priority group pgroup belongs
pgroup	Priority group to which new value and priority are being added
value	Literal value that is being assigned added to pgroup
sname (Oracle7 only)	Not used

Exceptions. The DROP_PRIORITY_<datatype> procedure may raise the following exceptions:

Name	Number	Description
missingprioritygroup	−23336	Priority group pgroup does not exist
missingrepgroup	−23373	Replication group gname does not exist
nonmasterdef	−23312	Calling site is not the master definition site
paramtype	−23325	Datatype of value is not the same as the datatype for priority group pgroup

Restrictions. You must call DROP_PRIORITY_<datatype> from the master definition site.

Example. You can specify the member to be dropped by its data value rather than its priority (as was done with DROP_PRIORITY). In the following example, we drop the member of the PG_PRODUCTION_STATUS priority group whose value is CONCEPT:

```
BEGIN
    DBMS_REPCAT.DROP_PRIORITY_VARCHAR2(
        gname  => 'SPROCKET',
        pgroup => 'PG_PRODUCTION_STATUS',
        value  => 'CONCEPT');
END;
```

As with DROP_PRIORITY, this change takes effect after DBMS_REP-CAT.GENERATE_REPLICATION_SUPPORT has been run for any object in the replication group.

Site Priority Groups with DBMS_REPCAT

The site priority group technique resolves conflicts by accepting the data that originated from the site with the highest priority.

About Site Priority Groups

The procedures for creating and maintaining site priority groups are almost completely analogous to those used for priority groups. The similarity arises because a *site priority group* is actually a special case of a priority group in which the range of data values is the range of global names in the replicated environment. In fact, Oracle stores the information about priority groups and site priority groups in the same data dictionary views (DBA_REPPRIORITY_GROUP and DBA_REPPRIORITY). However, unlike in the priority group technique, you should base site priority group rankings on your confidence in the data from each site, as opposed to the business rules associated with a workflow.

Use the following programs to maintain site priority groups:

    DBMS_REPCAT.ADD_SITE_PRIORITY_SITE
    DBMS_REPCAT.ALTER_SITE_PRIORITY
    DBMS_REPCAT.ALTER_SITE_PRIORITY_SITE
    DBMS_REPCAT.COMMENT_ON_SITE_PRIORITY
    DBMS_REPCAT.DEFINE_SITE_PRIORITY
    DBMS_REPCAT.DROP_SITE_PRIORITY
    DBMS_REPCAT.DROP_SITE_PRIORITY_SITE

Creating, Maintaining, and Dropping Site Priorities

DBMS_REPCAT's DEFINE_SITE_PRIORITY and DROP_SITE_PRIORITY procedures allow you to create and drop site priorities. Use the COMMENT_ON_SITE_PRIORITY procedure to maintain the comment on the site priority.

The DBMS_REPCAT.DEFINE_SITE_PRIORITY procedure

The DEFINE_SITE_PRIORITY procedure creates a site priority group. You can add sites to this group later. Specifications differ for Oracle7 and Oracle8 as follows.

Here is the Oracle7 specification:

```
PROCEDURE DBMS_REPCAT.DEFINE_SITE_PRIORITY
    (gname IN VARCHAR2 := '',
    name IN VARCHAR2,
    comment IN VARCHAR2 := NULL,
    sname IN VARCHAR2 := '');
```

Here is the Oracle8 specification:

```
PROCEDURE DBMS_REPCAT.DEFINE_SITE_PRIORITY
    (gname IN VARCHAR2 := '',
    name IN VARCHAR2,
    comment IN VARCHAR2 := NULL)
```

Parameters are summarized in the following table.

Name	Description
gname	Name of the replication group containing the site priority group
name	Name of the site priority group
comment	Comment, visible in DBA_REPPRIORITY_GROUP data dictionary view
sname (Oracle7 only)	Not used

Exceptions. The DEFINE_SITE_PRIORITY procedure may raise the following exceptions:

Name	Number	Description
duplicateprioritygroup	−23335	Site priority group name already exists
missingrepgroup	−23373	Replication group gname does not exist
nonmasterdef	−23312	Calling site is not the master definition site

Restrictions. You must call DBMS_REPCAT.DEFINE_SITE_PRIORITY from the master definition site.

Example. The following call creates a site priority group called SP_NORTH_AMERICA:

```
BEGIN
    DBMS_REPCAT.DEFINE_SITE_PRIORITY(
        gname   => 'SPROCKET',
        name    => 'SP_NORTH_AMERICA',
        comment => 'Site Priority for North American Locations');
END;
```

These changes take effect after the next call to DBMS_REPCAT.GENERATE_REPLICATION_SUPPORT for an object in the SPROCKET replication group.

The DBMS_REPCAT.DROP_SITE_PRIORITY procedure

The DROP_SITE_PRIORITY procedure drops an existing site priority group that is no longer in use. Specifications differ for Oracle7 and Oracle8 as follows.

Here is the Oracle7 specification:

```
PROCEDURE DBMS_REPCAT.DROP_SITE_PRIORITY
    (gname IN VARCHAR2 := '',
     name IN VARCHAR2,
     sname IN VARCHAR2 := '');
```

Here is the Oracle8 specification:

```
PROCEDURE DBMS_REPCAT.DROP_SITE_PRIORITY
    (gname IN VARCHAR2 := '',
     name IN VARCHAR2)
```

Parameters are summarized in the following table.

Name	Description
gname	Name of the replication group containing the site priority group
name	Name of the site priority group
sname (Oracle7 only)	Not used

WARNING   As with the DROP_PRIORITY_GROUP procedure, do not attempt to drop a site priority group that is acting as an UPDATE conflict resolution handler for a column group. First, use DROP_UPDATE_RESOLUTION to drop the conflict handler for the column group.

Exceptions. The DROP_SITE_PRIORITY procedure may raise the following exceptions:

Name	Number	Description
missingrepgroup	−23373	Replication group gname does not exist
nonmasterdef	−23312	Calling site is not the master definition site
referenced	−23332	Site priority group is used by existing conflict resolution method

Restrictions. You must call DBMS_REPCAT.DROP_SITE_PRIORITY from the master definition site.

Example. The following example shows how to drop a site priority group that is no longer in use:

```
BEGIN
    DBMS_REPCAT.DROP_SITE_PRIORITY(
        gname   => 'SPROCKET',
        name    => 'SP_NORTH_AMERICA');
END;
```

The DBMS_REPCAT.COMMENT_ON_SITE_PRIORITY procedure

The COMMENT_ON_SITE_PRIORITY procedure creates or replaces the comment field in the DBA_REPPRIORITY_GROUP data dictionary view for the specified site priority group. Specifications differ for Oracle7 and Oracle8 as follows.

Here is the Oracle7 specification:

```
PROCEDURE DBMS_REPCAT.COMMENT_ON_SITE_PRIORITY
    (gname IN VARCHAR2 := '',
    name IN VARCHAR2,
    comment IN VARCHAR2,
    sname IN VARCHAR2 := '');
```

Here is the Oracle8 specification:

```
PROCEDURE DBMS_REPCAT.COMMENT_ON_SITE_PRIORITY
    (gname IN VARCHAR2 := '',
    name IN VARCHAR2,
    comment IN VARCHAR2)
```

Parameters are summarized in the following table.

Name	Description
gname	Name of the replication group containing the priority group
name	Name of the site priority group
comment	Comment
sname (Oracle7 only)	Not used

Exceptions. The COMMENT_ON_SITE_PRIORITY procedure may raise the following exceptions:

Name	Number	Description
missingpriority	−1403	Site priority group name does not exist
missingrepgroup	−23373	Replication group gname does not exist
nonmasterdef	−23312	Calling site is not master definition site

Restrictions. You must call DBMS_REPCAT.COMMENT_ON_SITE_PRIORITY from the master definition site.

Example. The following example shows how to replace a comment on a site priority group:

```
BEGIN
    DBMS_REPCAT.COMMENT_ON_SITE_PRIORITY(
        gname   => 'SPROCKET',
        name    => 'SP_NORTH_AMERICA',
        comment => 'Comment added on '||sysdate|| ' by '|| user);
END;
```

Maintaining Site Priorities

Once you have created a site priority group as described in the previous section, you can add and drop sites (with ADD_SITE_PRIORITY_SITE and DROP_SITE_

PRIORITY_SITE) and modify their priority values (with ALTER_SITE_PRIORITY and ALTER_SITE_PRIORITY_SITE).

You can query the data dictionary table DBA_REPPRIORITY for information about site priority group members and their priorities.

The DBMS_REPCAT.ADD_SITE_PRIORITY_SITE procedure

The ADD_SITE_PRIORITY_SITE procedure adds a new site to a site priority group. Specifications for Oracle7 and Oracle8 differ as follows.

Here is the Oracle7 specification:

```
PROCEDURE DBMS_REPCAT.ADD_SITE_PRIORITY_SITE
   (gname IN VARCHAR2 := '',
    name IN VARCHAR2,
    site IN VARCHAR2,
    priority IN NUMBER,
    sname IN VARCHAR2 := '');
```

Here is the Oracle8 specification:

```
PROCEDURE DBMS_REPCAT.ADD_SITE_PRIORITY_SITE
   (gname IN VARCHAR2 := '',
    name IN VARCHAR2,
    site IN VARCHAR2,
    priority IN NUMBER);
```

Parameters are summarized in the following table.

Name	Description
gname	Name of the replication group to which site priority group name belongs
name	Name of the site priority group
site	Global name of the new site
priority	Priority designated to site
sname (Oracle7 only)	Not used

Exceptions. The ADD_SITE_PRIORITY_SITE procedure may raise the following exceptions:

Name	Number	Description
duplicatepriority	−23335	Another site is already designated with priority specified by priority parameter
duplicatesite	−23338	Site is already in the site priority group name
missingpriority	−1403	Site does not exist
missingrepgroup	−23373	Replication group gname does not exist
nonmasterdef	−23312	Calling site is not the master definition site

Restrictions. Note the following restrictions on calling ADD_SITE_PRIORITY_SITE:

• You must call the ADD_SITE_PRIORITY_SITE procedure from the master definition site.

• The new priority must be unique within the site priority group.

Example. This example adds four sites to the site priority group SP_NORTH_AMERICA:

```
BEGIN
    DBMS_REPCAT.ADD_SITE_PRIORITY_SITE(
            gname       => 'SPROCKET',
            name        => 'SP_NORTH_AMERICA',
            site        => 'D7OH.BIGWHEEL.COM',
            priority    => 10);
    DBMS_REPCAT.ADD_SITE_PRIORITY_SITE(
            gname       => 'SPROCKET',
            name        => 'SP_NORTH_AMERICA',
            site        => 'D7NY.BIGWHEEL.COM',
            priority    => 20);
    DBMS_REPCAT.ADD_SITE_PRIORITY_SITE(
            gname       => 'SPROCKET',
            name        => 'SP_NORTH_AMERICA',
            site        => 'D7HI.BIGWHEEL.COM',
            priority    => 30);
    DBMS_REPCAT.ADD_SITE_PRIORITY_SITE(
            gname       => 'SPROCKET',
            name        => 'SP_NORTH_AMERICA',
            site        => 'D7CA.BIGWHEEL.COM',
            priority    => 40);
END;
```

TIP   As with the ADD_PRIORITY_<datatype> procedure, it is a good
             idea to use multiples of 10 or more for the priority values so that
             you have some flexibility for future changes and additions.

After making these calls, we can query DBA_REPPRIORITY to confirm that Oracle added the sites.

```
SQL>  SELECT    gname,
   2            priority_group,
   3            varchar2_value      site_name,
   4            priority
   5  FROM      dba_reppriority
   6  WHERE     priority_group = 'SP_NORTH_AMERICA'
   7  ORDER BY  priority;
```

```
GNAME       PRIORITY_GROUP       SITE_NAME              PRIORITY
--------    --------------       ---------------------  --------
SPROCKET SP_NORTH_AMERICA        D7OH.BIGWHEEL.COM            10
SPROCKET SP_NORTH_AMERICA        D7NY.BIGWHEEL.COM            20
SPROCKET SP_NORTH_AMERICA        D7HI.BIGWHEEL.COM            30
```

Although DBA_REPPRIORITY reflects the changes from the ADD_SITE_PRIORITY_
SITE call, you must call DBMS_REPCAT.GENERATE_REPLICATION_SUPPORT for
an object in the replication group for the changes to propagate to the other master sites. This is the case for all of the DBMS_REPCAT procedures pertaining to
site priority groups.

The DBMS_REPCAT.DROP_SITE_PRIORITY_SITE procedure

The DROP_SITE_PRIORITY_SITE procedure removes a site from a site priority
group. Specifications for Oracle7 and Oracle8 differ as follows.

Here is the Oracle7 specification:

```
PROCEDURE DBMS_REPCAT.DROP_SITE_PRIORITY_SITE
   (gname IN VARCHAR2 := '',
    name IN VARCHAR2,
    site IN VARCHAR2,
    sname IN VARCHAR2 := '');
```

Here is the Oracle8 specification:

```
PROCEDURE DBMS_REPCAT.DROP_SITE_PRIORITY_SITE
   (gname IN VARCHAR2 := '',
    name IN VARCHAR2,
    site IN VARCHAR2);
```

Parameters are summarized in the following table.

Name	Description
gname	Name of the replication group to which site priority group name belongs
name	Name of the site priority group
site	Global name of the new site
sname (Oracle7 only)	Not used

Exceptions. The DROP_SITE_PRIORITY_SITE procedure may raise the following
exceptions:

Name	Number	Description
missingpriority	−1403	Site priority does not exist
missingrepgroup	−23373	Replication group gname does not exist
nonmasterdef	−23312	Calling site is not the master definition site

Restrictions. You must call DROP_SITE_PRIORITY_SITE from the master definition site.

Example. Here we drop D7TX.BIGWHEEL.COM from the SP_NORTH_AMERICA site priority:

```
BEGIN
    DBMS_REPCAT.DROP_SITE_PRIORITY_SITE(
        gname    => 'SPROCKET',
        name     => 'SP_NORTH_AMERICA',
        site     => 'D7TX.BIGWHEEL.COM');
END;
```

As with the other site priority procedures, you must call GENERATE_ REPLICATION_SUPPORT for an object in the replication group to propagate this change to other master sites.

Can I Drop a Site Priority Referenced by Priority Level?

You may have noticed that there is no procedure that will drop a member of a site priority referenced by priority level—that is, there is no analog to DBMS_ REPCAT.DROP_PRIORITY. Perhaps the team at Oracle decided that a procedure name like DROP_SITE_PRIORITY_PRIORITY is too cumbersome.

However, you can use DBMS_REPCAT.DROP_PRIORITY to drop a site priority referenced by priority level! Pass the name of the site priority to the pgroup parameters, and the priority value to the priority_num parameter.

Site priority groups really are priority groups in disguise.

The DBMS_REPCAT.ALTER_SITE_PRIORITY procedure

Just as you can change the priority of a value in a priority group, you can change the priority of a site in a site priority group. Use the ALTER_SITE_PRIORITY procedure to do this. The specifications for Oracle7 and Oracle8 differ as follows.

Here is the Oracle7 specification:

```
PROCEDURE DBMS_REPCAT.ALTER_SITE_PRIORITY
    (gname IN VARCHAR2 := '',
     name IN VARCHAR2,
     old_priority IN NUMBER,
     new_priority IN NUMBER,
     sname IN VARCHAR2 := '');
```

Here is the Oracle8 specification:

```
PROCEDURE DBMS_REPCAT.ALTER_SITE_PRIORITY
    (gname IN VARCHAR2 := '',
```

```
    name IN VARCHAR2,
    old_priority IN NUMBER,
    new_priority IN NUMBER);
    site IN VARCHAR2);
```

Parameters are summarized in the following table.

Name	Description
gname	Name of the replication group to which the site priority group name belongs
name	Name of the site priority group
old_priority	Site's current priority
new_priority	Site's new priority
sname (Oracle7 only)	Not used

Exceptions. The ALTER_SITE_PRIORITY procedure may raise the following exceptions:

Name	Number	Description
duplicatepriority	−1	Priority new_priority already exists for the site priority group name
missingpriority	−1403	Priority old_priority is not associated with any sites
missingrepgroup	-23373	Replication group gname does not exist
missingvalue	-23337	Value old_value does not already exist
nonmasterdef	-23312	Calling site is not the master definition site
paramtype	-23325	Parameter new_value is incorrect datatype

Restrictions. Note the following restrictions on calling ALTER_SITE_PRIORITY:

• You must run this procedure from the master definition site.

• The new priority must be unique within the site priority group.

Example. In this example, we move D7NY.BIGWHEEL.COM (from a previous example) to a higher priority, between D7HI.BIGWHEEL.COM and D7CA.BIG-WHEEL.COM:

```
BEGIN
    DBMS_REPCAT.ALTER_SITE_PRIORITY(
        gname           => 'SPROCKET',
        name            => 'SP_NORTH_AMERICA',
        old_priority    => 20,
        new_priority    => 35);
END;
```

And, querying the DBA_REPPRIORITY data dictionary view again, we see the changed data (shown here in boldface):

```
SQL>  SELECT     gname,
  2              priority_group,
  3              varchar2_value      site_name,
  4              priority
  5  FROM        dba_reppriority
  6  WHERE       priority_group = 'SP_NORTH_AMERICA'
  7  ORDER BY    priority;
```

```
GNAME     PRIORITY_GROUP       SITE_NAME              PRIORITY
--------  -------------------- --------------------   --------
SPROCKET  SP_NORTH_AMERICA     D7OH.BIGWHEEL.COM          10
SPROCKET  SP_NORTH_AMERICA     D7HI.BIGWHEEL.COM          30
SPROCKET  SP_NORTH_AMERICA     D7NY.BIGWHEEL.COM          35
SPROCKET  SP_NORTH_AMERICA     D7CA.BIGWHEEL.COM          40
```

This shows D7NY.BIGWHEEL.COM with its new and higher priority.

The DBMS_REPCAT.ALTER_SITE_PRIORITY_SITE

The ALTER_SITE_PRIORITY_SITE procedure is analogous to the DBMS_REP-CAT.ADD_PRIORITY_<datatype> procedure; use it to change the site name for an existing named site in a site priority group. The specifications for Oracle7 and Oracle8 differ as follows.

Here is the Oracle7 specification:

```
PROCEDURE DBMS_REPCAT.ALTER_SITE_PRIORITY_SITE
   (gname IN VARCHAR2 := '',
    name IN VARCHAR2,
    old_site IN VARCHAR2,
    new_site IN VARCHAR2,
    sname IN VARCHAR2 := '');
```

Here is the Oracle8 specification:

```
PROCEDURE DBMS_REPCAT.ALTER_SITE_PRIORITY_SITE
   (gname IN VARCHAR2 := '',
    name IN VARCHAR2,
    old_site IN VARCHAR2,
    new_site IN VARCHAR2);
```

Parameters are summarized in the following table:

Name	Description
gname	Name of the replication group to which the site priority group name belongs
name	Name of the site priority group
old_site	Global name of the site currently associated with the priority level

Name	Description
new_site	Global name of the site that is to replace old_site at old_site's priority level
sname (Oracle7 only)	Not used

Exceptions. The ALTER_SITE_PRIORITY_SITE procedure may raise the following exceptions:

Name	Number	Description
duplicatesite	−1	new_site is already in the site priority group
missingpriority	−1403	Site priority group name does not exist
missingrepgroup	−23373	Replication group gname does not exist
missingvalue	−23337	old_site is not in the site priority group
nonmasterdef	−23312	Calling site is not the master definition site

Restrictions. Note the following restrictions on calling ALTER_SITE_PRIORITY_SITE:

* You must call this procedure from the master definition site.
* The new site must be unique in the site priority group.

Example. In this example, we replace the site associated with priority level 10 with D7TX.BIGWHEEL.COM:

```
BEGIN
    DBMS_REPCAT.ALTER_SITE_PRIORITY_SITE(
        gname       => 'SPROCKET',
        name        => 'SP_NORTH_AMERICA',
        old_site    => 'D7OH.BIGWHEEL.COM',
        new_site    => 'D7TX.BIGWHEEL.COM');
END;
```

And again, we can see the change in DBA_REPPRIORITY:

```
SQL>  SELECT    gname,
  2             priority_group,
  3             varchar2_value    site_name,
  4             priority
  5   FROM      dba_reppriority
  6   WHERE     priority_group = 'SP_NORTH_AMERICA'
  7   ORDER BY  priority;

GNAME     PRIORITY_GROUP        SITE_NAME             PRIORITY
--------  --------------------  --------------------  --------
SPROCKET  SP_NORTH_AMERICA      D7TX.BIGWHEEL.COM           10
SPROCKET  SP_NORTH_AMERICA      D7HI.BIGWHEEL.COM           30
SPROCKET  SP_NORTH_AMERICA      D7NY.BIGWHEEL.COM           35
SPROCKET  SP_NORTH_AMERICA      D7CA.BIGWHEEL.COM           40
```

Assigning Resolution Methods with DBMS_REPCAT

Once you have configured your column, priority, and/or site priority groups, you can assign conflict resolution techniques to your replicated tables.

About Resolution Methods

In addition to column groups, priority groups, and site priority groups, the advanced replication option includes eleven other built-in resolution methods to handle update and uniqueness conflicts (see Table 16-14). You can also write your own resolution handlers. In particular, if you require a delete conflict handler, you must write your own because Oracle does not supply one.

Table 16-14. Built-in Conflict Resolution Methods

Conflict Type	Method Name	Comments
Update	MINIMUM	Data from the row having the minimum value for the designated column prevails. Data is guaranteed to converge if the value is always decreasing, or if there are fewer than three master sites.
	MAXIMUM	Data from the row having the maximum value for the designated column prevails. Data is guaranteed to converge if the value is always increasing, or if there are fewer than three master sites.
	EARLIEST TIME-STAMP	Data from the row having the earliest timestamp for the designated column prevails. Data is guaranteed to converge if there are fewer than three master sites.
	LATEST TIME-STAMP	Data from the row having the latest timestamp for the designated column prevails. Data is guaranteed to converge if the value is always increasing, or if there are fewer than three master sites.
	OVERWRITE	Intended for a single master site with one or more updateable snapshot sites. Data from the site originating the update prevails. Convergence is not guaranteed with more than one master site.
	DISCARD	Intended for a single master site with one or more updateable snapshot sites. Data from the site originating the update is discarded. Convergence is not guaranteed with more than one master site.

Table 16-14. Built-in Conflict Resolution Methods (continued)

Conflict Type	Method Name	Comments
Uniqueness	ADDITIVE	Intended for use with a column group con-sist-ing of a single numeric column. Oracle deter-mines the new value of the column by adding the difference between the old value and new value at the originating site to the current value at the destination site. Convergence is guaran-teed for any number of master sites.
	AVERAGE	Intended for a single master site with one or more updateable snapshot sites. Oracle deter-mines the new value of the column by averag-ing the current value at the destination with the value from the originating site. Convergence is not guaranteed with more than one master site.
	APPEND SITE NAME	Oracle resolves unique key violations (DUP_VAL_ON_INDEX) by appending the global name of the destination site (up to the first '.') to the offending column. The column must be a CHAR or VARCHAR2 type. Convergence is not guaranteed with more than one master site.
	APPEND SEQUENCE	Oracle resolves unique key violations (DUP_VAL_ON_INDEX) by appending a generated sequence number to the offending column. The column must be a CHAR or VARCHAR2 type. Convergence is not guaranteed with more than one master site.
	DISCARD	Oracle resolves unique key violations (DUP_VAL_ON_INDEX) by ignoring (i.e., not insert-ing) the new row. Convergence is not guaran-teed with more than one master site.

You'll use the following procedures to manipulate the conflict resolution methods associated with a given table:

```
ADD_<conflicttype>_RESOLUTION
DROP_<conflicttype>_RESOLUTION
COMMENT_ON_<conflicttype>_RESOLUTION
```

<conflicttype> can be UPDATE, UNIQUE, or DELETE. Therefore, the complete set of procedures in this category follows:

```
ADD_UPDATE_RESOLUTION
ADD_UNIQUE_RESOLUTION
ADD_DELETE_RESOLUTION
DROP_UPDATE_RESOLUTION
DROP_UNIQUE_RESOLUTION
DROP_DELETE_RESOLUTION
```

COMMENT_ON_UPDATE_RESOLUTION
COMMENT_ON_UNIQUE_RESOLUTION
COMMENT_ON_DELETE_RESOLUTION

The DBMS_REPCAT.ADD_<conflicttype>_RESOLUTION

The ADD_<conflicttype>_RESOLUTION procedure adds a conflict resolution type to a table. The value of <conflicttype> can be UPDATE, UNIQUE, or DELETE. Here are the specifications:

```
PROCEDURE DBMS_REPCAT.ADD_UPDATE_RESOLUTION
    (sname IN VARCHAR2,
     oname IN VARCHAR2,
     column_group IN VARCHAR2,
     sequence_no IN NUMBER,
     method IN VARCHAR2,
     {parameter_column_name  IN dbms_repcat.varchar2s, |
     parameter_column_name IN VARCHAR2,}
     priority_group IN VARCHAR2 := NULL,
     function_name IN VARCHAR2 := NULL,
     comment IN VARCHAR2 := NULL);

PROCEDURE DBMS_REPCAT.ADD_UNIQUE_RESOLUTION
    (sname IN VARCHAR2,
     oname IN VARCHAR2,
     constraint_name IN VARCHAR2,
     sequence_no IN NUMBER,
     method IN VARCHAR2,
     {parameter_column_name  IN dbms_repcat.varchar2s, |
     parameter_column_name IN VARCHAR2,}
     comment IN VARCHAR2 := NULL);

PROCEDURE DBMS_REPCAT.ADD_DELETE_RESOLUTION
    (sname IN VARCHAR2,
     oname IN VARCHAR2,
     sequence_no IN NUMBER,
     {parameter_column_name  IN dbms_repcat.varchar2s, |
     parameter_column_name IN VARCHAR2,}
     function_name IN VARCHAR2 := NULL,
     comment IN VARCHAR2 := NULL);
```

Parameters are summarized in the following table.

Name	Description
sname	Name of the schema containing the replicated schema. Defaults to current user.
oname	Name of the replicated table.
column_group	ADD_UPDATE_RESOLUTION only. Column group for which the conflict resolution method is being defined.
constraint_name	ADD_UNIQUE_RESOLUTION only. Name of the constraint name or unique index for which the conflict resolution method is being added.

Name	Description
sequence_no	Number indicating when this conflict resolution method should be applied relative to other methods defined for the same column group or priority group.
method	The conflict resolution method. Valid values are, • PRIORITY GROUP • SITE PRIORITY • USER FUNCTION or one of the methods in Table 16-14.
parameter_column_name	Comma-separated list of columns to be used to resolve the conflict (if VARCHAR2) or a PL/SQL table of column names. If column_group is passed, the column(s) passed to parameter_column_name must be in the group. A '*' indicates that all columns in the table or column group should be passed to the conflict resolution function, in alphabetical order.
priority_group	ADD_UPDATE_RESOLUTION only. If using a priority group or site priority group, the name of the group.
function_name	If designating a user-defined conflict resolution method, the name of the user function.
comment	Comment on the conflict resolution method, visible in the DBA_REPRESOLUTION data dictionary view.

Exception. The ADD_<conflicttype>RESOLUTION procedure may raise the following exceptions:

Name	Number	Description
duplicatesequence	−1	Resolution method already exists with sequence number sequence_no for this column or priority group
invalidmethod	−23340	Resolution method method does not exist
invalidparameter	−23342	Column(s) specified in parameter_column_name invalid
missingcolumn	−23334	Specified column(s) do not exist in table oname
missingconstraint	−23344	Constraint constraint_name specified in ADD_UNIQUE_RESOLUTION does not exist
missingfunction	−23341	User-defined function function_name does not exist
missinggroup	−23331	column_group does not exist
missingobject	−23308	Table oname does not exist in the replication group
missingprioritygroup	−23336	priority_group does not exist
nonmasterdef	−23312	Calling site is not the master definition site
typefailure	−23319	Datatype of one of the columns specified in parameter_column_name is not appropriate for the resolution method

Restrictions. Note the following restrictions on calling ADD_<conflicttype>_RESO-LUTION:

* You must call this procedure from the master definition site.

* After this call, you must generate replication support for the table passed to oname.

Examples. The following examples illustrate how to assign various conflict resolution methods to replicated tables. These examples use the products table used in earlier examples; for convenience, we've included its description here again.

```
Sql>desc products
Name                        Null?          Type
-----------------------      ---------      ---
PRODUCT_ID                  NOT NULL       NUMBER(9)
PRODUCT_TYPE                NOT NULL       NUMBER(6)
CATALOG_ID                  NOT NULL       VARCHAR2(15)
DESCRIPTION                 NOT NULL       VARCHAR2(30)
REV_LEVEL                   NOT NULL       VARCHAR2(15)
PRODUCTION_DATE             NOT NULL       DATE
PRODUCTION_STATUS           NOT NULL       VARCHAR2(12)
AUDIT_DATE                  NOT NULL       DATE
AUDIT_USER                  NOT NULL       VARCHAR2(30)
GLOBAL_NAME                 NOT NULL       VARCHAR2(20)
```

Examples of ADD_UPDATE_RESOLUTION. Assume that we have created a priority group PG_PRODUCTION_STATUS and have designated priorities to the full range of values for the column PRODUCTION_STATUS. The following call implements this priority group as the conflict handler that Oracle invokes first (because sequence_no = 1) when an update conflict occurs.

```
BEGIN
    DBMS_REPCAT.ADD_UPDATE_RESOLUTION(
        sname           => 'SPROCKET',
        oname           => 'PRODUCTS',
        sequence_no     => 1,
        method          => 'PRIORITY GROUP',
        priority_group  => 'PG_PRODUCTION_STATUS',
        comment         => 'Update Res. 1 added on '||sysdate);
END;
```

This next call assigns the column group CG_PRODUCT_MFG_COLS as the second update conflict resolution handler for table products. Oracle invokes this resolution method if and only if the first method failed to resolve the conflict.

```
BEGIN
    DBMS_REPCAT.ADD_UPDATE_RESOLUTION(
        sname                  => 'SPROCKET',
        oname                  => 'PRODUCTS',
        column_group           => 'CG_PRODUCT_PRICE_COLS',
        method                 => 'LATEST TIMESTAMP',
        parameter_column_name  => 'PRODUCTION_DATE',
```

```
          comment                 => 'Update Res. 2 added on '||sysdate);
END;
```

The following example assigns a third update conflict resolution handler to the products table. This handler would simply ignore an update if the first two conflict handlers failed to resolve it.

```
BEGIN
    DBMS_REPCAT.ADD_UPDATE_RESOLUTION(
          sname                   => 'SPROCKET',
          oname                   => 'PRODUCTS',
          sequence_no             => 3,
          method                  => 'DISCARD',
          comment                 => 'Update Res. 3 added on '||sysdate);
END;
```

Examples of ADD_UNIQUE_RESOLUTION. Uniqueness conflicts may occur during inserts; for example, two different sites may insert a record with the same primary key. While you can guard against this sort of conflict by partitioning primary key values among your sites, this design is not always possible. Note that if you wish to use the APPEND SITE NAME or APPEND SEQUENCE NUMBER methods, the column with the unique constraint must specify a character datatype (CHAR or VARCHAR2). This choice of datatype may not be appropriate for a primary key column.

The following example configures the products table to discard records that result in uniqueness conflicts:

```
BEGIN
    DBMS_REPCAT.ADD_UNIQUE_RESOLUTION(
          sname                   => 'SPROCKET',
          oname                   => 'PRODUCTS',
          constraint_name         => 'PK_PRODUCTS',
          sequence_no             => 1,
          method                  => 'DISCARD',
          parameter_column        => 'PRODUCT_ID',
          comment                 => 'Unique Res. 1 added on '||sysdate);
END;
```

Examples of ADD_DELETE_RESOLUTION. As we have mentioned, Oracle does not provide any built-in conflict resolution techniques for delete conflicts. In fact, Oracle recommends that applications that use the advanced replication option avoid delete entirely, and simply use a status column to flag records as deleted. However, if you must delete rows, you can write your own conflict resolution method and assign it to your table. See the "User-defined methods" section later in this chapter.

The following function serves as a delete conflict handler for the products table. It
forces a delete against the table.

```
CREATE OR REPLACE FUNCTION products_delete_handler (
        old_product_id          IN OUT NUMBER,
        Old_product_type        IN OUT NUMBER,
        old_catalog_id          IN OUT VARCHAR2,
        old_description         IN OUT VARCHAR2,
        old_rev_level           IN OUT VARCHAR2,
        old_production_date     IN OUT DATE,
        old_production_status   IN OUT VARCHAR2,
        old_audit_date          IN OUT DATE,
        old_audit_user          IN OUT VARCHAR2,
        old_global_name         IN OUT VARCHAR2,
        ignore_discard_flag     OUT BOOLEAN ) RETURN BOOLEAN IS

BEGIN
    DELETE  FROM products
    WHERE   product_id = old_product_id;

    ignore_discard_flag := TRUE;

    RETURN TRUE;
END products_delete_handler;
```

This final example designates the function products_delete_handler from the previous example and a user-defined delete conflict handler for the PRODUCTS_
TABLE:

```
DECLARE param_col_list DBMS_REPCAT.VARCHAR2S;
BEGIN
    param_col_list( 1) := 'PRODUCT_ID';
    param_col_list( 2) := 'PRODUCT_TYPE';
    param_col_list( 3) := 'CATALOG_ID';
    param_col_list( 4) := 'DESCRIPTION';
    param_col_list( 5) := 'REV_LEVEL';
    param_col_list( 6) := 'PRODUCTION_DATE';
    param_col_list( 7) := 'PRODUCTION_STATUS',
    param_col_list( 8) := 'AUDIT_DATE',
    param_col_list( 9) := 'AUDIT_USER',
    param_col_list(10) := 'GLOBAL_NAME',

    DBMS_REPCAT.ADD_DELETE_RESOLUTION(
        sname                   => 'SPROCKET',
        oname                   => 'PRODUCTS',
        sequence_no             => 1,
        paramekter_column_name  => param_col_list,
        function_name           => 'PRODUCTS_DELETE_HANDLER',
        comment                 => 'Del handler 1 added on ' || sysdate);
END;
```

User-defined methods

User-defined methods must meet the following criteria:

1. Must be a PL/SQL function.

2. Must return BOOLEAN TRUE if successful, FALSE otherwise.

3. Must not perform DDL.

4. Must not perform transaction control (e.g., ROLLBACK).

5. Must not perform session control (e.g., ALTER SESSION).

6. Must not perform system control (e.g. ALTER SYSTEM).

7. Update handlers accept old, new, and current column values for columns specified in parameter_column_name parameter of ADD_UPDATE_RESOLU-TION. Old and current column values are IN parameters, new column values are IN OUT parameters.

8. Delete handlers accept old column values as IN parameters for all table columns.

9. Uniqueness handlers accept new values as IN OUT parameters for columns specified in the parameter_column_name parameter of ADD_UNIQUE_RESO-LUTION.

10. Last parameter is ignore_discard_flag OUT BOOLEAN, which is set to TRUE if new values are to be discarded, or FALSE if they are to be accepted.

The DBMS_REPCAT.DROP_<conflicttype>_RESOLUTION procedure

The DROP_<conflicttype>_RESOLUTION procedure removes a conflict resolution type from a table. The value of <conflicttype> can be UPDATE, UNIQUE, DELETE. Here are the specifications:

```
PROCEDURE DBMS_REPCAT.DROP_UPDATE_RESOLUTION
    (sname IN VARCHAR2,
     oname IN VARCHAR2,
     column_group IN VARCHAR2,
     sequence_no IN NUMBER) ;

PROCEDURE DBMS_REPCAT.DROP_UNIQUE_RESOLUTION
    (sname IN VARCHAR2,
     oname IN VARCHAR2,
     constraint_name IN VARCHAR2,
     sequence_no IN NUMBER) ;

PROCEDURE DBMS_REPCAT.DROP_DELETE_RESOLUTION
    (sname IN VARCHAR2,
     oname IN VARCHAR2,
     sequence_no IN NUMBER) ;
```

Parameters are summarized in the following table.

Name	Description
sname	Name of the schema containing the replicated schema. Defaults to current user.
oname	Name of the replicated table.
column_group	Column group for which the conflict resolution method is defined.
constraint_name	For procedure DROP_UNIQUE_RESOLUTION only. Name of the constraint name or unique index for which the conflict resolution method is defined.
sequence_no	Number indicating when this conflict resolution method is applied relative to other conflict resolution methods defined for the same column group or priority group.

Exceptions. The DROP_<conflicttype>_RESOLUTION procedure may raise the following exceptions:

Name	Number	Description
missingobject	–23308	Table oname does not exist in the replication group
missingschema	–23306	Schema sname does not exist
nonmasterdef	–23312	Calling site is not the master definition site

Restrictions. Note these restrictions on calling DROP_<conflicttype>_RESOLUTION:

- You must call this procedure from the master definition site.

- After this call, you must generate replication support for the table passed to oname.

Example. In this example we drop the delete handler (created in a previous example) from the products table:

```
BEGIN
    DBMS_REPCAT.DROP_DELETE_RESOLUTION(
        sname       => 'SPROCKETS',
        oname       => 'PRODUCTS',
        sequence_no => 1);
END;
```

The DBMS_REPCAT.COMMENT_ON_<conflicttype>_RESOLUTION procedure

You can use the COMMENT_ON_<conflicttype>_RESOLUTION procedure to create or replace a comment for a given resolution type. You can see this comment in the DBA_REPRESOLUTION data dictionary view. Following are the specifications for the three values of <conflicttype> (UPDATE, UNIQUE, DELETE):

```
PROCEDURE DBMS_REPCAT.COMMENT_ON_UPDATE_RESOLUTION
    (sname IN VARCHAR2,
     oname IN VARCHAR2,
     column_group IN VARCHAR2,
     sequence_no IN NUMBER,
     comment IN VARCHAR2);

PROCEDURE DBMS_REPCAT.COMMENT_ON_UNIQUE_RESOLUTION
    (sname IN VARCHAR2,
     oname in VARCHAR2,
     constraint_name IN VARCHAR2,
     sequence_no IN NUMBER,
     comment IN VARCHAR2) ;

PROCEDURE DBMS_REPCAT.COMMENT_ON_DELETE_RESOLUTION
    (sname IN VARCHAR2,
     oname IN VARCHAR2,
     sequence_no IN NUMBER,
     comment IN VARCHAR2) ;
```

Parameters are summarized in the following table.

Name	Description
sname	Name of the schema to which object oname belongs
oname	Name of the object
column_group	Name of column group for which conflict resolution method is defined
constraint_name	Name of unique constraint the method resolves (COMMENT_ON_ UNIQUE_RESOLUTION only)
sequence_no	Sequence number associated with the resolution method
comment	Comment

Exceptions. The COMMENT_ON_<conflicttype>_RESOLUTION procedure may raise the following exceptions:

Name	Number	Description
missingobject	−23308	Object oname does not exist
missingresolution	−23343	No resolution method exists for column_group and sequence_no
nonmasterdef	−23312	Calling site is not the master definition site

Restrictions. Note the following restrictions on calling COMMENT_ON_<conflicttype>_RESOLUTION:

* You must call this procedure from the master definition site.

- After this call, you must generate replication support for the table passed to oname.

Example. This example replaces the comment on the unique resolution method created in a previous example:

```
BEGIN
    DBMS_REPCAT.COMMENT_ON_UNIQUE_RESOLUTION(
        sname                => 'SPROCKET',
        oname                => 'PRODUCTS',
        constraint_name      => 'PK_PRODUCTS',
        sequence_no          => 1,
        comment              => 'New comment added on '||sysdate);
END;
```

Monitoring Conflict Resolution with DBMS_REPCAT

Oracle can audit successful calls to your conflict resolution handlers so that you have insight into the frequency and nature of the conflicts that occur.

About Monitoring

If you enable the auditing of successful calls to your conflict resolution handlers, you can review this information in the DBA_REPRESOLUTION_STATISTICS data dictionary view.

Use the following programs to enable, disable, and purge these statistics:

> DBMS_REPCAT.REGISTER_STATISTICS
> DBMS_REPCAT.CANCEL_STATISTICS
> DBMS_REPCAT.PURGE_STATISTICS

The DBMS_REPCAT.REGISTER_STATISTICS procedure

The REGISTER_STATISTICS procedure enables the collection of data about the successful resolution of update, uniqueness, and delete conflicts. This information is visible in the DBA_REPRESOLUTION_STATISTICS data dictionary view. Here is the specification for this procedure:

```
PROCEDURE DBMS_REPCAT.REGISTER_STATISTICS
    (sname IN VARCHAR2,
     oname IN VARCHAR2);
```

Parameters are summarized in the following table.

Name	Description
sname	Name of the schema to which the replicated table belongs
oname	Name of the replicated table

There are no restrictions on calling REGISTER_STATISTICS.

Exceptions. The REGISTER_STATISTICS procedure may raise the following exceptions:

Name	Number	Description
missingobject	−23308	Table oname does not exist
missingschema	−23306	Schema sname does not exist

Example. This call enables the gathering of conflict resolution statistics for the products table:

```
BEGIN
    DBMS_REPCAT.REGISTER_STATISTICS
        sname   => 'SPROCKET',
        oname   => 'PRODUCTS');
END;
```

The DBMS_REPCAT.CANCEL_STATISTICS procedure

The CANCEL_STATISTICS procedure disables the gathering of conflict resolution statistics. Here's the specification:

```
PROCEDURE DBMS_REPCAT.CANCEL_STATISTICS
    (sname IN VARCHAR2,
     oname IN VARCHAR2);
```

Parameters are summarized in the following table.

Name	Description
sname	Name of the schema to which the replicated table belongs
oname	Name of the replicated table

There are no restrictions on calling CANCEL_STATISTICS.

Exceptions. The CANCEL_STATISTICS procedure may raise the following exceptions:

Name	Number	Description
missingobject	−23308	Table oname does not exist
missingschema	−23306	Schema sname does not exist
statnotreg	−23345	Statistics have not been registered for object oname

Example. This call disables the gathering of conflict resolution statistics for the products table:

```
BEGIN
    DBMS_REPCAT.CANCEL_STATISTICS(
        sname    => 'SPROCKET',
        oname    => 'PRODUCTS;);
END;
```

The DBMS_REPCAT.PURGE_STATISTICS procedure

If you are collecting conflict resolution statistics, you can purge this information periodically using the PURGE_STATISTICS procedure. Here is the specification:

```
PROCEDURE DBMS_REPCAT.PURGE_STATISTICS
    (sname IN VARCHAR2,
     oname IN VARCHAR2,
     start_date IN DATE,
     end_date IN DATE);
```

Parameters are summarized in the following table.

Name	Description
sname	Name of the schema that owns oname.
oname	Table whose conflict resolution statistics are to be deleted.
start_date	Beginning of date range for which statistics are to be deleted. If NULL, all entries less than end_date are deleted.
end_date	End of date range for which statistics are to be deleted. If NULL, all entries greater than end_date are deleted.

There are no restrictions on calling PURGE_STATISTICS.

Exceptions. The PURGE_STATISTICS procedure may raise the following exceptions:

Name	Number	Description
missingobject	−23308	Object oname does not exist
missingschema	−23306	Schema sname does not exist

Example. This example purges all records collected for the products table between 01-Jan-1998 and 01-Feb-1998:

```
BEGIN
    DBMS_REPCAT.PURGE_STATISTICS(
        sname       => 'SPROCKET',
        oname       => 'PRODUCTS',
        start_date  => '01-JAN-1998',
        end_date    => '01-FEB-1998');
END;
```

17

Deferred Transactions and Remote Procedure Calls

Oracle's advanced replication option relies primarily on deferred transactions and remote procedure calls (RPCs). When you commit a transaction against a replicated table, for example, the replication support triggers queue a deferred transaction to do your bidding in one or more remote databases. In addition to providing many of the underpinnings for the advanced replication option, the packages used to create and manipulate deferred calls are available for direct use in your applications. You will use the packages described in this chapter for deferred transactions and RPCs.

DBMS_DEFER_SYS
> Performs administrative tasks such as scheduling, executing, and deleting queued transactions.

DBMS_DEFER
> Builds deferred calls.

DBMS_DEFER_QUERY
> Provides access to parameters passed to deferred calls, primarily for diagnostic purposes.

NOTE   Users must have explicit EXECUTE privileges on DBMS_DEFER in order to create deferred calls.

About Deferred Transactions and RPCs

This section provides some basic information you'll find useful in using the packages described in this chapter.

About Remote Destinations

Every remote procedure call has to be executed *somewhere*, and Oracle offers several methods of specifying where.

If you are using the advanced replication option, you have implicitly named the destinations for deferred RPCs and transactions by creating master sites. Whenever a user performs DML on a table, the transaction is applied locally and is queued for delivery to all other sites where the table is replicated; these sites are listed in the DBA_REPSITES data dictionary view. Similarly, replicated procedure calls are also queued for all master sites in the replicated environment. Refer to Chapter 15, *Advanced Replication*, for details on using DBMS_REPCAT, which performs most replicated environment administration operations.

If you are not using the advanced replication option, then the destination site(s) are determined by one of the following means, listed in order of precedence:

1. The sites specified in the nodes parameter in the call to DBMS_DEFER.CALL, described later in this chapter.

2. The sites specified in the nodes parameter to DBMS_DEFER.TRANSACTION, described later in this chapter.

3. The sites specified in the DEFDEFAULTDEST data dictionary view, described later in this chapter (Table 17-4).

If Oracle cannot determine a call's destination by any of these methods, or if you specify differing destinations in the DBMS_DEFER.TRANSACTION and DBMS_DEFER.CALL procedures, the deferred call will raise an exception.

Data Dictionary Views

There are eight data dictionary views (see Table 17-1) that contain data about deferred transactions and RPCs. You can query these views to determine information such as the destination of RPC calls, error messages, and scheduled execution times. Most of the packages associated with deferred calls reference and/or modify the data in these views.

Tables 17-2 through 17-9 provide details about the contents of these views.

Table 17-1. Data Dictionary Views Associated with Deferred Calls

View Name	Description
DEFCALL	Contains information about all deferred RPCs. Queries SYSTEM.DEF$_CALL table.
DEFCALLDEST	Contains the destination database(s) for each deferred RPC in DEFCALL. Queries SYSTEM.DEF$_CALL, SYSTEM.DEF$_DESTINATION, SYSTEM.DEF$_CALLDEST, SYSTEM.DEF$_ERROR, and SYSTEM.REPCAT$_REPPROP.
DEFDEFAULTDEST	Contains the default destinations for deferred RPCs. Queries SYSTEM.DEF$_DEFAULTDEST.
DEFERROR	Contains error information for deferred calls that could not be applied at their destination. Queries SYSTEM.DEF$_ERROR.
DEFERRORCOUNT	Contains the count of errors for each destination. Queries SYSTEM.DEF$_ERROR.
DEFSCHEDULE	Contains information about the scheduling of deferred jobs. Queries SYSTEM.DEF$_DESTINATION and SYS.JOB$.
DEFTRAN	Contains information about all deferred calls. Queries SYSTEM.DEF$_CALL and SYS.USER$.
DEFTRANDEST	Contains the destination database(s) for each deferred transaction. Queries SYSTEM.DEF$_CALL, SYSTEM.DEF$_DESTINATION, SYSTEM.DEF$_ERROR, SYSTEM.DEF$_CALLDEST, and SYSTEM.REPCAT$_REPPROP.

Table 17-2. Columns in DEFCALL Data Dictionary View

Column Name	Description
CALLNO	Unique ID of call at deferred_tran_db
DEFERRED_TRAN_DB	Global name of database that originated the call
DEFERRED_TRAN_ID	Unique ID of the transaction
SCHEMANAME	Schema that owns the package
PACKAGENAME	Name of the package
PROCNAME	Name of the procedure within the package
ARGCOUNT	Number of arguments passed to the procedure

Table 17-3. Columns in DEFCALLDEST Data Dictionary View

Column Name	Description
CALLNO	Unique ID of call at deferred_tran_db.
DEFERRED_TRAN_ID	Unique ID of the transaction. Note that each deferred_tran_id has one or more calls.

Table 17-3. Columns in DEFCALLDEST Data Dictionary View (continued)

Column Name	Description
DEFERRED_TRAN_DB	Global name of database that originated the call.
DBLINK	Global name of the destination database.

Table 17-4. Columns in DEFDEFAULTDEST Data Dictionary View

Column Name	Description
DBLINK	Global name of the destination database

Table 17-5. Columns in DEFERROR Data Dictionary View

Column Name	Description
DEFERRED_TRAN_DB	Global name of the database that originated the RPC
DEFERRED_TRAN_ID	ID of the transaction originating or copying the deferred RPC
CALLNO	Unique ID of call at deferred_tran_db
DESTINATION	Database link used to specify the destination database
ERROR_TIME	Time the error occurred
ERROR_NUMBER	Oracle error number
ERROR_MSG	Error message text

Table 17-6. Columns in DEFERRCOUNT Data Dictionary View

Column Name	Description
ERRCOUNT	Number of errors in deferred RPC calls to destination
DESTINATION	Global name of destination database

Table 17-7. Columns in DEFSCHEDULE Data Dictionary View

Column Name	Description
DBLINK	Global name of the database for which pushes of deferred RPC calls is scheduled
JOB	Number of the job (job column in DBA_JOBS)
INTERVAL	Date expression that determines how often the job runs
NEXT_DATE	Next time the job is scheduled to run
LAST_DATE	Last time the job ran
DISABLED	Y if propagation to destination is disabled, otherwise N
LAST_TXN_COUNT	Number of transactions pushed last time job ran
LAST_ERROR	Oracle error number from the most recent push
LAST_MSG	Error message text from the most recent push

Table 17-8. Columns in DEFTRAN Data Dictionary View

Column Name	Description
DEFERRED_TRAN_ID	ID of the transaction that originated or copied the deferred RPCs.
DEFERRED_TRAN_DB	Global name of the database that originated or copied the deferred RPCs.
ORIGIN_TRAN_ID	ID of the transaction that originated the deferred RPCs.
ORIGIN_TRAN_DB	Global name of the database that originated the deferred RPCs.
ORIGIN_USER	USERID of user originating deferred RPC calls.
DELIVERY_ORDER	SCN of the deferred transaction in the queue.
DESTINATION_LIST	R if destinations are determined by the DBA_REP-SCHEMA data dictionary view. D if destinations were specified in DEFDEFAULTDEST or the NODE_LIST parameter to the DBMS_DEFER.TRANSACTION, DBMS_DEFER.CALL, or DBMS_DEFER.COPY procedures.
START_TIME	Start time of the origination transaction.
COMMIT_COMMENT	User-supplied comments.

Table 17-9. Columns in DEFTRANDEST Data Dictionary View

Column Name	Description
DEFERRED_TRAN_ID	ID of the transaction to propagate to database specified by dblink
DEFERRED_TRAN_DB	Global name of the database that originated the deferred transaction
DBLINK	Global name of the destination database

DBMS_DEFER_SYS: Managing Deferred Transactions

The DBMS_DEFER_SYS package provides a number of programs for administrative tasks associated with deferred transactions.

Getting Started with DBMS_DEFER_SYS

The DBMS_DEFER_SYS package is created when the Oracle database is installed. The *dbmsdefr.sql* script (found in the built-in packages source directory, as described in Chapter 1, *Introduction*) contains the source code for this package's specification. This script is called by *catrep.sql*, which must be run to install the advanced replication packages. The wrapped sql script *prvtrctf.sql* creates the public synonym DBMS_DEFER_SYS. No EXECUTE privileges are granted on DBMS_DEFER_SYS; only the owner (SYS) and those with the EXECUTE ANY PROCEDURE system privilege may execute the package.

DBMS_DEFER_SYS programs

Table 17-10 lists the programs available in the DBMS_DEFER_SYS package.

Table 17-10. DBMS_DEFER_SYS Programs

Name	Description	Use in SQL?
ADD_DEFAULT_DEST	Adds a destination to the DEFDEFAULTDEST data dictionary view	No
COPY	Creates a copy of an RPC with a different destination	No
DELETE_DEFAULT_DEST	Deletes a destination from the DEFDEFAULTDEST data dictionary view	No
DELETE_ERROR	Deletes an error from the DEFERROR data dictionary view	No
DELETE_TRAN	Deletes a transaction from the DEFTRANDEST data dictionary view	No
DISABLED	Returns a BOOLEAN indicating whether deferred transactions from the current site to the destination site are disabled	No
EXCLUDE_PUSH	Acquires a lock to disable deferred pushes	No
EXECUTE	Executes an RPC immediately	No
EXECUTE_ERROR	Reexecutes an RPC that failed previously	No
EXECUTE_ERROR_AS_USER	Re-executes a failed RPC under security context of connected user	No
PURGE	Purges transactions that have been propagated from the deferred transaction queue	No
PUSH	Pushes queued transaction to destination node	No
REGISTER_PROPAGATOR	Makes designated user the propagator for the local database	No
SCHEDULE_EXECUTION	Schedules automatic RPC pushes between a master or snapshot site another master site	No
SCHEDULE_PURGE	Schedules automatic purge of transactions that have been propagated from the queue	No
SCHEDULE_PUSH	Schedules automatic pushes to destination node	No
SET_DISABLED	Disables deferred transactions between the current site and a destination site	No
UNREGISTER_PROPAGATOR	Complement to REGISTER_PROPAGATOR; revokes privileges granted to make user the local database's propagator	No
UNSCHEDULE_EXECUTION	Stops automatic RPC pushes between a master or snapshot site and another master site	No

Table 17-10. DBMS_DEFER_SYS Programs (continued)

Name	Description	Use in SQL?
UNSCHEDULE_PURGE	Complement to SCHEDULE_PURGE; unschedules automatic purge of transactions that have been propagated to the queue	No
UNSCHEDULE_PUSH	Complement to SCHEDULE_PUSH; unschedules automatic pushes to destination node	No

DBMS_DEFER_SYS exceptions

The DBMS_DEF_SYS package may raise the following exception:

Name	Number	Description
crt_err_err	−23324	Parameter type does not match actual type

DBMS_DEFER_SYS nonprogram elements

The following table defines the constants defined in the DBMS_DEFER_SYS package. These constants are used internally in the package.

Type/Name	Description
CONSTANT parm_buffer_size	Size of long buffer used for packing parameters (= 4096)
CONSTANT default_alert_name	VARCHAR2(30):= ORA$DEFER_ALERT

Adding and Deleting Default Destinations

The DBMS_DEFER_SYS package's ADD_DEFAULT_DEST and DELETE_DEFAULT_ DEST procedures add and delete records in the DEFDEFAULTDEST data dictionary view.

The DBMS_DEFER.SYS.ADD_DEFAULT_DEST procedure

The ADD_DEFAULT_DEST procedure adds records in the DEFDEFAULTDEST data dictionary view. Adding a record to this view effectively specifies a default destination for deferred RPCs. The specification is,

```
PROCEDURE DBMS_DEFER_SYS.ADD_DEFAULT_DEST
    (dblink IN VARCHAR2);
```

where dblink is the global name of the destination site being added.

There are no restrictions on calling ADD_DEFAULT_DEST.

Exceptions. The ADD_DEFAULT_DEST procedure may raise the following exception:

Name	Number	Description
None	−23352	Specified destination is already in DEFDEFAULTDEST data dictionary view

Example. The following call adds the default destination named D7NY.BIG-WHEEL.COM to DEFDEFAULTDEST:

```
BEGIN
    DBMS_DEFER_SYS.ADD_DEFAULT_DEST('D7NY.BIGWHEEL.COM');
END;
```

Of course, the appropriate database links must be in place for deferred transactions to reach your intended destinations. Also, remember that the DBMS_DEFER package queues RPCs to the locations in DEFDEFAULTDEST if and only if you have not passed the nodes parameter to DBMS_DEFER.CALL or DBMS_DEFER.TRANSACTION.

NOTE   Changes you make to DEFDEFAULTDEST affect future calls only,
              not calls that may already be queued.

The DBMS_DEFER.SYS.DELETE_DEFAULT_DEST procedure

The DELETE_DEFAULT_DEST procedure deletes records in the DEFDEFAULTDEST data dictionary view. Deleting a record effectively removes a default destination for deferred RPCs. The specification is,

```
PROCEDURE DBMS_DEFER_SYS.DELETE_DEFAULT_DEST
    (dblink IN VARCHAR2);
```

where dblink is the global name of the destination site being deleted.

There are no restrictions on calling DELETE_DEFAULT_DEST, and the procedure raises no exceptions.

Example. The following example removes the default destination named D7OH.BIGWHEEL.COM from DEFDEFAULTDEST:

```
BEGIN
    DBMS_DEFER_SYS.DELETE_DEFAULT_DEST('D7OH.BIGWHEEL.COM');
END;
```

As with other DBMS_DEFER_SYS programs, these deletions affect only future calls.

Copying Deferred Transactions to New Destinations

If you want the deferred RPCs that are already in the queue to be propagated to the newly added destinations, you can use the DBMS_DEFER_SYS.COPY procedure to make a copy of the existing deferred transaction(s).

The DBMS_DEFER_SYS.COPY procedure

The COPY procedure copies a specified deferred transaction. Oracle queues the copied transaction to the new destinations that you specify. Here's the specification:

```
PROCEDURE DBMS_DEFER_SYS.COPY
    (deferred_tran_id IN VARCHAR2,
     deferred_tran_db IN VARCHAR2,
     destination_list IN dbms_defer.node_list_t,
     destination_count IN BINARY_INTEGER);
```

Parameters are summarized in the following table.

Name	Description
deferred_tran_id	ID from DEFTRAN data dictionary view to be copied
deferred_tran_db	Global name of the originating database
destination_list	PL/SQL table listing global names of databases to which the transaction is to be sent
destination_count	Number or entries in destination_list

There are no restrictions on calling COPY.

NOTE   This procedure is available only in Oracle7.

Exceptions. The COPY procedure may raise the following exception:

Name	Number	Description
NO_DATA_FOUND	–1403	Specified deferred_tran_id does not exist

Example. Suppose that you have a new site in Hawaii, and you want to include it as a destination for RPCs that are already queued. First, add the Hawaiian site to the list of default destinations like this:

```
BEGIN
    DBMS_DEFER_SYS.ADD_DEFAULT_DESTINATION('D7HI.BIGWHEEL.COM');
END;
```

Next, query DEFCALLDEST to get the transaction ID of a the queued RPC(s). You need this information to copy the transaction:

```
SQL> select * from defcalldest;

                 Deferred Deferred
                 Tran     Tran
Call No          ID       DB                   DB Link
-------------    -------- -------------------- --------------------
6631429919536    2.59.13  D7CA.BIGWHEEL.COM    D7OR.BIGWHEEL.COM
6631429919536    2.59.13  D7CA.BIGWHEEL.COM    D7WA.BIGWHEEL.COM

2 rows selected.
```

Now, use DBMS_DEFER_SYS.COPY to queue this transaction to the destination named D7HI.BIGWHEEL.COM:

```
DECLARE
    vNodes DBMS_DEFER.NODE_LIST_T;
BEGIN
    vNodes(1) := 'D7HI.BIGWHEEL.COM';
    dbms_defer_sys.copy( '2.59.13', 'D7CA.BIGWHEEL.COM', vNodes, 1);
END;
```

Maintenance Procedures

There are several maintenance procedures available in the DBMS_DEFER_SYS package. These procedures round out the deferred RPC repertoire by providing a means of cleaning up errors and temporarily disabling queue pushes.

The DBMS_DEFER_SYS.DELETE_ERROR procedure

The DELETE_ERROR procedure allows you to delete transactions from the DEFERROR data dictionary view. The procedure also deletes the related entries from DEFCALL, DEFTRAN, and DEFTRANDEST. Use DELETE_ERROR if you have manually resolved a transaction that initially failed.

Here is the specification:

```
PROCEDURE DBMS_DEFER_SYS.DELETE_ERROR
    (deferred_tran_id IN VARCHAR2,
     deferred_tran_db IN VARCHAR2,
     destination      IN VARCHAR2);
```

Parameters are summarized in the following table.

Name	Description
deferred_tran_id	ID from DEFTRAN data dictionary view of transaction to be deleted from DEFERROR. If NULL, all entries for the specified deferred_tran_db and destination are deleted.

Name	Description
deferred_tran_db	Global name of the originating database. If NULL, all entries for the specified deferred_tran_id and destination are deleted.
destination	Global name of the destination database. If NULL, all entries for the specified deferred_tran_id and deferred_tran_db are deleted.

There are no restrictions on calling DELETE_ERROR.

Exceptions. The DELETE_ERROR procedure may raise the following exception:

Name	Number	Description
NO_DATA_FOUND	−1403	Specified deferred_tran_id does not exist, specified deferred_tran_db does not exist, and/or specified destination does not exist

Examples. The nice thing about the DELETE_ERROR procedure is that you can pass NULL to any or all of the three parameters to treat it as a wildcard.

Here's how to delete all errors:

```
BEGIN
    DBMS_DEFER_SYS.DELETE_ERROR( null, null, null);
END;
```

Here's how to delete all errors having D7NY.BIGWHEEL.COM as a destination:

```
BEGIN
    DBMS_DEFER_SYS.DELETE_ERROR(null, null, 'D7NY.BIGWHEEL.COM' );
END;
```

Here's how to delete all errors from RPC calls that originated at D7CA.BIG-WHEEL.COM:

```
BEGIN
    DBMS_DEFER_SYS.DELETE_ERROR(NULL, 'D7CA.BIGWHEEL.COM', NULL);
END;
```

The DBMS_DEFER_SYS.DELETE_TRAN procedure

The DELETE_TRAN procedure deletes deferred transactions. You might want to do this if you have applied the call manually or if you remove a node from your environment. The procedure deletes the call from the DEFTRANDEST data dictionary view and also from DEFCALLDEST (if it is an RPC). If the original call has been applied to all other destinations, then the procedure also removes the entries from DEFCALL and DEFTRAN.

As with the DELETE_ERROR procedure, DELETE_TRAN also treats NULL parameter values as wildcards (see the examples under DELETE_ERROR).

Here is the specification:

```
PROCEDURE DBMS_DEFER_SYS.DELETE_TRAN
    (deferred_tran_id IN VARCHAR2,
     deferred_tran_db IN VARCHAR2,
     destination      IN VARCHAR2);
```

Parameters are summarized in the following table.

Name	Description
deferred_tran_id	ID from DEFTRAN data dictionary view of transaction to be deleted from DEFERROR. If NULL, all entries for the specified deferred_tran_db and destination are deleted.
deferred_tran_db	Global name of the originating database. If NULL, all entries for the specified deferred_tran_id and destination are deleted.
destination	Global name of the destination database. If NULL, all entries for the specified deferred_tran_id and deferred_tran_db are deleted.

There are no restrictions on calling DELETE_TRAN.

Exceptions. The DELETE_TRAN procedure may raise the following exception:

Name	Number	Description
NO_DATA_FOUND	−1403	Specified deferred_tran_id does not exist, specified deferred_tran_db does not exist, and/or specified destination does not exist

The DBMS_DEFER_SYS.DISABLED function

The DISABLED function returns the BOOLEAN value TRUE if the deferred RPC calls to the specified destination have been disabled (with SET_DISABLED), and returns FALSE otherwise. The specification is,

```
FUNCTION DBMS_DEFER_SYS.DISABLED
    (destination IN VARCHAR2) RETURN BOOLEAN;
```

where destination is the global name of the destination database.

There are no restrictions on calling the DISABLED function.

Exceptions. The DISABLED function may raise the following exception:

Name	Number	Description
NO_DATA_FOUND	−1403	Specified destination is not in the DEFSCHEDULE data dictionary view

The DBMS_DEFER_SYS.EXECUTE_ERROR procedure

The EXECUTE_ERROR procedure forces execution of a transaction that originally failed, leaving a record in DEFERROR. You might call this procedure if you have repaired the error (for example, a conflict in the advanced replication option) and you now wish to re-attempt the transaction. If another error occurs during EXECUTE_ERROR, the attempt is aborted and the last error encountered is returned as an exception. Upon successful completion, the procedure deletes the entries from the DEFERROR data dictionary view. If the original call has been applied to all other destinations, then the procedure also removes the entries from DEFCALL and DEFTRAN.

As with the DELETE_ERROR and DELETE_TRAN procedures, you may pass NULLs to indicate wildcards.

Here is the specification for this procedure:

```
PROCEDURE DBMS_DEFER_SYS.EXECUTE_ERROR
   (deferred_tran_id IN VARCHAR2,
    deferred_tran_db IN VARCHAR2,
    destination      IN VARCHAR2);
```

Parameters are summarized in the following table.

Name	Description
deferred_tran_id	ID of transaction in DEFERROR data dictionary view
deferred_tran_db	Global name of database that originated or copied the transaction originally
destination	Global name of destination database

Exceptions. EXECUTE_ERROR may raise the following exception:

Name	Number	Description
None	–24275	Destination is null, or deferred_tran_id and deferred_tran_db are neither both NULL nor both NOT NULL

If execution stops because of an exception, the EXECUTE_ERROR procedure raises the last exception encountered.

Restrictions. Note the following restrictions on calling EXECUTE_ERROR:

- The destination parameter may not be NULL.
- The deferred_tran_id and deferred_tran_db parameters must either both be NULL or both be NOT NULL. If they are NULL, all transactions in DEFERROR destined for destination are applied.

Example. For an example, see the *fixdefer.sql* file on the companion disk. The example lists all deferred transactions that have encountered errors, and generates calls to DBMS_DEFER_SYS.EXECUTE_ERROR to reexecute the calls.

The DBMS_DEFER_SYS.SET_DISABLED procedure

The SET_DISABLED procedure disables or enables propagation to the specified destination. If you are managing a replicated environment, you might want to disable propagation to a given site while you perform maintenance.

NOTE   If you disable propagation while RPCs are being delivered to the destination database, the delivery will be allowed to complete.

The specification follows:

```
PROCEDURE DBMS_DEFER_SYS.SET_DISABLED
    (destination IN VARCHAR2,
     disabled IN BOOLEAN := TRUE);
```

Parameters are summarized in the following table.

Name	Description
destination	Global name of the destination database
disabled	Flag indicating whether calls are to be disabled (TRUE) or enabled (FALSE)

Exceptions. The SET_DISABLED procedure may raise the following exception:

Name	Number	Description
NO_DATA_FOUND	−1403	Specified destination is not in the DEFSCHEDULE data dictionary view

Restrictions. You must execute a COMMIT after a call to the SET_DISABLED procedure for the changes to take effect.

Example. The following example disables propagation of deferred RPCs to D7NY.BIGWHEEL.COM:

```
BEGIN
    DBMS_DEFER_SYS.SET_DISABLED('D7NY.BIGWHEEL.COM', FALSE);
END
```

The following example enables propagation:

```
BEGIN
    DBMS_DEFER_SYS.SET_DISABLED('D7NY.BIGWHEEL.COM', TRUE);
END;
```

Propagating Deferred RPCs

The DBMS_DEFER.CALL procedure, which we'll discuss later in this chapter, neither executes nor pushes transactions to the destination databases: it simply queues them. In order to propagate the deferred call to the destinations and to execute it there, you must use the DBMS_DEFER_SYS package's EXECUTE procedure. Use SCHEDULE_EXECUTION to schedule execution at prescribed intervals, and UNSCHEDULE_EXECUTION to stop propagation.

NOTE   We describe the EXECUTE, SCHEDULE_EXECUTION, and UNSCHEDULE_EXECUTION procedures here because they are a part of the DBMS_DEFER_SYS package. However, because the discussion assumes knowledge of the DBMS_DEFER.CALL procedure (and related procedures), you may find these sections more understandable if you first read the subsequent DBMS_DEFER package section.

Scheduling strategies

The granularity of the DBMS_JOB facility is one second, so you could schedule propagation of your deferred RPC calls for once per second if you wanted to. However, such an aggressive schedule is not advisable. In fact, scheduling propagation to occur more often than once every five minutes is rarely wise. Of course, your ideal schedule is a function of your application, business requirements, and resources. Nevertheless, a lengthy interval is seldom justifiable. Why the restrictions?

Efficiency

You don't go to the grocery store every time you need a particular item; you add items to a list and wait until you've accumulated a list that justifies the trip to the store. Shopping in this way uses less of your time and resources. Similarly, it is far more efficient to accumulate transactions in the DEFTRAN queue, and to propagate several to a given destination than it is to check the queue frequently and/or make several calls to the remote database to deliver only one or two transactions. You should be sure, however, that the time it takes to deliver n transactions does not exceed the time it takes for n transactions to accumulate.

Redo volume

Whenever an SNP background process wakes up to check the job queue for work to do, Oracle updates the table SYS.JOB$ to reflect the fact that the queue has been checked. This update, as with all updates, generates redo log entries. We have found that scheduling a job that does *nothing* to run once per minute generates more than one megabyte of redo per hour. Do not incur the overhead of these redo log entries unnecessarily.

Resources

If you schedule a job to run once per minute, you must also set the *INIT.ORA* parameter JOB_QUEUE_INTERVAL to 60 seconds or less, because the job can run only as frequently as the background processes wake up to check them. However, just as redo activity increases, so does CPU utilization for the SNP background processes that check the job queue.

In short, you should avoid the temptation to schedule deferred transactions to be propagated on a subminute interval unless your application truly requires it. Five-minute intervals are the shortest that Oracle Corporation recommends.

The DBMS_DEFER_SYS.EXECUTE procedure

The EXECUTE procedure propagates a deferred call to the destination database and executes it there. Here is the specification:

```
PROCEDURE DBMS_DEFER_SYS.EXECUTE
    (destination IN VARCHAR2,
     stop_on_error IN BOOLEAN := FALSE,
     transaction_count IN BINARY_INTEGER := 0,
     execution_seconds IN BINARY_INTEGER := 0,
     execute_as_user IN BOOLEAN := FALSE,
     delay_seconds IN NATURAL := 0,
     batch_size IN NATURAL := 0);
```

Parameters are summarized in the following table.

Name	Description
destination	Global name of the destination database.
stop_on_error	If TRUE, execution of queued transactions stops if an error is encountered. If FALSE (the default), execution continues unless destination is unavailable.
transaction_count	If > 0, maximum number of transactions to execute.
execution_seconds	If > 0, maximum number of seconds to spend executing transactions.
execute_as_user	IF TRUE, the execution of deferred transactions is authenticated at the remote system using the authentication context of the session user. If FALSE (the default), the execution is authenticated at the remote system using the authentication contexts of the users that originally queued the deferred transactions (indicated in the origin_ user column of the DEFTRAN data dictionary view).
	This parameter is obsolete in Oracle8, which executes transactions under the context of the propagator.

Name	Description
delay_seconds	If > 0, routine sleeps for this many seconds before resuming when there are no more transactions to push to destination.
batch_size	The number of deferred transactions executed before committing. If batch_size = 0, a commit occurs after each deferred transaction. If batch_size > 0, a commit occurs when the total number of deferred calls executed exceeds batch_size and a complete transaction has been executed.

There are no restrictions on calling the EXECUTE procedure.

Exceptions. If execution stops because of an exception, the EXECUTE procedure raises the last exception encountered.

Examples. Although the EXECUTE procedure includes several parameters, you can use it in its simplest form to push all queued transactions to a given destination. For example, to send the transaction that was queued to D7TX.BIG-WHEEL.COM in the example of DBMS_DEFER.TRANSACTION, we would simply make this call:

```
BEGIN
    DBMS_DEFER_SYS.EXECUTE('D7TX.BIGWHEEL.COM');
END;
```

This call propagates and executes all deferred RPCs bound for D7TX.BIG-WHEEL.COM.

The EXECUTE procedure includes various optional parameters (described in the next section) to accommodate applications that may queue tens or hundreds or thousands of deferred RPC calls. The advanced replication option has this potential. (In such cases, you may need to control the rate and volume of transactions, privilege domains, and error handling.)

Advanced usage: using the EXECUTE parameters. The items in the following list describe in greater detail how you use the EXECUTE parameters:

NOTE   If you are queuing a relatively low volume of deferred RPC calls,
              these additional parameters controlling the volume and timing of
              deliveries are not especially relevant. They are provided for fine-tun-
              ing the behavior and performance of automatically scheduled RPCs,
              such as those associated with the advanced replication option.

---

stop_on_error

Setting the Boolean parameter stop_on_error to FALSE (the default) causes Oracle to continue propagating and executing deferred RPC calls at a destination even if one or more of the calls encounters an error. Setting this parameter to TRUE causes execution of deferred RPCs to stop if an error occurs.

transaction_count and execution_seconds

These two parameters are usually used in tandem. They cause propagation of RPCs to the destination to cease after transaction_count transactions or execution_seconds seconds, whichever comes first. These parameters provide a method of throttling the time and resources that are consumed during any one call to the EXECUTE procedure. Since these settings may cause the propagation to stop before all deferred RPCs are sent, it is your responsibility to monitor the DEFTRANDEST data dictionary view and/or to schedule automatic propagation at intervals. The default for both of these parameters is 0, which means that no such limits are set.

execute_as_user

This parameter determines the privilege domain under which the procedure call executes at the destination. Setting execute_as_user to FALSE (the default) causes the call to execute under the privilege domain of the user who queued the call originally, as seen in the ORIGIN_USER column of the DEFTRAN data dictionary view. Setting the parameter to TRUE executes the call under the privilege domain of the session that calls the EXECUTE procedure. The user in execute_as_user refers to the user calling EXECUTE, not the user who queued the call.

delay_seconds

This parameter causes EXECUTE to sleep for delay_seconds seconds before returning when it finishes propagating the queued transactions to the destination. The primary purpose of this parameter is to delay the next call to EXECUTE; the idea is that more transactions will have a chance to accumulate. It is more efficient to propagate five deferred RPCs with one call to EXECUTE than to issue five separate calls. This parameter is relevant only if you have scheduled automatic propagation.

batch_size

This parameter is the number of deferred calls to execute between COMMITs. The default is 0, which means that a commit should occur for each deferred call that is propagated.

The DBMS_DEFER_SYS.SCHEDULE_EXECUTION procedure

If you are using the advanced replication option, or if your application queues deferred RPC calls on a continual basis, then you should schedule the calls to the

DBMS_DEFER_SYS.EXECUTE procedure at prescribed intervals for each destination. The SCHEDULE_EXECUTION procedure does just that by placing calls to the EXECUTE procedure in the job queue. Here is the specification:

```
PROCEDURE DBMS_DEFER_SYS.SCHEDULE EXECUTION
    (dblink IN VARCHAR2,
     interval IN VARCHAR2,
     next_date IN DATE,
     reset IN BOOLEAN default FALSE,
     stop_on_error IN BOOLEAN := NULL,
     transaction_count IN BINARY_INTEGER := NULL,
     execution_seconds IN BINARY_INTEGER := NULL,
     execute_as_user IN BOOLEAN := NULL,
     delay_seconds IN NATURAL := NULL,
     batch_size IN NATURAL := NULL);
```

Parameters are summarized in the following table.

Name	Description
db_link	Global name of the destination database
interval	Frequency with which to execute the RPC
next_date	First time to execute transactions queued for db_link
reset	If TRUE, then last_txn_count, last_error, and last_msg are nulled in DEFSCHEDULE data dictionary view for this db_link
stop_on_error	If not NULL, value is used by the call to EXECUTE
transaction_count	If not NULL, value is used by the call to EXECUTE
execution_seconds	If not NULL, value is used by the call to EXECUTE
execute_as_user	If not NULL, value is used by the call to DBMS_DEFER_SYS.EXECUTE (obsolete in Oracle8)
delay_seconds	If not NULL, value is used by the call to EXECUTE
batch_size	If not NULL, value is used by the call to EXECUTE

This procedure looks like a cross between DBMS_JOB.SUBMIT and DBMS_DEFER.EXECUTE, because it is. The interval and next_date parameters behave in exactly the same way as the parameters by the same names passed to DBMS_JOB.SUBMIT; the parameters stop_on_error, transaction_count, execution_seconds, execute_as_user, delay_seconds, and batch_size are passed directly to the DBMS_DEFER_SYS.EXECUTE call that is put in the job queue (dblink is passed to the destination). Setting the reset parameter to TRUE sets columns LAST_TXN_COUNT, LAST_ERROR, and LAST_MSG to NULL in the DEFSCHEDULE data dictionary view.

The SCHEDULE_EXECUTION procedure does not raise any exceptions, nor are there any restrictions on calling this procedure.

Example. The following example shows how to schedule automatic propagation of deferred RPC calls to D7WA.BIGWHEEL.COM. These calls will be propagated every 15 minutes, starting at midnight tonight.

```
BEGIN
DBMS_DEFER_SYS.SCHEDULE_EXECUTION( -
     db_link      => 'D7WA.BIGWHEEL.COM', -
     interval     => 'SYSDATE + 15/1440', -    /* 1440 minutes in a day*/
     next_date    => TRUNC(SYSDATE + 1), -
     reset        => TRUE);
END;
/
```

For additional examples, see the *defsched.sql* and *jobs.sql* files on the companion disk. The *defsched.sql* example lists RPCs that have been scheduled with DBMS_DEFER_SYS.SCHEDULE_EXECUTION, including last and next execution times in hours, minutes, and seconds. The *jobs.sql* example lists all jobs in the job queue, including last and next execution times in hours, minutes, and seconds, aslong with the package call that is being executed.

The DBMS_DEFER_SYS.UNSCHEDULE_EXECUTION procedure

When you need to stop the propagation of deferred calls to a given destination, you can do so with the UNSCHEDULE_EXECUTION procedure. The specification is,

```
PROCEDURE DBMS_DEFER_SYS.UNSCHEDULE_EXECUTION
     (dblink IN VARCHAR2);
```

where dblink is the global name of the destination database.

Calling this procedure is analogous to calling DBMS_JOB.REMOVE to remove the job that DBMS_DEFER_SYS.SCHEDULE_EXECUTION scheduled. The job is removed from the queue, and automatic propagation to the database specified by dblink ceases.

There are no restrictions on calling UNSCHEDULE_EXECUTION.

Exceptions. The UNSCHEDULE_EXECUTION procedure may raise the following exception:

Name	Number	Description
NO_DATA_FOUND	−01403	Specified destination is not in the DEFSCHEDULE data dictionary view

Scheduling Propagation (Oracle8 only)

Oracle8 uses a slightly different mechanism to propagate transactions to remote databases. Instead of deleting transactions from the local queue as soon as they are delivered to a remote site, Oracle purges the queue as a separate process. This strategy enhances performance because there is no need for a two-phase commit when transactions are propagated. In addition, Oracle8 includes support for parallel propagation, which means that multiple transactions can be delivered to the destinations simultaneously if they are not dependent on each other.

NOTE   The Oracle8 documentation refers to scheduled propagation as "scheduled links."

Here are the DBMS_DEFER_SYS programs that support propagation in Oracle8 are:

    DBMS_DEFER_SYS.EXCLUDE_PUSH
    DBMS_DEFER_SYS.PURGE
    DBMS_DEFER_SYS.PUSH
    DBMS_DEFER_SYS.REGISTER_PROPAGATOR
    DBMS_DEFER_SYS.SCHEDULE_PURGE
    DBMS_DEFER_SYS.SCHEDULE_PUSH
    DBMS_DEFER_SYS.UNREGISTER_PROPAGATOR
    DBMS_DEFER_SYS.UNSCHEDULE_PURGE
    DBMS_DEFER_SYS.UNSCHEDULE_PUSH

The DBMS_DEFER_SYS.EXCLUDE_PUSH function (Oracle8 only)

The EXCLUDE_PUSH function acquires a lock to disable deferred pushes. The specification is,

```
FUNCTION DBMS_DEFER_SYS.EXCLUDE_PUSH
    (timeout IN INTEGER) RETURN INTEGER;
```

where timeout is the time to wait to acquire a lock that disables pushes. Specify DBMS_LOCK.MAXWAIT to wait indefinitely.

The EXCLUDE_PUSH function may return the values shown in the following table.

Value	Meaning
0	Normal successful completion
1	Timed out waiting for lock
2	Unsuccessful due to deadlock
4	Lock is already owned

The DBMS_DEFER_SYS.PURGE function (Oracle8 only)

The PURGE procedure purges transactions that have been propagated from the deferred transaction queue. Here is the specification:

```
FUNCTION DBMS_DEFER_SYS.PURGE(
    purge_method IN BINARY_INTEGER := purge_method_quick,
    rollback_segment IN VARCHAR2 := NULL,
    startup_seconds IN BINARY_INTEGER := 0,
    execution_seconds IN BINARY_INTEGER := seconds_infinity,
    delay_seconds IN BINARY_INTEGER := 0,
    transaction_count IN BINARY_INTEGER := transactions_infinity,
    write_trace IN BOOLEAN := FALSE )
    RETURN BINARY_INTEGER;
```

Parameters are summarized in the following tables.

Name	Description
purge_method	1 = purge_method_quick (not necessarily complete, but faster) 2 = purge_method_precise (complete purge)
rollback_segment	Which rollback segment should be used
startup_seconds	Maximum number of seconds to wait for the completion of a previous push to the same destination
delay_seconds	If > 0, routine sleeps for this many seconds before resuming when there are no more transactions to push to destination
transaction_count	Maximum number of transactions to push per execution
write_trace	If TRUE, record result in a trace file

The return values for PURGE are listed in the following table.

Value	Meaning
0	Normal completion after delay_seconds expired
1	Terminated by lock timeout while starting
2	Terminated by exceeding execution_seconds
3	Terminated by exceeding transaction_count
4	Terminated at delivery_order_limit
5	Terminated after errors

Exceptions. The PURGE function raises the following exceptions:

Name	Number	Description
argoutofrange	−23427	A parameter value is out of range.
executiondisabled	−23354	Execution is disabled at destination.
dbms_defererror	−23305	An internal error occured.

The DBMS_DEFER_SYS.PUSH function

The PUSH function pushes a queued transaction to a destination node. Here is the specification:

```
FUNCTION DBMS_DEFER_SYS.PUSH(
    destination IN VARCHAR2,
    parallelism IN BINARY_INTEGER := 0,
    heap_size IN BINARY_INTEGER := 0,
    stop_on_error IN BOOLEAN := FALSE,
    write_trace IN BOOLEAN := FALSE,
    startup_seconds IN BINARY_INTEGER := 0,
    execution_seconds IN BINARY_INTEGER := seconds_infinity,
    delay_seconds IN BINARY_INTEGER := 0,
    transaction_count IN BINARY_INTEGER := transactions_infinity,
    delivery_order_limit IN NUMBER := delivery_order_infinity )
    RETURN BINARY_INTEGER;
```

Parameters are summarized in the following table.

Name	Description
destination	Global name of the destination database
parallelism	Degree of parallelism: 0 = serial (no parallelism) 1 = parallel propagation with one slave N = parallel propagation with N slaves
heap_size	If > 0, maximum number of transactions to examine simultaneously for parallel scheduling computation If 0, compute this number based on parallelism parameter
stop_on_error	If TRUE, then stop on the first error, even if not fatal
write_trace	If TRUE, record result in a trace file
startup_seconds	Maximum number of seconds to wait for the completion of a previous push to the same destination
execution_seconds	Maximum number of seconds to spend on the push before shutting down; defaults to seconds_infiinity (i.e., unlimited)
delay_seconds	Shutdown push cleanly if queue is empty for this many seconds
transaction_count	Maximum number of transactions to push per execution
delivery_order_limit	Shut down cleanly before pushing a transaction with delivery_order > delivery_order_limit

Return values for PUSH are listed in the following table.

Value	Meaning
0	Normal completion after delay_seconds expired
1	Terminated by lock timeout while starting
2	Terminated by exceeding execution_seconds

Value	Meaning
3	Terminated by exceeding transaction_count
4	Terminated at delivery_order_limit
5	Terminated after errors

Exceptions. PUSH raises the following exceptions:

Name	Number	Description
incompleteparallelpush	−23388	Internal error
executiondisabled	−23354	Execution is disabled at destination
crt_err_err	−23324	Error creating DEFERROR entry
deferred_rpc_quiesce	−23326	The system is being quiesced
commfailure	−23302	Communication failure
missingpropagator	−23357	A propagator does not exist

The DBMS_DEFER_SYS.SCHEDULE_PURGE procedure (Oracle8 only)

The SCHEDULE_PURGE procedure schedules the automatic purge of transactions that have been propagated from the queue. Here is the specification:

```
PROCEDURE DBMS_DEFER_SYS.SCHEDULE_PURGE(
    interval IN VARCHAR2,
    next_date IN DATE,
    reset IN BOOLEAN := FALSE,
    purge_method IN BINARY_INTEGER := NULL,
    rollback_segment IN VARCHAR2 := NULL,
    startup_seconds IN BINARY_INTEGER := NULL,
    execution_seconds IN BINARY_INTEGER := NULL,
    delay_seconds IN BINARY_INTEGER := NULL,
    transaction_count IN BINARY_INTEGER := NULL,
    write_trace IN BOOLEAN := NULL );
```

Parameters are summarized in the following table.

Name	Description
interval	Frequency with which to execute the call
next_date	First time to execute the purge
reset	If TRUE, last_txn_count, last_error, and last_msg are nulled in DEFSCHEDULE data dictionary view
purge_method	1 = purge_method_quick (not necessarily complete, but faster) 2 = purge_method_precise (complete purge)
rollback_segment	Which rollback segment should be used
startup_seconds	Maximum number of seconds to wait for the completion of a previous push to the same destination

Name	Description
execution_seconds	Maximum number of seconds to spend on the push before shutting down; defaults to seconds_infiinity (i.e., unlimited)
delay_seconds	If > 0, routine sleeps for this many seconds before resuming when there are no more transactions to push to destination
transaction_count	Maximum number of transactions to push per execution
write_trace	If TRUE, record result in a trace file

The DBMS_DEFER_SYS.SCHEDULE_PUSH procedure (Oracle8 only)

The SCHEDULE_PUSH procedure schedules automatic pushes to the destination node. Here is the specification:

```
PROCEDURE DBMS_DEFER_SYS.SCHEDULE_PUSH(
    destination IN VARCHAR2,
    interval IN VARCHAR2,
    next_date IN DATE,
    reset IN BOOLEAN := FALSE,
    parallelism IN BINARY_INTEGER := NULL,
    heap_size IN BINARY_INTEGER := NULL,
    stop_on_error IN BOOLEAN := NULL,
    write_trace IN BOOLEAN := NULL,
    startup_seconds IN BINARY_INTEGER := NULL,
    execution_seconds IN BINARY_INTEGER := NULL,
    delay_seconds IN BINARY_INTEGER := NULL,
    transaction_count IN BINARY_INTEGER := NULL );
```

Parameters are summarized in the following table.

Name	Description
destination	Global name of the destination database
interval	Frequency with which to execute the call
next_date	First time to push transactions queued for destination
reset	If TRUE, last_txn_count, last_error, and last_msg are nulled in DEF-SCHEDULE data dictionary view for this destination
parallelism	Degree of parallelism: 0 = serial (no parallelism) 1 = parallel propagation with one slave N = parallel propagation with N slaves.
heap_size	If > 0, maximum number of transactions to examine simultaneously for parallel scheduling computation; if 0, compute this number based on parallelism parameter
stop_on_error	If TRUE, stop on the first error, even if not fatal
write_trace	If TRUE, record result in a trace file
startup_seconds	Maximum number of seconds to wait for the completion of a previous push to the same destination
execution_seconds	Maximum number of seconds to spend on the push before shutting down.; defaults to seconds_infiinity (i.e., unlimited)

Name	Description
delay_seconds	If > 0, routine sleeps for this many seconds before resuming when there are no more transactions to push to destination
transaction_count	Maximum number of transactions to push per execution

The DBMS_DEFER_SYS.UNSCHEDULE_PURGE procedure (Oracle8 only)

The UNSCHEDULE_PURGE procedure is the complement to the SCHEDULE_PURGE procedure. This procedure unschedules the automatic purge of transactions that have been propagated to the queue. The specification is simply:

```
PROCEDURE DBMS_DEFER_SYS.UNSCHEDULE_PURGE;
```

The DBMS_DEFER_SYS.UNSCHEDULE_PUSH procedure (Oracle8 only)

The UNSCHEDULE_PUSH procedure is the complement to the SCHEDULE_PUSH procedure. This procedure unschedules automatic pushes to the destination node. The specification is,

```
PROCEDURE DBMS_DEFER_SYS.UNSCHEDULE_PUSH(dblink IN VARCHAR2);
```

where dblink is the global name of the database to which pushes are to be unscheduled.

Exceptions. UNSCHEDULE_PUSH raises the following exception:

Name	Number	Description
NO_DATA_FOUND	-100	No pushes to dblink exist

The DBMS_DEFER_SYS.REGISTER_PROPAGATOR procedure (Oracle8 only)

The REGISTER_PROPAGATOR procedure makes a designated user the propagator for the local database. The specification is,

```
PROCEDURE DBMS_DEFER_SYS.REGISTER_PROPAGATOR
    (username IN VARCHAR2);
```

where username is the name of the account to which privileges are to be granted.

Exceptions. REGISTER_PROPAGATOR raises the following exceptions:

Name	Number	Description
missinguser	−23362	User username does not exist
alreadypropagator	−23393	User username is already the propagator for this database
duplicatepropagator	−23394	Database already has a propagator account

The DBMS_DEFER_SYS.UNREGISTER_PROPAGATOR procedure
(Oracle8 only)

The UNREGISTER_PROPAGATOR procedure revokes the privileges granted to make a particular user the local database propagator. The specification follows:

```
PROCEDURE DBMS_DEFER_SYS.UNREGISTER_PROPAGATOR
    (username IN VARCHAR2,
     timeout  IN INTEGER  DEFAULT dbms_lock.maxwait);
```

Parameters are summarized in the following table.

Name	Description
username	Name of the account to which privileges are to be revoked
timeout	Number of seconds to wait if the propagator account is in use when the call to UNREGISTER_PROPAGATOR is made

Exceptions. UNREGISTER_PROPAGATOR raises the following exceptions:

Name	Number	Description
missingpropagator	−23357	User username is not a propagator
propagator_inuse	−23418	The propagator account is in use, and timeout seconds have elapsed

TIP   We recommend using the same username as the propagator at all database sites. Also, make sure that the account is the same as the replication administrator (REPADMIN) account.

DBMS_DEFER: Building Deferred Calls

The DBMS_DEFER package builds deferred remote procedure calls.

WARNING   DBMS_DEFER can execute procedures at remote sites under a highly privileged account, such as the replication administrator account. Therefore, EXECUTE privileges on DBMS_DEFER should not be widely granted. As a general rule, you should restrict it to DBA accounts. If you want to provide end users with the ability to create their own deferred calls, you should create a cover package and grant EXECUTE on it to end users or end user roles.

Getting Started with DBMS_DEFER

The DBMS_DEFER package is created when the Oracle database is installed. The *dbmsdefr.sql* script (found in the built-in packages source directory, as described in Chapter 1) contains the source code for this package's specification. This script is called by *catrep.sql*, which must be run to install the advanced replication packages. The script creates the public synonym DBMS_DEFER. EXECUTE privileges on DBMS_DEFER are not granted. The following procedures grant EXECUTE privilege on DBMS_DEFER to the specified grantees:

DBMS_REPCAT_AUTH.GRANT_SURROGATE_REPCAT
DBMS_REPCAT_ADMIN.GRANT_ADMIN_ANY_REPGROUP
DBMS_REPCAT_ADMIN.GRANT_ADMIN_ANY_REPSCHEMA
DBMS_REPCAT_ADMIN.GRANT_ADMIN_REPGROUP
DBMS_REPCAT_ADMIN.GRANT_ADMIN_REPSCHEMA
DBMS_REPCAT_ADMIN.GRANT_ADMIN_ANY_REPGROUP

DBMS_DEFER programs

Table 17-11 lists the programs available in the DBMS_DEFER package.

Table 17-11. DBMS_DEFER Programs

Name	Description	Use in SQL?
CALL	Defines a remote procedure call	No
COMMIT_WORK	Commits deferred RPC transaction	No
<datatype>_ARG	Adds parameter of specified datatype to a deferred call; <datatype> may be CHAR, DATE, NUMBER, RAW, ROWID, or VARCHAR2	No
TRANSACTION	Marks a transaction as deferred	No

DBMS_DEFER exceptions

The DBMS_DEFER package may raise any of the exceptions listed in Table 17-12.

Table 17-12. DBMS_DEFER Exceptions

Name	Number	Description
bad_param_type	−23325	Parameter type does not match actual type
deferred_rpc_quiesce	−23326	Database is quiescing
dbms_defererror	−23305	Generic internal errors
malformedcall	−23304	Argument count mismatches, etc.
updateconflict	−23303	Remote update failed due to conflict
commfailure	−23302	Remote update failed due to communication failure

Table 17-12. DBMS_DEFER Exceptions (continued)

Name	Number	Description
mixeddest	–23301	Destinations for transaction not specified consistently
parameterlength	–23323	Parameter length exceeds limits (2000 for CHAR/VARCHAR, 255 for RAW)
executiondisabled	–23354	Deferred RPC execution is disabled

DBMS_DEFER nonprogram elements

Table 17-13 lists the constants and other nonprogram elements defined in the DBMS_DEFER package. The DBMS_DEFER.NODE_LIST_T element is a PL/SQL table whose first entry is always placed in row 1. It is filled sequentially, with each subsequent entry placed in row DBMS_DEFER.NODE_LIST_T.LAST + 1.

Table 17-13. DBMS_DEFER Other Elements

Type/Name	Description
CONSTANT arg_csetid_none (Oracle8)	Internal Character Set ID. Value = 0. Includes types DATE, NUMBER, ROWID, RAW, and BLOB.
CONSTANT arg_form_none (Oracle8)	Internal Character Set ID. Value = 0. Includes types DATE, NUMBER, ROWID, RAW, and BLOB.
CONSTANT arg_form_implicit (Oracle8)	Internal Character Set ID. Value = 1. Includes types CHAR, VARCHAR2, and CLOB.
CONSTANT arg_form_nchar (Oracle8)	Internal Character Set ID. Value = 2. Includes types NCHAR, NVARCHAR2, and NCLOB.
CONSTANT arg_form_any (Oracle8)	Internal Character Set ID. Value = 4.
CONSTANT arg_type_num	Used in arg_type column of def$_args table. Value = 2.
CONSTANT arg_type_char	Used in arg_type column of def$_args table. Value = 96.
CONSTANT arg_type_varchar2	Used in arg_type column of def$_args table. Value = 1.
CONSTANT arg_type_date	Used in arg_type column of def$_args table. Value = 12.
CONSTANT arg_type_rowid	Used in arg_type column of def$_args table. Value = 11.
CONSTANT arg_type_raw	Used in arg_type column of def$_args table. Value = 23.
CONSTANT arg_type_blob (Oracle8)	Used in arg_type column of def$_args table. Value = 113.
CONSTANT arg_type_blob (Oracle8)	Used in arg_type column of def$_args table. Value = 112.

Table 17-13. DBMS_DEFER Other Elements (continued)

Type/Name	Description
CONSTANT arg_type_blob (Oracle8)	Used in arg_type column of def$_args table. Value = 114.
CONSTANT arg_type_blob (Oracle8)	Used in arg_type column of def$_args table. Value = 115.
CONSTANT repcat_status_normal	Signals normal successful completion. Value = 0.0.
TYPE node_list_t	Table of VARCHAR2(128).

Basic RPCs

The simplest RPC calls use default destinations and take no parameters. The basic procedure for building a parameterless deferred transaction or a deferred remote procedure call is to follow these steps:

1. Call DBMS_DEFER.TRANSACTION (optional).

2. Make one or more calls to DBMS_DEFER.CALL.

3. Issue a COMMIT with DBMS_DEFER.COMMIT_WORK.

The following sections describe in some detail how these procedures work. Later sections describe more complex RPC calls.

The DBMS_DEFER.TRANSACTION procedure

The TRANSACTION procedure allows you to specify destination sites for the ensuing call(s) to the DBMS_DEFER.CALL procedure. There are two main reasons why you might wish to identify destinations this way:

- You might wish to override the destinations in the DBA_REPSITES data dictionary view.

- You might be making several calls to DBMS_DEFER.CALL and not wish to specify the destinations in the nodes parameter individually each time.

The TRANSACTION procedure is overloaded such that the nodes parameter is optional. You can specify either,

```
PROCEDURE DBMS_DEFER.TRANSACTION;
```

or:

```
PROCEDURE DBMS_DEFER.TRANSACTION
    (nodes IN node_list_t);
```

If specified, nodes is a PL/SQL table containing the list of nodes that should receive the RPC call. If you do not specify the nodes parameter, the ensuing

call(s) to DBMS_DEFER.CALL will queue the calls to destinations in DEFDEFAULT-
DEST. If you do specify the nodes parameter, you must populate it with the global name of target destinations.

Exceptions. DBMS_DEFER.TRANSACTION may raise the following exceptions:

Name	Number	Description
malformedcall	−23304	Transaction is not properly formed, or transaction terminated
ORA-23319	−23319	Parameter value is not appropriate
ORA-23352	−23352	node_list_t contains duplicates

Restrictions. You can call the TRANSACTION procedure only in conjunction with
DBMS_DEFER.CALL.

Example. At the end of the DBMS_DEFER section (in the COMMIT_ WORK subsection) is an example that incorporates the TRANSACTION procedure and the
other DBMS_DEFER procedures.

The DBMS_DEFER.CALL procedure

The CALL procedure queues a call to the destination specified in the DEFDE-
FAULTDEST data dictionary view. Here is the specification:

```
PROCEDURE DBMS_DEFER.CALL
   (schema_name IN VARCHAR2,
    package_name IN VARCHAR2,
    proc_name IN VARCHAR2,
    arg_count IN NATURAL,
    {group_name IN VARCHAR2 := ''|
    nodes IN node_list_t});
```

Parameters are summarized in the following table.

Name	Description
package_name	Name of the package containing the procedure that is being queued.
proc_name	Name of the procedure being queued.
arg_count	Number of parameters being passed to the procedure. You must have one call to DBMS_DEFER.<datatype>_ARG for each parameter.
group_name	Optional. Reserved for internal use.
nodes	Optional. List of destination nodes (global_names) where the procedure is to be executed. If nodes is not specified, destinations are determined by the list passed to DBMS_DEFER.TRANSACTION.

Exceptions. The CALL procedure may raise the following exceptions:

Name	Number	Description
malformedcall	−23304	Number of arguments in call does not match value of arg_count
ORA-23319	−23319	The parameter is either NULL, misspelled, or not allowed
ORA-23352	−23352	The nodes list contains a duplicate

Restrictions. The procedures used in deferred RPC calls must be part of a package; it is not possible to queue standalone procedures.

Example. At the end of the DBMS_DEFER section (in the COMMIT_WORK subsection) is an example that incorporates the CALL procedure and the other DBMS_DEFER procedures.

For an additional example, see the *defcall.sql* file on the companion disk. The example lists all entries in the deferred call queue (DEFCALL), including the originating database and the package name.

The DBMS_DEFER.COMMIT_WORK procedure

The COMMIT_WORK procedure issues a COMMIT command to commit the transaction constructed by the preceding TRANSACTION and CALL procedures. The specification is,

```
PROCEDURE DBMS_DEFER.COMMIT_WORK
   (commit_work_comment IN VARCHAR2);
```

where commit_work_comment is a description of the transaction. The comment may be up to 50 characters.

There are no restrictions on calling COMMIT_WORK.

Exceptions. The COMMIT_WORK procedure may raise the following exception:

Name	Number	Description
malformedcall	−23304	Number of arguments in the CALL procedure does not match value arg_count; or missing calls to the <datatype>_ARG procedure, or the TRANSACTION procedure was not called for this transaction

Example: The DBMS_DEFER.TRANSACTION, CALL, <datatype>_ARG, and COMMIT_WORK procedures work together to construct a deferred transaction or deferred RPC call, as described in the following examples.

Using DBMS_DEFER.TRANSACTION. To illustrate the way that you might use the TRANSACTION procedure, consider the following example. The schema

SPROCKET has a package called PriceMaint, which contains procedure TenPctIncrease. This package exists at all sites in the DEFDEFAULTDEST data dictionary view. The TenPctIncrease procedure increases the wholesale and retail prices of products in our PRICES table by 10%.

```
CREATE OR REPLACE PACKAGE PriceMaint IS
        PROCEDURE TenPctIncrease;
END PriceMaint;
/

CREATE OR REPLACE PACKAGE BODY PriceMaint IS
    PROCEDURE TenPctIncrease IS
    BEGIN
            UPDATE  prices
            SET     price_wholesale= price_wholesale * 1.10,
                    price_retail    = price_retail * 1.10;
    END TenPctIncrease;
END PriceMaint;
/
```

Now, suppose that we wish to make a 10% price increase at all of our locations (i.e., all locations in the DEFDEFAULTDEST data dictionary view). We could create a procedure that queues a call to PriceMaint.TenPctIncrease to all of these sites. In this case, we issue the TRANSACTION call without parameters:

```
CREATE OR REPLACE PROCEDURE TenPctPriceHike IS
BEGIN
    DBMS_DEFER.TRANSACTION;
    DBMS_DEFER.CALL(    schema_name => 'SPROCKET',
                        package_name=> 'PRICEMAINT',
                        proc_name   => 'TENPCTINCREASE'
                        arg_count   => 0 );
    DBMS_DEFER.COMMIT_WORK(commit_work_comment=>'No nodes or args needed');
END;
```

Because the nodes parameter isn't specified in either the call to TRANSACTION or the call to CALL, Oracle resolves the destinations by using all sites in the DEFDEFAULTDEST data dictionary view.

Here is how you might use the TenPctPriceHike Procedure.

Confirm the default destinations:

```
SQL> SELECT * FROM defdefaultdest;
DBLINK
--------------------
D7NY.BIGWHEEL.COM
D7OH.BIGWHEEL.COM
D7OR.BIGWHEEL.COM
D7WA.BIGWHEEL.COM
D7TX.BIGWHEEL.COM

5 rows selected.
```

Now use TenPctPriceHike to queue the RPC to all five destinations:

```
SQL> EXECUTE TenPctPriceHike

PL/SQL procedure successfully completed.
```

Figure 17-1 graphically illustrates how a deferred call is queued.

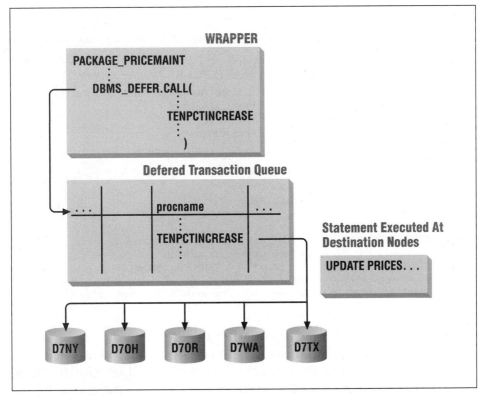

Figure 17-1. Queueing up a deferred call to TenPctIncrease

Now check the entries in DEFTRAN (this call was made from D7CA. BIG-WHEEL.COM):

```
SQL> select * from deftrandest;

DEFERRED_TRAN_ID           DEFERRED_TRAN_DB          DBLINK
----------------------     ------------------        -------------------
2.44.13                    D7CA.BIGWHEEL.COM         D7NY.BIGWHEEL.COM
2.44.13                    D7CA.BIGWHEEL.COM         D7OH.BIGWHEEL.COM
2.44.13                    D7CA.BIGWHEEL.COM         D7OR.BIGWHEEL.COM
2.44.13                    D7CA.BIGWHEEL.COM         D7WA.BIGWHEEL.COM
2.44.13                    D7CA.BIGWHEEL.COM         D7TX.BIGWHEEL.COM

5 rows selected.
```

For an additional example, see the *deftdest.sql* file on the companion disk. The example queries the DEFTRANDEST data dictionary view and lists destination databases for deferred RPC calls.

NOTE   Procedure TenPctPriceHike queues the deferred RPC only if the owner of the procedure has EXECUTE privileges on DBMS_DEFER.

Specifying nondefault destinations with TRANSACTION. What if we wanted to apply the 10% price hike only to our West Coast sites (i.e., D7CA.BIG-WHEEL.COM, D7OR.BIGWHEEL.COM, and D7WA.BIGWHEEL.COM)? The following example does just that by specifying the nodes parameter in the TRANSACTION procedure:

```
CREATE OR REPLACE PROCEDURE TenPctPriceHikeWest IS
vNodes DBMS_DEFER.NODE_LIST_T;
BEGIN
    vNodes(1)  := 'D7CA.BIGWHEEL.COM';
    vNodes(2)  := 'D7OR.BIGWHEEL.COM';
    vNodes(3)  := 'D7WA.BIGWHEEL.COM';

    DBMS_DEFER.TRANSACTION( vNodes );
    DBMS_DEFER.CALL(     schema_name  => 'SPROCKET',
                         package_name => 'PRICEMAINT',
                         proc_name    => 'TENPCTINCREASE'
                         arg_count    => 0 );
    DBMS_DEFER.COMMIT_WORK(commit_work_comment=>'West Coast Price Hike');
END;
```

Committing deferred RPC calls with COMMIT_WORK. Notice that the last two examples include a call to DBMS_DEFER.COMMIT_WORK. All deferred RPCs queued with the CALL procedure *must* be followed by a call to COMMIT_WORK; an explicit COMMIT or COMMIT WORK is not sufficient. The reason for this restriction is that COMMIT_WORK not only commits the transaction, but also updates the commit_comment and delivery_order field in the DEFTRANS data dictionary view. The commit_comment is updated with the optional string passed to COMMIT_WORK, and the delivery_order field is updated with the transaction's SCN.

Remember that the TRANSACTION procedure is not required to queue deferred calls. It is used only to specify destinations. The real power and flexibility of deferred transactions is in the CALL procedure.

For an additional example, see the *defcdest.sql* file on the companion disk. The example queries the DEFCALLDEST data dictionary view and lists the destination databases of all calls in the deferred call queue.

Parameterized RPCs

The preceding sections describe the simple version of building deferred RPCs with the DBMS_DEFER package. We saw in those sections that the DBMS_DEFER.CALL procedure is the program that actually queues deferred RPCs. Most of the examples we have seen so far use it in its simplest incarnation, without the nodes parameter and with an arg_count parameter of 0. This is fine when making deferred calls to procedures that take no parameters, and when the default destinations are acceptable, but sooner or later you will want to defer calls to procedures that require parameters, and you will want to specify the destinations for each call individually. The steps to accomplish these more complex operations follow:

1. Specify the destination nodes, either with DBMS_CALL.TRANSACTION or by supplying the nodes parameter to DBMS_DEFER.CALL.

2. Execute DBMS_DEFER.CALL, supplying the schema name, package name, procedure name, number of arguments to the procedure, and (if you do not use DBMS_CALL.TRANSACTION) the nodes parameter.

3. Call DBMS_DEFER.<datatype>_arg arg_count times, where arg_count is the value passed to DBMS_DEFER.CALL. The order in which you call DBMS_DEFER.<datatype>_arg must be the same order as the parameters are listed in the procedure definition.

4. Call DBMS_DEFER.COMMIT_WORK with an optional comment.

The DBMS_DEFER.<datatype>_ARG procedure

This procedure specifies an argument for a deferred call. The argument is of the datatype specified in <datatype>. Here is the specification:

```
PROCEDURE DBMS_DEFER.<datatype>ARG (arg IN <datatype>.
```

specifications differ for different datatypes, depending on whether you are using Oracle7 or Oracle8. <datatype> can be one of the following:

NUMBER
DATE
VARCHAR2
CHAR
ROWID
RAW

NVARCHAR2 (Oracle8 only)
ANY_VARCHAR2 (Oracle8 only)
NCHAR (Oracle8 only)
ANY_CHAR (Oracle8 only)
BLOB (Oracle8 only)
CLOB (Oracle8 only)
ANY_CLOB (Oracle8 only)
NCLOB (Oracle8 only)

The arg parameter is the value to pass to the parameter of the same datatype in the procedure previously queued via DBMS_DEFER.CALL.

The various alternatives are listed here.

The following specifications apply to both Oracle7 and Oracle8:

```
PROCEDURE NUMBER_ARG (arg IN NUMBER);
PROCEDURE DATE_ARG (arg IN DATE);
PROCEDURE VARCHAR2_ARG (arg IN VARCHAR2);
PROCEDURE CHAR_ARG (arg IN CHAR);
PROCEDURE ROWID_ARG (arg IN ROWID);
PROCEDURE RAW_ARG (arg IN raw);
```

These specifications apply only to Oracle8:

```
PROCEDURE NVARCHAR2_ARG (arg IN NVARCHAR2);
PROCEDURE ANY_VARCHAR2_ARG (arg  IN VARCHAR2 CHARACTER SET ANY_CS);
PROCEDURE NCHAR_ARG (arg IN NCHAR);
PROCEDURE ANY_CHAR_ARG (arg IN CHAR CHARACTER SET ANY_CS);
PROCEDURE BLOB_ARG (arg IN BLOB);
PROCEDURE CLOB_ARG (arg IN CLOB);
PROCEDURE ANY_CLOB_ARG (arg IN CLOB CHARACTER SET ANY_CS);
PROCEDURE NCLOB_ARG (arg IN NCLOB);
```

Exceptions. This procedure may raise the following exception:

Name	Number	Description
paramlen_num	−23323	Parameter is too long

Example. The following scenario describes how to perform the steps required to construct a deferred RPC that takes parameters.

Suppose that we have a PRODUCTS table and a procedure that adds new products to it, as follows:

```
SQL> desc products
 Name                          Null?        Type
 --------------------          --------     ----
 PRODUCT_ID                    NOT NULL     NUMBER(9)
 PRODUCT_TYPE                  NOT NULL     NUMBER(6)
 CATALOG_ID                    NOT NULL     VARCHAR2(15)
```

```
DESCRIPTION          NOT NULL    VARCHAR2(30)
REV_LEVEL            NOT NULL    VARCHAR2(15)
PRODUCTION_DATE      NOT NULL    DATE
PRODUCTION_STATUS    NOT NULL    VARCHAR2(10)
AUDIT_DATE           NOT NULL    DATE
AUDIT_USER           NOT NULL    VARCHAR2(30)
GLOBAL_NAME          NOT NULL    VARCHAR2(20)
```

Procedure ProductMaint.AddProduct populates this table. We will queue deferred calls to the this procedure.

```
CREATE OR REPLACE PACKAGE ProductMaint IS
    PROCEDURE AddProduct(product_type_ININ NUMBER,
                    catalog_id_IN    IN VARCHAR2,
                    description_IN   IN VARCHAR2,
                    rev_level_IN     IN VARCHAR2,
                    production_date_ININ DATE,
                    product_status_ININ VARCHAR);
END ProductMaint;
/
CREATE OR REPLACE PACKAGE BODY ProductMaint IS

PROCEDURE AddProduct(product_type_ININ NUMBER,
                catalog_id_IN     IN VARCHAR2,
                description_IN    IN VARCHAR2,
                rev_level_IN      IN VARCHAR2,
                production_date_IN  IN DATE,
                product_status_IN   IN VARCHAR) IS
BEGIN

    INSERT INTO products (product_id,
                product_type,
                catalog_id,
                description,
                rev_level,
                production_date,
                production_status,
                audit_date,
                audit_user,
                global_name )
    VALUES (seq_products.nextval,
            product_type_IN,
            catalog_id_IN,
            description_IN,
            rev_level_IN,
            production_date_IN,
            product_status_IN,
            SYSDATE,
            USER,
            DBMS_REPUTIL.GLOBAL_NAME);
END AddProduct;

END ProductMaint;
```

Since the procedure ProductMaint.AddProduct accepts parameters, we must supply values for these parameters when building a deferred call. The following procedure does just that:

```
CREATE OR REPLACE PROCEDURE qAddProduct IS
vNodesDBMS_DEFER.NODE_LIST_T;
BEGIN
----------------------------------------------------------------------
-- 1. Specify the nodes to which the deferred RPC call is to be queued.
----------------------------------------------------------------------
    vNodes(1) := 'D7NY.BIGWHEEL.COM';
    vNodes(2) := 'D7OH.BIGWHEEL.COM';
    vNodes(3) := 'D7OR.BIGWHEEL.COM';
    vNodes(4) := 'D7WA.BIGWHEEL.COM';
    vNodes(5) := 'D7TX.BIGWHEEL.COM';


----------------------------------------------------------------------
-- 2. Execute DBMS_DEFER.CALL, supplying the schema name, package name,
--    procedure name, number of arguments to the procedure, and (if you do
--    not use DBMS_CALL.TRANSACTION) the nodes parameter.
----------------------------------------------------------------------

    DBMS_DEFER.CALL(schema_name=> 'SPROCKET',
            package_name=> 'PRODUCTMAINT',
            proc_name=> 'AddProduct',
            arg_count=> 6,
            nodes   => vNodes );


----------------------------------------------------------------------
-- 3. Call DBMS_DEFER.<datatype>_arg arg_count times, where arg_count is
--    the value passed to DBMS_DEFER.CALL.  The order in which you call
--    DBMS_DEFER.<datatype>_arg must be the same order as the parameters
--    are listed in the procedure definition.
----------------------------------------------------------------------

    DBMS_DEFER.NUMBER_ARG( 10 );                          -- product_type
     DBMS_DEFER.VARCHAR2_ARG( 'BIKE-0018' );               -- catalog_id
     DBMS_DEFER.VARCHAR2_ARG( 'Mens 18 Speed Racer');     -- Description
     DBMS_DEFER.VARCHAR2_ARG( '19971031-01' );             -- Rev Level
     DBMS_DEFER.DATE_ARG(to_date('31-OCT-1997','DD-MON-YYYY'));   --Date
     DBMS_DEFER.VARCHAR2_ARG( 'PLANNED' );                 -- status


----------------------------------------------------------------------
-- 4. Call DBMS_DEFER.COMMIT_WORK with an optional comment.
----------------------------------------------------------------------
    DBMS_DEFER.COMMIT_WORK(commit_work_comment=>'5 Nodes, 6 args');
END;
```

Let's see what happens when we execute AddProduct:

```
SQL> execute qAddProduct

PL/SQL procedure successfully completed.
```

Note that even though this deferred RPC call is destined for five different databases, there is only one entry in DEFCALL:

```
SQL> SELECT        callno,
  2  deferred_tran_db,
  3  deferred_tran_id,
  4  schemaname,
  5  packagename,
  6  procname,
  7  argcount
  8  FROM          defcall
  9  /
```

Call No	Deferred Tran DB	Deferred Tran ID	Schema Name	Package Name	Procedure Name	Arg Count
6631429922096	D7CA.BIGWHEEL.COM	2.125.13	SPROCKET	PRODUCTMAINT	AddProduct	6

The DEFTRANDEST data dictionary view, on the other hand, includes all of the destinations for this call:

```
SQL> SELECT        deferred_tran_id,
  2  deferred_tran_db,
  3  dblink
  4  FROM          deftrandest
  5  /
```

Deferred Tran ID	Deferred Tran DB	DB Link
2.125.13	D7CA.BIGWHEEL.COM	D7NY.BIGWHEEL.COM
2.125.13	D7CA.BIGWHEEL.COM	D7OH.BIGWHEEL.COM
2.125.13	D7CA.BIGWHEEL.COM	D7OR.BIGWHEEL.COM
2.125.13	D7CA.BIGWHEEL.COM	D7WA.BIGWHEEL.COM
2.125.13	D7CA.BIGWHEEL.COM	D7TX.BIGWHEEL.COM

```
5 rows selected.
```

DBMS_DEFER_QUERY: Performing Diagnostics and Maintenance

Occasionally, you may want to see details about deferred RPCs in the queue, such as what procedure and parameters are used. The DBMS_DEFER_QUERY package contains procedures to display this data.

Getting Started with DBMS_DEFER_QUERY

The DBMS_REPCAT_QUERY package is created when the Oracle database is installed. The *dbmsdefr.sql* script (found in the built-in packages source directory, as described in Chapter 1) contains the source code for this package's specification. This script is called by *catrep.sql*, which must be run to install the advanced replication packages. The wrapped sql script *prvtrctf.sql* creates the public synonym DBMS_REPCAT_QUERY. No EXECUTE privileges are granted on DBMS_REPCAT_QUERY; only the owner (SYS) and those with the EXECUTE ANY PROCEDURE system privilege may execute the package.

DBMS_DEFER_QUERY programs

Table 17-14 lists the programs available in the DBMS_DEFER_QUERY package.

Table 17-14. DBMS_DEFER_QUERY Programs

Name	Description	Use in SQL?
GET_ARG_TYPE	Returns the type of a parameter in a deferred call	No
GET_CALL_ARGS	Returns information about parameters in text form	No
GET_<datatype>_ARG	Returns the value of a parameter whose type is <datatype>; values can be CHAR, DATE, NUMBER, RAW, ROWID, or VARCHAR2	No

There are no exceptions defined for this package.

DBMS_DEFER_QUERY nonprogram elements

Table 17-15 lists the nonprogram elements defined for the DBMS_DEFER_QUERY package.

Table 17-15. DBMS_DEFER_QUERY Other Elements

Name/Type	Description
TYPE type_ary	Table of NUMBER
TYPE val_ary	Table of VARCHAR2(2000)

The PL/SQL tables type_ary and val_ary are both used in parameters to the procedure GET_CALL_ARGS; type_ary is an output array for RPC parameter datatypes and val_ary is an output array of the parameter values. Table 17-16 shows the mapping of numbers to datatypes in type_ary.

Table 17-16. Mapping Numbers to Datatypes

Datatype	Numeric Value in type_ary
BFILE (Oracle8 only)	114
BLOB (Oracle8 only)	113

Table 17-16. Mapping Numbers to Datatypes (continued)

Datatype	Numeric Value in type_ary
CFIL (Oracle8 only)	115
CHAR	96
CFIL (Oracle8 only)	112
DATE	12
NUMBER	2
RAW	23
ROWID	11
VARCHAR2	1

Before examining the details of the individual procedures, let's look at a basic example of how they are used. Suppose that we have queued a call to the Pro-ductMaint.AddProduct procedure, as described in an earlier example.

```
SQL> EXECUTE qAddProduct
PL/SQL procedure successfully completed.
```

We now have an entry in the DEFCALL data dictionary view:

```
    1   SELECT      callno,
    2               deferred_tran_db,
    3               deferred_tran_id,
    4               schemaname,
    5               packagename,
    6               procname,
    7               argcount
    8*  FROM        defcall
SYSTEM@D7CA SQL> /
```

Call No	Deferred Tran DB	Deferred Tran ID	Schema Name	Package Name	Procedure Name	Arg Count
9929966326029D7CA.BIGWHEEL.COM	3.58.14		SPROCKET	PRODUCTMAINT	AddProduct	6

```
    1 row selected.
```

Here we see that the procedure ProductMaint.AddProduct is queued, and that it has six parameters. To determine what these parameters are, first determine their data types with the GET_ARG_TYPE procedure, and then determine their values with GET_<datatype>_ARG. Alternatively, you can use GET_CALL_ARGS, which returns all the information in a single call. The examples in the following sections illustrate the use of each technique.

The DBMS_DEFER_QUERY.GET_ARG_TYPE function

You can use this function in conjunction with the GET_<datatype>_ARG or GET_CALL_ARGS functions to determine information about the deferred RPCs in the queue. GET_ARG_TYPE returns a number corresponding to the argument's datatype. Here is the specification for GET_ARG_TYPE:

```
FUNCTION DBMS_DEFER_QUEUE.GET_ARG_TYPE
    (callno IN NUMBER,
     deferred_tran_db IN VARCHAR2,
     arg_no IN  NUMBER,
     deferred_tran_id IN VARCHAR2)
 RETURN NUMBER;
```

The following table shows the mapping of datatypes to return values.

Argument Datatype	GET_ARG_TYPE Return Code
BFIL (Oracle8 only)	114
BLOB (Oracle8 only)	113
CFIL (Oracle8 only)	115
CHAR	96
CFIL (Oracle8 only)	112
DATE	12
NUMBER	2
RAW	23
ROWID	11
VARCHAR2	1

Notice that the datatypes here are limited to the Oracle-supplied datatypes; you cannot, for example, defer a call to a procedure that accepts a PL/SQL table as a parameter.

Parameters are summarized in the following table.

Name	Description
callno	The CALLNO of the RPC, as stored in the DEFCALL data dictionary view
deferred_tran_db	Global name of the database deferring the call (also stored in DEFCALL)
arg_no	The position of the argument in the RPC
deferred_tran_id	The deferred_tran_id for the call (also stored in DEFCALL)

There are no restrictions on calling GET_ARG_TYPE.

Exceptions. The GET_ARG_TYPE function may raise the following exception:

Name	Number	Description
NO_DATA_FOUND	–100	Specified argument does not exist for specified RPC call

Example. This example shows how you use the GET_ARG_TYPE function to determine the datatypes of a queued call:

```
 1   DECLARE
 2       vDataType NUMBER;
 3   BEGIN
 4       vDataType := DBMS_DEFER_QUERY.GET_ARG_TYPE(
 5                   callno => 9929966326029,
 6                   deferred_tran_db => 'D7CA.BIGWHEEL.COM',
 7                   arg_no => 3,
 8                   deferred_tran_id => '3.58.14');
 9       dbms_output.put_line('Datatype for arg 1 is '|| vDataType);
10*  END;
SYSTEM@D7CA SQL> /
Datatype for arg 3 is 1

PL/SQL procedure successfully completed.
```

Here we see that the third argument passed to ProductMaint.AddProduct is of type VARCHAR2. Now you can use the GET_VARCHAR2_ARG function (described in the next section) to determine the value passed.

```
 1   DECLARE
 2       vArgValue VARCHAR2(80);
 3   BEGIN
 4       vArgValue := DBMS_DEFER_QUERY.GET_VARCHAR2_ARG(
 5                   callno => 9929966326029,
 6                   deferred_tran_db => 'D7CA.BIGWHEEL.COM',
 7                   arg_no => 3,
 8                   deferred_tran_id => '3.58.14');
 9       dbms_output.put_line('Argument 3 is '|| vArgValue);
10*  END;
SYSTEM@D7CA SQL> /
Argument 3 is Mens 18 Speed Racer

PL/SQL procedure successfully completed.
```

Here we see that the actual value passed was "Mens 18 Speed Racer."

The DBMS_DEFER_QUERY.GET_CALL_ARGS procedure

The GET_CALL_ARGS procedure allows you to obtain the datatypes and values for all arguments passed to a procedure in a single call. This is the easiest way to obtain information about the datatypes and values of all passed parameters. Here is the specification:

```
PROCEDURE DBMS_DEFER_QUERY.GET_CALL_ARGS
   (callno IN NUMBER,
```

```
startarg IN NUMBER := 1,
argcnt IN NUMBER,
argsize IN NUMBER,
tran_db IN VARCHAR2,
tran_id IN VARCHAR2,
date_fmt IN VARCHAR2,
types OUT TYPE_ARY,
vals OUT VAL_ARY);
```

Parameters are summarized in the following table.

Name	Description
callno	The CALLNO of the RPC as stored in the DEFCALL data dictionary view
start_arg	First argument to fetch
argcnt	Number of arguments to fetch
argsize	Largest size of a returned argument
tran_db	Global name of database deferring the call (also stored in DEFCALL)
tran_id	The deferred_tran_id parameter for the call (also stored in DEFCALL)
date_fmt	Date format mask
types	Output array for argument types
vals	Output array for argument values

There are no restrictions on calling the GET_CALL_ARGS procedure.

Exceptions. GET_CALL_ARGS may raise the following exception:

Name	Number	Description
NO_DATA_FOUND	–100	Specified argument does not exist for specified RPC call

Example. The following example illustrates the use of the GET_CALL_ARGS procedure:

```
 1  DECLARE
 2      vTypes DBMS_DEFER_QUERY.TYPE_ARY;
 3      vVals  DBMS_DEFER_QUERY.VAL_ARY;
 4      indx NUMBER;
 5  BEGIN
 6      DBMS_DEFER_QUERY.GET_CALL_ARGS(
 7              callno => 9929966326029,
 8              startarg => 1,
 9              argcnt => 6,
10              argsize => 128,
11              tran_db => 'D7CA.BIGWHEEL.COM',
12              tran_id => '3.58.14',
13              date_fmt => 'DD-Mon-YYYY hh24:MI:SS',
14              types => vTypes,
15              vals => vVals );
16      FOR indx IN 1..6 LOOP
```

```
17              dbms_output.put_line('Arg '|| indx || ': Datatype '||
18                   vTypes(indx) || ' Value: '|| vVals(indx) );
19      END LOOP;
20* END;
SYSTEM@D7CA SQL> /
Arg 1: Datatype 2 Value: 10
Arg 2: Datatype 1 Value: BIKE-0018
Arg 3: Datatype 1 Value: Mens 18 Speed Racer
Arg 4: Datatype 1 Value: 19971031-01
Arg 5: Datatype 12 Value: 31-Oct-1997 00:00:00
Arg 6: Datatype 1 Value: PLANNED

PL/SQL procedure successfully completed.
```

The DBMS_DEFER_QUERY.GET_<datatype>_ARG function

The GET_<datatype>_ARG function returns a value of a certain type (specified by <datatype>). The type of the returned value corresponds to the value of the argument specified by arg_no in the deferred RPC corresponding to callno.

There is one variant of the GET_<datatype>_ARG function for each of the Oracle-supplied datatypes. Here is the specification:

```
FUNCTION DBMS_DEFER_QUERY.GET_<datatype>_ARG
   (callno IN NUMBER,
    deferred_tran_db IN VARCHAR2
    arg_no IN NUMBER,
    deferred_tran_id IN VARCHAR2 DEFAULT NULL)
RETURN arg;
```

<datatype> can be one of the following:

CHAR
DATE
NUMBER
RAW
ROWID
VARCHAR2
NCHAR (Oracle8 only)
NVARCHAR2 (Oracle8 only)
BLOB (Oracle8 only)
CLOB (Oracle8 only)
NCLOB (Oracle8 only)

Therefore, any of the following are valid:

```
FUNCTION DBMS_DEFER_QUERY.GET_CHAR_ARG...
FUNCTION DBMS_DEFER_QUERY.GET_DATE_ARG...
FUNCTION DBMS_DEFER_QUERY.GET_NUMBER_ARG...
FUNCTION DBMS_DEFER_QUERY.GET_RAW_ARG...
FUNCTION DBMS_DEFER_QUERY.GET_ROWID_ARG...
```

```
FUNCTION DBMS_DEFER_QUERY.GET_VARCHAR2_ARG...
FUNCTION DBMS_DEFER_QUERY.GET_NCHAR_ARG...
FUNCTION DBMS_DEFER_QUERY.GET_NVARCHAR2_ARG...
FUNCTION DBMS_DEFER_QUERY.GET_BLOB_ARG...
FUNCTION DBMS_DEFER_QUERY.GET_CLOB_ARG...
FUNCTION DBMS_DEFER_QUERY.GET_NCLOB_ARG...
```

Parameters have the same meanings described for the GET_ARG_TYPE procedure.

Exceptions. The GET_<datatype>_ARG function may raise the following exceptions:

Name	Number	Description
NO_DATA_FOUND	−100	Specified argument does not exist for specified RPC call
WRONG_TYPE	−26564	Specified argument is not of type <datatype>

Example. Assuming that argument number 3 in the deferred call has CALLNO = 8 and DEFERRED_TRAN_ID = 45.12.3 in the DEFCALL data dictionary view is of type CHAR, follow these steps to determine the argument's value:

```
VARIABLE vChar CHAR;

BEGIN
    vChar := DBMS_QUERY.GET_CHAR_ARG(callno => 8,
                                     deferred_tran_db=> 'D8CA.BIGWHEEL.COM',
                                     arg_no => 3,
                                     deferred_tran_id => 45.12.3);
END;
/
```

What's on the Companion Disk?

The disk that accompanies this book is a Windows disk containing the Oracle Built-in Packages Companion Guide, an online tool designed by RevealnNet, Inc., to help you find additional resources. The guide offers point-and-click access to approximately 175 files of source code and documentation prepared by the authors. The goal of providing this material in electronic form is to give you a leg up on the development of your own PL/SQL programs. Providing material on disk also helps us keep the size of this book under (some) control.

Installing the Guide

In a Microsoft Windows environment (3.1, 95, NT 3.5, or NT 4.0), you begin installation by double-clicking on the *setup.exe* file to run the installation program. If you are working in a non-Windows environment, please visit the RevealNet PL/SQL Pipeline Archives (*www.revealnet.com/plsql-pipeline*) to obtain a compressed file containing the examples on this disk.

The installation script will lead you through the necessary steps. The first screen you will see is the install screen shown in Figure A-1.

You can change the default directory in which the files will be placed. Once this step is complete and the software has been copied to your drive, an icon will appear in the folder you specified. Double-click on the icon to start using the Companion Guide. You will then see the main menu shown in Figure A-2.

Figure A-1. Installing the Companion Guide

Figure A-2. The main menu

Using the Guide

The four buttons on the main menu take you to the companion information for this book.

About the Companion Guide

A brief description of the contents of this disk.

About the Indexes

An explanation of the information provided for each file: name, chapter reference, and description. Filenames highlighted in blue indicate that the files are encapsulations of underlying packages or programs (Chapter 1, *Introduction* explains encapsulation.) The displayed information also explains the meaning of the various file extensions (e.g., *spp, sp, sql*).

Source Code Index by Filename

The guide gives you point-and-click access to each of the files on the companion disk. Here the files are listed alphabetically. Source code listings in the book begin with comment lines keyed to these filenames on the disk. Figure A-3 shows a portion of the Source Code Index by Filename.

File Name	Chapter	Description
apinex1.sql	7	Examples for SET_ACTION, SET_CLIENT_INFO, and SET_MODULE procedures
apinex2.sql	7	Example for SET_SESSION_LONGOPS procedure
apinex3.sql	7	Uses LONGOPS package to set long ops data
aq.spp	5	A package that encapsulates DBMS_AQ and DBMS_AQADM, allowing developers to more easily create and manage queues.
aqadmset.sql	5	Issues DDL statements to set up an account as an Advance Queuing Administrator
aqbrowse.sp	5	Demonstrates "browse" mode in AQ: read contents of queue without removing the message from the queue.
aqbrowse.tst	5	Test script for the aqbrowse.sp procedure.
aqcorrid.spp	5	Package demonstrating use of correlation identifier to dequeue selected messages.
aqcorrid.tst	5	Test script for the aqcorrid.spp pacakge.
aqcremq.sql	5	Creates a multiple consumer queue.
aqcrepq.sql	5	Creates a prioritized queue.
aqcreq.sql	5	Creates a normal queue based on an object type.
aqcrerq.sql	5	Creates a normal queue based on the RAW datatype.
aqdata.sql	5	Defines the message object TYPE used in many examples.
aqdeq1.sql	5	Demonstrates simplest form of dequeue operation.
aqdeq2.sql	5	Demonstrates use of browse and remove dequeue modes.
aqdeq3.sql	5	Dequeues and displays message information.
aqdeq4.sql	5	Demonstrates dequeuing by message ID.
aqenq1.sql	5	Demonstrates basic enqueue operation.
aqenq2.sql	5	Demonstrates enqueuing with specification of non-default sequence.
aqfor.sql	5	Issues DDL statements to set up an account as an Advance Queueing User.

Figure A-3. The Source Code Index by Filename

Source Code Index by Chapter

Here the files are listed in chapter order to make it easy for you to move between the book and the guide. Figure A-4 shows a portion of the Source Code Index by Chapter.

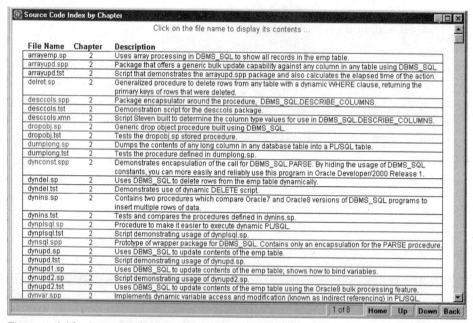

Figure A-4. The Source Code Index by Chapter

Index

Symbols

% (multiple-character substitution), 351
<datatype>_ARG procedure (DBMS_
    DEFER), 877, 885–896
=> (named notation), 310
_ (single-character substitution), 351

A

ABORTED_REQUEST_THRESHOLD
    procedure, 640, 644–645
absolute file numbers, returning, 501
action names
    registering, 427
    returning, 423–424
action procedure, 432
ADD procedure, 700, 706
ADD_<conflicttype>_RESOLUTION
    procedure, 795, 838–842
ADD_DEFAULT_DEST procedure, 855,
    856–857
ADD_DELETE_RESOLUTION
    procedure, 838–842
ADD_GROUPED_COLUMN
    procedure, 795, 807–808
ADD_MASTER_DATABASE
    procedure, 732, 763–765
ADD_PRIORITY_<datatype>
    procedure, 795, 817–819
ADD_SITE_PRIORITY_SITE
    procedure, 795, 829–831
ADD_SUBSCRIBER procedure, 306, 315

ADD_UNIQUE_RESOLUTION
    procedure, 838–842
ADD_UPDATE_RESOLUTION
    procedure, 838–842
addname procedure, 549
ad-hoc query generation, Method 4
    dynamic SQL used for, 121
administrator accounts, 727–731
administrator role (AQ), 283
Advanced Queuing (see AQ)
advanced replication, 724–793
    account creation, 725–731
    administrator accounts, 727–731
        granting privileges, 729–730
        revoking privileges, 730
    propagator accounts, 727
    remote destinations and, 851
    user accounts, 726–727
        granting privileges, 726
        revoking privileges, 726–727
    (see also entries under replication)
ADVISE_COMMIT procedure, 253, 255
ADVISE_NOTHING procedure, 253, 255
ADVISE_ROLLBACK procedure, 253, 255
agents, 275
    object type for, 287–288
    (see also consumers; producers)
alerts, 211–231
    locking and, 215
    names for, 213
    registering, 213–214
    removing, 214

About the Authors

Steven Feuerstein is considered one of the world's leading experts on the Oracle PL/SQL language. He is the author of *Oracle PL/SQL Programming* and *Advanced Oracle PL/SQL Programming with Packages* (both from O'Reilly & Associates). Steven has been developing software since 1980 and worked for Oracle Corporation from 1987 to 1992. As Chief Technology Officer of RevealNet, Inc., he has designed several products for PL/SQL developers, including the PL/SQL Knowledge Base, PL/Vision, and PL/Generator. Steven hosts RevealNet's "PL/SQL Pipeline," an online community for PL/SQL developers (*www.revealnet.com/plsql-pipeline*) and can be reached through email at *feuerstein@revealnet.com*. Steven is President of the PL/Solutions training and consulting company (*www.plsolutions.com*). He also serves as codirector of the Oracle Practice at SSC, a Chicago-based consulting firm (*www.saraswati.com*). Steven shares a Rogers Park, Chicago Georgian with his wife, Veva, his youngest son, Eli, two cats (Sister Itsacat and Moshe Jacobawitz), and Mercury (a Congo Red African Gray parrot). His older son, Chris, is busy making music and creating art nearby. Steven is a member of the Board of Directors of the Crossroads Fund, which provides grants to organizations in Chicago working for social change.

Charles Dye is the Database Architect for Excite, Inc. (*www.excite.com*), where he is responsible for the design and implementation of the databases that supply content to some of the world's busiest web sites. Prior to joining Excite, he was the Senior Database Administrator for The Dialog Corporation. Charles also operates a small yet thriving consultancy with clients in the San Francisco Bay area and Hong Kong. Once upon a time, before fleeing the East Coast for California skies, Charles taught math and physics at the Georgetown Day School in Washington, DC. Charles is a frequent speaker at regional and national Oracle conferences such as Oracle Open World and IOUG-A Live. He also writes for the Northern California Oracle Users Group newsletter, and is an active contributor to the Oracle internet list server. Look for Charles' upcoming O'Reilly title, *Oracle Distributed Systems*. Charles lives in Los Altos, California with his wife Kathy, daughter Natalie, and labrador Jed. You can email him at *cdye@excite.com*.

John Beresniewicz is currently a Product Analyst at Savant Corporation (*www.savant-corp.com*) responsible for design and development of the Q Diagnostic Center for Oracle. Prior to joining Savant, he was an Oracle DBA with eight years' experience in large corporate client-server environments. Developing the Q product's server-side PL/SQL engine has given John extensive and unique experience with using Oracle built-in packages to develop large package-based applications. John is also known in the Oracle user community as a frequent speaker on DBA and PL/SQL topics and an active participant in various Oracle online discussion groups. He has presented papers at numerous conferences, and at ECO '97 he received the "Outstanding Speaker" award for his talk on using the PL/SQL built-in packages, DBMS_PIPE and DBMS_LOCK. John lives with his wife Arlene in Gaithersburg, MD, where they enjoy going to the $2 movie theater. He can be reached by email at *jberesni@savant-corp*.

Colophon

Our look is the result of reader comments, our own experimentation, and feedback from distribution channels. Distinctive covers complement our distinctive approach to technical topics, breathing personality and life into potentially dry subjects.

The animal appearing on the cover of *Oracle Built-in Packages* is a centipede. Centipedes (class *Chilopoda*) are flattened, elongated, carnivorous arthropods, bearing one pair of legs per body segment. There are numerous orders of centipedes and over 2,500 species. Most of these are small, but some range up to 10 inches in length. Lifespan also varies among species, the longest being about 6 years. Centipedes generally live in moist habitats, including household basements, and are usually nocturnal or underground dwellers. Most species lay eggs in soil during the warmer months and live through the winter as adults.

Though the name implies a hundred legs, the actual number varies from 15 to well over a hundred depending on species. The first pair of legs immediately beneath the mouth is modified into a set of venom-bearing jaws with which the centipede kills its prey (live insects and other small animals) and which are only occasionally used to bite humans, resulting in minor pain and swelling. Centipedes are usually considered household pests, though they are more of a nuisance than a threat, and eat unwelcome insects and other household pests.

Edie Freedman designed the cover of this book, using a 19th-century engraving from the Dover Pictorial Archive. The cover layout was produced with Quark XPress using the ITC Garamond font. Whenever possible, our books use RepKover™, a durable and flexible lay-flat binding. If the page count exceeds RepKover's limit, perfect binding is used.

The inside layout was designed by Nancy Priest and implemented in FrameMaker 5.0 by Mike Sierra. The text and heading fonts are ITC Garamond Light and Garamond Book. The illustrations that appear in the book were created in Adobe Photoshop 4 by Robert Romano. This colophon was written by Nancy Kotary.

More Titles from O'Reilly

Database

Oracle PL/SQL Programming, 2nd Edition

By Steven Feuerstein with Bill Pribyl
2nd Edition September 1997
1028 pages, Includes diskette
ISBN 1-56592-335-9

The first edition of *Oracle PL/SQL Programming* quickly became an indispensable reference for both novice and experienced PL/SQL developers. Packed with examples and recommendations, it helped everyone using PL/SQL make the most of this powerful language.

Oracle8 presents PL/SQL programmers with new challenges by increasing both the possibilities and complexities of the language. This new edition updates the original book for Oracle8, adding chapters on the new PL/SQL object features (object types, collections, object views, and external procedures). It also contains a much-requested chapter on tuning PL/SQL, as well as expanded discussions of debugging and tracing PL/SQL execution. A companion diskette contains the Companion Utilities Guide for Oracle PL/SQL Programming, an online tool that includes more than 100 files of source code and documentation prepared by the authors.

Even if you've already read the first edition of *Oracle PL/SQL Programming*, you'll find an enormous amount of new and revised information in this second edition and on its companion diskette. If you're new to PL/SQL, you'll soon find yourself on the road to mastery.

Oracle8 Design Tips

By Dave Ensor & Ian Stevenson
1st Edition September 1997
130 pages, ISBN 1-56592-361-8

The newest version of the Oracle DBMS, Oracle8, offers some dramatically different features from previous versions, including better scalability, reliability, and security; an object-relational model; additional datatypes; and more. To get peak performance out of an Oracle8 system, databases and code need to be designed with these new features in mind. This small book tells Oracle designers and developers just what they need to know to use the Oracle8 features to best advantage.

Mastering Oracle Power Objects

By Rick Greenwald & Robert Hoskin
1st Edition March 1997
508 pages, Includes diskette
ISBN 1-56592-239-5

Oracle's new Power Objects is a cross-platform development tool that greatly simplifies the development of client/server database applications. With Power Objects, you can develop applications for Windows, Windows 95, Windows NT, and the Macintosh in a remarkably short amount of time; for example, you can build a master-detail application that can add, update, and select records via a user interface—all in 30 seconds, with no coding!

This is the first book that covers Power Objects Version 2. It's an in-depth work, aimed at developers, that provides detailed information on getting the most from the product. It looks thoroughly at the most advanced features of Power Objects, covering specific application issues such as lists, reports (using both the native report writer and the Crystal Reports product), built-in methods, moving data, implementing drag-and-drop, etc. It also focuses on the use of object-oriented principles, global functions and messaging, OCXs, debugging, and cross-platform issues. The book also includes chapters on using PL/SQL with Power Objects and integrating the World Wide Web with the product. It provides a wealth of developer tips and techniques, as well as understandable explanations of the internal workings of Power Objects. The accompanying disk contains practical and complete examples that will help you build working applications, right now.

Oracle Design

By Dave Ensor & Ian Stevenson
1st Edition March 1997
546 pages, 1-56592-268-9

This book looks thoroughly at the field of Oracle relational database design, an often neglected area of Oracle, but one that has an enormous impact on the ultimate power and performance of a system. Focuses on both database and code design, including such special design areas as data models, enormalization, the use of keys and indexes, temporal data, special architectures (client/server, distributed database, parallel processing), and data warehouses.

Database

Advanced Oracle PL/SQL *Programming with Packages*

By Steven Feuerstein,
1st Edition Oct.1996, 690 pages,
plus diskette, ISBN 1-56592-238-7

Steven Feuerstein's first book, *Oracle PL/SQL Programming*, has become the classic reference to PL/SQL, Oracle's procedural extension to its SQL language. His new book looks thoroughly at one especially advanced and powerful part of the PL/SQL language—the package. The use of packages can dramatically improve your programming productivity and code quality, while preparing you for object-oriented development in Oracle technology. In this book, Feuerstein explains how to construct packages—and how to build them the right way. His "best practices" for building packages will transform the way you write packages and help you get the most out of the powerful, but often poorly understood, PL/SQL language.

Much more than a book, Advanced Oracle PL/SQL Programming with Packages comes with a PC disk containing a full-use software companion. Developed by Feuerstein, RevealNet's PL/Vision Lite is the first of its kind for PL/SQL developers: a library of thirty-plus PL/SQL packages. The packages solve a myriad of common programming problems and vastly accelerate the development of modular and maintainable applications.

Oracle Built-In Packages

By Steven Feuerstein
1st Edition April 1998 (est.)
600 pages (est.), Includes diskette
ISBN 1-56592-375-8

This new book focuses on one particularly important aspect of PL/SQL—the use of Oracle's built-in packages. Built-ins are packages (collections of PL/SQL objects, such as procedures, functions, tables, etc.) built by Oracle and made available to developers. They extend the power of the language in significant ways.

The Windows disk included with the book contains the Companion Utilities Guide, an online tool developed by RevealNet, Inc., that provides point-and-click access to the many files of source code and online documentation developed by the authors.

Oracle Performance Tuning, 2nd Edition

By Mark Gurry & Peter Corrigan
2nd Edition November 1996
964 pages, Includes diskette
ISBN 1-56592-237-9

The first edition of *Oracle Performance Tuning* has become a classic for programmers, managers, database administrators, system administrators, and anyone who cares about improving the performance of an Oracle system. This second edition is a complete revision, with 400 pages of new material on new Oracle features that will be helpful whether you are running Oracle6, Oracle7, or Oracle8. It updates all the original information, incorporating new advice about disk striping and mirroring, RAID, client-server, distributed databases, MPPS, SMPs, and other architectures. It also includes new chapters on parallel server, parallel query, backup and recovery, the Oracle Performance Pack, and more.

The book comes with a PC disk containing all of the SQL and shell scripts described in the book, as well as additional tuning scripts that can help monitor and improve performance at your site.

Oracle Scripts

By Brian Lomasky & David C. Kreines
1st Edition May 1998 (est.)
200 pages (est.), Includes CD-ROM
ISBN 1-56592-438-X

Database administrators everywhere are faced with the ongoing job of monitoring Oracle databases for continuous reliability, performance, and security. This book provides the first central source of previously created, tested, and documented scripts for performing these monitoring tasks. The accompanying Windows CD-ROM contains all of the scripts discussed in the book.

O'REILLY™

TO ORDER: **800-998-9938** • *order@oreilly.com* • *http://www.oreilly.com/*
OUR PRODUCTS ARE AVAILABLE AT A BOOKSTORE OR SOFTWARE STORE NEAR YOU.
FOR INFORMATION: **800-998-9938** • **707-829-0515** • *info@oreilly.com*

How to stay in touch with O'Reilly

1. Visit Our Award-Winning Web Site
http://www.oreilly.com/

★ "Top 100 Sites on the Web" —*PC Magazine*
★ "Top 5% Web sites" —*Point Communications*
★ "3-Star site" —*The McKinley Group*

Our web site contains a library of comprehensive product information (including book excerpts and tables of contents), downloadable software, background articles, interviews with technology leaders, links to relevant sites, book cover art, and more. File us in your Bookmarks or Hotlist!

2. Join Our Email Mailing Lists
New Product Releases
To receive automatic email with brief descriptions of all new O'Reilly products as they are released, send email to:
listproc@online.oreilly.com
Put the following information in the first line of your message (*not* in the Subject field):
subscribe oreilly-news

O'Reilly Events
If you'd also like us to send information about trade show events, special promotions, and other O'Reilly events, send email to:
listproc@online.oreilly.com
Put the following information in the first line of your message (*not* in the Subject field):
subscribe oreilly-events

3. Get Examples from Our Books via FTP

There are two ways to access an archive of example files from our books:

Regular FTP
- ftp to:
  ftp.oreilly.com
  (login: anonymous
  password: your email address)
- Point your web browser to:
  ftp://ftp.oreilly.com/

FTPMAIL
- Send an email message to:
  ftpmail@online.oreilly.com
  (Write "help" in the message body)

4. Contact Us via Email
order@oreilly.com
To place a book or software order online. Good for North American and international customers.

subscriptions@oreilly.com
To place an order for any of our newsletters or periodicals.

books@oreilly.com
General questions about any of our books.

software@oreilly.com
For general questions and product information about our software. Check out O'Reilly Software Online at **http://software.oreilly.com/** for software and technical support information. Registered O'Reilly software users send your questions to: **website-support@oreilly.com**

cs@oreilly.com
For answers to problems regarding your order or our products.

booktech@oreilly.com
For book content technical questions or corrections.

proposals@oreilly.com
To submit new book or software proposals to our editors and product managers.

international@oreilly.com
For information about our international distributors or translation queries. For a list of our distributors outside of North America check out:
http://www.oreilly.com/www/order/country.html

O'Reilly & Associates, Inc.
101 Morris Street, Sebastopol, CA 95472 USA
TEL   707-829-0515 or 800-998-9938
       (6am to 5pm PST)
FAX   707-829-0104

O'REILLY™

International Distributors

UK, EUROPE, MIDDLE EAST AND NORTHERN AFRICA (EXCEPT FRANCE, GERMANY, SWITZERLAND, & AUSTRIA)

INQUIRIES
International Thomson Publishing Europe
Berkshire House
168-173 High Holborn
London WC1V 7AA
United Kingdom
Telephone: 44-171-497-1422
Fax: 44-171-497-1426
Email: itpint@itps.co.uk

ORDERS
International Thomson Publishing Services, Ltd.
Cheriton House, North Way
Andover, Hampshire SP10 5BE
United Kingdom
Telephone: 44-264-342-832 (UK)
Telephone: 44-264-342-806 (outside UK)
Fax: 44-264-364418 (UK)
Fax: 44-264-342761 (outside UK)
UK & Eire orders: itpuk@itps.co.uk
International orders: itpint@itps.co.uk

FRANCE

Editions Eyrolles
61 bd Saint-Germain
75240 Paris Cedex 05
France
Fax: 33-01-44-41-11-44

FRENCH LANGUAGE BOOKS
All countries except Canada
Telephone: 33-01-44-41-46-16
Email: geodif@eyrolles.com
English language books
Telephone: 33-01-44-41-11-87
Email: distribution@eyrolles.com

GERMANY, SWITZERLAND, AND AUSTRIA

INQUIRIES
O'Reilly Verlag
Balthasarstr. 81
D-50670 Köln
Germany
Telephone: 49-221-97-31-60-0
Fax: 49-221-97-31-60-8
Email: anfragen@oreilly.de

ORDERS
International Thomson Publishing
Königswinterer Straße 418
53227 Bonn, Germany
Telephone: 49-228-97024 0
Fax: 49-228-441342
Email: order@oreilly.de

JAPAN

O'Reilly Japan, Inc.
Kiyoshige Building 2F
12-Banchi, Sanei-cho
Shinjuku-ku
Tokyo 160-0008 Japan
Telephone: 81-3-3356-5227
Fax: 81-3-3356-5261
Email: kenji@oreilly.com

INDIA

Computer Bookshop (India) PVT. Ltd.
190 Dr. D.N. Road, Fort
Bombay 400 001 India
Telephone: 91-22-207-0989
Fax: 91-22-262-3551
Email: cbsbom@giasbm01.vsnl.net.in

HONG KONG

City Discount Subscription Service Ltd.
Unit D, 3rd Floor, Yan's Tower
27 Wong Chuk Hang Road
Aberdeen, Hong Kong
Telephone: 852-2580-3539
Fax: 852-2580-6463
Email: citydis@ppn.com.hk

KOREA

Hanbit Media, Inc.
Sonyoung Bldg. 202
Yeksam-dong 736-36
Kangnam-ku
Seoul, Korea
Telephone: 822-554-9610
Fax: 822-556-0363
Email: hant93@chollian.dacom.co.kr

SINGAPORE, MALAYSIA, AND THAILAND

Addison Wesley Longman Singapore PTE Ltd.
25 First Lok Yang Road
Singapore 629734
Telephone: 65-268-2666
Fax: 65-268-7023
Email: daniel@longman.com.sg

PHILIPPINES

Mutual Books, Inc.
429-D Shaw Boulevard
Mandaluyong City, Metro
Manila, Philippines
Telephone: 632-725-7538
Fax: 632-721-3056
Email: mbikikog@mnl.sequel.net

CHINA

Ron's DataCom Co., Ltd.
79 Dongwu Avenue
Dongxihu District
Wuhan 430040
China
Telephone: 86-27-3892568
Fax: 86-27-3222108
Email: hongfeng@public.wh.hb.cn

ALL OTHER ASIAN COUNTRIES

O'Reilly & Associates, Inc.
101 Morris Street
Sebastopol, CA 95472 USA
Telephone: 707-829-0515
Fax: 707-829-0104
Email: order@oreilly.com

AUSTRALIA

WoodsLane Pty. Ltd.
7/5 Vuko Place, Warriewood NSW 2102
P.O. Box 935
Mona Vale NSW 2103
Australia
Telephone: 61-2-9970-5111
Fax: 61-2-9970-5002
Email: info@woodslane.com.au

NEW ZEALAND

Woodslane New Zealand Ltd.
21 Cooks Street (P.O. Box 575)
Waganui, New Zealand
Telephone: 64-6-347-6543
Fax: 64-6-345-4840
Email: info@woodslane.com.au

THE AMERICAS

McGraw-Hill Interamericana Editores, S.A. de C.V.
Cedro No. 512
Col. Atlampa 06450
Mexico, D.F.
Telephone: 52-5-541-3155
Fax: 52-5-541-4913
Email: mcgraw-hill@infosel.net.mx

SOUTH AFRICA

International Thomson Publishing South Africa
Building 18, Constantia Park
138 Sixteenth Road
P.O. Box 2459
Halfway House, 1685 South Africa
Telephone: 27-11-805-4819
Fax: 27-11-805-3648

O'REILLY™

TO ORDER: **800-998-9938** • **order@oreilly.com** • **http://www.oreilly.com/**
OUR PRODUCTS ARE AVAILABLE AT A BOOKSTORE OR SOFTWARE STORE NEAR YOU.
FOR INFORMATION: **800-998-9938** • **707-829-0515** • **info@oreilly.com**

O'REILLY™

O'Reilly & Associates, Inc.
101 Morris Street
Sebastopol, CA 95472-9902
1-800-998-9938

Visit us online at:
http://www.ora.com/
orders@ora.com

O'REILLY WOULD LIKE TO HEAR FROM YOU

Which book did this card come from?

_____

Where did you buy this book?
- ❏ Bookstore
- ❏ Direct from O'Reilly
- ❏ Bundled with hardware/software
- ❏ Computer Store
- ❏ Class/seminar
- ❏ Other _____

What operating system do you use?
- ❏ UNIX
- ❏ Windows NT
- ❏ Other _____
- ❏ Macintosh
- ❏ PC(Windows/DOS)

What is your job description?
- ❏ System Administrator
- ❏ Network Administrator
- ❏ Web Developer
- ❏ Other _____
- ❏ Programmer
- ❏ Educator/Teacher

❏ Please send me O'Reilly's catalog, containing a complete listing of O'Reilly books and software.

Name _____ Company/Organization _____

Address _____

City _____ State _____ Zip/Postal Code _____ Country _____

Telephone _____ Internet or other email address (specify network) _____

Nineteenth century wood engraving of a bear from the O'Reilly & Associates Nutshell Handbook® *Using & Managing UUCP.*

BUSINESS REPLY MAIL

FIRST CLASS MAIL   PERMIT NO. 80   SEBASTOPOL, CA

Postage will be paid by addressee

O'Reilly & Associates, Inc.
101 Morris Street
Sebastopol, CA 95472-9902